SCRI...
A BIOGRAPH...

Faubion Bowers

SECOND, REVISED EDITION

DOVER PUBLICATIONS, INC.
Mineola, New York

To Jane Gunther
Music Lover and Muse

Bibliographical Note

This Dover edition, first published in 1996, is a corrected and revised republication in one volume of *Scriabin: A Biography of the Russian Composer, 1871–1915,* originally published in a two-volume set by Kodansha International Ltd., Tokyo, and Kodansha International/USA Ltd., Palo Alto, California, 1969.

The Dover edition incorporates numerous corrections and revisions, including the relocation of some illustrations in Volume Two. The original discography, now outdated, has been omitted.

Library of Congress Cataloging-in-Publication Data

Bowers, Faubion, 1917–
    Scriabin, a biography / Faubion Bowers.—2nd, rev. ed.
      p.   cm.
    Rev. ed. of: Scriabin : a biography of the Russian composer, 1871–1915.
    "Catalog of Scriabin's works": p.
    Includes index.
    ISBN-13: 978-0-486-28897-0 (pbk.)
    ISBN-10: 0-486-28897-8 (pbk.)
    1. Scriabin, Aleksandr Nikolayevich, 1872–1915. 2. Composers—Russia—Biography. I. Title.
ML410.S5988B7   1995
786.2′092—dc20
[B]   95-44705
                                                    CIP
                                                    MN

Manufactured in the United States by RR Donnelley
28897808   2015
www.doverpublications.com

CONTENTS

Illustrations in Volume One appear on p. 12 and following p. 160. Volume Two—which begins after p. 342 *but is paginated from its own page 1—*includes illustrations on pp. 2–6, and after p. 80 and p. 192.

VOLUME TWO

INTRODUCTION TO
THE DOVER EDITION

ONCE WHEN I pointed out an error in Sir George Sansom's seminal *A Short Cultural History of Japan*, he sighed, "So many mistakes you never notice until a book is out!" When my *Scriabin* appeared nearly thirty years ago, the errata reached out from the pages and grabbed me by the throat. Thankfully, the Dover edition has enabled me to correct my most humiliating bloopers.

Scriabin has had a curious history. In 1967, despite the fact that no authoritative work on the subject existed in English, publishers still rejected the manuscript. During my despair, the Japanese writer Mishima Yukio chanced to visit New York. In the course of our reminiscences about good old days in Tokyo, he casually mentioned that the publisher Kodansha wanted to expand its English-language catalogue. "Do you know any book going begging?" I did.

Kodansha published *Scriabin* lavishly, slipcased and with gold and vermilion covers at $45 a copy—quite pricey in those days for a book aimed at music students. After two uncorrected editions, the two-volume set drifted into the limbo of out-of-print. Meanwhile I wrote a smaller update, *The New Scriabin: Enigma and Answers*, published in 1974 by St. Martin's Press and later translated into Italian and Japanese. The distinguished Japanese authority on Russian pianism, Sato Taiichi, translated the book and appended an exhaustive Scriabin discography that extended from early 78 rpms to the most recent CDs.*

---

* Copies of the discography may be had from The Scriabin Society of America, Penthouse D, 44 West 62nd Street, New York, NY 10023. Also available from the Society is Luigi Verdi's extensive bibliography of books and articles about Scriabin. Mr. Verdi is Professor at the Martini Conservatory, Bologna, Italy.

Although I once wrote that Scriabin shifted in the public's mind from being half-forgotten to being half-remembered, I cannot write so diffidently today for much has happened in the world of Scriabiniana. In 1971, on the occasion of the centennial of his birth, USSR put the composer's picture on a 10-kopek stamp. In the same year, Margarita Fyodorova, Professor at the Moscow Conservatory, played from memory Scriabin's entire pianoforte *oeuvre* in five recitals. Vladimir Horowitz spearheaded a reconsideration of Scriabin in America. Sviatoslav Richter played all-Scriabin concerts worldwide, as has pianist-conductor Vladimir Ashkenazy, playing all ten sonatas and conducting all five symphonies. Becoming something of a fad, the composer had become so fashionable that a renowned teacher at The Juilliard School said to me, "If one more student asks me to teach the Tenth Sonata, I'll shoot myself." Several asked, but my friend died a natural death subsequently.

After Scriabin's death, in 1915, Russian pianists held a monopoly on playing him, both stylistically and technically. (The axiom in those early days about Scriabin players was: "Those who can't, do; those who can, don't.") With the composer's resurgence, that snide remark is no longer accurate, the exclusively Russian copyright expiring as European, American and Asian Scriabinists flourish: Alan Gampel, Dmitry Rachmanov and Robert Taub (United States); Roberto Szidon (Brazil); Marc-André Hamelin and Anton Kuerti (Canada); Gordon Fergus-Thompson (England); Nakai Masako (Japan); HaeSun Paik (Korea); and Håkon Austbø (Norway) are among the first who come to mind.

Indeed, Scriabin has come into his own. Now, that vain composer, born 125 years ago, can truly rest in his grave on the heights of Sparrow Hills cemetery in Moscow, where he has lain uneasily for eighty-one tortuous years.

FAUBION BOWERS
New York City, 1996

AUTHOR'S NOTE

THIS IS the story of one man at one period of history. Aside from the guideline of my opinions arrived at over a lifetime's study of Scriabin, and from living with his music and studying his surroundings, I have in this biography tried to let the composer speak for himself or be spoken for by his contemporaries, those who actually heard and touched him. These friends and sometimes enemies, in all their confusion, conflicting feelings, and often innocence of what they were really disclosing, add up to certain contradictions. Truth, it seems to me, lies here in the this *and* that, the either *and* or, rather than in the thinner line of simplification which a more winnowed, clarified narrative produces. The picture of Scriabin builds like children's blocks into shapes of enigmas, riddles of complex life—insoluble and absorbing.

The Russian spellings here vary erratically because I have followed common usage in individual cases. "Chaikovskii" looks strange to us. "Taneieff," "Sabaneeff" and others preferred to be spelled abroad this way, rather than transliterally Tanyeyev or Sabanyeyev. On a single page it may be distracting to see successive inconsistencies, such as "Zverev," "Prokofiev," "Nicolai," "Eugene Onegin," and "Serge Koussevitzky," or Kommissarzhevskaya and Komisarjevsky within one sentence. However, I have yielded, perhaps confusingly, to custom, familiarity and to their (and my) personal choice. I have left Nikolai as Nikolai, Ksenia not Xenia, Kyril not Cyril, but Aleksandr looks affected. And I find it impossible to call Vassily Safonoff "Basil."

I have put dates after names only on their first appearance. The period covered by the lives of these many Russian musicians is split by the Revolution, its turmoil in the home country and confusion of émigré life that some of them chose abroad. Many records were destroyed or lost, and certain facts were never recorded. Regretfully, despite every effort on the part of Soviet, European and American scholars, a number of ancillary dates, particularly terminal ones, are missing and undiscoverable.

Five books, none of which has ever been translated from the Russian before, constitute the bedrock of Scriabinic lore and knowledge. I have quoted from them copiously, and my debt, for all its occasional disagreement and doubt, is overwhelming:

A. V. Kashperov, *A. Skryabin Pis'ma*. 746 letters collected and edited by A.V.K. and introduced by V. Asmus, Muzyka, Moscow, 1965. (My particular indebtedness to Alexei Vladimirovich Kashperov is immeasurable. His formidable and detailed annotations to each Scriabin letter, drawing from every source in Russia, Europe and America, interpret and widen the whole area of Scriabin knowledge. His *Chronicle of Scriabin's Life and Creative Work* (Letopis' Zhizni i Tvorchestva Skryabina), a further collection of source materials, is long-awaited. That one of the leading musicologists of the USSR should devote his inexhaustible attention to Scriabin not only signifies the importance of this composer, but also removes the stigma of vagueness and carelessness which has characterized, heretofore, so much Scriabin material.)

B. F. Shletser, *A. Skryabin*. Vol. I "Personality and Mysterium," "Grani" Publishers, Berlin, 1923. (There is no Vol. II or III.)

Leonid Sabaneeff, *Vospominaniye o Skryabinye*. (Reminiscences of Scriabin) Muzsektor, Moscow, 1925.

Sbornik. (Memorial Collection.) 25th Anniversary of Death of Alyeksandr Nikolayevich Skryabin. State Music Publishers, Moscow and Leningrad, 1940. Edited by E. Beichek, there are important articles and memoirs by L. Scriabina, L. Limontov, M. Pressman, O. Monighetti, O. Sekerina, A. Scriabin (a first cousin), E. Bekman-Shcherbina, R. Plekhanova, L. Danilevich, N. Kotler, N. Volter, A. Alshvang, S. Markus, S. Skrebov, T. Shaborkina, V. Yakolev, and two compositions—exquisite little preludes—by Scriabin's son, Julian, who wrote them at ten years of age, a year before his death.

Yuri Engel, *Muzykal'nyi Sovremennik* (Musical Contemporary) Vols. 4 and 5. (Dec. and Jan.) Magazine of Musical Culture (edited by A. N. Rimsky-Korsakoff, I. Lapshin, Vyacheslav Karatygin, Alexander Ossovsky, Peter Suvchinsky (founder of the magazine in 1915), and Yu. Beisberg), Moscow, 1916. (The combined issues are devoted to Scriabin with adjunctive articles by Nemenova-Lunz, Kashkin, Abraamov, Karatygin, Sabaneeff and Schloezer.)

To other invaluable monographs from which I have repeatedly drawn,

I refer by the author's name, such as the three important Soviet critics B. V. Asafiev (pseudonym, Igor Glebov), A. Alshvang, and L. Danilevich, and pianists Mark Meichik and Anatol Drozdov.

Chekhov wrote in 1890, "I've already stolen much thought and knowledge from the books of others which I shall pass off as my own. It is impossible to do otherwise in our practical age." And Stravinsky said, "I steal the music of Mozart, and I feel I have the right to steal it because I love it." In this spirit I acknowledge my borrowings.

My debts of gratitude extend in other ways too. Heartfelt thanks go to the following for their unstinting help: Donald Keene, Mishima Yukio, Donald Garvelmann, Vera Kovarsky, Joan Cook, Gorham Munson, who fathered this book, Edwin Hymovitz, Dr. Alexander Scriabine, Mrs. F.R.T. Evreinow, Goddard Lieberson, Martin Bookspan, Mme. Djane Lavoie-Herz, Elena T. Mogilat, Gershon Swet, and Harold C. Schonberg; to Tatyana Shaborkina, late Director of the Scriabin State Museum in Moscow, particularly for generously giving me photographs and photostats of the final music sketches of the *Prefatory Action*, including fragmentary notes and chords Scriabin wrote on his deathbed; and most especially to Mme. E. N. Alekseeva, former Director of the Glinka Museum in Moscow, who obliged me with microfilms of Scriabin's unpublished letters.

Profoundest gratitude for moral encouragement and material assistance I offer to Katrine Arthur, Gerald Freund and the Rockefeller Foundation, Joy Chute and P.E.N., and Carolyn Kizer and Saunders Redding of the National Foundation on the Arts and Humanities.

It would be convenient for the reader to remember that the ruble (100 kopecks) was roughly the equivalent of 50¢, one German mark (two to one ruble) equaled around 25¢, and there were during most of Scriabin's lifetime 5 French and 4 Swiss francs to the American dollar. Throughout, I have given amounts of money in the coin of the time and country.

All translations from the Russian, French, Japanese, and German have been made by me except when expressly stated otherwise and I am responsible for errors.

VOLUME ONE

Scriabin's favorite photograph of himself, one he often gave to admirers. Taken in Paris in 1905 prior to a concert tour. (Courtesy of Djane Lavoie-Herz.)

BOOK I

*. . . Scriabin . . . Where does he come from?
And who are his forebears?*

IGOR STRAVINSKY in *Poetics of Music*

KALEIDOSCOPE OF
RUSSIAN MUSIC

☞ I ☞

ORIGINS

THERE IS much to make us think of Mother Russia or Holy Rus as ancient, so it comes as a shock to discover how recent is its music. It is new, of course, in content and form, subject matter and treatment, in its attitudes and phraseologies. As histories of music go, that of Russia is astonishingly young. Fashion nowadays in the voice of Richard Leonard dismisses this fact as a "half-truth,"[1] but it would be hard to be wholly honest and regard it otherwise. Scholar James Billington refers to the "elusive and neglected area of early Russian music."[2] Before 1836 the music we think of as Russian did not exist.

James Bakst found music—"during ceremonies, receptions, festivities, and hunts"—in Kiev of the tenth century, and "one musical art . . . bell ringing" in the fourteenth-fifteenth centuries in Novgorod, and "historical songs . . . described the successes of the tsar" in the sixteenth, "songs of freemen" and "lyrical songs" in the seventeenth century[3]. Still there is no doubt that Russia was, to say the least, backward in the sense that everything musical had been consumed by the Church.

The earliest days of any country lack developed music. However, the introduction of Christianity in the ninth century by the converting fathers from Byzantium insisted upon church music. This and some folk music were all there was to be heard until centuries later in Russian his-

---

[1] Richard Anthony Leonard, *A History of Russian Music*, Jarrold's, London, 1956.
[2] James H. Billington, *The Icon and the Axe*, An Interpretive History of Russian Culture, Alfred A. Knopf, New York City, 1966.
[3] James Bakst, *History of Russian-Soviet Music*, Dodd, Mead and Co., New York, 1966.

tory. As in painting, so in music; the profane must not exist. An incipient interest in Palestrina (1516–94) was snuffed out by Ivan IV (1530–84), the first "tsar," and the first to be called "the Terrible."

When other foreign music, that from Italy and France and Germany, began infiltrating Russia in the seventeenth century at the request of Tsar Alexis "the Most Quiet" (1629–76), there was still a secular blank in the land of Rus . . . and an upheaval. In 1649, the Patriarch of the Orthodox Church ordered six wagonloads of musical instruments burned. Anyone caught playing on a musical instrument of popular use, as opposed to church bells and unaccompanied choral singing, was banished to the provincial borders.

The resultant impoverishment was still reflected after Peter the Great (1672–1725) and his schism with the Church. In a withering letter dated 1694, the Secretary to the German Ambassador had this to say:

> Though the Muscovites have no information about music, their musical accord nevertheless fascinates. The foreign artists that dwell among them please the Muscovites only so long as they play; but no sooner have they satisfied them by their playing, than the patrons of these artists become stingy and the Muscovites are never willing to make a yearly budget for a pleasure that lasts only a few hours.[1]

However, with Peter had come dances at court, and with dances came music—from abroad like everything else. To orient ourselves musically, let us recall that Monteverdi (1567–1643) and Lully (1633–1687) were already dead, their work accomplished; and Bach (1695–1750), Rameau (1683–1764) and Handel (1685–1759) about to begin their careers.

A century later all music outside the Church was still Western. In 1802 the violinist virtuoso Louis Spohr (1784–1859) reported while on tour in Russia that all his audiences were foreigners, and the only good piano teachers there were the Italian Muzio Clementi (1752–1832) and Irishman John Field (1782–1837).[2]

One further century along, Peter Tchaikovsky (1840–1893) truthfully declared, "Russian music is tied to the tail of more cultured Europe,"

---

1 B. V. Asafiev, *Russian Music*, Translated by Alfred Swan, American Council of Learned Societies, J. W. Edwards, Ann Arbor, Michigan, 1953.

2 James Lyon, editor, *The American Record Guide*, from the sleeve jacket of Monitor Record MC2068 and MCS2068, Taneieff's Trio Op. 22.

and thereby incensed his compatriots. However, he failed to mention the then dramatic, lightning fast changes, many of which were due to him himself, and to no one else.

Russian music rose from minuscule beginnings. Once started, it quickly fledged. Moreover, the line sustained itself despite occasional flagging and failure, and it still shows little sign of exhaustion. Russia accomplished this feat in less than a century's span. No other country can make such a claim. America, for example, has yet to produce a body of indigenous, creative musicians in comparable bulk and of equivalent merit. Japan, to cite another instance, may possess the world's oldest counterpoint and chordal combinations in the Gagaku orchestra of the Imperial Palace in Tokyo, whose concerted patterns antedate Bach by a thousand years, and her musical vanguard ferment of the present day may also begin to command world attention; however, nothing anywhere matches the successive outbursts of geniuses skyrocketing to the heavens of Russia's golden period, the nineteenth century.

The first internationally viable, creative Russian music was the work of Mikhail Glinka (1804–1857). There had been other musicians. Recently rediscovered Ivan Khandoshkin, for example, who died the year Glinka was born. But Glinka was the father and fountainhead of Russian music, Russia's first "composer." Yet, as a pianist, which is how he was originally known, he was always asked to play concertos by Johann Nepomuk Hummel (1778–1837), Mozart's pupil, who rivaled Beethoven. Hummel was not, though, the maker of the best art; neither does he entirely deserve the obscurity that now enshrouds him.

The date 1836 is immortal in Russia for being the première year of Glinka's patriotic, historical opera *Ivan Susanin* (subtitled "A Native, Tragi-heroic Opera"), so named after the peasant hero who sacrificed his life in 1612 to prevent Polish invaders from reaching Moscow... Hired as a guide, Ivan Susanin leads the Poles into a wintry, icy impasse. He is murdered, but the word "Motherland" is on his lips, and the enemy soldiers freeze to death.

Glinka retitled his opera *A Life for the Tsar* in order to secure Court favor and pass the rigorous censorship which objected to scenes depicting Poles. After all, the "Time of Troubles" (1612) was when Poles occupied Moscow. Poland was a province of Russia now, under the "King of Poland"—the tsar. The country had revolted in 1830, and soon after the opera's appearance there would be another bloody insurrection. For obvious reasons, the Soviets returned the opera to its first designation, and it is this work which annually opened the Bolshoi Theater.

The same year, 1836, saw Nikolai Gogol (1809–1852), the "father" of both the Russian novel and realistic drama, produce his important first play, *The Inspector General*. Its comic plot, a satire on bureaucracy and corruption among officials in government, had been suggested by yet another Russian "father," that of poetry, Alexander Pushkin (1799–1837). *The Inspector General* marked the turning point of Russian drama into its own autochthonous naturalism.

Glinka, curiously enough, awoke to his Russian heritage while living abroad. In Italy, his memoirs inform us, "homesickness nudged me into the idea of composing something in Russian."[1] He did; but this was still no instant passport home, nor was it a *carte d'identité* there either. Ivan Turgenev (1818–1882), for example, attended the first performance of *A Life for the Tsar* and wrote, "I was simply bored. The music of Glinka at any rate I ought to have been able to understand."[2] Turgenev was stubbornly unwilling to recognize the genius of Russian music. Literature yes; music no. Of Balakirev (1837–1910) he later said, "*Kein Talent, aber ein Character*" (No talent but a character). The truth was Balakirev had talent and lacked character in the sense Turgenev meant.

A grand duke, another time, buttonholed Franz Liszt (1811–76), who was performing in Petersburg, and asked, "*Est-ce que c'est une mauvaise plaisanterie à vous de trouver Glinka un génie?*" (Are you making some sort of bad joke when you call Glinka a genius?) His Highness went on to recount how generals sent their officers to Glinka's operas—for punishment. Decennia after this, Count Lev ("Lion") Tolstoi (1828–1910), dictator of taste within Russia of his day and "perhaps the most celebrated man in the world at that time," according to Ernest J. Simmons[3] (who is possibly the most famous Russian scholar in our own period), viewed Glinka's music suspiciously. That incredibly bright and sunny music, he said, was "the work of a man unclean and sensual."[4]

---

1 M. I. Glinka, *Memoirs*, edited by A. N. Rimsky-Korsakoff, State Music Publishers, Moscow, 1930.
2 David Magarshack, *Turgenev: A Life*, Grove Press, New York, 1954.
3 E. J. Simmons, *Chekhov, A Biography*, Little Brown and Co., Boston, 1962.
4 M.D. Calvocoressi and Gerald Abraham, *Masters of Russian Music*, Tudor Publishing House, New York, 1944.

Posterity and Pushkin ("I smell Russia in his music") esteemed Glinka. Musicians following him in rapid, tumbling succession worshiped, imitated, copied him, and recopied themselves. The really extraordinary fact is that Glinka, whose own only opera experience at the Bolshoi in Moscow and the Maryinsky in Petersburg consisted of hearing dry works by François-Adrien Boieldieu (1755–1834), Luigi Cherubini (1760–1842) and Etienne-Nicolas (1763–1817), was still able to invent Russian music for Russians—and us.

Vladimir Stassov (1824–1906), revered polemist on behalf of Russian music, its first propagandist, wrote, "Each picture of Glinka's is full and whole; each incarnates a century and a people."[1] He was not the first, however, as one might suppose, to use Russian themes.

Carl Maria von Weber (1786–1826) had written nine variations on the theme *Schöne Minka* Op. 40. And Ludwig van Beethoven (1770–1826), twenty-odd years before Glinka, composed three Razumovsky Quartets Op. 59, two containing Russian themes. Count (later Prince) Razumovsky was the Russian ambassador in Vienna from 1793 to 1809, and he spent money prodigally for music.

But Glinka's music *is* Russian and was the first so written by a Russian. The USSR accorded Glinka canonical sanctity. Doctrinaire Marxist musicologists avowed that the War of 1812, the beginning of Russian pride and the "fight to the death against Napoleon, played the decisive role in the formation of the thought and art of Glinka:"[2]

> Deeply national in its source, full of light and optimism, masculine and life-affirming, the music of Glinka—like the poetry of Pushkin—reflects all the gigantic, inexhaustible might of the awakening powers of Russia and the Russian people.

This opinion is not without accuracy, nor is it indisputable. Glinka's music now sounds to us for all its peasant choruses and unprecedented novelties, rather Italianate.

Glinka (like Tchaikovsky later) spoke of what little native music there

---

[1] V. V. Stassov, *Collected Works*, Vol. III, SPb 1894.
[2] *History of Russian Music*, Vol. III, Muzgiz, Moscow, 1960, edited by N. V. Tumanina. Official text of the Moscow Conservatory and approved by the Ministry of Culture.

was around him as "a jay bedecked with other birds' plumage."[1] He carefully excepted his own, but in reality the description fitted him too. Ten years before *Ivan Susanin* he was writing like a complete foreigner. He incorporated into his music melodies not only from Russia, but from the Ukraine, Poland, Georgia, Tatary, Arabia, Finland, Spain and Scotland, and feathered his nest with pickings from the wide world. He introduced Oriental dances in his second opera *Ruslan and Ludmila*, performed in 1842 on the same day as the première of his first, 23 November. He peopled his operas with "exaggerated, hyperbolic, esthetically heightened characters," as the Soviets admitted. We find them sometimes stiff and not-so-Russian, but nevertheless fascinating by their faroff and distant delineation.

Glinka's personal friends and acquaintances abroad were none other than Weber, Schubert, Chopin, Berlioz, and towards the end, Liszt. What amateur would not succumb to their influence? Who could resist their musical definition? Yet, Glinka was a master. He held much of his own. He founded a school, and more, graced it with unique embellishments.

Glinka is also noteworthy for travel postcards or "masquerades," as he called them, disguises such as he himself liked to wear to masked balls. His Spanish music, *Night in Madrid* and *La Jota Aragonaise*, for instance, captures another first discovery for the West—the wholetone scale. Here he forecast Nikolai Rimsky-Korsakoff (1844–1908) and his *Spanish Caprice*, both being monitory of Debussy.

The images we derive of Spain from Glinka's music—and his own country too, except for the underlying sentiment and their purest passages—may be fanciful or even inaccurate. But are they any more so than say, the later de Falla-approved, French-composed *Ibéria* or *Rapsodie Espagnole* by Debussy and Ravel respectively? All music of this genre is, after all, impressions rather than photographs. Fanciful postcards. "Nations create music: composers only arrange it," Glinka is supposed to have said. Alas, if only he had, and it were true.

Glinka blazed. At last Russia had its own music, for whatever it was and whatever it represented in the hearts and minds of men.

"Russia first became acquainted with secular singing and secular instru-

---

1 M. Montagu-Nathan, *A History of Russian Music*, William Reeves, London, 1918.

mental music not in life, but in spectacles," quotes Dr. Billington[1]. He cites here a German pastor in 1672 who introduced baroque music to accompany one of his plays. So, it is not surprising that music in Russia even before Glinka, lay with opera. The very grandeur of the Bolshoi structure, built over the years 1821–1825, emblazons this enduring preference, as does the Maryinsky Theatre of 1860. From the eighteenth century, Russian musical taste turned towards Italian opera, with a little French here or there, although the first piece of Western opera ever heard there was by Neapolitan Francesco Araja in 1736, *The Force of Love and Hate*. In 1775 Russians performed in Russian opera, but this opusculum's theme was Greek and its composer was . . . Araja again.

Opera was imported from abroad like a commodity, and even domestic brands were in the hands of aliens. Resident composers in Russia were Italian, Spanish, German, French, or English. They had come to Russia as hired tutors, teachers or performers, and remained in tenure to churn out uninspired facsimiles of the operatic music they first brought from their homelands. Catherine the Great (1729–96), an aspirant librettist (she fancied revising Shakespeare), invited Araja to Russia personally.

The most exceptional among these ragged composers was Catterino Albertovich Cavos (1776–1840). He was the conductor of the Petersburg opera house and would later have the historical honor of conducting Glinka's *A Life for the Tsar*. On his own, he was significant for incorporating local folksongs as themes. Before Glinka, he had composed incidental music to a two-act play on the Ivan Susanin story (Glinka's took five acts and six scenes), and this was his greatest success. P.H. Lang observes that Cavos' "harmonizations were entirely incompatible with the nature of the tunes. Yet, we might say that Cavos set the model for the rising school of Russian composers, a school composed of well-to-do dilettanti."[2]

A host of unknown early operas have been discovered in Leningrad. They were written by Italians, performed once, then forgotten. No hidden geniuses lurk there, according to trustworthy reports, although such names as Baldassare Galuppi (1706–1784), maestro to Catherine's court, and Domenico Cimarosa (1749–1801) appear in the roster.

---

[1] *Op. cit.*
[2] P. H. Lang, *Music in Western Civilization*, W. W. Norton, N.Y. 1941.

Foreign musicians in Russia were called Varangians in an historical reference to the ninth century when the disorganized Slavic peoples voluntarily submitted to the strong Northmen, Normans, Variags, or Varangians. As Russian musicians began to copy this alien Varangian music, they were promptly dubbed "Semi-Varangians," or "native-born foreigners." Many tried like Cavos to create Russian music, but most of their work remained "arrangements" of a scarcely dignified degree. Vaudeville was current, and the word in Russian meant a mixture of songs, dances and comic skits—Varangian-type opera, so to speak, in one spoken and sung act. Audiences of the upper stratum, because they bought tickets, controlled all theater programs. They demanded their loves—either foreign, Varangian opera, or vaudeville. They got them.

— This penchant for "opera" persisted in Russia. Eventually it refined itself. By 1870 Petersburg would have the distinction of the world première of Verdi's *La Forza del Destino*. In 1871 the annual Italian opera company touring Russia starred no less a celebrity than Adelina Patti (1843–1919).

When censorship was lifted from Pushkin's dramatic poem *Boris Godunov*, its first staged representation in 1871 set the keystone for the arch of Russian opera to come, such as Glinka could never have conceived —authenticity, emotional veracity, and the destruction of the last Varangian overtone. Meanwhile, popular opera troupes would sometimes sing Russian folk stories in Italian; just the reverse of conditions today where *Floria Tosca*, for example, (under that title) is always heard in Russian.

During the splendid years from Glinka to the Revolution, when jays doffed their borrowed plumage and their ties to foreign tails were cut, Russian composers still put their finest music in opera. Tchaikovsky wrote ten of them, and they were his chief source of income. His tenderly intellectual *Eugene Onegin* (the heroine reads books), based on Pushkin's strong verses, is magnificent. So is *Queen of Spades*, also from a Pushkin novel. It strangely brews a combination of high society and black superstition, casting auras of eeriness and elegance.

Rimsky-Korsakoff wrote a dozen richly spectacular operas—*Sadko Snow Maiden, Kashchei, May Night, The Tsar's Bride, Tsar Saltan, Kitezh,* the glorious sun-worshiping *Golden Cockerel,* and on and on. Borodin's *Prince Igor* and Mussorgsky's *Boris Godunov* and *Khovanshchina* crown Russia's panoply of opera.

Modest Mussorgsky (1839–1881) was the Russian among Russians, the country's least disciplined composer and its least trained. Yet, his is the one Russian work standing most steadfastly year after year in the repertory of opera houses in Europe and America. While performances of Tchaikovsky are usually poor abroad, *Boris* is often passably played.

Most leading Soviet composers have attempted at least one opera. None has really succeeded. Perhaps the glory of the tradition defeats them. Although Prokofiev (1891–1953) in *Love for Three Oranges* and *Angel of Fire*, and Shostakovich (1906–1975) in *Lady Macbeth of Mzensk* (*Katerina Ismailova*) and *The Nose* wrote fine works, and Prokofiev's *War and Peace* is, to my mind, a semi-masterpiece, internal reports of Soviet music conferences,[1] with their haranguing discussions of policies and aims, reveal how operatic failure nags at the Russian conscience. Still, opera occupies priority on the composing agenda.

There is often a disparity between certain art forms and the inherent ability of their admirers to actualize them. This applies to individuals and nations alike. Despite all the past operas of genius in Russia, the country's nature still resides more in the static cantata or oratorio. (This may be an inheritance from Slavonic church music.) These forms are little appreciated in the impatient West, although Liszt and Wagner (1813–83) both wrote commemorative *pièces d'occasion* with choruses, but have always drawn full glare of attention from Russian musicians.

The dry magnificence of Sergei Taneieff (1856–1915), archimandrite of Russian music (unperformed outside Russia), is best exhibited in his virtually stationary platform opera-trilogy *Orestes*. Before this he had contemplated an oratorical opera *Danton and Orestes*. Anton Arensky's (1861–1906) first work was a cantata, *The Forest Tsar*, and he won a gold medal at the Conservatory for it. Even the greatest Russian operas suffer from patches of motionlessness and they compensate only by sheer beauty of music. Act V of *Ivan Susanin* is a case in point. Here is a vast chorus and the listener finds himself enjoying a costumed concert.

Russians are also disposed towards memorializing with choruses and clustered groups of singing. They accompany their writers with music, but they also paeonize them in their own words and set this to music. Any occasion can elicit musical commemoration. The twenty-fifth or thirty-fifth anniversary of a debut, for example. The sculptor Mark

---

[1] Alexander Werth, *Musical Uproar in Moscow*, Turnstile Press, London, 1949.

Antokolsky (1843–1902) (carver of Peter the Great) was celebrated in music jointly written by Glazunov (1865–1936) and Liadov (1855–1914). Tchaikovsky composed a choral "Welcome to Anton Rubinstein," when he returned from his triumphal tour of America; Glazunov, a "Prologue in Memory of Gogol"; Rachmaninoff (1873–1943) conducted a vast musical "Letter to Stanislavsky" at the time of the twenty-fifth anniversary of the Moscow Art Theater in 1912: Chaliapin soloed.

Prokofiev's cantata honoring the twentieth anniversary of the Bolshevik Revolution was completed in 1937, but displeasing Stalin because of its unmelodious modernity and in spite of its concluding "Ode to Stalin," had to wait twenty-nine years for a performance. (Even then the "Ode" was deleted.) The limited purpose of such tributes prevents them, usually, from being performed more than once. But workmanship and an affinity with opera, stationary and statuesque or not, are nonetheless evident.

Once Russian opera was firmly recognized, a torrent of symphonic music began to flood the country and thence flowed into the mainstream of world music. This too rose from Glinka. He drafted a "Cossack Symphony on Ukrainian Themes," and had he finished, it would have been the first Russian "symphony." Instead, twelve years after his epochal opera, he composed in 1848 an "Overture" for orchestra, based on a popular wedding-dance tune and rhythm known as the "Kamarinskaya." From here, as Tchaikovsky himself perceptively averred—"as the oak is in the acorn" —all subsequent symphonic music of Russia derives. In it is found that Russian transparency of instrumentation, a free and intelligent embodiment of native materials, and most of all, Russia's first confidence in employing the European symphony orchestra as a rightful and independent part of her heritage.

Russia's first real symphony and called as such, appeared late in 1865. Poorly written by a then callow and ambitious Rimsky-Korsakoff, nonetheless it launched the form. Glinka's *Kamarinskaya Overture* eventually culminated in Stravinsky's (1882–1971) *Les Noces*. Rimsky's First Symphony evolved as far afield as, say, Shostakovich's "Leningrad" or Seventh Symphony with its tedious hundred non-stop bars of drumrolls.

Here at midway point we must come to Scriabin (1871–1915). Arthur Lourié (1891–1966), Russian composer and writer, asserts that "until Scriabin arrived Tchaikovsky was the only symphonist in Russian music."[1] This observation is basically correct, although it slights Borodin's (1834–87) two successful symphonies written in the 1880's. Some agree with the critic Sabaneeff (1881–1967), who commented that Scriabin's five orchestral pieces and poems are "false symphonism"[2] or a pseudo-orchestration of unsymphonic ideas and sources. The German authority, Clemens-Christoph von Gleich, however, categorically propounds that, "The most important monuments of Scriabin's symphonic work, the "Poem of Ecstasy" and *Prometheus* still await acceptance by larger circles of the musical world. The performance of *Prometheus* with the keyboard of colors is one of the heavy obligations on the future."[3]

More than to any other Russian, the symphony belongs, obviously, to Tchaikovsky. It is his domain. Who has not loved the Sixth Symphony, the *Pathétique*? But why "pathetic"?

Since this word arises often in Russian music, it is necessary to digress. There is the first, Glinka's "Trio Pathétique" written in 1826, and also Scriabin's famous Etude in D♯ minor, Op. 8, marked *patético*. Curiously too, his Prelude, Op. 59, No. 2 which we know by its marking *sauvage et belliqueux* (savage and bellicose) with its explosions and answering roulades is explained by Russian critics as "pathetic and agitated."

It must be pointed out that Russian *pafos* is not our "pathos." Admitting that Modest Tchaikovsky (1850–1916), the brother, proposed *Pathétique* in French as a subtitle for the symphony, we must still acknowledge its Russian meaning (which is closer to the Greek, "away from suffering," rather than our sense of "pitiful" or wallowing in pain).

Tchaikovsky alone among composers left masterworks in every genre of musical composition. The Moscow Conservatory, where he taught painfully and nervously from its founding in 1866 until 1878, is "named after Tchaikovsky"—the Soviet fashion of honoring their great.

---

1 Arthur Lourié, *Sergei Koussevitsky and his Epoch*, Translated by S. W. Pring, Knopf, New York, 1931.

2 Leonid Sabaneeff, *Scriabin*, State Publishing House, Moscow, 1923.

3 Clemens-Christoph von Gleich, *Die Sinfonischen Werke von Alexander Skrjabin*, A. B. Creyghton, Bilthoven, Holland, 1963.

Early musicians explored other areas than the symphony. Borodin in 1870 produced a stunning string quartet, Russia's first. Overtures, tone-poems, ballets mounted in number. Piano pieces of every form and dimension appeared, among them, that pyrotechnical showpiece by Mily Balakirev (1837–1910), *Islamey*, a piano fantasy and, incidentally, Liszt's favorite piece of Russian music. At the other end of the pole were Scriabin preludes, some "briefer than a sparrow's beak, shorter than a bear's tail."

Concertos flamed into the repertoires of world pianists, and there they have remained. This lineage too was continuous: from Tchaikovsky's three pieces in the genre (one over- and the other two under-played), through all five of Rachmaninoff's velvety "piano symphonies," as he himself spoke of them, to today's modern concertos—honey-tongued Shostakovich, Dmitri Kabalevsky (1904–1987) and Aram Khachaturian (1903–1978).

Additionally, the exponents of Russia's musical literature have been and are peerless. No country has ever established so abundant a roster of performers. At random, let us name: Singers Feodor Chaliapin, the rollicking basso; P. Stravinsky, another popular bass and now best known for his composer-son; Galina Vishnevskaya, Bolshoi soprano; Zara Dolukhanova, contralto; Conductors Serge Koussevitzky, Gennady Rozhdestvensky, Kyril Kondrashin, Evgeny Svetlanov; Violinists Leopold Auer (Hungarian by birth but a professor at the Petersburg Conservatory), Mischa Elman, Efrem Zimbalist, Bronislaw Huberman, Jascha Heifetz, Nathan Milstein, David and Igor Oistrakh, Leonid Kogan; Cellist Mstislav Rostropovich (husband of Vishnevskaya); and pianists galore, various Rubinsteins from Anton on, Josef Hofmann (pupil for two-and-a-half years of Anton Rubinstein in Dresden), Annette Essipoff (a Leschetizky wife), Rachmaninoff, Scriabin, Ossip Gabrilovich, Mark Hambourg, Josef Lhevinne, Vladimir Horowitz, Emil Gilels, Lev Oborin, Sviatoslav Richter, Dmitri Bashkirov, Vladimir Ashkenazy, Lazar Berman, Nicolai Petrov . . . and dozens of others representing every department of musical performance.

With regard to the Russian school of pianism and composing for piano "that came forth from Imperial Russia," Arthur Loesser observes the paradox that "in 1910 Russian piano production and consumption amounted to less than six percent of that of the United States, thus revealing the relative insignificance of the prosperous urban middle class in the vast empire." But *where* the pianos were truly counted.

Russian music, whether pre- or post-Revolution, local or émigré, had arcane rarefactions, not only in expatriate experiments such as Stravinsky's serialism, but even in the miscegenations of politics and art encouraged by the Soviets. Electronic music too grew in the USSR, and there are also pieces of immense complexity only now being played and listened to.

One nearly incomprehensible and extraordinary product is the music of Nikolai Obukhov (1892–1954), an outgrowth of Scriabin. He wrote scores in red ink for blood, and notated hisses, shrieks, and screams as well as tones. His *La Livre de Vie* (Book of Life), a forerunner of Olivier Messiaen (1908–1992) and perhaps Gunther Schuller (b. 1925), both of whom according to Wilfred Mellers, "are still under the spell of Scriabinic sonorities,"[1] is based on "sounds which by their purity and absolutism attain, as it were, a sacred character."[2] The chords are dodecaphonic and use the twelve tones simultaneously. Spiritually "Universalist" in concept, the music was supposed to recall Christ to Earth . . . literally.

This outlandish thinking reached American shores too. Scriabin, for instance, developed a doctrine (*uchenie*) not unrelated to a Kantian *Conceptus Cosmica* or a Swedenborgian *Arcana Celestia*. Pianist Katherine Ruth Heyman introduced Scriabin's thought and music to Charles Ives (1874–1954), and he understood both, as a piece such as "The Unanswered Question" *inter alia* indicates. Perhaps all this was in turn-of-the-century air.

---

[1] Alec Harman and Wilfred Mellers, *Man and His Music*, Vol. III, Barrie and Rockliff, London, 1962.
[2] Nikolai Obouchoff, "*L'Emotion dans la Musique*," *Révue Musicale*, Paris, May 1927.

II

ATMOSPHERE

To ENLARGE our picture of musical Russia, let us return to its heydays and observe the country's atmosphere historically.

Perhaps the most determining factor in Russia's pre-Petrine history was a scar—the invasion and long domination by Tatars. Genghis Khan began life as a petty chieftain of an obscure Mongol tribe, but by 1222 he had dispatched his grandson, Batu Khan, from as far east as Mongolia and the borders of China to as far west as European Russia itself. In 1240 a nephew of the Khan crushed Kiev. For two hundred years, until Muscovite Grand Duke Ivan III (1440–1505)—the first ruler to be called by history "the Great"—refused to pay tribute in 1480, these Tatars ruled intensively. Even after, in 1572 the Tatars burned Moscow, as they had also done in 1382 and would do again in 1409. Ivan the Terrible actually surrendered his throne and title, Tsar, to the Tatar Khan in 1575.

Mongols were the "Scourge of God," but their Tatar khanate was so magnificent, with tents so lavishly accoutered on the banks of the Volga that the word "Golden Horde" spread both in acknowledgment of the wealth and the color of their skins. Beyond these masters lay reinforcements in Central Asia—the Blue Horde.

Tatar power in the course of the fourteenth to sixteenth centuries dwindled into a loose control system over a gradually diminishing territory. However, Russia still existed in the name of the khan. Khans were Tatar leaders, descendants of Genghis. They employed Jews, Armenians, and Chinese to collect taxes, register the subjected Russians, and administer punishments along with the nation's affairs. One day Russian orthodoxy would, perversely enough, thank the Tatars for saving it from the theological distortions of Western Europe. A play written in the nineteenth century even shows an attentive Ivan the Terrible being educated by a khan. *Ex oriente lux.*

Humiliation at Tatar hands stained the Russian mind. Dostoevsky invariably refers to them as "The Unclean." The word for "hypocrisy" in Russian is *khanzhenstvo* or "khanishness." The word for "darkness" or "unenlightenment" (*t'ma*) is Tatar for "military district." Hair pulling, breast beating, as well as the prostration where you touch your forehead to the floor, were all Asiatic rather than Western customs, and Russia used them for its own extremes of emotion.

Doubtless the origin of anti-semitism dates from the time of the Tatars. The word *pogrom*, after all, is Russian—meaning "destruction." The kremlins which dot the center of most main cities of Russia are also reminders of subjugation. Originally these were anti-Tatar fortifications with fourteen-foot walls and dozens of lookout towers, and offering refuge in time of siege by the atrocious enemy whose collaborators were so deceptive.

Count Hermann Keyserling (1880–1946), a German philosophical writer of tremendous importance during post-World War I, was the first to mention publicly that Russians by race are the only Slavs with an admixture of Asiatic blood. "Scratch a Russian to find a Tatar." Even Lenin referred to "our Asiatic and barbarous land," as did other soul-searching, self-lacerating Russian intellectuals of the nineteenth century. Gogol had been the first to bemoan this split between the East and West.

In the 1830's the Slavophiles appeared. No more "liberal sniggering" at Russians, they cried. Now Russia glorified herself as the leader of mankind. Why? Because they, as Slavs and Russians, stood between the East and the West. On one hand they "preached the erection of a sort of spiritual Chinese Wall around Russia and sought the economic salvation of this vast country in the primitive agricultural commune of the Russian peasants and the no less primitive cooperative associations of Russian handicraftsmen."[2] On the other, these Russians wanted to infuse Europe with the "fresh and powerful sap of the Slavic East." Russia had escaped the curses of Europe—violence and competition, they said. These ardent pan-Slavists believed that Westernization was a deviation from the true course, and Tatarizing a part of a negligible past.

---

[1] David Magarshack, *op. cit.*

Slavophiles glorified Russia's indigenous specialities of autocracy and orthodoxy. They wanted to convert the Godless West. Turgenev, "the greatest European of his time," as David Magarshack perhaps denigrates him, caustically described one leader of Slavophiles as "that clever Muscovite . . . who raves about old Russian palaces and ancient Russian princes, expects regeneration from his skullcap, eats turnips, curses the peoples of Western Europe." This same Slavophile dressed "nationally" with an embroidered skullcap for authenticity, and the joke went round Moscow that people in the street took him for a Persian.[1]

In the 1840's, a reaction of "Westernizers" flourished. Still later, an even more extreme form of Slavophilism was to rise, Eurasianism. It reaffirmed that true Russia, the real Russia, stemmed from the Tatars of Asia, that Russia's roots were in Mongol Asia, and by virtue of this special fact the country was unique. Light from the East, they shouted as watchword. How the Muslim religion of the Tatars could be harmonized with Russian orthodoxy defies the rational mind. But it was all part of *sobornost'* (communality), the union of all within the one.

Scriabin, like many of his contemporaries exploiting this speciality of Russia rather than remaining ashamed of it, embraced Eurasianism. At the expense of God, of course, and even of Asia. He was most proprietary: "*I* am more truly Asian than Hanako," he said after seeing Rodin's Japanese mistress dance, and promptly played a most sophisticated and cosmopolitan Poem (in F# major, Op. 32). Nor was he disturbed by the "rising yellow race." When Japan defeated Russia in 1905 on the fields and in the war waters, he recognized it as a process of natural events, without losing a shred of patriotism. "This is only the beginning . . ." he said, expecting the apocalypse, and for him, *that* came with World War I.

He was also desirous of having his final composition performed in India. He was unaware of the absence of taste for serious Western music there. He thought it a Theosophists' wonderland. Such pro-Asiatic attitudes of Eurasianists were subscribed to by other coevals of Scriabin, the celebrated painter Vasily Kandinsky (1866–1944), for one. He boasted that

---

[1] *Ibid.*

his father was Siberian and his great-grandmother a Mongolian princess.[1] The distinguished literary critic, Prince D. S. Mirsky, was an Eurasianist as late as 1931.[2] Eurasianism even turned into pan-Asianism. Dostoevsky in his famous speech of 8 June, 1880, claimed Pushkin alone among writers had the ability to embody the genius of foreign peoples. "His *Imitations from the Koran* are Mohammedan: his *Egyptian Nights* are the ancient world as it was," he avowed (most incorrectly), and the audience cheered (most foolishly). The first piece of music five-and-a-half-year-old Prokofiev wrote was a "Hindu Galop."

Simultaneously, an antithetical aspect emerged—the "Universalists," pan-humanists, members of omni-humanity. These were spearheaded by Russia's greatest and almost only philosopher, Vladimir Solovyov (1853–1900). No more magnitudinous star exists in Russian thought, yet he dreaded a "pan-Mongolism" resurgence, and mortally opposed the Slavophiles. He exhorted Christian Russia to unite with Christian Europe to stave the potential resurrection of another Golden Horde. His acolyte in this too was Dostoevsky, who sometimes felt that brotherly love could cure the world's ills. Make no mistake, the Universalists meant Europeans—Aryans and Christians only. All these mystical principles and theories based on geographical determinism have since been discredited, but their unsated specters reappear in contemporary politics in many guises and with varying degrees of force.

Communism in politics also shouted an earth-encompassing song. Nikolai Berdyaev (1874–1948), philosopher and anti-Soviet emigrant, pointed out, perhaps regretfully, how the whole history of the Russian intelligentsia from the middle of the nineteenth century to the beginning of the twentieth "prepared for Communism."[3] Reactionary, Francophiliac Turgenev wrote of revolutionary forces in every novel. Nor were musicians aloof.

The Marxist *History of Russian Music* seized on these facts. Without deviating from the truth, the dialectically materialistic musicologist,

---

[1] Kenneth C. Lindsay, "Kandinsky in Russia," Kandinsky, A Retrospective Exhibition, The Solomon R. Guggenheim Museum, New York, 1962.

[2] D. S. Mirsky, *Pushkin*, Introduction by George Siegel, Dutton and Co., New York, 1963.

[3] Nikolai Berdyaev, *Origins and Significance of Russian Communism*, Paris, 1955; also *The Mind of Modern Russia (Historical and Political Thought of Russia's Great Age)*, Harper Torchbook, The Academy Library, Harper, New York, 1955.

Y. Kedysh, emphasized his point:

> Russian classical music developing in close consort with the social life and literature of its time reveals itself as one of the indefeasible aspects of our chief national culture. It reflects a common idea for all democratic peoples ... All paths of development in Russian classical music are linked without a break to the growth of the liberation movement in Russia ... The creativity of the great Russian composers of the past was nourished by the noble and patriotic ideals of serving the people and struggling for their freedom from autocratic, land-owning, and bourgeois oppression. Finding themselves in the center of the main interests of contemporary social activity, the composers heatedly and immediately answered the call of all significant events in the homeland's life.

The thought lasted well beyond its time. Here is Boris Pasternak (1890-1960) singing in 1943:

> ... Moscow is dearer than the whole wide world
> ... at the primal source
> Of all with which the century shall flower.

Progressive Russians charged the Orient in them for many of their unpleasant inheritances—their extended use of corporal punishment, the knout, seton, kowtowing, the tyrannical patriarchy of the family system, the adhesive and superstitious religious practices that so deformed Russian orthodoxy, the imposition of reform autocratically from the top without concern for the human cost below, as well as the exclusion of women from mixed company, as prescribed in the *Domostroy* book regulating behavior.

But credit is also due for the feeling of world unity for instance, international and interracial brotherhood that the name Eurasia implies. Musically, the fact of Asia-in-Russia proliferated as compositional sources of inspiration. It paved an aesthetic road for Oriental themes, exotic program-plots, and fabulous tonal colorations. What more provident recourse for flamboyance in music could there be?

One has only to glance at the titles of Russian compositions, or read the synopses of their ballets, to find an intimate association with the historical past of Southern, Eastern and Asiatic geography. Stassov himself wrote of "the Oriental element ... Nowhere in Europe does it assume such an important role as it does among our musicians. This is not surprising when one considers the totality of Oriental influences and characteristic colorings in manifestations of Russian life."[1]

What was Alexandrine Russia like in mid-nineteenth century? There had been many opportunities of military conquest. Take the Crimean War (1845–1855). It was a push to the West, a bid for European power; Russia needed an outlet to the Mediterranean Sea. England and France wanted to defeat the giant and keep her slumbering. This was their belated revenge against Tsar Paul I (1754–1801), who had plotted with Napoleon to strike at England via India.

Internally, there was the long conquest of the Caucasus (1857–1859). The Turkish Wars, all of them as far as 1877 were also successful, though the outsider, Field Marshal Count von Moltke (1800–1891) called them "conflicts between the one-eyed and the blind." Ostensibly the Russians wanted to protect Christians from persecution by heathen Turks. The result was her free access to and hold over the Bosphorus and the Dardanelles. The one-eyed won.

At home, the remaining Tatars had become vagrants, itinerant pedlars selling hand-embroidered dressing gowns and soaps along the Volga riverside. Chekhov tried a newspaper exposé of how Russians lorded over them and kept them uneducated. Half of Russia's entire population —23,000,000 serfs—had been liberated in 1861 (before the American Civil War, note), with the ensuing economic adjustment. Landowners had to pay for labor for the first time in their lives.

Traffic in selling male serfs, enumerated by the word "souls" (as British sailors are counted in "bodies"), was discontinued with still further disruption of the economy, as Gogol's *Dead Souls* presaged. Until mid- and late nineteenth century, people such as Turgenev's mother had the legal right—and she exercised it—to beat a serf to death. On city streets however, His Gracious Majesty the Tsar had in a grand concession finally permitted smoking for his people. But command performances at the opera were sparsely attended. People feared on such nights bomb-plots against the monarch. You could still occasionally see a stark naked man emerging from a tavern where he had pawned his last item of clothing for a drink. Or, more infrequently, a woman might cool off, naked, outside one of the ubiquitous bathhouses.

---

[1] James Bakst, *op. cit.*

In the intellectual world, Pushkin, Gogol, and Mikhail Lermontov (1814–1841), lyric poet and novelist, had all made their mark and passed on. Dostoevsky and Turgenev were rising. So was Tolstoi. He began his writer's career as a war reporter in the Crimea. Soon, Chekhov would depict the "gray life" of the end of the nineteenth century. Glinka-originated and Glinka-anchored music flourished. The azimuth of Russia's musical individualism was set. Meanwhile, all sophisticated life for all of Asiatic and European Russia—that span of ten thousand miles—fluctuated between two large, rival cities—St. Petersburg and Moscow—four hundred miles from each other.

St. Petersburg was begun in 1703. Six-foot-eight in height, and even taller in mind, Peter the Great, after growing up in the "foreign suburbs" of Moscow and after an eye-opening journey incognito into Europe itself, built this artificially conceived, precisely executed capital on the marshy banks of the Neva River. Its gridiron layout is still unique in Europe. He sited it in the north, remote from any Tatar hint, and smack on the formerly Swedish-held shores of the Gulf of Finland.

When not frozen in winter, Petersburg's waters open into the Baltic Sea and from there to the Western Europe of Holland, France and England. Peter hired Italian architects for his buildings. The stones themselves were imported too, from Finland. The Italians painted them and their plaster rococo handiworks in colors of fantasy—apple greens, soft russets, rose, pale pinks, and turquoise blue. The city was and still is miraculously beautiful. In truth, Pushkin's immortal poem about Peter, *The Bronze Horseman*, says "To cut a window into Europe" (*V Evropu prorubit' okno*), and this is what St. Petersburg did.

Slavophiles and their successionist Eurasianists, who preferred inward living behind shut doors and closed windows, excoriated Peter's enforced Europeanization. Old-fashioned Russians considered their beards "passports to heaven" (like Chinese pigtails), and Peter threatened his boyars with shaving, to make them obey. He outlawed long coats merely because they looked oriental. A terrible flood the year of his death proved to the orthodox his evil-doing. However, Elizabeth (1709–62), Peter's youngest daughter and really reaper of the Petrine cultural harvest of things Western, founded the country's first university (in Moscow in 1755) and in St. Petersburg an Academy of Sciences.

Catherine "the Great, Wise, Mother of the Fatherland" followed both their leads into fulfillment. She forcibly propagated potatoes (as Peter had introduced smoking) from Europe, and to celebrate her smallpox vaccination she declared the date an official feastday. Through the "window" Russians looked westward for civilization, culture, conveniences, progress, learning, medicine, and social reform as a whole. By means of these, they could divert attention away from the Tatar-impoverished, Asiatically backward south and west.

Thanks to both the man and patron of Petersburg, the phrase *na zapadu* —it lingers, and means "to the West"—became rampageous fashion. Yet the West was the very area Peter the Great had vowed his country would "one day put to shame." The upper classes vacillated between being put to shame by Western superiority and vindicating themselves against the West in the West. There had always been feeling against Europe, though. After all, the "medicine" known as vodka had arrived in the fourteenth century, and in the fifteenth, the "Latin sickness" or syphilis—both from abroad. Still, the first real Russian poetry, for example, sprang from Thomas Gray's "Elegy" translated by Vasily Zhukovsky (1788–1852), who became an olympian poet himself and forger of the Russian language. The first translations, however, had been earlier—Aesop's fables.

Many Russians merely succumbed and aped the West. They found there the only life suitable for them. Russia was intolerable. They became "spreading whortleberries," the sour fruit that springs up everywhere on any soil and requires no planting or care. These were the words, the epithet, for Russians who moved abroad and headquartered themselves in Europe.

Even Glinka was embarrassed by his country's backwardness. He left Russia in search of "peace of mind, music, and self-respect." After crossing the border, he stopped the carriage and spat—towards the Russian side. Turgenev wrote his good-byes from abroad in his *Reminiscences*, "I hated the very air I breathed . . . leave me in peace a little while longer! I shall come back to your steppes!"[1] Both Turgenev with his *Sportsman's Diary* and Gogol with *Dead Souls* claimed they could not have written these first works (picturing Russia, mind) without having left for abroad,

---

[1] David Magarshack, *op. cit.*

to put a certain distance between themselves and their enemy, Russia (their word). "Farewell, unwashed Russia . . . " cried Lermontov. Turgenev professed later love for his country calling it *"cara patria,"* like that, in Italian. Borodin writing from St. Petersburg to his Belgian friend, Countess de Mercy-Argenteau, and first patroness of Russian music abroad, depicted Russians to her as "eaters of tallow candles, Polar bears, too long consumers of foreign products . . . "[1] And Chekhov was nearly arrested for calling Russia "swinish."

While Slavophiles spoke of Russia as the regenerator of the world, going abroad *na zapadu* remained obligatory for the landed, the aristocratic, the intellectual, the ill, the politically minded, and the *zapadniki* (the Westernized ones). Sometimes these journeys were impelled by a feeling of being "superfluous," otiose, that curse of idleness described in several Russian novels. Goncharov's *Oblomov* (1857) was the first work to show the indolence of an intelligent gentleman with no place or energy in his homeland. Sometimes travel was to escape the sickness of boredom, alysosis, another scourge of Russian life transmuted into literature, art and music with piercing strokes of genius.

Russia was short of amusements, save for gossip, parties, and alcohol. Boys' fistfights in the street were popular spectator shows. So were dwarfs, puppeteers and beggar minstrels. One sport was to set fire to drunkards' beards as they lay in the street. But such silliness could not absorb the talents or emotions of the Westernized "returnees." Dostoevsky compared a Russian's trip outside Russia to "hating and beating your mother at the same time." His *Idiot* ends with an indictment, "We abroad are a delusion."

But Dostoevsky too, like all the rest, voyaged restlessly. His Slavophilism was scorched half-a-century later by Trotsky (1879–1940), who called it the "Messianism of backwardness." It was also an inversion of inferiority. Tolstoi in *War and Peace* recites a telling musical moment when Natasha sings particularly well. Her German music master, Dimmler (an actual Varangian of the time—the detail is authentic), living in the Rostov household, exclaims to her mother, "Ah, Countess, that's a European talent. She has nothing to learn. What softness, tenderness, and

---

1 Rosa Newmarch, *The Russian Opera*, Dutton, New York, 1906.

strength . . . "[1] This inferiority before the West seemed endemic to Russia. A German apostrophized Peter the Great's father to his face as, "the incomparable Tsar who loves our German people more than Russians."[2]

St. Petersburg, abbreviated popularly into SPb (on coins and elsewhere) or "Piter" in conversation (Pushkin apotheosized it as "Petropol"), retained this appellation until World War I. Then the hateful German "burg" (Dutch really, from Sankt Piter Bourkh) was Russified into the Slavonic "grad," and the city renamed Petrograd. It was "Peter's City" still, but no longer after the saint in heaven but now the sanctified Peter the Great, brave founder, patron, and protector on earth. Afterwards, the city became Leningrad, so-called after yet another Westward-looking scorner of the West. The biographies of many musicians in encyclopedias read: Born in St. Petersburg, grew up in Petrograd, and died in Leningrad. Now it is St. Petersburg once again.

The city of Peter in mid-nineteenth century has been well described with its glimmering boreal clime, endlessly long white nights in summer when the sun never sets, alternating with stingingly sharp, damp and cold winters. Rivers and canals linked the streets of the city and froze regularly. They became additional routes for sleighs. Tarantasses, *drozhki* or *isvoshchiki* pulled by troikas of horses and smelling of leather and furs glided passengers along iced-over streetways. Ladies' sleighs were trimmed in red satin. Horses wore foxtails for decorations. Gentlemen rode sitting in gold-studded saddles.

Double-windows and two-doors of houses shut out the zero weather and muted the city's noises, which had already been blanketed by the falling snow into cottonlike quiet. Outside, eternal shouts of foul-mouthed drivers lured fares, and whores brazenly called to passers-by. The "Passage," famous in journalism and literature, was an arcade for prostitutes. You could purchase children there—either for adoption or a night's fornication. In the city's outskirts, residents of SPb hunted wild goats, wolves and foxes. The Petrine "Thaw" was annually blamed by doctors for "shattering the nerves" already exacerbated by the long winter.

The center of life there was the tsar. The word derives from "Caesar,"

1 Leo Tolstoi, *War and Peace*, Translated by Louise and Aylmer Maude, Simon and Schuster, New York, 1942.
2 James Billington, *op. cit.*

and was used to establish superiority over the Roman Catholic Church, rival of the Greek and Byzantine Orthodox Church which Russia had perfected into rigidity. The tsars traced their lineage back to Emperor Augustus Julius Caesar (63 B.C.–A.D. 14). This did not seem unlikely either, since Odessa, the southern port on the Black Sea, derived from the even older Odysseus.

The tsar's court was alluded to exaltedly as "The Spheres," relating it to the galactic, heavenly bodies of princes and princesses surrounding the sun and moon of tsar and tsarina.

St. Petersburg was thus the social and administrative capital of the country. Its officials high and low arbitrated decorum as far as the provinces. Their number was legion and legendary. Generals and admirals wore uniforms of silver and purple with sashes and cross-ribbons of gold and crimson. So did clerks at a ministry. Rising in these government circles, however, was hard for any person with a non-Slavic name.

Behind the façade of the city, life balefully teemed. Arriving travelers by sea or train had to procure police clearance to take a cab anywhere in the city. Everyone carried passports, even for inland travel. Moscow-born Dostoevsky, who perceived the total of Russia with a frightening acumen, gives St. Petersburg one passingly devastating sentence: "There are few places where there are so many gloomy, strong and queer influences on the soul of man as in Petersburg."[1] Symbolist poet and novelist Andrey Biely (1880–1934) wrote half a century later of it still as the "city of insomnia, cigarettes, and alcohol. . . . "[2] So did acmeist poet Osip Mandelstam (1880–1938): "Living in Petersburg is to sleep in a coffin,"[3] he wrote.

Inland, the other capital, the Asiatic capital, lay thousand-year-old Moscow. So different; so similar and twice the size of St. Petersburg. This is

---

[1] F. Dostoevsky, *Crime and Punishment*, Translated by Constance Garnett, Macmillan, New York, 1929.

[2] Andrey Biely, *St. Petersburg*, Translated by John Cournos with an introduction by George Reavey, Grove Press, New York, 1959.

[3] Translated by Robert Lowell. Cited by Olga Carlisle, Book Week, New York Herald Tribune, 9 January, 1966.

Moscow as Napoleon saw it in 1812 from Sparrow Hills (later Lenin Hills) and entered it to spend overnight and then depart: "*Moscou, la capitale asiatique de ce grand empire, la ville sacrée des peuples d'Alexandre, Moscou avec ses innombrables églises en forme de pagodes chinoises*"[1] (Moscow, Asiatic capital of this great empire, sacred city of Emperor Alexander's people, Moscow with its countless churches shaped like Chinese pagodas).

"Moscow," wrote Mussorgsky, "the world has never produced such rogues and beggars . . ."[2] He, the one exception among musicians who never traveled outside Russia, addressed his letter to Balakirev, strange, great musician who almost singlehandedly kept Russian music Russian when St. Petersburg's "window into Europe" was letting in too much light. "Oh Moscow," said Tchaikovsky to his brother, "the instant one arrives, one is expected to get drunk."[3] Chekhov in a letter dated 13 August, 1888, railed, "Moscow with its cold, its rotten plays, restaurants, and Russian thoughts terrifies my imagination. I would willingly live the winter as far as possible from it."[4] Traditionally, as Dr. Billington finds, there were "two of the most widespread moral irregularities of Muscovite society: alcoholism and sexual perversion."[5]

Moscow, like Rome or San Francisco, is built on seven hills. It was surrounded by six fortified monasteries manned by "black" or celibate and military monks. At its heart—the heart within the heart—is that pentagon built by Italians in 1580, the Kremlin. The outskirts are little changed today, and give an impression of what all Moscow was once like. Streets of "asphalt made of sunflower seeds, roads with goosegrass in the cracks, dark elms and silver-grey birches . . ."[6] Russians invented prefabricated houses in the seventeenth century, because of the enemies of frost and fire, and today's little wooden homes are still warped by the dry extremes of alternate cold and heat. They look as if they had been crazily blown by Siberian winds sweeping clean across the plains. They are painted too,

[1] Quoted in Tolstoi's *War and Peace, op. cit.*
[2] M. D. Calvocressi and Gerald Abraham, *op. cit.*
[3] Catherine Drinker Bowen and Barbara Von Meck, *Beloved Friend*, Random House, New York, 1937.
[4] E. J. Simmons, *op. cit.*
[5] *op. cit.*
[6] Konstantin Paustovsky, *The Story of a Life*, Translated by Joseph Barnes, Simon and Schuster, New York, 1964.

but the blue has faded. Bright paper cutouts of flowers and animals are pasted on the windows. Even now, rugs and tapestries hang gaudily outside windows on festival days as if to cancel the dead whiteness of winter.

Moscow has been epitomized as "the city of forty times forty churches." It is still speckled with golden onion-shaped domes, zigzag crosses, peppermint canes of gaily striped columns. Church bells "boom," as remarked by Avrahm Yarmolinsky, "so different from the thin chimes of Western churches."[1] Moscow was called the "Third Rome," implying that the true faith had fled from the Pope, through Byzantium or Constantinople, to Moscow.

Ivan the Great at the end of the fifteenth century was assured by the pious monk Filofei, "two Romes have fallen . . . there shall be no fourth!" This was what gave him superstitious and false courage to suspend fealties to the Tatar khanate. Religious observance was such that orthodox Greek visitors called living in Russia "suicide, for no one except Russians could remain standing for such long hours at church services and remain almost without food during the seven weeks of Lent."[2] Until the Revolution, going to church for a Muscovite meant that an ardent believer could attend a service a day, each day in a different place, and such piety could take months, and often did. So hidebound was orthodoxy in the seventeenth century that correcting translation errors in the Bible, in particular the gross misspelling of Jesus' name, caused a major schism with the "Old Believers."

Leonid Sabaneeff contrasts the two cities succinctly as Moscow "city of landowners and merchants," and St. Petersburg a city of "aristocracy and officialdom." However, Moscow had its grand dukes invested with their titles and their power by the Tatar khans and supported by the wealth of the boyars or lesser nobles around them. These were "Great Princes" (*velikiye knyazy*) with all their subtitles—"the Proud," "the Terrible" (meaning "stormy," not evil), "the False." Peter was one; so was Ivan the Great. However, Muscovites referred like awed peasants to the tsar in St. Petersburg as "Father" (*batyushka-tsar*), as if they could

1 Avrahm Yarmolinsky, *Dostoevsky*, Grove Press, New York, 1934.
2 Arthur Voyce, *Moscow and the Roots of Russian Culture*, The Centers of Civilization Series, University of Oklahoma Press, Norman, Oklahoma, 1964.

never aspire to "The Spheres." Petersburgers themselves and the intelligentsia would never use so crude a form of address.

Maxim Gorky (1868–1936) apostrophized Moscow as "the broad heart of all Russia." Having no window, Moscow looked entirely within itself or southeastwards to the Tatar yesterday. The city winds itself around its namesake, the Moscow River, crossed by hunchback bridges, and connecting quickly in tribute to the Oka and to the wide Volga. Mother Volga cleaves Russia in two: European and Asiatic Russia, Western and Eastern. The longest river in Europe, it meanders for more than two thousand miles to the south and empties eventually into the Caspian Sea, famous for its sturgeon and fine-grained caviar. The land there smells of roses and black earth, and yields perpetual summer fruit. The inhabitants include Persians, Turks, gypsies, and remnants of Tatar tribes. When the Moscow River flooded, as it used to from year to year, dust, a curse of Moscow, turned to mud. Streets became impassable. Papers and valuables within houses were often water-soaked and ruined.

Oskar von Riesemann (1880–1934), German musical writer and correspondent for the *Moskauer Deutsche Zeitung* (Moscow German News), who spent from 1899 to 1917 in Russia, once called Moscow "a State within a State, a world unto itself."[1] However, since it was Russia, it shared similarities with St. Petersburg. Ice rinks were meeting places for lovers. Trams were drawn by horses. Schools shut down when the thermometer sank too low. Tap water was contaminated. Tchaikovsky committed suicide by deliberately drinking a single glass of unfiltered water, it is said.

Cholera raged epidemically. Adults were subject to children's diseases —diphtheria, scarlet fever, mumps—and died of them. Houses reeked from being scrubbed with carbolic acid. Garbage was flung into the open streets helterskelter for sometime collection. The stench from pothouses was, those who remember say, unbearable. At night both cities stank of gas and kerosene, bedsheets and sex. Electricity was still a novelty, although a Russian, Alexander Ladygin, had invented its use in 1874. In 1892 Rachmaninoff made his debut at the first Electric Exposition. Even then illumination was from crude oscillating carbon arcs. As for

---

1 Oskar von Riesemann, *Rachmaninoff's Recollections as told to Oskar von Riesemann*, Translated by Mrs. Dolly Rutherford, Macmillan, New York, 1934.

theater, both cities before the turn of the century had seen a major hit, *Lear*, played in German with Ira Aldrige, a Negro, acting the lead.

In summer, St. Petersburg and Moscow were infested with flies. Flocks of pigeons hovered ceaselessly over the Kremlin and palaces, soiling them with droppings. Everyone who could afford it deserted to the country-side. Serial publication of novels in the magazines, customary at the time, was discontinued, because no one was in town to read them and the mails were unreliable.

"What can be worse than Moscow in the summer?" moaned Rachmaninoff to his poetess and lady correspondent, Marietta Shagynian.[1] The country, near and far, meant birch woods, ponds or sea, bathing and *cures d'eau*, boating, croquet, borzoi dogs, estates with their own vast parks of shrubs and peopled with nude statuary. Middle-class Russians rented half-brick, half-wooden houses with sun verandas, or caretaker huts, and some even converted peasant dwellings, whose windowless kitchens still had the "black half," the area where light from the door never reached, into *dacha* summer cottages. Dogcarts hauled provisions from village stores. Peasants chewed sunflower seeds incessantly.

Thunderstorms shaking the countryside's complacency announced the end of summer. Mushrooms disappeared, and the national recreation of picking them stopped. Summer's over. Return to the city. For musicians, country life was vital. It was then that they could practice or compose undistractedly without the winter pressure of earning their keep by teaching, proofreading, copying, or other employment. Summertime was worktime, but at what they found pleasurable.

Common to the social life of both capitals was extravagant entertainment. A special breed of man played host. This was the maecenases or wealthy patrons of art and artists. They gave banquets which lasted from midnight to dawn. The circumstances would be special and lively when a protégé returned from abroad *na zapadye*, or if a new piece of music by an acquaintance was performed privately, publicly, or even to be published. Guests "trans-cognacked" or "trans-champagned" themselves, meaning they drank to unconsciousness, in Mussorgsky's words. String quartets and their performers were launched in alcohol, like ships christened in champagne.

---

1 Victor I. Seroff, *Rachmaninoff*, Simon and Schuster, New York, 1960.

At ordinary dinner parties, of a mean dozen courses say, invitees spent whole nights playing "commercial cards," or less delicately put, they gambled for high stakes. Gogol once sighed, "The card table—solace of all Russia." People danced mazurkas at cotillions, drank barley coffee, drew tea water from samovars and sweetened it with jam. They talked high ideas from the depths of their soul, sitting in high-back "Voltaire chairs." Such inner scrutiny saved life after life from emotional and mental collapse, while the riotous party-going hastened physical and psychic deterioration.

In St. Petersburg rich men shaved their beards to look Westernized. Peter the Great removed the Church Patriarch's edict making shaving a heresy. In Moscow among the nationalists, the maecenases sported long, hanging beards and they wore ankle-length greatcoats of sable and bearskin. Maecenases acted as they pleased. They flouted custom or yielded to it at their whim. Their fortunes were established by their fathers or grandfathers. They had only to administer their inheritance. Nor were they bound by social decrees from "The Spheres." Church and State looked to them for support, rather than they looking there for protection. They used this money-bought power and freedom for good.

The expansive emotionalism of the Russian maecenas is unique in history. Turgenev pointed out that, "Only in Russia is the maecenas amusing, incredible, yet actually existing." They were not just the rich, supporting necessitous artists. They were knowledgeable and held to a clear sense of private taste. Their generosity was truly selfish.

Beethoven expressed the artist's problem well. "It is good to mingle among aristocrats," he said meaning the rich, "but one must know how to impress them." But maecenases took delight in exercising their own ideas and inclinations. If some of their swans turned out to be geese, there was still honor in the mistake.

Chaliapin spoke warmly of the Russian maecenas of his generation, "How good he was . . . a protector of art in the fullest sense . . . He loved art with his heart and soul . . ."[1] Dozens of them existed in both capitals by the end of the nineteenth century. Their names form a veritable history of Russian art, and their houses and palaces were often preserved as museums under the Soviets: Belaieff, adored timber merchant, early

[1] Feodor Chaliapin, *Pages From My Life*, Translated by H. M. Buck, Harper's, 1927.

publisher of Russian music; Tretyakov, Mayor of Moscow, who gave the city his collection of Russian paintings, (Siloti married a daughter) Mamontov, who spent his railways fortune (much income derived from pilgrimage or penitential trains to monasteries) on an opera company of his own; Ushkov, entrepreneur of tea and chemicals, whose money made Koussevitzky's career possible; Polyakov, collector of paintings and founder of the publishing house "Scorpion" and editor of "Scales"; Solodovnikov, a merchant's son who built the present Moscow Conservatory for 200,000 rubles; Sabbas Morozov, who supported the Moscow Art Theater and whose estate was as lavish as the Vatican, according to Chekhov, and Varvara Morozova, his wife, whose favorite charity was a "Committee on Literacy"; Shchukin, art collector and intimate of French impressionists, who founded with his brother the Museum of Russian Antiquities, and supplier of the core of the Hermitage Museum's modern masterpieces; Sabashnikov, who used his wealth to publish books; Bakhrushin, collector and creator of Russia's first Theater Museum; Alexeyev, industrialist and father of Konstantin Stanislavsky, whose money eventually created the Moscow Art Theater; and, in even better remembered times, Sergei Diaghilev (1872–1929).

These men were not artists, but like their protégés they wept over an artistic failure as if it were their own, and grew arrogant in a success of music. In their manses they wreathed the busts of artist-friends with laurels, and on great occasions of fame abroad they and their guests burnt candles before them like living ikons. Their manners were copied even in Soviet Russia. Yevgeny Yevtushenko (b. 1933) and Khachaturian are masters of the maecenas' technique of the grand gesture.

Basting the fabric of St. Petersburg and Moscow together was the life of foreigners and foreignisms, although it was only in 1850 that a railroad was built connecting the two cities. Foreigners in Moscow originally were confined to a district northeast of the Kremlin, called German suburb, and long after English goldsmiths and Swedish merchants had joined the foreign community, the original name stayed.

Now in both cities, Germans appearing at every turn were chemists, doctors, clockmakers (they also introduced the pipe organ to Russia), private secretaries, bandmasters, mercenaries, and music teachers. They put weathervanes atop the Russian orthodox jagged double-crosses.

The French occupied posts as governesses, restaurateurs, *pension* keepers, dancing masters, instructors in decorum. There were English Clubs, operated by Russians; and a permanent French Theater, patronized by Russians but with French actors.

Among better-off families, German and French were spoken in the house to children, employees, and to each other. Russian was reserved for the serfs, with devastating effect on the relationship between language and its superiority-inferiority connotations. "None But the Lonely Heart" was effortlessly written by Tchaikovsky to German words. His *Queen of Spades* slips into French arias in natural conformance with Russian upper-class thought and experience. Glinka's librettist for the patriotic *Ivan Susanin* was, unpatriotically, a German baron named Rosen, secretary at the tsar's court. He clipped his scant Russian to fit Glinka's already composed, skintight music. Pushkin tried to help Glinka with his Russian by telling him to study it from the Moscow women who bake bread for communion services. Theirs was the purest, the most Russian.

Official censorship was stultifying. Turgenev had been held under house arrest in the country for calling Gogol in an obituary "great." His play *A Month in the Country* was banned for "immorality" . . . a woman's unrequited love for a younger man. The cities tolerated these controls to the limits of their endurance. The alternative was exile away from the two centers of Russian life.

The Romanoff dynasty, beginning with Michael in 1613 and including its founder Peter the Great, could not be represented on the stage. Tsarist and grand ducal predecessors might, however, be allowed in serious tragedies, but not in opera, comedy, or satire of any sort. Paul I banned the words "citizen" and "society," after his anti-English flirtation with Napoleon failed. Nikolai I (1825–1855) proscribed the word "assassinate." Plays about Roman emperors, including *Julius Caesar*, suffered plot obscurities.

Musicians had to manipulate their librettos carefully. Rimsky-Korsakoff's simpleton tsars were altered to grand dukes. His tsar in *The Golden Cockerel* forecast Russia's defeat by the Japanese, but, like so many other operas and ballets at that time, this theme was couched in the obliquity of fairy-tale fantasy. Borodin chose characters whose station in life was so equivocal and set so far back in time that they passed invulnerably (Prince Igor, for example).

Of course, revolutionary scenes of any kind were excised. Less expectedly, so were religious processions and representations of ikons and priests. In this, Mussorgsky's *Boris Godunov*, another far-back grand duke *cum* tsar, with scenes of religious worship was daring for more than its music. Russians abroad flocked to any theater representing Christ or saints on stage.

Sometimes censorship was merely silly or mistaken, such as when Knut Hamsun's books were confiscated for being thought to be about the "knout," or when the acid crystals of grapejuice, cream of Tartar, were eschewed in food for being too close to "Crimean Tatars." Anton Rubinstein's (1829–94) music was once seized at the border, not for its poor quality, but because some official thought its notes were a kind of revolutionary code. If one signed a letter "love," it must not imply insubordination to one's primary love of God or tsar.

Every department of Russian life was either shadowed by obedience to orthodoxy or seething with reaction from it. Church and State, those "black beasts," as Mikhail Bakunin (1814-1876), that early Westernized revolutionary called them, were inseparably yoked, and they dragged Russia along behind them. Their stranglehold was likened to *rogatki*, spiked collars used for medieval torture. The more one strained or shouted, the greater the pain. There was a Ministry of Spiritual Affairs, and in religious schools the hypotenuse of a right triangle was taught as God's mercy descending through Jesus Christ.[1] Even Tolstoi spent his lifetime attacking Church and State. Only his popular stature prevented his imprisonment.

The tsar was sacred. His coronation was literally a sacrament equal to those services accompanying christening, marriage, and extreme unction. Many educated Russians as well as peasants were religiously strict with themselves. They made the sign of the cross when they said goodnight to one another. Corpses were kept on view and friends kissed the lips and forehead of their dead for days. They blessed each other's shoulders and forehead with the sign of the cross. They kissed each other regardless of sex on the mouth or three times on the cheek, and still do. Every regiment had a priest, who in wartime advanced with the soldiers.

---

1 James Billington, *op. cit.*

During Lent all music and theater ceased. Butterweek, however, the seven preceding days, was something of an artistic and social saturnalia. At all hours of the day or night you could find a concert in some maecenas' house, or a *bliny* party where you spread pancakes with caviar or herring, or *blinchiki* with sweetened cloudberries, washing each mouthful down with gulps of vodka.

The price for orthodoxy and tsarism was high, and it was paid in infinite, sometimes contrary forms. Some people became confirmed atheists. Debased Byronism took Don Juan as a model against convention. Others became "self-destructive transcendentalists," as Avrahm Yarmolinsky put it, essaying to become God himself, like Scriabin or Dostoevsky's Kirillov in *The Possessed*.[1] Eschatology was a keynote of pre-World War I Russia, as it had been throughout most of Russia's religious history. Apocalypticism made the "Book of Revelation" the most quoted, painted, sung, and set-to-music section of the Bible. Everyone predicted the end of the world, earth-shattering changes (*potryasenia*), upheavals (*perevoroty*); "unheard of events," said symbolist poet Alexander Blok (1888–1921), "world conflagration," shouted Scriabin, "the end of history," intoned Solovyov. Even Liadov stopped talking long enough to write an "Apocalypse Suite."

Chekhov sounded the theme too, but more sensibly: "The time is at hand, an avalanche is moving down upon us, a mighty clearing storm which is coming is already near and will soon blow..."[2] By 1906 Gorky's "Storm Messenger," a story symbolizing the approaching storm of successful revolution, had become a young people's bible, and its theme song was Scriabin's D# minor Etude, Op. 8.[3] Nikolai Berdyaev, the philosopher, writing of Scriabin said somewhat cooly, "Scriabin prophesies the new world-epoch, but in him we feel a sense of foreboding and unconquered chaos..."[4]

Many of the devout who feared the future fell into hateful, blackhearted

---

[1] *Op. cit.*

[2] A. Chekhov, *Three Sisters*, Translated by Constance Garnett, Modern Library, Random House, New York, 1928.

[3] A. Drozdov, "Reminiscences of Scriabin," Sbornik Sovietskaya Muzyka, No. 1 Muzgiz, Moscow, 1943.

[4] N. Berdyaev, *The Meaning of the Creative Act*, Translated by Donald A. Lowrie, Collier Books, New York, 1962.

sects. Sadism and cannibalism were practiced by a few. Nikolai Sperling (1880–1915), painter and friend of Scriabin, drank human blood and ate human flesh at the front during the War in an effort to derive mystical experience. But this was scarcely out of tradition. After all, Tolstoi in the Caucasus had relished cocktails made of vodka, gunpowder and congealed blood. Satan was worshiped in blasphemous, perverse and even sexual "Black Masses." The Anti-Christ, dreaded by some, sought by others, was admitted by all. The practices were discussed in secret. In those days before psychoanalysis, the living devil within man was scrutinized quite subtly, and sometimes with an ecstatic religious rapture. "God and the Devil are at war," Dostoevsky wrote in *The Brothers Karamazov*, "and the battlefield is the heart of man."

Russians passed time tabletipping, asking questions of ouija boards, rasputinizing themselves to this holy man or that. Tsar Nikolai II (1868–1918) was elegantly tattooed with crosses and religious signs. Only because of royal hemophilia was the young tsarevich left unadorned. Newspapers of the day record instances where, in the name of religious faith, groups of people and even whole villages committed suicide by starving themselves to death or burning themselves up in caves.[1]

Voluntary castration in some sects was practiced so as to enable the faithful to live more like Christ. The self-castrators (*skoptsy*) worshiped Peter III (1728–62), the impotent tsar. Circumcision, borrowed from the Jews and Tatars, was adopted as a conscious and willful mortification of the flesh. Dr. Billington mentions Scriabin as introducing "the mystic chords of the flagellants into his music . . . "[2]

Anti-Semitism, that special problem of Christianity, was contradictorily condoned and condemned. Many Russians actually believed that Jews were born with a blood spot on their chest. Russians allowed Jews residence in the capital cities, if they studied or worked in government institutions. Happily for musicians, the Conservatory was one. But Jews in general were not so permitted unless they were baptized Christians (*perekresty*). Mischa Elman (1891–1967), the violinist, at his debut in Odessa was not permitted to have his family in the audience, and Leopold Auer,

---

1 Elizabeth Wormeley Latimer, *Russia and Turkey in the XIX Century*, A. C. McClung and Co., Chicago, 1897.
2 James Billington, *op. cit.*

(1845–1930), his teacher, threatened to resign, before Elman was permitted to live and study in SPb, the tsar's capital. Only apostates could play in the Bolshoi orchestra. These stipulations were revised somewhat by the government in 1903, when Hippolytus Altani, a Jew, became conductor. The census of 1897, the first reliable one, revealed that Russia had half the Jews of the world, 5,000,000, within her borders.

Tolstoi publicly stated that there was "something Jewish in Dostoevsky's blood," and the fantasy of this remark was never noted except by young Gorky. When Gustav Mahler (1860–1911) played his works in Russia, one newspaper headlined the review, "Music by the Jew Mahler." Stanislavsky astounded Russian audiences by playing Shylock with a Yiddish accent. As late as 1911, a leading Moscow newspaper criticized Vsevolod Meyerhold's (1874–1930) production of *Boris Godunov* (the drama) for being "more Jewish than Pushkin." While Prokofiev was writing an overture on Jewish themes, his friend the portrait painter Konchalovsky, would ask jokingly, "How are all your Jews today?" Contemporary attitudes towards race in general are part make-believe, but Russian forthrightness was obnoxious and damaging.

How peculiar Russian life was as we view it now. A statute in law books forbade "educating the children of cooks," as late as 1884. "Class rights" were spoken of as casually as Americans assume "civil rights." Doctors used leeches, let blood, and prescribed at best change of scene, at worst seton, a crude form of acupuncture. Alcohol was used like tranquilizers for mental illness. When miraculous ikons failed, as a last resort swans or captured birds were brought to the bedside of a dying person.

Borodin, the musician-scientist, fought both for music and women's right to study, though not practice, medicine. The ugly phrase Turgenev used for suffragettes was "mentally developed women." Conversations of the period spoke euphemistically of "the woman question." "Apollo" and "Romance" were common, everyday men's names, and many, too many girls were called "Love" or "Hope" (even in French as "Aimée"). One wonders how many old maids died with "Lyubov" on their lips, and too, the bitter irony of crabby Balakirev having as his first name "Sweet." Gay blades spitefully autographed their young ladies' memory books with a well-known aphoristic caution: "Woman! Remember it was *I* who brought *You* into being." One popular epitaph on tombstones was "Love of Truth."

"Moscow was small . . . everyone knew everyone else," Marietta Shagynian wrote recollecting the 1880's. She meant simply that everyone minded everyone else's business. Gossip between St. Petersburg and Moscow and against one another, was delicious, malicious, and traveled underground fast as a grass fire. The two cities were rivals even in ill will. When Tchaikovsky left St. Petersburg to work in Moscow, he was coldly received on each return visit. Rachmaninoff, to cite a later instance, wanted to study with Rimsky-Korsakoff in St. Petersburg. He dared not, however, flout his Muscovite loyalty.

Despite a constant interflow and exchange of musicians, the lineup on sides was (and still is to a certain extent) clearly staked. St. Petersburg exulted in Glinka, Dargomyzhsky, Balakirev, Borodin, Cui, Mussorgsky, Rimsky-Korsakoff, Grechaninov, Liapunov, Tcherepnine, and later Prokofiev, Stravinsky and still later Shostakovich. Moscow gloated gleefully over its Tchaikovsky, Taneieff, Arensky, Ippolitov-Ivanov, Scriabin, Rachmaninoff, Vassilenko, Kalinnikov, Koreshchenko, Medtner, and later Myaskovsky, Rebikov and Kabalevsky. The dividing line was where the composer was born, but also, in principle at least, where he worked and held his affinities.

But what of the music and its men in these two nineteenth-century centers of Russia's world?

III

HISTORY

CATHERINE THE Great, Voltaire's friend and correspondent (he had written a biography of Peter the Great), created and conferred the title "Free Artist." But this applied only to architects (so valuable to growing Russia) and painters (as essential then as photographers today). The Court did not use musicians particularly, although Alexis, Peter's son, had astonished everybody by ordering music for his second marriage. Musicians were ignored as objects of honor. Catherine, for all her Arajas, pared operas down to two acts and no more. Even after Glinka's dawn, an entrenched attitude spurning music prevailed all over Russia, just as it had in the beginning. In the nineteenth century von Riesemann explored this question. He found it a matter of "class prejudice." Russians expressed it this way, in French: "*Pour un gentilhomme la musique ne peut jamais être un métier mais seulement un plaisir*" (Music must never be a means of livelihood for a gentleman, only an enjoyment). Rimsky-Korsakoff's father translated this sentiment for his son: "Music should be regarded merely as a pleasant pastime, preferable to cards or drinking."[1]

Music was looked down on for being "proletarian." Even governments were embarrassed by the wide attendance at operas and music halls. To salve conscience, all taxes derived from music were given to charity and education. Later, music became respectable, but its amateur aspect persisted. Grand Duke Michael composed an "Influenza March" while ill in 1907 and played it on the piano at a concert in aid of the English Cricket Club in Staffordshire. His brother, Tsar Nikolai II, composed

---

[1] Nikolai Rimsky-Korsakoff, *My Musical Life*, Translated by Judah A. Joffe, Alfred A. Knopf, New York, 1936.

a song or two and sang privately in a high tenor voice.

In 1802 St. Petersburg had organized the country's first orchestra. Its purpose was to aid widows and orphans. Joseph Haydn (1732–1809) was invited to be honorary president. The orchestra neither played Russian music (there was none) nor allowed a Russian (even had there been an able one) to conduct. The bill of fare was Pergolesi and Mozart, and, oh yes, Haydn. He had accepted.

Other orchestras were eventually formed with serfs as the players. Sometimes aristocrats joined in briefly for the fun. Serf boys made up the Imperial choirs and their foreign kapellmeisters beat them if they sang a false note. Glinka's uncle, a nobleman, had his private serf orchestra, and Glinka used it like a toy. Balakirev, also nobly descended, but with more of his Tatar blood showing from under his dark skin and almond-eyes, availed himself of a neighbor's orchestra in the country. This was his chief childhood diversion. These serf orchestras were not so different from the *ospedali* or foundling homes where musical training was compulsory, in eighteenth century Venice. Nicolai Malko in his recollections[1] says his father knew a serf who was a graduate of the Paris Conservatoire, having been sent there by his owner.

Virtually all Russian composers belonged to that very leisured, upper class—princes, nobles, gentlemen, generals and admirals—who scoffed at any serious respect for music. The military in Russia was considered high ranking by virtue of education—a scarce asset in old Russia. Cadets who were sent to school as part of their training were screened on the basis of snobbism first and intelligence second. Dostoevsky pointed at this: "The rank of general is the acme of Russian happiness," he moaned. Sure enough, foreign nannies in wealthy homes were taught to sing in Russian:

> You'll be happy, darling, rich and gay,
> You'll a general be one day.

A familiar toast and greeting was "God grant you health and . . . a general's rank." Chekhov's manservant called him "General" after he was elected to the Pushkin Academy. Although life was hard—any mili-

---

1 Nicolai Malko, *A Certain Art*, William Morrow and Co., New York, 1966.

tary officer could be demoted in rank for one unsatisfactory dress parade—nevertheless 8,000 generals were on the payroll in 1870. Their wives were addressed as "Her Excellency."

Art confined to high social level had to be dilettante. Glinka's contemporaries called him delightedly, "the enlightened dilettante." Rimsky-Korsakoff of his professorship at the St. Petersburg Conservatory wrote, "I was a dilettante and knew nothing. This I frankly confess and attest before the world." The lack of professionalism among the self-taught Russian dilettanti tormented them, desiccating their natural gifts.

Glinka's immediate successor, Alexander Dargomyzhsky (1813–1869) supplemented his talent with aesthetic criteria. "Truth in sounds ... I want the tonal note to be the direct representation of the word ... truth and realism, that is the secret."[1] But how to achieve such a grand goal with incomplete and imperfect training? Art is truth, as we all know, but truth is not art. His opera *The Stone Guest* is successful for its motivating slogans and its near-misses as much as for actual achievements. It is dry, a little dull, but exactly set word for word to Pushkin's text of four scenes on *Don Juan*. It lasts less than one hour and a half.

Musical amateurism was simply an accepted fact, until Tchaikovsky. Dargomyzhsky accommodated to it in 1866, for instance, by composing a "Tarentella Slav," a piano duet "for persons unable to play the piano." The bass consists of repetitions of a single "A." Later, Rimsky-Korsakoff, Cui, Borodin, etc. did the same for "Chopsticks." They dignified its notes with the title "Paraphrases. Music for the untutored." Such was the longing, and such the absence of method.

In the 1860's dilettantism perturbed the first group of musicians to appear in body. These five men, all from St. Petersburg, were the *moguchaya kuchka* ("powerful handful" or derogatively "mighty heap") variously rendered in English as Mighty Five, Invincible Band, sometimes as the Balakirev Circle, or still more imprecisely, the Russian School. Its members are now household names to musicians—Balakirev, Cui, Mussorgsky, Borodin, and Rimsky-Korsakoff. Soon after, their designation was made diminutive to *kuchkisty*. The implication was still more pejorative, "sturdy little fistful." S. W. Pring gives it as "potent little crowd." The uncomplimentary denigration of this St. Petersburg group,

[1] M. D. Calvocoressi and Gerald Abraham, *op. cit.*

of course, began in Moscow. It denoted Muscovite contempt and Russian incredulity in general at indigenous musical ability.

Russia was struggling for her musical voice. Stassov, intimate of the Five and himself a dilettante, being a lawyer by profession and critic by choice, wrote bitter memories of the era:

> Nothing new coming from a change with the past—whether it is good for nothing, or just good, or even a perpetuation of an old *status quo*—is established without stubborn resistance all round. Such art can gain its place only after doing battle. To fight for rights has to be a heart-breaking struggle. But nowhere ever before has a new art encountered such hostility and opposition, such ferocious and bedeviling persecution as with us in those days. It was nothing less than an Inquisition.[1]

All this stormy drama was merely because sufficient talent had at last emerged. A professional, valued and valuable place for Russian music composed by Russians had been demanded and achieved. Nothing more, in effect, than the consolidation of Glinka's earnest.

These "Five" composers wrote from inspiration without rubrics to guide them. All were still dilettanti. Four of them worked at other posts than music: Borodin was a doctor; Rimsky-Korsakoff a naval officer; Mussorgsky a clerk in the Communications Ministry; Cui a general in the Engineers Corps, professor of Fortification, and really more of a pamphleteer than a composer, despite his ten operas on paper.

When Borodin met Liszt, he said apologetically, "I am only a Sunday composer." The Abbé-flatterer instantly retorted, "Then Sunday is a feast day." Liszt wrote Borodin in 1877 these gentle and prophetic words, "Through all Russian music flows a current of life that will inescapably endear it to other countries in time." But Liszt too was troubled by Russian ignorance. He knew that only solid musical grounding could stabilize. He taught his Russian pupils with particular love.

Balakirev, the head of the group around whom all this Russian music first clustered, lived by music alone. He quelled amateurism by brute genius. Genius wanes; technique sustains. Art needs craft for fulfillment. The informality of Balakirev's studies and their incompletion made him compose with agonizing slowness.

---

1 *History of Russian Music, op. cit.*

He was so unabashedly arrogant too, he discouraged his adepts from learning. "Study nowhere other than through me . . . Actual practice of the art is the only way to learn," he would say to disciples thirsting for technical equipment. Such remarks flung them squarely back into Glinka's dilettantism. As inspiring as Balakirev was spiritually to his friends in the clique for a while, his dismissal of theory rejected with one hand while the other one, the weaker, succored.

His symphonic poem *Russia* is remarkably crude and rough-hewn music. A program holds it together. It starts with Russia's paganism, an inspiration source for *Rite of Spring*, later. Balakirev conceived it in 1862 as a "Second Overture on Russian Themes," but revised it in 1882, renaming it *Russia*. It tells in story form of princes and popular government, Cossack institutions (he was on their side), and ends with a curse on Peter the Great, who deformed by reforming "nationalistic and religious tendencies."

Until 1871 anybody wanting to study composition in Russia was at a loss. Tchaikovsky's *Manual of Harmony*, the first of its kind in Russian, appeared only then. Rimsky-Korsakoff's *Principles of Orchestration*, an equally important first came a few years later. His definitive *Practical Guide to Harmony* saw the light of print in 1884. Nikolai Kashkin (1839–1920) wrote one of the earliest textbooks on basic theory. And Taneieff's monumental work in counterpoint showing the mathematical possibilities and permutations of melodic combinations, was published in 1908. It took ten years of labor, for there had been nothing on the subject before. The title of its thousand-long pages has been variously translated, *Horizontally Movable Counterpoint*, *Invertible Counterpoint*, *Movable Counterpoint in the Strict Manner*, and simply, *Treatise on Counterpoint*. This book crystallized a lifetime's teaching and standardized the Russian basis of contrapuntal forms. Before it, Tchaikovsky had had to depend only on his intuition. "I always hear another melody to go with the one I'm putting down . . . " This was scarcely polyphony.

As the tendrils of the "Five" reached out, growing strong through practical experience, an event of epoch-making consequence took place in 1862. Russia's first music school, the Conservatory in St. Petersburg, was established. Unfortunately, it was not for the nationalistic "Five," but rather for those who looked westward. In any case it was an incredible step forward towards musical competence. The founder was Anton Rubinstein, whose financial, spiritual, and social patroness was the Grand Duchess Helena Pavlovna, a powerful and intelligent maecenas. She had discussed the possibility of a conservatory with Clara (1819–1896) and Robert Schumann (1810–1856) as early as 1844, inviting them to teach—in the event the idea was consummated.

Graduation diplomas now for the first time for musicians could be given and inscribed "Free Artist". What magical words they were. At last a man could write "Musician" as his occupation on travel papers, census reports, and even in the important religious records of baptism and confirmation for his children.

Anton Rubinstein was a leonine-looking Polish Jew born in Bessarabia (now Rumania), with long pompadoured hair. In common custom he was baptized a Christian at birth. He soon became a colossal virtuoso pianist, the piano titan of his time, whose only rival was Liszt. He played the world over in major cities everywhere. His tour of America in 1872 with Polish violinist Henryk Wieniawski (1835–1888), two singers and an instrumental ensemble, consisted of two hundred and fifteen concerts in the space of a couple of months.

Joint recitals of instrumentalists, pianists and singers were the demand of concert managers then, regardless of the greatness or popularity of any one performer. William Steinway and Maurice Grau had to be persuaded and Rubinstein had to throw a fit of temperament before "Ruby," as the Americans called him, was permitted to play a solo recital—the first in America. The reason was not so much the barbarity of audiences demanding variety to accommodate their short attention span, as starved and thirsting eagerness to ingest all culture possible. Rubinstein's share of the American tour was $60,000 (he had been guaranteed $40,000), both amounts being unprecedented for any artist. He declined a later offer of $125,000 for only fifty concerts. The travel conditions for artists, he said, were too primitive in America. Nor was he fond of barnstorming.[1]

---

1 Milton Goldin, "The Great Rubinstein Road Show," *High Fidelity Magazine*, Great Barrington, Mass., Vol. 16, No. 9, September, 1966; also Arthur Loesser *op. cit.*

Rubinstein's aim at the St. Petersburg Conservatory where his heart lay was primarily discipline, "to train a living army of performers," he said, to produce "orchestras of generals." For this he invited Theodor Leschetizky (1830–1915), the great Polish pedagogue, to head the piano department. He hired other foreigners, English, Italian, Polish, to teach aesthetics, history, theory, instruments, and composition.

Rubinstein achieved all worldly goals in his rich lifetime except one, creativity. He was a true Varangian, a foreigner who wrote operas. All the baptisms of Holy Russia could not change this. The operas were fair enough in their day, but today they are boring, relieved only intermittently by charm.

Worse than anything, Rubinstein was an epigon (from Greek, "the one who came later"), an eclectic, an imitator of other people's music. His compositions—and they passed the one-hundred mark—were "helpless and watery," as Asafiev notes. Sabaneeff dismisses him altogether as a "musical feuilletonist." Sadly, he himself lamented in a private paper posthumously published that "neither as a man nor as a composer am I fish, flesh, or fowl." However, by the end of his life at the age of sixty-five he had been decreed a nobleman by the tsar, soloist to Her Majesty, had received the Supreme Order of Vladimir, been made Councilor of State, and most governments of Europe decorated him.

The Conservatory for all its own musical blessings caused a ruction with the "Five" and their protagonists. Such was the temper of musical Russia then. Alexander Serov (1820–1861), lawyer-composer-critic, friend of Dostoevsky and Wagner, cracked puns and sneeringly called it the "Jewish Conservatory." "Not a Russian in the lot," others said acerberously and rather accurately. They attacked Rubinstein's weakness in composition. They called him "foreign" and "alien." The fact that one of their own, Cui, was half-French and Lithuanian, and quite as vacuous a composer, was ignored.

Rubinstein himself, unfortunately, had provoked this opprobrium. In 1855 he wrote in the Viennese periodical, *Blätter Für Musik*, soon translated and published in Russia, some inflammatory statements. Here is a sample—an epigon's cry: "No one in his right senses would attempt to compose a Japanese opera. Therefore, to write a Russian opera merely argues want of sanity. Every attempt to create a national music activity is bound to lead to one result—disaster."[1] How could any musical nationalist ever forgive an attitude so hostile to native aspirations and one so barefacedly false? One of Rubinstein's better efforts to escape "nationalism" was *Feramors*, based on Irishman Thomas Moore's (1779-1852) "Lalla Rookh," an Oriental narrative set in Bokhara. This was translated into German and thence into very Western, non-Russian music.

Anti-academic, anti-foreign and anti-Jewish Balakirev challenged Rubinstein and the Conservatory by setting up a rival institution, the Free School of Music (*Bezplatny*, "without paying"). Rosa Newmarch (1857-1940), one of the few outsiders who knew Balakirev personally, defined its purpose as "defending individual tendencies whilst upholding the cause of national music." Asafiev pinpoints a more central contest between the two schools: "Balakirev's aim was to implant musical literacy by means of concerts and choruses accessible to all." The Free School in all its democracy and nationalism lasted only a few years. As it finally failed, the Conservatory ruled the day.

Four years after the founding of the Petersburg Conservatory, Anton Rubinstein commissioned his brother, Nikolai (1835-1881) to establish a similar institution in Moscow. Peter Jurgenson (1836-1904), wealthy merchant, first music storekeeper and music publisher in Russia—Tchaikovsky among others—helped in financing this project of 1866.

Nikolai Rubinstein was a piano virtuoso in his own right and of exceptional caliber. Anton invariably said that his brother was the better of the two. Whatever Nikolai's brilliance, the public glory of Anton overshadowed. Greatness is not always the equivalent of popularity, and how destructively this was demonstrated by the Rubinstein brothers.

Nikolai was administratively and musically wise, but irresponsible. He came to classes drunk, died early, burnt out and worn. When the news reached Anton, there was no sorrow. Tchaikovsky reported only that Anton looked "as if a load of lifetime worries had been lifted from him."

A rival to the Moscow Conservatory appeared in 1883, and endured. The Philharmonic School of Music was founded by a pianist-conductor,

---

1 Yuri Arnold, *Reminiscences*, Moscow, 1891-1893. Arnold, a Russian of English extraction, was a leading music critic in St. Petersburg.

Pyotr Shostakovsky, pupil of Theodor Kullak (1818–1882), a German pianist of exceptional powers and a Liszt disciple. The school was small but boasted nominal, grudgingly granted favors from the government. Its teachers, all of local provenance, were less renowned than those of the Moscow Conservatory, and the pupils consisted at first of Conservatory rejects. Among these, Serge Koussevitzky (1874–1951).

A basic item in the curriculum differentiated the Philharmonic. Drama was compulsory. Ostensibly the aim was to improve the standard of Russia's ever-loved opera. But the teaching affected theater at large. The instructor was Vladimir Nemirovich-Danchenko (1858–1943), nobleman, playwright, director, critic, and co-founder with Stanislavsky of the Moscow Art Theater. Among his first pupils were two shining geniuses: Olga Knipper (1868–1959), actress and later Chekhov's wife (the Soviets named a street after her); and Vsevolod Meyerhold (1874–1942), prodigious avant-garde director and producer of Vladimir Mayakovsky's (1894–1930) superb plays.

Now that Russia had government-supported and privately endowed schools of music, dilettantism became intolerable. The only impediment to musicians would be their own indolence, a trait Turgenev found distastefully prevalent in Russian character, terming it harshly, "want of will." However, Russian music showed no lack of energy. In fact, it could not be contained. Knowledge in every ramification spread with the blaze of wildfire.

The first pamphlet on Russian music, *Musique en Russie*, was written by Cui in 1880. The first biography of any musician by a Russian, *New Biography of Mozart* by Count Oulybyshev (1794–1858), again in French, because "I have no great hope of interesting my compatriots," was written in 1843 and only translated into Russian in 1890. Prince Nikolai Yussupoff printed in 1856 a "Luthomonographie" on violin-making. 1873 saw the first newspaper, *Musical Leaflet*, started by Vasily Bessel (1843–1907), a wealthy Russian of German descent, publisher of Mussorgsky's music and fellow-student of Tchaikovsky. The resplendent weekly *Russian Musical Gazette* began in 1894, and the first history of Russian music appeared in 1895, both the work of the Russian musicologist and editor, Nikolai Findeizen (1868–1928).

Peter Sokalsky (1832–1887) issued his *Fundamental Book of Russian Folk Songs* in 1888. The hungry nationalists scoured its pages for themes and examples. Mitrofan Belaieff (1836–1903), the best music publisher of exclusively Russian music, established his firm in 1884.

As the music of the 1860's and 1870's turned into that of the 1880's and 1890's, Balakirev's Circle vanished. Belaieff's Circle emerged. Rimsky-Korsakoff, transitional survivor, distinguished the difference between the two: The former was "Revolutionary;" the latter, "Progressive."[1] But he was not entirely happy with the more recent crop of composers. In a letter of 1890 to critic Simeon Kruglikov (1851–1910), he bickered:

> New times—new birds, someone has said. New birds—new songs. How well this is said! But our birds are not all that new, and they sing new songs that are worse than the old ones . . .[2]

He was speaking of Glazunov, Liadov, Scriabin—Belaieff's pet composers. History would prove Rimsky mistaken.

Into this burst of spontaneous musical activity at home paraded the West's greatest names from afar. Russians now paid visiting artists munificently. Eager audiences hungered for any music from abroad, no longer just opera. Those nationalists who eschewed study abroad were nevertheless exposed to the light from the West.

Richard Wagner in his Russian series of performances astounded spectators by facing the orchestra and conducting with his back to the audience. What impoliteness! He also floored them by conducting without a score. He directed his operas also while standing on a podium in the pit. The traditional method had been for the conductor to sit in a chair behind the prompter's box. However, he still wore white gloves for visibility and respect. When a Russian conductor dispensed with gloves, Tsar Alexander II (1855–1881) ordered one at least back on, as if he were a butler serving plates of food. Wagner's reforms came into permanent effect only when Rachmaninoff accepted the conductorship of the Bolshoi Theater in 1905. He added one of his own innovations by forbidding smoking at rehearsals. Liszt's farewell concert on retirement from the world was played in Kiev. Clara Wieck also toured Russia, accom-

---

[1] N. A. Rimsky-Korsakoff, *Literary Works and Correspondence*, Vol. I, Muzgiz, Moscow, 1955.

[2] A. N. Rimsky-Korsakoff, *Life and Works of N. A. Rimsky-Korsakoff*, Moscow, 1936.

panied by her husband, Robert Schumann. (He was asked, "Are you musical, too?") She surprised Russians by playing without the notes before her on the piano rack. (It was considered disrespectful to composers.) Johann Strauss (1825–99) conducted in Moscow in 1863. Riccardo Drigo (1846–1930), known mostly for his sweetheart "Serenade," moved to Russia permanently in his twenties to conduct the Maryinsky ballet orchestra. He was close to Tchaikovsky and lived with him for a time. Hector Berlioz (1803–69) in 1867 stunned Russians with his music and his personal disagreeableness.

Camille Saint-Saëns (1835–1921) in 1876 brought back to Europe the first piano score of Mussorgsky's *Boris Godunov*. In 1881 Sara Bernhardt played at the Bolshoi. Ferruccio Busoni (1866–1924) taught at the Moscow Conservatory during the year of 1890–91. In 1891 the tsar personally invited Dame Nellie Melba and the de Reszke brothers (tenor and baritone) to sing at the opera in St. Petersburg. Richard Strauss (1864–1949) appeared in 1909. Even Claude Debussy (1862–1918) reached Russia, first in 1879 as a music tutor to Baroness von Meck's family (she was Tchaikovsky's benefactor and confidante); and again in 1913, under Koussevitzky's auspices, he conducted a cycle of his compositions, including *La Mer*. The exposure, in other words, to the best of the West was continuous over a sustained period of time.

Russia was flourishing. Music had taken root. Its parched ground was watered from abroad. But the seed was good, and the soil fertile. Through music the Russians spoke their hearts universally. "Art is a means of conversation with people, not a goal . . ." Mussorgsky wrote.

This then was the musical geography flowering within intellectual Russia in St. Petersburg and Moscow. The rest of the nation was provincial and existed only for summertime or, further south, as a source of thematic material, nothing more.

One inexplicable contradiction appears. St. Petersburg, the "window into Europe," gave rise to the nationalist "Five," those patriot-musicians who despised visitors, shrank from foreign influence, who talked, breathed and lived egoistic Slavophilism. In contradistinction, Muscovy, that preeminently Russian area developed the international school. Here were the "Cosmopolitans," "Universalists," "Occidentalists," "Denationalists" who sometimes barely escaped the palling accusation of epigon. Tchaikovsky, for example, adored the West and it worshiped him. Early Scriabin splintered straight from the foreign graces of Chopin and Liszt. Rachmaninoff straddled the two: he structured himself on Tchaikovsky, but worked on nationalist themes, at least until his flight from the USSR.

IV

MALAISE

THE BROAD field of Russian music by the completion of the nineteenth century had unleashed and embraced irreconcilable elements. There were magnificent scores of music. Within their panoramic vistas appeared the personalities and private lives of the men who created them. The seamy side of any country, city or coterie can be ferreted, but in Russian musical history two salient points astonish first by their existence, and second, by ubiquity. They clamor for mention, because too often in the past they have been relegated to black holes of dark secrecy.

Partisans of the healthy, sunny view of Russia's musical heritage can parry all they will; however, mental instability often to the point of madness and misogyny, even in the form of homosexuality, preponderate. This view beyond music into biography reveals sicknesses that were more than a climate of troubled, pre-revolutionary Russia. Often these illnesses are compounded by dipsomania. Was alcohol the cause or the manifestation? It once was a joke to reduce old Russia into "two classes" —those who drink and those who sell it. In regard to the great composers, the statement loses mirth.

Mental illness was dismissed by Russian doctors as "brain fever." They used the phrase as mechanically as they said "galloping consumption," "the vapors" or "humors." Brain fever extenuated every mood from lassitude, depression, irascibility, erethism, to alysosis—all clinical ailments which are today taken seriously and treated. In pre-Freudian days "neurasthenia" or "nervous breakdown" was a handy label pasted on any malaise, lack of ease, or dis-ease of the mind. So, imprecisely termed, the symptoms and syndromes of psychic disturbance were too often woefully in evidence. Artists often smelled of Valerian drops, a strong sedative. Many misjudged the number of glasses of champagne "to calm nerves" before going onstage or sitting down to compose, put a bottle of cognac on the desk or piano.

Many nineteenth and twentieth century personalities in Russian music were exemplars of rectitude, may it be said at the outset. Some let abstention exceed the Plimsoll line of reasonable virtue. While secret life forms a curiously reiterated note in the lives of Russia's composers, it was a forbidding time. Discretion imposed a silence. The punishment for homosexuality, for instance, was ten years imprisonment and exile to Siberia. Instances of anomaly in the personal lives of Russian musicians are too frequently documented, hinted, or suggested, to be banished by the magic wand of mere wish. The psychic causes, even if they were amenable to psychiatric probing in retrospect, have been engulfed by ignorance of the past and its contemporaries.

The majority of people leave no written details of their sexual life. Turgenev was the exception. His letters tell how his mother paid a serf girl when he was fifteen to service him and he records how many times a month he had intercourse. Mussorgsky makes a few tortured references to masturbation in his letters. But for the most part, the specific nature of this subject has to be guessed hazardously. Inference can be offered, and of course, caution is essential in implying details of a musician's private life, but not at the expense of truth. A number of suppositions are verifiable behind smattering references, oblique innuendoes, innocent comments by unknowing coevals, and more bluntly, from hearsay, private conversations, but rarely, by open confession. The upper-class rule of morality in Russia was: "Any vice in private; none in public."

Glinka submits in his *Memoirs* that he was a hypochondriac of boundless proportion. Stassov, who knew and loved him, spoke of Glinka's "fainting fits and nervous depressions . . . He was neurotic, with hallucinations."[1] An out-and-out "nervous breakdown" in 1823 took him to the Caucasus mountains in the far South for the hot, sulphurous water cure. In various contemporary reminiscences, note is made of how Glinka amused his cronies with female impersonations and singing the heroine roles of Mozart operas "in an exquisite *castrato* voice."[2]

---

1 V. V. Stassov, *Collected Articles*, Muzgiz, Moscow, 1926.
2 Glinka, *Memoirs*, Introduction by A. N. Rimsky-Korsakoff, *op. cit.*

Pushkin wrote a humorous poem, *The Little House in Kalomma*, where a widow and her daughter hire a cook who later, much later, turns out to be a transvestite who shaves. This became the plot of Stravinsky's opera *Mavra*. "If born a man," Pushkin moralizes, "futile to masquerade in petticoats." But this was traditional. Empress Elizabeth loved and encouraged masked balls called "Metamorphoses," where the men came as women and women as men.

Glinka, by his own deposition, preferred the company of women as friends to any sort of clubbiness with men. His several marriages were unsuccessful, frivolous, and little more than irresponsibly conducted affairs. The combination of all these several factors would suggest some sexual malfunctioning.

Tchaikovsky was the most famous homosexual in Russia. Shortly after his death his photograph, along with Proust's, and by mistake Alexander Siloti's, was published in Germany to illustrate a caption, "Famous Perverts of Our Era." Not until 1935 did the Soviets publish his self-revelatory letters. Mental crises periodically disturbed Tchaikovsky, and he poignantly outlined them, particularly in his letters to his brother Modest, who was also, conveniently, a pederast. Both referred to their affliction as "*Eto*" (That), and used the code letter "Z" in their private diaries. How they suffered to keep it secret!

Tchaikovsky often thought his head was falling off whenever he conducted an orchestra in public. He could not shake off such seizures. His abortive, unconsummated, week-long marriage ended with him in flight. His wife had hoped that marriage to a homosexual would save her from the insane asylum and her own insurmountable problems.

Tchaikovsky's emotional upheavals sharpened his vision of others. He wrote to Baroness von Meck about Arensky, ". . . strange, unstable, and he is nervous unto sickness."[1] Arensky died at the age of forty-five of "acute alcoholism." In the course of his tormented life he had never married nor formed any known attachment of a romantic nature with a woman.

Rimsky-Korsakoff, paragon of sensible behavior, suffered at one period from "mental depression." He was forty-eight years old when suddenly all composition and his usual pursuits ceased. How terrified he must have

---

[1] P. I. Tchaikovsky, *Correspondence with Nadezhda von Meck*, Vol. I, Moscow, 1934.

felt when he collapsed in front of his students at the Conservatory. "Just an attack of nerves . . . it will pass," one of them said consolingly. "Nerves, nerves," he replied in agony from the floor, "this is only the first symptom." The doctors diagnosed "brain fever" first, and amended it to "neurasthenia cerebro-spinalis."[1] Rimsky's own description of his symptoms is an almost clinical portrait of involutional melancholia, a vague modern term for "unspecific depression".

Mussorgsky's psychasthenic decline has been widely publicized in several biographies. His excesses were fierce. He drank beyond oblivion into annihilation. He suffered from misogamy and had "a physical horror of marriage,"[2] and like Glinka, Turgenev, and others he experienced an obsessively alternating morbid fixation on and revulsion towards his mother. He wailed to his friends of his compulsive onanism. He wrote to Balakirev at the age of twenty, "my nervous disorder is not just the result of masturbating . . . but because of it my body has not developed in pace with my brain . . ."[3]

His first mental collapse felled him when his mother died. His autobiographical notes were sometimes disorientedly written in a remote third person. Mussorgsky's life was spent on a maniacal pendulum riding high in society, then being discovered in rags, drunk, in the company of the most disreputable and lowest louts. The stronger pull in his life was not upward to musical ambition, but down toward immersion in physical, emotional and sexual degradation.

His last alcoholic paroxysms in a sanitarium are sadly recalled by Rimsky: "Suddenly Mussorgsky would pass into a mad delirium . . . his powerful organism proved to have been completely undermined by alcohol." He died when barely forty-two years old.

Rimsky also consigns Arensky's life to a handful of sad words: "According to all testimony, his life had run a dissipated course between wine and card playing, yet his activity as a composer was most fertile . . . He had been a victim of a nervous ailment . . . He will soon be forgotten."[4]

---

1 Rimsky-Korsakoff, op. cit.
2 M. P. Mussorgsky, Letters and Documents, Collected by A. N. Rimsky-Korsakoff, Muzgiz, Moscow, 1932.
3 Ibid
4 Judah A. Joffe's translation.

The story of clumsy, hulking Alexander Glazunov has only recently been revealed. Glazunov was so nervous and fearful of contagion he would leave a carriage if the horse sneezed. He never moved from the home where he was born, nor left his mother, until he was an old man. He was also an alcoholic whose binges of one to two weeks' duration were chronic. Often he would flee to his sister's house. (She had been disowned by the mother.) Glazunov, for all his liquor they say, never missed a technical oversight such as parallel fifths, harmonic inconsistencies, and even drunk he played the piano well with a fat cigar between his fingers.[1]

Imperturbable, good-natured, normal Borodin was oddly mismated. His wife slept all day and stayed awake all night. Richard Leonard after scanning new material recently published describes Borodin as "actually an extremely nervous man," not least of which part was that he was "prey to minor ailments."

Rachmaninoff once wrote Marietta Shagynian openly about himself, "And I? I am mentally ill." He again recollected that period to Asafiev: "From 1897 for three years I composed nothing. I was like a man who had been struck a blow and who for a long time loses the use of his hands and—his head."[2] Rachmaninoff also disclosed that for ten years he wallowed "in apathy and drink." He found surcease only in the care of and eventual cure by a professional hypnotist, Dr. Nikolai Dahl, who was very much in vogue in Moscow at the time. For a year of post-hypnotic suggestions, Rachmaninoff was told, "You will compose a concerto . . . it will be very good . . ." Roused from his "paralyzing apathy," he composed the C minor Concerto No. 2, and dedicated it to his "doctor."

A whole vocabulary—confirmed bachelor, misogynist, gynophobe, misogamist, and woman-hater—existed as a social commonplace in Russia. Femininity in a man as such, however, carried no *arrière pensée* (anymore than in Asia), nor even an ulterior snicker as it does now. To many Russians of standing, delicacy betokened civilization, a smoothing-out of the crude, boorish, aggressive roughness of overmasculine Russian men. There was always, as there is everywhere, a circle of homosexuality.

One flagrant group revolved around the musician Nikolai Zverev

1 N. Malko, *op. cit.*
2 B. V. Asafiev, *Selected Works*, Vol. II, Muzgiz, Moscow, 1954.

(1833–1893). He was Moscow's most fashionable piano teacher, and society's darling because of his elegance and charm. He went to the houses of the rich, where he "safely" taught the daughters and wives. To his own home came the boys, and he selected some of them as boarders to live with him. Through his hands passed the most dazzling pianists of his day —Scriabin, Rachmaninoff, Goldenweizer, Siloti . . .

One wonders how farfetched it is to make persons guilty by situation and opportunity . . . if there is guilt at all. The indications are that Zverev was active and insistent. He paraded his adolescents in *le beau monde* so flagrantly, that even in those innocent times, wags called his ménage the "harem," "monastery," and "zoo" (from *zver*, meaning animal, and implying the "bestiality" of sodomy). The boys, of course, guarded Zverev's secret for their own protection. But Moscow, being Moscow, people whispered.[1]

Such matters were spoken of behind ivory and lace fans, when ladies separated after dinner to powder their necks and faces, or in the blur of smoke when men in ruffled and pleated shirt fronts pulled out pipes or cigarettes at the table. Still Zverev was received in society. Those daughters who knew him by daylight had parents who invited him by night, to regale the company with gossip and name-dropping anecdotes as they sipped Georgian wines and played cards.

Nikolai Strakhov (1828–1896), social commentator and Dostoevsky's first biographer, portrayed Moscow and St. Petersburg as being cities where "religious or spiritual vileness was reckoned strictly and subtly, while carnal vice mattered not a whit." Only open scandal was remonstrable. Gentlemen of the upper classes were usually immune to either sexual exposure or punishment. High birth inspired awe in the lower classes. Equals protected each other. Over all lay silence. As Gorky wrote too, "It is difficult to live in Holy Russia! It is difficult. They sin here disgustingly, they repent their sins even more disgustingly."

Even today within these post-Freudian latitudes, to impute homosexuality—latent, passive or ultimately triumphed over, as it was in Scriabin's case, in my opinion—seems offensive to some. Bearing this in

---

1 This period in Rachmaninoff's life is recorded by Victor Seroff in *Rachmaninoff, op. cit.* Despite any pain it caused and litigation, the book is an honest portrait of Russian musical life. To Seroff and Sabaneeff goes credit for pulling up the ostrich head of society's moral silence.

mind, still it would be recreant to shirk a rather homosexual interpretation of Scriabin's life. Incontrovertible proof cannot now be dredged up
from the past, but so many signposts there seem to be.

Through Scriabin's actions coursed femininity. "Refined ... wom-
anish ... effeminate ... delicate ... exquisite ... tender ..." These words
crop up repeatedly. Scriabin was brought up by women, and Yuri Engel
(1868-1927) wrote with open heart, "Ties to all these women left a
certain mark of femininity on Scriabin. Made, one might say, his very
nature effeminate, as was demonstrated throughout his life by his personal
appearance and his mode of expression ... He himself deplored the lack
of masculine elements in his early life ..."[1] Of course Scriabin's contemporaries did not necessarily link the formative years or the effect of
such models with the mind and emotions of the man, although his letters
to Modest Altschuler (1873-1963) read like a little girl writing to a lover.

It is remarkable how there was invariably a male pattern laced with
his contacts with women. Wherever he loved, there was a brother, husband, or son close at hand. His deepest attachments were with huge,
massive, gruff men, totally contrasting from himself. All his six known
heterosexual affairs were marked with undue publicity and scandal, as
if to advertise himself ... and counterbalance.

Or take his career. Scriabin disliked talking about sex, even in male
company. He was prudish and ladylike. He never used a coarse word.
He called homosexuality, when speaking of others, "that which cannot
be mentioned." Sabaneeff says that "We never heard a vulgarism from
him. Never did he talk pornography. All *that* was intrinsically foreign to
his elegant soul ..." Yet his music was openly erotic.

Wagner wrote love-night and love-death music or gardenfuls of
voluptuous temptations. But he sang about passion and romantic love,
the mental overwhelming of vast love emotion. Scriabin on the other hand
wrote erotic music in a physical sense. He used titles and designations,
such as "Sensual Delights," "Danced Caress," "Desire," "orgiastic,"
"voluptuously" and "with ravishment." In his later music, he called his
extraordinary chord constructions and changes *oshchushchenia* (sensations),
not male or female, but the thrill itself.

In 1907, when Scriabin appeared in America, his effeminacy was well

---

[1] Yuri Engel, "Musical Contemporary," *op. cit.*

marked by the reviewers. The critic of the Chicago *Sun* noted: "In appearance Scriabine is small, fidgety, finical, and saved from the suggestion of effeminacy only by the beard and mustache. When he takes his seat at the piano and commences to play, however, the hint of effeminancy—if there is any—vanishes. You realize that here is a man at work, though he exploits the poetic and the suggestive, rather than the heroics, of music."

The Chicago *Inter-Ocean*'s music critic, Glenn Dillard Dunn, also wrote, "Virility is the last attribute which Mr. Scriabine's art suggests, and various rather effeminate mannerisms in playing emphasize this fatal weakness." Only routinely did critics mention the warmth of the audience.

The artist's personality cannot be heard, always, in his art. Where is perversion in Tchaikovsky's 1812 *Overture*? Anti-semitism in Balakirev's *Tamara*? Or neurasthenic apathy in Rachmaninoff's first concerto? But for all the two wives and seven children, had there not been a homosexual core in Scriabin could his life have been as tortured? Could he have spawned a delusive identity with Christ? Or striven for the supremely male heights of believing himself God the Father and the one who was to seize the world as he would a woman? Would he have overblown his symphonies and certain piano preludes with magniloquence?

Philosophically, Scriabin considered women as the personification of materialism, the power of inertia, the female principle in matter. Creativity with them can only begin with the help of man. Sabaneeff once asked him, "Can a woman be a composer?" He quickly answered, almost as if vexed by the question, "Of course not."

"Why do you think not?"

"Why can't you and I make a baby together?" he sharply retorted.

But wives—they had to be dark and Jewish, like his father's second— were vital to Scriabin's heterosexuality, though they themselves were anti-Semitic and baptized.

Scriabin loved the epicene as he grew older. He liked dissolving the line between the masculine and the feminine. He adored the cover design of his *Prometheus* symphony. It showed a sexless face surrounded by cosmic symbols, nebulae of clouds, spiraling comets, and was drawn by his Belgian friend, Jean Delville (b. 1867), a bachelor, professor of Fine Arts at the Royal Academy, and President of the National Federation of

Artists and Sculptors. Looking at that cover of the androgyne or her-
maphrodite, Scriabin said, "In those ancient races, male and female were
one . . . the separation into poles hadn't yet taken place."

Sabaneeff repeats a conversation where Scriabin confesses his effeminate-
ness. "It's in us all," he said, "but I could not have become what I am
without *fostering* the masculine side of me and suppressing the feminine."[1]
If so, then how can we understand one night? Here is Sabaneeff's graphic
picture of the occasion:

> I almost never saw him "drunk," only high-spirited. He was very strong with
> regards to drink. Once in the summer of 1912, we were talking late and
> repaired to the Ampir Restaurant at the Petrovsky Railway Station . . .
> Scriabin, Podgaetsky, Dr. Bogorodsky, Baltrushaitis and I. We were there a
> long time and drank a lot.
> Scriabin was tipsy. When the waiters had blown out the candles, he took me
> by the hand and led me unsteadily through the darkened restaurant. He began
> kissing the few male guests still sitting around at tables alone, and introduced
> himself as a count, and me with some absurd double-barreled name. In his
> "langorous" voice he said, "The hour has come for us to know all about each
> other."

Balakirev, Dargomyzhsky, and Taneieff never married, nor even
flashed a beam of infatuation. Taneieff sublimated any eroticism he may
have felt into abrasive virtue. He was impeccably pure. For this morality
he was renowned, perhaps in contrast to the familiar dissoluteness of
the others. Tolstoi's wife was frankly in love with Taneieff. He requited
her advances with cordial friendship. He lived alone with an old serf
housekeeper. Only she who served him all his life knew his personal
life and, uneducated, she could not write, and being a serf, her gossip
reached no ears of importance. His life was as rigid as a contrapuntal
construction, and probably devoid of passion.

Of course, many Russian musicians did marry but even here they
showed faint gleams of maladjustment. Considering the anti-Semitic
tenor of the day, it is observable that a large number of them married
Jewesses. Were these philo-Semitic marriages and liaisons no more than
relationships of guilt and atonement for the savagery of pales, pogroms,
tsar-condoned school restrictions and residence quotas? Were they what

---

[1] Leonid Sabaneeff, *Reminiscences of Scriabin, op. cit.*

Theodor Reik calls "flights forward," efforts to replace fear by confronting reality? Or was it an effort of demoting, a raising of masculinity by default, where sexuality need not be tested in the crucible of equality?

Other composers conversely, married close relatives, almost as if their sexual inversion or shyness could not expand further afield. Nikolai Medtner (1879–1951) was "quiet, delicate, quite like a little girl and not of this world, really," in the frank words of a friend.[1] He married his brother's wife, while her sister married yet another of Medtner's brothers. Rachmaninoff late in life took his first cousin in marriage. Koussevitzky, his own niece.

Anatol Liadov suffered terrible and disabling headaches all his life. He was "very secret and withdrawn, and painfully guarded his inner world."[2] In his classroom he often tediously pared his fingernails, and more often suffered from logorrhea and chattered uninterruptably. He was given to unaccountable spells of high humor and practical jokes. Mussorgsky, of all people, found him "extraordinarily nervous and high-strung."[3] He "could not even swat a fly, but was powerfully attracted to Superman, that creation of another gentle and ill man, Nietzsche."[4] But when he finally married late in life he refused to let his closest friends— not even his intimate next-door neighbor Belaieff—meet or see his wife. There were no celebrations. All was covert. "With his friends in art," Rimsky observed resignedly, "he wished to remain, as it were, of the bachelor estate as before."

Of all Russian composers, Balakirev rates as the oddest. Nothing is known of that icy bachelor's sex life, nor can it even be surmised. Rosa Newmarch wrote, "So few strangers ever came in contact with Mily Balakirev that I may be excused for giving my impressions of this remarkable man . . ." and she proceeds uninformatively. Balakirev, as von Riesemann more boldly said, "had deteriorated into gloomy bigotry and misanthropic introspection." Rimsky called him "an implacable Jew-hater."[5]

1 A. V. Ossovsky, *Reminiscences of Rachmaninoff*, Vol. I, Muzgiz, Moscow, 1957.

2 A. I. Kandinsky in *History of Russian Music*, Vol. III, *op. cit.*

3 Mussorgsky, Letter to Stassov, *op. cit.*

4 I. I. Lapshin, *The Legacy of Scriabin's Thought*, Central Cooperative Publishing House, Petrograd, 1922.

5 Rimsky-Korsakoff, *My Musical Life*, *op. cit.*

His inability to create music as he grew older seemed to stifle him with hate and corrode his life with religious mania.

When visitors on rare occasions called, if they were allowed in, Balakirev would make them cross themselves. "For my sake . . . it may do *you* good." Or he would sometimes break into other people's houses at night and light ikon candles which had burned down, disregarding the hazard of fire. He was a member of the fearsome "Black Hundred," an arch-reactionary, secret, police-indulged and monarchist organization of violence. Balakirev appreciated its religious and racial platforms and approved of their instigations of pogroms. He glossed his diseased life with fanaticisms of good behavior. He ate no meat, wore no furs, smoked nothing, and drank only water. At night he held solitary séances and induced nightmarish visions of punishments for his real and imagined sins.

So much madness there was in music, and how at crosspurposes it seems, particularly when you consider that early musician, King David, who used the art of sound as a cure for mental disorders. Today's student looking back on these men and their times can only wonder at the inner torment, the human misery and personal dissatisfaction their lives represented. At what emotional cost did they surmount these debilitating confusions in their private lives? What led such unhappy and strange people into the clarity of art? Art was to many of them a savior they sought, but it could not save them. Many died of drink, committed suicide, or went insane.

These Russian musicians seemed to live life with a layer of protective skin removed. Every blow crushed them, just as every labor of art revived . . . for a while. They were raw nerves and the edges of their feelings were precipice high. How complex, sickly, broken they were. Yet how great their art. Fortunately, the psychic storms blustered and spent themselves. Even when this inner weather did not abate, and abject life remained their daily occurrence, some of them cowering in shadows still kept their art radiant and sublimated their sorrow into brightness.

Although today's psychiatric sciences show that insanity and a functioning being are not inconsonant, the question will always occur in connection with Scriabin. Was he insane? The question has been asked ever since he rose to fame. If he was, how can we esteem him?

Sabaneeff who knew him well, but not invariably saw him in his best light, wrote in a retrospective article titled "About the Composer Scriabin and his Musical Fate,"[1] "To my regret," he said, facing the problem head on, "after much wavering I must admit that Scriabin was psychically ill." So?

How much was romantic indulgence of self and society? As we tolerate the mad scientist for the good of humanity, so did Victorians and Alexandrines forgive and even encourage the "artist" . . . odd, wild, irresponsible, not of this world, but worth it. Scriabin for example, wove a spell of charm over all who met him. But once this was gone, the outrageousness and extremes of his ideas and his personality often struck and embarrassed those very converts. His genius, however, was imperturbable and cannot be impugned.

Tolstoi in *War and Peace*[2] noted a "vague and quite Russian feeling of contempt for everything conventional, artificial, and human—for everything the majority of men regard as the greatest good in the world . . . this strange and fascinating feeling . . . that wealth, power and life . . . all that men so painstakingly acquire and guard—if it has any worth has so only by reason of the joy with which it can all be renounced. It was the feeling that induces a volunteer recruit to spend his last penny on drink, and a drunken man to smash mirrors or glasses, for no apparent reason and knowing that it will cost him all the money he possesses: the feeling which causes a man to perform actions which from an ordinary point of view are insane, to test, as it were, his personal power and strength, affirming the existence of a higher, nonhuman criterion of life." Tolstoi, for all his vagueness and inexactitude in this particular thought, comes close to describing a major fact of Russianism, and one which makes many of the composers, otherwise inexplicable and unendurable, understandable.

1 *"Novoe Russkoye Slovyo"* Newspaper, New York, 12 January, 1964.
2 *op. cit.*

SCRIABIN

✐ I ✐

FOR AND AGAINST

SCRIABIN. Scriabine. de Scriabine. Skriabin. Skrjabin. Skryabin.
Whatever the spelling of the name—s-k-r-ya-b-i-n transliterates the
Russian—and however said—scree-*yah*-been is the correct pronunciation
—Alexander son of Nikolai (Nikolaevich) is *the* Scriabin. He signed himself abroad as "Alexandre Scriàbine" in the French manner, and once had
a fashionable card engraved in Paris: Alexandre de Scriabine, 5, rue de
la Neva; but the dust of fashion has settled and the spelling "Scriabin"
has slipped into habit by its simplicity.

The name crops up internationally. One Scriabin was a member of the
USSR Academy of Sciences—one of the world's foremost parasitologists.
There is a cobbler in Nice called Scriabin; and a Scriabina danced with
the Moiseev ballet.

Scriabin's son-in-law Vladimir Sofronitsky (1901–1963), professor at
the Moscow Conservatory, frequently concertized—often on Scriabin's
own piano. His records afford a cross-sampling of the music.[1] The first
recordings, however, of major Scriabin were commissioned by a Japanese
Music Society in 1928, processed in Germany, and performed by a Pole,
named Sinkiewicz. They included the most advanced last three sonatas.

A Scriabin daughter was active in Palestine and Israel. An old cousin,
Monsieur le Général de Scriabine lived quietly in Paris amid his gene-
alogical archives. A great grandnephew is a pharmaceutical expert in
Philadelphia, Pennsylvania, and has inherited the handsomest of typical

Scriabin features—cleft chin, upturned nose, marmoset-soft eyes set in a broad Slavic face wreathed in bronze-glinted brown hair.

Who was he, this central Scriabin? A composer, pianist, poet, mystic, solipsist, and a semi-, neo-, theo- philosopher. All these disparate talents, facts, dreams, concepts and fantasies combined in the cauldron of his genius. The brew was potent music-magic. He was a musical thaumaturge and mystagogue, and he earned for his name a quota of immortality. Not all the overtones of his personality were entirely pleasant, yet every note of the music is splendid.

Alexander Scriabin lived from 25 December, 1871 (7 January, 1872, new style of Russian calendar reckoning) to 14 April, 1915 (27 April, 1915). Now, a century since his birth and half that from his death, there has been time enough for retrospection and perspective. When he was born, Bruckner and Tchaikovsky were composing their second symphonies. By his demise, Stravinsky had written *Rite of Spring*, Webern *Five Pieces for Orchestra*, Ravel *Daphnis and Chloë*, and Sibelius, a Fifth Symphony. Scriabin himself had by then electrified the world.

Scriabinists, noting that, like Christ, Alexander Nikolaevich Scriabin was born on Christmas and died at Easter, make much of these dates. During Scriabin's lifespan of forty-three years, four months, six days and six hours, he did nothing to discourage an homology with the Messiah, though he could hardly have foreseen that final seal of Easter.

Without any question Scriabin was the most unusual composer ever nurtured on Russian soil. He ranks among the greatest of any country as a rare innovator of music. He was, however, and is still enveloped in clouds of contention, vast mists of misunderstanding. Both pro-Scriabinists and rabid opponents impede his evaluation. Numbers of books in Russian about him begin in words of this prefatory vein: "No composer has had more scorn heaped or greater love bestowed. . . ."[1] The Great Soviet Encyclopedia puts it modestly, "Scriabin's path of creativity was fraught with controversy . . ." And certainly, such phrasing sets the stage accurately.

Vyacheslav Karatygin (1875–1925), critic, teacher, and a pioneer in propagandizing Scriabin (and later Prokofiev), wrote in one of many

---

[1] L. Danilevich, Great Russian Composers Series, *A. N. Scriabin*, Muzgiz, Moscow, 1953.

early monographs: "No name in Russian music has awakened more passionate or more condemnatory interest. For some the name Scriabin is linked to memories of fearsome madness. For others, and each year there are an increasing number of us, he signifies the daring innovations of genius . . . yet he was bayonetted for this very newness . . ."[1] Evgeny Gunst announced in the first biography of Scriabin, "He was our greatest musical genius ever . . . He died at the beginning of the twentieth century, and with this the eclipse of Russian music begins."[2]

Arthur Lourié spoke of the year 1908: "The most brilliant and prominent name in Russian music at that time was Aleksandr Nikolaevich Scriabin. He was in the fullest sense the master of the minds of the younger Russian generation, and the idol of all who were in the front line of Russian culture."[3]

Oskar von Riesemann as translated by Princeton philosopher, Geoffrey Gibson, had this to say: "A genuine theory of divine right is perhaps rare. Meager is the order of composers who can be elevated to such height. Still the book of Scriabin is not closed. It stands. But whatever the ultimate answer, no one can take from him the fact that he launched an aesthetic theory of unheard-of boldness, grandeur and color. No artist before him so dared. He was unquestionably one of the most interesting artistic personalities ever, and one who forever will characterize the international musical scene at the close of the nineteenth century."[4]

England's critics and musicologists were especially vociferous. M. Montagu-Nathan commented in 1917 that "Scriabin's output, having emerged from the condition of being the most discussed, is now the most performed music of the day."[5] A year later he claimed Scriabin to be "the most notorious product of the Russian school,"[6] and elsewhere, ". . . he recalls the appearance of Wagner on the musical horizon . . ."[7]

England's worshipers were highpriested by Dr. A. Eaglefield Hull.

---

[1] V. G. Karatygin, *Scriabin*, Contemporary Art, Butkovsky Publishers, Petrograd, 1915.

[2] Evgeny Gunst, *Scriabin and his Creative Work* (2nd edition), Jurgenson, Moscow, 1915.

[3] Arthur Lourié, *op. cit.*

[4] Oskar von Riesemann, *Prometheische Phantasien*, Deutsche Verlags-Anstalt, Stuttgart and Berlin, 1924.

[5] M. Montagu-Nathan, *Contemporary Russian Composers*, Cecil Palmer, London, 1917.

[6] M. Montagu-Nathan, *A History of Russian Music*, William Reeves, London, 1918.

[7] M. Montagu-Nathan, *Handbook to the Piano Works of A. Scriabin* (2nd edition), J. and W. Chester, London, 1922.

After years of heartfelt application, he wrote a biography of Scriabin. In it he proclaimed, "Scriabin's work brought about an artistic revolution unequaled in the whole history of the arts . . . he wrote the greatest sonatas since Beethoven . . ."[1] Alfred Swan (1890–1970) followed with another biography. "Let us rejoice," it ends, "in the heritage left to us by this messiah."[2] Even before this wave of affection in the 1920's, Rosa Newmarch publicized Scriabin with the catchwords, ". . . new . . . ideal . . . deeply moving."[3]

Considering the obscurities and musical and emotional inaccessibilities of much of Scriabin's later music, read this astonishing comment by Herbert Antcliffe, an English critic then writing for America: "With regard to Scriabin there is much to be admitted in the arguments of those who claim him as one of the few on high Olympus because of the direct appeal to the larger public of even his most elaborate and modernist as well as his most subtle works . . . The music of Scriabin offends the listener whose small or great technical knowledge makes him analyze rather than feel the music. It delights the crowd which knows not how to analyze but which does feel its deep impelling emotion."[4]

In another part of the world, Japan's pioneer composer, Yamada Kosaku, would write in his autobiography of hearing a Scriabin "poem" in 1913 in Moscow: "Scriabin's music! I listened to it ardently. Why did I feel I too lived in his special musical world? Because inside his sounds I could see my own face reflected."[5]

Attacks and counterattacks of musical artillery outrange international boundaries. These shells of dispute fell everywhere and each enthusiast, measured or cautionary, had his opposite number equivalently antipathetic to Scriabin's music. Arthur Bliss (1891–1975), the composer, gave the fracas short shrift: "You can have your Scriabin poems of earth, fire and water . . . Give me *Sacre*."[6] Aldous Huxley wrote a scabrous

---

1 A. Eaglefield Hull, *Scriabin*, (Fourth impression), Kegan Paul, London, 1927.

2 Alfred J. Swan, *Scriabin*, John Lane, Bodley Head, London, 1923.

3 Rosa Newmarch, "Scriabin," *Musical Times*, London, June 1915.

4 Herbert Antcliffe, "The Significance of Scriabin," *The Musical Quarterly* (Vol. X, No. 3), G. Schirmer, New York, July 1924.

5 Yamada Kosaku, *Autobiography, Search into Distant Youth*, Nagashima Publishers, Tokyo, 1951.

6 "Interview," *The Observer*, London, July 3, 1921.

essay in which he called Scriabin "the voluptuous dentist."[1] I believe he regretted this, after his experiments in drugs revealed that Scriabin had already arrived, by other means, at the combination of sensory responses Huxley sought.

Herbert Antcliffe quotes a critic who spoke in noisome phrases before the Musical Association of London in 1924 about Scriabin's "hectic erethisms ...sugared clamminess...the very mire of hysterical emotions ..." A Dutch ladies' paper commented on "the dadaisms of Scriabin."

M. D. Calvocoressi from his early days as musician in Russia through his journalism in France frankly "loathed Scriabin out and out...I was repelled ... and I have never changed...Conceited music of colossal self-aggrandisement,"[2] A dozen years later he charily softens: "Given a normal maturing of his powers and deepening of experience, Scriabin might have become a real master...As a miniaturist...the equal of any..."[3] This phrasing was Gerald Abraham's, whose own earlier opinion of Scriabin had been: "works of incredible egomania... insane imagination."[4] Alexander Werth, erstwhile BBC commentator, editorialized antagonistically about Scriabin "...if ever there was a composer who suffered from all vices...neuropathic...antipeople."[5]

America echoed the uproar. Lazare Saminsky propounded in one breath that Scriabin was composed of "formal anaemia...strength-sapping literary fancy" and a "creator of greatness...with cosmic insight."[6] Or take the historian Wilfred Mellers, who wrote of Scriabin's "obsessively 'introverted' harmony."[7]

Of all detractors, Constant Lambert was most vicious in his shrill diatribe. He charged Scriabin with "opulent vulgarity...his waves vainly beat at the breakwater of our intelligence...Those who were swept off their feet by Scriabin, and they included some of our most level-headed critics, thought nothing of referring to Mozart as a snuffbox composer in comparison with the cosmic master."[8]

1 Aldous Huxley, *Essays Old and New*, Harper's, New York, 1926.
2 M. D. Calvocoressi, *Musicians Gallery Recollections*, Faber and Faber, London, 1933.
3 M. D. Calvocoressi and Gerald Abraham, *op. cit.*
4 Gerald Abraham, *A Hundred Years of Music*, Knopf, New York, 1938.
5 Alexander Werth, *op. cit.*
6 Lazare Saminsky, *Music of Our Day (Essentials and Prophecies)*, Crowell, New York, 1939.
7 *op. cit.*
8 Constant Lambert, *Music Ho! A Study of Music in Decline*, Faber and Faber, London, 1934.

And listen to Nicolas Nabokov's dyspeptic apostasy:

> ...came a serious and protracted case of esoteric mumps: the music of Alexander Scriabin. It began mildly ... Gradually it spread in area and intensity and I began to revel in the more "transcendental" sonatas of his later period until in my passionate *Flucht in die Krankheit* (flight into illness) I became addicted to the esoteric orgasms of such numbers as the *Poème de l'Extase*, *Vers la Flamme*, and *Prometheus*. Scriabin's music kept me in total subservience for at least three years but then left me abruptly. One morning I woke up with the realization that Scriabin's eroticism was good only for high-strung adolescents, that his orgasms were fake, and that his musical craft was singularly old-fashioned, dusty, and academic.[1]

Repeatedly, voices protest Scriabin, then other minds spur his defense citing him favorably, according him his due. A cult of Scriabin has always been with us, not always articulate, and often sporadic or evanescent. But the thread of Scriabin appreciation has proven remarkably durable.

Let us go to the early beginning. Ernest Newman, once revered dean of England's music critics (*London Times* and the *Manchester Guardian*), recorded this remarkable judgment on a second hearing of Scriabin's Fourth Symphony, the "Poem of Ecstasy."

> ...just as a piece of orchestral music, it must strike even the most casual listener as a masterpiece among masterpieces. It not only takes us into a sphere that was previously unexplored territory for music, but guides us through it with an uncanny certainty, making us almost forget the newness of it all and be conscious only that here some of the most secret and mystical of our dreams have become reality.
> This is what one cannot sufficiently admire and wonder at—Scriabin's perfect command of an absolutely new musical language...[2]

Now, skip down nearly fifty years to Harold C. Schonberg, the *New York Times*'s music critic emeritus.

> This listener had not heard the Scriabin "Poem of Ecstasy" for quite a few years. It is a curious score, and a strangely attractive one. There is even a section

---

1 Nicolas Nabokov, *Old Friends and New Music*, Little Brown and Co., Boston, 1951.
2 Ernest Newman, "Music in London," *Manchester Guardian Weekly Edition*, 31 October, 1919.

that anticipates Stravinsky's "Firebird." . . . Scriabin's spirit must have been a very sensual one. The music is lush and as sexy as music can get.
But it is not post-Wagnerian. Scriabin's harmonic ideas were too advanced for that, and his language is very original. Perhaps a re-examination of his work is in order.[1]

Soon after, Schonberg expressed more fully developed, second-thoughts:

Not only is the composer out of favor, but there seems to be active resentment when his music is played. Let a pianist present a group of early Scriabin preludes and etudes, and critics will go out of their way to condemn the music as nothing but diluted Chopin. Let one of the late piano pieces be programmed, and the musical intelligentsia are up in arms, inveighing against Scriabin's diffuseness, vagueness and fake philosophy.
Thus it is with some diffidence that I set my piping treble against the great roars of his detractors. I happen to adore his music, all of it . . . those graceful, melodic aristocratic, perfectly proportioned piano pieces, up to about the Fourth Sonata, belong in every pianist's repertory.
The really significant contribution of Alexander Scriabin, however, comes with the later works . . . Scriabin has been largely ignored outside of Russia . . . This grieves those of us who consider Scriabin one of the most original, fascinating, enigmatic, revolutionary—and, yes, rewarding—composers of the century.[2]

(Of another performance of the "Poem of Ecstasy," a major critic, Alan Rich, simply said, "I hated it."[3]) However, in between the time distance from Newman to Schonberg, another critic during the second decade of the twentieth century, Lawrence Gilman, kept his eye cocked at "the only Russian doing something new . . ."[4]

Others have been consistently appreciative. Nicholas Slonimsky, leading protagonist for Russian music in America, calls Scriabin "a great composer, and prophet of metaharmony."[5] Composer Aaron Copland praised him for being "often magical . . . the best examples I know of

[1] Harold C. Schonberg, "Music; Maazel Returns," New York Times, 26 March, 1965.
[2] Harold C. Schonberg, New York Times, 11 April, 1965.
[3] Alan Rich, World Journal Tribune, 19 January, 1967, New York City.
[4] Lawrence Gilman, "Mystical Tone Poet," North American Magazine, June 1922.
[5] Nicholas Slonimsky, Music Since 1900, W. W. Norton, New York, 1937.

'pure' inspiration."[1] And Ned Rorem, the composer, with considerable fancifulness has spoken well of him.[2] Among international musicologists, Adolfo Salazar wrote:

> The last six sonatas for piano by Scriabin probably represent the most important music of this type written in Europe between 1908 and 1913 and we may even add that, after this date, in the years between the First World War and the Second, there have been no sonatas written for solo piano worthy to be placed beside them.[3]

Salazar goes on to speak of the music's "chordal hypnotism." Music critic Irving Kolodin perspicaciously stated that Scriabin "is not merely of today, but emphatically of tomorrow."[4]

Vladimir Horowitz was the celebrated exponent of Scriabin in America. He signed a notable statement in 1956: "The time has come for a rehearing of this man who has so vastly enriched our piano literature,"[5] and promptly issued an all-Scriabin record. Certainly Horowitz enriched our comprehension of Scriabin.

In Horowitz's youth, his talent was submitted to Scriabin—so great was his name then—for approval or sanction. Here is Horowitz telling the story of his first meeting with the master:

> I played for Scriabin in Kiev, before one of his concerts, when I was a boy of ten. Just three months before he died, at the age of forty-three. My uncle, the brother of my papa,[6] was an accomplished pianist and musicologist, a music critic, and the greatest friend of Scriabin, so when he told Scriabin he had a very talented nephew, Scriabin probably hated to do it, to listen to me play, *just before his own concert!* But he probably said to himself, "I *have* to do it." So my parents took me, and I played some Chopin, some Paderewski, some other things, and he told my parents, "Don't make of him a sectarian pianist; make him a cultured musician."

---

1 Aaron Copland, *Our New Music*, McGraw-Hill, New York, 1941.

2 N. Rorem, *Paris Diary*, George Braziller, New York, 1966.

3 Adolfo Salazar, *Music in Our Time* (Translated from the Spanish by Isabel Pope), W. W. Norton, New York, 1946.

4 Irving Kolodin, Program Notes to the Vladimir Horowitz Anniversary Recital Commemorating the Twenty-fifth year of his American Debut, Carnegie Hall, 1953.

5 Sleeve of Vladimir Horowitz's all-Scriabin record, RCA-Victor LM 2005, 1956.

6 Alexander Horowitz (1877-1927), professor of piano at the Conservatory in Kharkov, and Scriabin's pupil.

Another pianist was not so happily received. Seventeen-year-old
Artur Rubinstein (1897–1982) appeared at the door, and Scriabin said of
himself: "I was once a Chopinist, then a Wagnerist, now I am only a
Scriabinist." When young Rubinstein mentioned Brahms, Scriabin was
annoyed, "How can you come to me wanting to be a Scriabinist and
yet praise Brahms?" Later Rubinstein would be the first to introduce
Scriabin's Fifth Sonata to London.

The push and pull of partisanship over Scriabin is extraordinary. Why
were (and are still) voices of animadversion so raucous? What crime does
Scriabin's music commit?

Boris Schloezer (1881–1969), biographer of Scriabin, his brother-in-
law and translator of Dostoevsky into French, was one of the first to
express his astonishment. He was struck when he went abroad by the
inimical attitude toward Scriabin. He attempted an exclamation:

> Every Russian musician leaving his own country to live on the continent is
> amazed at the complete lack of recognition which the Occidental world gives
> to Scriabin. Indeed, the indifference of France even takes the form of hostility
> toward an art of which, nevertheless, Parisians know little enough.
> In Russia, the influence of Scriabin is so far-reaching that there is scarcely one
> young composer who has escaped it. Many copy him directly, others seek
> new fields along the road taken by him late in his life, still others attempt to
> react against him, trying to create in an opposite direction, and yet proclaiming
> their "anti-Scriabinism," and invoking Rachmaninoff or Medtner, even they
> cannot deny the charm of the author ... and Scriabin's power in Russia ...
> The forces which have made Scriabin the unquestionable master of young
> Russia also account for the paralysis of his effect elsewhere. The spirit of his
> music finds no alliance with the spirit of postwar Europe where one perceives
> the need of calm, stability, a desire for order, a fear of experiments in every
> field, in politics, literature, poetry and music. In France, especially, the reigning
> tendency is traditionalist in the largest sense of that word, embracing nearly all
> the arts, providing a setting in which Scriabin appears old-fashioned, a démodé
> anarchist. Scriabin's restlessness, his over-reaching desire, his ecstaticism are
> felt as vain agitation, weakness and lack of discipline. His work is a mighty
> explosive, without effect where the conditions for its reception are unfavorable.
> The spirit of Scriabin believes in music as a special magic, and he dreams of
> a godlike art whose function is to remake man and transfigure nature.

But one might well ask, why should Scriabin the *artist* remain a stranger?[1]

American critic Paul Rosenfeld offered an explanation: "The complete eclipse of Scriabin's fame, by no means honorable to the musical profession or advantageous to musical culture, was largely the snobbish concomitant of one of those changes in musical fashion . . ."[2]

Artur Rubinstein, the pianist, attributed this anti-attitude, the neglect of Scriabin, to our times. "He was a romantic lyricist," he said in private conversation with me in 1961. "He always has emotion and feeling, even underneath his most *schablone*—patterned and schemed—music. The public wants coldness, not warmth. Look at this vogue for pre-Bach! Look at those moderns who are popular. Where's the lyric sweep? The heart? No, today *rejects* Scriabin and his romanticism."

Pablo Casals (1876–1973), from another area, in a letter of 1967, expressed bewilderment. The two had met in 1914: "He was one of the most renowned composers and his works were played all over Europe. I keep a warm souvenir of his distinguished and sensitive personality. I admired him then, as I do now. How I regret that his music is not much played." And clever Seroff found the hostile nerve not in Scriabin but in Scriabinists:

> Scriabin's musical mysticism was considered the only doctrine of musical evolution with a future and the one true aesthetic fate . . . To prove one was advanced you waxed enthusiastic over Scriabin whose musical mysteries and ecstasies were the fashion (other music could be disposed of by elevating the nose) . . . The wheel of time has passed over Scriabin more rapidly than one would have expected . . . If Scriabin should have a renaissance, which is probable, for his purely artistic qualities are too great to fall into oblivion, it will never be maintained that his doctrine is the only possible salvation for the future of music . . .[3]

Today, the pessimism has changed. Scores of pianists have recorded Scriabin's music and many conductors have recorded all five symphonies. Scriabin at last may be said to be in vogue!

---

1 Boris de Schloezer, *Scriabine, The League of Composers' Review*, Vol. 1, No. 3, November 1924.

2 Paul Rosenfeld, *Discoveries of a Music Critic*, Harcourt Brace and Co., New York, 1936.

3 V. Seroff, *op. cit.*

✐ II ✐

AMONG THE SOVIETS . . . FOR A WHILE

FOR GEOGRAPHICAL and cultural reasons, Scriabin's widest body of railers and ralliers has always been in Russia. Immediately on his death in 1915 a large Scriabin Society was organized. And there has also been a consecutive line of superlative pianists continually performing his music: Heinrich Neuhaus (1888–1964), founder of the Soviet school of pianism, Prokofiev himself, Sofronitsky, Feinberg, Bekman-Shcherbina (1882–1951), Lev Oborin (1907–1974), Margarita Fyodorova, and master of all, Sviatoslav Richter (b. 1915).

Alexander Goldenweizer (1875–1961), late Director of the Moscow Conservatory (Vladimir Horowitz's teacher), spoke on the subject of Scriabin: "I was among the first to play Scriabin," he said, "that man of genius . . . The West is indifferent to him, and his marvelous piano works are never played by foreign pianists; and yet they accept our present day modernists as their own . . .."[1] Soviet musicologist D. Zhitomirsky expresses the present official attitude categorically: "Scriabin was a daring thinker and innovator who will always be counted dearly in the culture of mankind as a whole."[2] So does Mikhail Mikhailov: "Scriabin anticipated stereophonic effects in his placement of audiences or performers, he forecast electronic instruments in his use of noise-sounds . . . and science fiction in the colors cosmonauts see while they hear music . . . All forward-looking men must cherish him and rejoice forever."[3] But matters have not always been easy, even in the homeland.

---

[1] Alexander Werth, *op. cit.*

[2] D. Zhitomirsky, *Conversations about Modern Russian Composers*, Soviet Composer, Moscow, 1960.

[3] M. Mikhailov, *A. N. Skryabin*, Muzyka, Moscow & Leningrad, 1966.

After the October Revolution of 1917, a reaction set in against Scriabin. Mystical prophets were suspect. By 1923, virulence towards Scriabin was open. The All-Soviet Association of Proletarian Musicians (VAPM) and the All-Russian Association of Proletarian Musicians (RAPM), musical OGPU's so to speak, wanted "simplification" in music. They denounced Scriabin. L. Lebidinsky, their chief, saw in Scriabin what he also saw in Liszt and Chopin, "...the agitation of men incapable of fighting for socialism. Worse! They are all *enemies* of socialism." Even Tchaikovsky was indicted for "criminal pessimism."

Stalin persisted, "The composer must learn to master all musical resources for the complete musical expression of the ideas and passions motivating Soviet heroes."[1] VAPM and RAPM were Stalin's musical arms. How could Scriabin with his morbid complexities and fantastic, personal and private heroics fit? Young Shostakovich mimicked Stalin: "Scriabin is our bitterest musical enemy," he cried at home and abroad. Finally, under total pressure from Russia's musicians, in April, 1932, the two organizations were liquidated. Scriabin's ghost was reprieved from its prison of hate. Again it began to haunt memories.

Reinstatement is always more difficult than denunciation. Scriabin's hushed proponents had to invoke another god before their god could reascend. Lenin had said, "I can't listen to music too often...it affects my nerves." His favorite piece, according to Maxim Gorky, was the *Appassionata Sonata* of Beethoven. "Superhuman music," he called it. Nevertheless, Lenin had written during the revolutionary confusion when no one was certain of what stand to take or what was acceptable, "To associate certain great artists with the Revolution may at first seem strange and forced... Great artists still reflect in their works something of the essence of our Revolution... A reflection cannot exist independently of what it reflects..."[2] Thereupon, he signed and sealed the famous proclamation of 30 July, 1918. According to it, "Doers in the Arts and Sciences" of Russia's past regardless of their ideological associations were decreed to be protected and preserved. The protocol listed Alexander Nikolaevich Scriabin.

1 Martin Cooper, *Russian Opera*, Max Parrish, London, 1951.
2 V. I. Lenin, *Leo Tolstoi as a Mirror of the Russian Revolution*, Collected Works, Vol. XII, p. 331.

Still another god was summoned to Scriabin's support, Georgy Plekhanov (1856–1918), father of Russian Marxism.[1] He was, of course, inimical to Scriabin's ideas (not his art), but he nevertheless had spoken the truth when he wrote: "Scriabin was of the very flesh and blood of our Russian intelligentsia . . . He was a son of his times expressed in sounds."[2]

Anatol Lunacharsky (1875–1933), first People's Commissar of Education and Minister of Culture, the aesthetic arbiter of all Soviet art, and inventor of the phrase "socialist realism," was a brilliant intellectual. He kept the cultural keel during the tumultuous changeover period between revolution and high Stalinism. He said, "Scriabin is near to us because he embraces in his work the fascination of revolution . . ."[3] Soviet critic Alshvang added his weight squarely placing Scriabin in the new Russia: "While clearly not understanding the events of the Revolution, Scriabin still marvelously expressed the heroic energy of revolutionary consciousness and its proud will to conquer."[4]

Around this time too, Isadora Duncan, (1878–1927) who had become a self-converted Red, wrote her accompanist, Vitya Seroff, "Are you playing beautiful music? Think of me and play Scriabin."

So, the Scriabin apartment was designated a museum in 1922. As a State Museum it was restored exactly as it had been in Scriabin's lifetime. Furniture that had been sold to buy food was traced. The fine copies of Correggio's Jupiter and Venus bathing in the nude were hung again on either side of his narrow bed. They had been considered erotic and therefore hidden after his death. Blavatsky's *Secret Doctrine* (in French), the score of Debussy's *La Mer* ("He shouldn't have stolen from our Russian music," was Scriabin's only known comment on Debussy), Strauss's *Heldenleben*, volumes of autographed poetry from the "decadents," the symbolist poets, books of philosophy were repurchased and returned to the bookcases. Scriabin's favorite Chinese figurine of the Goddess of Mercy was put back on his composition writing desk. The little circle of light bulbs for music-color experiments, built by his friend

---

[1] Samuel M. Baron, *Plekhanov*, Stanford University Press, Stanford, California, 1963.
[2] Letter from Plekhanov to Dr. Bogorodskii, *Memorial Collection, op. cit.*
[3] Anatoly Lunacharsky, *Revolutionary Silhouettes,*, Hill and Wang, New York, 1968.
[4] A. Alshvang, *Classics of Russian Music—Scriabin*, Muzgiz, Moscow ,1945.

Professor Alexander Mozer, was reconnected. The esoteric, mystical painting of a saint by Sperling was put back in its frame. Various documents, manuscripts (including sketches for the preamble to the Mysterium), photographs, letters were all collected for safekeeping. Everyone who had ever been close to Scriabin at any time was commissioned to write their reminiscences. These are stored in strongboxes in the basement.

Today when you climb the flight of stone stairs to the apartment house in the Nikolo-Peskov Lane, lovingly cared for by its present protectrices, Bachstein, you enter Scriabin's life. The lingering rays of his presence flicker. A continuous tape recording plays all seventy-four of his opuses. His piano stands open, and you may play on it. It is a gathering place for youth. Electronic composer Vladimir Ussachevsky, among others, finds it a most congenial spot for learning what Russian youth is thinking about, feeling, and doing in musical Russia.

Scriabin is, as Richter says, "in the mainstream of Russian life and music. We are exposed to him from childhood. He forms some of our earliest musical memories." Several music schools or *tekhnikums* bear his name. (Composer Kabalevsky graduated from one.) Entrance and exit examinations at conservatories sometimes include such questions as "What are the three periods of Scriabin's creative work?" "Outline his five symphonies." International piano competitions, including the Grand Tchaikovsky Prize, prescribe a Scriabin sonata, along with Beethoven or Chopin.

Soviet government subsidies contributed substantially to Scriabinic knowledge. From 1927 to 1929 the Musical Sector of the State Publishing House (Muzgiz) in Moscow republished Scriabin's complete works, including posthumous music as well. Even the alternate version of the famous D♯ minor Etude, Op. 8, was issued (in 1949), which shows how it was conceived and should be played. All the music was carefully annotated, minutely corrected.

The editorial commission consisted of the USSR's highest names—composers, professors, pianists and critics—all of whom knew Scriabin or had heard him perform: Alexander Goldenweizer, Mark Meichik, Leonid Sabaneeff, Alexander Khessin, Anatol Alexandrov, Nikolai Zhilaev, Nikolai Myaskovsky, Victor Belaieff, and A. Efremenkov. Their work was expert and judicious.

From 1939 to 1940 V. Zhdanov assembled a large number of letters written by Scriabin, but the project was abandoned with the proofs of the proposed book filed in the Scriabin Museum archives. The monumental achievement of collecting all Scriabin's letters waited until 1965.

GIMN, the State Institute of Musical Sciences under the direct auspices of the Academy of Arts and Sciences, evolved a system called "biometrics." They devoted thousands of manhours to Scriabin, counting the number of times given "type-elements"—chords, distribution of harmonies, figurations, tonalities, meters, melody sequences, duration of certain harmonies, etc.—appear in his music. They found, to cite one instance, the dominant seventh with an augmented fifth (V_7 plus 5; C, E, G$\#$, B flat), an appropriate departure point for measuring his music biometrically. By adding the number of times it appears with the length of time it is actually held and heard, then multiplying and dividing the results proportionately on a basis of total number of pieces written and examined, they arrived at this table:[1]

Scriabin:	1st period	Opp.	1–24	67 units
	2nd period	Opp.	25–48	1,456 units
	3rd period	Opp.	49–74	560 units

The same chord in other music proportionately:

Wagner	72 units
Mozart	12 units
Bach	10 units
Beethoven	2 units

From this, you deduce that such a harmony was frequently employed by Scriabin, but in his later works he evolved away from it. Stylistically, you also see his harmony is closest to Wagner and furthest from Beethoven. A comparison with Tchaikovsky or Debussy, more pertinent and to the point, has yet to be published. The biometrical principle carried to ultimate lengths investigates every aspect of music, harmony, counterpoint, distribution and duration of tone, phrase, and speed.

Georgy Konyus (1862–1933), an important professor of theory at the Moscow Conservatory, invented "metro-techtonic analysis," a system of

---

[1] *Pro Musica Quarterly*, "The Biometrical Method in its Application to Question of the Study of Style," Leonid Sabaneeff, Translated by S. W. Pring, December 1927.

scientific measurement to record symmetry in musical forms. He published his researches in part. They discover hidden proportions of equilateral phrasings in old masters and certain moderns, not evident from bar markings alone. This balancing of four musical rather than metrical measures with four, or six with six, etc., looks diagramatically symmetrical, but was arrived at by composers intuitively. Konyus's methodical system cannot substitute for inspiration in composing, any more than biometrics can. The occasional examples of symmetry in harmony which I have cited in this book were arrived at independently and are meant to indicate a possible formula for the idiosyncratic effect of Scriabin's music.

The Soviets also studied Scriabin's tempi. Taking only melodies and counting their metronomic speed as marked by the composer, Soviet musicologists discovered that 60% of his music is "fast," 30%, "slow," and 10%, "medium." His music had, in their official though romantic words, an "impetuosity to match the feverish tempo of his spiritual life." This result is the opposite of say, Rimsky-Korsakoff (60% slow and 30% fast), and strikingly different from gloomy Mussorgsky (66% of whose melodies are slow, and a mere 30% fast). Tchaikovsky turned out to be the most equanimous of all: 36% slow, 34% medium, and 30% fast.[1]

Another group of biometricists collected statistics as to the relative choice of major or minor keys. Forty-six percent of Scriabin's first thirty opuses use the minor key. (A similar study of Mozart yields 12% in the minor key.) As for accidentals, chromatic sharps and flats that is, after the tonality is set, raising and lowering the pitch of notes so as to color the music into higher complexity, Scriabin's first thirty opuses averaged a high 45% as contrasted with Haydn, or more surprisingly, Grieg, who kept their alterations at 20% and 24% respectively.

Germans too have devoted close analytical attention to the structure, harmony and form of Scriabin's music. One book of brilliance, *The Symphonic Works of Alexander Scriabin*,[2] breaks down the detailed structure of every Scriabin orchestral work. Measure by measure Clemens-Christoph von Gleich traces main and subsidiary themes, developments, reprises, recapitulations, codas, as well as each rhythmic and harmonic device employed. He even finds one identical passage common to De-

---

1 I. I. Lapshin,*op. cit.*
2 *Op. cit.*

bussy's *La Mer*, Scriabin's "Poem of Ecstasy" and Stravinsky's *Firebird*. The book also has a detachable appendix with 173 musical examples—Scriabin's symphonies in thematic nutshells—and an extraordinary diagrammatic picture of *Prometheus* with its eleven themes symbolically represented like a score of electronic music. Another useful work is by Hans Steger.[1]

Scriabin's only recorded piano performances were seven pianoplayer rolls for Phonola and the Welte-Mignon Company in Leipzig. Welte-Mignon invented in 1903 a contraption to be attached to a special piano which paper-recorded a performance by means of the keys puncturing holes. Studying these is like analyzing a writer's personality from his typescript. True, something can be told, but imponderables and impalpables, the speed or slowness of depressing the key, its release, the mystery of flesh against ivory and ebony cannot, of course, be found.

Mechanical speeds can, however, and the general sense of a piece. One Soviet musicologist[2] deciphered the exact speed of each passage as played by Scriabin. He wanted to capture the secret of his famous *rubato*, called by some his "arhythm," by others, "capriciousness." The finding is that Scriabin performed well within "the framework of an extraordinarily measured and strict rhythmic skeleton. Although he always played freely, his *accelerando* and *ritard* eventually compensated one another. Unfailingly Scriabin sets a steady and regular, metrical inner pulsation throughout each piece, although the specific metronomic speed changes every so many measures.

For example, in the Poem in F# major, Op. 32, marked on the music at Maelzel's Metronome 50, Scriabin played the first two groups of five measures slowly at MM 49, the next twenty-four measures at MM 50; he played the first ten measures of the reprise faster at MM 52, and the next twenty-four measures again at MM 50. The peg on which the speed framework hangs, obviously, is as Scriabin originally marked it, 50.

---

1 Hans Steger, *Der Weg der Klaviersonaten bei Alexander Skrjabin* (The Path Taken in Alexander Scriabin's Piano Sonatas) published in Munich, 1966, by the Staatliche Hochschule für Musik (Government Academy of Music).

2 Skrebkov, "Certain Data Concerning the Agogics of Scriabin's Own Performances," *Memorial Collection, op . cit.*

Another Soviet musicologist waded through every critique ever written during Scriabin's lifetime of concerts. She sought the secret quality of his playing. Her means was to sort all the comments and descriptions into words and add the number of times each appears. The most often repeated comments were, in this order: "arhythmical," "nervous," "magical," "wizard-like colors," "pedalization," "tonal lights," "pauses," "silences full of thought . . ."[1]

In 1919, shortly after the discovery of Scriabin's secret notebooks, the editors of the M. and S. Sabashnikov Publishing House in Moscow printed them as Volume VI of a series, *Russkiye Propilei* ("Propylaea," derived from the entry-porch at the Acropolis, means "gateway," implying the opening into thought), subtitled "Materials for the History of Russian Thought and Literature." Scriabin shares the volume with Pushkin's early sketchbooks of poetry, an instance of how seriously he was taken as a writer and thinker.

The critical editor of the *Memorial Collection*, Stanislav Markus, undertook the extraordinary labor of scanning every book ever owned or borrowed by Scriabin. He noted all the underlinings and marginal comments made by Scriabin. This resulted in a lecture read at the Scriabin Museum in Moscow on 22 December, 1939, under the title "Concerning the Particularities and Sources of Scriabin's Philosophy and Aesthetics." For the first time the seriousness of Scriabin's philosophical studies was described without the whitewash of mysticism.

Among the most enlightening facets of Soviet scholarship have been the researches of Professor Ivan Lapshin (1870–1952) of Leningrad University, who concentrated on the combination of Scriabin's "philosophy of music" and his "psychology of musical creation."[2] He sets aside Scriabin's hocus-pocus mysticism to make room for the music and philosophy:

> Stupid proponents of Scriabin during his lifetime were inclined to wrap him in the mantle of a prophet, or better put, in the cloak of a charlatan. They preferred above all else his theosophic delirium, theurgic tricks, and thaumaturgic manipulations. This was nothing less than consummate ignorance and a salon type snobbishness of a most frightful tone . . .
> Scriabin's philosophical world-understanding was merely a convenient plat-

---

1 T. Shaborkina, "Notes on Scriabin the Performer," *Memorial Collection, op. cit.*
2 I. I. Lapshin, *Artistic Creation*, Petrograd, 1923.

form from which he fleshed out his artistic, intuitive world-view. We must look at his *works* for the key to his artistic feelings about the world, and not to his philosophy. Music alone is expressible in sounds. No system of thought is.[1]

The sweep of Lapshin's objection strikes at the very kernel of Scriabin and his music. The connection between thought and feeling, philosophy and art, world-feeling and world-understanding was most real to Scriabin . . . and to today's Russians after perestroika. Alshvang asserts that there *is* a bridge between the two and furthermore, "Scriabin walked over it as straight as man can." Scriabin consciously sought to create a spiritual experience intellectually and to do so by means of intensifying musicality and musical sounds. The power of Scriabin's reputation rests on the degree to which he succeeded.

Today in America, in Europe, and in musical Asia, Scriabin is being freed from nepenthe. The restoration is not complete, but he is now half-remembered, rather than half-forgotten. He answers something, particularly for young people.

Van Cliburn, virtuoso idol of musical youth, plays Scriabin warhorses as encores. Other pianists in America also air Scriabin music with notable distinction: Raymond Lewenthal, distinguished pioneer in obscure and unusual areas of music, Ronald Turini (Horowitz's pupil), Anton Kuerti (Serkin's pupil), Daniel Kunin (Michelangeli's pupil), Edwin Hymovitz (Barere's pupil), Paul Schoenfield, Ronald Taub, Peter Serkin, Dmitry Rachmanov, Ruth Laredo and other stars have risen well in contact with the Scriabin azimuth.

A college tour of "young society on campuses" in America showed a preference for talking about Scriabin.[2] Some of this is the vogue for consciousness expansion, the increasing of sensibilities, the psychedelic, and perhaps drugs. But this is only part of the aesthetic journey. Scriabin by his own imagination was the first to conceive symphonies of glances, touches, perfumes, fluttering wings, settings of incense, columns of smoke, music and color to be simultaneously performed. Fire, flame, light was to burst from his music. He spoke of a sonata based on the pain of a toothache, of choruses which dissolved into orchestral music and

---

[1] I. I. Lapshin, *op. cit.*
[2] Leonard Spiegelglass, *The Scuttle Under the Bonnet*, Doubleday, New York, 1962.

vanished. A melody begun in song was next heard . . . as an aroma. His art embraced all the arts—sound in all its forms, movements and dance, voice and choruses and declamation.

He inspired Yves Klein (1928–1962), who painted in fire and attempted to fly. Scriabin conducted flying experiments with his second wife, and considered this physical dematerialization as important in the body as in his music. He wanted his Prelude, Op. 74, No. 2, to be hot as a scorched desert, and passages of his "Poem of Fire" to *sound* as slow as eternity's ticking. His last work (unfinished) was to have bells suspended from clouds. The melody they were to chime was sketched on his deathbed. This would summon spectators and participants—although all would be performers. Scriabin, in brief, began the present-day art and cult of multi-media, spectacles, the assault on all the senses.

Much has been written about mystic experiences felt during his music. Katherine Ruth Heyman, founder of the Scriabin Circle in New York in 1936, wrote eloquently of her visions at hearing his music—waves of light, golden ships floating on seas of violet radiance.[1] Others have recorded similar reactions of total mystic excitements and agitations.[2] Many of these testimonies came from Theosophists, who are predisposed to suprasensory art. But rationalist and positivist Sabaneeff—Scriabin often reproached this Boswell for his anti-mystical stand—wrote about the magic:

> As Scriabin played his secret liturgical acts for people, even a passive listener began to feel currents stretching out to touch his psyche. This was not simply an artistic experience, but something more irrational, something that shattered the frontiers of art . . .

In my own particular case, on two occasions I have seen radiant flashes of blinding colors and lights during performances of Scriabin's music. I neither prepared for them, nor was I able to repeat them a second time. They happened; I saw light unexpectedly and for no explicable or useful purpose. The experiences lasted for not more than a few seconds and were gone. They were quite different from a thrill of sensation, tears

---

1 Katherine Ruth Heyman, *The Relation of Ultramodern to Archaic Music*, Small Maynard and Co., 1921.

2 Eugene Cosgrove, *Letters to a Disciple*, Ashram Press, Chicago, 1935.

of pleasure, or usual emotions associated with beautiful music. I was more surprised than pleased. They have not recurred. But I have not forgotten them.

Olivier Messiaen explained this absence on my part as an "increasing insensitivity," whereas he, for instance, had only to read a page of Scriabin to see colors. Strangely, these colors are different from the ones he saw when he heard the same Scriabin passage actually played. Circumferentially it might be said that as Messiaen invokes light, colors and perfume in his music as did Scriabin, he, however, goes one step backward with his reproductions of bird calls and one step further with his insertion of precious stones and their sparkle in music. The religiosity of both men, another denominator between them, psychologically may be attributed in the one case to the fact of being born on the same day as the Messiah and in the other, the name "messiah" itself.

Or, to cite another deponent of Scriabin's peculiar effect in music, take this passage from Henry Miller's *Autobiography*. Surely it describes something of the extraordinary and extravagant effect Scriabin's music has exercised at large.

> You call it talk, eh? Listen, do we still have the *Poème de l'Extase*? Put it on, if you can find it. Put it on loud. Scriabin's music sounds like I think— sometimes. Has that faroff cosmic itch. All fire and air. The first time I heard it I played it over and over. Couldn't shut it off. It was like a bath of ice; cocaine and rainbows. For weeks I went about in a trance. Something had happened to me. Now this sounds crazy but it's true ...[1]

Such experiences convince me that Scriabin's music adjusts and manipulates sensitivities in sound barely ever explored in music. It taps sources still poorly documented or recognized. Scriabin was wrapped more in a prophet's mantle than a charlatan's cloak. Detached, impartial opinion resulting from a study of his life and especially its crystallizations into music of unique sounds and extravagant conceptions affirms the strange music ... and delight. He crosses, even transgresses, accepted musical experience. He induces visions and paints them with tones. But the source of this genius will always be a riddle, a *zagadka* or "guessing game." All it is safe to say is that examination by the heart shows it to be there.

---

[1] Henry Miller, *Nexus*, Grove Press, New York, 1945.

The enigma of Scriabin is the mystic process by which his madness—not the harsh insanity of today but a softer nineteenth century imbalance in the practical or rational side of the mind—turned into genius. His sick self-thought becomes some of the finest, most exquisite pages of music ever conceived. What happens can only be likened to another enigma—the pearl. That grain of sand is an irritation, a wrong, an evil, and the oyster oozes its shellac over and over to seal and ease the irritant within itself, to heal the scratch and grating harshness, and over and over it seeps its sticky mucus, and suddenly—lo, the pearl. Man's precious gem, so rare, so unique, so lustrous, and glowing with light garnered from the black darkness of the bottom of the sea. Yes, that is Scriabin's music, and its enigma.

BOOK II

. . . Scriabin, that's who it was. Yes, Scriabin could derail me for days . . . the divine Scriabin.

HENRY MILLER in *Nexus*

✐ I ✐

FAMILY

I

"I come from a noble and military family," Scriabin always pointed out in answer to questions of his origins. Like the Pushkins, Turgenevs, Dostoevskys, and other Russians of this specific class before the Revolution, Scriabins were proud of being "hereditary nobles" (*dvoryanye*) and "of the military," although the significance had dissolved into the vague concept of being "wellborn."

The family of Alexander Nikolaevich Scriabin, the composer, traced its ancestry back to the thirteenth century when Russia was under Tatar rule. The name itself derives from *skriba* or "scribe." The first known Scriabin is listed as a "boyar," a Mongol title which meant "Exalted One." Russians who rendered the invading Tatars services—perhaps in this case, of a stenographic nature initially and only later militarily—were rewarded not only with this title but given lands, money, serfs or slaves and, oddly, dignity. To have derived genealogically from the boyars marked a distinction of merit. As the powers of the Asiatic foreigners waned with time, the social and economic structure of boyars stood fast. They and their boyarinas were, in short, gentry. As they left or lost the lands, some served the court and became aristocracy, belonging to part of the *dvoryanstvo* or nobility.

By the sixteenth century boyar-Scriabins had quit their native place near Nizhny-Novgorod (once named Gorky, after the Revolutionary writer). They delegated the management of their village—Skryaba—to overseers and straightway moved to Moscow. This was a national and perpetual failing for Russians. They replied to the lure of fashionable and lively Moscow, and neglected the source of their incomes, until every resource was pilfered, appropriated, or abandoned. By then they were uprooted,

alien to country estate and fatally acclimated to the giddy atmosphere of
Moscow. Even without money they remained there and, because of prestigious birth, their good name continued. They were "upper class."

The conservative, respectable, impoverished but upstanding Scriabins
inveterately accommodated themselves to each period of history and its
slowly changing demands. Thus they turned to the new military, now
a "profession." After all, the army required a modicum of aptitude and
minimal intelligence. Only one other gentlemanly means of livelihood
was open to them, diplomacy. Therefore, in the eighteenth century we
find a single mention of the Ambassador to Switzerland, one Scriabin, and
the court annals list a certain General Scriabin. These are, in brief, the
composer's only known distant forebears.

By the middle of the nineteenth century, Russia was sufficiently Westernized that the purlieu of decent occupation was opened to both law and
medicine. Trade or physical labor remained anathema. These lacked direct control over human life, and therefore were unsuitable to gentlemen.
Most Scriabins until the very end of tsarist Russia remained steadfastly
devoted to the military. For elder sons the army was compulsory as a
lifetime career. For the others, a Cadet Corps schooling, that is the equivalent of gymnasium or junior and high school, was obligatory.

The entire nineteenth century of Russian wars had offered opportunities for military advancement. Yet, for all this, no "noble and
military" Scriabin rose to the ancestral rank of general. The turbulence
of Russian history did, however, thin their numbers.

The composer's immediate family begins with the grandfather, Alexander Ivanovich Scriabin (1811–1879). By the time of his retirement, he had
been knighted with the Order of St. George and attained the rank of
Colonel in the Tsar's Artillery. The preponderance of artillery in Russian
military history goes back to Ivan the Terrible, and more than one Scriabin
chose it as his special field of service. Alexander Ivanovich's younger
brothers were scattered over the country in minor training outposts.

According to those few who remembered Alexander Ivanovich, he
was quiet, not much given to speaking, gentle-seeming, and absent or
preoccupied in both manner and thought. He preferred the company of
children to adults. When they grew up, he changed for the worse. He
became autocratic, and even treated his own family like subordinates in
an army platoon.

Somewhat late in life and career, at 35, he acceded to a marriage arranged by his parents. They had selected a girl twelve years his junior and the daughter, fittingly enough, of a naval lieutenant, Elizabeth Ivanovna Podcherkova (1823–1916). Part of the bargain, and old-fashion-. ed marriages of this sort were full of clauses and counter-expectations, included the acceptance of Elizabeth's older sister, a spinster, Maria (1822–1908) in the Scriabin household for life. They rented a small house or *domik* near the Pokrovsky Cantonment where Alexander Ivanovich was stationed. Here on the edge of suburban Moscow at the Pokrovskie Gates, where carpenters and lumber markets were centered, the Scriabins remained until long after the old colonel's retirement. Close by was the Novospasky monastery whose archimandrite was a visitor. Over the walls the monks' music was well within hearing.

In the space of eighteen years eight children were born. First came Vladimir (1847–1915) who was the first to vindicate the family aspirations, for after long service as Colonel Instructor and Tutor, Company Commander of the 2nd Moscow Nikolai I Imperial Cadet Corps, he was promoted to the rank of general and retired. The cost of Vladimir's devotion to the Army was perhaps marriage late in life to a woman even older and duller than himself. From this marriage came two sons, one a naval captain and the other a lieutenant in the Rostov Grenadiers, and a daughter.

The second of Alexander Ivanovich's sons was Nikolai (1849–1914), father of the composer. Then came an only daughter, Lyubov (1852–1941), and in well-spaced succession five more sons: Alexei (1853–1916), made a general in 1911 and later appointed Commander of the Omsk Military District; Alexander (1855–1918), officer of the 1st Ulansk Regiment in St. Petersburg and a Privy Councilor; Nil (1861–1934); Peter (1864–1918), who became a colonel in the artillery; and Dmitri (1865–1928), whose career ended as Major-General of the 2nd Mikhail Artillery and Instructor at the Artillery Academy. The imprint of the father was strong on these sons and it visited unto the final generation. All had at least one son who served Russia either in the army or navy.

The unique daughter became plainer the older she grew. Her wide-apart eyes, framed in ringlets of mouse-brown hair, gave her face a vacuous expression, one almost of stupidity. She never married. Her life centered itself in constant devotion and amiable attendance upon her family. She lived in happy bondage to them all, as a self-effaced person.

Fortunately she wrote her *Memoirs* (unpublished) for posterity, and they are at once openly sentimental and unconsciously piercing in brave asides. Her single reference to Alexander Ivanovich is passingly adequate to disclose the tyranny under which the children lived. "Ours was an extremely patriarchal family... All my brothers had to return home for the Christmas and Easter holidays... from wherever they might be and whatever their age... " For sons living at home, such as little Dmitri, for instance, or those old enough to be boarding at the 1st or 2nd Moscow Cadet Corps in cantonments, this was simple. It was for Vladimir, stationed a horse-pulled tramway's ride across town from the Pokrovskie Gates in the garrison of Lefortovo (from the French *le fort*), a spacious, gracious park of lawned squares, red brick buildings, clean barracks, and with large private apartments for officers permanently billeted there.

As time passed and the sons reached their majority and married, the act of returning home became difficult, particularly for Nikolai, who was to journey far afield in his life. Still he obeyed the patriarch, and when he became head of a family himself, he exercised his parental rights to demand reunions. His own son, Scriabin the composer, always called him formally "Nikolai Alexandrovich" when speaking about him, although to his face, he was *papasha*.

The Scriabin household bustled at such times. Excitedly the old Colonel, his wife, her sister, and the one daughter awaited the returning men. The little house shook with voguish, dilettante music of the day and Yuri Engel paints the picture rosily, "Perhaps the standard of homemade music was not very elevated and the repertoire limited, but Scriabins spent whole days in its merriment. They played and sang and danced together with delight. Everything and everyone was gay and friendly." Even the family cat was musical, the only animal in the *domik*, and he would sit under the piano when it was played.

The Cadet Corps taught music, and some of the sons valiantly played in military bands: one the flute, another the clarinet, still another the cornet. One of them attempted the violin. When at home, they pounded and strummed the little upright piano which was Lyubov's single solace at the time. Nikolai was even able to pick out melodies with one finger.

Music was popular in those days, but the majority of it had to be made in the parlor. Gogol propounded the dictum that music's purpose was for "a wife to furnish moments of agreeable relaxation to her husband." Hence, Lyubov, before being relegated to spinsterhood, had been given a daily half-hour's quota of piano lessons over a number of years.

Nikolai was the first son to break with Alexander Ivanovich's military indoctrination. He persuaded his father to let him study law. Respectably enough, for his last year at the Cadet Corps he shifted to the Fourth Gymnasium. He then entered—with difficulty and a good deal of family influence—Moscow University itself, making jurisprudence his major subject.

By 1870 Nikolai was twenty-one with two years of University life to his credit. As usual he spent his summers in the country visiting friends. This time he was at the Bernovs, who had a small piece of land and a *dacha* perched midway along the Nikolaevsky railroad line (later called "October," after the 1917 Revolution) connecting Moscow and Petersburg. (The four-hundred-mile trip could take up to twenty hours.) There was also another houseguest his same age, a girl named Lyubov, like his sister, but who played the piano seriously. Nikolai fell in love.

Lyubov Petrovna Shchetinina (1849–1873), daughter of the respectably employed but hardly wealthy Director of the State Decorative Porcelain Factory outside Petersburg, was chaperoned that summer by her brother, a painter. He was soon to die, as was his sister, but he, according to L. Danilevich, was "unredeemably alcoholic and unstable." As an irony, his talent had just begun to be recognized. He had received some commissions for portraits. One is a large oval painting of Lyubov Petrovna, and from it we see his sister as a sweet woman of ash-blond hair with contrasting, rather heavy black eyebrows, with a stern look and tight mouth of determination to countermand her frail health. His painting reveals more than her single photograph, but both would be cherished by her son until his death.

Remarkable for her day and sex, Lyubov Petrovna was one of the first lady-musicians of Russia. She graduated in 1867 from the Petersburg Conservatory with honors—the Great Gold Medal—and the diploma of Free Artist. She knew Anton Rubinstein as "Little Papa," and he replied equally intimately, "Little Daughter." Her piano teacher was no less than Theodor Leschetizky, the most lauded pedagogue of Europe. He rated

Lyubov as . . . "among ladies, the greatest." Grand Duchess Helena Pavlovna attended the graduation recital. So did Alexander Borodin, and in the artists' room he warmly complimented her. Subsequently she concertized in both SPb and Moscow.

Nikolai Kashkin, theory and history professor at the Moscow Conservatory, recalls the gist of a conversation he once overheard between Tchaikovsky and the critic, Hermann Laroche (1845–1904). Both of them agreed "that Shchetinina girl is a true virtuoso, but lamentably, her physical stamina precludes any extensive career . . ."

Nikolai and Lyubov Petrovna were married precipitously in autumn of 1870. Nikolai is depicted by his contemporaries as "strong, energetic, severe to the point of despotism, despite an innate goodness of heart." "Whatever he demanded had to be given," says Engel pointblank. He had ignored the all-important family consultations which were the heartbeat of the ladies at home and the law of the patriarch.

In the spring term of 1871, again Nikolai was to act wilfully. He stopped taking classes at the University. He was not doing well and promptly swept off to Saratov, a large city on the Volga more than a thousand miles by river from Moscow and half as much again from the Caspian Sea itself. He planned, with Muscovite condescension towards anything provincial, to set himself up as an advocate. His scant smattering of two-and-a-half years of jurisprudence was enough for the unsophisticated South, he assumed. They had spent the dowry money. A baby seemed on its way. If they had to be poor, Nikolai argued, at least the climate would be clement and healthful fruits abounded.

Nikolai worked all summer as a lawyer. He went into legal partnership with a certain Skripitsin. His wife, impelled by her own ambitions, pressed her concert career. Nikolai's law partner also had a musical wife, a soprano. One program still extant, fancily printed on yellow silk is dated 30 October, 1871—Lyubov was seven months pregnant—and shows a joint recital given by the ladies. Charity made the occasion thoroughly respectable. The proceeds were to be donated for the building of the first "shelterhouse for juvenile delinquents in Saratov."

Lyubov played a full program, tersely listed in the fashion of the day as Scarlatti Sonata; Chopin Ballade and A minor Etude; "piece" by Leschetizky; Schumann, *Warum*; Wagner, "Evening Star;" Verdi-Liszt, *Rigoletto*; Gounod-Liszt, *Faust*, and "Scherzo" by Lyubov Petrovna

Scriabina. This last piece, the first music created by anyone named Scriabin, no longer exists. The local reviews left no description beyond the fact. In between this piano section, the soprano inserted her program of songs, arias, and lieder. This shows astounding endurance on the part of Saratov audiences.

Indefatigably, or compulsively, Lyubov played a solo concert on 20 December, five days before the child was born. Her program this time was less audacious—Bach, Fugue; Chopin, Berceuse and Etude; Anton Rubinstein, Nocturne; Schubert-Liszt, *Erlkönig*, and Liszt, Hungarian Rhapsody.

Next morning the couple left Saratov . . . for good. It had been reckless for Lyubov to perform these difficult pieces in public, and also to corset herself tightly in evening dress with a baby imminent and to delay their departure. They had to reach Moscow in time for the confinement (in patriarchal style) at the house of the husband's parents. Besides, the holidays for Alexander Ivanovich started on Christmas Day precisely.

The railway ride was joggling with sporadic stops at all hours of day and night. The cold grew extreme the further North they went. The train was frightfully overheated, and Lyubov, suffering, stifling, fretful and frightened paced each platform she could. Finally, she "breathed the frost" and caught cold. On the morning of 25 December the couple reached Moscow. Her cough was racking. She was so ill, Lyubov Alexandrovna remembers, that Nikolai and his brothers had to carry her up the tiny flight of stairs to the bedroom.

2

CHRISTMAS DAY, 1871, in Moscow was as always a gaudy, noisy celebration. Church- and party-goers plied the streets all day dropping in on friends to eat little cakes or rolled pancakes. The churches in this city of one hundred and sixty churches rang cannonades of bells for each of the three solemn Christmas Day masses. Golden cupolas in the sunlight steepled the skyline with flashing pinpoints and luminous bulbs of light. Snowcrusts on rooftops and windowsills crackled and snapped as the sun shone steadily. The freezing cold was dry, crisp, stimulating.

Inside the Scriabin *domik* clouds of anxiety hushed the exuberance of assembled relatives. No music that Christmas, only silent waiting. It has generally been stated that the composer was born at two in the afternoon. However, an unfinished draft of a letter to an astrologer who was asked to prepare Scriabin's horoscope gives the information exactly. Written from the Welbeck Hotel in London where Scriabin was staying in March, 1914, it says to a "*Cher Monsieur*" that "I have the pleasure of telling you that I was born on the 25th December, 1871. The hour I can tell you approximately, between noon and one in the afternoon. As for the place, Moscow." While Scriabin's sense of time and inaccuracy in dates on letters was notorious, perhaps in matters mystic he may be trusted.

Aunt Lyubov Alexandrovna now begins the heart of her *Memoirs*: "From the moment Shurinka—I always called him that—entered the world, my memory is vivid. I am now seventy and my mind often fails me, but when I recollect my life, that day of his birth springs first into my head . . ."

On New Year's Eve, propitiously, the infant was christened at the Church of the Three Bishops in the respectable district of Kulishki, literally, "world's end." The grandfather and Maria his sister-in-law stood as godparents, somewhat unusually. In honor of the old patriarch, the child was named Alexander, and his patronymic was automatically Nikolaevich, after his father.

Turning from the child, the family now began discussing Nikolai. He was back in the fold. He had failed in Saratov. He should never have gone. He was a father and husband. Nikolai suggested he might try the diplomatic corps, but this meant first that he would have to return to the University. Still he refused the army, and the patriarch yielded again. The compromise between his past and present was to major in "diplomatic jurisprudence."

The baby's mother grew worse by the day. The Scriabins hired a wet nurse, Arina, a serf, who remained with the family long after her milk had dried. Ten days after the birth the doctor discovered that Lyubov Petrovna's lungs were grievously inflamed. To prevent contagion, Elizabeth the grandmother transferred the baby and nurse to her room temporarily. Later, expecting the worst, the grandmother put Shurinka into the nursery with her young Peter and Dmitri, sons who were then seven and a bare six. This remained a permanent arrangement, and "Thus it was," wrote Aunt Lyubov, "that little Shurinka became our property . . ."

Lyubov Petrovna improved, surprisingly. With her husband away at the University all day and the sons returned to their posts, she would falter downstairs and practice the piano briefly. She spoke of playing a concert in the future. Together the two Lyubovs worked at four-hand arrangements of Beethoven symphonies. The pianist Lyubov taught sister-in-law Lyubov an easy sonata, early Beethoven. She played it for her brothers, and Alexander Alexandrovich, the third son, later remarked "It wasn't well played, but not badly either."

Gloom enveloped the Scriabins again. As in-laws are wont to do, they discussed endlessly how Nikolai shouldn't have gone off at half cock and married Lyubov Petrovna who was congenitally weak, how there had been many stillbirths in that Shchetinina family, how "galloping consumption" had whisked many of its members off to untimely demises, and after all, look at how early that painter brother had died. As hope for the mother diminished, solicitude for the infant Shurinka grew.

The doctor finally despaired. He recommended that Nikolai take his wife, as a last desperate hope, to Europe where the climate was merciful. In September, 1872, without registering for the fall term at the University, he and his Lyubov set out for Arco, a tiny town in the Dolomites. (Arco lies at one edge of the beautiful Lake Garda, a resort for Russians seeking health cures, and so popular that Russian could meet Russian and never depart for a day from his native language. Rimsky-Korsakoff, for instance, wrote the final pages of his recollections there.)

Within a bare seven months of this idyllic life, Lyubov Petrovna died at the age of 23. "There she died, and there she was buried," Aunt Lyubov wrote, "Nikolai came back to Moscow to us, alone." She continues:

> My devotion to Shurinka grew. In truth, all the strength of my love for the other members of my family fastened onto him alone. I even forgot that I was young and that I could still bear a child of my own. Whenever a proposal of marriage was expressed, I had only to take a look at that infant and realize that I would be separated from him. I could not face such loneliness, however rosy the future might seem.

By 1875 the young widower Nikolai completed his four years' stint at the University. He had a diploma, but it had been earned without distinction. Now he expressed a desire to study oriental languages. Again there was patriarchal confabulation. Was this again an excuse to get as far as possible from Alexander Ivanovich? The School for Oriental Languages was in Petersburg. His idea was approved whatever the motivation, because much of Russia's military and political focus turned toward the Near East.

The School for Oriental Languages screened its candidates carefully. The standard of instruction was superlative. Only ten students a year were admitted, and each had not only to be wellborn but gifted. Nikolai, surprisingly, showed linguistic aptitude. Within two years he had a working command of both Arabic and Turkish. This gift of a sensitive ear and an obedient tongue may have been part of the composer's musical heritage, although it is usually only the mother's musicianship which is credited.

On graduation, Nikolai was dispatched as official dragoman or interpreter to the huge Russian Embassy in Constantinople. To Russians, however, this Turkish city was "Tsargrad" (now Istanbul). Through Nikolai's language passed all Russian communication with the Ottoman Court. Once every three years he was allowed four months' home leave. For three of these months, he gallivanted over Europe, holidaying "in civilization," as he called it.

One month he had to spend in Moscow with his family and his son. Aunt Lyubov points out in a mixture of asperity and loyalty how Nikolai "did not help with the material comforts of his own child until the death of Alexander Ivanovich; however, he did send presents."

3

"Two GRANDMOTHERS and an aunt," was how Alexander Scriabin himself telescopically simplified his childhood in later years. He was referring to the *babushki*, Elizabeth the grandmother, and Maria the grandaunt, and, of course, Lyubov. Engel describes this childhood in sentimental tints, as one "passed amid a gently soft and feminine atmosphere set in an old patriarchy of yesterday." The truth was that without anyone noticing it, the Scriabin patriarchy had turned into a matriarchy of formidable sorts. For little Shurinka or Sasha, it was a houseful of doting women. Glinka had been so reared. He wrote of his early life as "a kind of fragile mimosa-like upbringing." Tchaikovsky was called "a glass child," because he was so carefully and cautiously babied. All three had been "born in a shirt," and kept in cotton batting long beyond an appropriate time.

Originally, Elizabeth was autocratic about the baby. She would not entrust her grandchild even to her own daughter, although Lyubov was fresh from experience with her youngest brothers. She had been thirteen when Dmitri was born. Lyubov's attachment to her nephew rapidly reached a state of exaltation. She wrote that when he was a mere one-year, "his face was so extraordinary, not from beauty, but by his welcoming expression and smile, that no one could pass near him without touching him." When she practiced the piano she either propped Shurinka in her arms or laid him on a pillow at the pedals. If he cried in the nursery, Arina would bring him to the piano. "She loved him too, more than her own son," Lyubov generously allows.

There is a sharp moment in the *Memoirs* when Lyubov rebuffs her critics. "Someone who hadn't bothered to learn about the Scriabins mentioned 'those ignorant little aunts.' There was only *one* aunt. I! For my time I was sufficiently well educated . . . I felt secure in undertaking full responsibility for Shurinka's total welfare." Indeed she had studied daytimes at a French *pension* finishing school where young ladies of breeding went to learn a modicum of information and a maximum of decorum. She had piano lessons there under Moses and Krall.

Nikolai taught Lyubov history in his spare time. At fourteen she had at her own request subscribed to a concert series of the newly established and elite Moscow branch of the Imperial Russian Musical Society, abbreviated to IRMO or RMO. Later she spent three years at the Elizabeth Institute for Girls, where she studied "classics." This was more education than many females could boast at the time.

When Shurinka was three and his aunt twenty-three, Lyubov confronted the old ladies with a demand. She had decided to devote her life to the child. Nikolai had approved the idea and she rationalized her desire by saying that it would free the *babushki* "for their more pressing duties within the household." What these could be, aside from Peter who was soon to become a day boarder at his brother's Corps, or the younger Dmitri (Mitya or Misha), is hard to imagine. Lyubov added in her *Memoirs* a final suasion, "Both the child and I were now ready for one another." The grandmothers acquiesced. The boy was given her like a precious and delicate toy.

Now Lyubov waxed euphoric. "Shurinka's love of music showed from the cradle. He bore the piano such a tender feeling that he seemed to think it human." His first words had been "Auntie sit," which meant for Lyubov to play. By now he was making "his own noises," and these moments were his most prolonged spans of attention. The uncles too, whenever they visited the household or the ladies' *dacha* in summer, knew to bring only musical presents—a toy hurdy-gurdy, drums, fifes, and pipes. The house now had a new guitar and dozens of clay reedpipes which Shurinka scattered everywhere in the otherwise tidy rooms.

Until Scriabin was ten years old, almost all his summers were spent in Svidlovo village, an easy drive from Moscow, but cool, quiet, and clean enough to count as a country antidote to the city. There peasants wandered in and out of the *dacha* without knocking. They too brought gifts to Sasha. Always they were "things that made sounds." One favorite was an earthenware bird, and Sasha blew on it, top force, for days on end. Lyubov said that it sounded like "the pipes of Pan," but Vladimir, less enrapt, finally used it for skeet shooting.

Scriabin was able to play the piano by the time he was five, and with both hands. If organ-grinders came begging in the courtyard, he could reproduce their tunes. In Moscow, the archimandrite would sit Shurinka at the piano and listen to him play. That senior monk wanted to satisfy his secret love for secular, even profane music. He hid this taste from his novices. Surely, the playing of a little child, he reasoned, was "blameless."

Lyubov took her ward to the RMO concerts. One season all the Scriabins took a loge for a season of Italian opera at the Bolshoi Theater. His glowing eyes followed the orchestra rather than the singers. His cheeks flushed the moment the music sounded. During intermissions he remained seated studying the instruments the musicians had laid aside.

In town or country, Alexander Ivanovich required an after-lunch walk "for his digestion." In Moscow these family strolls took them from Pokrovsky past the Mikov music store near the Kuznetsky Bridge. Shurinka always ran in there, opened the one grand piano on display, and played little pieces he had heard or improvised. The owner liked children, but a weary grandfather, the *babushki* and aunt had to entice the boy away.

He wouldn't leave until the piano was closed, "so it would not spoil between visits." At night in his own home, he would not go to bed until he had kissed the little upright, quite unlike other Russian children who kissed ikons.

Scriabin himself remembered his earliest childhood only in three phrases: "Love of fairy stories. Strong imagination. Religious."

4

WHEN THE Turkish War of 1877 broke out in April, Vladimir, Alexei and Alexander Alexandrovich—all three military sons—were mobilized for battle. Two were assigned to the stylish Izmailov Guards Regiment. Since Catherine the Great's time this was the most snobbish of regiments. The children, Shurinka and twelve-year-old Mitya, were taken to the station to see the heroes off. Just as the train started moving, the military band burst into a lively quadrille, *Byushka*, in 6/8 time. That night at home Shurinka pounded out the fastest and loudest part of the dance, quite from memory. Then he picked up a toy violin and repeated the same passage. Next day, he worked out the entire piece in all its sections. He played it all day long, first on the piano then on the violin.

At seven Shurinka began to make toy pianos. First he used cardboard, thread, pins, pieces of silk. Later he worked with wood, wire and nails, and borrowed his grandfather's fret saw. In the course of the year he constructed ten such pianos, complete with sounding boards, pedals that worked, legs, lids that opened and closed, keys that moved, wires that stretched and grew thicker in the bass. He always gave them away to the first visitor who admired them. And as soon as he completed a perfect one, his interest lapsed.

In summers, Lyubov always rented a piano for Shurinka. He insisted on it, though it was an extravagance the Scriabins could ill afford. The Mikov music store shipped the same little piano each time, and when it arrived, Shurinka would bossily take over. "Put it here . . . Pull the ropes now . . ."

The education of Shurinka and his literary interest developed side by side with music. At five he had asked his Aunt to stop reading fairy tales.

"They're all false and untrue, Auntie . . . don't read them . . ." She introduced him to the popular literary tastes of Russia then, translations of Dickens and Scott. At six, unnoticed, he copied out a book of alphabet letters given him by his grandmother, and he loved to leaf through illustrated editions of Shakespeare and Molière. He spent much of his time in the corner of his and Mitya's room, now that Peter had gone to the Cadet Corps, at a little table and chair—a present from his father in Turkey.

Above all else at home Shurinka was fascinated by his aunt's embroidering. She gave him pillowcases and napkins with stenciled patterns to work on, but he always devised other designs. For years Lyubov preserved his needlework, scrapbooks, and letters from his father, but one of Moscow's great floods destroyed the ground floor of the *domik* where all these memorabilia were kept.

Shurinka also wrote playlets. When he was seven he would get a notebook and ask his aunt to bind it in cloth first, then he inscribed the title, and afterward wrote the play itself. The plots—in verse always—were always tragic, and classical in five acts. Occasionally they were gory and bloody, so that by the third act all the characters would end up killed off. Then, he would shriek with sadness, "Look Auntie Lyuba, there's no more anyone in the play. They're all finished . . . what can I do now?" He would insist, "All there was for them to do is die."

One comedy, however, brightened the household. Lyubov had read at the family's evening reading session Gogol's short story, *The Nose*. It delighted Shurinka and he adapted it as a playlet. *The Nose*, very much to Russian but not international taste, tells the weirdly comic and satiric story of a barber who finds a nose in his morning breakfast roll.

Shurinka begged for a toy theater. He then made puppets, his own décor and scenic effects. For one play, he sewed scraps of blue gauze together to contrive a sea with rolling waves. On Sunday afternoons uncles and wives from Lefortovo lunched at the *domik*, and afterwards Shurinka performed. He wrote out admission tickets, placed his little theater on a table and set up a row of chairs.

One performance, Lyubov remembers, was laced with songs and music, composed, sung, acted and played by him. He declaimed in various high and low voices, simultaneously watching his audience and his toy characters. "No one is crying," he suddenly burst out. He expounded on the sorrow in the play. Next performance, all the Scriabins wept noisily and Shurinka was offended. "No one in a real theater cries that loud . . . your tears are fake," he shouted, then *he* began crying.

As much as Shurinka filled his aunt's life with joy, he also occasioned her worry. Lyubov was baffled that in spite of all her solicitude, he was fearfully nervous, thin, delicate, subject to illness, and unhappy. There was nothing in the world, according to her, to cause it. When he was seven she took him to Dr. Grigory Zakharin (1829–1897), physician, professor at the Therapeutic Clinic of Moscow University, and specialist in nervous disorders. He assured her that there was nothing specifically wrong, but "good nourishment, summers out of Moscow, and clean air might calm him."

Because he was an only child in a house of old people, Lyubov particularly wanted him to make friends with children his own age. He went to a children's party, one day, and met a little girl his same age, seven, Lisa Ivanova. Shurinka surreptitiously gave her a lace handkerchief which his father had just sent him from Constantinople. Lisa's mother, unnerved by so forward an advance, returned it with rather unpleasant words to Lyubov. The children were forbidden to see each other, but he kept her in his memory and composed a playlet called *Lisa*, later turning it into a little operetta.

Still the boy preferred Lyubov's company, his grandmothers and his uncles. Lyubov frets, "I only wished that at least in the summertime he would play and run about with children his own age. There were so many little boys among our neighbors. They invited him, but he never consented to go."

Another time, when he was nine, the country children created an orchestra of whistles, drums, a barrel organ, and tambourines. They asked Shurinka to conduct, since he was the only one who had ever been to the opera. He agreed. He put a box in the yard to stand on and got a branch for a baton. He decided to teach them a waltz. But they blew so hard, buzzed and howled in their own way so obstreperously that he fled in a state of upset. He and his sensitive ears, Lyubov explains, avoided them ever after.

Young Shurinka was always a very serious child. He never laughed or played games, except when the uncles came. They would throw him in the air, pass him from hand to hand. But Shurinka was never like other children. Nor was he ever mischievous. Perhaps in Russia this was less strange than it would be elsewhere. Both Dostoevsky and Rachmaninoff have stated that as children they were never known to have laughed out loud . . . even once.

Lyubov continued: "Except for his beloved junior uncle Mitya, Shurinka was always with us grownups and females. He studied without stopping all day—at the piano or writing. No rest. He said at night that his thoughts wouldn't let him sleep. He became so very nervous, afraid to be alone in any room, and in bed would even deliberately stay awake so that I couldn't leave him. It disturbed me very much to see him live a life so little befitting a child.

"His only sport was jumping. He would leap from the top of the piano to the floor with ease, giving us all a fright. Sometimes he amused us by imitating ballerinas turning en pointe . . ."

Lyubov realized that music was his sole love, so she now wanted to train him correctly. She was certain that his natural talent would speed him through the groundwork, but he lacked patience. He preferred guessing to reading notes. Worse, he liked only to play by ear and improvise. Lyubov insisted on accuracy. He balked. It was the first time he had ever been "commanded."

As she had taken him to Dr. Zakharin, so she now took him to the supreme adjudicator of musical talent, Anton Rubinstein in St. Petersburg. He (who himself at an early age had been presented for an opinion from Felix Mendelssohn [1809–1847]) assessed the boy's perfect pitch, exceptional memory, his outstanding ability to imitate anything by ear, and he listened to some improvisations. He nodded sagely when Aunt Lyubov told him the boy preferred the piano to toys. "Don't push him," he advised. "Allow him to develop freely, for everything will surely come to him of its own accord . . ."

Long after his career as a pianist was established, Scriabin confessed that he still could not "sightread a Kuhlau sonatina."

II

CADET CORPS

DEATH ALWAYS disrupts sooner or later a family's established way of being. The patriarch died in 1879. The walls of the *domik* seemed to shrink drastically. One by one the sons had all left, but this time the seigneur made his departure.

Vladimir as a result of the Russo-Turkish War was a captain. He now became head of the household. Alexander found a job as Inspector of Taxes and would end up a resident of Petersburg, with a wife. Nil was soon to graduate from the Cadet Corps. From there he briefly embarked on law, sufficiently to become a Justice of the Peace. He moved to a small estate midway between Vilnius (Lithuania) and Minsk, close to the Polish border.

Peter and Mitya, fifteen and fourteen, had already spent several years at the 2nd Moscow Cadet Corps. Military life suited them. Shurinka suffered especially when Mitya left. He had been his last companion, in that house of diminishing occupants. No one had been so close to his own age. Shurinka was too frail in his family's opinion to join him.

Still, the matter of education was irksome. Lyubov had exhausted her book information. Three times a week they worked on history, grammar, composition. The child no longer babbled, "Auntie sit." He pleaded instead, "Auntie, let's study." Shurinka never tired or got bored at lessons, Aunt Lyubov emphasizes, because "his mind was active and occupied." He was quick—too fast—grasping everything she taught. His answers were clear. His attitude, advanced and inquisitive for a nine-year-old. "I realized instinctively that one could not talk to him as one would to another child." He was soon beyond her reach, and she floundered.

Sometime during the year of 1880, Nikolai wrote the family a long and detailed letter. It had been eight years since his wife died, and he had been a year in mourning for his father. He had now removed the black band from his arm. More, he had remarried. The woman, a pretty, dark-featured and vivacious brunette named Olga Fernandez (1862–1959) was thirteen years his junior, close to the same age as his first wife when he married her, and only ten years older than his son, Sasha. They met when Nikolai had first arrived in Constantinople. She was of Italian descent, he was at pains to point out, despite her Spanish name, her accentless Russian and, no doubt, her Jewish blood. She also played the piano ingratiatingly. Sasha was to call her "mamotchka," like that, in Roman letters, not Russian ones.

Nikolai continued the letter by speaking seriously of Sasha's education. He had not seen his son for a year, briefly on emergency leave for the patriarch's funeral, but he had been displeased. He insisted Lyubov send the boy to the *Lycée Français* in Moscow, the most fashionable and expensive school for sons of "noble and military" families. Otherwise his worst fear would be realized—the child was growing up *neobrazovanny*, uneducated, and without discipline. He did not want Sasha to attend the Cadet Corps. He had hated his own life there.

For all the love and recent marriage, Nikolai's heart had not changed. He had become more autocratic, and somehow empoisoned. He weltered with antipathies. He had been promoted, yes, but too slowly. From dragoman-interpreter to vice-consul, then consul, but as his rank rose, the posts themselves grew smaller. He worked in remote places—Bitola, a monastery in Albania (now part of Yugoslavia); Adrianople, then Russian, and now belonging to Turkey; Yannina, Southern Albania (now Ioannina in northern Greece)—all places where Turkish was the *lingua franca*. Briefly he was senior Russian official on the island of Crete.

When he finally attained the title consul-general—and there would never be a higher position for him—he was little aggrandized. The post was in Erzurum, Turkey.

Nikolai's lack of intellect obstructed his advancement, and his temperament could never "accommodate to superiors," as Engel says. The less his promotions actualized his ambitions, the more embittered and self-enclosed he became. And turn he did, sourly against his own country. "The manners of Asiatics," Engel explains, "were the only ones that suited him. In Turkey, Bessarabia, and South Central Europe, people bowed their heads when the Russian Consul walked abroad, but in Moscow he was treated like everyone else." He could not bear the city's conceited indifference to him.

"Here they brush against you on the sidewalk," Nikolai complained. When the Japanese defeated the Russians in 1905, he had a scapegoat. "Before Port Arthur, this could never have happened," he would say of every inconvenience and discomfort anywhere in Russia. Except for that triennial month in Moscow, he spent holidays in Europe. There too Russians received special, if wondering, attention.

Nikolai grew older and got fat. Like all Scriabins he was tiny, even minuscule and now looked dumpy. He wore long "military mustaches" with twirled ends. He never lost his Cadet Corps carriage and bearing. His bulldog chin heightened this impression of strength. His pride kept his head high, nose in air. It was false, this pride, and the strength a mask.

Leonid Sabaneeff describes Nikolai in his later years, "a man really without gifts, a severe despot and actually quite stupid." Scriabin his son once said that his family consisted of "really awfully good little military people and absolutely, *absolutely* dry of ideas. They prefer drinking and . . . doing that other thing . . . to thought. My father is a reactionary. In such soil I have been unable to take root. He has convictions which are . . . how shall I put it? . . . simply Black Hundred. And when you argue, Nikolai Alexandrovich can never concede . . ." Sabaneeff summed up Scriabin's family as "reactionaries of the harmless well-meaning type so prevalent in those old days of the military nobility."

Nikolai and Olga produced a family of four sons and one daughter. Their first son, born a year after the marriage, was named after the father Nikolai (1881-1905); then came Vladimir (1884-1914) named after the then senior Scriabin; now a girl Ksenia (1889-1959); followed by Andrei (1891-1941) and Kyril (1899-1941). All Nikolai's sons—the composer's half-brothers—were destined for military deaths.

6

SHURINKA begged off going to the *Lycée*. He still must equip himself by "studying the sciences." Music promised no livelihood, and Sasha eventually would have to assume financial responsibility for himself. There were no inheritances among the Scriabins, only pensions for Army widows.

Uncle Mitya fired Sasha with passion for the Cadet Corps on his weekends and holidays at home again. Everything outside the *domik's* doors was lived by Shurinka vicariously, either dully through his aunt, or excitingly through this young uncle. Mitya probably confided in him. As Engel states, "They even slept in the same room, and, as always happens with a difference in age, Sasha tried to copy Mitya in everything."

The finical old women had begun to smother Shurinka. Only Mitya eased Sasha's life, perhaps in several ways. *"Le cousinage c'est dangereux voisinage"* (Cousinship is a dangerous proximity) was a familiar axiom in Russia, with several meanings. Sabaneeff declares that Scriabin said to him in all seriousness that, "At nine I was mentally and physically in love in the utmost sense of the word." Who but Mitya could this have been?

The Scriabins were astonished when Sasha announced his decision to attend the Cadet Corps. They acknowledged that the Corps provided the necessary academic education and more, its standard was high in Moscow. Three uncles were already there; so it would be a second home. He would also have access to the piano in Vladimir's capacious apartment. In 1882 Sasha took the entrance examinations. Out of seventy cadets accepted, Shurinka topped the list . . . scholastically.

How sad Lyubov was to see him dressed in cadet uniform. It was sky-blue with silver and blue epaulettes, and a white leather belt. The shiny black, leather-visored cap swamped his face. He was so little and fragile, she says, his clothing hung from him. He himself was happy. He would carefully place the uniform on the back of an armchair to keep the epaulettes stiff, and would brush it thoroughly day after day. "This was the first time he had ever taken care of any belonging . . . I was sad, but also glad that at last he was distracted from music. Music had seemed to act perniciously on his nervous system."

With Shurinka's departure the three lonely old women gave up the *domik*. They divided the furniture among the brothers and promptly moved into Vladimir's bachelor apartment. He needed women's company, they said. The truth was they could no longer afford the rent, and Lyubov wanted to be near Sasha.

The Director of the Cadet Corps was General A. Albedil, a portly, cultivated man, an amateur musician. His daughter, on whom he doted, lived with him on the cantonment grounds and played the piano prettily. Vladimir apprised Albedil both of Sasha's talent and physical shortcomings. Together they connived to excuse him from heavy duty, military drill and even marching.

Sasha was the only cadet of the Russian Army never to carry arms throughout five years of training. Regulations required the boys to hold their twelve-pound rifle by two fingers at all times, even when going to class. How could piano fingers endure this strain? Sasha had only to take a daily half-hour's light calisthenics as substitute. He was permitted two hours a day free time to practice piano. Albedil was delighted. His daughter had a companion-in-music. How could it matter if the barracks lacked a comrade-in-arms?

Cadet life was hard for someone of young Scriabin's mansuetude. The Cadets' only ideals were strength and physical prowess. In Sasha's first year, 1882–83, a certain Grisha was the strongest, handsomest, most agile, and the leader of the class in all sports. His neatest trick was to somersault in the air and land in a pit of sand. One cadet composed a poem to Grisha, "In science he is dumb, but in athletics supreme . . ." The author was Alexander Kuprin (1870–1938), later a much translated author whose first novel, *The Duel*, condemns army life.

Grisha, poor Grisha, even his last name is unknown, but he was Sasha's hero. Sasha used to watch his gymnastics, in ecstasy every time Grisha leapt in the air or landed hard, and bursting out in shrill, nervous laughter. Sasha gave him his ration of milk, which the doctors had specifically prescribed to build up Sasha's strength. By popular acclamation Grisha sat at the head of the table, while Sasha sat at the foot, far from his idol. All the strong boys had to show derring-do. One, for instance, used to stick a needle in his tensed bicep. Sasha would shudder. "How horrible . . . look, look," he would say and not take his eyes away for a second.

The cadets had their own system of ratings. Each new "hazel hen" had to fight against someone of equal weight and height. Grisha awarded the numbers. Sasha's "total absence of muscle" put him at the bottom of the list. Upset, he decided to avenge himself against the smallest boy in the class, but unhappily, the smallest boy was one of a pair of twins who were intensely devoted to each other. No sooner would Sasha lure one away, than the other would come to the rescue. Sasha always had to run from the fray.

The cadets also took their toll of Sasha, because of his special privileges. They called him "Accidental Cadet," "Cadet by Happenstance," and a score of more unpleasant reminders of his weakness and being a misfit. Cadet hazing was the practice, and its particular victims were invariably the sissies in the group. Sasha was forced to drink ink. Some nights he went to bed on a soaking wet mattress.

Sasha tried to establish his worth, but with dreadful lack of success. He told the cadets how clever he was, how he had made little grand pianos that worked. The result: he was teased out of his wits, brutally called "Liar," "Braggart," and "Fibber." Even Grisha kicked and punched him.

Fortunately, one cadet would leave the pack riding down on Scriabin. Leonid Limontov, who later distinguished himself as an actor, has written a chapter of memoirs. He begins with sad-sweetness, wisdom grown tender with retrospect:

> Almost sixty years have come and gone since I met a pale, thin, delicate, boy with hazel eyes. He was standing alone on the parade ground. If I had known this unlikely cadet would one day be the composer we all have heard of, I would never have been so severe in my judgment of him.
>
> At first sight then, I exulted and gloated simply because of his weak face which seemed twisted with sickness. I mocked his small, thin hands and their long fingers.

Limontov and Sasha were both nephews of Corps' instructors, and they had music in common. "In fact, it was not altogether surprising that Scriabin became my beloved friend, for I too was musical with a good ear and an exceptional memory...." Limontov checked with Captain Scriabin whether young Scriabin had ever made toy pianos. The story was true. "We became friendlier..." he wrote.

6

NOVEMBER 8, 1882, unexpectedly elevated Sasha at the Cadet Corps. Each year the Corps celebrated its "holiday," a dutyless and class-free weekend. This always began with a fund-raising concert, a patriotic Moscow event to benefit the cantonment, which always needed money. The artists appearing on the program were fairly famous.

On that eventful day, General Albedil appeared in full dress on the stage. Trailing behind him was the diminutive Sasha in uniform. The captive audience of cadets burst into spontaneous applause, more in relief after the string of fat women and red-faced men performers. Sasha blanched at their rowdy greeting and pinched the bridge of his nose. While Sasha played the piano, Albedil sat beside him on the piano bench. This debut performance at ten was impressive enough to make Limontov's "heart swell with pride . . . and surprise."

The Corps' holiday had also coincided with father Nikolai's leave from Turkey. This was his first return home since marrying. His new wife played in Vladimir's apartment, and Sasha, who still had never had a proper piano lesson, mimicked her two fortes by ear—Mendelssohn's "Gondolier's Song," and a Bach Gavotte. So he played them at the Corps.

Lyubov sat in the front row with her new sister-in-law. All Scriabin hearts, for sure, were swelling along with Limontov's way at the back behind the officers and invited guests. Lyubov informs us of a minor, momentary mishap. "Shurinka was so excited he forgot the ending of the Gavotte," she recollects. "He paused an instant and improvised the rest with his own made-up chords. We who knew the piece were delighted at his inventiveness." Those who didn't were still thrilled at his command. The cadets were uproarious. Their "accidental cadet" really could play . . . in front of people, too.

After the concert the Corps gave a ball. Only daughters of officers, young sisters, or distaff relatives of the cadets were invited. For many cadets, this was their first contact with the opposite sex (apart from the street women who camped outside the barracks), and their first social occasion. Girls accompanied by a related cadet were called "personals." That night, all the "personals" ignored their escorts to surround the boy who played so well. Sasha was asked to lead the cotillion, and, Limontov remarks with cadet-like envy, "Sasha danced all eight mazurkas that night . . ."

Now, a new torment started for Sasha. After this triumph the cadets assumed he could play all their favorite dance tunes. Anytime they caught Sasha going to the library for a book, they dragged him to the adjacent recreation room. The piano was an old, reddish upright, with half its strings broken or yanked out. They demanded sets of quadrilles, waltzes, mazurkas, and polkas, and treated him like a hired musician. If he refused, they tickled him. That, as they had learned on his first day, was what he hated most. So Sasha played while the cadets danced. He produced melodies and tunes they had never heard before, but the rhythms were right. This dance element will often appear in Scriabin music.

One Christmas vacation Limontov and Sasha went to the heart of town on their own, to the Bolshoi Theater. The matinée offered a fairy-tale ballet—a form beloved of Russians—called "The Enchanted Pill," full of songs, dances, declamation, and sudden scenery and costume changes. The evening consisted of Tchaikovsky's *Eugene Onegin*. The boys stayed on. These visits to the Bolshoi became holiday rituals of Gounod's *Faust* and Massenet operas.

Once Aunt Lyubov, Limontov recalls, gave Sasha enough money to eat at the Metropole Restaurant across from the Bolshoi. Dressed in their bright blue uniforms, they boldly walked up to the door, but began giggling and dashed away. Neither had ever eaten in a public place. "So it was once again," muses Limontov, "we saw the evening show with hungry stomachs. That time, however, we were rich enough to buy tea and lemon and a couple of cakes from the buffet in the foyer."

In March, 1881, Alexander II was assassinated. The following year, Alexander III was to be crowned in fullest pomp and holy circumstance. A Cossack Honor Regiment came from Petersburg bringing an entire platoon of mounted trumpeters and drummers. They drilled on the cadets' parade ground. Limontov was bewitched by the metallic clanging resonances. He swore to himself he would create a brass choir for the Corps.

The Cadet Corps at this time lacked a military band, and after ransacking the storeroom Limontov found fourteen cornets, three horns, two clarinets, two flutes, one trombone, and a kettledrum. He tried to convert this into a Turkish drum, such as the Cossacks beat from side to side in their saddles to regulate the riding speed, but the transformation failed.

Limontov wrote a score for his brass band, but Sasha refused to look at it. He knew nothing about instrumentation. Limontov broke into "tears of rage" and accused him of a "lack of friendship." Limontov rounded up twenty-two cadets who rehearsed, while Sasha "frowned and visibly suffered at the racket." Since military music was part of the official curriculum, Limontov and his co-cadets played for General Albedil. He listened. "Friends, you are bad, bad . . . Try to do more than cater-wauling." The group practiced, and they petitioned for a second hearing. Albedil found them "too squawky." Sasha sprang into battle.

"But look what they're playing with. There's not a band in the whole world all horns and a single trombone," he cried.

Albedil gave the cadets good marks, and drew from discretionary funds money to buy all the instruments needed for a proper outfit.

Limontov scored all the latest dance crazes for the new band. He begged Sasha to clarify the middle melodies. He then drew the best from the group and called them "The Gay Dozen." Sasha was asked to conduct, but he declined. Albedil gave permission for the cadets to borrow the instruments over Christmas. So "The Gay Dozen" drove in *drozhkis* into Moscow, and stopping at street corners played while pedestrians danced in the snowy open air. They earned all their Christmas money. Sasha stayed back with his family at Vladimir's apartment, or at friends, but when the "Gay Dozen" returned, he would listen to their adventures with excitement. "When we told him this or that he would spin around the room like a ballet dancer, and he would laugh outright."

Limontov also provides us with the earliest report on Scriabin's creative process:

> Sasha was alone in his uncle's apartment. The room was all dark, except for a fringe-shaded table lamp which lighted some music paper and his pale, pale face. I had, as usual, entered without knocking. He jerked up, frightened.
> He was composing some music of his own. His eyes glowed. His face was white as a sheet. He was scribbling sharps and flats and seemed to be in some sort of creative paroxysm. The fit pervaded his whole being. He continued in this wise for a long time, occasionally leaning back in the armchair and closing his eyes. He would burst out again with ideas, leave the table where he had been writing and walk to the piano.
> "Do you like it?" Sasha asked softly.
> "Yes, what is it?"
> "My Sonata . . . I have just composed it."

Limontov introduced Sasha to the Monighettis, a warm, educated, intellectual family headed by the father, Ivan, a wealthy man and oc-casional doctor for the Corps whose large house was quite near Lefortovo. He was Russian, but descended from an Italian opera musician of the

18th century. The wife, Elizabeth, was a Detroville, from a Russian family of French extraction.

The large-hearted Monighettis adored young people, and opened their home on Saturdays and Sundays to them. Naturally for most cadets the chief lure was the presence of two adequately handsome daughters, Zinaida (1867–1950) and Olga (1869–1952). They were clever, stimulating, and eligible. There was also an attractive younger brother, Vladimir or "Vova." The Monighettis added a new affectionate nickname for Sasha—they called him "Skryabochka."

Limontov fell in love with nineteen-year-old Zinaida. Sasha copied, with seventeen-year-old Olga. At sixteen in 1887, Sasha's last year at the Corps, as it would turn out, he proposed marriage. Sensibly, she refused. However, over a period of twenty years, the Monighetti children and Scriabin remained friends.

Meanwhile, Sasha continued with his studies. In his first two years he won all the Corps' prizes. The tutors asked, for his third year, that his name be dropped from competitions. Honors were designed as incentives for those who would be making military careers for themselves.

Only one report card has been preserved—for the year 1885, his third at the Corps. Sasha was again first in the class. He averaged 9.8 out of a perfect score of twelve. His marks were: 12 in French and in Natural History Science; 11 in Bible (God's Law); 10 each in German and Geometry; 9 in Algebra; 8 in Painting and Geography. To this score, the Head Instructor appends a cautionary note: "Good, but in the strict sense, not good. This year he has shown far less interest in his work." Perhaps Sasha had been discouraged by being withheld from competition.

In this same year, several cadets had come down with measles. When the infection struck frail Sasha, he fell gravely ill. Measles developed into what they called "watery dropsy." His whole body tumefied with serous fluid. Dr. Monighetti called in specialists, including Dr. Zakharin. After due consultation, they declared their helplessness. He was close to death.

There was one last chance, a final remedy. Lyubov says only this: "The doctors risked a cure." Engel too is elliptical: "The doctors tried one extreme measure. It worked." The treatment was the seton. They made a slot in the flesh at the back of Sasha's neck. They then drew a handkerchief-size strip of gauze cloth back and forth to force a discharge of liquid and cause extreme pain to the point of unconsciousness.

The Tatar theory was that anguish in one area of the body diverts the course of a disease and turns it from death into health. The agony shattered Scriabin. His lifelong conviction that sickness was avoidable, his mortal dread of ill health found a source here.

After summer and recuperation, Sasha returned to the Cadet Corps, alive and even more of a hero for it. Russians were awed by anyone who had undergone the seton. Too, none of the other cadets had been face to face with death, although they were training, in a sense, for death on the battlefield.

✒ III ✒
MUSIC

7

AFTER SASHA's auspicious debut at the Cadet Corps, he asked Aunt Lyubov for formal music lessons. Nothing was done until the summer vacation. The Scriabin ladies customarily rented a *dacha* in the vicinity of Moscow, this time at Khovrino, a village encircled by ponds with picturesquely wooded banks and tiny beaches, where hundreds of nightingales sang, day and night.

By great good fortune that summer of 1883, one of the neighbors was Georgy Konyus. Barely turned twenty-one, this budding artist was already backed with the highest credentials. He had been a pet of Tchaikovsky and Taneieff, and now Arensky adored him. The eminent Paul Pabst (1854–1897), a Prussian and Liszt's best pupil then in Russia, taught him piano. Georgy wanted to compose, but his music was, as described by Alfred Swan, "pretty but timid, and hardly independent."

Tchaikovsky admired Georgy's music sufficiently from his Op. 1 orchestral suite, "From Children's Life," to recommend him for the Tsar's stipend of 1,200 rubles given each year to a worthy musician for life. Georgy's talents lay in teaching, textbooks, and research. He graduated from the Moscow Conservatory with honors, and himself became a long-standing professor there.

The Konyus family reaches back to the times of the Napoleonic Wars when a family of French musicians named Conus migrated to Russia. Abroad, their descendants reverted to the ancestral French: "Georges Edouard Conus will appear in recital . . ." Georgy was the eldest of four brothers—Yuly (or Julien) (1869–1942), violinist and composer; Lev (or Léo) (1871–1944), pianist, and Victor, who, in exile, earned his living teaching French. (Rachmaninoff's only daughter married Boris Conus, son of Yuly.)

Lyubov called on Konyus as was proper among summer neighbors, but she had a further purpose. Konyus' own words describe the moment: "A woman I did not know came to me and asked if I would give an eleven-year-old some lessons on the piano. It turned out to be a certain Sasha Scriabin. He lived with some old ladies who were, to put it mildly, infatuated with him." The impecunious Georgy accepted. Lyubov herself speaks only of the end of the summer, crisply, "I was very pleased when, finally, Sasha learned to read music."

Engel asked Konyus to record his impressions and he wrote with particular, acerbic charm: "What a puny boy he was! Pale, short, looking far younger even than his years. He played the piano neatly and fluently, but weakly. The first piece I gave him was Weber's 'Perpetuum Mobile' Op. 24 and, though he played it fast enough, he hadn't the physical stamina to make it anything more than something ethereal, and therefore monotonous. All that summer of 1883 I taught him, while the old ladies constantly told me how talented his mother had been."

Lessons continued into winter. Every Thursday afternoon at 4:00, Sasha made the hour-long trip across Moscow to Konyus' furnished rooms. The sun would have set by the time of his return. "I forget what I taught him now. Probably easy Cramer études, little Mendelssohn 'Songs Without Words,' short Chopin pieces, how to read, but mostly I gave him scales and arpeggios to practice in all the different keys. I lost sight of him, for a time, sometime in the spring of 1884 . . ."

Under Konyus' aegis, Sasha began to compose in a somewhat disciplined manner. His first kept effort was a short two-page Canon, more of a canonical prelude, in D minor (published by Muzsektor, Moscow, in 1928). It controls the musical inspiration and makes its beauty within rules. The charming counterpoint is bold, but already Scriabin is thinking in vertical rather than linear impulses.

Sasha determined to enter the Moscow Conservatory. Vladimir went to the Commandant of All-Moscow, Major-General Nikiforov, a friend of Taneieff, Head of Piano Department and next year in 1885, destined to become Director of the whole Moscow Conservatory.

Already by the time Sasha entered his life, Sergei Taneieff, at the age of twenty-eight, was a powerful factor and leading figure in Russian music. In person, he was short and dumpy, square and squat. His benign face, with its short beard and its bright cornflower blue, slightly crossed eyes, reflected a soul that was pure, however dour and honest and dry.

Taneieff lived all his life on the "Street of the Dead," in a provincial-style, wooden *domik*. Its unseasoned lumber was warped and the house lacked running water and electricity. Outside hung a permanent sign to discourage visitors: "I am not at home." But visitors came—Ysaÿe, Nikisch, Hans Richter, Godowsky, Pugno, Hofmann, Rosenthal, von Sauer and Busoni.

Taneieff was essentially a pedagogue, but he was also a composer of thorough, unromantic, pristine music. No one could write a connecting passage as well, or create as smooth a logic and flow of phrase.

Nikolai Rubinstein first prevailed on him to help with counterpoint classes at the Conservatory. Later, since his dispassion was so wide, and his capacity for impartiality so deep, Tchaikovsky asked him to take over the piano department. He complied as an act of friendship.

Taneieff believed in the obligation of fostering talent. Once he spent seven hours writing Tchaikovsky a letter of details, corrections, and criticisms of his Fourth Symphony. And so it was with young Sasha. He accepted him as a pupil to prepare him for the Conservatory: "I taught him a little privately . . . acquainted him with the rudiments of form, placement and disposition of voices, phrasing and the like. He brought me several charming pieces. A real talent, he was."

Among these pieces was a Nocturne in A flat major (published in *Muzyka* Magazine, No. 13, Moscow, 1911). It shows the master as a child. Perhaps it smacks of Chopin, and probably it uses pretension to cover ignorance. We find sharps instead of flats and these enharmonic complexities later would have reason in Scriabin's works, but not at this time.

9

TANEIEFF WAS a colossal pianist; but he was not interested in a career. The piano was a means to compose. He advised Sasha, therefore, to prepare himself in piano with Nikolai Zverev. This tutelage guaranteed entry to the Conservatory.

Zverev could either extract talent or inculcate proficiency. Strangely, he himself never played in public. At best, his pupils heard no more than a snippet of demonstration from him. Possibly there was one exception, Alexander Siloti. This Zverevian alumnus, who later studied with Anton Rubinstein and then moved on to Franz Liszt, claimed Zverev had played for him: "Very elegant it was, with an unusually beautiful tone."

Zverev's story is formidable. At fifty-one, when timid, twelve-year-old Cadet Scriabin walked into his elegant private house near the Smolensk market place, Zverev was the most adulated piano teacher of Moscow's high society. For fourteen years he had been auxiliary teacher at the Conservatory with privileges of choosing his own pupils. He augmented his fame and purse by going to the mansions of princes and fashionable hostesses to instruct privately. He also gave lessons once a week at the finest ladies' gymnasium.

He was a flagrant homosexual with a half-dozen choice boys living as *pensionnaires* in his house, and he was a gentleman, a *barin* to be exact. Already by then the word was somewhat old-fashioned and excessive, meaning "a man nobly born." Classically, servants addressed their masters as "*barin*," in the way generals are called "Excellency." Zverev with his fine and chiseled features, his steel-grey hair neatly combed, his straight-backed bearing, good looks and spotless wardrobe, could make a better-born host deferential.

Zverev's father had indulged his son in music lessons on condition that he remain a decent person despite music's deleterious effects, and that he keep it a pastime. Zverev violated both behests. Zverev's two teachers were the greatest in Russia of the 1840's. Both were typically "resident foreigners," or Europeans attracted by the valuable ruble.

Alexandre Dubuque (1812–1898) taught Zverev first. This Frenchman had actually touched the hand of Beethoven in 1823. He had also given Balakirev ten piano lessons—all the learning that man ever submitted to. Dubuque belonged to a second generation of expatriates living in Russia, musically. His teacher had been John Field, who had invented the "nocturne," those rambling moods which Liszt borrowed for his "love-dreams," subtitled *notturno*, and Chopin later exploited so well. Dubuque drank himself to death and probably corrupted more pupils than Zverev.

Zverev's other instructor was more respectable, Adolf von Henselt (1814–1889), a Bavarian noble and virtuoso in the anti-Beethoven faction led by Johann Hummel. Henselt also set a standard of magnificence for

Russia's musical lineage as "Chamber Pianist to the Tsarina" in Petersburg.

Zverev first worked in the government at a ministerial sinecure created expressly for *bary* who had through improvidence lost their family estates. His salary was one hundred rubles a month. His carousing crony, Nikolai Rubinstein, persuaded him to switch to teaching music. Within three months Zverev trebled his income. He left the Ministry and joined the Conservatory on steady salary. Unbelievably, he inherited a fortune from a distant relative whom he had never met. At this point, with music as profession, a fortune in the bank, Zverev grew bolder.

Zverev's *pensionnaires* had to be superlatively talented and of excellent family. They paid nothing for board, room or daily lessons. Moscow's most prominent tailor, an Englishman, personally outfitted them in special uniforms of tight-fitting dash.

No boy could be idle. Each had French and German lessons, learned dancing on the premises, practiced bowing to guests and addressing ladies by their titles—*knyazhna* for an unmarried princess, *knyaginya* for a woman married to a prince, and so forth, down to generals' wives and various other "Her Excellencies." Zverev determined to make gentlemen out of them. Without personal grace and taste, he would ask, how can your music have these qualities?

Zverev believed in strict convictions and correctives. The boys were not allowed to contact members of their family, even if they came to Moscow or passed by the neighborhood, for fear that compliments would spoil them or undermine discipline. They had to rise at 6:00, clean their rooms, and start practicing. There were three grand pianos on the top floor and two downstairs in the drawing rooms. Three hours was the acceptable minimum. While Zverev's maiden sister supervised the housekeeping, he listened to his pupils. "Stop improvising!" "Don't smear the notes! . . . Clear, clean . . . clear, clean . . ." he would call out from the adjoining rooms to prevent bad habits from developing at the keyboard.

Zverev's bookshelves were filled with presentation copies, autographed first editions, and the best of the world's literature. No *pensionnaire* could be pretentious, either. If he mentioned the title of a book, he must first have read it. Zverev tested them and many of them were forced through more Tolstoi or Dostoevsky, Stendhal or Renan than they liked. They developed intellectually, and Zverev's pupils ended up cultivated in the finest sense.

When Zverev attended Italian opera at the Bolshoi in his *bel étage* box, or saw Duse, Salvini, Sarah Bernhardt there, or attended the latest play by one of the Tolstois at the Maly Theater (where he also kept an ostentatious box), his "harem" stood at attention stiffly behind him. They removed their gloves and applauded when he did, and for no longer a period than he. Murmurs went around, but not all the boys by any means accepted their counselor's sexual blandishments. Not all lived *en pension* with him either.

As the young protégés passed puberty into adolescence, Zverev continued educating. He guided them to the right restaurants, taught them how to order and what to order. He selected the best vodka. He showed them how to get drunk, and how *not*. He was even cicerone to the fifteen-, sixteen-, seventeen-year-old boys, according to their development, and took them to the nightclub quarters along the road out of town to Moscow's race track. There the plutocracy met with gypsy entertainers and prostitutes. In summertime, a few of the most select and youngest boys went with him to an estate in the Crimea where a maecenas host shared Zverev's predilections for very young, talented, and wellborn boys.

Zverev was also a tyrant and subject to hysteria. He sadistically punished boys for the slightest infractions, for a wrong note, for inattention. There were also humiliations for the boys. They had to light his constant cigarettes, carry an ashtray around for him, and arrange his chair wherever he sat. He forbade any form of athletics for fear of an injury to their hands. Yet he beat them and threw vases at them recklessly. He screamed when Rachmaninoff, for example, at sixteen tired of two roommates, asked for a room to himself. For all this, no place in Moscow was more conducive to music. The *pensionnaires'* idea of relaxation was to compose oriental marches, or improvise four-hands on two grand pianos.

Sunday was the official rest-from-work day. It was also the one evening of the week when guests (male only) were invited. These occasions began with a formal concert performed by one of the students. Here they received their first sensations of terror and thrill playing before an audience. They also heard their first critical words of advice from an outsider. Taneieff, for instance, once croaked out after a mechanically and technically perfect performance, "Boy! Where was the *music?*"

Dinner would be announced at eleven. The evening's boy-of-honor then took the guest-of-honor's coattails and, following behind, accompanied him into the dining room where he draped the tails at the sides of the chair when the guest sat down. Meals were lavish, long, abundant with wines and meats, and as delicious as those of *bary* in the old days. Guests often included Tchaikovsky, the Rubinsteins, Kashkin, Paul Schloezer, piano professor, Gutheil, the German publisher of Russian music, Remezov of the Philharmonic School, Shimanovsky, director of Moscow's schools, and leader of the medical profession, Dr. Sadkyevich. When in town, Dostoevsky too appeared.

Zverev's *pensionnaires* of 1884 were Rachmaninoff; Alexander Goldenweizer; Leonid Maximov (1873–1904), whose early death at thirty-one, from typhoid, ended two careers, one of concert playing and one of music criticism; Matthew Pressman (1870–1937); and two shimmering stars of pianism, Fyodor Keneman (1873–1937) and Semeon Samuelson.

There were other students who counted as dilettanti. Kyril Chernayev, for instance, Sasha's best friend among the *pensionnaires*. He relinquished the piano and later became a critic on the staff of the *Russian Musical Gazette (RMG)*. Dukhovsky was another. He became, fifteen years later, Moscow's public prosecutor for the High Court. Yuri Sakhnovsky (1868–1930) was a wealthy amateur who tried composing, conducting and reviewed for the *Courier* and *Russian Word*—vociferously decrying Scriabin's later music. Ten years after Scriabin's day, there were the Sabaneeff brothers, one who became professor of organ at the Conservatory, and the other, Leonid, to whom Zverev bequeathed his priceless musical library.

One of Zverev's earlier *pensionnaires* who left as Scriabin arrived, was the affable Emil Rozenov (1861–1935). Despite a ten-year difference in age, they became friends. Scriabin often visited Zenino, Rozenov's summer *dacha* in Lyubertsy. They overlapped again at the Conservatory, but Rozenov ultimately directed his energies to the theoretical side of music. In 1904, he founded the "Moscow Scientific and Musical Society," where he frequently lectured on subjects such as "The Living Creation of Fugues and Inspiration in the Writing of Counterpoint," "New Ways of Hearing," or "The Significance between Science and the Art of Music."

Emil Rozenov has explained Zverev's ability as a teacher well. "He could analyze what was wrong and rectify it," and in final tribute he said," He loved his pupils, and attended to us like a father."

Scriabin expressed this in a letter to Siloti (1911): "Fate willed us pupils of that dear Nikolai Sergeevich to come together, and how right it is that all is due to the kindness of yet another one—his most loved pupil of all." He was referring to Pressman.

10

"SUNDAY MORNINGS, talented but poor pupils came. Scriabin, I remember, a little cadet from Moscow Military College." In this way, Rachmaninoff noted the occasion. That early October, 1884, Aunt Lyubov had crossed the city holding Sasha's hand—he was not allowed out alone—patiently enduring the forty-five minute tram ride. She presented Sasha to Zverev, and Zverev lined up his *pensionnaires* to introduce the newcomer.

Arrangements were for Sasha to be delivered into Zverev's hands by Lyubov, then after lunch one of the pupils would accompany him to Taneieff's house a square away. After studies there, Taneieff had promised to return Sasha in person to Vladimir's apartment.

"Why did Taneieff play this governess' role?" asks Engel. No one knows, but all winter long and longer, he apparently did and did not seem to mind.

Pressman noted in his *Recollections* that Sasha was "weakly, delicate, small-featured, eyes full of life, walked somehow fussily . . ."

Zverev affectionately dubbed the new pupil "Skryabusha," a diminutive of a diminutive. This roused envy, although the other pupils had to admit, as Pressman did, "Zverev immediately spotted Sasha's extraordinary gifts. He endeared him with 'Skryabusha's.' How gladdened was this teacher's heart when pupils showed such passion for music."

Each Sunday Sasha arrived with his assignment, a brand new, big composition, prepared. He could play any étude within an hour. He looked at the notes once, glanced at the page again, practiced the main technical problem or difficulty at the piano, and then played it by ear, never to look at it again. Sasha was jealous of Zverev's pupils, most of whom could read even an orchestral score at sight.

Zverev goaded his *pensionnaires* with Skryabusha this and Skryabusha that, and how beautifully he played a piece. Pressman remembers one occasion vividly: "After a private session Zverev flung open the doors to the drawing room and summoned us all. He asked Skryabusha for the Haydn 'Variations' in F minor. We were simply stunned. He played excellently from a technical point of view, but such a work requires genuine artistic maturity, and he possessed it." Another week Zverev asked him to look over the *Wanderbilder*, Op. 17 by Adolf Jensen (1837–1879), a German composer then much in vogue. He turned up with all twelve of the "forest scenes" memorized. "For any of us in those green years to prepare so big an assignment on a week's notice was stupendous. Sasha played each 'picture' sensationally. He gave each its own coloration."

Skryabusha reciprocated Zverev's devotion. He dedicated a little Nocturne in F# minor to him. Eight years later when it was printed as Op. 5 No. 1, there was no dedication—a policy which Scriabin followed for all his published music throughout life and against the custom of the day. (Russian violinists frequently play it in an arrangement by A. Mogilevsky.)

When Zverev accepted this Nocturne he responded graciously. However, he had no intention of letting Skryabusha compose. He fed him Chopin nocturnes, waltzes, mazurkas and études not as models for composition, but to perfect his brilliance as a concert-performing, world-touring pianist like his other stars. If Zverev neglected Rachmaninoff, it was because he and all the rest of musical Moscow expected him to be a composer and not a pianist.

Skryabusha fell in love with Chopin. He slept with his music under his pillow at night. He carried it in his book bag to Corps classes. In the first decade of Scriabin published opuses, there are nineteen mazurkas, nine impromptus, three waltzes, three nocturnes, one polonaise and scores of preludes and études. Chopinesque titles, but, let it be said immediately, not a page plagiarizes. Scriabin once reduced to tears blurted out, "What if my music does sound like Chopin?! It's not stolen. It's mine . . ."

He continued to astonish by his virtuosity, particularly at this period with Schumann's "Etude on a Paganini Caprice in E flat," Op. 10. Strangely, for all the Chopin influence, there is no information as to how he actually played him, and very few pieces of Chopin music are listed in his early programs. While Taneieff encouraged Sasha's composition, Zverev maneuvered Skryabusha, now thirteen, before the public as piano soloist. He hoped the sound of applause (so often denied a composer) would embed the idea of a concert career and divert him from the solitudinous and less secure road of composition.

Toward the end of the Conservatory year, April, 1885, the advanced students gave a grand grab bag of a concert in the Great Noblemen's Hall (now the Hall of Columns and acoustically one of Europe's finest auditoriums). This annual event was in no sense an examination. Patrons, critics, maecenases, composers and performers all gathered simply to hear what was going on at the Conservatory, that is, the future of Russian music. Skryabusha neither belonged to the Conservatory nor was he listed on the program, but he appeared wearing his uniform.

He looked "keyed up but happy," and played Schumann's *Papillons*. The audience was enchanted, and Lyubov reports the near-disaster. Her Shurinka missed every one of the bass d's and the high, tower clock chime at the end. "I laughed and leaned over to my friend. 'My Shurinka is doing badly.' She answered me, 'If he played *nothing* but wrong notes, you would still know that he is true talent.'" This was Scriabin's debut before qualified musicians.

Not long after this concert, Aunt Lyubov went visiting. Shurinka ventured to buy some music at the Mikov Music Store downtown near the Kuznetsky Bridge. "A horse carriage ran him down, and he fell, crushed," Lyubov tells us remorsefully. "They brought him home. His right hand hung limply from his body at the side. The older ladies were calm. The neighborhood doctor put him to bed and said he had broken his collar bone . . . From that moment onward, I vowed I would never leave his side even for an instant. Long after he was grown, if I myself could not accompany him, I would arrange for some friend of his to fetch him and return him to us safely!"

Over the years 1883 to 1887, Sasha composed inordinately. Many of these compositions are preserved, half-written, roughly jotted in pencil in little, pocketsize black notebooks of score paper. He sometimes drafted substantial amounts of ambitious pieces and titled them: rondo for orchestra, suite for strings, fantasy-sonata, ballade, variations in F minor on a theme of Egorova's, scherzo, and, most atypically, Hungarian rhapsody. All were full of "felicitous melodies and fiery dramatics."

A Waltz in D flat major, written when Scriabin was fifteen (Muz-Sektor, Moscow, 1929) bears a French dedication "A Mlle. Vera Gambourzeff." She was one of the "eligibles" Sasha had met in the carefully supervised household of the Shaikeviches. Sasha's best friend at the time, the same age as himself, was "Tonichka" (Anatol), son of Samuel Shaike-vich (1842–1908), a well-known lawyer and amateur violinist who gave private recitals twice a week which friends were expected to attend, before the meal would be served. "He gets worse each time," Scriabin once wrote in a letter. He was also a maecenas art-collector with a mansion on Poluektovy Street in the Arbat, a district where "nests of gentry" housed themselves. The son, Tonichka, wanted to become a professional cellist, but he took up law eventually. Later the family moved to Paris, and the mother became Proust's close friend.

The Gambourzeff Waltz does not exist in Scriabin's handwriting, but from the sound of it and the two separate versions found in different places—Rozenov's and Shaikevich's—its authenticity as a Scriabin souvenir cannot be doubted. Scriabin was already able at "practical" music, and if Mlle. Gambourzeff wanted to waltz, she could, but he was also sensible enough not to publish these works written à la mesure.

In that same year of 1886, Scriabin composed one masterpiece, if so large a word can be applied to a miniature of less than three minutes duration. The popular Etude in C♯ minor, Op. 2 No. 1 is almost Scriabin's signature in the West. It is a contemplative, melancholy, searching piece whose simple ascending melody is underlined with plangent chords. It elicits a feeling of Russian expanse, of steppes, tundra . . . loneliness. A wondering note sounds: a repeated question expressed by a falling interval of a minor third at each phrase end. There is no reply. The mood comes from a maturity far beyond its author's youth, and is a diffuse sorrow.

At fifteen, Scriabin's creative process was forming so that he would need companionship. Lyubov writes, "His babushki and I would sit on the divan in the drawing room, for him to work the better. Finally, we brought pillows and simply turned the divan into a bed. We never slept so soundly as when his music was filling our ears . . . and dreams of sleep."

Conservatory time was drawing near. Target date was 1887. Sasha would be sixteen, having completed the general educational requirement of five years, and musically, three years with Zverev and, intermittently, four with Konyus and Taneieff.

Kashkin gives us one last view in 1887 of Zverev's Skryabusha. He still had not lost his baby-face, his smallness, his delicate constitution. "But in his eyes," Kashkin notes, "was an adult look, a quiet conviction. It was sympathetic, and he conversed with a smile that was indefinable and somehow caressing. Sometimes he smiled ironically, or even smirked. This did not go with the half-childishness of his face. When he talked he looked you straight in the eye. Behind the calm, clear gaze, you felt he was sizing you up, figuring you out.

"He was by no means deferential to persons older than himself, nor to authorities in his own field. He defended his opinions staunchly. It was not that stubbornness which limited men exhibit and which is so exasperating. He would always see the right in the other person's point of view, even when it opposed his own . . ."

II

SCRIABIN WAS developing in other, secret ways. His talents overflowed beyond the world of music. We find a fragment of his first poem, dated 1887, a penciled caption for his unfinished ballade:

> O country of visions!
> How different from this life
> Where I have no place
> But there, I hear voices,
> A world of beatific souls
> I see . . .

One phrase of this music is found in the prelude Op. 11 No. 4, and it sounds the thoughts these words imply. He is lost in life. He sees visions, and suffers and longs to escape. These feelings will steadily increase.

Another literary statement written around the same time was discovered between the pages of the family Bible. Sasha had hidden a single leaf of paper inscribed in indelible ink and cautiously formed script with his declaration—a *profession de foi*. It is his first ratiocination on paper, foreshadowing his persistent soul-probings—what Dostoevsky called "walking round yourself and watching"—which sometimes tormented him and occasionally preceded a burst of creative activity. Here he tries to clarify religious mysteries with logic. He wants to solve the heart by means of the head.

Naturally, he embraced the orthodox Church. He was still young enough for those eminently satisfying answers. They had served him since the age of ten, as he himself would record in a sheet of autobiographical notes found after his death. There he wrote of the Cadet Corps days:

> FULL BELIEF in the tutors and in priests.
> Naive faith in Old Testament.
> Prayed devoutly.
> Had deep sense of Holy Communion.

Now he progresses to the New Testament and lauds Christ and extols His morality. Of this period in his life, he would call himself in those same notes, "remarkably unanalytical."

Aunt Lyubov says that she "never made Shurinka pray and never discussed religion with him." His attendance at Church had been ordinary for a Russian—Sundays, Christmas, Easter, funerals and weddings. But here, certainly, is a hosannah to Christ.

> God, in the general sense of this word, is the cause of all phenomena, *in toto*.
>
> Jesus Christ speaks of God in part only. He posits God as an inexplicable reason. This leads to the concept and precept of what we call morality.
>
> Since the concept of morality is ONE with the total, He speaks of the one true and eternal God. It dwelt in Him (as appearance) and He moved in it (life, actions).
>
> To believe in God means to believe in the veridity of this morality and to obey.
>
> Prayer is an *élan* towards God.
>
> Religious feeling is awareness of the divine within one's self.
> Here is the essence of the teaching of Jesus Christ: Be honest, good, righteous, love thy neighbor as thyself. Matthew 5: 14.
>
> He was the first to speak these Holy words full of eternal significance. He was the first to open the eyes of mankind to the good and the true, the first to give them true happiness, and therefore He was right in saying: I am the light and the truth and life!
>
> And how are we who are indebted to Him for all our happiness to regard Him?
>
> Should we not raise the banner of Christ with joy, and cry out with pride we are Christians?

Let us hear within ourselves this holy figure of the suffering Christ and let us dwell in Him, in His teaching, in Him and in our one true and eternal God.

Later at the height of his career Scriabin wrote a passage—at once the same and dissimilar:

> Like the word of Christ
> As the deed of Prometheus
> I clothed thee, O world of mine,
> With a single glance,
> And by my one thought.

✒ IV ✒

CONSERVATORY

12

SASHA'S ACCEPTANCE at the Conservatory entailed changes for the Scriabins. Lyubov and the *babushki*, abandoning Vladimir, quickly found "a *gemütlich* little apartment"—walking distance from the Conservatory—right in Ostozhenka, a fashionable section of town where ballerinas and later, Isadora Duncan, lived. She set up a *kabinet* or study room where Shurinka could work undisturbed. "He needed to work without interruption and there had been just too many people at the Corps. Besides it was noisy there . . ." and, Lyubov adds, "for all of us began a most happy life . . . Indeed, the entire apartment was always cheerful, gay and comfortable."

His actual enrollment was delayed until mid-semester, January 1888. Lyubov had him to herself during that first part of winter for the first time in six long years. He turned seventeen, and still she cared for him hand and foot.

Scriabin now was almost handsome, wide-eyed with eyes far apart, his long upperlip as yet naked, cleft chin showing, his nose still upturned, and his oval face tilted as if to say, "I am aware of my gifts." He sometimes dressed in Cadet uniform, and sometimes rather foppishly in tight-fitting suits, foulards of white silk, and high button shoes in souvenir of Zverev. Summertimes, he liked to pin tiny bouquets of wildflowers to his coat's wide lapel.

Sasha skipped the entrance examinations to the Conservatory. Vassily Safonoff (1852–1918) had been Head of the Piano Department's Higher Division since 1885, and the man who would succeed Taneieff as director in 1889. Ever since that *Papillons* debut four years earlier, he had earmarked

Sashkina, as he called him. He deferred his entry for his own pleasure. During the beginning semester of 1887, Safonoff was on tour in the provinces with the cellist Karl Davydov (1838–1889), an outstanding and well-educated musician from the Petersburg Conservatory. The two artists would not return to their respective capitals until Christmas.

Moscow Conservatory was then a converted mansion, rented from Prince Vorontsov. The ballroom served for concerts or assemblies; classrooms were former bedrooms. Teaching methods were by and large informal. Professors usually held "collective classes," seminars of several students, rather than private instruction even in piano. Sashkina's lessons, however, were always given in Safonoff's home. They lasted into meal-times and past Safonoff's naptimes.

The training of a musician at the Moscow Conservatory took five years. Basic fundamentals included a year each of theory, solfeggio, harmony; one year of counterpoint and fugue together; and two final years of free composition. A student majored either in an instrument or in composition. He could also undertake a broad curriculum called "Encyclopedia," a hodgepodge schedule of work covering theoretical and academic subjects, such as history of music, aesthetics, composition analysis, and musicology.

The student who ranked highest in his major and showed distinction in all his other subjects received the "Little Gold Medal." If he topped the class in two major subjects and showed remarkable ability, he won the highly coveted "Great Gold Medal." Taneieff had been the first ever to be awarded that honor at the Moscow Conservatory. The next recipient would be Rachmaninoff, Scriabin's classmate.

The piano faculty of the Higher Division shone lustrously, as professionals and as performers. They were required to tour—it was part of a musical schedule to educate the provinces—and each had to teach not less than twelve pupils. (These rules still apply today.) In Scriabin's years at the Conservatory, the senior pianist was Paul Schloezer (1848–98). He played brilliantly and on this side of superficiality. Paul Pabst was youngest of the faculty. (His father taught at the Philharmonic School. Since father and son both had been Liszt's pupils, their pupils referred to themselves proudly as "grandsons of the masters' master.") The great Karl Klindworth (1830–1918) had left, but the respected, if uninspired Nikolai Shishkin (1857–1920), and Alexander Siloti, were there.

Taneieff had invited Siloti from Saint Petersburg that year of 1887, in order to bolster the piano department. This infuriated Safonoff, who was a law to himself, and within four years, he ousted him. Siloti was enormously tall, with a small head. His face was dotted with moles from which long hairs flourished. He cultivated these as assiduously as a mandarin tends his little fingernail. The family of Silotis, aristocrats from Genoa, had a century earlier settled in the Crimea.

All these professors were unanimous in training their students for fingers of steel and meters of iron. Lisztian music as far as the *Grand Galop Chromatique* dinned like shod horses from practice rooms. Brilliance and marvel sparkled everywhere. Astride, stood Safonoff—tall, muscular, with close-cropped hair, pointed beard and severe, pale blue eyes, gruff, giantismic, a Cossack general's son. His pianism was antithetical to Liszt's bravura and to his own personality.

Safonoff had studied with Alexander Villoing, a pioneer pianist of French descent, born in Petersburg and dying there in 1878, who taught both Rubinsteins. Safonoff's technique then was meticulously forged by Leschetizky. Scriabin's mother and he were fellow students at the SPb Conservatory. However, Safonoff's most determining instruction came from Louis Brassin (1840-84), a Belgian who taught in Russia during his last years. Brassin had been a pupil of Ignaz Moscheles (1794-1870), the first to use "touch" as a means modifying tone, in diametric difference to the later Lisztians, who regarded the piano as an orchestra.

Safonoff married Barbara Vyshnegradskaya (1863-1921), a mezzo-soprano and daughter of Ivan (1831-95), the powerful Finance Minister of Russia from 1887-92. At thirty Safonoff had already been an instructor in piano at the Petersburg Conservatory for five years. He transferred to Moscow with the rank of full professor. Taneieff stabilized the rocky Conservatory finances with the help of the wealthy singer Fyodor Kommissarzhevsky. However, it was Safonoff who raised the funds for a new Conservatory—the magnificent building we see today on Herzen Street with its "Big" and "Little" concert halls—and ensured stable and continuing Government support.

Vassily Safonoff was nicknamed far behind his back, "Gun Butt". His career strutted with harshness and even abusiveness. Any description of him vacillates between respect and censure. Engel, calling him a superb pianist and professor and remarking how well he conducted and organized

SCRIABIN 143

symphonic programs, also says that his aggressively energetic handling of
his subordinates in the pit or on his administrative staff, his despotism
and difficult nature, led "to a whole series of rows and personal collisions
at the Conservatory . . . He would not listen to his colleagues. His stern
temperament could not allow him to . . ."

Victor Seroff excoriates Safonoff for "idiosyncracies bordering on
foolhardiness." One example occurred in January, 1888, when he refused
Koussevitzky entry to the Conservatory, probably, it was said, because
he was Jewish and not talented enough. He gave the reason that no one
could enroll mid-term. However, he kindly never failed to distribute his
autographed photographs to each member of every orchestra he conducted everywhere.

The school year 1887–88 had been tense and rivalrous for piano
teachers. Zverev hated Safonoff. He found him autocratic without aristocracy, and saw to it that as many of his students as possible went to
other teachers at the Conservatory. He sent Rachmaninoff, Keneman,
Goldenweizer to Siloti.

Although Safonoff had a *droit de seigneur's* first choice, he resented not
getting Rachmaninoff, and wickedly discouraged him at every opportunity throughout his years at the Conservatory. "I know your interests
lie elsewhere," he would say to Rachmaninoff whenever he played the
piano. Von Riesemann reported how Rachmaninoff felt Safonoff's
"suggestive power" over him. Its dreadful effect, he claimed, deadened
his creative powers.

The last word, however, came from Siloti. He gave a concert in London,
not long after being driven from Safonoff's Moscow, and introduced
Rachmaninoff's Prelude in C# minor, which soon became one of the
most famous pieces of music in the world. This christened Rachmaninoff's
tremendous worldwide reputation, and began his ultimate retaliation
against Safonoff.

13

DURING THOSE early years Scriabin's wildest shore of self-esteem was
reached by the coddling of this otherwise reproving and stern man. Safon-

off tendered nothing but affection to Sashkina. An entire repertory of stories developed to demonstrate Sashkina's genius. Engel says Safonoff indulged him "on every score and loved to reminisce about the so-called lessons . . ." Safonoff told him, for instance "I was teaching him at home and was very tired. 'Work on your own,' I said, 'I'm going to rest a bit.' Just as I began to doze I heard something not quite in C# minor and yet it was not in A major. Sashkina was improvising. This was one of the highest pleasures of my musical life."

According to Safonoff, Scriabin had already attained the pianist's chief aim: "to make the piano *not* sound like a piano . . . That was what I always told my pupils. I taught Sashkina many things, but he had his own rare and exceptional gifts—tonal variety, pedaling refinement . . . Under his hands the instrument fair breathed . . ." He told students to "watch his feet, not his hands." One, Josef Hofmann, heeded. He borrowed several Scriabinic pedal tricks for coloring effects.

Professors closely watched Sashkina. Paul Schloezer made an ambiguous remark in the staffroom which became much quoted, "One never knows who is passing through our hands." He was recognizing that Scriabin's talent ranged far beyond Conservatory ken and that of conservative musicians.

Students from their first year appeared in concerts, and Scriabin always stood out. Lyubov states that the instant he walked on stage a kind of animation spread over the audience. When he played, professors would "prick up their ears, glance at one another, and mumble words of amazement and approbation."

Terminating his first semester in May, 1888, Scriabin played three pieces for his examination: Mendelssohn's "Serenade" (probably one of the "Songs Without Words"), G minor Ballade by Chopin, and again, *Papillons*. Davydov had been invited from SPb to sit on the jury. He wrote his short verdict: "Earnest money of genius."

The examination in harmony started at nine and students had until five to work. Two tasks to be written at the desk without recourse to a piano were: a prelude of sixteen to thirty measures illustrating a specific series of modulations and including a tonic and dominant pedal point at the end; and a four-part harmonization of a Haydn melody. It was Taneieff's Sasha, rather than Safonoff's Sashkina, who sailed through these within a couple of hours.

The Conservatory was severe, and Sasha was lazy, slow getting to classes, lackadaisical about his attendance.

"He was always extremely able," Taneieff said to Engel, "and he wrote what was demanded of him note for note, but he demonstrated little love of work. On his own, he lacked initiative. He always tried to simplify and shorten the problems I assigned. Sometimes his effort to save himself work, and still be precise, took curious forms. He always picked the shortest theme for a canonical imitation, and while this meant fewer measures of actual writing, the solution asked for far more actual work. Longer themes; easier imitations. Anyone knows that."

Scriabin was willful at the piano, but Safonoff never minded. Classmates noted with distress that he appeared to listen to Safonoff's instruction, but when the time to play came, either in class or on stage, he changed it. Annoyingly to others, Safonoff, even if he envisioned a piece otherwise, never tampered with a Sashkina performance. "Everything that that pupil did, *he* pronounced good," one disgruntled student complained.

His work habits were desultory. Shurinka would rush back from Safonoff's saying he had to learn a new piece. He would go to the piano and labor hard . . . for a while. Suddenly he would break off, think a moment, strike a few chords, and start off on his own tangent. He would continue this until Lyubov intervened. "Then he would jerk himself up, as if awakened from some deep slumber. He would walk about the room a bit, thinking, then sit down again, this time to the appointed task."

Both Safonoff and Taneieff felt genuine friendliness for Sasha. They often came to the Scriabin apartment to eat, to make music, and the meetings generally ended in amiable argument over some musical point. Taneieff's second-year class bored his pupils, so the teacher devised tricks to get his favorites to work. He invited Sasha to his house, gave him the problem, and locked him in a room. If the room was on the ground floor, Sasha would crawl out the window and run home. It would be hours before Taneieff, who was absent-minded, noticed. Sometimes Taneieff sent his cook with a *cantus firmus* to the Scriabin apartment. He would sit in the kitchen waiting until the counterpoint was done.

In the fugue class of 1890, only Scriabin and Rachmaninoff really interested Taneieff. In Scriabin's case it was vital that he work, because the intertwinement of melodic strands and counter lines in orderly progression was not instinctive. Taneieff succeeded in implanting a certain grounding of craft. Whenever emotion, intuition or inspiration flagged, Scriabin could fall back on these as a sustaining device. Rozenov discovered among his Scriabin souvenirs one pencil sketch for a five-part fugue. It was probably designed to conclude the Fantasy for orchestra and piano (published posthumously for two pianos by Oxford University Press, 1940), and the idea was later incorporated in the finale of the First Symphony.

Other students in Taneieff's class were Seidenberg, a clarinetist, who afterwards graduated to the Bolshoi orchestra; a lady-pianist, Elisabeth Kashperova (d. 1936), aunt of the great musicologist to come, Alexei; and two Germans—Weinberg, who played the bassoon in the Bolshoi orchestra to support himself while at the Conservatory; and Lidak, a handsome, quiet man, a specialist in horn and trombone.

Scriabin wrote a charming piece for Lidak, "Romance for Waldhorn." That horn was really a hunting horn, a length of brass thrice coiled and without valves. Scriabin's "Romance" is played today on the less difficult French horn. Its music is affectionate.

The Conservatory supplied Scriabin with a lifetime of friendships, more friends than he had ever known before. Music bound his coterie together tight as an embrace. One group of intimates nicknamed him "Kitten," "Kitty" or "Pussycat" (kiska, kiski, kisynka), because of his feminine or feline ways, but it was said without malice. Medtner was a Safonoff pupil also, and the dour Konstantin Igumnov (1873–1948) studied with Paul Schloezer, but the most brilliant pianist of all in a special way was the ethereal and willowy Vsevolod Buyukly (1873–1921). He studied with Paul Pabst (so did Olga Monighetti, who had been accepted at the Conservatory on a provisional basis), and was "eccentric," a circumlocution for homosexual. Sabaneeff described him as being "of enormous queerness," and Engel said that "for all his strangeness, there was something amazing and grandiose about him..." Legend had it, most unlikely, that he was an illegitimate son of Nikolai Rubinstein. Scriabin was particularly close to a dark-haired and energetic violinist, Nikolai Averino (1872–1948). He was abbreviated to "Kolya" or, more often, Mavr meaning "Mars."

"His friends came to us in vast numbers," Lyubov says. "Some came almost every day, until I decided to control matters. We made it a rule that anyone who wished to see him must do so in the evening and take late tea with us. In this way he could have some rest from the ardor of his studies. When guests came he was always cheerful and gay. Sometimes the boys would laugh together all evening long."

Limontov also joined the group. He recounts his last year at the Corps and the thoughts of the future which troubled him. He even tried to enter the Philharmonic School (already he felt drawn to drama), but was rejected. He talked about his dilemma with Sasha, who took him to Safonoff. Limontov described the moment vividly:

> Safonoff took the manuscripts, looked at them, and spoke very tenderly to Sasha.
> "Who wrote the second voices?"
> "He did, dear professor. Them and the whole score . . . alone."
> Safonoff handed me the music and said, "Tell your parents that I will accept you in my classes free of charge."

In 1890, Kolya Averino and Kyril Chernayev (from Zverev days) took a furnished room together near the Kuznetsky Bridge. At eighteen and nineteen they were old enough to live on their own without a chaperon. Sasha asked to join them. He went nervously to his Auntie Lyuba. He emphasized it was to be only for the wintertime.

"I was not perturbed in the least by his announcement," Lyubov wrote deceitfully, "however, my mother was in despair." None of the old ladies felt he would be able to function in an atmosphere of romping, rowdy boys. Lyubov herself thought that his health would never allow him to exist even a few streets away from her. Pretending to be calm, she pointed out that he was no longer a child. "Live life as you see fit," she said, "only come to see us every day. Thus, Shurinka and I parted from each other—momentarily."

In his absence, Lyubov tidied up his little room, made it even more charming with curtains, flowers and bric-à-brac. She kept his piano open wide and dusted it regularly, just as if he were there. Finally, she could resist no longer. Less than a month after his departure, she made an appointment to call one afternoon.

The boys greeted her with much fuss, fed her coffee and cakes. When she inquired about the sleeping arrangements, "Averino announced loudly that he had given Sasha his bed and that he himself was sleeping on the piano. I glanced at Shurinka and saw that he was laughing with the rest . . . but not quite so heartily." Lyubov saw with her own eyes that the disorder of such living arrangements upset him, affected his nerves. She brought him home with her that very day.

He ran to his piano, played on it, and could not tear himself away. He asked Lyubov to go fetch his things home for him. "Never again did Shurinka speak of separate living arrangements," Lyubov sententiously concludes the episode.

14

AT THE Conservatory Scriabin appeared more frequently in concert than any other student, both at Safonoff's behest and by popular demand. One neatly scripted, hand-drawn program shows his solo recital of 4 January, 1891, in the Little Hall:

> Prelude and Fugue, Bach
> *Variations Sérieuses*, Mendelssohn
> *Papillons*, Schumann
> Nocturne, Etude, Mazurka, Scherzo, Chopin
> Concerto in E flat major, Liszt (without accompaniment)

Soon after, the RMO sponsored a gala Sunday evening concert by the Conservatory's finest students in the Great Hall, 24 February, 1891. Admission was charged and the proceeds went to the Conservatory's "Necessitous Comrades." Student Scriabin had senior billing—the big Henselt Concerto in F minor.

The longer the students were at the Conservatory, the more ambitious they became. Samuelson learned Bach's complete *Well-Tempered Clavier*. Scriabin set about memorizing all the Beethoven sonatas. He stopped at the tenth . . . from boredom.

He decided to study Beethoven as a composer. He looked for a formula, a plan, a system that governed his modulations in his statements, expositions, and developments. Was there a common denominator of interrelated progressions among the sonatas? He thought he found a pattern. Later he would call all Beethoven's seesaw of tonalities, tonic to dominant or sub-dominant, major to related minor, "unbearably monotonous . . . the work of a muscleman with biceps."

Meanwhile Scriabin was steadfastly composing his graciously elegant, exquisitely mannered early pieces, vest-pocket music. They were attracting attention by their refinement and charm. That agony which accompanied their creation was the opposite of the tranquility many of them expressed.

Lyubov describes how Scriabin suffered prior to each bout of composing. "He was a martyr to his muse," she begins grandly. Actually, it was the other way around. His muse, by absorbing his intense, nervously destructive inner life, made sanity possible.

> When Shurinka was inspired, he was truly tormented. He became another person entirely, speaking to no one, not answering when spoken to. On these days I would not quit his side.
> Shurinka really couldn't be left alone. In the middle of the night he would have hallucinations—would turn ice-cold. I would have to hold his head in my hands, hard. At last he would quieten. These moments of the night always ended in bitter tears for some reason. After this, he would drop off to sleep, and sleep through the following day until four in the afternoon. He would rise, take up his work instantly, and seem somewhat at peace with himself.
> These attacks of nerves invariably appeared before he composed a new work. The doctors said his physical organism was too sensitive and weak to uphold his colossal mental activity. And for sure, as he grew older and his bodily strength improved, these states lessened bit by bit.

From 1891 well into 1900, Scriabin hovered on the brink of nervous breakdown, sometimes toppling, only to recover and again hang perilously in self-dread by some thread of life. The true peculiarities of his nature—both invisible to the outside and perhaps even unvoiced within—combined a neurasthenia of the mind and neuralgia of the body. Scriabin was imprisoned within himself. His only exit was music.

In 1891, calamity struck and nothing could have taxed his nervous system more. At the last lesson of the school year, Safonoff asked Sashkina to "deepen his tone . . . sink into the keys, don't skitter over them." Scriabin had been much impressed that year with Josef Lhevinne. He decided to emulate him in virtuosity, and with the same "Don Juan Fantasy" Lhevinne had played so spectacularly.

When the summer vacation began the *babushki* rented two farmstead houses on the banks of the Klyazma river, a connecting tributary between the Moscow and Volga rivers. One house had four rooms, for the ladies and Shurinka. The other, with seven rooms for Vladimir with his family . . . at last he had married.

Scriabin learned new pieces of music in secret. He said he wanted no one, not even Aunt Lyubov, ever to hear his mistakes. However, that summer, since Lyubov and her brother spent the days outside picnicking in the surrounding forest or paddling in the river, Shurinka left the house wide open. From the river, from deep within the forest, the music of Mozart as viewed by Liszt resounded. He pounded and pounded mercilessly repeating every difficult passage over and over. Pressman points out that "not possessing a tremendous technique by nature, he played *through* and *over*played." The result was a severe hand strain. Of course, Safonoff, had he known, would have forbidden attacking anything so relentlessly. When he saw him at the end of the summer with his useless right hand dangling limply, he cried, "Are you mad?"

Safonoff prescribed *oleum rizini* to cure Sashkina's hand. This referred to a medicinal purgative, and he meant by it, that Sashkina should work very lightly on Mozart's D minor Concerto.

"This," said Safonoff, "will relieve your indigestion from Don Juan's hot spices." But the nostrum failed. Sashkina's tendons and inflamed muscles burned and ached. The doctor ordered him to abstain from all practicing, and prognosticated the end of his career as a public performer. Restless and despairing, Scriabin practiced with his left hand. He developed a phenomenally independent and proficient left hand. This "sinistrality" underlines all his music of shimmering sub-surfaces.

Scriabin for the rest of his life was always nervous about his hand. He constantly tested and checked his fingers for strength and speed. While talking to people—particularly when bored—he would poise his hand on a table, on his knee or crook his left arm before him like a keyboard. Then he slowly flexed each finger. Gradually he moved into trills. He would cock his head to one side and observe his fingers closely. He had regained their once lost, light automatism, but this habit often annoyed and perplexed strangers.

In 1894 three years after the catastrophe he wrote two compositions for left hand alone, a Prelude and Nocturne, published as Op. 9. They are original, ostentatious and luscious.

Scriabin also worked out a left-hand paraphrase of a Johann Strauss waltz. It entranced his friends. No manuscript exists, but Rozenov often heard this "Composition after the Manner of Strauss" in 1894, and wrote that "God alone could count the virtuosic tricks it contained."

Towards the end of that fateful summer of 1891 Lyubov tried to distract Shurinka. She took him on a long trip South to Kiev, the capital of the Ukraine. He could see his Uncle Alexander, the tax-inspector Scriabin who had been stationed in Petersburg and now had turned landowner. The *babushki* were pleased to come along.

Alexander, at the age of forty, bought a good-sized place just outside Kiev, in Karostyshev. There he spent summers with his wife and children in a large house surrounded by a pine forest. The house, like all the others in Kiev and environs, was plagued with flies. Everyone had to drape cloth over the windows to keep them out, and the cool in. On hot days, Alexander's pine forest weighed the air down with a clean, medicinal scent.

Shurinka and the party of ladies arrived in Kiev. Alexander had made arrangements for them to spend the night at one of the local hotels before sending horses and a carriage. The train arrived unexpectedly early, so aunt and nephew walked all day sightseeing. The grandmothers remained in their room. The sight of southern beauty—the chestnut trees, the flower-beds planted along the sidewalks to bloom in the Ukrainian national colors of red and blue, and of course the eleventh-century great "Golden Gate" (Mussorgsky's "Pictures at an Exhibition" describes it)—thrilled young Scriabin. It was his first trip away from Moscow.

Although Sasha had promised to rest his hand, he began to compose. That day he rented a piano to be sent to Karostyshev. He worked for the rest of the summer "without taking a bit of fresh air, and there was a pile of manuscript paper on the floor by the end," says Lyubov.

The first letter of Scriabin ever preserved dates from this summer. It is addressed to Vladimir, the Monighetti son. "Dear Friend Vova, I am writing you a few lines with my left hand as the right is all bandaged— And so I limit myself to only a few words to give you my address and to ask you to write me how you all are, even if in only a few lines. Well, goodbye," he continues, "when I am able again I will write all my news." He forgets to sign the letter and omits the date.

Scriabin met with another disaster during the Conservatory session of 1892. This time a personal clash in Free Composition class. Anton Arensky was twenty-one when he accepted a post at the Moscow Conservatory. His teaching was erratic, but still he taught for thirteen years from 1882 to 1895—harmony, counterpoint and free composition. Taneieff, who once took over when Arensky was recuperating from a drunken bout, asked the class to define a fugue. The students had spent nearly a semester with Arensky, but were unable to answer.

Arensky produced a variety of compositions during his forty-five years, although his temperament and musical knowledge was undisciplined and his inspirations fitful. He casually scribbled arabesques and waltzes—beautiful ones—and he completed two full-bodied symphonies and several operas.

Asafiev dismisses Arensky's music as "elegant and gracious, soft and flabby, merely a sympathetic lyricist." His personality contradicts his music. As a person, he was hot-tempered, given to outbursts. He quarreled with his fellow teachers and his students—all the way from Grechaninov to Scriabin. Safonoff, for any number of reasons, refused to promote him to rank of full professor even after he had served so many years. Arensky quit the Conservatory in high dudgeon, and took the post of Director of the Court Chapel and Choirmaster (easy sinecures) in SPb. Engel attributes Arensky's aversion to Scriabin as jealousy, "an inability to recognize rival talent in a composer." Kashkin offers a charitable word. "Arensky was the nicest and most delicate person *by nature*. But in class he was nervous and irritable. He offended Scriabin by his acerberous sallies."

Scriabin, nervous from a half-healing hand and uncontrollably irritable (erethismic), invited many of Arensky's attacks on him. "You are conceited and arrogant," Arensky screamed at his outright disobedience once. To Keneman he said, "That Scriabin is a wild man. Give him one thing and back he comes with another." Arensky announced that he would fail Scriabin for the year of 1891 unless over the summer he brought back ten perfect fugues. He returned with one "Fugue-Nocturne" full of startling harmonies in its *stretto*. (Reproduced in *Musical Contemporary* magazine, 1916).

On another occasion, Arensky ordered his class to write an orchestral scherzo. Scriabin's story is that he actually wrote it, but would not accept

Arensky's alterations. Another version has it that he wrote the beginning of an opera instead. No sketch of the scherzo exists in Scriabin's papers. However, Rozenov found a manuscript in Scriabin's handwriting of an unharmonized aria from an opera titled *Keistut and Peirut*, a Lithuanian love story. Rachmaninoff remembers this well. When he was ill, Sasha called to comfort him with music. "I was extraordinarily pleased, particularly by Scriabin's aria. I think I would still be pleased, were I to hear it again today," Rachmaninoff recalled in America.

Engel attributes the poem to Lyubov. Its phrasing is certainly clumsy, but the thought—escape to other worlds and other heavens—is unmistakably young Scriabin:

> Tell me, tell me, who art Thou?
> Can such beauty find shelter in the skies?
> Thy throne is not here,
> But amid the deathless gods,
> Encircled with perpetual roses in bloom. . . .

Arensky's advanced class in composition consisted of his favorite, Rachmaninoff; Scriabin; Nikita Morozov (1864–1925) (no relation to the maecenas Morozov); Ivan Alchevsky (1875–1917), later a leading tenor at the Maryinsky Theater in SPb; Lev Konyus, as well as those two brass players, Weinberg and Lidak. A congenial group, but Arensky made it torment for Scriabin . . . and he for him.

The trouble started when Siloti left the Conservatory. It would be absurd for his pupil Rachmaninoff to begin a last year of piano with another teacher. Moreover, Rachmaninoff fell ill with "intermittent fever." He asked Arensky if he might graduate that year, after only four years' study. Arensky agreed. Scriabin asked competitively for the same privilege, and Arensky flew into a rage. No.

The final examination in composition (April, 1892) was to compose a one-act opera, and to treat a given and quite intricate theme either as a *fuga reale* or *fuga de tono*. Rachmaninoff completed his *Aleko*, text by Pushkin as adapted by Nemirovich-Danchenko, in seventeen days. Scriabin never even began. The fugue disrupted the Conservatory seriously. Scriabin solved the problem according to Safonoff's understanding. Arensky judged it incorrect. The rumor went around that Rachmaninoff had overheard the argument, and then sent in his answer.

The final examination in piano was held before a large invited audience in the Little Hall. The aged Anton Rubinstein came from St. Petersburg. Each graduating student was required to perform one difficult and one easy piece. The pain in Scriabin's hand returned acutely before the examination. When he came on stage, he waved his hand pathetically before the judges, as if to say, some said, "Look how I am suffering. Mercy on my performance today."

For his easy piece he played his own little E major Mazurka, Op. 3 No. 4. Rubinstein was enchanted and went on stage to improvise a series of variations on its theme. Scriabin performed as his main work, like an angry gesture in the face of fate, the "Don Juan Fantasy." He played it brilliantly. The judges, on Safonoff's recommendation, accepted this as his final year and awarded him the Little Gold Medal. Rachmaninoff won the Great Gold Medal for excellence not only in piano but in composition.

Safonoff went to Arensky to ask that Scriabin also be given honors in composition and leave the Conservatory now with a Great Gold Medal. Arensky flatly refused, and Scriabin left the Conservatory anyway. Engel writes with irony: "And so it happened that this composer who brought such glory to his alma mater never received a diploma in composition. This same Conservatory has since honored tens of others who are scarcely names to us now."

Scriabin had ended four years at the Moscow Conservatory as he had begun . . . an exception to regulations and under a cover of controversy. But he was nevertheless a "Free Artist."

V

REPUTATION

16

A YOUNG musician must build the house of his career. He needs recognition. Sasha, no longer moored at the Conservatory, was adrift. At twenty-one, Scriabin began swimming in the sea of life. Engel pictures the distressful situation in universal terms, "Midst the dizzy atmosphere of a Conservatory establishment, gifted artists have their lives arranged for them, for good or ill. There they are evaluated, but out in the wide world, they are in a new arena where each step is a struggle. The public must first meet the artist personally; then it must go hear him. However, audiences are recalcitrant. They only go whither they are habituated to do so."

Scriabin had to move among the rich and powerful—the Moscow society that patronized the arts. He socialized, went constantly to parties. He was also almost invariably drunk. What a paradox he presented. And everyone noticed it. Engel remembered his mixture of self-assurance and soft and delicate manners: "The first few minutes you felt he was timid or embarrassed. Yet, in the same breath, he was someone Rimsky could call 'presumptuous,' and for sure, his pride throughout his life was titanic."

Modest Altschuler, then studying cello with A. von Glen at the Moscow Conservatory, specifically remarks how Scriabin was regarded at the time "as an attraction to women." Yet he was not handsome. Down sprouted on his chin, and although the fashion was for Free Artists in the musical world to be clean-shaven, like their Western confrères, Scriabin was impatient for hair. He believed in the Russian superstition that a beard prevents toothaches, as he says in a sincere letter (13 July, 1893),

"Unfortunately women lack the best prophylaxis against tooth decay—a bushy beard, or even one not so bushy." He grew mustaches in the Army-officer style, and later waxed their tips.

Scriabin added new affectations to his dress. In the evenings, he fancied full-dress clothes with long, starched cuffs and very high collars. Frequently he appeared wearing bright red woolen sleeves—painfully and obviously homemade. The *babushki* had knitted them to keep his damaged hand warm, and they showed under his jacket and reached down half covering his hands. Sabaneeff remembers this as most "striking to the eye and distracting to the ear." Before he would play at a party or salon, he waved his poor hand at the gathering, reminding them of "Don Juan." His trousers were macaroni tight. His boots, specially fitted to his feet, had, unusually, elastic sides. He began walking, and even sat, like a ballerina, with his toes turned out. In short, he attracted attention.

Rozenov believed Scriabin's "excessive gregariousness" was due to his embarrassment at asking people to his own apartment. There he was dominated by elderly women and he had grown ashamed of his situation in their life. The air in the apartment was old-fashioned. It precluded social entertainment. "Parties" to the Scriabins meant family gatherings, nothing more, where the entrenched idiosyncrasies of its various members were understood, catered to, and no one looked askance. Such people were hardly suitable for the gay, expansive world Scriabin now had to function in. Still, he had to present his music to society and Engel adds, "he preferred to show it to us anywhere, save *chez lui* . . ."

In the spring of 1892, Scriabin played a large private program for the "Circle of Music Lovers," in the mansion of the wealthy patron of young artists, Eugene Gunst. Among the guests was Boris Jurgenson (1868–1935), son of the founder of the great music publishing house in Germany, Peter Jurgenson and Co. Lyubov sat next to him by design. She proposed that he submit some of Shurinka's compositions to his father for publication. Home pianists and amateurs would surely delight in such easy little pieces, she argued.

Jurgenson responded coolly. However, he proposed gross terms of contract: A Waltz in F minor (composed in 1885) and thirteen other pieces (including the celebrated Etude in C♯ minor, Op. 2, No. 1 written when Scriabin was fifteen) to be "given without any remuneration whatsoever."

The company published the waltz first, and by 14 July Scriabin had proofs. He was also informed that music stores in three cities, Leipzig in Germany and Vienna and Gmunden in Austria had each ordered one copy. "This gives me great pleasure," Sasha commented in a letter. Apparently an unwritten stipulation required Lyubov to pay for her vanity. She received a bill at the end of the year to cover a deficit of ten rubles.

Today many of these first pieces—ten Mazurkas, Op. 3, composed in 1889 and two Nocturnes, Op. 5, composed in 1890—sound like faded valentines. Of the nocturnes, Taneieff merely remarked, "They end badly . . . open fifths sound empty." Originally, these compositions were published without opus numbers. His reputation was too small for the dignity of enumeration.

The following year, 1893, Jurgenson gave Scriabin another, somewhat better contract. He paid Scriabin fifty rubles—his first musical earnings, aside from salon fees for little concerts—for four Impromptus in mazurka form. Two of these, composed the year before, became Op. 7. The other two (earlier works, when he was seventeen) became companion pieces to Op. 2. Particularly interesting is Op. 2 No. 2, now called Prelude, a greeting to the morning sun, fresh and clear music. The "*Impromptu à la mazur*" which follows it contains (twenty-four measures from the end) Scriabin's first suggestion of a chord built in fourths instead of customary thirds.

17

ON LEAVING the Conservatory Scriabin began his most socially useful summer vacation. In May, 1892, he found Moscow "insufferable and dusty" and spoke of the little excursions in the environs as "not country at all and boring to extinction." He went horseback riding with friends. They took walks to oak groves and explored subterranean passages overgrown with grass, and sealed with intertwining tree roots.

He finds a "traveling companion." Scriabin never reveals his name and only describes him in a letter to his sweetheart, Natalya Sekerina (1877–1962), as "an adventure lover . . . I fear he will get caught in something he can't get out of. He spent a whole night on one of the deserted islands

in the Gulf of Finland. But he is companionable and a poet. He loves
free verse. That means poems without either meter or rhyme. Because
of this his poetry is different, at least. Well, God forgive him his poetry,
if that's his only defect . . ."

Together the boys set out for St. Petersburg, where they stay with
Uncle Alexander, who will not leave for his Kiev house until later that
summer after Uncle Mitya marries on 18 July. Early June, Scriabin and
his unknown friend visit Finland together. They see Vyborg, Finland,
several monuments dating back to the Russo-Swedish War (1741–3), a
Gothic castle perched atop a rocky island in the middle of the Gulf,
and Fort Transmund and Fort Mon Repos. The greatest sight of all is
the Imatra waterfall, renowned for being a place where lovers commit
suicide. The trip, Scriabin's first abroad, was spoiled by intermittent rain.
He counted its "starting and stopping for 22 times." He describes his
impressions to Natalya. He is twenty and she, fifteen:

> I have just come back from the falls filled with strange emotion. They are
> beautiful. But they overpower life. There are no bird songs. You cannot hear
> people's voices. The tranquility necessary for the human soul is absent. Imatra
> reigns supreme and alone. Its gigantic whirlpool and ever-seething waters are
> like the vortex of vain, human life . . .
> Swift streams of water plunge from its heights and crash on the rocks and
> crags . . . Today for ten or fifteen minutes the whole waterfall was covered
> with fire-colors. The setting sun tinted the clouds, and the clouds cast a reflec-
> tion. It was like a smile on the face of a gloomy giant—a ray of hope in the
> midst of despair. Finland is beautiful, but my soul is restless here. There is
> something desolate and comfortless, and my heart grows heavy.
> Papa reproaches me sometimes for a lack of patriotism. "You want to go to
> Italy," he says, "and you don't know Russia yet. There's beauty here, and in
> Finland, too."
> Maybe so. But am I to be blamed for being attracted to nature's luxuriance?
> To the glow of warm waves? To palms and lovely flowers? Am I to be censured
> for loving flowers so much?
> I'm not sure I'll ever get to Italy, but I will doubtless reach the Caucasus. My
> military service comes up in August.

Scriabin returns to Petersburg and exhausts all its sights again—gardens,
walks, and he finds, like a Muscovite, Petersburgers are "fun-loving but
of little interest." Fun in summer consists of deformed jesters doing the
same tricks over and over again, and concerts of Hungarian and Ukrainian

music in the open-air parks. Scriabin prejudicedly dismisses it as "Yakut," meaning "primitive," music. He also notes that the abundance of water in SPb makes the *dachas* better, more country-like than those in dry Moscow's suburbs.

On the last day of June he again writes Natalya:

> What climate they have here! If, as they say, talking about the weather is the occupation and only possession of fools, then Petersburg at the moment is inhabited exclusively by fools. Everyone dreams of the sun and its bright, warming rays. But these are dreams only, and will remain so. It rains from dawn to dusk, from dusk to dawn, and winter's leaden clouds are impervious to sun and cannot be pierced.
>
> I would have fled long ago had my relations with whom I am staying not watched me so zealously. One often hears that Petersburgers are neither kind nor hospitable. My own experience has been quite to the contrary. Everyday I am convinced of the opposite by my good friends and relatives. They seem to keep their wits sharpened by devising interesting places to visit.
>
> Now the stock of amusements has begun to dwindle . . .

In July Scriabin takes his first sea voyage. He spends two-and-a-half days going to Latvia, where he visits two wealthy maecenas families who have summer residences near Riga: Nikolai Mamontov (1836–1896) (no relation to the railways and opera Mamontov) was a wealthy manufacturer and terrible amateur singer, whose wife and two daughters became Scriabin's private pupils; and Sergei Yakolev (1838–1906), one of the directors of the Moscow RMO.

Scriabin enjoyed the sea. It lifted his sense of acute loneliness at leaving his traveling companion and family in Petersburg. He was fascinated by the ocean's "limitlessness." Scriabin's poetic powers overwhelm him in this next letter to Natalya:

> Everything glowed with magnificent majesty on the horizon. First a clear purple, then it turned rose-colored, and finally silvery flecks stained the surface of the sea. Meanwhile the wind awoke the waves and brought the sea to life. Then it became even more gorgeous. The green of the sea blended with the blue reflection of the sky. The sun scattered its golden rays on the rising waves. There was such a play of colors and shades as I've never seen. It was a picture, a triumph of colors, a festival of truth. The sea sparkled; the air shimmered; the world was filled with daylight's enchantment.

However, the boat began to rock. Scriabin became seasick.

Meeting with the Mamontov family at Dubbeln, outside Riga, was pleasant. Olga (1872–1897) in two years would marry Kolya Averino. She also would die within another two. Her story from the beginning was sad. Her father, Hermann Laroche, the once celebrated, now hated, ultra-conservative music critic, had led a life, according to Rimsky-Korsakoff, of "grimace and gesticulation, lies and paradoxes." At last become indigent, he simply abandoned his children, and the musically gifted Olga was adopted by the Mamontovs. She studied piano with Paul Pabst and graduated from the Moscow Conservatory with some distinction.

The happy group of Mamontovs and Yakolevs, with Sasha in the center, took long walks, ice-skated in the evenings, and made music all the time. They waltzed, and on "operetta night" a fifteen-piece orchestra hired by Mamontov arrived to accompany him in hideous songs. Illuminations and fireworks—"Just fancy what a variety of pleasures!" Scriabin wrote— brightened the night sky. But Scriabin had to return home. He had promised Auntie Lyuba to go with her to the Taneieff summer home for two weeks at Demyanovo, near Klin, some fifty miles north of Moscow ... before his military service.

18

VLADIMIR TANEIEFF (1840–1921), lawyer, brother and sixteen years older than Sergei, was the chief landowner of the district, and owned a whole series of *dachas*-to-let, Demyanovo village itself with a hundred serfs, and of course, all the district park and its adjacent, rather tatty buildings.

Sergei Taneieff appeared only on weekends and rode the three miles from the train station on horseback, preempting the animal—as was his right—from the first peasant he encountered. When Sasha was there he amused himself by posing contrapuntal conundrums, the answer to which would spell out some musical or literary allusion.

Vladimir Taneieff was eccentric. "An exceedingly queer fellow," Scriabin described him. Unlike his calm and chaste brother, Vladimir

Scriabin's pianist-mother, Lyubov Petrovna Shchetinina-Scriabina, pupil of Leschetizky and pet of Anton Rubinstein.

Little Shurinka, as he was then called, at the age of two, taken in 1874.

Lyubov Alexandrova Scriabina, the devoted aunt who was responsible for Shurinka's upbringing after his mother's death in 1873.

A unique picture of the entire Scriabin family. The patriarch, Artillery Colonel Alexander Ivanovich Scriabin, sits in the center with his wife, Elizabeth Ivanovna, her arm around the three-year-old composer-to-be, Alexander Nikolaevich. On his left her sister, Maria Ivanovna Podcherkova, hand on table, stands between the elderly couple. On their right is the only daughter Lyubov. At her feet is the youngest brother, Dmitri. Reading from right to left, Alexander Ivanovich Scriabin's sons are: Nil, Vladimir, Alexei, Alexander, Nikolai and Peter.

The six sons, most of whom followed in the father's ▷ military footsteps. From left to right, top to bottom: Vladimir, Alexei, Nikolai (Scriabin's father), Alexander, Nil and Dmitri.

Sasha, now a cadet in the 2nd Moscow Corps, photographed with his father on leave from translation duties in Turkey. Taken in 1883, Scriabin had already composed the Canon and early Nocturne.

Nikolai Zverev, Moscow's most fashionable piano teacher and notorious homosexual with his adored class of 1884. Sitting, from left to right: Scriabin, or Skryabusha as Zverev dubbed him, Zverev, Chernayev, Pressman; standing, Samuelson, Maximov, Rachmaninoff and Keneman.

Scriabin on graduating from the Moscow Conservatory in 1892 and beginning his "socializing" era.

Scriabin's diploma from the Conservatory making him a "Free Artist" and awarding him the Little Gold Medal. Dated 28 May, 1892, his grades are "Excellent" in piano, theory, esthetics; "Very Good" in music history and academic subjects; and only "Good" in instrumentation. The diploma, issued in the name of the Imperial Russian Music Organization, is signed by Grand Duke Alexander, Safonoff and the Artistic Committee of Kashkin, Shishkin, Pabst, Schletser, etc., but Arensky's name is absent.

Mitrofan Petrovich Belaieff, Scriabin's devoted admirer and publisher, taken in 1895 at the time of their first trip together abroad.

Natalya Sekerina, Scriabin's first lady-love in 1894.

Poster for the Petersburg concert of 7 March, 1895. He played on a Becker similar to the piano Belaieff gave him.

Scriabin wearing the ivory and gold cuff links he bought in Paris, in 1898, the year of his tour with Vera.

Vera Ivanovna Issakovich, Scriabin's first wife whom he married in 1897 against the wishes of his aunt, his benefactor the music publisher Belaieff, and his own misgivings.

Vera in 1899, with their first child Rimma, Scriabin's favorite and soon to die... in 1905.

Scriabin with his graduating pupils in May, 1902, his next to last year at the Conservatory. From left to right: A. Loiko, Alexander Horowitz, O. Esaulova, Scriabin, Yuri Pomerantsev, A. Malinovskaya, and Maria Solomonovna Nemenova-Lunz.

was a storm of nihilism, after the fashion of Turgenev's hero, Bazarov. But he was an anti-Bazarov Bazarov. He had participated in the Polish Insurrection of 1863–64 against his own countrymen, and he harbored those far-out, secret revolutionaries, Nechayevists, in 1871. These actions were not only dangerous, they were progressive beyond the liberal pale.

Scriabin describes Vladimir to Natalya, in a letter of early August, 1892: "He is petty with people and extremely rigid. Tidiness is the supreme principle in his world. 'When I walk along an avenue,' he openly admits, 'and I see a cigar butt far down at one end, my head spins and I begin to gasp for breath.' When he lends you a book from his library, he begs you not to get it dirty. If you return it with a spot on it, not to mention a tiny dog-ear of a page, he puts on the nicest expression and asks you most sweetly to give him the book as a present. This makes you feel most awkward. If, however, you fail or forget to get him a new copy (or pay for it) he says, 'All the same, I am quite, quite, most grateful to you.' He kills you this way . . . with these merciless thanks."

Sasha was still conventionally religious, and religion was repulsive to the older Vladimir.

"You believe in God . . . no matter what?"

"Yes . . . regardless."

Vladimir would then stretch his arms out in despair, turn on his heel and walk away leaving the younger Sasha provoked, speechless, and without redress.

To get back at Vladimir, Scriabin practiced his only sport—jumping. He leaped over the wide flowerbeds of Demyanovo Park, grazing the roses and columbines. Vladimir would run after him like a woman shooing chickens. No flower was ever harmed, Lyubov swore, but once Shurinka sprained his ankle and Lyubov kept him in bed for a week. "All his young friends came to comfort him. This kept him from composing, and thus he rested well . . ."

Demyanovo was full of Moscow youths Sasha's age. He singles out his next door neighbor, a certain Boris Shervut (a Russianization of the English family name, Sherwood), son of an architect and painter.

Boris is another poet in Scriabin's life. He too is a "peculiar person . . . I take walks with Boris while he recites his poems to me. Some of them are alive and pellucid. Others do not quite satisfy me. He loves abstract poetry, and this makes his images elusive. It is a mistake of his to follow this abstract line. It leads him into a dark hole and no beam of light can guide him out. He constantly sacrifices content and form for succulence."

Scriabin signs his letters to Natalya, "Your poor common soldier," anticipating his round of duty. Compulsory military service seemed inescapable. Uncle Vladimir busied himself day after day trying to secure him a place of least hardship. It was essential, he agreed, that maximum time be spent in music. Vladimir summoned his nephew to Moscow several times, and they spent whole days at various military posts throughout the city. "I'm in a vile mood," Sasha wrote Natalya, "you can't imagine what a fuss there is over my being drafted. So many papers have to be filled out. So many petitions to be presented."

One day Sasha called on an officer who was "most unbearable . . . He immediately wanted to learn how to compose. I explained that, assuredly, art worked from laws that enable one to create, but that something else was also required and that something cannot be taught . . . My explanations were fruitless. He then asked me not only to teach him harmony and counterpoint, but he also proposed that I give lessons to the colonel's daughter. 'She loves music to eat by,' he said, and she likes playing the 'pianofortes.' Most of all, 'she loves dancing.' I am sure all of them would much prefer it were I to teach dancing!"

Uncle Vladimir's efforts all were wasted. Scriabin wrote Natalya in mid-August: "I am freed from military service. I tell you of this most important event in my life. In a few days I receive the official confirmation from the conscription board. This all happened so unexpectedly that I am in a state of shock." Scriabin fails to mention that he was rejected on the grounds of poor health and "unsuitability."

Back in Moscow for the winter season, Scriabin's social life and activities resume. He sees old friends. He went to the Monighettis when he was tired or upset. Often he sat "remorsefully silent for long periods." Olga, his ex-light-o'-love from Cadet Corps days, remembers that "once in a while he would speak up: 'How good it is to be here! . . . How quiet! . . . Life is a great gift of happiness. It should be and must be a festival of rejoicing. And look what people do with it! Probably I myself don't know how to make it what it is . . .'"

Olga's sister, Zinaida, argued with Scriabin about his compositions. "You're not Scriabin, again," she said if a piece sounded Chopinesque to them, or "Here you're making music according to Safonoff's chemistry book . . ." If it was advanced in harmony or conception, Olga joined in, "You're being crafty as Odysseus again . . ." Sasha would then reply, "You don't understand . . ."

Among his new acquisitions of the winter was the friendship of Alexander Rakhmanov, a young Muscovite of "a good and well-to-do family." Scriabin introduced him to Rozenov and the three became pals. The Rakhmanov mansion had a billiard room, and Scriabin reveled in this new sport. "He was," Rozenov wrote, "terribly friendly in the Rakhmanov house, and indulged in all kinds of funny pranks . . . He dissipated a good deal. Sometimes the Rakhmanovs could not get rid of him."

Scriabin visited the homes of professors, as he had in the Conservatory days. Sergei Taneieff organized a "seminar against Wagner." His most brilliant students, post-graduate and present, gathered together: Scriabin, Rachmaninoff, Goldenweizer, Igumnov, Georgy Catoire (1861–1926) (composer and mathematician, of French descent), and Sabaneeff. Wagnerism had become the fashion. But Taneieff and Tchaikovsky, the supreme authorities in Russia were in dead antipathy toward Wagner. To them, to imitate his music was a composer's worst sin.

Taneieff called Wagner "trash," but said to his students, as he distributed copies of *Tristan*, "we will study the villain thoroughly." Rachmaninoff, sitting in a corner with his legs curled under him and munching on a cabbage roll, cracked one of his rare jokes as he flipped through the score, "Good! Only fifteen hundred pages left to go."

One night in the winter of 1893, Sabaneeff found himself sitting next to Scriabin at Taneieff's. This was their first encounter. Sabaneeff reacted unfavorably. "He was supercilious towards the room, and the cleft in his chin turned me against him. He looked too distracted for my taste, and he didn't even seem particularly intelligent. When Sabaneeff asked Scriabin what he thought of Wagner, he got an unwilling and curt answer. "Formless. Doesn't interest me." Sabaneeff then observes that he sensed Scriabin's "self-love. He was opinionated. Others too looked at him with skepticism and reservation . . ."

Scriabin dropped in on Safonoff more than anywhere else. His evening parties were a mixture of late food, music and mysticism, that persistent fashion of Russian life before the Revolution and now, after the recent changes. Scriabin always arrived late, around two in the morning. Invariably he looked pale and tired, worn out. No one ever knew where he had been, or what had kept him, or why he was late.

People spoke of this as Sasha's "period of adventure." Safonoff, like a tender father, ignored his late arrivals or his abstracted appearance saying, "Sashkina is not with us tonight," or "He is devising something in his head." Sabaneeff felt that there was a "touch of joking irony" in the tone of his voice. But there was no doubting his seriousness when he ordered Grechaninov to go out and buy Scriabin music, or said, "He is very, very great . . . a great pianist and a great composer . . ." or, as he rebuked some eager students, "You learn all the classics from Taneieff and you skip the new life—Sasha Scriabin . . . He is cleverer than Chopin ever was."

Occasionally, Scriabin and Safonoff would sit in the Hermitage Restaurant in downtown Moscow and drink away the night. The waiters locked the doors on them and went home. Others opened them in the morning and let the pair out. Sabaneeff once asked Safonoff in later years about Scriabin's drinking. "Yes, indeed," he answered, "Sashkina drank a lot. In fact he drank so much then that he was drunk for the rest of his life . . ."

Lyubov too was aware of the dissoluteness. She called this his period of "incautious existence and injudicious life." Drink had taken tenacious hold of Scriabin. Boris Schloezer explains that "in the 1890's his body was so frail that alcohol got the better of him . . . He used liquor as a means to awaken creative forces in himself and to extend the limits of his personality. He sought its liberation, albeit transient . . ."

Scriabin himself recalled for Sabaneeff, after he had finally overcome his dependence on alcohol, "In those days I needed such external excitement, physically that is. Now I do not. I have other ways and means. I have conquered all that, not by asceticism, but by overcoming. Now I am always drunk, but not physically, never coarsely . . ."

Scriabin saw a lot of Buyukly. In later life Scriabin loved to recount to Sabaneeff how "peculiarly Buyukly acted in the good old days." Sabaneeff comments that he "felt from these stories that Scriabin himself did not lag far behind in contriving extravagant doings."

Safonoff, at one midnight session in those long ago days, composed a rhyming acrostic on Scriabin's name. He proudly read it to guests, and improved it on successive nights.

"Isn't it good?" he would ask, and then recite:

*S*trong a creator's sight
*C*arries all to heaven's height
*R*adiant sound of sweetest light
I a fountain of delight
*A*ll life's plan
*B*y man is won
*I*n the end, I am
*N*o doubt, a holy man.

Safonoff particularly liked the "no doubt a holy man" part and the phrase "fountain of delight."

"Why a holy man?" Sabaneeff asked.

"Ah, you do not know him. Among us he is a holy person. Granted his personal life is far from saintly, but all the more reason why he'll end up a priest. All priests commence in sin; whence they proceed to holiness. You haven't really talked to him. He's Nietzschean and a *mystic* . . ."

To Scriabin, his path at this time was neither Nietzsche nor mysticism, but Arthur Schopenhauer (1788–1860). In his autobiographical sketch he had written: "At 21: First acquaintance with philosophy. Something of Schopenhauer."

That "something" was *The World as Will and Idea*. Phrases such as, "The world is my idea," and "the world is my will," incubated in Scriabin's mind. They recur like *da capo* arias in his thought. Seeds of Eastern mysticism too were well watered by Schopenhauer's extravagant claims for "Vedanta philosophy" and "wise men of India."

Scriabin in 1892 was also reading French philosophy. Especially taken was he with aristocrat-philosopher Ernest Renan (1823–92), a man who had disturbed public peace in France by calling Christ "incomparable, but an incomparable *man*." Scriabin spent part of his twenty-first birthday writing a thank-you letter on a Renan theme to Natalya's older sister, Olga:

Everything dissolves into and abides in eternity. So said Renan. With this as a foundation, everything that lives even if only for an instant, lives forever and therefore, it follows, for all eternity.

As you see this theory opposes what you propound: Mankind is here on earth only to make a choice, to accept this over that and not to accept that other thing over this.

Isn't it better to think about why *this* is eternal and *that* perishable? That is why I do not say to you that eternal gratitude lives in me. I say only to you that as long as I live, this feeling of gratitude towards you lives in my memory and good wishes.

Scriabin's conversation often flowed along philosophical directions. One night at Safonoff's, he developed the theory that "it is much harder to do *all* that you want to than *not* to do all you want to." Therefore, he deduced, it is nobler and even preferable to do as you like for as long as you wish, and take as much of it as possible. Whereupon, surely, he must have downed another glass of vodka.

Paul Schloezer also invited Scriabin. Safonoff had made the first introduction to the professor himself. "I have brought you my treasure," he announced. Thereafter, Scriabin attended Schloezer soirées on his own. This would have far-reaching and intimate consequences on his future, as we will see.

Schloezer was a bachelor, living with an aggressive and disagreeable spinster sister, Ida. She relished intrigue, and used her brother's position as senior professor at the Conservatory to launch rockets of venom. Neither of these Schloezers were liked. Sabaneeff called Paul "a loquacious gadfly." Barbara von Meck scorned him for being the same kind of musician as Artur Nikisch, the conductor. Both would do anything and teach anyone for money.

No one denied his abilities, but Sabaneeff described him vividly: "To say the least, he was comically boastful. He would reminisce by the hour about purely imaginary triumphs." Scriabin in those days was generally considered as a pianist, rather than a composer. Yet, one day, Schloezer began speaking of the "fine and superb composer, Scriabin." It seems that he had shown him the manuscript of an Allegro Appassionata (later published in 1894 as Op. 4). Schloezer took this as a dedication, and responding to the presumption, was flattered. He called him his "pupil," and continued to make remarks such as "He's a real composer, not like that Rachmaninoff who copies Wagner and thinks he's Tchaikovsky . . ."

Schloezer and Rachmaninoff disliked each other, and the quarrel dated back to Zverev days. At one Sunday supper there, the guests celebrated the first publication of young Rachmaninoff's first composition. Schloezer remarked on its high cost. "For that much money you can buy a whole Chopin concerto," he said. Rachmaninoff retorted instantly, despite Schloezer's being twenty-five years his senior and the strictness of Zverev's table, "And why pay two rubles for your two little études when you can get twelve of Chopin's for one ruble?" Part of the hostility towards Schloezer was anti-Semitism. He spoke clearly and simply of being Jewish. He pronounced his name "Shletser," in Russian. His brother, Fyodor (1842–1906), a lawyer, however, married a Belgian, Marie Boty, and lived in Brussels. Their children claimed to be aristocrats descended from a Baltic baron, and called themselves "von Schloezer," and later, in exile, "de Schloezer."

On 6 December, 1893, Paul Schloezer arranged a memorial concert to Nikolai Rubinstein. One of his pupils, a girl named Vera Ivanovna Isa-kovich (1875–1920), a Karaim Jewess (baptized) from Nizhny-Novgorod then living with the Schloezers and being chaperoned by them while she attended the Conservatory, performed on the program. Another of the Schloezer boarders was Vera's best friend, Nadezhda Mirotvortseva (b. 1873), who would later marry Lev Konyus.

Vera herself looked rather like Scriabin's stepmother, with dark hair, rather glowing, piercing black eyes, and a thin mouth. She also played the piano well. A little hard and coarse in tone, some said, but after this concert Scriabin paid a compliment: "While you were playing, I thought to myself, here is at last a woman to whom I can listen with pleasure . . ." Ida Schloezer began matchmaking.

By coincidence, the ten-year-old niece, Tatyana Fyodorovna Schloezer (1883–1922), visiting from Belgium for the Christmas season, was also in the house. One day she too would become Scriabin's common-law wife.

19

WHILE IN his twenties, Scriabin began keeping notebooks or journals in which he jotted random thoughts, poetic musings, and philosophical speculations. This practice continued side by side with musical sketchpads he carried with him. He was erratic and inconsistent with both. What remains of the "literary" notebooks occupies a splendid place not only for reconstructing Scriabin's world of secret thought, but to place his ideas in the context of Russian philosophy, if such they can be called.

Scriabin was careless with everything. Auntie Lyuba still tied his gloves together, so he wouldn't return home with an oddfellow. But he handled his notebooks with attention and caution. He covered their bindings each with a different colored cloth. He marked them with alphabetical code letters, although they contain scarcely a personal or indiscreet word. They were inviolate. He was suspicious and secretive, as if an outsider might invade his soul, were he to see them.

He kept the notebooks under lock and key, hidden from strangers and friends alike. If a servant, or later his wife and children, happened by while he was writing, he would shove the notebook into a drawer and slam it angrily. He lost his temper, if anyone suggested that these notebooks existed. If he misplaced a volume, he literally could not rest until it was found and safely put away. Boris Schloezer likened this attitude to that of "an ashamed love."

The earliest of these notebooks, belonging to the years 1891 and 1892, traces his emotional life directly from the hand injury to its sublimative expression in his first major work, the First Sonata, Op. 6.

At twenty: Gravest event of my life . . . Trouble with my hand. Obstacle to my supreme goals—GLORY, FAME. *Insurmountable*, according to doctors. This was my first real defeat in life.
First serious thinking: *Beginning of self-analysis. Doubted*, however, that I would NEVER recover, but still my darkest hour.
First thinking about the value of life, religion, God. Still a strong faith in Him (Jehovah rather than Christ). I prayed from the bottom of my heart, with fervor, went to church . . .
Cried out against fate, against God. Composed First Sonata with its "Funeral March."

Even before, Scriabin had written his first schematic outline or "plan," as he called these guidelines. Here is the First Sonata in "program" form, although he himself at first was unaware of the connection. While his mind sorted out the ferment and agony within him, at another level in the unconscious, music formulated itself.

I. Good. Ideal. Truth. Goal outside myself.

(Belief in God who placed striving within me. Who gave me the ability to attain. Through Him and His strength.)

II. Disappointment at failure to reach I. Tirade against God.

III. Search for these ideals within myself. Protest. Freedom.

IV. Scientific basis for Freedom (Knowledge).

V. Religion.

This outline begins and ends in religion, like a circle come full round. Musically, the First Sonata begins its burst of mighty drama and inner tragedy with the striving towards the goal of Good or God, and ends with death. Throughout there is fiery upheaval, "pathos" in the Russian sense, a controlled sadness which exudes discontent.

The First Sonata in F minor was actually Scriabin's third attempt at the sonata form. There had been a light little Fantasy Sonata of 1886, which Limontov and Rozenov heard (*Soviet Music*, issue No. 4, 1940). An Allegro Appassionata had been intended as an opening movement to a sonata begun in 1887 and completely revised in 1892. In response to Rozenov's plea, he finished a Presto third movement (published in Vol. I of Scriabin's Collected Works, Muzgiz (1947). The First Sonata, however, after a year's emotional gestation was completely written the first few months of summer, 1892, a surprisingly short space of time.

The opening theme (*allegro con fuoco*) surges up from its bass undertow. The nuclear chord is symmetrically formed—major seconds separated by a major third (F G—B C# (D Flat), and governs the phrase's thought. The waves sink into the *meno mosso* theme with a downward pull, instead of breaking. The bugle-like third theme in A flat ascends again and expands into the first *ff* and the widest distance between bass and treble on the keyboard. This first movement is conventional in form with a proper development, thematic elaboration and a short recapitulation. From its loud beginning in the minor key, it ends, contrastingly, in major, *pppp* . . . a soft hint of optimism?

The second movement begins as a meandering, contemplative chorale. A filigree spins itself decoratively into the texture. The shadowy beginning in the key of C minor resolves, as in the first movement, into a clarification—C major.

The third movement is a *presto* tour de force of incessant left-hand octaves. They throb against steady, chordal beats of the right hand. Scriabin called these *ropoty* (murmurings, defiant cries), grovelings before God and fate. Unexpectedly, the searching *meno mosso* theme of the first movement returns like a flash of reason within turbulence. The restless, headlong rush resumes and stops abruptly *fff*. A recitative intervenes, as if asking a crucial but unanswerable question.

This passage arches into the last movement, the "Funeral March." Here bells toll in the bass. Over this, a melodic line, broken and crushed by the death of the heart, sighs. Midway, a processional of unearthly four-part harmony (played at half-pedal with half-depth of the piano keys for ghostly coloration) interrupts. It intones the life beyond, the hope of salvation. A human cry interrupts (*a piacere*), bespeaking grief. The funereal pace resumes and as the marching passes the sound fades. The concluding measure suddenly sounds a loud question mark: three compelling notes.

Scriabin will rarely accept death again. He himself played the First Sonata only once, in Petersburg on 11 February, 1894, although he used the "Funeral March" alone at a small concert in Paris at the Salle de Journal on 10 July, 1900. Perhaps it embodied too many painful memories. Hearing the First Sonata today one realizes how conventionally romantic it is. Such sonatas are no longer written, nor would Scriabin himself continue to write them.

Meanwhile, Moscow society was welcoming Scriabin as a rising new celebrity. Rozenov played the Allegro Appassionata in the Conservatory's Little Hall in 1893. In heart, the piece was dedicated to him. On 31 May, 1895, Keneman performed the First Sonata at the Great Hall of the Conservatory for the graduating students.

Scriabin, in sober moments of the evening, in salons and professors' houses, was himself performing again. His intimate tone was charming. His pianissimo remarkable. His coloring bordered on the fantastic.

♪ VI ♪

LOVE

20

Aunt lyubov now speaks the word "love" for the first time. "I don't know for a fact if Shurinka was ever in love while at the Conservatory. However, he received letters from various girl students, inviting him to many a rendezvous . . . Shurinka always brought them to me, and he would smile. I know that he never accepted any of them, because I watched him at the appointed hour. The time would come and go. He was still working in his room . . ." Then she reveals his first love. Scriabin scholar Kashperov called it "youthful and platonic," but Lyubov wrote more strongly: "Shurinka met a beautiful and clever, most gifted girl. He became more and more enamored of her. When at last he was invited to her house, he was very happy. He would return home cheerful. Sitting down at my feet, his head in my lap, he would recall every word she said. He reported his answers and asked me if he had replied correctly, or could he possibly have given offense? They were both so fine and young, I wished their attachment could have lasted."

For reasons the past sometimes obeys, everyone referred to the affair obliquely. Lyubov omits the girl's name. Rozenov contents himself with saying that once in 1893 when Scriabin was staying with him, some pressed flowers came in the mail. He kept them next to his heart and took them out from time to time to kiss them.

Only in 1922 was the mystery solved and the love openly known. Scriabin's love letters to Natalya Sekerina were found in the desk drawer of one of her several, subsequent husbands—I. Gurlyand, member of the Foreign Affairs Council under the Department of External Affairs, whose documents were confiscated by the "Commission of Enquiry into

Unlawful Acts Committed by the Tsar's Government." Still more letters were turned over to the Scriabin Museum by Natalya's older sister, Olga. She recounts that in 1891 Zverev, who came to the Sekerin house once a week to give piano lessons, gave them tickets to a concert as part of their musical education. Skryabusha was playing at the Conservatory. The girls, accompanied by their mother, were enraptured. A student sitting nearby offered to introduce them. Next day, both boys called on the girls formally.

Olga describes Scriabin of that year. "He may have been in cadet uniform, but there was nothing military in his bearing. He was awkward I must say. Behind it you could see all the wonderful softness which feminine care and upbringing had left on his manners..." Zverev, hearing of the meeting, fostered it by bringing Skryabusha with him to Natalya's next lesson. The girls expressed interest in his ménage of *babushki*. The following Sunday at the Church of Sts. Athanasius and Kyril, Scriabin pointed out his aunt, the grandmother and her sister from a distance.

Natalya and Olga invited Scriabin to ice skate, since that was their chief pastime and only respectable way of seeing him without stirring gossip. But he did not know how to. Natalya worked out a system whereby Scriabin sat in a chair and the party took turns pushing him around over the ice. Scriabin also hid outside Natalya's school, the Fourth Gymnasium for Young Ladies. He saw her as she entered and left. They nodded or bowed covertly.

Twice a month on Wednesdays, the Sekerina sisters entertained. When Scriabin came, their favorite game of musical chairs always ended with him on the floor. Olga is clear when she writes that "he never showed his infatuation for my sister, except sometimes I would catch a certain light in his eyes as he looked at her." The girls subscribed to the RMO symphony concert series that winter at Zverev's insistence. To their amazement Scriabin's seat was right beside them. He had wangled this with a friend at the box office. During intermissions he delivered lessons on music appreciation.

One night when he was sleeping at Kolya Averino's apartment, Scriabin woke his friend up, "I've just written a poem for Natalya," he shouted, "Listen!"

Were I by sweet dreaming
To dwell within thy soul
But for a moment,
Were I with impassioned flight
To trouble the peace of thy soul,
Were I to turn thy fair head
To great thoughts of creation,
I would, dear friend,
Reveal to thee
A universe of delight.

Averino went back to sleep. He was again awakened. Scriabin had now set it to music. "It was junk," Averino commented in recalling the incident many years later, and next day asked him to improve the music. Rozenov too spoke harshly about the song. He called it "weak and officerlike," which meant "affected and posing." Actually it is a lovely page, subdued and graceful. Scriabin titled it "Romance."

(The manuscript was found after Scriabin's death. Nina Koshetz, whose career as vocalist and actress ended many years later in Hollywood, sang it *in memoriam* in 1915. Natalya herself never heard the Romance. Nor had she the courage to ask if he had set the poem [which she did see] to music.)

Some time in March, that year of 1891–2, Natalya's German maid found a note in her pinafore. She took it straight to Mme. Sekerina. It sounded businesslike enough, asking only that if the Sekerinas were observing the custom of "No Amusements First Week of Lent," would he still be able to come and call?

Natalya's mother sent for Scriabin. She intended to explain that "feelings" may not be addressed to a girl of fifteen. Before she could open her mouth, Scriabin burst out, "I think I am within my rights ... Natasha and I consider ourselves engaged to be married and have so for some time." Scriabin was forbidden ever to enter the house again.

Olga continues her narrative:

> Next day, *I* received a letter by messenger. He begged me to meet him. I flung on some clothes and sneaked out of the house. He rushed towards me, trembling all over as with fever. His voice shook. "Don't take away my little Natasha. Don't deprive me of my muse. I love her with that pure, ideal love with which one loves only once in a lifetime. Indeed, I have felt for the first

time happiness, happiness in love . . ."

I just didn't know what to say. I calmed him by saying that all he needed was patience—two years. I told him that Natasha had fainted dead away when she saw his letter in Mama's hands. The doctor had to be called. He took this as proof that his love was requited. It made him quite happy.

After that he left secret messages underneath the garden gate.

21

THE SCRIABIN-SEKERINA correspondence consists of a total of sixty-seven, more long than short, letters. Scriabin wrote primarily during summers (when they could not meet) covering a period from December, 1891, to December, 1895. None of Natalya's replies is preserved, since Scriabin never kept correspondence from anyone.

All his letters, from first to last, begin formally "Respected Natalya Valeryanovna," and are signed "A. Scriabin." Each ends too, regardless of his habitual nervous haste, with a long phrase requesting Natalya to transmit his respects, cordial regards, to her mother and sister.

Both Sasha and Natasha considered themselves passionately in love. Face to face they used each other's diminutives. Ordinarily thoughtless, Sasha never once in almost five years, forgot her saint's day.

Whenever Natalya fails to write often enough, Scriabin is not afraid to whine—"Perhaps you will pity your Scriabin who is dying of loneliness. . ." ". . .will give him a few words. . ." ". . .From one who awaits word from you with frightful impatience. . ." or "For God's sake, write!" Once he sent a telegram, which, of course, openly exposed their correspondence to her family and caused needless trouble.

Sanguine evidence that Scriabin loved her is also in the completeness of his letters sharing experience with her. No other correspondent of Scriabin's lifetime ever received such abundant detail of weather, description of scenery, thoughts, caustic comments on fellows and fellow-travelers, recitals of what doctors said and what happened in daily life.

Scriabin wrote as fast as he thought, illegibly, and often with all kinds of errors in spelling. "Forgive my chicken scratches." He would beg, over and over again, but he never recopied, edited, or reread for corrections, nor even dated his letters.

At the end of summer in 1892, Scriabin mentions to Natalya that he will be going abroad in January, 1893. The trip, a concert tour to be arranged by Safonoff, is postponed because his hand troubles him, as he starts to practice more.

Scriabin remains in Moscow in despair over the recurrent pain. Natalya has been whisked away to Polevaya Station just outside Kursk, some two hundred miles from Moscow, one of the two Sekerina estates. He projects his own fears and warns Natalya in a letter postmarked 30 May, 1893, not to ride her "Pegasus," a horse which once threw her.

> Don't ride him like a whirlwind . . . Leave such skullcracking to those who feel about themselves as I do. God! What blackness I live in. The doctors have not yet given their verdict. Never before has a state of uncertainty been such torture for me. Oh, if only I could see some light ahead. If it were possible to believe blindly in the future! Then, then can a man take firm and steady steps towards the goal he loves. Then, then life unfolds enticingly. Alas, there is too much in life that destroys faith, *no matter how much* I want to believe.

Dr. Zakharin was called into conference. Scriabin fears he will detain him in Moscow near his clinic. That is how he cured Safonoff's sister, Anastasia, who had likewise overworked at the piano. To dramatize his suffering, Scriabin adds, "I have even forgotten how to hold a pen. I've written no one all winter. . ."

Later that month, Scriabin gives Natalya a detailed report of his interview with the doctor:

> His examination lasted a long time and touched every facet of my life. First of all, I had to tell him in detail how I spend each day from the time I get up to when I go to bed, what and when I eat and drink, when I sleep, how much I play the piano, compose and write, etc. It seemed there was not a single stone he left unturned.
>
> Naturally, he found everything I told him bad. I am forbidden everything in the future. This is the superficial part of the consultation.
>
> Then he brought up the question of my moodiness. How unnatural it was, he said, for me to change so quickly up and down. This affects me horribly. So much volatility works on the nervous system. In brief, he dressed me down. Then he passed sentence on me: A quiet life in the Caucasus and bathing in the Black Sea. He promises that this treatment will restore my hand . . .
>
> I hasten to share this joy with you. I can leave horrid, summertime Moscow . . .

Scriabin wants to go to Kislovodsk, in the Caucasian mountains where

Safonoff summers. However, he has misunderstood Zakharin. There is
another specialist to be consulted, Dr. Alexander Belyaev, chief physician
at the Surgical Clinic of Moscow University.

Both doctors agree that the cure for both Scriabin himself and his
hand is "a regular and tranquil life, a diet of kumiss, bathing in sea water."
However the question devolves on "where?" The choice, finally, is
between "the south, with its marvelous country and unusual, variegated
scenery, or east to the boring plains of dry grass and steppes."

Kumiss, a Tatar remedy for "nerves" of every kind, is a lightly intoxicating, health-giving drink made from fermented mare's (or camel's)
milk, and though available in both areas, is inferior in the Caucasus.
Caucasian air too is damp, not nearly as "beneficial as the Slavic air of
the east." The doctors settle on the hot and sweating east—Samara
(later Kuibyshev), a large port city three hundred miles down the Volga
from Moscow and renowned for its sanatoria. Sea bathing, of course,
meant afterwards in the Crimea. To keep their spiritual connection
even closer, he asks Natalya to "write exactly when you practice and I
will share the sounds of your piano exercises in my thoughts and over
the great distance."

Lyubov describes Samara: "The sanitarium is uninteresting, the
weather fearfully hot, but we were not too enervated to take walks."

Scriabin writes Natalya, 28 June, 1893:

Odious Samara! Here I am installed for already a week with a very nice family
in a dacha two miles out of town. I have two little rooms, one of which is my
bedroom and the other where I receive guests. Up to now, outside of the son
of the house and his dog "Nero," I have received no one. I sit hours on end
alone, enjoying the lovely view from my window overlooking the garden,
and sometimes I work.

Just as you place my letters on your piano, I put yours by my music paper and
pencil. But I must admit that work of any kind's rarely possible during the
kumiss cure. One clever inmate here calls the treatment "harmless alcoholism,"
and says it was invented by the Kirghiz people to circumvent the law forbidding
them spiritous drinks. It is quite true that the second bottle has some effect and
after the third it is simply impossible not to doze. I sleep twelve out of the
twenty-four hours. The rest of the time I eat and drink. So go the days here.

True, there are some people who bring variety into this existence. I'll tell you
first of all about one of them, a lady in striped morning dress . . . "Lydia of the
stripes." Her face has the expression of a question mark with a very prominent

nose on the end of which fate has willed two warts. Unheeding destiny has furnished one of them with three red hairs. The lady places all her moral strength in these hairs and therefore never trims them.

This woman is bad, spiteful, and irritable. Her favorite theme of conversation is her warts, which have led to the most improbable adventures.

Here is her favorite episode: Moved to tears at some group for reading sentimental poetry, she took out her handkerchief to blow her nose. She accidentally got one of her warts and let out a screech or made some sort of odd sound which broke the deep silence and made her look as if she were terribly ill-mannered. Now since good breeding is the highest of virtues to this lady, from that day on she set about destroying the warts. Every day she cauterized them. This did not stop the growing. It only changed their color.

She is very famous in meteorological and medical circles, and she even plays an important role among residents here. Her warts forecast the weather by turning dark blue and brown in rain and cold, and bright red in clear weather and heat. The doctors prescribed kumiss for her, and she is to drink it until she becomes beautiful! Enough of this woman.

There is one more subject here, and he is most interesting . . . He is an artist, but one hindered by details. He sees only minutiae and embellishments in everything. For example music is most impressive to him when it has grace notes and sequences or *gruppetti*. He has only to hear a piece with two or three *gruppetti* one after the other and he is reduced to tears.

I will tell you one episode which characterizes his personality. To do so I must revert once again to the lady in the striped morning dress. She said she was desirous of having her portrait painted in oils. The artist's face lit up, his eyes burned, and a word of agreement slipped from his lips. Here was something on which he could expend the full brilliance of his talent. The sittings began. After the fourth the artist gave the portrait its final reworking of "details," and on the following day, with a look of triumph he submitted his labor to the criticism of all us residents.

The portrait was magnificent! True, the face was rather hidden and didn't look like her, but all the details and embellishments stood out in relief and struck the eye instantly. First of all there were two bright purple warts looking like balls of fire, and on one of them he had painted three huge red hairs, and on the other sat a fly. Her birthmark over her left eye looked like an ink blot with whiskers tough enough for a sergeant-major. There is no human language with sufficient vocabulary to express the fury of the lady when she saw how scandalously she had been painted. She grabbed the first knife she saw and poked the eyes of her own portrait and cut it, and threw it over the terrace. There, some street urchins picked it up and added insult to injury. They took a dead toad and tied it to the picture. Finally, they fastened it to a post of the summerhouse where "Lydia" had gone to down some more kumiss. I think she will stay away from us in the future. And for some inexplicable reason the painter is *also* sulking.

I talk too much. Goodbye. I must now drink three bottles . . . Don't forget your harmless but still alcoholic A. Scriabin who wishes to bring you and your sister all the countless flowers in the garden . . .

Another letter (13 July, 1893) tells more about his Samara life:

> My beard has sprouted in all kinds of unmatching bunches and queer shapes. It looks quite like the marshy steppes. So it must go, I fear, but before, I'm asking my artist friend to immortalize it. It ought to please him to work out its peculiarities on canvas.
> Natalya Valeryanovna, if only you knew how I wanted to escape from here. I am sick of kumiss. I sometimes cheat and just don't touch it. I used to drink six bottles a day.

Scriabin's last letter from Samara, 19 July, 1893, gives news of Averino. Kolya, it seems, has severely strained his hand at the violin. He has left Russia to see the greatest of specialists in Paris, Jean Charcot (1825–1893), neurologist, hypnotist, and influence on Freud. Drs. Zakharin and Belyaev were unable to promise him a cure.

Scriabin hears from Kolya again in August. Charcot died just as Kolya reached Paris. Another expert examined him lengthily and prescribed electricity and massage. "Nothing new," Scriabin writes Natalya: "So that is the latest, most advanced school! They just look at the bony structure and study *how* people injure themselves, instead of serving the true, the good, and the artistic. They just count the numbers of people who suffer because of music. No one protests. No one tries to abolish this. Statistics! . . . if the hand doesn't right itself . . . without music, he will turn into a garden vegetable . . ."

August and September find Scriabin in that celebrated peninsula of the Ukraine which hangs like a pendant into the Black Sea. It combines the rare marvel of mountains and immediate sea. The countryside is redolent with vineyards, orchards of cherry, pyramidal mulberry, almond trees, vegetable and flower gardens. The woods are thick and beautiful. In the hills, with their fine views of the sea, still stood Tatar villages and settlements of Karaim Jews. Along the beaches gentled by breakwaters, good-sized ships docked at the port and pearl of the Crimea, Yalta.

Scriabin on 25 August, 1893, pictures for Natalya the resort town on the south coast where he is staying:

Gurzuf is nice, but somehow I cannot take full delight in its natural beauty. The Crimea makes a totally different impression on me from what I expected. The Crimea is like a personality who wants to appear better than he is. In all justice I must admit it admirably succeeds on the outside.

It is a showoff boasting of cypresses, laurels, pomegranates, magnolias, and other southern plants, although in winter they wrap them in mats and keep them under glass to protect them from frost. Still, the personality gloats over "subtropical" nature.

In the next letter, 17 September, Scriabin is "frightfully bored."

If I didn't hope to leave this prison of torture soon, I don't know what I'd do . . . Thank God I have only five more sea baths and then this matter is done with . . .

22

SCRIABIN IN the letters to Natalya shows particular interest in nature, "that tender mother of mankind." As his ideas progressed, he would see nature more as man's mind turned inside out. But its presence where flowers bloomed, fountains flowed, and birds sang, was always there affording him an opportunity to intellectualize, to philosophize, to poeticize.

Here are random samples of his responses to nature. Each of these written thoughts predicts future music. They read too like a cornerstone for his later philosophy of man's dominance, and dominion.

From Finland on 15 June, 1892:

Disgusting weather fogged us in, going up the Saimas Canal. Only when we were close to the banks could we see the luxuriant countryside and Finland's valiant battle—the struggle of Northern Man against Savage Nature. In this country, the human being can proudly raise his head and say:

"I have conquered you, Nature. I have converted your impossible masses of forests and your crags and stones into parks of pathways, grottoes, arbors, bridges. I have curbed Thee, mountain streams, and forced Thee to serve me. Everything that surrounds me has been subdued by my will, by my reason . . ."

14 June, 1893:

The trip down the Volga to Samara has already done me good. Yesterday, there was something special, something inexplicable in Nature.

Over the whole view lay a mood, a wonderful feeling which I cannot communicate. Each blade of grass, each flower, seemed to understand its importance in just being. Everything stopped shock still in reverent attention and harkened to some secret, sweet whispering of divine inspiration. I could almost hear a voice say:

Creatures, you are endowed with life, but never think that the world exists for you or you for the world. You were not, and the World was. You will not be, and the World will remain. Do not try to isolate yourself. You are a part of it. Do not try to grasp the secret of your being, or to possess the World which is already possessed—by Thought.

Just as your body once constituted a single atom of a mass and was swallowed up by this mass, so will your thoughts, your soul be swallowed up by the creative idea. Thus it will be forever. Thus the earth will be sucked back into the sun to create a new planet. Evaporating drops of moisture fall into the sea as rain, only to evaporate once again. In this way Nature herself attests the truth of the manifested, material world.

As a sinful thought seizes the hitherto pure soul, so did a black, leaden, heavy cloud move and cover the earth with ominous gloom. Soon there was a majestic and terrifying procession of fiery sky darts, splendidly refulgent, and with claps of thunder. And meanwhile, on the other side of the heavens, the sun itself still glowed with blinding luster. I couldn't help thinking, Why the protest? Why the struggle? And then came all those petty, insignificant drops . . . The rain came and I was forced to take cover. I left the deck of the boat and went to the lounge.

19 July, 1893, now in Samara, Scriabin develops an interest in design and pattern.

I am now engaged in serious work classifying musical forms. This morning I read a remarkable book on flora of this planet and the relation of tropical flower forms and patterns to those in other latitudes. My imagination led me to some fantastic considerations.

I took our present-day music as representing the flora of temperate latitudes. Then I carried each form to its ideal, that is, to its fullest development and considered this the musical equator. Then I compared this with what is already found in tropical latitudes and related it to the forms found in the middle latitudes.

In other words, from our latitude to the ideal, is there a relationship such as exists between the flora of the middle latitudes and the tropical ones? The boundless possibilities of this are unimaginable.

One cannot but think that the realist-artists are right, and that the whole realist school—with Balzac as the grandfather and Gustave Flaubert as the father—alone triumphs in the end of ends. In consequence, all artists must draw their inspiration from Nature and life exclusively. Only this way can they ever forget themselves and their subjectivity.

At the beginning of vacation 1894, in Moscow he writes Natalya on 9 June:

When one returns to one's country place where one has passed an entire childhood, the heart is filled with acres of emotions. The whole world of childhood dreams is awakened. That aura of shining silver dust quivers with fantastic beings of beauty and monstrosity. It brings to mind that time when one loves and doesn't know why one loves.

Again, on the other hand, one is proud of awareness: The world of light in which man walks with firm steps along a clear path towards a certain, specific goal.

20 June, he sends deeper ruminations still, writing from Rozenov's country estate:

How many thousands of years have people contemplated the beauties of Nature? How many poets have sung the charm of moonlit nights? And still we send up eternal thanks to the moon, our eternally young satellite. What fantastic number is it? Those to whom it has given pleasure?! And the moon showers down on earth its clear and awakening light gently stroking our nerves. It rules the world for a short time, secretly with caressing radiance, and every object washed in the light seems larger and takes on added significance. Then finally it grows effeminate and langorous, floating in its background of ash-colored light. There is always something new to investigate in it.

On such nights the mind—this fearsome mind, to which everything is rotten, analytical, critical, and destructive—is silent, and, although not for long, one can give oneself up to contemplation and quiet.

Oh how an intellectually exhausted and morally enfeebled person today needs this pause! It sometimes seems that Nature itself, that tender mother of mankind, calls him to salvation. She whispers, "Come to me, you pale, dying creature. Cast off your false veil of knowledge."

In September he reproaches Natalya as his father had earlier rebuked him:

> Is it possible that you are not attracted by our open, simple and melancholy Russian landscape? It is impossible to love truth. Nature in the South with its boasting, glittering exterior still conceals another self behind it.

Finally, he wrote Natalya on 24 May, 1895, from Heidelberg, and here made one of his last extended declarations on the subject of nature:

> I have to admit that as nice as Europe is, still, for the Russian nothing can take the place of his native countryside. It has a special charm of some kind whose basis is in its breadth and sweep. I couldn't last a week living in a mountainous country. A mountain range is beautiful but immobile, and therefore it wearies, finally it oppresses. To keep continually refreshed one ought to change one's locale constantly, that is, live a nomadic life. In Russia we are so used to our plains we don't even see them anymore.

> At Safonoff's once I met a missionary who told us of the terrifying effect the steppes produced on a person who left his mountains for the first time and came to Russia. He was so frightened by the expanse of the spacious heavenly vault above him, he kept closing his eyes to try and get used to it. I remember that so well.

> The plains must make a deeper first impression on the mountaineer than mountainous country makes on a plainsman. Therefore, as I said before, I love the sea very much and long for it. That is where space really is, not to mention an infinity of colors and forms.

23

WINTER OF 1893–94 saw Scriabin's hand worsen. He was rested physically; the kumiss-drenched summer had induced some calm. But the brutalizing hurt to his hand followed him everywhere. Pain had spread from the fingers up his arm. The second year of misfortune had begun and Scriabin's agony turned into the terror of uncertainty. His fear expressed itself as excessive, irrational irritability.

When Natalya returned to Moscow she heard that Scriabin could no longer play. She and her sister met him at the symphony series and were shocked at the sight. "He had changed beyond recognition. He was driven to distraction by his ailment. He said many pianists suffered the same thing and that it would leave him, but his nervousness at this time was incredible," Olga said.

In 1893 Zverev died. Scriabin asked to become Natalya's teacher, but for all Natalya's entreaties the mother decided on Igumnov, to Scriabin's fury. He again demonstrated how overwrought he was at the next concert. A young physics professor joined the Sekerina girls in the foyer. Scriabin suddenly "ran about, rubbed his hands together, and simply did not know how to stop my sister and the professor from talking. He chivvied us back to our seats ahead of time. After that we always entered and left the concert hall by way of the artists' entrance . . . obscurely, avoiding the crowd."

Another flareup occurred. The trio attended Josef Hofmann's debut recital in Moscow in 1894. Natalya was most impressed and this displeased Scriabin. He refused to let them meet, but Natalya learned that Hofmann was an expert ice skater and "on view" every afternoon at two in the Lazarik Rink. Natalya asked Scriabin to join her there. A Zverev pupil introduced her to Hofmann and they sailed around the rink "gaily chatting while Scriabin became fearfully depressed . . . He winced everytime Hofmann called her 'Fräulein' or paid her a compliment."

Natalya's class at the gymnasium decided to give a grand school ball. As was customary, professional theatrical personnel—N. Musil, a young actor of the Maly, and Olga Knipper of the Moscow Art, in this instance—were charged with the arrangements. They decorated the auditorium with artificial flowers and ribbons, ordered supplies of confetti, and hired an orchestra and some dancers to lead the dancing, in case the girls themselves faltered. Scriabin, who had not danced since the cotillion at the Cadet Corps, and would not again in his whole life, attended. He sat near the wall with Olga. Natalya's seat nextby was vacant. She danced every dance . . . "even the newest ones with amazing grace. My sister had become a 'young lady'," Olga thought, "she was beautiful and shapely . . ." Scriabin found the sight "unpleasant." His head began to ache, and he went home, ill.

One of the messages left at the garden gate—the only one saved— voices a heartbreaking cry of Scriabin's soul. Its poignancy could be the melancholy motto of the First Sonata. The torment of that winter is painfully expressed.

> Hear me out! Listen to this voice of a sick and tormented soul. Remember and pray for the man whose entire happiness is yours and whose entire life belongs to you.

With the resilience of youth, there were also happy times. Scriabin turned up, uninvited, at excursions to Sparrow Hills. He and Natalya "frolicked, capered, joked, and breathed the autumnal air." Sundays the pair also met in the gardens of the Cathedral of Our Savior. New Year's was celebrated in Russian custom "by visiting in costume." Olga dressed as Grandfather Frost. Natalya disguised herself as a clown. Making the rounds in hired *drozhki* and *troikas*, they encountered a gracious Spanish lady and a clown—Sasha and Kolya. Olga observes: "Scriabin was unusually gifted in acting the part of a woman, and all of us laughed outright with pleasure. In one house Mama was also a guest, and that 'Spanish lady' dared sit on the divan beside her and even fan her . . ."

Scriabin and Natalya read the life of Beethoven together. He instructed her in the meaning of the American Constitution. He wrote an étude (Op. 8 No. 8 (*Lento, rubato*) in A flat major) for her and asked Igumnov to teach it to her. Its form is in three repeated sections, varied by first having two notes to a beat, then three, and finally four notes to the still steady, single beat. Full of wandering tonalities, hovering constantly between major and minor key, the piece breathes Russianism and romance. It proved to be one of his most popular pieces, and second to the D♯ minor *patético*, he played it more frequently than any other of his études.

He gave this music on manuscript paper bordered with hand-drawn flower wreaths and exquisitely wrapped in colored paper. He sent Olga a Waltz in G♯ minor (which was absorbed into the Fantasy Sonata—the 3/4:3/2 section of the first movement). He explained to Olga that Natalya "creates my mood, and I create the music." He apologized for not sending white roses, his favorite flower, for fear of interception.

The summer of 1894 began dully enough. Scriabin was still in Moscow and wrote Natalya on June 9, "I pass my time monotonously. I spend it all with Safonoff. He seems to be my only acquaintance in Moscow. Evenings we take walks or go on drives out of town."

Scriabin visits his aunt and *babushki* who are staying with Uncle Vladimir in Povarovo, a sub-station platform not far from the city on the Moscow-Petersburg railroad line. He takes Rozenov, "that marvelous and indefatigable walking companion," with him.

They are flustered by news of the great earthquake in Constantinople. "Although it broke more dishes than actually cost lives," Scriabin writes in a letter 30 June, 1894, to Natalya: "What surprises Nature provides! All the same I would like to be present during such a phenomenon, so I could see how I feel. They tell me that for the first several seconds the survivors thought they were dead. Then some became apathetic. Others began running for cover and forgot every safety precaution. It was haste that made them victims. What a sorry spectacle it must be!"

On Scriabin's return to Moscow, rumors reach Natalya (she is five days by letter away) that Scriabin was seen walking in a park—one of their own haunts—holding hands with a girl. He protests his innocence: "Being of sound mind and firm memory, I can testify I have held hands with no one except Alexander Kabat, and he by no means can be taken for a woman." (Kabat, a mutual acquaintance of the Sekerins, later was board member of the State Noblemen's Bank).

Scriabin visits Rozenov in September at Zenino. An invitation comes from Natalya. Scriabin accepts with pleasure, "provided I am assured that my presence will not upset anyone . . ." He then tells her Rozenov has taken up embroidering. "He makes his own designs in magnificent oriental style and he chooses the silks himself. The results are astonishing."

Scriabin hints that he cannot visit Natalya unless the invitation is confirmed by the mother. This is not forthcoming. Scriabin, when he says goodbye to Rozenov heads, therefore, straight for Safonoff, a thousand miles further south. There he is at last in the heart of the mountains, with snowcaps for a view, amid fir forests, wild animals—martens, leopards, roebucks, ibex—and radioactive, curative hot springs. Scriabin passes the time listening to band concerts twice a day, eating flaming Caucasian shashlik and bathing again and again in the thermal waters, particularly the sulphurous ones. Safonoff himself has gone back to Moscow to prepare for opening the Conservatory. Scriabin is happily and healthily left with the ladies.

He writes Natalya that he is still upset about the state of his nerves and attributes it to the amount of work he did while he stayed with Safonoff earlier in the summer in Moscow. "I gave myself unstintingly and my nervous system reached such a point of irritability as to make me unbearable in company. I cannot begin to tell you how hard it was for me to deprive myself of the pleasure of seeing you—I've dreamed so often of it—yet at the same time I realized how undesirable my appearance would be for all concerned."

24

AT THIS point, we skip to the conclusion of the Natalya affair. Scriabin's letters will continue for the following year, but the romance really ends here, on a note of upset at not being accepted by the mother.

Natalya's life apart from Scriabin held much happiness. She had been taken abroad on the grand tour, partly to forget Scriabin. Her beauty, and the ambition of her mother, brought her to the attention of Grand Duchess Elisabeth Fyodorovna. She was presented at Court. When she was eighteen, she married Nikolai Markov, a judge and Palace Chamberlain. They produced one son, Leo. She divorced Markov in 1908 and married Gurlyand. At her salon, dignitaries and statesmen of the era gathered—Sturmer, Protopopov, Kokovtsev, Khvostov. After the Revolution, Gurlyand fled. Natalya left in 1925 and lived in France for ten years. She married a third time, to Usachov, a Cossack colonel. They went to Paraguay, according to the obituary of Natalya Sekerina-Markova-Gurlyanda-Usachova published in *New Russian World* (New York) 11 February, 1962.

In 1930, Natalya herself volunteered a letter of clarification. She addressed it to the Scriabin Museum in Moscow, and captioned it with a line of poetry, "Our curly locks are white, like morning snow:"

> Now when one whose great love has long lain in the grave, I want to say what I have never said to anyone before now. There never was a break with Scriabin. He came less frequently to us after a very serious conversation which caused me not a little emotional tension . . .
> One night, Scriabin again reiterated his proposal of marriage. I said, "I am not worthy of marrying you, because I love you less than I did at first." He said

nothing, did not argue. I went up to my room, contrite and desolate and confused and nearly out of my mind for having said it.

I have kept this a secret because I never wanted the world to know that Scriabin had ever suffered a rebuff of any sort. But was this not a natural and basic refusal? That beloved man could never have had happiness, if I had been afraid to say "No" to him. And what kind of wife would I have made him, a genius? My subconscious truly pointed the right path and led me to a correct decision.

In 1955 Colonel Usachov died. Natalya moved to Washington, D.C. with her son, and lived quietly until her own death at the age of 85.

Two pages in a notebook show an entry belonging to 1894. Scriabin is beyond the despair of the First Sonata; his hand is getting better; Natalya fades. He is persistently affirming to himself a desire to be healthy, a wish to live and live in health and happiness. A new Scriabin now expresses himself: the Scriabin of victory, the triumphant man who overcomes and conquers. This is Scriabin's famous "What Then?" credo. It will serve him for most of the rest of his life, as both a philosophical and musical platform of vantage.

To be an optimist in a real sense, one must suffer doubt and conquer it .

Not by my own wish have I come into this world. Well, what then?

In tender youth, full with illusions of desire and hope, I delighted in shining glories.

I awaited a revelation from Heaven. It came not. Well, what then?

I sought eternal truth and asked of people. Alas, they knew no more than I. Well, what then?

I sought eternal beauty, and found it not. Like buds which never bloom, my feelings were stilled. The rain of night dimmed the bright day.

I sought solace in the new spring, new flowers, but nowhere found it. I strove not to change what was, but to return to the already spent, to recall the already experienced.

Into each person's life, springtime can come but once. How people rush beyond these divine dreams, those enchanting delusions!

At last I took comfort in memories. But once used to them, they vanished. Well, what then?

Whoever you may be, you who laughed at me, who plunged me into dark depths,

Whoever you were, you who mocked me, cast me in prison, ravished me to disillusion, gave in order to steal back, caressed in order to torment,

I take my leave of you and ask no further redress.

I am alive. I love life. I love people. I love them all the more because through *you* they have suffered.

I will proclaim to all people that I have triumphed over you, over myself. I say that they can place no hope in you, that they can expect naught from life except THAT WHICH THEY CREATE BY THEMSELVES ALONE.

I thank you for all the fears which your trials and tribulations aroused. You made me know my endless power, my unlimited might, my invincibility. You gave me the power of creativity.

I will tell them that they are strong and mighty, that it is needless to lament, that there is no loss, that they must not fear doubt which alone gives birth to true triumph.

Powerful is he! Mighty is he! He, who feels defeat and overcomes it!

The music which accompanied these words are the brightest gems of his early period, the twelve brilliant, passionately exuberant Etudes, Op. 8. They range widely in subject matter—major thirds, minor sixths, octaves, a ballade, a love *Lento* to Natalya. . .

✐ VII ✐

MAECENAS

25

MUCH HISTORY of Russian music is the story of multimillionaire music publisher Mitrofan Belaieff. Without him, there could be no Scriabin as we know him today. Speaking of this incongruous pair of men—one nearing sixty, the other barely twenty when they met; one a giant, the other elfin—Lyubov writes simply, "Belaieff loved Shurinka and Shurinka in his turn loved Belaieff."

Belaieff and two younger brothers, Yakov and Sergei, were heirs to the largest timber fortune in Russia and Siberia. Mitrofan entered his father's office in Petersburg as a regular employee at fifteen. His parents arranged a conventional marriage for him on coming into his majority. Since no children came of this, again conventionally, he adopted a girl, Valentina. (She eventually married the celebrated painter, Sergei Ivanov [1846–1910].)

Mitrofan Belaieff was an amateur viola player, and performed in a little private orchestra of "SPb Music Lovers" directed by Anatol Liadov. Fairly late, at forty-eight, Belaieff changed the course of his life, retiring from business altogether and diverting his vast capital to music. He was genuinely a maecenas-patron, and aimed to make Russian music known throughout the world. He surpassed Jurgenson and Gutheil.

His first step was to publish music clearly on fine quality paper. In 1884 he bought a factory in Leipzig. It was not only cheaper to engrave plates in Germany and more efficient, but it provided copyright protection, since Russia had not signed the convention protocol. The heart of the firm beat in Russia, and Belaieff's chief distribution in Russia was through the large chain of Jurgenson music stores.

By 1895 the Belaieff catalog listed 1,200 compositions; by 1914, the number doubled. Belaieff discovered Russian composers and helped them. Alexander Glazunov was his first, a sixteen-year-old boy in gymnasium uniform at the time. He bought out contracts of Russian composers being published elsewhere.

Belaieff also established the prestigious Glinka Prize giving substantial amounts of money to the best Russian compositions each year. The date of the award coincided with the anniversary of Glinka's first opera performance and Belaieff's own nameday, 27 November. He also created a series of symphony and chamber music concerts to rival those of the RMO, devoted exclusively to Russian music and providing a venue for Russian performers, whom, however, he regarded as of low order, because they were not "creative." Belaieff paid performers at his concerts a flat fee of 50 rubles, which was indeed low.

Never entirely sure of his own amateur judgment, in 1885 Belaieff set up an Advisory Board of professionals for the firm, composed of Rimsky-Korsakoff, Liadov, and Glazunov. They passed on each composition to be published. The house of Belaieff accepted works only on the basis of merit. The Board rejected any thought of subsidization or vanity publishing. Their terms were generous, though not as high as those paid by European houses: 200 rubles for a sonata; 50 rubles a prelude; and 100 rubles a song. Final payment was given a composer after second proofs were corrected and returned. As a result, the number of errors caused by haste—particularly in Scriabin's case—was great. Belaieff himself was a man of meticulosity and businesslike punctilio. (Nearly all dates on Scriabin's letters were written in by Belaieff on receipt.)

A full-length portrait by Ilya Repin (1844–1930), greatest of Russian painters, depicts Belaieff as a huge man with long-flowing, pompadoured hair, sparse beard, and sensuously intelligent eyes. His photographs, on the other hand, show a rather ugly, coarse-featured man, debauched with deep circles under his eyes, and, surprisingly, cruel. Few men have ever had more adoring friends than Belaieff. Each described him variously as "brusque," "full of personal crotchets," "a rough diamond," "implacable," but each loved him. He was "strong and appealing," according to all.

Lyubov wrote to him on 8 March, 1897, saying, "I know you look upon women as enemies..." Engel calls him "a woman-hater," and Gerald Abraham and M. D. Calvocoressi agree in their fine book, *Masters of Russian Music,* to dub him "a confirmed misogynist." However, his distaste for women did not extend so far as musicians. He created a fund—the first of its kind—for their widows and orphans.

One of several immortal tributes was paid Belaieff in 1886, a "Surprise" string quartet. Its theme was three notes punning his name—b-a-f (in Russian, B-la-f or Be-lya-yef). Rimsky composed the first movement, Borodin the second, Liadov the Scherzo, and Glazunov the Grand Finale. Its first performance took place on Belaieff's nameday and on a famous "Friday."

Belaieff entertained in his mansion on Fridays throughout the winter. "Suppers generously laced with abundant libations . . . and chamber music," Rimsky said, and they were a Petersburgian tradition. "The hospitable instigator of Quartet Fridays," as Asafiev called him, was invariably at his viola. He was never ill. Unlike other members of the quartet who were frequently replaced or substituted for, he never missed a performance. The quartet started originally by playing all the chamber works of Haydn, then moved on to Mozart, followed by all of Beethoven. Gradually, the evenings turned predominately Russian. Much of the music Belaieff printed was baptized first at these social gatherings.

The great Kashkin said, "These Fridays were interesting because everybody went. Whenever I happened to be in Petersburg, I tried to attend too." By everybody he meant the soul of Russia's musical activity.

Tchaikovsky was often seen there drinking more than was good for him. Glazunov, too, when he was barely out of school. And there were the three Stassov brothers (particularly Vladimir, "ideologist" of Russian music who, like Tolstoi, always wore Russian clothes everywhere, and both his beard and shirt were always stained, again like Tolstoi's). Nikolai Sokolov (1859–1922), professor at SPb Conservatory; Nikolai Artsybushev (1858–1937), lawyer, composer, pupil of Rimsky and later on the Advisory Board of the Belaieff firm; Josef Witohl (1863–1948), composer and critic; Felix Blumenfeld (1863–1931) (and his brother), conductor of the Maryinsky Theater then, formerly pupil of Rimsky in composition and Alexander Stein in piano, and in later life would teach successively at the Petersburg, Kiev, and Moscow Conservatories; Victor Evald (b. 1860), professor at the Institute for Civil Engineering in Petersburg, cellist, permanent member of Belaieff's Quartet; Alexander Winkler (1865–1935), Russianized German, professor at the Conservatory in "Special Subjects" and "Required Piano"; Vladimir Shcherbachov (1889–1952), wealthy dilettante and composer of salon pieces such as "Zigzag" and "Papillons"; Nikolai Lavrov (1861–1928), piano professor at the Conservatory; Vasily Kalafati (1869–1942), composer and professor; Findeizen; Dütsch; and others *ad infinitum.*

Women were excluded, because, the host explained, men would not be able to smoke freely. Evenings began at 11:00. Food was served at 2:00 in the morning. Guests never dispersed before 3:00, and even then, pockets of them adjourned to hotel restaurants and continued their musical carousing until after dawn.

Safonoff on a visit to SPb in May, 1894, brought Belaieff some Scriabin music. Jurgenson's idea of publishing the light, short, and easy pieces was not at all what Safonoff had in mind for his Sashkina's future. Except for the left hand pieces (Op. 9) and two impromptus (Op. 10), Safonoff left all those floating serenades and preludes at home in Moscow. He introduced Belaieff straightway to the large Allegro Appassionata and the First Sonata. Belaieff liked them enormously, even the Allegro's bombast, and asked for a photograph of Scriabin.

Belaieff trusted Safonoff's musical competence. Still he had to obey his own rules. The manuscripts were shown to the Board, and while Rimsky and Glazunov opposed a firm commitment to publish all future Scriabin music, Liadov differed. With two against two, Scriabin was accepted and became Belaieff's favorite and most favored composer.

Before summer was out, Lyubov went to Petersburg to negotiate the business particulars. Belaieff paid 150 rubles for the fifteen-page Allegro. He proposed a monthly stipend of 100 rubles to be given for life for exclusive rights to all of Scriabin's music. In addition, Scriabin would receive bonuses for particularly distinguished and noteworthy work. To prove this point he paid 400 rubles for the First Sonata, double the usual rate, which naturally irritated Belaieff's board, each of whom was also a composer and being paid less.

To give an idea of what this money signified, here is a random scale showing cost of living. The average student lived on 30 rubles a month. A family of four managed modestly on 100. Tuition at Moscow University cost 100 rubles per annum. German housemaids were paid two or three rubles a month, the equivalent of an opera ticket. A brothel cost a man 50 kopecks an hour, the same price as the cheapest seat at the opera or a piano recital, and what, in fact, a pianist had to pay for the *Allegro Appassionata* when it reached the counter as sheet music.

Lyubov returned in ecstasies. She brought with her the precious proofs of the *Allegro Appassionata*, a sum of money, and a letter from Belaieff to Scriabin. The terms, as she explained them, were simple: "He would pay by the month, and Shurinka would write only when he wished. . . . Material matters did not exist for Shurinka. He turned the Belaieff money over to me and forgot it was there . . . However, we were able to undertake more extensive travels during the summers . . ."

Life in general for the old ladies was easier. Nikolai had begun paying for Shurinka's clothes. He also contributed along with the other brothers to a common purse for the support of the ladies' household where Shurinka lived.

Lyubov tells how "Belaieff wanted to know all manner of details concerning Shurinka's personal life and work . . ." She obliged, until direct contact was established between the two when Scriabin writes his first letter in September, 1894:

> Accept my sincere gratitude for your kind trust in me. I shall endeavor to justify your faith by devoting all the power of my mind and will to the service of my beloved art. *I thank fate which has sent you into my life.*

Thus begins Scriabin's most voluminous and sustained correspondence. Still the two have not met. The photograph has, however, been sent . . . to Liadov by mistake.

Scriabin was unusually nervous about his first proofs, was afraid of losing them. When the corrections were finished he wrote Natalya excitedly: "I now feel like a little boy just released from school. Thanks to Safonoff, who helped me very, very greatly, the corrected proofs of the *Allegro Appassionata* have gone to Petersburg. Now that they are off, I have not touched pen to music paper, although ideas and themes are piling up inside my head. Along with a sense of freedom, I have a feeling of moral satisfaction. I want to share my little success with you, but I will forbear, knowing the egotism of such a desire . . ."

26

FROM 1894 to 1903 Scriabin wrote Belaieff one hundred eighty-four letters. Again we have an oddly one-sided picture emerging from reading answers and only rarely the eliciting letter. Innuendoes, consequently, abound.

In the first couple of months nothing goes smoothly and matters will roughen with the passing of time. However, the relationship is steadily deepening on both sides and neurotically so. Here are extracts of Scriabin's early letters, full of apologies and implicit with misunderstandings. He lives in terror of Belaieff being "angry" with him or of "finishing with" him. He begs to be scolded, as if that would purge his guilt. ("I feel the better for it.") Over and over again he speaks of his *rasseyannost'* (absent-mindedness), and his eternal *bezalabernost'* (carelessness). (He even misspells this word as *bezolabernost'*!)

December, 1894

Don't be angry with me, for heaven's sake, because of the proofs. Don't blame it on laziness or messiness. I simply cannot see my own mistakes. I cannot begin to thank you enough for your catching the errors. I beg you to convey to Liadov my sincere gratitude. I must have caused him many unpleasant minutes.

However, what use are words? In future I will endeavor to show gratitude by my deeds. Please continue to be severe with me, otherwise I will think you are angry.

4 January, 1895

Will send the Impromptus today. I put metronome marks as you suggest, although it is virtually useless to do so. In the second one, the tempo constantly changes.

11 February

As childishly helpless as I am, there is still some consideration in me. I would never trouble you with the chore of *arranging* my concert, only with setting the date. Nothing more.

In any event, I will come to SPb at the end of the first week of Lent. I wouldn't dream of inconveniencing you, so I dare not accept your kind offer to put me up . . .

24 February

I leave for SPb on Saturday by express train, but I implore you not to meet me. That would be too kind. I will come straight to you from the station, although I am most embarrassed to avail myself of your kind hospitality.

Forgive this dreadful handwriting . . .

Businessman Belaieff realized that Scriabin must be launched not only in print, but in person and in public. He arranged a debut for 7 March, 1895, at the small, conveniently located hall of the Petrov School of Commerce. Prior, he introduced his protégé privately on two successive "Fridays," 25 February and 2 March. In addition, on Saturday the 3rd, Scriabin rehearsed the recital publicly. For this Belaieff invited the subscription members of his amateur Society of Chamber Music Lovers. Belaieff in other words saturated Petersburg with Scriabin.

Kashkin describes one soirée. "I was delighted to see a Muscovite amid all those Petersburgers. Scriabin with his unaffected conduct made a most agreeable impression on Belaieff's guests. He was simultaneously free and reserved. He sat down to play at 1:00 A.M. and did not stop until supper was announced. His success with all of SPb was decisive. Everyone spotted his remarkable talent both as composer and as pianist. Belaieff was in ecstasy, just as he had been with Glazunov . . ."

Stassov gives a different version of another "Friday," and felt constrained to write Belaieff on 26 February:

I was astounded *last night* at the program to see so many people attack Scriabin!!

First, Cui said that Scriabin was not just bad but *monotonous*, nothing special, nothing to him. I reproached him, "You had better listen more carefully." He got angry.

Second, Markovich [Vice-President of RMO] talked much in the same way and Bessel [editor of *Musical Leaflet*] supported him. They agreed, "Yes, Scriabin, Scriabin. We all heard him and there is nothing there. Chopin . . . monotonous . . . everything one and the same, that is all . . ."

This means those toadstools will abuse him in print before the 7th of March and that will keep the public away . . .

Nikolai Findeizen's diary corroborates Stassov's enthusiasm: "This morning I went to the office and Stassov told me of a newly rising star—

pianist and composer Scriabin. On Friday he played at Belaieff's and Stassov had been invited. Rimsky-Korsakoff, Liadov, Blumenfeld, Lavrov and Belaieff and Stassov sat side by side. Stassov said, 'At first he played his Nocturne. Very well, it was all right. And I thought, if this is all, then there's nothing new or fine to expect from him. Then he played his Fantasy [presto of the Fantasy Sonata] and Lord, he did well!!! We all shouted and had him repeat it instantly.'"

Findeizen himself attended both the public rehearsal and the 7 March concert: He reviewed the program for his own *Russian Musical Gazette* (*RMG*), sensibly, with reservations, and while noticing the lavish attention Scriabin received—his well-wisher Belaieff sent several crowns of laurel leaves to the stage, the equivalent of flowers—he cautions:

> . . . albeit somewhat prematurely. It depends entirely on him whether he will from now on deserve such laurels.

> We have heard this very young pianist-composer twice. He almost passed by unnoticed, but it would have been most undeserved. The appearance of any composer-pianist implies something new, curious, and should stir interest.

> All the pieces on the program sounded like improvisations of a very high order of talent. The best, with real strength and beauty, was the D# minor Etude. It is full of power and thought.

Most unexpected of all Scriabin's press after his SPb concert is the review in *Week*, written by César Cui.

> Such is my joy in devoting these few lines to A. N. Scriabin, an unquestionably great talent for composition.

> He is still quite young, only 22, and unless I am mistaken, he has written only for piano and small pieces at that. He played fifteen of these in much refined taste, elegance, beauty, expressiveness, feeling . . . depth of thought and feeling . . . transport, passion, and power . . .

> They are nervous pieces, and by their prevailing minor key bear some of the marks of sickliness.

> When you listen to a number of his compositions, you think you are hearing Chopin's unpublished opuses. You can only rejoice that such a great artist of genius, such a poet of sound, serves as a point of departure . . .

> All the pieces were very pianistic and written most gratefully for the instrument.

As a pianist his playing is nervous, arhythmical, and at times unclear. He exaggerates soft and loud contrasts. His left hand is stronger than his right and sometimes smothers it. He played better with one hand in the Nocturne than he did with two hands in the other pieces.

Regardless of the unsatisfactory performance, he had considerable success. In this case, in contrast with what usually happens, the composer carried the performer. May success always accompany Mr. Scriabin and facilitate the prickly path he has chosen . . . that of composing.

In the midst of all this public exposure, the artistic adjutant to Tsar Nikolai II suggested that Scriabin play at Court, "any day of your convenience." Aunt Lyubov overheard Scriabin's reply: "Please do not ask me. If you do I will have to say no, I'd rather not." She feared repercussions from his curtness, but there were none.

Scriabin did, however, accept Tolstoi's invitation to play for him. After hearing one prelude Tolstoi said to his private secretary, Valentin Bulgakov (1887–1966), "How *sincere* it is, and sincerity above all is truly precious. From this single piece you can tell he is a great artist . . ." Tolstoi invited him to Yasnaya Polyana to play again and said he regarded musicians as "priests and their art the highest in the world."

(A nod from Tolstoi was enough to make Tchaikovsky some years earlier fly into raptures. "I am now a very important bird . . . I have met Count Tolstoi," he wrote his brother. Tolstoi was also once asked to comfort Rachmaninoff at the nadir of nervous depression. He spent the interview hour belittling Beethoven, Pushkin, Lermontov—all gods. Rachmaninoff related this sad conversation to his friend Chekhov, who replied, "Tolstoi's just like a stomach-ache. Nothing to do but ignore it.")

27

SCRIABIN RETURNED to Moscow riding the wave of success. He formally appeared on 11 March, 1895, before the Muscovites. The RMO arranged an extra concert in the Great Noblemen's Hall for Karl Scheidemantel (1859–1923), baritone with the Dresden Court Opera (creator of the role of Amfortas in *Parsifal*), violinist Yuly Konyus, and Scriabin, who performed a set of solo pieces.

Typical of the newspaper reviews was Kashkin's important one in the *Russian Gazette*: "His music is rich and unusually appealing. He has refinement of harmony and sincerity of feeling. All these qualities combine with his noble piano style and make him a total stranger to the usual run-of-the-mill music which draws upon or imitates Liszt."

Ten days after this concert the anxious Belaieff finally heard the results. Scriabin wrote, "The concert in Moscow exceeded all expectations and went excellently . . . Safonoff too, wrote definitely: "Scriabin played his compositions with great success and attracted considerable attention in a very positive way. This was his first debut in Moscow, and as such it may be called in every sense a success."

Belaieff answered Safonoff on 22 March with a clear-headed appraisal of his protégé:

> As a performer he is regarded more mistrustfully, and it seems to me that this is not without foundation. Is this a result of his nervousness? Or is it because he always plays solo and never with partners? Sometimes he ruffles up his pieces and confuses the listener. The performance is often to the detriment of the music, and you can't assimilate either the rhythm or the melody. There is much feeling in his compositions, but his method of expressing it leads him sometimes into studied affectation. This is neither inherent in his nature nor desirable in its effect.
>
> My desire is that he play his compositions so superbly that his performances will form the basis of a future tradition.

All the rest of March Scriabin worked over the Etudes, Op. 8, as the following letters show. He had promised them early in January. Belaieff would have settled for six instead of twelve, but Scriabin saw them as a group, a lucky dozen. Scriabin habitually miscalculates the date he will complete a piece of music. Kashperov attributes this to Scriabin's "exigent standards," his desire to release only perfect music. Scriabin would, in time, send off packets of less than polished music.

16 March

> For two whole days I have sat over the études without rising from the table once. I still have not finished. Forgive me if I hold them a day or two longer.

20 March

You are angry with me! And quite rightly. But surely I deserve some leniency. I work all day long. As soon as I get up I sit down to write and don't rise again until evening. I don't even take walks. You imagine I am composing something new? Not at all. Those études, still. You won't recognize several of them, I have changed them so much.

29 March

I have included two different versions of the D♯ minor. I don't feel like publishing either just yet. Let it rest a while on your desk. There is something in it that doesn't satisfy me.

6 April

You surprise me telling me there are mistakes in the études. I looked them over very carefully. Rozenov too found nothing wrong. Are the mistakes in the second version of the D♯? It needn't be printed anyway for the time being.

Today it seems as if I have done everything I should have. Why be angry with me?!

P. S. Mitrofan Petrovich, I have a request to make of you. If it doesn't inconvenience you, send me a "rainbow" to fortify my scanty means. Forgive me for this decision to bother you.

"Rainbow," meaning a hundred rubles, was the first of a long series of circumlocutious requests for "money." Usually he called money "that contemptible metal" or "filthy lucre," and abbreviated this to "cont. me.," as if even the spelling out of the word pained him. Other times he calls it cryptically, "the aforementioned," or "ray of hope," and openly, "purse," "finances," "capital," "pocketbook," "coffers," almost any word, in fact, except blunt "money." Sometimes he leaves the crucial word out altogether—"If it doesn't inconvenience you, send me now," he once wrote Belaieff.

28

BELAIEFF INVITED Scriabin to spend Easter and the first week of April, 1895, with him. He declines, "for reasons too complicated to write, but I will tell you in person about it," referring to complications in his Natalya affair. Belaieff suggested a trip abroad to clear his head of her. It would also be useful, since he would see and feel Europe before actually playing there in concert.

Both Belaieff and Safonoff agreed on Europe as the logical next step for the artist Scriabin. Safonoff had written to Baudoux, manager of the Salle Erard, music publisher and music store owner in Paris. Scriabin, just twenty-three and desperate, tries to decide what he should do. Force the issue of marriage with Natalya? He brings the matter to the two older men. They have identical reactions. He should not marry. He should take a trip abroad.

Belaieff insists that Sasha get his papers in order. Belaieff also wanted him to consult a European specialist about his "nerves." He found his many symptoms worrisome. On 29 March, 1895, Scriabin gives excuses, "I can't get my passport until they give me my domestic passport first. Will they hold that up?"

(A domestic passport was needed in order to travel within Russia. A passport to go abroad was a document of political security, showing that the bearer was not a revolutionary. Both passports were necessary before any Russian could venture outside the country.)

On 3 April, Scriabin writes Belaieff a long and intimate letter. His suspicious nature (part of his nervous illness) makes him couch it obscurely. He mentions no specific name. He sends his letters to Belaieff's office rather than his home, for secrecy, and although he formally asks to be remembered to Belaieff's wife, he rather regularly gets her patronymic wrong.

Don't be angry with me, dear Mitrofan Petrovich. No news has come from you for so long. I think that you no longer wish even to know me. Well, you are right! When I do come, scold me, punish me, only just don't be angry.

I spent all day yesterday with Safonoff. I had not seen him in more than two weeks. I grieved him very much by telling him something about myself and that too keeps me here over the holidays away from you. We talked and argued for a long time and in the end, we each stood our ground just as we were. It would interest me very much to hear your opinion (when we meet) and I will give you all details, unless it is disagreeable for you to enter into my private life.

You once wrote me that I was helpless. You know, I am really an utter child in so many respects. I cannot take a step with certainty. And oh, my extremes of mood! Suddenly it seems that my strength is unlimited, all is conquered, everything is mine. Then, next second, I am aware of my utter impotence. Weariness and apathy seize me. There is never any equilibrium in me.

I explain this by saying that my heart treats my reason the way an intelligent artist treats a music critic. He listens to him and then goes about his business. The critic tries desperately in review after review with warning after warning, and all for what?! That's the disharmony. But after all, man has to contain two opposing poles within himself. But I for one don't know which will win out in the end.

Within a week, Belaieff wins this battle of indecision. Scriabin is back with him in the whirl of Petersburg, composing a new prelude and writing to Natalya.

14 April, 1895

I remain in Petersburg for a few days and then set out for a further journey. Thus, it follows, if I do not hear from you now, then I shall be deprived of the pleasure for a long time, and I have not the strength to endure that. Forgive me this short and unlovely missive, but I am frightfully flustered. Liadov and Sokolov are playing Wagner with four hands in the next room, and Belaieff is summoning us.

✒ VIII ✒
ABROAD

29

SCRIABIN's first trip to Europe lasted from May to August, 1895. Lyubov resigned herself to three lonely months plaintively: "I prepared myself for the idea that my idyllic life with him had reached an end—his profession from now on would demand trips without me..."

In order to be as close to Europe as possible, she and the *babushki* descended on Nil, living on the Polish border. Lyubov waited patiently for Shurinka's return.

Scriabin's first letter from abroad goes to Natalya. He writes as soon as he gets off the train and settles into the Bristol Hotel early May (European time) in Berlin. "Europe greeted her guest with a wondrous spring morning."

He spends his first day calling on a descendant of Felix Mendelssohn who has "a great rarity...the original score of Beethoven's Fifth Symphony." He buys a ticket for a concert, but does not go, because in the afternoon on his way to the zoo, something gets in his eye. He goes on to Dresden, visits the picture gallery, and calls on Scheidemantel, the singer, and Emil Sauer (1862–1942), the pianist. Safonoff has given him a letter of introduction to this former pupil of Nikolai Rubinstein.

He takes a steamer to Bastei, a short evening's trip away from Dresden, picturesque with deep gorges and jagged peaks, of which Bastei, 1,500 feet high, is the most curious.

"Bastei makes a charming impression...I would like to take some music with me and go again, alone..." He visits it "with even greater pleasure the second time. I now know every stone there. I took my work with me, as I had intended, and made masses of music sketches filling a whole notebook and six sheets of paper," he rhapsodizes to Natalya on 5 May.

More important than Scriabin's letters are his musical postcards, those radiant travel preludes in Opp. 11, 15, 16 and 17. At Bastei he watches a rushing mountain stream pounding against rocky boulders, and promptly composes the powerful prelude (Op. 11 No. 14 in E flat minor). With this, his "account with Dresden is settled."

A badgering letter from Belaieff reminds Scriabin that he is not to neglect composing. To make certain that his "absent-minded and careless" Sasha understands, he makes him repeat instructions like a parrot. Although Scriabin for one of the few times in his life actually dates a letter, he writes "23 April," as if he were writing from Russia instead of Europe. On 5 May (Dresden calendar) Scriabin answers Belaieff:

> You ask me to write you where I am supposed to send my manuscripts. I will say first of all that I am frightfully ashamed of being so absent-minded. How I abuse your kindness! Best of all would be for you just to punish me, and let me not send you any music at all. Let me suffer, I beg you . . .

> Anyway, I know full well that I must send the music to Paul Yulevich Schloezer, House of Krumbyugel, Gnezdnikovsky Alleyway (Swedish corner), Moscow.

> Now I will answer your other question, a most delicate one. No, I won't trouble you for the moment, but I soon will. I will be asking for reimbursement indelicately. Here's why: I came without any summer clothes, and will have to do something about it.

Good news reached Sasha in Dresden. Lyubov informed Safonoff, who telegraphed Scheidemantel to tell Scriabin that his father is arriving momentarily. "I hadn't expected such a surprise . . ." he writes Belaieff, "we are together and are leaving for Heidelberg at 7."

On 16 May he writes Natalya from Heidelberg. At first Scriabin is unaffected even by the river or the mountain where Heidelberg is situated and only recalls the anxiety of waiting for Papa and the bad weather, but then:

> This time you catch me in a brighter frame of mind as I have just spent two pleasant days. Rain here doesn't fall like drops of water from above, but forms a cloud and that settles over the whole valley. It is quite like autumn in Petersburg.

So, fancy how I felt when I awoke yesterday and saw a bright blue expanse of heaven. A madness seized me. I gulped down my coffee, ran straight to the mountain where the Heidelberg Castle is. I walked on from the *kurhaus* for two hours without stopping

I was so conscious of freedom, the sense of it so filled my whole being, that I felt nothing else.

Nikolai made an appointment for his son to see Dr. Wilhelm Erb (1840–1921), the leading neuropathologist in Germany and professor at Heidelberg University in nervous disorders. Scriabin reports to Belaieff, also on 16 May: "First, he was very kind and listened to my entire repertoire of stories (we spoke French, of course). Second, he gave me masses of advice, and finally made his overall prescription, namely, hydrotherapy in Switzerland—a four-week course of this at Schoenke on Lake Vierwaldstättersee (Lucerne) and finally, sea bathing in Italy." Before he has spent four days with his father a telegram comes from Yannina saying that a Turkish dignitary is arriving and Nikolai must return briefly to interpret for the Consul General.

"Again I write from unhappiness," he says to Natalya next afternoon, "I have just parted from Papa. I had thought to spend a whole week with him, but fate decided not to allow me such a gift . . ."

I am sitting all alone gazing on Heidelberg Castle. It is wrapped in grey mist and sad-looking. Even in this weather, how beautiful it is! Wherever you look, you see the meaning of those terrible and magnificent centuries now vanished into eternity. Compared with this soul of the past the practicality of contemporary civilization seems outrageous. How vile those iron railings on the edge of the precipice. How vulgar the signboards advertising restaurants. How ridiculous the ubiquitous posts with their pointing fingers. And how offensive are these fat, red-nosed guides who imbibe beer immoderately and forever intrude their services.

Sorrow seems to be a prevailing wind in Scriabin's life. On 24 May he writes Belaieff :

Yes, only now do I begin to understand the meaning of the word "alone" . . . How brave I act. I struggle to look outside myself. But there are times when I am so terribly, terribly depressed for reasons I cannot fathom, and my head aches. It aches all the time these days. I was so frightened I shaved all my hair off and now I am quite bald. I look even worse than usual, if you can imagine!

How I wish these frightful headaches would leave me. They torment me so. Maybe they'll disappear when I go to Erb again. They stopped after I was with him last time . . .

Belaieff sent Scriabin needed money, and surprised him with the news that he will join him. This was doubly astonishing, since he hated "abroad," found Europeans "tiresome," inferior to Slavs, and nothing more than "an obligation for reasons of health or art."

> If only you could know how happy you make me with the news that you are coming abroad. You cannot imagine what a pleasure it will be for me or with what impatience I await your arrival. Write me ahead of time and tell me where you will live and I will go there and wait . . .

During his thirteen days in Heidelberg, Scriabin wrote six pieces: Impromptu, Op. 12 No. 2; and Preludes, Op. 11 Nos. 3, 19, 24; Op. 15 No. 5; Op. 17 No. 5. He leaves for the water cure in Switzerland, as he tells Natalya, "in the best of spirits . . . I have found here what I have long searched for—monuments and ruins of past epochs. This interests me more than anything else."

30

SCRIABIN finds Schoenke "the most boring place on the whole shore-line" of Lake Lucerne and within two days he begins to wander. He stays in three different places in five days. At last he settles on the Hotel du Parc in Witznau, a charming little village of wooden chalets close to Lucerne, the city, and on the water. It is not, however, a spa, and he cannot undergo the necessary *cure d'eau*.

He tells Belaieff that at Schoenke "the cheapest pension is fifteen francs . . . impractical because of the expense . . . besides, only people with nervous disorders stay there and to see such abnormal people constantly is, to says the least, disagreeable. I could not last more than two days . . . Were I to spend a month in such an atmosphere, I would become totally unhinged . . . . I have now settled here to await your arrival . . . Here the air is clearer, the table not bad, and the manager a dear old soul."

He tells both Natalya and Belaieff that he has met friends from Moscow (he does not name them), and together they take all the excursions around Lake Lucerne—"to all the inhabited places"—including Rigi-Kalbad, where in June there was still springtime snow on the ground. One morning he rises at five to motor across the lake to Pilatus and contemplate the mountain there. "Marvelous days . . . Magnificent nature . . . I haven't had so pleasant a time anywhere else . . ." He has some Swiss acquaintances too, the families of Homell and Tushaus. He admits to a "special partiality" for Mme. Homell. She knew his mother, heard her play in concert many times. "She has told me much about her. We take long walks together, and I am glad to say this keeps time from dragging . . ."

In his letter to Belaieff he asks him "*not* to mention my new work to anyone except Liadov . . ." For the five weeks he waits in Witznau he composes prolifically: Impromptu, Op. 12 No. 1 (the last he will ever write); Preludes, Op. 11 Nos. 12, 17, 18, 23; Op. 14 No. 2; Op. 16 No. 2.

Even with this hefty portfolio of musical souvenirs of Switzerland, Belaieff asks for more.

"I am not lazy," he tells Belaieff, "in five months you will see . . ." On 18 June, 1895, he writes more strongly. "I am *not* wasting my time. But I will say once more in answer to your remark about burying my talents, I promise you that I am striving to extract *everything* there is in me. By 'everything' I mean of course, the best possible . . ."

And the friends whose names he at first concealed? Kolya Averino, on holiday to celebrate becoming a "Free Artist" (his graduation had been delayed, because he failed in piano as a second instrument), and honeymooning. Scriabin tells Natalya that Olga deserves full credit for Kolya's success. "She worked and suffered so much to make her disobedient husband get down to work . . ."

In answer to Belaieff's direct questioning about health, Scriabin speaks frankly and distressingly in a letter belonging to mid-June:

> Physically there is nothing I could possibly complain of. It's only my frame of mind—queer, somehow not good. I myself cannot define it. A sort of uneasiness, an expectation of something horrible lives inside me and torments me continuously.
>
> I want to renounce everything and live a simple life, but I can't. Forgive me for being so open, but it is only with you that I am.

He adds a postscript informing Belaieff that Witznau has no hydro-therapeutic facilities, but he is bathing in the lake as a substitute.

Scriabin asks Belaieff for money a second time. "Again I have to speak as follows: My finances are not quite exhausted, but I am so ter-rified of being without. It might be wise to send me another hundred rubles. Forgive me for being so bold, but the Heidelberg disaster frightened me. You know, however far we exile money from our thoughts, still it is awkward without it on foreign soil . . ."

Belaieff was kept in Petersburg until the tenth anniversary celebrations of the founding of his publishing house on 20 June. He soon left thereafter, and on 2 July, 1895 the two reunite in Witznau. Belaieff accompanies him on the second part of Dr. Erb's prescription. On 7 July they are in Genoa. From there their itinerary takes them to Nice, Geneva, Basel, Mannheim, Heidelberg (to see Dr. Erb again), Frankfurt, Liège, Brussels, then to Aachen (Aix-la-Chapelle) where they will rest for a few days, before returning to the homeland.

Belaieff also tried another nerve cure for Scriabin. He initiated him into heterosexual relations with a German woman "somewhere en route . . ." the wife of some sculptor, according to Engel who apprises us delicately of the story. "I was too young to appreciate the remarkably mature soul of this older woman," Scriabin himself said.

The travelers spend the week of 15 August in Berlin where the im-portant, international Anton Rubinstein contest for pianists is being held. Three of their friends are contestants—Lhevinne, Igumnov and Kene-man. "We heard Igumnov play his solo piece magnificently," Scriabin wrote to Natalya. The voting was not easy for the judges. At first count, Lhevinne, Igumnov, and Staub from Vienna tied for the prize. On the second ballot Lhevinne won. Igumnov received an honorable mention.

Igumnov, who was also writing Natalya, provides her with a terrifying portrait from Berlin: "Alexander Nikolaevich seemed emotionally unstrung and shattered . . . He gives the impression of a person who has nothing in the future, very little at present, and for whom everything belongs to the past. He says he is the happiest person in the world, but this doesn't stop him from saying in the next breath that it is time for him to retire, that he wants to die more than anything else, etc."

After this two-month *voyage à deux*, Scriabin and Belaieff part at the

Russian border town, Minsk. Belaieff went directly to Petersburg where Scriabin would soon follow for a farewell week.

Aunt Lyubov describes Shurinka's homecoming at Nil's: "Finally that happy day came. . . . Nil spoiled Shurinka by arranging his room and picking flowers for him. Nikolai joined us too. So we were quite a group to greet his return. We did so noisily and gaily."

Mid-September Scriabin joined Belaieff. He played the first "Friday" he was in SPb, 20 September, and Stassov again sings praises. He wrote Semyon Kruglikov (1851–1910), Director of the Moscow Philharmonic School in Moscow, and notable critic: "We heard Scriabin again after his return from Switzerland. His various new things for piano are just delightful! Do try and make his acquaintance . . ."

Lyubov finds a new apartment for them all in Moscow. Its address, Scriabin teases in a letter to Belaieff, is quite to Liadov's liking—No. 1 Middleclass Street (*meshchanskaya*—bourgeois, or even philistine) and across from a Church, "The Trinity in Droplets." In a thank-you note to Belaieff, Sasha speaks of "hospitality and generosity . . . kindness and goodness . . ."

Scriabin also wrote another letter to Liadov, October, 1895. He is already on intimate terms with him from Petersburg (he calls him *ty* or "thou"), and apparently from the veiled references in this letter, Liadov is a friend of the Sekerin family. Primarily, Scriabin shows himself here in a rarely deferential mood, musically. Still in difficulties with that Fantasy Sonata, and at a crossroads of schematicism, he turns to the wiser Liadov for aesthetic arbitration:

I am working very hard, and enjoying myself. Not really enjoying myself but simply going out a lot and socializing to revitalize my nerves.

I have found all your dear friends here well and happy and apparently pleased to see me.

In the first place I am growing even more insane and am doing all kinds of stupid things. As far as composition goes, I am becoming a little orderly. The sonata is almost finished. There remain only certain details and doubts about procedure.

I have two ideas: One is better logically; but the other is more beautiful. Write me please, whether logic or beauty should have priority. Which do you prefer? Most musicians would say that which is more beautiful is more logical. But there are scores of things we call logical that can be explained otherwise.

How are you, my dear, my good one? Are you angry with me? You know how awful I am. But if you come to Moscow we'll have a very gay and cheerful time. Why don't you come just to get away from what is dull for you there?

The mental conflict he is asking Liadov to resolve is that which Debussy called "the alchemy of sound versus the science of the beaver." Unlike his letters to Belaieff which he continues to sign "A. Scriabin," he writes here, "Sasha Scriabin."

A grand concert in Petersburg is announced for Sunday morning, 15 October. All three Russian contestants from the Berlin competition will appear. Safonoff is to conduct, and he inches Scriabin onto the program. Scriabin writes Belaieff his hand is hurting, and he is emotionally too distracted to play. He tactlessly asks Igumnov to substitute for him and play his music.

Safonoff quickly rebukes Scriabin. "Safonoff says I am treating Keneman badly . . . in truth it was he who played the First Sonata with such love and so conscientiously. Nor do I need mention how he's making a lion of himself playing my études these days . . ."

Scriabin proposes to sacrifice and play his Fantasy Sonata himself. However, he continues asking Belaieff's advice, "If you don't want me to appear, I won't. It all depends on you . . . There is nothing so disagreeable for me as to hurt someone's feelings, and especially someone as sweet as Keneman."

Belaieff vetoes Scriabin's appearance. It would be intrusive of him at that particular concert. Belaieff has plans to introduce Scriabin in Europe; his Russian reputation can wait.

Scriabin now had enough money to buy a piano, a medium-priced Schroeder, for the new apartment. He calls it his "fine new piano." When Belaieff visits him in Moscow, he sends him a welcome-back-to-Russia handsel—a superb, concert grand Becker.

(Jakob Becker from the Palatinate had cornered the luxury market and from the year 1841 made the best pianos in Russia. Rubinstein and Hofmann toured with Beckers. No gift could have been more lavish.)

He took time to write a spontaneous and affectionate letter on 4 October, 1895:

First of all allow me to submit my official thanks for the piano. And now hear several unofficial words. How good you are! How kind! How happy you make me! I am not ashamed to tell you I burst out weeping. How comforting, how wonderful when one knows that there are people who truly love one. And here I am knowing how vile I am and still you think of me and love me.

However, Belaieff soon starts his reproaches again. On 10 October (neatly dated in his own handwriting) Scriabin answers: "Yes, henceforth I will date my letters. I am so ashamed of being absent-minded . . ." And he goes on to gossip: his cheek is swollen, so he cannot go out anymore; he will not see Igumnov, Keneman or Lhevinne before they leave for SPb.

"I have a few pupils now. I am working hard. The life I lead, I must confess, is most unhealthy. I go to bed as late as 4:00 A.M. and rise with a heavy head. I am nervous again. Oh well, I guess it is my fate to be so!"

Belaieff tries squeezing more work from Scriabin, and faster. He makes a wager that Scriabin cannot send him forty-eight preludes by April, 1896. Scriabin accepts, but he writes on 21 October, "These days I am working like a madman. Today I want to rest a little . . . I have nothing to send you at the moment, but as you can see, it is not laziness . . ."

November, Scriabin was working hard all the time. He completed Preludes, Op. 11 Nos. 1, 2, 9, 11, 18; Op. 13 Nos. 1, 3, 4; Op. 17 No. 4. He still lost the bet. He sends in forty-seven preludes, but the forty-eighth waits until 1897.

Kolya and Scriabin plan a concert on 8 December, appearing in a joint performance. Natalya and her sister insist on buying tickets for this "Mars" concert, and Scriabin yields to their "inflexibility" and lets them.

Kruglikov reviewed the concert for the daily *Russian Gazette*. He called it a "great success," and added:

Of most interest was the participation of Mr. Scriabin, that talented composer and pianist of unarguable merit. He played a group of his fine little pieces, miniatures in form, but valuable for their beautiful music, marvelous imagination, and originality.

In mid-November Scriabin has told Natalya that he must go to Petersburg. Now, on Tuesday, 12 December, he forces the issue of marriage. We have already read her version of the story. This state of affairs, or lack of an affair, can only be an indignity to them both, and a severe exacerbation of his nerves. On 13 December, Scriabin writes her these harsh lines with neither heading nor signature:

> Again I repeat that a lie is unbearable. There are some things which one must take seriously. You must act simply and openly, if you are to be respected. And if the occasion for a lie comes up, then you must *explain why the lie was necessary*. I have too much respect to talk one way and act in another. I simply cannot understand why this shocking, needless, and unpleasantly dishonest situation has come about.

On the same date he wrote Belaieff that he will leave that Sunday with Safonoff for St. Petersburg. At last he is free to go on a concert tour abroad with Belaieff. They head straight for Paris.

Within a month he will fancy himself in love again, and Natalya will be married.

IX

TOUR

31

SCRIABIN AND Belaieff started the New Year of 1896 together on a train to Paris. There was no real reason for Belaieff to accompany Scriabin. He was forsaking his business and ignoring his own convenience in order to see that nothing went wrong during the European debut of "Scriabine, *pianiste-compositeur russe.*"

This time, Belaieff introduces him to the demimonde in Paris. They saw a belly-dancer at the Moulin Rouge in Montmartre where in a tiny room someone rattled a tambourine and a Negress played the piano, and there was the world of homosexuals where addiction to opium and ephebi was open.

Gustave Doret (1866–1943), a Swiss resident in France, composer and critic of considerable power, the first to conduct his friend Debussy's *L'après-midi d'un faune*, gave a musical party. Scriabin was astonished, he later confided in Rozenov, to encounter what he loosely called "decadence." One tall and lean young thing wore a lilac-colored necktie. His hair was so long and straggly that Scriabin swore it caught fire from a candelabrum on the piano.

"Lilac necktie" gave a hearing of his own music. Scriabin found it "cacophonous and trashy." In a cruel moment, he sat down and imitated it, but made improvements by softening the note distributions and fleshing out the disjointed harmonies of fourths. He put grace where there had been crudity.

"I don't worry about connections and transitions," the embarrassed "lilac necktie" said, "I just yield myself to the hypnosis of inspiration and colors."

"All that is very well, if you have God-given talent. But everything depends on that '*if*'," Scriabin sharply answered.

Scriabin played four measures of a Haydn sonata and asked the man to repeat it. He tried, got confused, and stopped. Later, they left the party together, Rozenov says, and on the way back to the hotel, he implored Scriabin, "Please don't harm me. What else can I do? *Je suis un pauvre diable.* I exist by the kindness of M. Doret, protector of decadents."

Scriabin made his European debut on 15 January, 1896, at the large and excellent hall, Salle Erard. Paris was then beginning to become capital of the musical world, and second only to Berlin as a starting point for musical careers. He played his bombastic new Concert Allegro, dramatic successor to the Allegro Appassionata, replete with octave thrusts and Conservatory flash, along with of preludes, études, impromptus and mazurkas.

At each concert Belaieff sat on stage in full view of the audience, "to give Sasha moral encouragement." Alshvang reprovingly reports that "he beamed as if pride itself were being tickled." The effect, however, was odd. "The huge, bulky shape of Belaieff alongside Scriabin's trim little figure looked as if someone had just taken a delicate mechanism out of its elaborate wrapping and set it ticking," according to Engel.

Scriabin's party-going in Paris paid off in reviews which reported his person as well as his art. The "protector of decadents" raved: "All his compositions disclose an indisputable personality. His playing exemplifies that peculiar and indefinable charm of the Slavs who are the greatest pianists in the world. Scriabin. Remember that name!"

He enchanted his listeners during the course of an hour and played a whole series of his pieces—very difficult, very exquisite, elegant and succinct ... *L'Echo Musicale*

... held a select audience for two hours under the spell of his controlled, precise, nervous, and richly colored pianism. Episodes of his music sound exceptionally powerful in his hands. His left hand is astonishing, and he plays the most difficult passages with rare ease ... *L'Art Moderne*

Other critics even mention his scarcely forming "philosophy." Eugène George of *La Libre Critique* (No. 4, 26 January, 1896) followed Scriabin to Brussels and reviewed his Saturday afternoon recital:

We encountered an exceptional personality belonging by nature to the élite, outstanding both as composer and pianist, and one who is as intellectual as he is philosophical. He is all nerve and a holy flame.

32

AFTER SCRIABIN'S Berlin recital, Belaieff returned to Russia, leaving Sasha to sightsee and continue the tour in Amsterdam and the Hague. But first, he interferes in a love affair. Mme. Homell has come to Berlin from Switzerland to hear the concert. She introduces the men to a certain M. K. F., "a ravishing girl, very intelligent and cultivated, a Russian," according to Engel. All that is known about her is that she lives in Düsseldorf, a German banking center and an elegant carnival city, with a family "S."

Scriabin falls in love at first sight, apparently, and proposes marriage. He is accepted. "After this decision," Engel says, "they quickly parted company." Belaieff must have spoken to the girl's parents privately, as considerable mystery and confusion surround the exact events. M. K. F. was supposed to join Scriabin in Amsterdam.

"My concert there," he wrote Belaieff, "was most useful from a *musical* point of view, but not otherwise . . . most harmful to the pocketbook!" He also performed at some Music Circle in the Hague with "terrific success before a small gathering, of course." In both places he complains, "I was driven to distraction by kindness. Today the theater, tomorrow a concert. It was absolute misery! Now I am alone and can concentrate and work seriously . . ."

On 3 February he wrote Belaieff about M. K. F. from Cologne: "I see from your letter she pleased you . . . Just think, Düsseldorf is only 45 minutes away!" But then bafflement spreads over the whole question. A worried Sasha writes Belaieff two days later:

> A word before I leave for Paris. Several matters remain unsolved. My affair has turned out to be most puzzling. Several of my suspicions were well founded. Namely, no one showed up in Amsterdam—she had already returned to Düsseldorf. I wrote to her father directly, but got a reply from her sister. I can reach no definite conclusion since the answer comes from a third person. To write to the person herself is impossible. All her mail is opened.

Scriabin returned to Paris, where M. K. F. promised to join him. (She did.) Meanwhile he sees his friend Tonichka Shaikevich. They stay together at the Pension Devies, run by the Blanchonnets at 18, rue Chateaubriand, just off the Champs Elysees. He informs Belaieff of his whereabouts and plans on 9 February:

> I am now in a place which is very quiet, nice, clean and cheap—10 francs for everything. I work wonderfully well.
>
> I will finish the preludes here, then rest with an easy conscience and enjoy the marvelous beauty. I know that if I budge even for an instant I'll put off working until doomsday . . .
>
> I have been to several concerts at the Salle Erard. I am now convinced that my own success was really quite exceptional.
>
> By now I have so many friends that I am tortured with visiting, lunching and dining.
>
> I met Lamoureux [Charles (1834–1899)]. He conducted when Lhevinne played the Rubinstein Concerto and three of my études so well.

Scriabin wrote six preludes in Paris: Op. 11 Nos. 8, 22; Op. 17 Nos. 1, 2, and two "strolling" preludes, even-paced little walks in the sun. Op. 15 No. 4, an *andantino* of wide leaps with tones seemingly drawn from the air, is particularly lovely. The bass mirrors and reverses the treble in strong symmetry. Op. 17 No. 3, a black key study, makes no distinction between its melody and harmony. Both spring from a single sonority.

Scriabin's voice here is now authentic. These Parisian pieces contrast strikingly with another hymnology of preludes—the chorales composed in the Russian winters of 1894, '95 and '96, Op. 13 No. 1, Op. 16 Nos. 3 and 4. In these you hear religiosity, Scriabin standing in a cathedral. The Paris preludes are secular, breathing with life, not belief. They belong to M. K. F.

33

BELAIEFF HAS grown less indulgent, although he increases the monthly allotment to 150 rubles while his protégé is abroad. He is querulous, carps about getting compositions in on time, and punishes Scriabin by remitting money slowly. The truth was he wanted Sasha to come home.

Pressman says: "The extraordinarily refined, sensitive, and effeminate Scriabin suffered under Belaieff's mentorship. Belaieff loved him and helped him materially, yes, but he treated him badly." And even Olga Sekerina takes posthumous sides against him: "He rushed Scriabin frightfully."

Scriabin had to account for every expense and beg for additional funds. Belaieff numbers his letters and forces Scriabin to do the same: "I have just received your letter no. 5 dated 31 March and I hasten to answer it," replies Scriabin. But where Belaieff interferes with Scriabin's method of composing, he is not so obedient. For all the weakness of Scriabin and the inequality between the two men, Scriabin is strong about music and matters of the heart.

Everytime Belaieff asks when he is returning, Scriabin deliberately treats the enquiry as a fatherly desire to know his plans. Belaieff tells Scriabin to come back to Russia by May at the latest. Finally, in June Belaieff orders him back. He goes to the seashore instead. Scriabin inflamingly speaks of it being *"very, very* difficult for me to leave . . ."* meaning that M.K.F. is now in Paris. Only in August, after seven months abroad and another Paris concert (making a total of seven public appearances) will he return.

The letters are stormy, filled with misunderstandings, griefs, confusions. Scriabin's destructive inner life becomes more visible. His handwriting deteriorates. His letters, always nervous, now are written in even more impatiently formed script. He writes a word over another and forgets to cross out the bottom one. He skips punctuation. He leaves words unfinished. Errors in grammar, however, are few.

Symptomatically, he cannot refuse invitations to parties. He is tired all the time. He begs to rest even while he is on holiday. (Belaieff ineptly used the word "laziness" for what was, sadly enough, chronic, psychic torpor.) Sometimes he wished himself dead. Often he falls prostrate from his head which "aches," "is heavy," "troubles me." Even his feet trouble him. "I have difficulty walking . . ." Something is awry in Scriabin's body and soul.

Scriabin cannot decide about the forty-eight preludes. How should they be arranged for publication and in what order? Letters fly back and forth inconclusively. Eventually, since Belaieff in any event has not that many preludes he published Op. 11 as four "notebooks" of six each. After all the fuss, they follow Chopin's pattern: up through the sharp keys, beginning with C, and down the flats, each interspersed with its relative minor.

"I must decide . . ." "I don't know . . ." "Tell me . . ." a refrain to many letters reveals a disarming dependency on Belaieff. Scriabin's contradictions and indecisions are astounding. Did he or did he not, for instance, mail the finished preludes when he swore he had. He was unconscionable about sending some impromptus, as we will soon see. Often he feels he has actually done something if only he thinks of doing it. He cites Tonichka to prove he dispatched the preludes. He says in the letter of 12 April that he has the postal receipt, and yet he fails to enclose it. Dostoevsky speaks of the Russian's "delicate reciprocity of lying," and Scriabin is a case in point. He had no receipt. And when he does send them, he grossly over-insures them for 3,000 francs. Belaieff snaps at him for extravagance.

Scriabin's bills of account make pathetic reading. How sad when he implores for clothes. How long a time lapses before he is properly dressed for springtime in Paris. He wrote early in March, 1896: "About money, I am faced with unforeseen expenses, namely a coat. They can't send my old one from Moscow, because customs does not allow used items through the mails. It is now impossible for me to continue going around in my winter surtout. Will you send a little more than I asked for? Tell me too, where should I go next? What excursion? I would like a month off, after I finish working. I am tired . . ."

Later in March, Belaieff objects not only to being asked for money but to the 10 francs a day at the pension. A dishonest whine rises from Sasha.

If my request was indelicate, forgive me. I asked you in full awareness that I could fulfill my obligation. You reproach me for laziness when never have I been less guilty. I am not lazy about composing. I do all I can. I ought really to hold myself back. As you know my constitution is not iron. I really am tired!

And why such haste? Surely writing 48 pieces of any kind, short or long, is no small or easy task. I have finished almost two months ahead of time. Do you think that I don't want to write two or three extra pages simply because of laziness? Why, oh why, such an opinion of me? I say again, although in my personal life I am slipshod, in the realm of composition I am very exact and fulfill my obligations. That is, at least I try to, I mean.

... To publish pieces which don't satisfy me myself is impossible. I simply cannot ...

You are displeased with my pension for 10 francs. But is it possible to find a cheaper place in all Paris? I cannot live indecently. It would be better just to quit Paris altogether. But my stay here is useful in so many respects.

The cooked goose doesn't fly into one's mouth, as you so rightly say. I know that, and I never thought otherwise.

Are you afraid that I will be corrupted by society if I taste too much of it? Are you thinking this is my reason for being lazy? You are wrong!

On 23 March, he received some money, but it is insufficient:

I want a rest from composing. I have not slept for six nights and am rundown, terribly rundown.

You ask me how much I need for clothes. A coat costs 120 francs, a summer suit the same, and besides, I need a hat, shoes, and yes, several shirts. That is all.

Life in Paris comes to 360 francs for everything, which equals 135–140 rubles a month.

More promises, pleas and apologies come on 29 March:

Today I send you four impromptus.

I don't understand what you say about the preludes you lack. Indeed, it is *you* who say that the creative urge mustn't be forced. If I wrote them, I would simply have to *wring them out of me* dry, because they do not exist *in* me. The ones I have but haven't sent are not right yet. I cannot let you have *sketches*.

You can't imagine how I want and *need* to rest. I would like to spend spring in Paris. It's divine here now. The trees are budding, the air is superb. They say it is late to go to Italy—Naples, that is.

Next day the crisis becomes intolerable:

How disagreeable to start talking about money right off, but I must. Imagine my predicament! It's Holy Week and soon the holidays begin. It's *boiling* in the courtyard. I go about in my long winter overcoat and everybody laughs at the very sight of me.

I could weep. And believe me, not a kopeck in my pocket. If only you would send me a little, otherwise I am lost. Well, what a holiday for me! Surely you have punished me enough. Give me surcease. There has already been enough sorrow in my life!

You ask me how much for clothes, hat and shoes. I can't go into a store and ask prices and *not* buy. You yourself know more or less what these things cost. Even were you to send me more than necessary, I wouldn't waste it. I'm so afraid of being embarrassed. It's so painful for me to tell you all this. I've grown so nervous over it that I am in a frightful state. Please send 450 rubles in *all* . . .

34

ON 6 APRIL, 1896, Scriabin writes twice. He is exuberant, because the money at last arrives, and thoughtlessly wastes postage by sending the letters separately. First he writes:

> Will send the impromptus tomorrow. They lie packed and ready in my suitcase.

> I promise you I'll keep busy (writing, that is) one hour every day. I'm composing nothing now and would not, even if I felt like it.

In the second letter he speaks of how he composes. However, when he says that the Second Sonata (Fantasy Sonata) is finished, he is expressing a wish. The manuscript of that year shows numbers of blank spaces where his inner hearing has halted. He will need to fill in and complete these soon. This custom remained with Scriabin for life. He often worked on several compositions at a time waiting for "lacking measures" to come to him. Belaieff has also, evidently, suggested in his letter that Scriabin jot down his compositions bit by bit as passages occur to him, and not carry them around in his head for so long.

> The method you propose doesn't suit me personally, and here's why: If a composition is revealed to me as a whole, then I can't stop until it's written down. If I have any doubts, however, then I can't write even when it is already conceived. This is because all that follows depends on what precedes. Naturally, I can force, but that's stupid.

> Now, noting down sketches. That's a different matter and cannot be dispensed with, especially for bigger compositions. I give you my promise. I will get a

bound notebook for jotting down ideas, and that way they won't get lost.

About the insurance. That wasn't up to me. They won't insure for less than 1,000 francs and that costs 12 francs itself. I am still at the pension, and can't find anything cheaper . . .

On 12 April he tenders Belaieff a humiliatingly detailed receipt:

Coat	120 francs	
Suit	120	
Hat	16	
Shoes	28	
3 shirts (4 francs each)	12	
2 shirts (6 francs each)	12	
Total	308 francs	
Sending preludes	20 francs and some centimes	
Sending impromptus	12 francs and some centimes	
Servant	32 francs	
Pension paid today	165	
Pension paid earlier	345	
Total	564 francs	

I have 98 francs left. And there are small expenses like shaves, ties, etc., that I have forgotten. I borrowed the money to pay the big bills, but have returned it . . .

Today yet another expense I had forgotten. Laundry for all this time cost 28 francs 60 centimes. I have 77 francs left. Less than for a week.

A man suffering from consumption has come to our pension. I am in grief! I must flee.

In all the hassle over money, Scriabin forgot until now to mention a concert. On 16 March, he played "with great effect" and "with great success" (*Le Guide Musical*, No. 12, 1896) at a program of Russian music arranged by the Euterpe Choral Society.

Belaieff reprimanded Scriabin for not keeping him *au courant*. He announces well in advance that he contemplates yet another performance. On 24 April: "I will risk a concert, but I don't know how it will turn out. I've been playing frequently at various salons, and I think everything will go well . . ." On 2 May: "As my concert is being arranged on the spur of the moment, I have many worries. To play as I should, to send out tickets, to call on people, in a word, I am overloaded with chores. The costs of the concert are negligible—320–340 francs all expenses included. And maybe, who knows? There might be a *sou* or two profit."

Scriabin gave a major solo recital at the Salle Erard on 5 May. Here he played for the first time the whole Fantasy Sonata, having completed or improvised the missing passages. He designates its key as "A flat" instead of "G#" on the program. He also makes the same mistake with the Prelude, Op. 11 No. 13, calling it F#, rather than G flat.

Scriabin writes Belaieff promptly on the night of the concert:

> You were partly right regarding my friends, but they are not to blame. I am. I gave out too many invitation passes. 900 francs worth of tickets were sold, and the hall was full.
>
> One day I would like to have a similar success in Russia.
>
> Dyomes [(1854–1908), music critic and impresario] told me that if I had not been so stupid and issued so many free tickets (I think more than a hundred) that I could have made more money. Well, no point in weeping over last year's snow. But it is important to have next year's concert guaranteed in a material sense.
>
> My expenses came to more than 400 francs. Balls and soirées cost me more than 200 francs (I had to go). And there were unavoidable expenses for clothes and laundry. I bought myself some small, gold, shirt studs as the bone ones kept falling out. These are on a chain. There were slippers for dancing, and trousers . . . you see? How many expenses! Out of this, I have a clear 260 francs. Is that so bad?

Belaieff was pleased. He planted a notice in the *Russian Musical Gazette*, June, 1896:

> The talent of Mr. A. Scriabin as composer and pianist is attracting more and more Parisian melomanes. They greeted him noisily and with pleasure at his recent concert . . .

35

THE MORE insistent Belaieff grows about returning to Russia, the more evasive Scriabin becomes. He speaks of concert offers. Nothing comes of them. "Today I received a letter from Daniel Mayer in London guaranteeing me *all* expenses for a concert. I must decide. I don't know. He can't be deceiving me, because the firm is reputable . . ."

He admits "I may be counting on trifles," but still he calls his stay in Paris "important." On 2 May, 1896, for example, he has written, "I don't know how much longer I will be abroad, but I must say that my being here is *very, very* useful. My biggest success here has been as a pianist, and that is because," he explains astonishingly, "I practice regularly an hour and a half a day."

A letter of salvation comes in early May. Nikolai invites Sasha to come to Rome, where the Scriabins will spend ten days. "I haven't seen my half-brothers in so many years . . ." Scriabin writes Belaieff on 4 May. "At last I could rest," and he enticingly adds, "I want awfully to go back to Russia this summer and be in those beautiful natural surroundings there. It is tempting, and I don't know what to do. How beautiful Paris has become! The chestnuts are blooming. So delightful! I go on an excursion almost everyday, and I know all the suburbs by heart."

After vacillating when to leave, what route, and whether to go at all, since it is now the Italian season for smallpox and fevers, Scriabin embarks. By the end of May he has reached the Hotel du Capitole, 15 Place de Venise in Rome. On 4 June, he wrote:

> Here I take walks, look at the sights, sometimes go into raptures, sometimes I have emotions of rather a different order. In general I am happy on this trip. Especially because the weather is clement. The warm days haven't come yet and the evenings are cool. I will stay here until the money you send arrives. Then I think I will go north. I am working a little, so the time is not fruitless . . .

> Papa leaves this evening, and I will be alone. I am a little frightened . . .

On 12 June he sends another missive of money troubles.

> I just don't know what to think. Are you ANGRY with me? Every day I go to the post office and find nothing there. I am alone, all alone, in Rome and I must admit I am sometimes bored, but only sometimes since I am working. This week I wrote a symphonic allegro for orchestra, and have begun its orchestration.

> The sonata is finished but I am not satisfied in the least with it, despite 7 rehashings. I need to forget it, it seems, for a while.

The weather is unendurably hot in Rome. I must move. My heart, I confess, turns to Paris . . .

The reference to a "symphonic allegro" sounds exaggerated. How could anyone draft a large orchestral piece in a week, particularly surrounded by family? The next letter, dated 20 June from Paris, says that he is not sending it, "because there are many unresolved questions, numerous erasures, and I want it all well-written and neat, and then I will *still once again* have to copy it over . . ." This means that the orchestration had taken only an additional week.

Here Scriabin is quite truthful. A rough pencil manuscript, now in the Scriabin Museum, shows his phenomenal speed in Rome.

Although Scriabin abandoned the symphonic allegro (his enthusiasm waned), it was complete enough to be published posthumously (in 1926 by Bessel) in a piano transcription by Sabaneeff, called *Poème en forme d'une Sonate*. Again in 1929, Nikolai Zhilaev (1881–1938) arranged it straightforwardly as Symphonic Poem.

One salience of the music is the bold theme of the *lento* introduction. Scriabin will use this in slightly different form as the powerful beginning of his Third Symphony, the "Divine Poem." Similarly, the main theme of the *allegro* will also appear in more finely wrought form in that symphony. The nervously syncopated rhythm or the triplet figure with dotted middle note is characteristic Scriabin, almost to the point of mannerism.

By 20 June he is back in Paris in a different, and presumably cheaper *pension de famille* at 31, rue Vaneau. He writes Belaieff, and dares ask a favor:

As you see I am writing from Paris. Rome became insupportable. While I was working time passed quickly, but as soon as work was over, oh what agony. I won't even tell you what happened. Then Paris. Here everything is different. For several days now I have been at peace and happy. I miss only those who are so far away and whom I so much want to see. You know, I thought of going *straight* to Petersburg. However, one, I hadn't the money for it, but you have probably sent it by now, although I have not received it yet. Two, four nights on the train—horrible! . . .

But please, dear Mitrofan Petrovich, for this time send it to me before the 12th *without waiting* for word from me. That'll prevent a muddle and I want to go to the seashore (Dieppe) and relax at last. Best of all would be if you would send me *two* months at once. That way I could have a month worry-free.

In fact I had to resort to all sorts of combinations in order to get here from Rome. OF COURSE *I alone am to blame for it all*, but the fact remains I am always either sunk in the mire or something else comes along I have to cope with . . .

Four days later money is forwarded from Rome, but Scriabin has difficulty cashing the check since it was made out in *lire*. Belaieff writes a stern letter. Crying for money not arrived, but already dispatched, irritates the older man. He feels and is put upon. And how, anyway, did he get to Paris without waiting for the money?

Scriabin's answer of 24 June, 1896, is sober, honest and full of self-justification.

> You upbraid me for a disrespectful attitude towards your letters. Your reproach is justifiable if you compare me to other people. But not if you look at me as I am.
>
> As for your questions, perhaps I disturbed you by saying that I *don't know when* I will return.
>
> As for the budget: Yes, I am continuing it. And despite my feeling of utter *revulsion* towards material matters, I will do everything *possible* to spend less. But unforeseen expenses come up, such as the trip to Rome. I spent 100 rubles over the budget, but that means only one month extra. In the future when planning my expenses I'll try to keep such eventualities in mind.
>
> Ah, dear Mitrofan Petrovich, even if I am 24, and am thoughtless and stupid, surely there are others who make worse use of you.

Belaieff urges and Scriabin complies, saying on 2 July that he will return "whenever you wish, but only after 5 August . . ." He goes on to say that he had actually planned to return to Russia earlier, "but now, you see, you are leaving to travel and so is everyone else in Moscow too." He also proposes, "Since I am so near the sea, I should make use of it for bathing. Isn't that so?" He and Tonichka have planned on Dieppe, four hours North to the English Channel. "Also since I will have acquaintances there, I will not die of loneliness. Write me what you think of this."

He annoys Belaieff by saying the Concert Allegro is still not ready for publication. Neither is the Fantasy Sonata. "They don't satisfy me, and both, though written down, need big revisions ... I'll do all this this autumn, but now for a month I will try to rest and live quietly."

> Please, if possible, don't withhold money this time. The fact is that my room is only a *thimble* of foul air, and the food in this pension is revolting. I can somehow manage until the 12th, then I must have fresh air. I will try to live more cheaply.

> What if you sent me two months all at once, since you'll be vacationing? However, do as you like about this. You know best.

He adds one new note. He may not be able to return after 5 August, "because of circumstances which I cannot explain to you yet." Here is another reference to the mysterious M.K.F., perhaps.

He writes Belaieff on 14 July from the Hôtel du Rhin et de Newhaven sur la Plage, Dieppe, although his acquaintance, Count Greffulhe, had a house there with " a hundred thousand geraniums."

> I have been all this time in Dieppe, but haven't yet decided to go bathing. The water is always cold.

> I am homesick and want to be with you in Petersburg as soon as possible.

At last Scriabin returns to Russia. He spends a week with Belaieff in September, then goes on to his aunt and *babushki*. Scriabin recalled this Parisian period in after years. In a letter of autobiography he wrote at the request of Nikolai Findeizen on 26 December, 1907, for the *Russian Musical Gazette*, he summarizes rhapsodically: "Splendid first tour abroad. Success everywhere; better even than the reviews indicated. Greatest success—Paris!"

However, Sabaneeff repeats a conversation with Scriabin, years later, which gives a different set of reasons for the allure of Paris.

> "Early in my life, in Paris, I led an extremely corrupt life ...

> "This was a period of my life when I tried everything. Strictly speaking a person must experience everything before he can surmount anything. I ... how shall I put it? ... I drowned myself in pleasures, and was put to the test by them. Without this there is no triumph. And now, none of that is necessary for me anymore.

"I don't turn my back on it when it comes my way by accident, but I take no particular pleasure in it anymore. I now experience these pleasures, but all on a higher plane . . .

"I have known since then that the creative act is inextricably linked to the sexual act. I definitely know that the creative urge in myself has all the signs of a sexual stimulation with me . . . And note, please, that the creative artist is square in the middle of this—the weaker he is in the sexual area, the weaker his art. Maximum creativity; maximum eroticism. Look at Wagner. *Tristan* is his maximum, and *Parsifal*, already it has dropped. It's the work of a worn-out old man.

The major work belonging to the Paris period is the Fantasy Sonata, a curious binary form. As late as August, 1897, (at the same time Belaieff tells Scriabin that the first printing of the twelve études Op. 8 is sold out— a thousand exemplars each), he exhorts him in one of the few saved letters to Scriabin: "Sasha, you've had the Second Sonata long enough. Don't fuss with it anymore." Two months later it is in his hands and published as Op. 19.

Unlike the four heavy movements of the First Sonata, this one is delicate. Scriabin appended brief program notes and regarded it as a vision of the sea remembered. "The influence of the sea," he wrote "and the first movement represents the quiet of a southern night on the seashore; the development is the dark agitations of the deep, deep sea. The E major middle section shows caressing moonlight coming after the first darkness of night. The second movement, *presto*, represents the vast expanse of ocean stormily agitated."

Later Scriabin would be more preoccupied with the problem of transmuting light into sound, and, palindromically, music into light. For "moonlight" in the Fantasy Sonata Scriabin transposes the main theme from G# minor to the brighter key of E major. (The same key that Rimsky-Korsakoff used in his seascapes. Rimsky and Scriabin both saw colors as sounds, and E major was to them a light blue or sea tint.)

Scriabin, caught in myths of ancient Greece, believed that the gods communicated by emitting lights and flashing sparks. As his music advanced, he dropped programmatic "imitation" or "description" of light. He was concerned with actually reproducing light in music palpably and visibly—like gods talking.

$\mathscr{S}$ X $\mathscr{S}$

MARRIAGE

36

BACK IN the crowded apartment at 1 Meshchanskaya, Sasha once again moves within a particular Moscow. Lyubov finds him "refreshed, saying how much he had missed us, and happy over the least little thing, grateful for all. Instantly our life became more active. We went everywhere together, to concerts, to Petersburg . . ." This was September, 1896.

Within a month Boris Schloezer met Scriabin for the first time at his Uncle Paul's. These impressions begin his long, unfinished biography of Scriabin: "I was struck by his frail and sickly appearance and by his extraordinary nervousness . . . His playing astonished me and was deeply moving. It was unusual and so unlike anything I had ever heard before. My memory was still vivid when I saw him next autumn of 1902, in Moscow . . . " Boris was fifteen years old at this time.

October and November were tempestuous months. Scriabin received word that M.K.F. was ill. "Sad news . . . I am unbearably worried. I can't remain in Moscow. I am torn, frightfully pulled there, and indeed you will understand. Don't hold me back. I can work there as well as here, even better there," he wrote to unresponsive Belaieff. Incongruously in the midst of this torrent of emotion, he says, "I am considering something these days, but just a bit." And then as if afraid to continue (he has conceived an idea for a concerto), he drones, "I am a little tired, and must take a little break, but I can't. I want everything finished up." The postscript reads, "It is very, very late in the morning. Perhaps they will telegraph me news."

Short letters pour out to Belaieff. Scriabin feels he must go to Düsseldorf, however, "I am busy with a concerto." He cannot make up his mind. "I think *too much* and this impedes making a decision. I am not a man, but some kind of a freak! Everything would be fine, if only it weren't for all these useless ratiocinations!..."

Belaieff knows that Scriabin's intention of marriage will founder. He goads him to state his plans "positively." Scriabin writes, "I very much regret being unable to give you a definite reply." He feels that M.K.F. is love-sick and that for her sake—her life is at stake—the parents will have to send for him. He awaits a telegram summoning him. He is so distraught he says he must come to SPb to talk personally to Belaieff. "Everything depends on what she decides . . . The concerto comes along bit by bit. The finale is almost finished."

On 22 October he tells Belaieff that he cannot visit him before two more weeks at least. He is waiting for a letter from her. He again asks for more money and says, "You are mad at me for something. I can tell from the tone of your letter. Don't be. When you know all, you will see I am not at fault." By 12 November, the concerto has won the tug-of-war. "It is finished, and I am orchestrating. I tried it out on two pianos at Safonoff's. Haven't heard from you in so long . . . You are probably through with me! And I am in low spirits. I no longer (for the time being) think about going abroad."

The M.K.F. affair ended definitely two days later. He wrote Belaieff: "I am prevented from coming to Petersburg by very grave matters. I am most grieved by this, as I was so wanting to see you. What can I do? I only tell you this: What I had planned on will not take place. Now the matter is clarified . . ." In short, M.K.F. is not dying of love; and her family refuses consent to the marriage. As consolation, Belaieff again invites Scriabin to celebrate his nameday, and on 22 November the two are together again for a week.

The next letter Scriabin writes on, 1 December after his return, uses the intimate *ty* or "thou" for the first time. They are also on a first name basis, Mitrofan (sometimes more affectionately, Mitrosha, or Belyasha) and Sasha. In European custom, even between intimates, the full name is used formally. "Dear Mitrofan Petrovich" heads each letter, but it is now signed "I kiss you and remain your loving A. Scriabin," a salutation which carries milder connotations than in English.

The trip to SPb did Scriabin worlds of good. His letters sparkle. "I am in a marvelous mood," he writes thanking him for the hospitality. "I am always hurrying. Sometimes I am filled with anxiety. Sometimes at the height of bliss. In moments I fall into the depths of despondency, but God be praised, these are not for long." Of the Concerto he writes cryptically on 17 December (after saying he needed extra money for a new suit of clothes), "I can say nothing about the Concerto for the present—innate doubt prevents me. My mood is grand, and if it weren't for a little ache in my hands, all would be perfect . . . I am so sorry you can't come to Moscow, not even for a day. No one comforts me the way you do. You can even scold me and I feel the better for it."

By December, Scriabin is determinedly in love again. He has proposed to yet another girl, Vera, the pianist at Professor Schloezer's. He has been accepted. She sparked her romance with Scriabin by asking him to teach her his music, some of which she already played.

A contrast marks this period of Scriabin's engagement. He works well on the Concerto, but his mood begins to plummet. He falls psychically ill again, and is plagued with doubts and hesitancy. However, he is implacable about marriage. (This "artist marriage" seems ideal to him.)

Lyubov recalls these events, placing the blame on Ida, Professor Schloezer's maiden-sister.

> Ida Yulevna came to us very often and also invited us over there. She loved Shurinka and she loved Vera, and decided to arrange a marriage. She would talk to Shurinka about Vera in front of me, describing her wonderful heart. He told me that indeed he liked her very much and could be happy with her.
>
> One night he came home very late and with a radiant face asked his *babushki* and me to love Vera, because he himself did.
>
> It was strange. He was so believing and trusting, but with Vera he was always in doubts. He thought he was incapable of fathoming any woman's nature.
>
> I would like to tell the truth here and say that Vera and I did not get along.

Lyubov's actual letters to Belaieff contradict some of her recollections. Her first letter to Belaieff was written the day after Shurinka's twenty-fifth birthday, 25 December, 1896, and it is astringent.

> Now I want very much to tell you some things about Sasha. There is no one save you really with whom I can discuss my anxiety.

I just don't know whether to want him to marry or not. His fiancée is a very good sympathetic sort of girl and loves him very much. However, I have not discussed him with her. My one question is how long will it last? If it were right for him, it would lead to a quiet and happy life. But does it?

Believe me, he comes back from her each day in a ghastly mood. He's excited, fretful, and of course tells me about his uneasiness. I take pains to say that he has no cause for worry. Surely, if it were another girl, he wouldn't let trifles be so personal and menacing!

To my horror I have arrived at the conclusion that he will never, not anywhere, ever, ever be happy or at peace. What is so sad is that he is young and already suspicious of people. Without trust in others, it seems to me, life in this world is very hard.

Her postscript is mock-jubilant, however. For the first time Shurinka has cut his own fingernails. He did it on Friday, without Lyubov reminding him.

Sasha also writes Belaieff the same night, at 2:00 in the morning. He sends season's greetings and, "Please do as I asked you to—scold me. I am in such a hateful mood, sometimes. The reasons are hardly important, and I myself don't understand any of it. What shall I do with myself? I am quite hopeless . . ." He writes Belaieff, 6 January, 1897, that he has been "prevented from normality," because Vera has been ill. He tries to give a second reason, he flounders. "I don't know, what I mean is, I am afraid to say it. My heaven for the first time it would seem, has been cloudless these past few days. Yet I am in excellent spirits and I give myself over to this feeling entirely, therefore, I cannot—well forgive me. How are you? How I want to see you . . ."

Spurred by these letters, Belaieff begins a line of mild attack. On 22 January, Scriabin replies, "My Concerto is finished. I have only to orchestrate it. My other affair goes well, just as before. Don't think it prevents me from working. On the contrary, she arranged the Concerto for two pianos, four hands (not six as I planned originally). We have already played it over . . ."

Belaieff published the Concerto the next year without even the slightest credit to Vera. "Arrangement for two pianos by the author," the sheet music reads. Poor Vera. This was probably the beginning cruelty, and she could not help feeling it. She said nothing.

As the engagement is fixed, Lyubov and Belaieff grow helplessly closer. He has asked her to tell him details. She writes on 25 January describing a terrifying picture of the "birth" of a piece of music. (The Prelude, Op. 22 No. 1, beginning in G# minor and ending unexpectedly in D# major, is a study in intensification. It moves from softest to loudest with a single melody and broken chord bass galvanized only by changes in volume and pitch. It is Russianism without ethnography, a never-ending expanse of steppes.)

Six nights ago he had a nervous attack. I have observed that this always happens before the birth of a new musical idea. I sat beside him all night. How hard it was to see his suffering. I calmed myself with the thought that this was not a chill and that next day it would be gone.

First he became ice cold, and I did not know how to warm him. Then his heart stopped. Mainly, it was his head that was affected. He says that not even I can understand how he is *not* sick, but at the time, the only way to soothe him was for me to grasp his head tightly in my hands.

The seizure ended in the morning with hysterical and bitter tears. He grew quiet, but didn't sleep for a second. He lay thus until four in the afternoon utterly exhausted. I talked him into getting hold of himself and going out for a breath of air. He obeyed, and of course set out for the Schloezers.

Hofmann, with whom he has long been close, was there. And despite his frightful night, and lack of sleep, he played all evening. They say he hasn't played so well in ages. This means the illness is a matter of nerves. He completely won over both Hofmanns, father and son. The latter began work next day on two mazurkas and two études in order to play them in SPb. You will, of course, hear them. Please don't fail to tell me if they are well performed.

I was not mistaken about the birth of something new. That evening when he came home he sat at the piano and played very softly, forgetting his promise to his fiancée to go to bed early. I dropped off to sleep at four, and he was still playing and continued all night. After it was daylight he was practicing his Concerto, and then he played something else with such a radiant and blissful face. I asked him if something new hadn't been born, and he assured me that good was resulting. I could see by his face that he was in a truly blessed state of grace.

You can't imagine, Mitrofan Petrovich, how mixed my emotions, my thoughts, my wishes regarding Sasha's marriage. I share your view with all my heart and soul. Such people should *not* marry. I am so fearful of the future that I cannot rejoice in his happiness. I know she is a good girl, but I feel I cannot judge her fairly. I am prejudiced, but I still love her because she loves Sasha. But I cannot love her for herself as she is.

Three weeks later, Lyubov still ponders the approaching marriage and turns once more to Belaieff on 14 February to relieve her anxiety and portray a shrewd analysis of the whole situation and personalities involved.

A rather sad emotion came over me today. After Sasha went out I sat for a long time and thought about him, and grew even sadder. Not one comforting thought entered my head. I think I really must talk with you a while about him.

It is true that what nature gives neither man nor life can alter. Sasha knows he is ruining himself with his injudicious life. But he can do nothing with himself. He loves his fiancée, and she entreats him to lead a more cautious existence. Her wisdom checks him for a week or two at most.

He has again lost weight, grown frailer, and today he went to the Schloezers only by forcing himself. He is a martyr. He will never find peace or happiness. He is always agitated and his face is marked with suffering. He has no reason to be sad. Neither God nor man has injured him. Everyone is warm to him. But his soul is searching for something intangible. Nothing contents him.

I don't think Sasha would be capable of hurting his wife. He is too big, too good for that. I am convinced that he would rather torture himself and hide his jealousy and all such feelings than do anything unpleasant to her. If his wife will love him and understand his soul's agitations, then it would be possible for her to live with him.

You ask if Vera has means of her own. I cannot answer for sure, but I can tell you my impression from meeting her father and from talking with the Schloezers who know Isakovich well.

Sasha like all the Scriabins did not think about money when he proposed. My father, as well as six out of seven of my brothers, married poor girls and this trait shows up in Sasha too. He talked about this with his fiancée and they decided they would both work. Vera really makes a good helper for him. She lost her mother when she was a child, and her father is a lawyer in Nizhny-Novgorod. They say he has means, but is so stingy and such a despot that his only son walked out on him and lives with a godfather in Samara. He is still only in high school too. I am told this, but I don't know how true it is.

Isakovich called on us when he was here. I found that he loved his daughter mentally, but not with his heart. He gave her a very Spartan education. Because of this, naturally, Vera is not spoiled, either by parental affection or by life. She buys clothes for herself by giving music lessons.

Frankly, this whole business has affected me most disagreeably. I hope that my opinion will be kept between ourselves. It all seems so typical of Jewish moneylenders. Needless to add, Isakovich is very intelligent, but when you talk to him you get the feeling that money is dearer to him than children or friends.

Vera naturally expects no help from such a father. I agree that it would be hard for Sasha to work if he lived with her family. I have long thought about this, and realize that music is a most thankless profession. If he falls ill, they are destitute. But what can I do? He dreads any reference to his sickly, helpless state. So I avoid mentioning it.

I have also thought maybe marriage will bring a world of the soul to him that will improve his health. Perhaps Vera will so assist him, his work will rocket to the skies. This may be fantasy, but the law of nature allows man patience and endurance . . . .

Lyubov in her desperation intrigues. She asks Belaieff (8 March, 1897) to lure Scriabin away from Vera and Moscow. Belaieff invites Sasha using his wife's nameday, the first week of April, Holy Week, as excuse. Lyubov also discusses different types of marriage possible in Russia. Civil marriage was tantamount to free love, but it was accepted, particularly by liberal-minded Russians who scorned orthodoxy. Lyubov preferred this for Sasha. It would leave him free, though not so respectable. Officially, of course, only church marriages were recognized, and divorce an impossibility, but civil divorces required no more than mutual agreement.

But first Lyubov thanks Belaieff for sending Scriabin a wonderful present—a set of his own compositions exquisitely bound. (Sasha had already written on 3 March, 1897, "I received the package of compositions. Wonderful! Wonderful! I kiss you and thank you endlessly . . .")

On Shrove Tuesday he returned home in such a state that I could have persuaded him to stop his marriage—had I had the courage to say so. But I couldn't say the word, because I am not fair enough or impartial enough to judge Vera and him.

I am accustomed to keeping my thoughts to myself, but the more I think, the more appalled I become. I don't like to meddle in affairs of his heart. But I will say to you that I think this is a mere passing infatuation, and *that* frightens me. If marriage is to be successful it must be mutual love. If you talked to him, you could make him realize this.

I have my sorrow, and here it is. I have always lived in the company of males. Until I was 15 I lived at home with my 7 brothers and their numerous men friends. I therefore cannot adjust to female society. I regret to say that I understand women only with difficulty. For a solid month I have studied Vera with every fiber of my being. I have impressions of her, but I do not understand her. Does she love Sasha or not?

I know, Mitrofan Petrovich, that you look upon women as enemies, and doubtless you have your reasons. I shan't defend my sisters-in-sex, but they are not always to blame for the witcheries of family life.

It used to be considered a disgrace to remain an old maid. But I deem it noble.

37

AFTER Petersburg Belaieff chides Sasha for not writing more about himself. His life is "monotonous." He spends his time with his fiancée. "... Vera Ivanovna sends greetings." He is "low" and he is "tired ..." He will not set a definite date for the wedding ... "probably July?"

Vera has entered Scriabin's life enough to save his letters. So, we have a letter from Belaieff, 12 April, 1897. The tone is petulant, mock-cross, and still it shows a man suffused with tenderness.

I am waiting not only for the first movement of the Concerto but the other things as well. It is more convenient for Rimsky-Korsakoff to work during the holidays. He has to have time, of which very little is left before the end of his duties at the Conservatory on the 25th of May. The parts can be copied and sent back to you. Everything must be done by the 20th of May, if Safonoff is to try the Concerto out on his pupils before vacation.

You see, you must work regardless of holidays, and *then* rest. As it is, I don't see how Safonoff can do more than play through the Concerto two or three times.

You mention my coming to Moscow. Yes, you have my promise. But if Liadov turns tail at the last moment, you won't see me either.

Your well-wisher and friend,

M.

P.S. Just received the first movement of the Concerto and I thank you for it.

The Concerto is turned over to Rimsky-Korsakoff, who speedily looks through it, is shocked at its disorder and inaccuracies of musical etiquette, and writes a personal letter to Scriabin. Scriabin did not show this to Vera—presumably it was scorching—but he answered quickly on 19 April, 1897.

> I have just received your letter which threw me into depths of depression. There is nothing I can say in justification except one minor matter which keeps me from concentrating in general and writing the score in particular. This is neuralgia, and I've been suffering from it for several days. I am so ashamed!! I will do *all that I can* to correct the rest of the concerto properly. I am conscience-stricken to trouble you. If, however, you are so good as to help me, then I will be infinitely indebted to you, and I will show my gratitude by *industriously* exterminating my carelessness.

He wrote that same evening to Liadov, thanking him for working on the score of the Concerto, mentioning the neuralgia, putting everything in the gloomiest of colors, and saying how embarrassed he was to have put Rimsky-Korsakoff out so. "What can I do with myself! I'll *try* to be more organized." He reminds Liadov of his promise to come to Moscow, and then he adds one of his tantalizing lines which denotes some situation of love, "I'd like to confide something to you, but I'm afraid it would be upsetting. I just don't know how to get myself out of this frightful fix."

In a supreme act of inattention, Scriabin mixes the envelopes. Rimsky was so insulted he walked into Belaieff's office and silently put Liadov's letter addressed to him on the desk, and stalked out. 30 April, Belaieff fired off a volley: "Is it possible that you find yourself blowing your foot when you mean to blow your nose? Your absent-mindedness and carelessness are simply phenomenal... Where is your head?!" He continues angrily, "You promised not to keep the rest of the Concerto and now you feed me 'tomorrows.' You are wrecking my stomach..." Belaieff threatens Sasha that if he doesn't rush with the orchestration of the second and third movements, "You'll neither get married *nor* go abroad ever again..." and as for the piano transcription, above all, "Don't imitate Balakirev whose transcriptions are laughed at by everyone."

The Concerto reaches Belaieff finally. Scriabin continues to suffer physically. "Some sort of head ailment has appeared and I can't sleep at night. On top of this my mollycoddling aunt paints a sad picture of the future... I have tried to watch myself so carefully and what has happened? A whole mess of mistakes!!!" Rimsky wrote critically about the rest of the Concerto. He wants to answer him, but has lost his address, "Please don't tell him as he might be offended again . . ."

On 14 May, Scriabin writes Liadov a revealing and sincere letter of tremendous dignity and good sense regarding his Concerto.

Yesterday I received a letter from Nikolai Andreevich [Rimsky] which grieved me. I am very grateful to him for his kind help, but has he wasted all this time on the Concerto only to say the orchestration is weak? Since he is so kind couldn't he have noted those places which seem to him most weak and explain why?

To orchestrate a concerto, you don't have to have written several symphonies as preliminary exercises. Nikolai Andreevich says that a concerto is very difficult to orchestrate and that it is easier to write for orchestra alone.

Let us suppose that all this is true. But that is for an *ideal* orchestration. What I want for my first try is a *decent* orchestration. This goal can be reached through advice and a little help from people who know. It is easy to say "study orchestration," but there is only one way and that is to hear one's own composition *performed*. Trial and error is the best teacher.

Now, if I don't hear my music, and nobody tells me anything, then how can I learn? I have read scores, am reading, and will of course continue to read them, but I always come up against the same thing . . . the need for wisdom's experience.

I am working every day, but it leads nowhere. I can make as many inventions and combinations as I like. I can create patterns Nikolai Andreevich himself never dreamed of. But *without practice*, this adds up to naught.

Forgive me for prattling on. But all this is rather painful for me. I had counted Nikolai Andreevich as good, good, and now I see he is only kind.

At any rate, I am *ashamed* to have bothered him and I will not repeat that mistake *in the future*. I will manage on my own. Advise me, please, what should I do? In any case send me the score (you have it). I will reorchestrate it and answer for it myself.

Sergei Ivanovich [Taneieff] is so generous, he wants to do everything to make the orchestration a success. He is working with me.

Forgive me, dear Anatol Konstantinovich, for my long chatter. I kiss you warmly and am WAITING with *impatience*. *Without fail, without fail, without fail*!!!!! Come to Moscow. You would be dreadfully unkind, frightfully unkind if you don't keep your promise. Lord, what would I do? Once again I embrace you . . .

What does it mean? Mitrofan Petrovich doesn't write me.

I will wait until tomorrow to write Nikolai Andreevich so as not to mix envelopes.

Rimsky's disapproval of the Concerto is well documented. After going over it completely, he handed it to Liadov with a covering note of remarkable harshness:

Look at this filth. *I* have! There is much I don't understand. It is beyond my powers. I am in no condition to cope with such a mush-headed genius. Best to let the composer publish it for two pianos and have someone else orchestrate it. Balakirev might do it with gold of Goldov. As for me, I have cleaner work to do. I have no time to scrub Scriabin.

As a postscript he asks Liadov to tear this note up, and informs him that he has written to the composer directly. In the note, Rimsky is being both anti-Semitic and sarcastic. "Goldov" is a pun on the name Vasily Zolotaryov (1873-1964), an anemic composer who had flunked Rimsky's own classes. He became a junior professor at Moscow Conservatory, however, and later in Minsk. To boot, Balakirev would not have worked with a Jew.

Rimsky peppered the score itself with comments: "Devil take it!" "To hell with this!" "Forte *or* piano?" "How sloppy to put rests *here*!" "Why *this* suddenly?!" "Two quarter rests instead of a single half?" After the first few pages, Rimsky gave up on the matter of sharps, flats and naturals which were omitted wholesale. Particularly acid is the one line penciled at the beginning of the second movement: "Fewer slips of the pen here. Almost no modulations."

Belaieff still sent the manuscript to Vasily Scholtz, a hack music copyist, who returned it with three pages of "errors." "Now," writes Belaieff smugly, "thanks to Herr Scholtz *all is correctly corrected.*" Belaieff enclosed a money order with the returned manuscript. Six hundred rubles for the Concerto, and an additional two hundred rubles as final payment for the now printed Fantasy Sonata (January, 1898).

There is no doubt Scriabin was careless and made many mistakes in his work. His speed with the Concerto had really been phenomenal. From its initial conception he had reached the third and last movement within five days. In two days short of a month he had drafted the entire orchestration. True too, he lost interest in a composition once it was down on paper and past a certain stage. And when he saw proofs, his inner hearing was so strong that he heard what he wanted to hear, rather than what appeared on the page.

Rimsky-Korsakoff called Scriabin a "star of first magnitude" in his autobiography, adding that he was "somewhat warped and self-opinionated." He also wrote, perhaps ominously, "Of Scriabin I shall speak later on." He never did. Here it should be noted that, for all the criticisms, their relations were affectionate underneath reserve and caution. Rimsky's final verdict would have been friendly. Scriabin always saw "Korsakoff" when he visited St. Petersburg, and Rimsky often conducted his orchestral works.

Valentin Asmus, learned philosopher and professor at Moscow University, in introducing Scriabin's letters, points out the fact that when Rimsky "passed judgment on the demerits and imperfections in Scriabin, they were the demerits and imperfections of a genius." Rimsky himself in one of his many moments of plunging self-honesty with his friend and secretary, Vasily Yastrebtsev (1866–1934), likened himself to Salieri, the great rival whom, it is commonly thought by some, poisoned Mozart. He said, "I found in myself clear indications of Salieri. To a degree, I am irritated by the success of Chaliapin, Scriabin, Nikisch, d'Alheim, and others. I behave more kindheartedly with a talented mediocrity."

It is interesting and surprising to compare the original manuscript with the final printed version of the Concerto. Aside from orthography, very few of Rimsky's roiling suggestions were taken. What is played today is very much the Concerto as Scriabin himself orchestrated it. At the end of all the dismay, he wrote to Belaieff, "While it isn't brilliant, at least it's something." He was headstrong about changes and he had, indeed, managed on his own. In correcting the proofs, Scriabin called in Safonoff for dynamic and agogic markings, but he ignored certain harmonic changes Safonoff proposed in the orchestral part. He left the queries in the solo sections unanswered.

38

SAFONOFF had pointed out as early as 1895 that Scriabin needed a concerto for his career. Appearances with orchestras were always a major means of making money and fame. The Concerto in F# minor, Op. 20, was Scriabin's unique effort in the genre. It was successful. Composers who long write for the piano usually have difficulty in transferring to the orchestra. Transition from the self-contained world of the piano to the large-as-life colors of the orchestra defeats many talents. Chopin failed. Conversely, Rimsky himself, who never really wrote for piano at all, also failed. How, however, to fathom Rimsky's distaste for the Concerto? It is inoffensive and domesticated music.

The Concerto is a chamber concerto of modest range. It glows with elegance, grace, and ineffable delicacy of craftsmanship. How adroit Scriabin seems. The melodies gleam with charm. Yet, the sweet mood never cloys as he spins his tunes. Fancy, writing a concerto for soloist and fifty other musicians with constant *rubato* or irregular rhythmic flow, and much of it to be played *con sordino*, with the soft pedal down as well. Yes, it is written in shade, as the opening horns announce, and few shafts of sunlight penetrate.

For a concerto, it is curiously aloof. Scriabin lived still at this time not far from the virtuosic Concert Allegro and soon the Polonaise (his only one), where display bursts in the air, would burgeon. But here, there is not even a cadenza. The pianistic difficulties, which are formidable, are, like intricate stitchwork, concealed. He resisted flamboyance. For this reason, pianists on the prowl for warhorses pass by this Concerto. An audience is left more charmed or bemused by it than roused to cheering. Most remarkable of all, perhaps, is the fact that nowhere is there a trace of Scriabin's personal life—neither the wrench from M.K.F. nor the love attendant on an engagement to Vera, neither his poor health nor any secret in his private life.

A pastoral, contemplative opening theme by the piano wanders uncertainly to set the initial mood of restraint, rather than thrust. The middle movement, a most beautiful water color, consists of four contrasting variations, full of ingenious melismata and crystalline figuration, on an affecting theme. It could be folk music, and here again the Russian soul speaks softly but audibly. This was Liadov's favorite passage in all Scriabin, and some of Liadov's own music copies it. The rondo finale, light as the wind, ripples and purls with roulades of arpeggios. The movement floats suspended, like a rainless cloud over tranquil earth.

The Concerto admits Scriabin's conscious schematicism. There have been other threads in this labyrinth—now we understand his drift. A bird sings a beautiful song. We enjoy hearing it. But it is devoid of thought. This then, is where man must rectify nature.

Scriabin has artificially formalized in the Prelude of "Threes," Op. 16 in E flat minor. It is twelve measures long, the diagrammatic presentation rigid: three sets of three measures each; three beats in each phrase. The melody consists of the first beat with one note, the second beat with two notes, and the third beat with three notes.

However, the Concerto's main first theme is far subtler. Its nucleus is three descending tones, like a classical melodic sequence. He marks these on the score with stresses: edc#; dc#b; c#ba; bag#; etc. This makes a rosalia pattern like wallpaper, better expressed to the eye by numbers: 10 9 8: 9 8 7; 8 7 6; 7 6 5; etc. In other words, Scriabin is seeking benchmarks of sound. He feels urgently impelled to arrive at logic, symmetry, a schema which celebrates man's perfectibility over nature's raw confusion.

Sabaneeff records a vital discussion with the mature Scriabin on this subject and his composing principle (*printsip*, a word which Scriabin often used and always mispronounced rather strikingly, *pruntsip*).

For this strange man of fantasy, how doubly odd it was that so much came "from his head." His creativity in music was half-intuitive, and half if not more, constructed as logically as geometry. He himself told me that he rarely "improvised" themes, that rather he formalized them. How he loved to show these "rational constructions" in his compositions, after they were written.

"Thought must always be present in composition and in the creation of themes. It is expressed by means of *principle*. Principle guides creation. I create my themes mainly by principle, so they will have concordant proportions.

"Take for example my Concerto. The bedrock of its design is the descending sequence of notes. Against this background the whole theme grows and unfurls."

He played me the theme of the Concerto and accented these descending steps richly, and the melody took on quite different meaning and sense.

"And here's a prelude from opus 11 erected like a diatonic edifice. You see, I was already doing this *then*, long ago. Later, when I became convinced that true creativity must always reflect a principle, just as the world of nature is founded on principles, then I began using this more consciously and on a broader scale . . ."

Such a methodical approach to music, one where the means surface to the consciousness, sounded stranger fifty years ago than now. Formalism is recognized, even in our yesterday of serialists and sets, composing by squaring binomials and permutations, or in our present of music-making machines and electronic cerebrations. No longer can these be regarded as a violation of romantic intuition or a cover-up for flagging inspiration. They are extensions of the composers' methods.

Scriabin's schematicism originated from his restless search toward law, order, the codification of life's disorderly play and chance. Around his formula for divine perfection he wrapped the heart's intuitive adjustments.

39

LYUBOV spread her machinations wider. She insisted that Sasha now invite Belaieff to Moscow. Her motives were direct, "I thought he would see through Vera better than we." At the end of May, 1897, Belaieff and his inseparable companion-in-work, Liadov, arrive. Inconvenient (and boring) as it was for them, they stayed with Vladimir Scriabin far out in Lefortovo.

Taneieff asked them to the final examinations at the Conservatory. Vera graduates and receives the Gold Medal in piano. She plays much Scriabin music for them, once at Uncle Vladimir's, and again at the small apartment in town.

Lyubov taxes Belaieff for a judgment at the end of his stay: "He didn't answer for quite some time. Then he said 'They don't suit each other. Alexander Nikolaevich should *not* marry. It would be a pity for him.'" Vera's father suffered a stroke paralyzing the right side of his face. She goes to Nizhny-Novgorod to be with him and make advance preparations for the wedding. It must, of course, take place at the house of the betrothed. Sasha, in abhorrence of ill health, waits behind in Moscow until the last minute. The *babushki* move to a big summer house in Maidanovo Village, a scenic, cool spot near the Volga dam and reservoir (Tchaikovsky had lived there).

Belaieff wrote on 7 June: "Give me the details of your engagement, its status, and your feelings." Sasha replies to the latter question only. "You ask about the state of my soul! I will say that it changes every day. Today I am well, very well. Yesterday, sour the whole day through." Belaieff, in guise of father confessor has written the fiancée herself and Scriabin is piqued: "Vera Ivanovna wrote me she had a letter from you, but didn't say what you said! I would be interested to know what you had to say to her?!" He ends his letter to Belaieff on a high note: "How good and kind you are! Please don't think if I sometimes seem short-tempered or sharp-tongued that I am ungrateful. I plainly don't know how to be sweet, but I want to be. How wonderful to be alive in this world today . . ."

Belaieff presses Scriabin for less emotional news. Snidely he mentions that letters to him can be freely written, neither revised nor changed after consultation, as he presumably had with Natalya and M.K.F. "I don't have to go to Nizhny until the father recovers," Scriabin answers.

Vera's father is better by 23 June. The wedding is set for 15 to 20 August, in full, five-day formality required by Russian orthodox services. Scriabin sends out gold embossed invitations.

A letter dated 30 June announced that Scriabin is in excellent spirits, and has "calmed down after the peregrination." He cautions Belaieff: "Say nothing in your letters Vera Ivanovna shouldn't know. I show them to her." The couple has decided to honeymoon in the Crimea for two weeks and then travel in Europe beginning October. Vera's dowry is 1,000 rubles but, "We will give joint recitals to earn our living . . ."

Belaieff bothers Scriabin about music. "When do the tempi change in the Concert Allegro?" "There isn't a metronome here, so I can't say," Scriabin replies. He and Vera, together with assorted relatives take a pre-nuptial boat trip down the Volga to Samara. They are gone for nine days. Scriabin meets her young brother there and persuades him to come work in Moscow after he finishes gymnasium.

Belaieff fires a fusillade. "Nizhny is not a village. If you make the slightest effort you can find a metronome . . . I don't want to publish your works in a mess . . . I have written you three or four times about the Allegro . . . I will not print it until you send me the proofs in fit and

proper order. Rimsky's lesson to you has sailed right over your head!"
Sasha answers, "Our trip to Samara was successful. Excellent weather
and plenty of fresh air. Now I can get a little work done . . ." He (or
Vera?) sends the metronome speeds. "Write me anything you wish. I
don't have to show my letters to Vera. About business or otherwise . . ."

During the spring and summer of 1897 Safonoff, as usual, was invited
to conduct various orchestras throughout Russia. He accepts one in
particular, and chooses it for the first performance of the Concerto. The
date is right, 11 October. The place convenient, Odessa, picturesquely
placed on the Black Sea where the Ukrainian steppes come to an end
and European trains set out for abroad. Nor was it far from the Crimean
honeymoon spot.

Safonoff wrote persuasively to the Odessa branch of the RMO:

> My pupil Scriabin has written a *remarkable* Concerto for piano. Since this youth
> is on his path to glory—he played with enormous success recently in Paris,
> Amsterdam, Brussels, and Berlin, and is leaving for abroad again in the autumn
> —I am thinking of taking advantage of his presence here (he leaves in October
> and may be abroad for a long time) and putting him on the program. His fee
> would be not more than 300 rubles, merely the cost of his transportation, and
> thus music lovers and the general public will be able to hear a *premier* [sic]
> which will be a veritable sensation in the music world. And the honor of
> having taken the initiative in all this will go to Odessa.

Odessa accepted the soloist. In the four sample programs accompanying
this letter, Safonoff placed the Concerto in the very heart of each. Scriabin
wrote Belaieff hurriedly: "We are in a frightful state of confusion . . .
The wedding now will end on 27 August, seven days later than planned."
He affirms the Odessa concert, gets the date wrong, and says, "And
that's all my news."

Belaieff arrives in Nizhny along with Lyubov and Vladimir the night
before the first service. Belaieff brings two magnificent wedding presents
—the complete works of Chopin bound luxuriously in a rare edition,
and a splendid Vuitton traveling trunk. "Vera greeted us tenderly,"
Lyubov found, and she thought Vera "sweet and good." Five days later
the married couple take the train for the Crimea. Thirty relatives and
friends are at the station.

Lyubov described her agonizing moment: "We stood on the platform, noisily talking all at once. I glanced at Shurinka. He was pale, his eyes looked sad, but he laughed along with the others. Until the very moment of the train pulling out, we did not exchange one word. Then I heard his voice, 'Auntie! Keep my grannies safe for me.' These words returned me to myself. I remembered indeed that there were others dear to me, for whom I must care, to whom I must give my love."

Except for one incident occurring in 1903, we now lose Aunt Lyubov's written words. She stops her reminiscenses when the one lighted candle of her life, blown out by the gust of marriage, leaves.

Scriabin's first letter from the Hotel Gubonia in Gurzuf is to Belaieff: "How wonderful it is here!! Although everything is so expensive and inconvenient." Belaieff replies, "I have had no music from you for some time . . ."

The day after the performance of the Concerto, 12 October, 1897, Scriabin informs Belaieff from a modest apartment in Khersonskaya Street, Medvedev district of Odessa, that all went well: "Safonoff will give you the details. He has the score. Four measures in the instrumentation of the finale are different. The rest sounds very good; so it can be printed. We changed some things during rehearsals . . ."

Safonoff writing Cui on the same day corroborates: "Yesterday the Odessa program went brilliantly. Scriabin had enormous success with his remarkable concerto . . ."

All the provincial critics were delighted to have a *première*, which they described as "that which is unknown in Petersburg." The consensus regarding the Concerto was that "the orchestra held the main role. Perhaps this was due to Scriabin's weakness of power." However, they all agreed that "the performance revealed the author's knowledge and talent, though the audience was somewhat cold except to the Variations. They applauded these vigorously and Mr. Scriabin played several encores, among them a nocturne for left hand . . ."

✒ XI ✒

SECOND TOUR

40

THE NEWLY married Scriabins rested a week in Odessa after the Concerto, sightseeing at the zoo and botanical gardens, safe from the early chill of the north. The two musicians bravely set out for Europe at the end of October, 1897, with high hopes and by slow train. In Vienna Vera wanted to absorb the atmosphere of Mozart, Beethoven and Schubert. Scriabin mailed the final manuscript of the Fantasy Sonata to Belaieff. He addresses the packet in French. Then he worries. Will the Austrians decipher it? Can the Russian post office cope?

They arrive in Paris and find a room at 5, rue de la Neva, a *pension* of small apartments catering to musicians. Surrounded on all sides by musicians, the couple rarely stay home. They diligently sightsee and socialize. Scriabin takes Vera on a pilgrimage to Chopin's grave.

Vera describes their Paris life in a long, prim letter to her former teacher in Nizhny-Novgorod, Vasily Villuan (1850–1922), then director of the Nizhny branch of RMO concerts, the local school of music, and enterpreneur of concerts. "We are not at all as you think. We are eager for knowledge. Be assured, Vasily Yulevich, we will see everything there is to see before we leave. The weather has been marvelous. We walk a lot and see Paris most conscientiously ... We arrived at the very worst of times. Paris, I believe, is charming in spring and summer when you saw it, but in winter it is depressing and boring, dark, grey, and our room is gloomy and dreary. I expected too much from Paris and was taken aback, unpleasantly so. Now I am beginning to get used to it. Good sunshine weather delights me much. I would like to remain here until spring when the whole city turns green, I am told."

At the time of this letter, 31 January, 1898, Vera had been abroad for a scant three months and for the first time in her life. There she was in her husband's beloved city, home of his first successes, and she turns patriotic: "In general, I find that a person is naturally better off living in his own country. I shall be happy to return to Russia. In my opinion we Russians are too modest and too little inclined to see all the things we have which are better than anywhere else."

She is far from unintelligent viewing the cultural status of Paris. "As for art, only painting blooms here. Paris is not very important in a musical sense. The time will soon come when the French will study in Russia. Many already talk in these terms. All the musicians here respect our conservatories and musicians most highly.

"We know conductors Lamoureux and Chevillard [Camille (1859–1923), successor to Lamoureux in 1897] very well and both are so devoted to Russian music they include something Russian every concert. They like Rimsky-Korsakoff especially. We heard three of his big works here. Chevillard like many others speaks with sorrow of present-day French composers. He says that all music here is in decline.

"We keep up with everything new and take out sheet music on approval. What is perfect here is the Lamoureux orchestra. I haven't heard the others. We attend these symphony concerts with the greatest of pleasure."

Belaieff's first letter reaches Scriabin in November, 1897. It is cold and firm.

I note the Second Sonata from beginning to end was in Vera Ivanovna's script. This means you have shifted that chore to her. I sent it next day to be set in print. There are, as usual, far too few markings. The metronome was not indicated. In the first measures should the octaves be repeated? They are marked with ties *and* staccato dots.

In the future, if you intend to write jointly cooperating with your wife, play the things over a few times for her. Let her insert the proper markings. These help a performer. I suggested Safonoff do this for you a long time ago but now you can do it under intimate circumstances . . .

His next letter, 21 November, maintains the faultfinding:

I have solemnly sworn not to print anything more of yours until the transcription for two pianos is in my hands. So I am waiting for you to send it. You have it doubtless, lying around somewhere in a mess.

Are you going to be a baby all your life? Will they have to wash your neck for you while you sit at the piano?

And a third, stern letter is written at the end of November. He encloses a "modest little Viennese review" which mentions Scriabin's compositions timidly.

You answer nothing about the two-piano reduction of the Concerto. You really ought to be concerned about it. This will open doors for you to conductors and augment your opportunities to appear as a pianist and composer.

Nobody publishes a concerto without also publishing the transcription of the orchestral part for piano at the same time.

Actually Scriabin is rushing frantically to find engagements for Vera and himself. Paris drawing rooms were less open to a couple than to an eligible young bachelor. He calls on Safonoff's friend, Baudoux of the Salle Erard. The hall has only one free date, 31 January, 1898. This will be their only concert appearance. As for salons, Mme. Samarina and Vera become fast friends.

In spite of Belaieff's petulance during this trip abroad, his maecenas-heart still beats. He raised Scriabin's stipend from 150 rubles a month to 200. He also suggests Scriabin submit his concerto to a contest in Vienna, arranged by Ludwig Boesendorfer (1835–1919), maker of magnificent Austrian pianos. Belaieff urges him by saying that no rights would be lost and he cannot publish it in any event until after the concerto competition.

Scriabin rejects this idea summarily. He had already performed it in public and was therefore ineligible, but the tone of his letter indicated that he was not interested in competing in public or being judged in relation to another. He adds that he is "working on my Third Sonata," and promptly forgets he has already told Belaieff of this work-in-progress.

Belaieff's next act of generosity was anonymous. The Glinka Prize was dispensed each year by that unimpeachable cognoscente, Stassov. (If the award went to Belaieff composers [and they almost always did], the honor would be suspect.) In November, Belaieff asks about Scriabin's "finances." The answer: "To tell the truth they are deplorable." Belaieff has Stassov write Scriabin on 25 November:

I have something very important for you. You have been *awarded* a prize of a thousand rubles for various compositions, but by *whom* I don't know . . .

Now, you must tell me: *Is it agreeable for you to accept this prize?* None of our composers in the past 13 years has refused, except once Shcherbachov and another, Balakirev. One other time I think Tchaikovsky excused himself on the grounds that he earned enough from his operas. But I wrote him in Paris, where he was at the time, that it would be unfortunate because it would look *disdainful* of those who love him, value him, and respect him. It would also *offend* those of his comrades-in-art who have already been so honored. After this he agreed and I sent him the money.

Scriabin's accepts so eagerly he writes the year "1879," instead of 1897. Stassov sends the money and itemizes the award. The trivial mazurkas are better rewarded than the masterful First Sonata.

Through all of Scriabin's letters from France one phrase recurs. Even in thanking Stassov he writes, "Of myself I will say I'm working sufficiently, but I do not feel well." To Belaieff: "I don't feel well. Everything makes my head ache . . ."

41

THE JOINT recital of 31 January, 1898, was advertised as" an audition of the works of Scriabine, Russian pianist-composer." The composer played first: Fantasy Sonata; Etudes, Op. 8 Nos. 8 and 2; and Nocturne for left hand. Vera then played after a brief intermission: Concert Allegro Op. 18; Prelude, Op. 15, F# minor; Etudes, Op. 8 Nos. 6 and 3; and Mazurka, Op. 3 in E major. Scriabin then reappeared with fourteen preludes in a row, presumably from Op. 11, which had been so popular two years earlier in Paris, and ended this second section with the two Witznau Impromptus, Op. 14.

Vera began the third section with two preludes, Op. 17 Nos. 7 and 3; the Impromptu, Op. 12 in B flat minor; and three Etudes, Op. 8 Nos. 9, 10, and 12. Scriabin concluded the program with a mazurka, Nocturne, Op. 5; and, for the first time, a long, loud Polonaise in B flat minor (later Op. 21).

The audience was distinguished with a mixture of money and celebrity, society and musical personalities. Vera wrote her Nizhny friend that the concert was "a fine success, but we were not entirely happy. The piano was bad. We were not able to give all we would have liked." She sent the program to Professor Schloezer the night of the concert.

Belaieff's instant cannonade: "Schloezer showed me your program. You played a polonaise. Recently finished?" Scriabin reports to him of "succeeding in an artistic sense," to which Belaieff replies understandingly, "If you write 'artistic success,' I know that means you paid for the recital out of your own pocket . . . I wish both artistic and material success for you, but the lack of the latter neither surprises nor troubles me."

In February, Scriabin answers, "I played the polonaise in concert, but it is far from being properly finished. Now I am working on other things." He also asks if he can put four new measures in the Fantasy Sonata. He is still mulling it over. He reminds Belaieff that he was permitted to insert some notes in the proofs of the Allegro Appassionata. Belaieff is sympathetic. "I can imagine the cares on your shoulders," he writes, "I notice that even the proofs of the Second Sonata are in Vera's handwriting." And the measures are added.

Scriabin continues about their recital, "By no means can it be called a financial success. Nevertheless, we made expenses and have a few francs left over. We are quite indifferent to the money aspect of our work. That's why I made no reference to it earlier. I am again rather to blame, as we worked with that frightfully unreliable Dyomes. He got us into all manner of unnecessary expense—500 francs for the hall, lights, ushers, etc. It could have all been done for 200." Dyomes obviously had also handled the critics badly, as only a brief, uninformative notice in *Le Guide Musical* mentioned "*les Scriabines.*"

Chevillard urged Scriabin to play the Concerto from proofs at his 15 March concert. Scriabin refers the matter to Belaieff, but first gives three negative reactions of his own: "One, he doesn't know the Concerto. Two, I am absorbed in interesting work and it would be difficult to leave it, in fact I DON'T WANT to. Three, my hand aches and I don't see how I could play decently. If *you* want me to I will. I would like to demur. But oh, how *he* wants me to appear!!! I would have to do the Concerto with only one rehearsal!!!" Belaieff, ambitious as he normally is for his protégé (and for his own enhancement), advised Scriabin to defer playing the Concerto: "It would be premature since Safonoff has made many more changes in it . . ." The real reason is that he wants the second performance to be under his aegis in SPb. (As it happens, it will not be.)

Belaieff, for once, it seems, is chatty and talks about his life. He is preparing a program featuring Glazunov's new ballet music, *Raymonda*. He invites Scriabin to contribute some music for a string quartet. He resumes his fatherly lecture: "I want you to hold on to your new compositions until they satisfy you. But I sometimes think that you work over them too long. The result is certain passages seem 'fabricated.' That's what happened with a couple of measures in the finale of the Second Sonata. They weren't that way originally . . ."

Belaieff now rags: "Sasha, the musician must set himself to 'black work' as *work* and not as a creative, inspirational activity. You've had the proofs of the Concerto for two months. Don't be so self-indulgent. Set aside a specific time each day to do nothing but this type of work . . ."

Scriabin has forgotten to designate the tempos for the Fantasy Sonata. He apologizes. "Liadov has heard me play it many times and I am sure he can guess at the speed. Moreover, the second movement depends on the performer's technique . . . its speed breaks the limits of the metronome . . ."

After a few weeks' silence from Belaieff, Scriabin withers. He writes on 12 March, "If you're mad at me, it's nothing deliberate on my part, only my absent-mindedness . . . I have sent you nothing for a long time, but don't think I have been idle. This summer I plan on sending you several things and one, maybe in a few weeks. What it is I won't tell you for the time being . . . I am longing for you very much . . . You never tell me anything about yourself, ever, ever . . . Forgive me for continuing in your debt for a while longer . . ."

The Third Sonata occupies Scriabin profoundly. He can think of nothing else, and plans to go to Lucerne to finish it in Switzerland's quiet. He tears himself away long enough to skim through the Concerto proofs and Vera's reduction for two pianos.

Life interrupts the Third Sonata even more, but nothing can halt its composing. Vera is seven months pregnant. Scriabin has not told Belaieff, but he hears from Vera's friends in Moscow. She is carrying the baby badly and is constantly ill. Her one desire is to return to the comfort of the Schloezers in whose house she wants the baby born. They leave Paris by train on 22 April.

Scriabin wrote Belaieff from Vienna, "Vera is not taking the trip well. She tires dreadfully. We stop everywhere and spend the night often as we can." He asks him to keep their return to Russia a secret. Secret? When all of Vera's world knew everything—even that Scriabin is drinking again. All the other Scriabins, including Nikolai with wife, three sons and a baby daughter, are to summer together in the house in Maidanovo.

On their arrival in Moscow, Vera and Sasha find the aged Professor Schloezer mortally ill. Death and birth cannot be juxtaposed. Nikolai orders the couple to come to Maidanovo. Belaieff wordlessly reduces the stipend from 200 to 100 rubles, without notification. Later he will say that Scriabin withheld already completed compositions too long and kept them from earning money for the firm. Scriabin rushes off the half-drawn polonaise and four drafted preludes, Op. 22 in panic. (No. 1, as it turns out, is one of the smoothest, most Russian pages of music ever written.)

The baby is due in July, and Scriabin was becoming a father without himself having grown up. He was assuming a posture of manhood, but beginning to feel how counterfeit, how confused between love and money, Belaieff's affection was.

Scriabin on 5 June expressed himself fully to Belaieff, and the letter makes shameful reading: "I must admit I simply do not know what to make of your silence. If you are angry at something, surely our relationship is such that you can be frank. Indeed, you do not skimp with reprimands when I deserve it. But more baffling than your silence is the change you have made about money. You are indeed the one who warned me never to let hardship befall my wife. Now at a time when you know how important material matters have become for me, you do not even give advance warning for me to adjust to the new situation. Of course you know that my sole source of income is composition. You know also that if I did not see a career ahead of me, that is, the ability to compose, I would never have accepted your terms. Please don't keep me in ignorance . . ." He lists the compositions he is sending forthwith.

Scriabin wrote again on 14 June: "You misunderstand me completely. I was not speaking of any obligation on your part, nor do I count on anything except that which was before. You sent me 200 rubles for many months. So it was natural for me to expect it, and to expect that if you

changed, you would give me notice and not fling me into awkward-
ness. As for terms, you know you can send me as much or as little as you
like. I am so sad that you have no faith in me. When I do not work, it
is because I am either ill or for some other equally grave reason . . ."

On 15 July, 1898—the month Professor Schloezer died—the baby is
born. It is a girl to everyone's astonishment, since Scriabins produced boys
in such abundance. Scriabin is delighted, and allows his stepmother to
name the girl, Rimma, à *l'italienne*, overriding Vera's choice. The house
rings loudly with the finishing chords of the Third Sonata. The lyric
second theme of the finale (*meno mosso* in A major) became the baby's
first lullaby. It was hummed and sung constantly by mother, step-
grandmother, and . . . joyous father, who is not clumsy in the slightest
holding the infant.

On 16 August he mails the Third Sonata to Belaieff. He omits the metronome speed marking again, but this time at least he knows he has. "There
is no metronome," he says, "but I am in a hurry to get this work off to
you . . ." Within three weeks he will have the proofs back, such is Belaieff's own haste . . . and delight. In eight-and-a-half months, through all
the changes of scene, Scriabin has finished a trajectory of inspiration
straight, continuous, direct and unswerving.

Two weeks later the Scriabin family moves back to Moscow. Vera has
found an apartment, No. 5, in the Shavykin house on Alexandrov
(later October) Street in the Maryinsky section. Behind it stands the St.
Catherine's Institute for Young Ladies, a boarding school of quiet refinement. Vera turns a tiny alcove into a *kabinet* or workroom for Scriabin
—not a nursery. She gives up practicing for a while. There is only one
piano, and when Scriabin is not using it, he needs quiet. Rimma cries a lot,
and he goes out a good deal, partying on his own.

Scriabin again meets Professor Schloezer's Belgian sister-in-law, Marie
Boty-Schloezer, with her fifteen-year-old daughter, Tatyana. Scriabin
learns that the mother had been a classmate of his mother's and a pupil
of Leschetizky. They speak of Mme. Homell in Switzerland. He notices
Tatyana, who is strikingly pretty, and very much to his taste for very
young dark women.

42

THE THIRD Sonata, Op. 23 in F♯ minor, already a favorite key for extended converse, is one of Scriabin's best-known and most widely played compositions. It is written in four long, consistent and coherent movements, simply marked *Dramatico* (he often referred to this first movement as *Allegro*), *Allegretto* (he called this an Intermezzo), *Andante*, and *Presto con fuoco*.

Sabaneeff, writing in his biography *Scriabin* (not the *Reminiscences*) says concisely that the Third Sonata is "where the real Scriabin shows his face . . . clear, powerful and all his own. Scriabin attached great signification to this sonata. Everything that had been embryonic, those individual flashes that had seen light in previous études and preludes—his affected tragedy, pathos, broken rhythms in which one feels a fearsome nervosity, eroticism, indisputable strength and color, refinement and elegance—all these and more were incarnated by it."

Rimsky had once expressed the fear to Yastrebtsev that "Scriabin would never break out of that magic circle of étude music for the piano." The Third Sonata disproved this. Scriabin now closed and locked the door on his early composition. Aromas of Chopin, Schumann, and Liszt dissipate themselves in thin air. He dispels his heritage, as the adult relinquishes his dependence on family. From now on, even if there are sprigs of preludes with vaporous melodies and diaphonous harmonies, the meaning and direction will be different.

Scriabin's first public performance of any part of the Third Sonata came late, 10 July, 1900, at a concert in the small (200 seats) Salle de Journal in Paris, where he played this curious program:

> Second Sonata // Seven Preludes in D major, E flat minor, B major, G♯ minor, F minor, D flat major, B flat minor / Impromptu, Op. 10 in A major / Polonaise // Intermezzo (*Allegretto*) and *Andante* from the Third Sonata / Five Mazurkas in B flat minor, E minor, E major, E flat minor, E major / Funeral March from First Sonata / Three Etudes, Op. 8, F♯ minor, A flat major, D♯ minor.

After the Third Sonata excerpts, the house that evening clamored, "Give us the finale!" Scriabin announced from the stage that his wife, Vera, would perform the Sonata *in toto* later that year.

He omitted the first movement partly because the openings of the Fantasy Sonata and the Third Sonata are similar. The finale demanded too much of him at the time. His hand ached again, and once in a letter to Vera he emphasized his diligence by saying, "I dare to practice that fourth movement." She with her greater fortitude coldly mastered it.

Buyukly gave the first complete performance of the Third Sonata on 23 November, 1900, in Moscow. Subsequently he toured with it throughout Russia. Critics raved: "He plays Scriabin better than Scriabin," and Scriabin called him "one of the greatest pianists in the world."

Scriabin himself played the Third Sonata in Moscow (1902) with no explanatory appendage. However, abroad in Brussels on 8 November, 1906, the program carries the following notes written not by Vera, ironically, to whom the Sonata rightfully belongs as common property of their first year of marriage, but by Tatyana, his second wife.

Scriabin subtitled the sonata, *Etats d'Ame,* or "soul-states." (This word, once in wide parlance, means "mood" or *nastroyenie,* but Israeli philosopher Martin Buber interprets rather than translates it as "a living through in oneself.")

I

The free, untamed Soul plunges passionately into an abyss of suffering and strife.

II

The Soul, weary of suffering, finds illusory and transient respite.
It forgets itself in song, in flowers.
But this vitiated and uneasy Soul invariably penetrates the false veil of fragrant harmonies and radiant rhythms.

III

The Soul floats on a tender and melancholy sea of feeling. Love, sorrow, secret desires, inexpressible thoughts are wraithlike charms.

IV

The elements unleash themselves. The Soul struggles within their vortex of fury. Suddenly, the voice of the Man-God rises up from within the Soul's depths.

The song of victory resounds triumphantly.
But it is weak, still . . .
When all is within its grasp, it sinks back, broken, falling into a new abyss
of nothingness.

Musically, the Sonata reverberates with proud, ponderous, noble
emphases of heavy chords. It spreads widely over the keyboard with large
intervals of space—windows for the sound to be heard through. Mixed
into this voyage of Soul are whiplashes of tempestuous winds and waves,
out of which bursts the Man-God. For all the Sonata's frowning black
shadows, Scriabin paints a positive smile on its face.

Certain recurrent themes anchor this vertigo of pianism leading us
emotionally through a cycle of grief, doubt, triumph, and then, in a last
flicker, back to sorrow. As the First Sonata sustained Scriabin through a
physical crisis, the Third Sonata carries him over the spiritual crisis of
his marriage. As emotional biography, it saves his soul. His achievement
left him exhausted. "I am _frightfully_ tired after the Sonata," he wrote
Belaieff on 24 August, 1898, eight days after he had sent the manuscript.

The third movement needs particular notice. Its theme is possibly the
most perfect melody he ever conceived. "Here," he said to a student,
"the stars sing . . ." He now has evolved into "starlight"—his second reference to light in music. The shimmering, transparent figurations literally
sparkle. Elena Bekman-Shcherbina pictured it as "lovers contemplating
an unending night sky of clouds and twinkling stars." Pianist Mark
Meichik describes how Scriabin himself played this passage: ". . . the
melody carried in the left hand sounded exactly like ringing silver bells
glinting in light."

Curiously this softly gentle theme ultimately becomes the Sonata's
strength. It is transmogrified into a climactic apotheosis—the Man-God's
hymn of triumph in the gigantic finale. A similar thematic transformation
also occurred in the First Sonata, but with this, ideas common to the two
pieces end. One is of the body; the other, of the soul. His next sonata
will be of spirit.

To Boris Schloezer, writing in _RMG_ (10 February, 1906) and fresh
from conversations with Scriabin, is due a last hermeneutical word:

Psychological reason for the crisis is easy to find: he became aware of himself.
He had to bring into full consciousness the liberating joy he had found within

himself... This joy lived deep within his soul, and it could not bear the light of day. It flickered, then went out. Byron was right when he said, "the tree of knowledge is not the tree of life . . ." But Scriabin was one of those few who summoned an ancient god from within the depths of his being and gave external consciousness to it. In short, this is the tragedy of a personality unable to bear his own deification into the Man-God. At the very moment he sounds his song of triumph, he sinks into the abyss. The world is deserted. The winds blow the dust of supermen into space.

If, as Schloezer and Scriabin himself claimed, Nietzsche was one of the influences on the Third Sonata, then one of Zarathustra's lines is prophecy: "That which will kindle lightning must for a long time be a cloud." The cloud of the Third Sonata, sure enough, changes into flashes of blinding light later.

✐ XII ✐
PROFESSORSHIP

43

OLD SCHLOEZER was scarcely dead before Safonoff began scheming for Sashkina. As Director of the Moscow Conservatory he wrote circumlocutiously to Professor Ivan Grzhimali (1844–1915), Head of the Violin Department, on 1 August, 1898: "Among youths who have graduated from the Conservatory several are talented, though immature, but they are fit, nevertheless, to teach as professors at some future date."

By the end of the month Scriabin is urgently writing Belaieff:

> Right off, I want to ask your advice about something very serious. Safonoff has suggested a professorship at the Conservatory for me with every possible advantage. I will have only advanced pupils, 12 in number, which means I would teach only 12 hours a week. My salary would be 1,200 rubles a year.
>
> I don't think this would interfere with my composing. In any event I would undertake the commitment for only a year, or until May, so I won't feel tied down.
>
> Of course the idea of giving piano lessons frightens me. I would not even consider it, were it not for that substantial salary. That now has very great significance in my life.
>
> Write me your opinion quickly. And please for the time being don't discuss it with *anyone*.

Belaieff answers by return mail, 1 September:

> You know full well that I have always been for a definite occupation which trains a person to regularity and which provides him with a sense of responsibility. From this point of view, you must say yes.

But what about your health? Are you physically well enough to assume professorial duties at the Conservatory without injury to yourself? I cannot decide this for you as I have not seen you for a long time.

In a week Scriabin tells Belaieff, "I accepted Vassily Ilich's offer. I begin work one of these days . . ."

As expected, Safonoff's invitation to the twenty-six-year-old Scriabin to an exalted professorship flabbergasted a number of persons. The hiring of another professor at the same time, James Kwast (b. 1852), Dutch pianist (and later Percy Grainger's teacher), caused no ripple of censure. Professor Stepan Smolensky (1848–1909) Choirmaster and Instructor in Church Music, told Findeizen in SPb simply that "Safonoff got young Scriabin a professorship by sheerest fluke!"

He was the youngest and greenest member ever on the staff. With courage, high head, and, as we will see, a great deal of dignity, Scriabin joined that group of athletes at the piano whose primary goal it seemed, was to tornado over the keys and to teach their pupils to keep pace. With the additional income, Vera looked for a better apartment closer to the Conservatory. She found one on Varsonofevsky Lane in a house owned by Prince Obolensky.

That month Belaieff fails to enclose a cheque. An oversight of course, but still . . . Scriabin sends him back his letter and envelope "to prove that the money was not sent . . . Perhaps you yourself forgot to enclose it? . . . I must rush now to the Conservatory . . ."

In October he accepts an invitation from Vera's friend in Nizhny to perform at the celebration of the twenty-fifth anniversary of the founding of the RMO there. Vera has already agreed to appear with other alumnae at a special concert on 14 November, 1898. At the last moment Scriabin cancels.

Ostensibly there are Conservatory duties. However, the real reason is that Belaieff and Liadov are coming to Moscow. Although they do not stay with him, they spend much time together. "Please don't dine anywhere but with me." And they don't. No sooner does Vera return to Moscow than Scriabin goes to Petersburg and Belaieff for two weeks. This time he plays his concerto. Here too, is a story of some complication and sadness.

Cui had invited Scriabin to debut his new Concerto in SPb on 28 November, 1898, at the RMO concerts with Safonoff as guest conductor. The fee would be 200 rubles, in addition to 50 rubles composer's royalty. Scriabin's prior promise, naturally, was to Belaieff's Russian Symphony series on 5 December. Scriabin suggests accepting both dates. Cui and Belaieff hesitate for Petersburg to have the same piece twice within a week, yet each wants to be first with the Concerto. When Scriabin learns that Rimsky has been scheduled to conduct the Belaieff date, he withdraws. He says instead he will play the Third Sonata in the middle of the orchestral program. "Undesirable," Belaieff snaps at this. "Of course all these discussions are to be kept *between us*," Scriabin answers.

Scriabin played on 28 November, but in the afternoon Safonoff's wife telegraphed twice to say that their daughter Nastya has fallen suddenly and fatally ill. Safonoff conducts the first half of the program through the Concerto, then, passing the baton over to concertmaster Leopold Auer, he rushes to catch the "Courier" night express to Moscow. Nastya is dead. Within a week another daughter, Sasha, dies of the same undiagnosed disease.

Scriabin forbids Vera to go near the Safonoff house for fear of contagion, but he sends a tender letter of condolence. "I was aghast at the news of your second loss. If my sympathy can be of any worth to you, know then that I weep with you as if your grief were mine and with all my heart." Later, when he sees Safonoff he is shocked at the change in him. Safonoff and his wife leave Moscow soon after "to get away in order to come back to themselves."

Scriabin gave Vera the details of the concert. "Safonoff was terribly upset by the unnerving news, and this, of course, showed in his accompaniment. (Don't tell him this.) During the first movement we were constantly chasing each other. The second and third movements went a little better." Scriabin played two encores, one a prelude, Op. 16, a bright, sunshine greeting as short as a "good morning." He said of the whole performance, "I am horribly dissatisfied with myself. But what can I do?"

The press blasted the Concerto and the performance. Findeizen reviewed it in his *RMG*:

It is virtually impossible to evaluate this composition because all the good—if there is any—was drained away by its bad rendition. As a performer Mr. Scriabin ranks below average. His weak, dry tone, his hard wooden touch, meager and mechanical, devoid almost of all nuance, made the piano sound insignificant against the accompanying voices of the orchestra.

The best movement is the first, since there is some semblance of order in it. The best part is the orchestration, which is beautiful and moreover, individual.

Ironically, some three months later on 12 March, 1899, Scriabin and Safonoff playing the Concerto for the first time in Moscow, met immediate success and the friendliest of press. Engel, for instance, reviewing for the *Russian Gazette* said, "Putting aside the countless excellences of the piano (especially the last movement, which is wonderfully constructed, and the theme and variations), it must be said how continually interesting the orchestration is . . . written by a master."

Prince Sergei Trubetskoi (1856–1905), music critic for the *Courier*, hailed the Concerto with a praiseful and thoughtful critique:

Scriabin's originality is not counterfeit. He already has definite artistic physiognomy, his own manner, his own style . . . Nor is he excessively complex . . . The compound meters, unusual filigree and pianistic intricacy, the difficulty in the music and its elaboration are neither artificial nor fabricated. He does not mask a lack of content with these, but rather, they issue as a natural result of musical ideas asking to be formulated and expressed in such truly complicated and complex concepts.

44

WHEN SCRIABIN went to SPb in November 1898, he brought a surprise present—a peace-offering—for Belaieff: a perfectly completed orchestral prelude, of seventy-six measures, nine pages, and three minutes playing time. For this miniature he still required a full scale orchestra of winds, brass, and strings. The form was simple, A B A and coda. The dynamics even simpler, soft-to-loud-to-soft, opening out and retracting, as if two cones were placed face to face. A *cantabile* in E minor hovers, scattering melodic fragments, trills, tremolos over ingenuously sweet harmonies of dominant sevenths with raised and lowered fifths.

Scriabin wrote this piece in total secrecy and without a word of advice. His Mitrosha was ecstatic. Rimsky came for tea one afternoon, played it over at the piano and thought it "delightful, wreathed in piquant harmonies and not badly orchestrated . . ." Scriabin wrote Vera happily, ". . . something pleasant to tell you. Except for some *divisi*, there was not a single mistake in the instrumentation of my prelude. It is now being copied and will be performed on the 5th . . ."

Belaieff decided that "prelude" was inappropriate for an orchestral title. They agreed on *Rêverie* in French, but further discussion ensued over the translation into Russian—*mechty* (daydreams) or *gryozy* (musings). Belaieff chose *mechty*. Both continued to say prelude. It was published as Op. 24.

Scriabin wrote, "Imagine my joy, the piece sounds very well. At the rehearsal on 1 December Korsakoff was *so* sweet. He had each section go through its parts separately and spent a whole hour on it . . ." *Rêverie* was immensely well received and Rimsky had to repeat it. The piece scarcely began before it was over, and the audience was taken completely by surprise. Immediately before the *Rêverie* (and after a spirited reading of Balakirev's *Tamara*) Scriabin played two Op. 8 études, six preludes, and an impromptu. When Safonoff conducted *Rêverie* in Moscow, 13 March, 1899, *RMG* wrote merely, ". . . not bad for a mood miniature. Felicitous sounding and charmingly orchestrated, but a nothing. It takes no hold. It leaves the memory as soon as the concert ends."

The visit to St. Petersburg was also financially gratifying. Scriabin won the Glinka prize again, this year for the Op. 8 études and the Op. 10 impromptus—500 rubles.

Scriabin writes faithfully whenever he is separated from Vera, and this correspondence (carefully saved by her) tells an extraordinary history of a marriage. Scriabin's inventiveness in finding diminutives surpasses even the characteristic Russian aptitude. He calls her by a different name in each letter—Vushka, Vushenka, Vushik, Vushunochka, Kulyochek (little sack), Zhuchenka, Zhuchka (little black dog), Kroshka (little crumb), variations on *zhuk* associating her with the lucky May Beetle—so lucky to Russians that a popular chocolate is shaped like one. When Vera is pregnant he calls her Lastochka or "little swallow." Only when he writes plain "Vera" or heads his letters "My good one," do we know the contents will be ominous.

He also gives himself an incredible number of nicknames, special only between the two of them—Tushka, Tukych, Tukenka, Tukik, Tuchkina, and finally, after Rimma's birth, "Papa Tuka." Only towards the end of the marriage does he sign himself "Sasha," and when he is angry, he omits his signature altogether. After the fiasco of the Petersburg concerto, he writes, "You know, they hurt your little Tuka by writing naughtily of him in the newspapers. You must comfort him. Write and tell him that it doesn't matter . . ." Sometimes he uses "we" instead of "I," as if he were literally plural personalities. Sometimes too everything is made affectionately small—"letterette," "worrylet," and "doggy-faces" meaning his "children."

His first letter is a reproach. He is in Moscow with Rimma (she is Rinochka, Rimusha, Rusinova, Runushka, "little face-maker," "suckling pig," etc.). Vera has left for the Nizhny concert. On 13 November, 1898, he writes before she has scarcely had time to arrive:

> I am very angry with you. I waited all day long for a telegram in vain. I go to bed with an uneasy heart, and probably will not sleep for hours . . . All of today has been unpleasant. My students never played so wretchedly. I even sent diligent Babchenko [Lyubov, b. 1876] out of the room. I couldn't hear her finish. I won't even speak of the rest. After the lessons, I myself left, because as you can see, I was terribly out of sorts.
>
> Lhevinne and I went to Jurgenson's to choose a piano. All they showed us were sluggish and uneven. I don't know what I'll do. And on top of this, Vushka offends me!

When we look back on a marriage, as we perforce must, as it is known to have ended in disaster, all seems bleak. Yet, there was love. His letters show it—sometimes through a veil—but it was always of a special and sickly kind. His demands for reassurance, for telegrams of safe arrivals, for writing him of herself, his worries about her health or her existence, these pleas become so repetitious in letter after letter that they almost discredit sincerity. The importance clearly was not for Vera, but for his peace of mind.

He loved her . . . "My glory, my joy . . . my treasure . . ." but again there was something spurious in their mutual and morbid dependence. He is terrified of being alone; so is she. When he goes to SPb, Aunt Ida moves in. Their letters exchange complaints, and she is like a whipping dog, who can, on occasion, bite back.

Often too, he writes her good, kindly and wise advice. From Petersburg, he says, "Don't be bored, my own, my little piece of gold. Work harder at music, occupy yourself with our little angel, and time will pass so fast you will not notice it . . ." At the same time he wickedly pretends to invite her to Petersburg—"We have the money now . . . Why not?"—knowing full well that she is preparing a Schumann Quintet for a chamber concert of the RMO and cannot possibly leave the city.

On her side too, Vera is capable of cruelty. When Scriabin traipses off to Europe in 1900 she simply neglects getting him a sleeping compartment on the train. "I didn't sleep a wink all night. You disobedient little pig. I told you to get a sleeper!" Or, on 28 December, 1904, he is in Paris and she in Switzerland, and he writes: "You're cruel not to want to send me a photograph of the children! You might just have *one* taken!"

One valuable aspect of these letters to Vera is their gossip. Picture, for example, 23 November, 1898, in Petersburg at the first Belaieff evening after Scriabin's arrival. The party was particularly complicated because Safonoff and Arensky were meeting for the first time in four years after their falling out.

> Mitrofan is very pleased with Tukynka. We chatted until breakfast, and I went to bed and slept until 5. I didn't feel well until evening. From 5 on guests had already begun to arrive, all people you would know. The last was, naturally, Safonoff, and horrors! he had to sit in the only free place, next to Arensky. I sat right across from them and could see everything. The first minutes were really terrible. They greeted each other coldly without looking at each other. Later they started talking. Over dinner there were a few somewhat successful witticisms.

> After dinner as usual the party broke into groups. Glazunov went to the drawing room to play his ballet, and Korsakoff, Sokolov, Safonoff, Liadov and I remained at table. You can imagine how the Petersburghers let loose on our old gun butt. Safonoff justified himself as best he could, but at the end of it all, he had to agree with the others.

> I must run. I'm going to see Kolya, whom I haven't yet apprised of my arrival.

Tushka plays on Vushka's interest in the highborn. In another letter he announces casually, "Tomorrow I shall probably go to Grand Duke Konstantin's palace." (This Romanov, Konstantin Konstantinovich [1858–1915] was intellectual, a poet, translator and, because of his musical inclinations, Vice-President of the RMO Board.) "He likes my music very much. He asked for all the music I played at the concert . . . If I play at his palace I'll be well paid . . ." Some while later, he observes in another letter that the "Grand Duke purchased copies of all my compositions yesterday. I don't know how he likes them or whether he will invite me to play. Yesterday at the palace I gave a good account of myself socially. This news must please you and that's why I apprise you of it."

45

NINE OF Belaieff's intimate friends decided to commemorate his nameday of 1898 with a massive, round-robin string quartet on an old Russian song, "How wearying the nights, and boring they are . . ." Each wrote a variation: Artsybushev, Witohl, Blumenfeld, Evald, Winkler, Sokolov, and the familiars Rimsky, Liadov, and Glazunov. Scriabin early in March had promised to join this distinguished assembly in homage to Belaieff.

On 22 December, Belaieff has to remind Scriabin. He answers, "I spent all day yesterday looking for the theme, but in vain. It must have fallen out of my pocket somewhere. Be so kind and ask Liadov to write it out again and send it to me." A month later Belaieff threatens: "I am not willing to wait another week for the variation . . ." and Scriabin sends it. Belaieff published it second after the theme, in a significant place of honor.

Again Belaieff has reason to be cross: "How is it possible for you to dawdle so long over a little four-hand transcription of your prelude. Either you've made some mistake or you're just procrastinating. Putting it off from day to day only holds up my printing it . . ." By way of apology, Scriabin writes that he is "completely embroiled in composing," but he does not reveal what. He adds that he is "being pulled hither and thither from this thing to that . . ." meaning his various Conservatory obligations. "I have completely lost my wits, and sit for 12 hours on end working. I am exhausted . . ." Belaieff blasts back, "If you've lost your wits, rush to the nearest police station, for you'll certainly never find them by yourself."

Belaieff asks Winkler, who needs money, to do the piano arrangement of *Rêverie* and he tells Scriabin he will deduct it from his fee. Is Belaieff spitefully ignoring Vera? Belaieff asks Goldenweizer to play the Concerto at one of his concerts, but he declines on the grounds that it is "too soon after the composer has played."

Scriabin's congenital absent-mindedness and carelessness, so tormenting to Belaieff (and to himself), should have extended to his Conservatory duties, a labor he could not have liked. However, they did not. Pavel Kon (Paul de Conne, b. 1874), a professor at the Vienna Conservatory, wrote to the Petersburg pianist, Sergei Bartenev (1863–1930), a revealing note in May, 1899, about Scriabin the pedagogue: "Safonoff asked me to participate in the Conservatory examinations and Scriabin asked me to visit his class and hear his students. I spent four most pleasurable hours and I am convinced that he is a solid teacher, attending to his work with great learning and love. I almost think him the best professor at the Moscow Conservatory..." One day Scriabin will also be invited to teach at the Vienna Conservatory, an honor which, despite dire need, he will reject.

Scriabin had twelve pupils his first year—1898–1899—of whom one, completing four years at the Conservatory, Natalya Margariti (b. 1878), formerly with Schloezer, graduated. Scriabin coached her diligently. Her program, performed at 9:00 A.M. on 22 May, consisted of the Grieg Concerto played with full orchestra, followed by the D# minor Prelude and Fugue from *The Well-Tempered Clavier*, Chopin's A flat major Impromptu, a mazurka by Liadov, and the C# minor "Moment Musical" of Schubert. Scriabin assisted helpfully at the rehearsal the night before.

In addition, since he was juniormost professor on the faculty, he was assistant examiner and during the school's final week, every day for nine hours, he listened to and passed on the entire roster of piano students at the Conservatory. The following year his teaching load increased to twenty-one students, five of whom were to graduate at the end of the 1899–1900 semester. During the week from 26 May to 9 June, 1899, he also agrees to be on the artistic advisory committee for the centennial of Pushkin's birth. These preparations and celebrations delay his summer holidays in the country.

As early as February, 1899, Scriabin has complained to Belaieff: "I can write nothing good about myself. I scream the whole time to keep things from interfering with my work. I have nothing finished except a little Andante for string orchestra [published in 1956 by Muzgiz, Moscow].

I'll send it with some other things. The Conservatory all the same, of course, keeps me from working, mainly by preventing me from concentrating. I hear too much music written by others . . ."

In April, he sends off nine dry mazurkas. Belaieff likes them. Short pieces sold well in the music stores. Scriabin, however, withholds the Andante, because, he says, it is not good enough. Belaieff invites him to take a steamer trip with him around Lake Ladoga, north of Petersburg and connecting the Neva River with the Gulf of Finland. Vera is pregnant again, and Scriabin declines. "How I regret not seeing you this spring. What pleasure to take a boat trip!" he writes on 20 May, 1899, "I have begun adding to the Symphonic Allegro, but otherwise I have no irons in the fire at the moment, nor do I anticipate any new opuses coming from me." And with this bold declaration, he asks Belaieff if he might have an extra 200 or 300 rubles—"I don't need them yet"—to tide him over the summer months when his earnings from the Conservatory cease. Belaieff says yes, most generously, and without argument.

Scriabin and Vera with their little face-making angel leave Moscow for the cooling country.

✍ XIII ✍

TWO SYMPHONIES

46

Scriabin now earned his living in winter to support his family. In summer, joining the ranks of ordinary Russian composers, he was free to do his own work, composing. In May of 1899 he rented a house in Podolsk, but at the last minute Vera wanted to be closer to her friend Nadezhda (now Konyusa). They took a remoter *dacha* in the little village of Darino, near Odintsovo, a junction town forty miles from Moscow along the Brest railway line to Europe.

Scriabin wrote Belaieff on 18 June, 1899, that he has dashed off a prelude (Op. 27, No. 1, another *patético*). He will send it with a mate, No. 2—a page-long, gliding, hovering, slow mood piece, like warm mist lying close over soft grass—exactly a year later. He closed off handedly: "Now I am working on a big composition for orchestra." Toward the end of summer on 21 September, he writes, "I am orchestrating a symphony; it has gone remarkably fast, but I cannot yet give the date I will finish."

His next letter to Belaieff reads, "I have composed a symphony in six parts with an end section. I am orchestrating it." In addition, he has completed an étude, nest egg of that miraculous set of eight, Op. 42 which will not hatch until 1903. "Oh yes, I forgot to tell you I have a Fourth Sonata for piano in G# minor, but it still has a long way to go." Part of the route is into the key of F# major.

Since Rome three years before, Scriabin had been toying with orchestral music. This time the results are more fruitful, and characteristically, Scriabin is obsessed with secrecy. "Please, I beg you, speak to no one about the symphony just yet. I will send it to you first thing, and I don't want to touch anything else while I am working on it." When it is finished (next year) he is in such hurry he does not even copy it in ink.

The Concerto nudged Scriabin into writing for orchestra. His exposure to symphonies at the Conservatory stimulated him too. Even Vera's chamber music-making affected his sense of ensemble away from the self-indulgence of the salon solo. The little trial *Rêverie* encouraged him further. His work poured from him, and before he could staunch its flow, he had finished six movements instead of the conventional three.

I   Lento   (E major)
II Allegro Dramatico   (C minor)
III Lento   (B major)
IV Vivace   (Scherzo)   (C major)
V   Allegro   (E minor)
VI Andante   (Tenor and Mezzo-soprano soloists)
            and Fugue (Chorus) (E major)

Lev Konyus recalled the love Scriabin bore this piece. "All summer long he kept saying this was his best music yet. He would write a measure and rush to the piano to make certain the sound was exactly as he wanted it. He took the score to bed with him at night. He began the instrumentation of certain sections while the music itself was still composing itself."

Skipping ahead in the narrative, let us observe the events concerning the actual performances of the First Symphony. Belaieff scheduled the premiere for 11 November, 1900, within a year of the first draft. Liadov conducted it without the finale of singers and chorus. (The SPb choral society had refused to sing gratis.) At rehearsal Scriabin was appalled by Liadov's "bad and flabby conducting . . . the tempi are all so slow," but still, he rejoices that "the symphony sounds excellently." He spent that evening telling Liadov how it should go. This late tact earned him a reproach the following year when his second symphony is performed. Belaieff wrote, "Please do not come only on the first day of rehearsal as you did for the First. Come a day or two ahead of time and tell Liadov exactly how you want it done beforehand . . ."

The symphony was a failure in SPb, eliciting boos and catcalls. Nevertheless, *RMG* (1900, No. 47, unsigned) reviewed it kindly, although Scriabin could only read damnation in the words:

We were dissatisfied with the composer's first attempt at the orchestra (the Concerto) and were therefore somewhat prejudiced at the prospect of hearing a symphony from him. Fortunately we were disappointed in a *pleasant* way.

> The Symphony is better, clearer, brighter and makes a most sympathetic impression on the listener . . . the contents are gratifying, artistic, and interesting. May his next symphony—even if it too is steeped in Wagner and Tchaikovsky —be no worse!

Scriabin in distress wrote Vera the day after this performance: "You can't imagine my agitation. To my shame, I must admit that I haven't myself in control yet. Now every vileness in life affects me! But all this shall be as I will it to be—Great! It is much comfort to me that fate has also sent me many admirers at the same time as it has served me this failure with the public at large . . ." He signed the letter as coming from "Your unwhimpering one."

Safonoff, immediately he had perused the manuscript at the end of 1899, wrote Scriabin, "I cannot begin to convey to you my rapture over your new symphony . . . it is divine creation." He conducted it in Moscow on 16 March, 1901, with combined choirs from the Conservatory and the Russian Choral Society. The soloists were the well-known mezzo-soprano Vera Zvantseva-Petrova (1876–1944) of the operatic theater, and tenor A. Shubin. "Safonoff had the look of a man opening a treasure and displaying it. He read the score with extraordinary zeal," Sabaneeff, who was present, recalled. At this rehearsal Scriabin kept running up excitedly and pulling on Safonoff's coattails and making various suggestions. But the results were no better than in SPb. The performance was another disaster; the audience again was cold; and the reviews were critical. Ivan Lipaev (1865–1942), one of the best *RMG* critics wrote:

> As is well known, Mr. Scriabin's symphony had slight success in SPb when it was played there. It was little more welcomed here, although the composer was applauded. The reason is the complexity of this brain child. The average man is not prepared for it.
>
> The first movement is beautiful on the surface and excellent in its quietude . . . However in the whole symphony there are only two variations of mood, and although they are skillfully wrought for the orchestra, like César Franck, the whole thing is a little monotonous . . .

On the evening of the Moscow concert, the public was large but the applause small. Scriabin was summoned to the stage only once. Kashkin, surprisingly, who had written an advance article in the *Moscow News* praising the symphony, now on actually hearing it, turned caustic: "Mr. Scriabin has composed a symphony without considering the orchestra . . . the mood of all six sections is monotonous."

Scriabin was again upset and saw only the bad. In his apartment next day, he threw a scene. Engel gathered one eyewitness report: "He beat his breast, and with a tearing cry said, 'So that's the way they want it! So be it!! If only I keep healthy, I'll show them! I'll show them I still have some things to say!!'"

The First Symphony now sounds frail. It is not a symphony, but a paper-thin suite structured on flimsy bits and pieces. Despite this, its thematic structure is rather formal. There are passages of subtle beauty, foretastes of the mystically mature author. Still it is laconic. Its short developments and expansions sound like musical shorthand.

The opening measures are eerie. The dark and cold second movement states a war between high violins and deep cellos. The brasses exhort, emphasize, and arbitrate. The third movement sounds of lassitude after struggle, surge upon surge, lift and fall, rising and sinking of melodies. The scherzo is delicate, full of fleetness, a swift careening in 9/8 time. The orchestration includes a glockenspiel. The fifth movement reiterates the drama of struggle.

At last, the sixth movement appears in a fragrance of Scriabin's harmonies. The mezzo-soprano and tenor sing antiphonally. (Their melodic line is somewhat wooden.) This evolves into a massive rejoicing in the chorus, a festival of art triumphant. To express this, Scriabin composed a fugue of iron consistency.

Contemporaries were quick to spot the finale's weakness. One called it "a Tausig exercise." Another sardonically praised its "extemporaneousness." The rumor spread that Rachmaninoff, however, had remarked after it that, "I thought Scriabin a simple swine, but it seems he's turned himself into a composer after all." Rachmaninoff disclaimed saying it.

The finale is Scriabin's own "Hymn to Art," and acts as text and program for the whole symphony. Its rhyming iambuses are as conventional as the schoolbook, glee club music which accompanies the words. The vocabulary is significant: "radiant," "dreams," "vision," "festival," "magical," "powerful," "soul," (all words which have a special import). The belief in the magic power of music is unshakable. It ends with trumpet calls, the soloists and chorus:

> Come, all peoples everywhere
> Let us sing praise to Art!
> Praise Art!
> Glorious Forever!

47

RETURNING TO the Conservatory year in which the First Symphony was being composed and readied for performance, an imbroglio rocked musicians all the way from Moscow to SPb. Safonoff was in its very eye. His antagonist was Georgy Konyus, fired from the Conservatory. Belaieff, eaten up with curiosity, asked Scriabin for full details. He perhaps worried that his protégé was involved. Scriabin replied clearly, accurately and fully on 26 October, 1899:

> Regarding the Konyus affair I *SIGNED* nothing, was not present during the Artistic Committee's sessions, and took no part whatsoever in any of it at all.
>
> Now, the following is *BETWEEN US*. As always in fights, both sides think they are right but as a matter of fact both are to blame. Konyus hates Safonoff and being impossible as a person, he has systematically pestered Safonoff for 3 years with petitions and has even complained to the Artistic Committee itself. I believe he had some legal grounds, but I cannot judge this since I don't know how the rules of the Conservatory work.
>
> The wrangle started over whether non-special students should have to take compulsory courses in instrumentation. As you can see, the subject is of no consequence whatsoever. However, Konyus and Taneieff disagree fundamentally with Safonoff on this matter. Taneieff said in the middle of an Artistic Committee meeting that it was impossible to teach under the existing compulsory rules. Safonoff cited tradition and stuck to his guns. The argument grew more heated and each side got more and more angry and disputatious.
>
> Konyus complained to the Committee, to the Direction, and even to the Central Board about Safonoff at every opportunity.
>
> On top of everything, Konyus pounced on Safonoff every chance he got. Once, he started lighting into him in front of me, but I stopped him saying that I subscribed to friendship in the ideal.

To my amazement Taneieff has not kept his nose clean in all this mess. It may be he is only angry, nothing more. Did you read his letter in the *Moscow Gazette*? Safonoff and Konyus will never be able to work under the same roof again, that's for sure; but I cannot, not by any stretch of my mind or with my hand near my heart, say that I approve of the *way* Konyus is being got rid of. The plan was drawn up asking for his dismissal, but those who signed it have no moral right at all on their side. They did it only to get in good with Safonoff.

My conscience bothers me that I did not study the matter in detail and go to the Artistic Committee myself to voice an opinion. But I must tell you that before I took on this professorship, I told Safonoff that I would *only* teach my classes and not meddle in any matters concerning the running of the Conservatory or get caught in the intrigues I heard about. I told him this would take too much time, and I haven't enough of that as it is. Also, it's no joke. Best to keep busy with one's music.

"Friendship in the ideal" ended Scriabin's long and good relations with Konyus and with Taneieff. He sided with Safonoff, right or wrong. Arensky, like Belaieff, had written for the inside story, and Taneieff replied to him, "From the moment I took up cudgels on behalf of Konyus, and incurred Safonoff's wrath thereby, Scriabin cut me off clean as a knife. He never comes around me anymore . . ."

Again Scriabin receives the Glinka Prize. In 1899 he is awarded 500 rubles for the Preludes, Op. 11 and Impromptus, Op. 12. His fame grew apace. The editor of the great compendium of musicians, Riemann, invited him to submit his *curriculum vitae* for his *Musiklexikon*.

In January, 1900, although Vera is momentarily expecting their second baby, Scriabin goes to Petersburg to be with Belaieff. Ostensibly he has to present him formally with the first finished manuscript of the First Symphony. "For heaven sakes, if there's the slightest indication of the awaited event, telegraph me, and I'll rush right on back," he writes her. "Belaieff is very sweet to me as always and spoils me so. I played the symphony for Liadov who liked the introduction and the finale with the chorus. He says the other parts are very complicated for him and he needs to hear them several times. Certain places please him (nearly all of these are themes). I haven't been able to work yet, since we play cards here . . . Tomorrow Belaieff is lending me his horse and carriage, so I can go calling."

Two days later he tells Vera that he received her postcard, calling it "shorter than a prelude by Tukynka . . ." It seems he might have caught cold. His throat was sore, and towards evening he ran a temperature. He stayed in bed for a day, and resorted to his own massage cure. It worked. Scriabin dreaded colds as others fear smallpox, but they reflect a psychic or psychosomatic pattern in his life. He has a cold every time he auditions a new composition. (When the First Symphony was to be performed later in the year, he wrote Vera: "What a hole Petersburg is! Merely look at it and you've already caught cold!") This time his illness prevented him from playing his symphony for Rimsky and Glazunov, who came that evening especially to hear it. He closed this letter saying "Liadov sends you greetings, but he's a terrible interruption. He hangs around the whole time and never once stops talking . . ."

Scriabin returned to Moscow. Belaieff is angry because Scriabin won't answer about arranging the symphony for four hands. He commissions Winkler again. Scriabin apologizes. Yes, Winkler's terms are acceptable. He has not written because he has not left the house a single time. On 6 February, 1900, "the wife gave me a little daughter. Praise God, all went well." They christened her Elena, and nicknamed her "Lyalya."

Two months later, April, 1900, Vera is pregnant for the third time. Scriabin mentions to Belaieff he is not composing, because he is "busy at the Conservatory." A series of angry exchanges begin. One is that money matters—checks, receipts, acknowledgments, and statements—are now handled entirely by Fyodor Groes, treasurer of the firm, so Belaieff will not be bothered. The First Symphony is bandied about. Belaieff says there are passages which are "simply too difficult." He sends a revised arrangement of the second movement, "so that it can be played." Scriabin replies that if Safonoff says it is unplayable as he has written it, then he will yield, "even though the composition will suffer. Those measures you mention are only *difficult*. There's nothing to get emotional over. They *are* difficult now, but 5 years from now they will be easy. Don't forget my piano pieces are also difficult."

Belaieff sends Scriabin a most petty letter on 22 April. "Well, little brother you've certainly come a cropper now!" Rimsky and Liadov have discovered that the vocal parts of the First Symphony are *both* too high and too low. However, Scriabin finds some singers who have no difficulty with the range. Still the score was printed with an alternative note for one high B flat.

Scriabin's mind, freed by the First Symphony, dreams of future projects. He conceives a symphony which is to start only with voices, then turn into a chorus, and finally become a purely orchestral composition. Belaieff's commonsensical reply is dated 5 May, 1900:

> I have decided to be forthright, to say something rather unpleasant to you . . . I will *not* publish such a composition. Forgive me for being so profane, but I must also say that I think your duet and final chorus pretend to be a 9th symphony and it's only your first. *Now* you want to write a 10th, beginning with voices and ending with an orchestra. I suppose your 11th will have a vocal number in the middle. Your saying emphatically that Mme. Polyakova found the vocal part *very easy* does not convince me for one second. I trust the experience of Nik. And. [Korsakoff] more than I do any Mme. Polyakova . . . Your symphony will be performed without the finale, and because of the chorus, it will probably rarely be played *in entirety*. What can one expect from such a composition which cannot even *be contemplated* without the assistance of voices? It will lie on the shelf as we have seen with the works of so many other composers. Write for the piano, for the orchestra, for voices, or for other instruments, but don't plunge into such a complex composition which demands huge musical resources which cost so much money.

> You've known the orchestra just a short time, and now, suddenly, without testing yourself in voice and orchestra, you swing from the *Rêverie* which was as short as the beak of a bird, and you dream up a huge composition. In it you make a mistake in the voice range right off. I tell you a soprano is not a mezzo-soprano. Such things are all right for geniuses, perhaps, but my friend, without denying your enormous talent, I rather see you as something less grand . . .

Scriabin answered with frigid acquiescence the day he receives the letter, 7 May. He cannot risk taking offense; so he pretends obtuseness: "You have said nothing unkind. What would be strange, to say the least, would be if I aspired to make you do something disagreeable for you or not to your liking. Of course you must publish only what you wish."

Belaieff's harsh words diverted Scriabin from his symphonic projects momentarily, but by 16 June he wrote Vera (not Belaieff) that he has begun a vaster project, "composing a little on an opera."

Belaieff's stomach ailment forces him to go to Europe for treatment. He invites Scriabin to accompany him. Scriabin decides to give a recital in Paris where the World International Industrial Fair is being held that summer of 1900. "It would be of great value for me to advertise my name now," he explains more to himself than to Vera. Vera and the two girls go to Nizhny for a long summer with her father. Her parting words are, "Don't overtip the Europeans . . . Avert your eyes when you give a servant a gratuity. Then you won't see their sour faces." Tuka promises. "Little Papka" waves goodbye to her. Alone in Moscow, Scriabin sees Buyukly, who sees him off. "Vsevolod wouldn't quit my side for a second . . ." he writes Vera. When Kashkin asked to see the score of Scriabin's symphony for his advance review, Buyukly the errand boy brought it.

Scriabin was abroad all of June and July, and he felt remorseful towards his family. "My dear, I'm so very sorry to have come alone. I'll take you traveling yet, my joy, my soul. I still haven't shown you Switzerland. I think of you everyday and can't forgive myself that all you little doggy-faces aren't with me."

48

VYUSHKA AND Tushka corresponded cheerfully during their separation in summer of 1900. "How are you, my little angel?" he wrote on 20 June, happy to be apart from her, ". . . We arrived at 4 in the morning and spent an eternity at customs. The Germans were too stingy to add a train so we virtually had to sit in each others' lap. Today I have been sightseeing like a crazy man . . ." He spends two days in Berlin, takes a little train to Grünewald, a colony of villas fringing the Havel lakes outside the city, goes to the Waxworks Museum, loses his umbrella, but consoles himself with a superstition that "it means long life . . ." Mindful of his career, he pays formal calls on Hermann Wolff (1845–1902), concert manager and publisher of the newspaper Neuer Berliner Zeitung ("He's terribly nice and promises me a Berlin recital . . ."), but Josef Hofmann is out of town taking the thermal waters. When he leaves Berlin the hotel overcharges him (as always with Russians), "But I kept my promise and did not overtip . . ."

Scriabin and Belaieff stayed in Paris near the Trocadéro at the Hotel du Longchamps. "I am directly under the roof, the 5th floor (the Russian seventh) and pay 6 francs a day for room alone!" They rushed off to the Industrial Fair first day and took in the art, music, and machinery exhibits.

"The Russian pavilion is pretty bad, to my regret." He contacted Dyo-mes. "You can't imagine how sweet he is. He's going to buy some con-certs for us in the provinces—Orléans, Lyons, Rouen, etc." These "pur-chases," a routine way of launching unknown artists in Europe, were never made.

Scriabin looked up his Paris friends. "I am doing no music at all and feel the better for it." His chum Shaikevich, now married with a four-month-old baby, "is just the same as ever ..." Gustave Doret has become "an important personage. He's conductor of a new symphony—a sort of third musical center in Paris." Saint-Saëns was president, Gabriel Fauré (1845–1924) vice-president, and the secretaries were Raoul Pugno (1852–1914), pianist, and Louis Bourgault Ducoudray (1840–1910), music his-tory professor at the Paris Conservatoire—all very impressive.

Scriabin also encounters numbers of Russians on holiday: Nikolai Kirshbaum, chairman of the Nizhny RMO; Nikolai Shishkin of the Moscow Conservatory; Boromir Korsov (1845–1920), baritone at the Bolshoi; and Michel Déline (1851–1914), whose real name was Mikhail Ashkenazy, an expatriate living in Nice, translator of Russian operas into French and correspondent for Petersburg papers.

"Can you imagine who is in Paris! Today I went into the hotel restau-rant and suddenly I see Ivan Oranovsky at a table! He's so queer, so gloomy, so silent. Because he was so unhappy, I made a big fuss over him. He came to life a bit ... I shall be seeing a lot of him (unfortunately)." Oranovsky, strange, young, wealthy, followed him everywhere—to Saint Cloud by boat where they look for a cheap place to live, only to realize that all they saved would be spent on transportation back into the city.

Ten days before the 10 July recital (mentioned earlier) at the Salle de Journal, Scriabin began practicing. Every day he trudged to Erard. Oranovsky tagged along. "My little child, don't worry. All is going well. I am preparing well ..." Simultaneously, he becomes eager for Vera to resume her career. Every letter carries advice: "Have you begun working? Look sharp! No laziness." "Glad you are practicing. Do not weaken!" He wanted Vera to enlarge her repertoire and concentrate: "Learn music *all* the way through ... *to the end.*"

He enquired about her father. "Any clashes yet?" However, he refers warmly and thoughtfully to his daughters. "You don't mention Lyalya.

Is it possible that you don't love her as much as Rimma? Just wait until I return. *I'll* cuddle her!" "I regret the children have no picture of me there . . . I would be dismayed if Rimma doesn't recognize me." "Is everything all right with the children? I suspect not. Take them outside more, to get them strong and let them profit from the summer . . ."

Out of homesickness he misses his own family, although he has turned over to Vera all burden of connection with them: "Aren't you writing to *mamotchka*? Do you know anything about my papa? Tell me about my aunt and the *babushki*. I was so wicked to leave everybody. Not a soul has written me a single word . . ." Again and again he asks for photographs of the children. In the last week of July, he receives one—with Vera. His only reaction: "What an awful picture of you!"

Dyomes buoyed Scriabin about the recital, so he wrote: "I am beginning to think my Paris trip will have fine results. Who knows? I might bring you back a million." However, his report of 11 July after the concert began: "Everything conspired against me financially." Although the hall, tickets, and programs cost 200 francs (a third of what they paid for their 1898 recital) and despite Shaikevich and Oranovsky rallying around and buying several tickets, only 240 francs worth of seats were actually sold. "My, you can't imagine how many free tickets one distributes in Paris!"

The weather was fine, "a pleasant 62° and just perfect for light playing, but it kept many people away, even with free tickets." The concert was a success in the artistic sense. The critics praised the Second Sonata highly. Many people came backstage to congratulate him. He himself deplored the fact that he "smeared the last page of the Polonaise, and it didn't go well . . .

"Dyomes is a swine. You know he's horribly lazy. Even his wife warned me of this. He's become even fatter and can barely move. He puts off going to Blondelle [General Manager of Erard] every day, simply because he can't bring himself to . . . But I did a good thing by the recital in Paris. The results for us will be very important . . ."

Scriabin went to Zurich, where Belaieff will rejoin him. He settled in Bendlikon, a tiny village ten minutes away, to wait. Oranovsky has followed.

He wrote Vera with some sarcasm, saying, "Your friend Belaieff arrives in 2 days," and later he cruelly exaggerated the wonderful time with Mitrosha: "We played around the whole time, gorging ourselves, taking trips to the mountains. The only flaw is the unbearable heat. It's stifling even high up . . ."

Finally on 26 July, 1900: "Tuka has spent everything he has and now must return to his homeland. If only I had some money. Tuka, however, would still come back to you." But he does not immediately. Instead, he joins his aunt at Uncle Nil's. Scriabin wants to ready a new apartment in Moscow for work in September. Someone had found for them a commodious and fashionable one in the Arbat district of nobles' mansions, ancient homes, and elegant residences. Theirs, however, was inexpensive: Apartment 57, in the Girsha (later Tito) Building at the corner of Merzlya-kovsky and Khlebny lanes. They will have to look for furniture, choose draperies, and set up the children's room for three instead of two.

Vera, however, first insists that he come in August to Nizhny, to fetch her (another difficult pregnancy), and pay his respects to her father. He complied. At last back in Moscow, he wrote Belaieff, "I am busy putting the new apartment in proper order. You can't imagine how boring it is to be in the throes of moving and unable to work. I hope we stay here for several years. It's more comfortable than all the others . . ." He will remain there until spring of 1904 when he leaves Russia for a long, five-year, self-imposed exile.

49

SCRIABIN TOOK on a new job to help ends meet—Inspector of Music at St. Catherine's Institute. His salary was 50 rubles a month. His duties were to teach a few young ladies "compulsory piano" once a week, and at the end of the year to hear some 350 girls play the piano. Also, in 1900–1901 the Conservatory proposed him for the Artistic Committee. In addition, he accepted another post—board member for the Moscow RMO concert series. When he left for that tumultuous First Symphony performance in Petersburg, 11 November, 1900, a number of persons were inconvenienced by his absence.

His chief concern was Safonoff. He begged Vera to smooth any ruffled feelings. When Vera answered that all was well, he wrote, "Bless Vassily for not being angry." He blames his delay in returning on Belaieff. "Little Bug, what can I do about Mitrofan? He does not give me a moment's freedom! He says that at home I have crying children and lessons to give. Here, I can rest quietly, far better than there. He would not let me leave on Monday . . . He says he will write you an affidavit attesting my good behavior, but we are late now for the symphony concert . . . I kiss you, my glory, my love, and give my little wailers a kiss from their absent father."

While in SPb Scriabin received 500 rubles for the Glinka Prize of 1900 (Preludes, Op. 17 and the Fantasy Sonata). He also managed to enjoy himself, although he was ill and nervous, as everyone noted. And he worked—composing sixteen stanzas of his opera libretto in one day.

His particular companion at the time was Alexander Bryanchaninov (1874–1918), a friendship in the pattern of the young and wealthy scions Scriabin collected, and also one belonging to those startling contrasts with his own person and personality. Bryanchaninov, who would never leave Scriabin's life, was according to Sabaneeff "coarse, short, thickset, a very rich gentleman, a big landowner, and square." He had vast lands in Pskov Province, and later he would marry a "Serene Highness" Gorchakova (daughter of the Prince Gorchakov who was Nikolai's classmate at the School of Oriental Languages, she signed her letters "Bryanchaninova née . . ."). He became a strange mixture of Slavophilia and Anglomania, and edited and published a progressive, mystically bent, intellectual and artistic journal, New Link. He was also, later, president of the patriotically Russian society, "Slavic Unity." Before World War I, he will move to England and until his death write on things Russian for the English and affairs of England for Russia.

In SPb at this time Scriabin gossiped with Vera about him: "Bryanchaninov has rented a studio and furnished it lavishly. He continues to try one thing after another in the manner of a true dilettante. Now he has gone and written a drama and given me a copy to read. Imagine my embarrassment. All the same, he is a capital fellow, a fine one, he is!"

Scriabin at last revealed to Belaieff that he is writing both an opera and a second symphony, and provoked another rebuke. Belaieff, however, contained himself until the Nikolaevsky railway separated them. Unlike earlier in the year, he now breaks the glass between Scriabin's inner world and outer reality. Scriabin in fury throws away this Belaieff letter of 20

November, and waits until 7 December to answer. The wound is open, and he begins, stingingly enough, by pointing out that Safonoff had been able to secure a chorus for his First Symphony without difficulty.

"I am most grateful that you write me so openly to tell me your frank opinion of me. But I must admit that I am surprised at your desire to undermine my courage and my faith in myself. *WITHOUT THESE* it is utterly impossible for me to function. You say that I want to try my hand in all different areas of art only because I long to equal and surpass others. This simply is not true. I do everything sincerely, and only that which I feel myself drawn to do."

His pain was so keen that he withdrew from Belaieff. He composed a major Fantasia without telling him a word. Some Moscow friends heard it and reported to Belaieff, who urged him to send it to him quickly. He lied at first, "I thought I had sent the Fantasia to you last week . . ." When Belaieff again asks, he answers coolly on 26 January, 1901, "I do not wish the Fantasia published at present. There is one episode which does not please me. I have not been able to right it yet." In a tone of ice he also asks, "Just please do not hurry me. I am now busy with other work . . ."

Nearly eight months pass stubbornly before Scriabin writes again. He does not even send the usual thank-you note for the 100 rubles which he continued to receive (from Groes). The 1,000 ruble payment for the First Symphony worked off much of his accumulated advances, and finally he dispatched the Fantasia without even a covering letter. Belaieff liked the music, a continuation of the Allegro Appassionatea and Concert Allegro. It is massively full of technique and pyrotechnics, soaring themes, resounding chords. The Fantasia, Op. 28 pleases the virtuoso and is today one of Scriabin's most likeable compositions. Its turgid and pompous flaws can be overlooked.

Goldenweizer introduced it with dazzling aplomb at a concert on 11 November, 1907. Scriabin himself never played it. He even forgot it. Sabaneeff tells how once in Scriabin's apartment he began idly strumming through its central theme at the piano.

"Who wrote that? It sounds familiar," Scriabin called from the other room.

"It is your Fantasia."

"What Fantasia?"

They searched his worn and incomplete stocks of music to prove its existence. It was not there. Yielding to assurances that he had written it, Scriabin covered up his confusion by explaining he was always in such haste to get compositions to Belaieff he had not even time to remember them. The haste, Sabaneeff remarks, was indeed evident in the enormous number of errors in the printed version, but Scriabin had taken his time with it. It belonged to a period of hurt between two friends.

The Fantasia made peace. Then Scriabin presented Belaieff with the Second Symphony as an accomplished fact. He wrote in an inflammatory manner, but Belaieff did not burn. He dated the letter 15 September, 1901, and underneath scribbled "See how I have reformed?" He excused his long silence: "I assumed you wanted to isolate yourself for a time and have a complete rest," and as if giving lie to the lie, "if you do not believe this ask Vera. I said so to her." He announced that he devoted his summer to the symphony. "It is very long and quite complicated. It will have only 5 parts, not 6 like the 1st Symphony, but it is bigger by far ... Incidentally, I think I'd like to conduct it myself. I have always wanted to direct an orchestra; so I might as well begin studying. Even if nothing comes of this idea, why not try it once? And who knows? perhaps the devil isn't joking with me after all! Write me what your opinion is ..."

Scriabin found an amateur orchestra willing to rehearse with him on Tuesdays. Referring to Safonoff's March performance of the First Symphony, maddeningly he teases, "I would have sent you the reviews, if you were interested, but I imagined you did not want to see them."

Belaieff remained silent. In October, Rimsky visited Moscow and called on Scriabin to hear this new symphony. He liked it and even asked him to play it through for him twice. "He'll tell you in person what he thinks of it ... It takes 40 or 50 minutes. I play it on the piano faster—37 or 38 minutes. I take all the tempi faster ... I read in the *Signale für die musikalische Welt* that Nikisch wants to do my First Symphony. Can you tell me when exactly he plans this?"

Belaieff replies to the question: "Nikisch writes me that the symphony is set for January, but everything depends on whether he can get a chorus and what kind of one at that. Now, do you see the wisdom of writing a 9th?"

Two months later on 11 November, 1901, after receiving the score of the Second Symphony and considerable thought, he answered the previous request for advice:

Regarding your conducting: I suppose you have made up your mind, but if you want me to speak truthfully, I must tell you I am against it. My conviction is that a conductor must be stable in rhythm. He needs to be, so as to hold unsteady rhythms together. I have not felt this requisite rhythmicality in you. If you try it, you may get in trouble.

The concert where we've scheduled your second symphony is to consist of new works exclusively. You'd flounder if you tried to conduct and consequently, your symphony would not stand up against the others. Trust Liadov to do all the needful.

If you itch to conduct, why don't you show me that you have a gift for it? I mean, get Safonoff to let you try, even if it is only the Conservatory orchestra. Such an experiment will prove if you really can.

We'll talk about it again when you write a Third Symphony!

By this time, Scriabin had already disbanded his amateurs and forgotten them. "I am fearfully tired . . . I need diversion!!"

Belaieff turned the Second Symphony over to Liadov who studied the first movement for twelve days. His comments were half-facetious, but they also indicate how strange that music must have originally been. "What a symphony, but what kind? Only the devil knows!! Scriabin boldly stretches out his hand to clasp Richard Strauss. But gentlemen, where is the music? Decadents write like this. Help, holy toadies!! Help!!! I am overwhelmed, like Don Quixote and the shepherds. And there's still a II, III, IV and V part to go. Help!!!! After Scriabin, Wagner lisps sweetly like a suckling babe. I think I'll take leave of my senses any minute now. But where can one hide from such music? Help!"

In less jocular vein, Liadov sent the score back to Scriabin complaining of its messiness. Scriabin was so flustered at the reproof that in answering he wrote the year "1892" instead of "1901". "Fancy my naiveté, and I thought I had never sent in a neater manuscript . . ." To Belaieff, however, he shifted the blame: "I wrote it in pencil because *you* said I wrote better in pencil. The 1st Symphony was in pencil . . ."

Today, one would think it impossible to find a more inaccurate description of the Second Symphony or a more inappropriate reaction than Liadov's. However, Arensky in writing to Taneieff after the first performance in SPb 12 January, 1902, bests it: "In my opinion the program erred when it said Scriabin's 2nd 'symphony.' They should have called it 2nd 'cacophony' because it or this (with your permission I will use the word) 'composition' lacks almost all consonance. For 30 or 40 minutes' duration, silence is broken. One dissonance after another piles up without a single thought behind any of it. I can't understand why Liadov consented to conduct such rot. Glazunov almost didn't go to the concert. Rimsky-Korsakoff, when I asked him to his face, told me that he could not understand how it was possible for Scriabin to flout consonance to such degree . . . I really want to laugh at it."

Scored with drum crashes, dense harmonic distributions, swirling chromaticism, hesitancies, changes of direction, langourous pauses for breath, and an almost Sibelian continuousness of climaxes, the Second Symphony, Op. 29 is crammed with lovely pages of music. Each of its five movements, really four—Andante (C minor), Allegro (E flat major), Andante (B major), Tempestuoso (F minor), and the finale Maestoso (C major)—is in a different key, mood and time. Each section is composed in highly evolved form. The whole, for all its length and variety, is homogeneous. The musical impulse sustained throughout is a formidable, conquering antithesis of the First Symphony. It is a strange symphony, sounding derivative without really being so. An elaborate counterpoint interweaves six simultaneous melodies and hints at times an infatuation for Strauss. (Scriabin would dispute this by remarking that "unlike Strauss all *my* voices can be heard," although he did admit he found Strauss's instrumentation "interesting.")

The opening theme is dark and tragic; the second movement darts impulsively, gathers tensions of momentum; the slow third movement, onomatopoetic with melismae and fioritura passages, depicts nature; the fourth movement menaces; the end pushes and swells. Suddenly the epilogue resolves into diatonic chords of dancing triads—bold trumpets exult in close, straightforward harmony.

This finale deeply disappointed Scriabin and logic had failed him. He chose C major and the triadic tonal system for translucence. The result was nobility and force, emotion rather than vision. "Instead of the light which I needed, I got stuck with a *military parade* on my hands. But fancy, even that long ago I was seeking light in music," he once said in after-years.

Sabaneeff recounts an incident of Scriabin's sensitivity on this score. Guests are sitting round the dining table late one night in 1911, over a supper of Georgian red wine and dry cake:

I said to Scriabin that the finales of both his first two symphonies were poor. It never occurred to me that my comment would be protested. He had gone so far beyond these early works and besides, he himself was very critical of them.

It was clear however that a "critical" attitude was only permitted the composer. "You see," he said, "I wrote the finale of the First Symphony in that style for a *purpose*. I wanted something *simple*, something *international*, common to all peoples. I could have composed it like the other sections . . ."

In time for his thirtieth birthday in 1901, he won the Glinka Prize of 1,000 rubles (Opp. 14 to 18) and Vera awarded Scriabin his third daughter, Maria.

50

EUGENE GUNST dramatized the evening the first performance of the Second Symphony on 12 January, 1902, in St. Petersburg in his biography of Scriabin: ". . . deafening noise of whistles and hissing and catcalls. It was so unusual to the auditors, so daring, so madly new that they cried out and could not contain their indignation."

However, the *RMG* review was measured:

> Far and away the most interesting and important composition of the concert was the new C minor Symphony by the young Moscow composer, A. Scriabin. On the basis of a single performance, which was unsatisfactory to begin with, it is difficult to estimate . . . It has good, even powerful moments, but there is also much that is harsh and ugly. The composer shows off his dissonances and, sadly, fills his symphony with so many of them that the ear begins to hurt. But this will pass, and trust me, you can lay your hopes on Mr. Scriabin . . .

It was one thing to have his music disliked (the First), and another to have stirred up a demonstration (the Second). Scriabin was hurt, and he resorts to irony, bitterly writing Vera the following day: "Zhuchek, you have probably read in the papers about my triumph. My, my what a festival it was! Well, thank the Lord it is over. Safonoff was at the concert and will describe the performance and its reception in detail. It was more or less a repetition of before, although the applause was a little louder and 5 or 6 voices even called for the composer. Of course I did not go to the stage. But my dear, I can't describe to you how friends are taking care of me. Belaieff orders all my favorite food every day. He doesn't wake me until lunchtime. He forces me to do gymnastics, etc. He has never been so kind."

Scriabin was inconsolably hurt. He even spoke ill—one of the few times—of his *babushki* and his children. "Mitrosha asks me to stay for a few more days, and I would rather like to rest up after all the rumpus. It's so quiet here. In Moscow I've got two old grumbling lemon peels and three suckling pigs who howl all day long."

During the Petersburg visit, Scriabin receives from Belaieff an assurance of extreme importance. Scriabin decided to leave the Conservatory, since the strain of alien work had begun to show on his nerves and in his composition. He reported Belaieff's reactions to Vera: "I have some very big news. Mitrofan was very happy when I told him about leaving the Conservatory. He guarantees me 200 rubles and more, according to my needs. If I compose more he will pay in proportion to my amount of composition. He fully agrees to do whatever is necessary to enable me to leave the Conservatory as soon as possible and to devote myself exclusively to composing. What a divine person he is! I can count on him like a rock." Scriabin exuberantly adds that he is lonely without Vera, and if she sees Safonoff, she is to lie and say that he is detained "on *business*." If she needs money she is to take it out of the savings bank, because he is bringing home with him his next month's stipend. "Farewell, my glorious!!" His thank-you letter from Moscow reads: "I had such a good time with you, dear Mitrofan, I forgot my artistic flop . . ."

In Moscow on 21 March, 1903, the failure of the Second Symphony repeated itself under Safonoff's hands (although Safonoff had at the first rehearsal waved the score at the musicians in the orchestra saying, "Gentlemen. Here is the new Bible!"). Hisses came after the first and last movements. *Russian Word* spoke of "stretching dissonances, chromatic harmonies, nervously syncopated rhythms, lifts and crying melodies, thick massive orchestra, such is the beloved language of Scriabin." *News of the Day* wrote unpleasantly too: ". . . extraordinarily decorative harmonies then unexpected banality . . . monotonous and clamorous orchestra . . ."

M. D. Calvocoressi in his book *Musicians Gallery* obliges with an anecdote. In 1907 in Paris he sat between Glazunov and Scriabin, whose Second Symphony had just been played. "Scriabin said to me casually, 'It's a very mediocre work.' As this represented my own opinion I felt very much embarrassed and contented myself with some kind of non-committal mumble. A moment later, Glazunov whispered into my ear with perfect gravity, 'You have offended him. He expected to be contradicted.'"

But when Modest Altschuler asked permission to perform the Second Symphony, Scriabin demurred. "I liked it while I wrote it," he said, "but now it doesn't please me anymore . . . the last part is banal."

✒ XIV ✒

PROFESSORSHIP
(continued)

51

SCRIABIN WAS accorded on 5 March, 1902, in Moscow's Great Noblemen's Hall his first all-Scriabin program of orchestral and piano music. Olga and Zinaida Monighetti contributed the rental of the hall and guaranteed expenses for the orchestra, in case ticket receipts were insufficient. A line from Scriabin exists asking them to set aside at the box office fifteen complimentary tickets and reminding them (Safonoff-like) to distribute forty copies of the program with his picture on it to members of the orchestra as souvenirs.

Safonoff conducted the First Symphony with chorus again. Scriabin played the Third Sonata. After the intermission, *Rêverie* followed, and Scriabin ended the evening with six preludes, four mazurkas, and the Polonaise. The concert succeeded magnificently.

One quarrel marred the event. Buyukly wanted to play the Third Sonata. Scriabin felt he alone should appear. Buyukly insisted, begging, "If you please, just give half the world to me. Surely we can divide it between us." Scriabin raged, "Take the whole world—if you think you can get it to go with *you!*" They never spoke to each other again.

Safonoff in a letter to Keneman reported that both the scherzo and *Rêverie* had to be repeated, and Scriabin himself played four encores. "I am so happy at this success for him. It lightens his grief over the Second Symphony in SPb." Still Safonoff dared not brave a hearing of the Second Symphony at this time.

Every newspaper and musical magazine covered the concert. Lipaev wrote favorably in the *RMG* of Scriabin's originality. Prince Trubetskoi again supported Scriabin in the *Courier*: "Major artistic worth . . . most excellent . . . exceptionally personal and refined . . . Scriabin is the first authentically Russian composer to have discovered a piano style which matches his truly lyric music mood . . ."

Scriabin's students at the Conservatory, in addition to flowers and laurel wreaths, presented him a large green writing set with blotter and pad bordered in silver. They engraved "5 March, 1902" on it with an ornate pattern of leaves.

Disinclined to become a professor, inexperienced and unwilling, Scriabin was what kind of a teacher? Like all musicians, he had taught daughters of millionaires, charging high prices and fussily demanding standards they were not prepared to meet. Barbara von Meck's sister came late to a lesson, having been to a luncheon party first. Scriabin demanded that she choose between parties or the piano. She quite naturally never returned to him.

The secret of teaching is to be systematic, grasping principles and rules of pedagogy. Scriabin lacked all these. Some students quit his classes. Teachers who heard his pupils remarked on "their inability to play in time." More and more, however, asked to study with him, those who felt an affinity; and in place of solid grounding, the Scriabin "method" became a way of communicating beauty through art. He demanded extraordinary work from the student. He wanted soul and a nervous impetus or lift. He instilled in them what he called "a technique of nerves."

Sometimes he "interpreted" music. Engel gives an example of this picture-painting. He assigned one student the slow C# minor étude by Chopin. "It is evening," Scriabin announced. "Someone is alone in a room. There is a longing for something. The window is open. The soft summer night is fragrant. The E major section needs a different touch, different pedaling. Everything must change here. Then, once again, the longing for the unknown as before."

He modernized Bach and Beethoven. "But he made you love them," Engel apologizes, "as if they were entirely new pieces written by another composer."

Margarita Morozova, (1873–1958) compared her two teachers: "When Scriabin played Beethoven he couldn't help coloring him with his own bright individuality . . . Medtner, on the other hand, would put himself

in the background. What emerged was not Medtner but Beethoven."
Here are some of Scriabin's most often repeated axioms and phrases,
as reported by his various pupils at various times.

> "No dry passages! Everything must live!" "Smear the difficult bits if you must,
> but if they end brilliantly, then you'll still have the impression of cleanness and
> splendor!" "Play it all . . . in one breath!" "The *thrill* (*upoitel'nost'*) before all
> else!" "The atmosphere of art above all!" "*Il faut se griser!*" (Get yourself
> drunk on it.) "This may seem like a passage to *you*, but to Mozart it was an
> *idea, a thought*." "You must draw sound from wood and steel as a miner
> extracts precious ore from the dry earth." "Don't play like you're washing
> laundry."

Maria Solomonovna Nemenova-Lunz's (1879–1934) rhapsodic
memoirs are particularly discerning. She had graduated from the Lower
Division in piano at the Conservatory, and in 1898 she learned that
Scriabin had joined the staff, but had "laid down impossible conditions
before accepting the post." She nevertheless opted for him as her teacher.

> The thought of revealing my slender ability plunged me into despair. I had
> been taught that "expression" or "interpretation" was the prerogative of the
> Higher Division. We had always been threatened when we showed originality.
> "You'll weep when *Professor* hears you."

> Feeling like a little girl going to school for the first time, I entered the class-
> room . . . That expression in Alexander Nikolaevich's eyes was so typical—
> a mixture of weary boredom plus a vain effort to hide it. I also remember his
> excessive correctness and politeness (whose meaning we were later to learn
> and to dread more than even his most stormy comments).

> I ran through, in the strict sense of the word, the C minor Fantasia of Mozart.
> It seemed endless to me. Fearing that Scriabin would stop me before I could
> finish, I was paralyzed and could give it no sort of interpretation. He asked me
> to play the introduction in another key and make some modulations. (I also
> played a little homemade piece of my own.) Finally he assigned me the Chopin
> F minor étude and the adagio from Beethoven's Second Sonata.

> At the next lesson, after the first two bars of the Chopin, Scriabin showed me
> how to hold my hands. He illustrated at the piano. "Everything is in the
> pressure of the hands on the keyboard," he said. We never got to the adagio
> because, as he explained, "if we don't understand the first principle we can
> never go on to the second."

> He was extremely nervous and active in moments of enthusiasm. It seemed as
> if he were emitting electric sparks. When he sat at the piano his whole body,

his hand gestures and movements of the head, so characteristic of him, seemed to translate the mood and meaning of music into action.

He guarded us against the ordinary and strove to keep every prosaic thing out of our playing. He awakened and developed our creative fantasy. He transformed insignificant places in music with comparisons, descriptions, and his own performance. Sometimes he would make a beautiful gesture with his hands, or characterize in words. "Flight" was one of his favorite terms, so was "fragrance." Later he would say, "*très parfumé*," meaning make it fragrant with this or that feeling. When I recall my lessons, it seems that Scriabin summoned from me everything of which I was capable.

52

THE LONGEST letter Scriabin ever wrote dealt with his devotion toward his students. In describing one stormy graduation session, he writes as if aflame with righteous indignation. "For the first time in my life I've managed to cover ten pages. You should treasure this letter!" he says to Vera on 15 May, 1902.

First, the background: Rimma has been ill, and after three weeks of waiting, worry and diagnoses, the doctors operate to remove her appendix. Vera, now seven months pregnant, has taken her and the other children early to the country to recuperate. That summer the Scriabins rented a gracious country house.

Obolenskoe, once part of Prince Obolensky's estate, now belonged to Mme. Kuzmina, mother of the talented Mikhail Kuzmin, who in 1907 would write a sensational and successful novel on homosexuality called *Wings*. It nestled in deep, tranquil, wooded country along the Moscow-Bryansk railroad line to Kiev, about sixty miles from Moscow, quite a distance for a pregnant woman and too far for friends to visit conveniently. Their nearest neighbors were the Leonid Pasternaks, of whom more will be written later.

Scriabin remained in Moscow because, as he wrote Belaieff earlier, he is frightfully busy with six graduating students "over whom I must take trouble."

"Little Bug!" Scriabin exclaims in this famous letter, "I am writing you the day after the examinations and I am in a most disagreeable state of mind." Here's why:

> The examinations went brilliantly. My pupils played well, each better than the one before. Pomerantsev forgot his fugue twice and hit a lot of wrong notes, but the others played impeccably. Horowitz [Alexander Ioachimovich Gorovits] played the Liszt concerto like an experienced virtuoso. Malinovskaya and Nemenova simply charmed everybody. All round me I could hear the most ecstatic praises for Nemenova. But, of course, the most obvious master was Horowitz. Never for one second did I doubt he would receive the gold medal.
>
> To my surprise and rage the committee split it between Nemenova and Malinovskaya, and left Horowitz out in the cold. I was fearfully angry. I sprang from my chair and said that the committee was unfair. Grzhimali looked offended and said that one has to accept the judgment of one's colleagues. He said that he had found himself in a similar position in regard to Belousov, his pupil. He had been passed over, that's true, but I interrupted Grzhimali to put the discussion of the basis of pure principle. I said that students and public believe in the infallibility of the judges' decision. The honor of the Conservatory is at stake.
>
> Safonoff backed me up and just as we were about to persuade the committee to vote again, Shishkin and, imagine! Konstantin Igumnov stood fast like asses, saying there's a rule against re-balloting.
>
> Well, the quarrel almost ended in blows. The meeting lasted until 1 in the morning. We had to yield as everybody rejected the idea of voting a second time on anything. The medal will be awarded differently in the future, so as to avoid this kind of mess; but I can't let the matter drop so easily as that. They have wounded my Horowitz, and I suffer. He came over just now, so pale, so sad. I comforted him as best I could.

The official records of the Committee make only a notation to the effect that Professor Scriabin expressed a wish to resign from the Conservatory.

The rest of the letter brings Vera up to date on Moscow happenings. Her father passed through and will go to Obolenskoe in a week. "Warmmest greetings from the Trubetskois. I spent the whole day with them, lunch and dinner. They are so sweet . . ." Princess Trubetskaya is teaching him "Latin, Greek and E N G L I S H, and so you'll be tormented all summer long with these. She speaks English like a native . . ."

Somewhat "less warm," he says, are remembrances from Margarita Morozova, whom he had invited to the examination as an alumna of his private classes. Some of Vera's students have asked when they can resume lessons. The Monighettis are leaving for the country and Scriabin spent Tuesday with them, as he had no lessons that day. He is troubled about his piano. He does not want to leave it closed up in the apartment during the heat of the summer. He asks about Rimma and cautions Vera to be very careful with her food. He noted that he has begun writing "like Bryanchaninov," leaving letters out of words in haste to get to the point.

He is looking forward to quitting Moscow for the summer. "I have worked hard for this day . . ." and for the first time he speaks of a Third Symphony he has obviously been laboring over. Nikita Morozov called and Scriabin played it for him. "He likes it more than the First or Second. As usual, everybody is wild about the *allegro* theme and that, of course, mortifies me somewhat." "I was so tired last night that I couldn't even drink at dinner. As a result I am unspeakably happy today."

On 24 May, 1902, he tendered his formal resignation from the Conservatory, making it a show of protest over Horowitz, though the more likely fact was as he had written Belaieff on 26 March: "In a word, I hear music every day from two in the afternoon until midnight. And I still have my composing to do at night. Ideas always come to me in spring. There seems to be some connection . . . Safonoff has asked me to stay on for another year but I will not, under any circumstance. I could manage 3 pupils (300 rubles), at the most. That wouldn't hamper me unduly. Three have to finish next year and want to continue working with me." Three turns into seven, but only two actually graduate.

Nemenova-Lunz talks about the music Scriabin taught. If it preyed on his mind as a danger, some of it he loved nonetheless. Even then, of course, he could be paralyzed with boredom.

One time, knowing that I had prepared some Beethoven and a piece by Liszt, Scriabin said before I had begun, "No Beethoven. I can't face it today. Give me Liszt." He could make all that was *real* flower from that music. From the first chord of the A flat major Etude, which Scriabin called *Poème d'Amour*, I decided that now was a time for me to listen. I think few have ever heard such Liszt.

One often hears from the school of "shattering pianism" how Scriabin lacked strength. It is true that he did not have a "frightening fortissimo." He did not much like "materialistic" sonority. He always said that the deepest *forte* must always *sound* soft. "This chord must sound like a cry of happy victory, not like a toppling chest of drawers," he told us.

He worried more than anything else about sound. "You must caress the keyboard. Don't pound it as if you hate it," he would say. He worked indefatigably on tonal shadings. He made us repeat one note forever. He helped us find ways of striking it to get separate colors. He kept us interested in the sound and life of the instrument. How valuable for technique! He wouldn't accept "music without rhythm." He made us think out every formal passage by likening it to speech or talking. His pedaling effects were literally beyond the piano's possibilities.

Our work never even stopped when high-ranking visitors arrived. I remember Safonoff once brought in a famous Hungarian pianist. After exchanging pleasantries, I played Bach's F minor prelude from the *Well-Tempered Clavichord* Book II. I was shy and could not concentrate. The first two measures upset Scriabin. He forgot the visitor and made me repeat them twenty times. I got into such a nervous state I simply could not play any more and fled from the room.

Scriabin's personal tastes and preferences never interfered with his fine and interesting instructions in Bach, Haydn, Beethoven, Mozart, Grieg, Saint-Saëns, Tchaikovsky, Arensky, Schubert, Schumann (one of his most poetic successes was *Kreisleriana*). The pieces he taught most unforgettably were: Beethoven's Op. 109 and the G major piano concerto, the driest of Bach preludes, a Schubert sonata, and Haydn's F minor Variations. This he played without pedal for style and transparency of sound. He drew all his colors from the naked keyboard.

Towards the end of our first year, Scriabin asked us all to learn one of the most common and frequently played Chopin waltzes. From the first of us who played, it was clear that we were slapdash and foolhardy, that we had fallen into bad habits from playing for and showing off to our friends. None of us will ever forget how Scriabin played this waltz. Students from other classes came to listen. Any hands but his playing at such "chronic high temperature" would have been dangerous....

We often talked about literature, about Chekhov's pessimism, which absorbed us at the time. Scriabin could not understand Chekhov's flabbiness, his "whine," as he expressed it. He compared him to those super-elegiac moments of Tchaikovsky. More than once he commented tartly on both men, "Can they *uplift?*"

Schloezer says that Tchaikovsky "actually caused Scriabin physical pain." Engel quotes him as calling Tchaikovsky "work-a-day" and "negative." However, Ivan Martynov, latter-day Soviet musicologist, developed a convincing thesis (*Soviet Music* Vol. 6, Moscow, 1945). "If Scriabin is

294 / SCRIABIN

not a Russian composer, then he is incomprehensible. If you take him out of the general historical process of Russian art and culture, he is obscure." He took that Russian of Russians, Tchaikovsky's "lyric rapture and turned it into passionate exaltation"; he changed Tchaikovsky's "power of broad expanse into nervous excitement and impulsiveness..." In the 1880's and '90's Tchaikovsky was the most played composer in Russia. Martynov finds direct melodic quotations between the main themes of Scriabin's Second Symphony and Tchaikovsky's Fourth, the "Divine Poem" and Tchaikovsky's *Romeo and Juliet*. As Nikolai Berdyaev said in another context, "After Dostoevsky man was no longer what he had been before"; so may the same be said of Tchaikovsky and Russian musicians.

But Scriabin's threshold of tolerance was low. Schloezer summed up this matter of "others' music" perceptively:

> Fundamentally, Scriabin was always bored but polite and hid his feelings. He was even bored when he had to listen to his own early compositions for any length of time. He would take interest in rare moments. One was the Lento and Andante of the First Symphony. He also liked the beginning Andante of the Second Symphony. As for the rest...

53

SCRIABIN FINALLY joined Vera at Obolenskoe, while Belaieff, who was ill again, went to Karlsbad for the waters. Scriabin wrote Belaieff on 17 July, 1902:

"For the present I am concerned solely with restoring myself to health. I devote myself exclusively to rest and physical exercises. I will resume my music in September, and then will finish all my compositions. The most important is the 3rd Symphony. One movement (*allegro*) is already finished and the others sketched. I want to work so badly, but I dare not allow it for fear of wrecking my health permanently. This spring I felt so badly that I began to doubt I would ever return to health. Now to my unlimited happiness, I see that I can and will once again be able to give myself over to art. I have dreamed of this for so long now. For the first time in my life I am resting in the real sense of the word. It has taken a month since the examinations for me to begin having good days when I feel even tolerably well. Such fatigue results from many years of frightful tension. If I had not decided finally to put an end to this state of affairs and give myself over completely to what I call the feat of inaction (I lie whole days in a hammock), then I really believe that I would have been dead within a couple of years."

This letter also told Belaieff to go ahead and pay Kalafati, the impecunious professor at the Petersburg Conservatory to whom Belaieff, this time without consultation entrusted the piano arrangement for four hands of the Second Symphony.

"Despite my monumental effort of will to think nothing and above all to avoid music," Scriabin went on to say to Belaieff "I have composed three little 'thinglets'—a mazurka, prelude, and étude—which step rather outside the usual category . . ." The mazurka, in the double keys of F# and C# major, eventually published as Op. 40 No. 2, is a willful (marked *piacevole*) moment of music—a half-waltz, perhaps a caught ray of fleeting morning light.

The prelude in C major (Op. 33 No. 3) is the first of those strange outbursts marked "bellicose" or "savagely." It is a chordal exercise mathematically punctuated: the leading figure appears first on the upbeat, then on the beat, and for each of the remaining two times—a rest and a double rest later; symmetrically reduced from four beats to triplets to twos and one.

The fragmentary étude appeared as Op. 42 No. 2. Its F# minor melancholy melody of three beats sounds the root or base note in upside down fashion, while the left hand flutters against it in a compound rhythm of five notes. The time signature is 2/4.

On 23 July, he wrote Olga Monighetti complaining that he has not heard from her. "I continue to indulge myself in laziness and am definite about doing nothing until I am fully restored to health . . . Already I feel better." He appended these lines:

The growing powers of nature's divinity
Rent my body weak and weary
Bade me forget all food, sleep and even drink
And rendered all for art's magnificence

Perhaps it was not wise to speak about indolence to patrons. Zinaida Monighetti has tactlessly spoken of "mental illness," and she draws Scriabin's fire on 8 August, 1902: "You completely misunderstood me about my health. I was only speaking of those illnesses from which I have suffered for many years, namely, overwork and unstrung nerves. Now, thank God, I begin to feel better and better, although I am still not entirely well. My mind, however, is clearer than ever. I have vowed not to start any work until my strength is back . . ." Even fate intervenes on Scriabin's behalf. The lid of the rented piano jams and he cannot open it to practice.

The birth of a new baby, Scriabin's fourth, approaches. On 1 August, 1902, Vera, together with little Maria, went to Moscow to be near the civilization of familiar midwives and wet nurses. Scriabin remained in Obolenskoe with the older girls and their serf nursemaid, Petrovna. Rimma cries, "Why did Mama have to go away?" Little Lyalya asks, "Why Mama go Moko?" Otherwise, "the children are beautifully behaved and healthy." The weather is marvelous. They spend all day in the open air, and often take walks together. Lyalya and Maria are minding their manners, although Rimma once was naughty at table and had to be sent to the nursery. Scriabin had a nightmare about Vera, so he sent an anxious letter: "Write *instantly* about your health, or else I shall fall ill."

Vera asked for her stepmother-in-law, Olga, to be present at this confinement. Scriabin was pleased. He trusted his mamotchka. "Set my mind at rest," he asked Vera, "notify me that she is with you." Lyubov, of course, was ineffectual.

Scriabin arranged (from Obolenskoe) for a wet nurse in Moscow. "Hire her immediately, you hear? *Now!*" he wrote. "More than anything else I worry about your being without a servant . . . If you wish, dear"— he calls her his "little swallow"—"we will all come to you the instant you give the word. God be with you, dear. I am thinking of you constantly. If you are unable to write, ask Aunt Lyubov to write for you . . ."

On 18 August, 1902, mamotchka's telegram informed Scriabin of the birth of a boy. He was so happy he "jumped, hopped, skipped, like a top-rank gymnast." When Vera wrote, he answered quickly: "My dear little child, thank you for your sweet, sweet letter . . ." He added that she had no idea how worried he had been, and he recites *his* household cares with the girls. He wanted her to bring little Lev, the new baby, to the country as soon as possible. He intended sending her some money by a local friend, Saltykov, but he did not go to Moscow as expected. Can she borrow the fare?

The weather has begun to change. Still it would be a pity to leave the country. The heat of summer was gone, and the sun still radiant. He was angry, because on his way to the station to post a letter to her, Saltykov latched onto him and would not let him go. "How to stop him?!" The train passed right before his nose, his letter clutched in his hand. He asked Vera please to express his gratitude to mamotchka for all her kindnesses.

Petrovna agrees to remain through next winter, provided she does not have to wash and iron. She does not mind the addition of Lev, but at her age she is afraid of tiring herself. "She's a miracle," Scriabin says, as he passes on this joyous solution to their servant problem.

Safonoff asked Vera for the Second Symphony. He was planning his performance of 21 March, 1903. "What do you think?" Scriabin answered. "Shall we send him the pencil copy in the sitting room cupboard?" If so, then Vera must go over every page carefully erasing Liadov's remarks in the margin. Scriabin wrote insistently: "You must do this yourself, Vera. Naturally only if you are well enough. Now don't turn this task over to mamotchka or Aunt Lyuba . . . Don't you dare!!! It would be better for me to do it myself when I come back to Moscow. However, Aunt Lyuba *can* be entrusted with delivering the score to Safonoff. She's often done that sort of thing for me in the past."

54

SCARCELY WAITING to see Lev or Vera, Scriabin set out for a two-week sea-bathing and grape cure in the Crimea the first week of September, 1902. At Dr. Zakharin's recommendation he remained there the whole month. He was ill, extremely cautious of himself, and seriously frightened about his health and his drinking.

He took the Kursk train, and by the time he reached Sevastopol he had made a friend of "an awfully sweet fellow from Tomsk. Tomorrow we will take the same boat to Yalta."

A misfortune occurred in Yalta. The boat arrived at sunset, the hour when the Muslim laborers stay home for prayers. The passengers were dressed and had eaten dinner. The temperature in the cabins was boiling, yet the boat stayed at anchor for more than half an hour. Scriabin was soaked through with sweat. In terror he rushed to the nearest hotel, the Russia. He found Yalta "an abomination which even the sea cannot prettify." His little single room cost an exorbitant four-and-a-half rubles, but there "I was able to take my usual steps against colds." He drank hot lemonade, climbed into bed, and covered himself with woolen blankets. He caught cold anyway, but did not run a fever. Rather than remain in Yalta, he hired a palanquin and was carried "by basket" into Gurzuf.

He had planned—"so that I would not be entirely alone"—to meet Oranovsky, who owned a house in Gurzuf. He had not arrived. Scriabin took the smallest room in the town at three rubles a day and immediately sent for the doctor who "vastly relieved me by saying that there was nothing seriously the matter with me. Still I should stay in bed for 2 days." Afterwards, Scriabin began sunbathing: "I baked for 3 hours in the sun . . . the heat is inconceivable."

Gurzuf, where Vera and he five years earlier had honeymooned, is now a sadder place: "You wouldn't know it, Vushka. There has not been a drop of rain this summer. All the vegetation in the Crimea is seared. Worse, that new city planning company that took Gurzuf over (may the devil send it back) has let the park grow wild. You remember those marvelous magnolias, mimosa, and the huge nut trees? All of them have withered. There are almost no roses at all, and the leaves have even fallen off laurel trees. There is no grass in the whole park! It is really very painful to see all this."

He asked Vera to send him twenty-five or thirty rubles, as he has had to spend so much on "miscellaneous things." He foolishly left what he called "my vast capital" at the Institute. He forgot to pick up some 46 rubles 98 kopecks due him. He suggested that Vera borrow money, from nurse Petrovna if she has it, or from Safonoff. It upsets him for Vera and him both to be without money. Next month when his part-time Conservatory duties resume, he reassured her, "All will be normal; there will be enough for everything. Meanwhile, borrow from all our good fairies. Keep yourself well dressed at all times, no matter what."

Oranovsky at last reached Gurzuf. Scriabin found him "the same as before only more so. He has the air of being an embarrassed guest about to take leave, even in his own house. When you excuse yourself to go, he clings to you. Fortunately, there was a local schoolteacher also present. We spent the whole time talking to each other, quite ignoring our host."

Scriabin gave Vera a further picture of Gurzuf. "The people here are most uninteresting. Aside from bathers, no one from Moscow or Petersburg is here. One general finds it so lonely he is leaving. Gurzuf is a very vulgar health resort, and to tell the truth, I am glad to be alone completely resting. I have mastered something great! I now know the art of going to bed early. Yesterday, I slept for 8 hours. You see how I chat with you for such a long time, and yet you keep me dangling from only a line or two. Write me about the children. I get very bored and nervous without all of you. Write me also if you know anything of my *babushki*. Have they found an apartment? Did you send the symphony . . . I have composed some excellent verses for my opera . . ."

In a later letter, 7 September, he thanks Vera for money and informs her that he will postpone his return. He must bathe ten more times and eat so many more grapes. "I feel better, but I pass the time most monotonously. I do everything as prescribed. There is a time to eat grapes and a time when to bathe. Day after tomorrow I start drinking kefir [liquor from fermented milk]. I no sooner turn around than the day is gone. What a pity it is so cold. The mornings are in the 40's."

He is worried again, because Vera told him the family is down with colds. His handwriting in this letter is particularly bad: "I am holding a bunch of grapes in my left hand and gobbling them the while." He visited the summer house where they had stayed. From there the view shows how "faded and dried everything is. Only the sea is beautiful . . ." He asked Vera to write, because her letters are his only diversion and comfort. He has not been allowed to walk, because the regimen must be strictly followed. "Once I start the kefir, I shan't be able to leave the park at all, and I am so bored with it already."

Of all the complaints he has for Vera, the most unpleasant of all was Gurzuf's park band. It played day and night. Scriabin could not even eat his grapes or get gently drunk on kefir in peace. The food was not too bad, although the butter was "sometimes vile."

A well and reasonably happy Scriabin returned to Moscow. On 26

September, 1902, he wrote Belaieff that the Crimean air and the sea bathing had been "most beneficial. Only Gurzuf's food damaged me. Yesterday I spent all day in bed with a terribly upset stomach, and still I am not right down there."

55

BACK AT the Conservatory, refreshed, Scriabin told Belaieff (22 October, 1902): "I work all this time, much and well. The Third Symphony moves along, also some small pieces, and yet another orchestral composition." He was also full of preparations for Safonoff's performance of the Second Symphony, and asked Belaieff to hurry, so that Safonoff can conduct from the printed score rather than a pencil manuscript.

He finally made good his promise to play in Vera's native Nizhny. On 22 November, his program consisted of the Second Sonata, C# minor étude, Op. 2, Etudes in F# minor and B flat minor from Op. 8, Nocturne for left hand, Concert Allegro, Mazurkas Nos. 1, 3 and 4 from Op. 25, No. 4 from Opus 3, two Preludes, Op. 27, and the Polonaise. As an encore he gave the rare but beautiful Prelude for left hand, Op. 9.

This was Scriabin's first recital in the provinces and the first of his so-called "provincial programs." In Europe, concerts were avenues for introducing his latest compositions. But with the Russian public beyond the capital cities, he was timid in his programs.

He risked only the Op. 27 among new works for Nizhny, and suffered, predictably. The *Volgan*, Nizhny's only newspaper, gave him a fine review, saying that it was essential "for a wider public to know the compositions of this unquestionably talented composer," but Scriabin himself offered Belaieff a better appraisal of the concert. "As I expected, the concert met a very mixed reception. The easy pieces elicited noisy approval and I had to repeat them. The rest were quite obviously perplexing and even Nizhny's biggest musician, Villuan, admitted that he was confused by them. The preludes were least well received of all . . ."

Scriabin's career thrived. Again he received the Glinka Prize. In 1902 it came to 1,000 rubles—300 for the Concerto, 200 for the four Preludes,

Op. 22, 200 for the Polonaise, and, remarkably, 300 for the nine Mazurkas, Op. 25. Scriabin still pretended: "Kindly transmit my great gratitude to my unknown benefactor . . ." He wrote Stassov once more hinting for the money to be hastened to him. Aged Stassov mislaid the receipt. "Ah . . ." he writes, "a misfortune!! . . . I have such a mass of papers here at the library it doesn't take much ingenuity for me to lose anything . . ."

He was invited to perform in Prague, but Vladimir Metzel (b. 1882), a journeyman pianist of the day, played an all-Scriabin concert in his place. The reviews were modestly good and Scriabin sent them to Belaieff. Safonoff planned for Sashkina to tour Europe with him playing symphonies and the Concerto.

The pianist and professor Anatol Drozdov (1883–1950) wrote a brief sidelight on these times in his Recollections:

> It so happened that the name and music of Scriabin first struck my ears at a time of social storminess. In 1902 I was living in Saratov and all the leading intellectuals there were undergoing deep political experience—workers frequently engaged in revolutionary activities, students agitated, and the government constantly panicked with ensuant reprisals.
>
> Into this oppressive atmosphere strode Vsevolod Buyukly, a shining pianist with an artist's individuality and a fiery temperament, playing Scriabin . . . In this playing we heard all the sobbing and shouting of social struggle. We felt the breath of our imprisoned heroes, the breaking of their chains, their perishing in labor but still not surrendering.

At Christmastime 1902, Scriabin wrote Belaieff about orchestrating the symphony. "This month I am working less, and worse. The symphony is complicated in its orchestration and requires every exertion . . ." A curious postscript reads: "You ask if I have quarreled with Safonoff. No, not even remotely." On New Year's he wrote: "I want to see you so badly. I won't be able to contain myself once the symphony is finished. I'll come flying to you for a few days. Will you chase me away?"

On 25 February, 1903: "You are probably worried, because I have sent you nothing. The reason is the symphony. It is fearfully big—350–400 pages. I cannot do a thing until I finish it. Over Christmas I started a big orchestral piece, but before I continue with that I want to put several small pieces in order. They have lain around for a long time . . . But only after the symphony." He reassured Belaieff that there would be no mistakes in the score of the symphony, because "Lev Konyus knows every note of it and will correct it with all his astuteness."

Belaieff sent a gentle but frightening letter on 15 March, 1903, which interferes with Scriabin's formulating plans: "Sasha, last year you informed me of your intention to give up the Conservatory and devote yourself exclusively to composition. You asked me to increase your advances *over the course of one year* from 100 rubles a month to 200. During this period you told me you hoped to get on your feet, as you put it. I began the increase in the advance on 20 May which means by your count, the 20th of April. During all this, I never questioned you, nor did you ever inform me of how you might manage any sort of *concrete* guarantee. Try to answer me clearly, and don't be a Muscovite and put it off interminably . . . Forgive me if I enclose an accounting according to *my* books. It is for *your* information."

Included in this letter was a document showing Scriabin's debt as of 1 January, 1903: 3,050 rubles.

CURRENT ACCOUNT OF A.N. SCRIABIN

Music in Hand		Money Paid Out	
	1900		
April:		Stipend for year	1,200 rubles
First Symphony	1,000 rubles	1 March for transcription	800
	1901		
September:		Stipend for year	1,200
Two Preludes, Op. 27	200		
Fantasia, Op. 28	200		
	1902		
August:		Stipend for year	2,000
Second Symphony	1,000	For Kalafati's transcription	150
	2,400		5,450

Scriabin never answered (*à la muscovite*), but the summer became one of panic and fervent activity.

Scriabin had taken Obolenskoe for a second summer in 1903, and his first letter is to Zinaida Monighetti late in August, 1903, about work. He reminded her of his "stupid absent-mindedness," how he had forgotten to mail a letter, but now he is changed. He has taken this letter personally to the train station to be posted to Moscow. "I would fly to you, just to spend a few minutes, but I cannot tear myself away from work. It is OBLIGATORY that I complete 30 compositions and settle accounts with Belaieff before I go abroad. I have LITERALLY sat at work all summer without lifting my head once. What are you doing in Moscow and are you en route somewhere? I want to see you terribly much. What a pity we live so far apart and I dare not ask you to come to us."

The Monighetti grandmother died while the family was vacationing in Hungeburg, Germany, and it returned to Moscow. Scriabin sent his condolences. "As for me," he adds, "everything depends on when I finish the piano pieces. I owe Belaieff 4,000 rubles [sic] and cannot even suggest an extension of my credit with him until I repay this debt. Although this leaves me with a great deal of composing to do, I still hope that in September I can arrange my affairs sufficiently so that I will be able to move abroad."

✐ XV ✐
OPERA
56

WHILE TWO symphonies strode into the world and a third was beginning to consume him, Scriabin was also working on a counterfoil, opera. Its intent was more philosophical than musical. From scattered references in his letters, he seemed to have worked on the libretto when ill or exhausted, and when he tried to restrain himself from the arduousness of music. In due course his passion for the Third Symphony eliminated the opera. After three years' intermittent preoccupation with it, he wrote Schloezer in July, 1903, "The libretto moves slowly..." Two months later he closed another letter with an exclamation, "Oh how I want to write the opera!"

On 7 December, 1903, he told Belaieff: "I was so happy all week I skipped around like a gymnast of the 2nd, no! 3rd class. I dashed to friends. I talked nonsense and acted tomfooleries, and I gamboled about until I nearly dislocated my spine. Now I'm ill. I'm bored with celebrating and have resumed my music and literature..." The occasion for this rejoicing was the completion of the first act text, which he cryptically called his "big work."

His joy also coincided with the Glinka Prize of 1903—1,500 rubles for the *Rêverie* (200), two Preludes, Op. 27 (100), Fantasia, Op. 28 (200) and the First Symphony (1,000). ("How endlessly I regret not knowing the name of the person who has expressed his sympathy for me in such a beautiful and noble fashion over so many years...") He paid all his debts and had enough left over to go abroad. "Isn't life good?" he asked Belaieff. Money and work had equal and excitant power over Scriabin's moods.

The whole project ended in nothing, abandoned and unfinished. The countless hours of writing the text and discussing its ideas were wasted. After Scriabin's death, a libretto of fragments was discovered in the Green Notebook. A line or two later found its way into the poem of the Poem of Ecstasy. Musical themes, leit-motifs, sketches, phrases for dramatic moments, scenes, chordal combinations were parceled out into preludes and études. One operatic melody came to rest as late as 1911 in a transient moment of the Sixth Sonata.

Friends have recorded enough of Scriabin's conversations so that it is possible to envision the opera fairly clearly. He talked a lot about it during the years 1901–3 and expounded its ideas in the course of normal conversation. Every posture of the philosophical Scriabin is indicated here, but something prevented its fulfillment.

Rozenov recalled that in January, 1902, Scriabin read him a "philosophical opera, . . . very high-flown, terribly pathetic, and completely devoid of any dramatic action . . . its characters were philosophical abstractions rather than living people." Scriabin, it seemed to Rozenov, made a distinction between what he called the "prose of life" (the hero's persecution and imprisonment) and the "poetry of idea" (his arias of thoughts, sung while the hero is seated in his study and visions, ideas, ideals, and ideates float past him). When Rozenov said what he frankly thought of the opera, Scriabin cooled and their relationship declined. "At any rate, I was living in the country and he soon left for abroad . . . We exchanged a few letters: I from the country; he, from Switzerland." With this, Rozenov leaves the composer's life and destroyed all the letters Scriabin wrote him through the years.

Boris Schloezer attributed major importance to the opera as a presage of Scriabin's ultimate concepts and subsequent magnawork. He began the main section of his biography with this picture:

Still living in me is the autumn of 1902 when I saw Scriabin for the second time. He was then a professor, father of a family, but he seemed tender, fragile, and strangely childlike.

We began to argue about philosophy, passionately and violently. Later we were to laugh about that evening. We had not really known each other well enough to engage in such altercation.

I remember vividly that we spoke of his opera . . .

The untitled opera centers around a nameless hero, designated abstractly as "Philosopher-Musician-Poet," in that order. Scriabin wanted to get away from the coldness of classical opera as well as the *verismo* of the Italian nineteenth century. He also felt that Wagner had exploited history as source material, and that he had turned to legends, tales, national myths, exhausting that soil too. Where was Scriabin to look, except to philosophy and the impersonality of a musical thought-drama? As Schloezer interpreted it, "The opera would be outside time and space, stripped of external reality, and denuded of all traits of ordinary existence. He thought this was how he would make a completely pure and transparent art form of general significance and universal character." The result, however, was "lifeless." He never discovered that "secret of artistic incarnation or the method of inventing mortal characters who are independent of their inventor . . ."

The hero was based on the Man-God first glimpsed in the Third Sonata and the *Übermensch*, Superman, the "Beyond Man" of Nietzsche. His motivation was Schopenhauer's "Will to Power," whose point was to attain freedom. This spurts from the hero's heart like blood from a gash. He "thirsts to be victorious over the world." He asserts his "I will" as an absolute, and so loves the world he absorbs it, fuses it with himself. This produces a state of bliss which soon Scriabin will call "ecstasy."

Total unity of the world was the fulcrum of the opera. On one occasion in 1902 Schloezer criticized the theme. "Unity of all humanity into one body is impossible and not even desirable," he said, and Scriabin was unusually sharp in his retort. He could, Schloezer says, "admit a composition was a failure, but he could not accept that this world with all its terrestial limitations was not in accordance with his own picture of unity and unification."

Against this central character and his goal of embracing the whole world in gladness, Scriabin sets the king's daughter, whom he calls Tsaritsa, or Queen-Daughter rather than "princess." In a fantastic scene of intellectual exposition, the hero seduces her. Sex becomes possible by means of philosophical excursus.

An Insurrection and Inquisition Scene (not in the Green Notebook) shows people who are "emotionally enslaved," resistant to the hero's gift of enlightenment and are "dark and stagnant forces" rising up against the hero. We are, once again, indebted to Schloezer for the description.

They throw him in a dungeon. They torture him: "Who art thou? Why has thou come to the people?" The hero answers in ringing, radiant tones . . . "I am Freedom!" Then, he uses his magical powers of thought and transfers "the vibrations of his will" from the dungeon up above onto the earth. He mentally summons the people who now obey him, storm the prison, and release their liberator.

Schloezer regarded this impersonal hero, dead as he may be as an operatic hero, as a "personification of the active, creative male principle of the world." The relation of the hero to the crowd of people is that of the active to the passive. The Tsaritsa becomes thus the symbol of the Eternal Feminine or mankind. She answers the superman's call. "The crown of their love is the erotic act, that is to say, bliss," Schloezer avowed.

The opera is socialistic, in keeping with the temper of the Russian time. There is no class distinction; the high are to be saved equally with the low. However, during the Insurrection, the hero maliciously ridicules the people. He is better than they. Their salvation can only come from him. There is never any question but that he is right and the people, all of them, are wrong. His purpose is to guide them from darkness into the light of his will. Toward the public, Scriabin's hero was as contemptuous as he was dependent. Without them there would be no recognition, no world to subdue, no ecstasy to impart. Symbolically, the hero stands as "unity" in opposition to "multiplicity," the one against the many.

Scriabin in the scene of the Nobles' Ball is equally cruel to the courtiers around the throne. The Tsaritsa rejects her father and her suitors for the Philosopher-Musician-Poet. This entire scene as Scriabin played it to Schloezer was a parody and he aimed lampoons and pasquinades of music at Tchaikovsky, Arensky and Glazunov. They personified to Scriabin "vulgarity and philistinism." In cold-blooded plagiarism he took their most banal melodies and drenched them in pompous harmonies.

Viewing the text of the opera and reinforcing it with hearsay descriptions, we are surprised at the absence of morality or moral conclusion. There is no good or evil, no duty or purpose in unifying the world, nothing but mere capricious will exerting itself towards bliss. The hero dies in ecstatic union with the Tsaritsa. He has triumphed through ideas. The mass of mankind has gathered together in felicity. For the last act the hero himself has composed a music-drama which is enacted on stage by the people as a kind of universal holiday. The world is unified, saved and happy. The hero and his lover are consumed in rapture. Extrasensorily they feel the general bliss enveloping their ecstasy and the world.

We encounter in the opera flabbergasting ideas: The unity of the whole world in one amicable, emotional brotherhood of festivity; the superheroic nature of an individual who commands crowds with a thought, who sexually seduces by a flick of a beauteous rumination; a stage character who lectures, boasts, and rules the world in the name of freedom, who composes his own work of art—the opera within the opera—of such melting exquisiteness that it accompanies the deaths of the hero and heroine in a titanic orgasm, a sex-death, a self-induced suicide *à deux*.

The opera is another chapter in Scriabin's evolution into megalomania. He creates the hero and then becomes it. The hero is a demiurge, a subordinate deity, but one who fashions the sensible world according to his divine idea. The world becomes a plaything of the mind. As in Nietzsche, only love and freedom carry man beyond the divisive categories of black and white, true and false, but Scriabin's freedom is a paste-diamond. Denial and annihilation are escape whereas freedom is assumption, implying choice. It insists on the renunciation of one thing in order to take responsibility for something else. The opera confers freedom in the name of ideas and love, and proposes them under appallingly patronizing and disengaged terms. The result is autistic illusion.

Here was Scriabin's philosophical, spiritual, and psychological misstep. For the sake of his private rapture, he turned from the rational being who says to himself that he exists in relation to an already created world, and joined irrational man who says that since he exists, the world exists through him. The suns he creates revolve around him.

However, whatever flaws in this opera or cantata of thoughts, the conception was unique. It might have worked as a study in the power of art over the forces of the stage—soloists, choruses, sets. Schloezer wrote wistfully summing up his conclusions:

> If only the Opera had been written in 1903 as planned. We would then have had today a large work, motley in styles, dual in ideas, devoid of wholeness or consistency, but abounding in musical and poetic beauties. However lacking it would have been in ultimate significance, it would still have been, in essence, a hopeful trial, a draft leading to the formation of something else.

57

The text of Scriabin's opera as written in the Green Notebook of 1901–1903, with clarifying directions added in parentheses:

(Scene I)
(THE SETTING)

> Dreaming in a beauteous garden
> Magic fires glow
> Revelry of feasting heard
> From shimmering distance.
> There, all is wonder
> There, luxuriant flowers take refulgent refuge
> There, choirs of birds
> Trill harmonies of praise to their Creator.
> There, plays a soft wave of sound
> With a plash of stroking light
> Filled with delight,
> Magic charms of welcome.

(DESCRIPTION OF THE QUEEN-DAUGHTER)

> But all these treasures
> Worthy of this picture divine only enhance
> The delicate form of the Tsaritsa
> She crowns the dream.
> She is all mortal hope,
> Idol of her subjects
> Her father proffers a sumptuous festival
> To her honor. It is her departure.

(Scene II)
(CRITICISM OF SYCOPHANTS)

> The dazzled throng of guests
> Enviously surround her
> They lavish praise.
> The Tsaritsa remains cold.

The noxious poison of their beguiling words
Does not move her prudent head.
She with passionless smile
Accepts . . . and rules.

(THE NOBLES' PARTY)

ONE OF THE GUESTS (A POET):
Stars of the Universe grow pale before you
Your brow is stamped with all heavenly beauty
Your baneful fascination rules all creation
O Goddess, command all on earth!

ANOTHER GUEST:
Songs of ravishment
Caress us,
Powers of captivating grace
Subdue us,
Each motion
Allows us joy,
Divine creation
Fiery genius
Rule over all!

(THE QUEEN-DAUGHTER'S REJECTION)

Not for her this brilliance. Clamorous revelry
Wearies her and lies heavy
Her heart cries out to freedom
From despised fetters
Her burning mind
Parched for perception
Her life spends itself
Feverishly searching.

QUEEN-DAUGHTER
He who pays me homage
With flattering speech
Will not receive my dream
But he who will have me must
Startle imagination
By magic enchantment of creation
Weave spells by his groping mind,
Quench thirst to know
His soul will mount higher than others—
He the fortunate bearer of genius!

(ARRIVAL OF THE HERO)

> A powerful miracle answered her dream
> Sending a young unknown
> Philosopher being a musician-poet.
>
> By chance she discovered
> His divine creations
> She read, and quickly gave the artist
> Her dream.
>
> No other wish exists
> In her enamored heart
> But to see her beloved friend, secretly.

(THE QUEEN-DAUGHTER CONQUERED)

> For the first time
> She knew
> Both life and world
> His flight of brave ideas conquered
> Quickly came the desire to discard
> Old oppressive outworn form.
>
> He with wise but simple words
> Subdued her science.
> He knew to gaze with pleasure
> Loftiness, brilliance, and beauty
> Into spaces of falling stars
> Knew to soar with free and winged thought
>
> In far distant epochs
> He embraced Eternity with ideas
>
> She listened with delight
> All to see, to know, to comprehend.
>
> The Tsaritsa kissed her god with gratitude for his wisdom.
>
> And now
> She wearies of the guests' chatter
>
> She wishes to forget
> In the sweet dance
> In vain

(THE BALL)

> DANCE-SONG:
> Dance of rapture

Give oblivion

With potent magic
Break my torture.

Life is suffering,
Life is doubt

Thou art dreaming,
Thou art pleasure.

Dance of enchantment
Give solace

With potent curative
Break my doubt.

(Scene III)
(THE QUEEN-DAUGHTER'S DEPARTURE)

The Tsaritsa is sad.
On a rock by the sea
At the garden's enclosure
Her idol sits, sits her solace!

Perhaps he grieves for her . . .

Stealthily she abandons the roistering crowd
Secretly filled with trepidation
Runs from the garden to the sea.

The enraptured poet hastens to meet the maiden
He speaks his passionate words
A song just composed.
He invites her to love's holiday.

(THE QUEEN-DAUGHTER SEDUCED)

Goddess, come
Here life awaits thee
All terrestial joys
Passionate breath of rapturous night
Mysterious whisper of warm waves
Magic delight of the wearying caress
Troubled dreams of burning love.
I reveal to you my passionate embrace,
Come to me, O dream Goddess!
I will exhaust you with my overpowering kisses
Now you will learn sweet felicity!

* * *

(Scene IV)

THE PHILOSOPHER-MUSICIAN-POET TO FESTIVE GUESTS:

I pity you unfortunate children of earth.
Your life is fearful pain
How piteous your existence,
You wander in a dark forest, aimless
Lacking faith in ideals, dreams, enchantments!

How can you live thusly?

You are a chance guest upon earth,
Around you all is closed by mystery
How pointless, the end!
How cowardly, the thoughts!

Where is valor?
Where the power of strengthened men
Going victoriously forward?!

Who holds the banner, who with wings
Leads to triumphant battle?!!

When, O King, will you learn
Of your will's might?
When, you slaves, will you
Escape your shameful chains by wish alone?

No one in this realm of desire and pain
Knows how replete is life
That paradise is not an empty dream
That strong wishing is worthy—

Only then, will happiness pour out its waves.

(THE HERO'S ARIA)

Sweet deceit of religion
No longer beckons
My mind is not clouded
By its tenderly shining mist
My reason is free always
And it affirms:
You are alone
You slave of cold chance

You in the power of the universe
Why do you entrust your destiny
To god?
O pitiful mortal
You can and you must of yourself
Bear on your radiant faces
The glorious imprint of victory.

(MISCELLANEOUS STANZAS FOR THE HERO'S ARIOSI)

I have long ruled the world
By the audacity of my powerful mind.

*

Take all, I demand no reward.

*

When my stars are aflame
And magic light embraces the earth
Then will my fire reflect
In the hearts of people
The world will understand the call.
I AM THE MAGICIAN OF A POWERFUL HEAVENLY
HARMONY
Who lavishes caressing dreams on mankind

With the POWER OF LOVE immeasurable and wondrous
I will make life's springtime for them
I will give them long desired peace
I, BY THE FORCE OF MY WISDOM.

People! Rejoice. After centuries
The awaited end of grief and sorrow has come.

(PERSUASIONS OF THE HERO)

I have felt the crushing deception
Of love's rebelling
Learned the feeling of tender friendship
And the veil of attraction.

*

He will rule the world, who by power
Draws people to himself
With dreams

You will come, enslaved
By a form of beautiful truth
By the delight of a caress.

*

I have come
Intending to speak.
For the herd
You must wisely make laws of the crowd.

And do not crush the glowing petals
Of flowers: love, work, and beauty

That in that modest covering
The divine spark be extinguished.

Everything changes, everything finds its fulfillment.
I am all desiring, ALL URGING, but for me desire is not longing—
it is my element—my happiness, it lives in me together with full certainty
of achievement.

ACT OF THE LAST ATTAINMENT

(THE DEATH IN ECSTASY)

*

(THE PEOPLE:)
You are the striving toward completion.
You are dreams, you the light, and joy,
Only he can know bliss
Who has tasted the sweetness of labor
Who has spent life
In search of charms
Who has found solace in
The might of knowing.

*

It has been accomplished; I go.

*

If I might give an atom of my felicity
I would be giving a world.

*

I am the apotheosis of world creation
I am the aim of aims, the end of ends.

XVI
PHILOSOPHY

58

WHERE DID Scriabin's extreme and inordinate ideas come from? What was responsible for his "supra-musical flights," as Engel asks? Books, sometimes. Friends, too. After Nietzsche died insane in 1900, that influence began to fade. His library now contained Goethe's *Faust*, Trubetskoi's *Study of Logos*, Solovyov's translation of Plato's *Dialogues*, Paulson's *Introduction to Philosophy*, Fulle's *History of Philosophy*, Sievegard's *Logic*, Kuno Fischer's *Kant*, Windelband's *History of New Philosophy*. Scriabin read and underlined, very often wrote extensive marginal notes, but for the most part he tailored ideas to fit his preconceptions, and shut these books to muse independently.

The impression is that Scriabin never read. "He derived his information from conversations exclusively . . ." (Engel) "I never saw a novel or short story in his hand." (Sabaneeff) "He had a low opinion of the arts of erudition." (von Riesemann) And Schloezer contradicts himself when he admits, "Sometimes when he was resting, he would take up a little book by Chekhov or a newspaper, but this was very rare." But here is only a half-truth.

Scriabin would have been an exception to his society had he not perused Brothers Karamazov at some point. The opera, for instance, courses with Dostoevsky's fever.

Scriabin's favorite character in Russian fiction was Kirillov in Dostoevsky's *The Possessed*. They both reasoned alike: "If there is no God then *I* am God." Both use death to prove divinity.

Part of the extravagance of Scriabin's ideas was no more than pollen in the Russian air. The titles in his library show influence from the West.

Freiherr Novalis (1771–1801), German mystic and pioneer of the Romantic movement, was known and read throughout intellectual Russia. In his novel of search for the famous "Blue Flower," *Heinrich von Ofterdingen*, he posed a question which Scriabin heard: "Cannot illness become the means towards a higher synthesis?" From here stems that conveniently evolved attitude of diffuse optimism after the terrible handstrain in 1891. When time and doctors failed to cure, Scriabin took over and filtered through the prismatic rays of his mind every consequence of life, each obstacle of fact.

German romantic philosophers flooded nineteenth-century Russia with their "thoughts from abroad" Georg Hegel (1770–1831) changed mid-century intellectual history in Russia more than any other single figure. His theory presented the human mind as moving from consciousness, through self-consciousness, reason, spirit and religion to absolute knowledge. God, in short, is thought thinking; the external world is as much intellectual conception as it is a fact of the senses. Hegel gave Russia its very visage of formal logic.

Similarly, Friedrich Schelling (1775–1854), darling of existentialists, equated philosophy and poetry, invented "metaphysical empiricism" making God an experience and a mystery. He believed Russia would redeem Europe's follies and heal her wounds. Schelling also agreed with Friedrich Schiller (1759–1805), the poet, that life was an "endless festival of creation," and reconciled nature and mind as the "creative act of genius." Every word here reverberates in Scriabin's vocabulary.

Scriabin was introspective, because he was Russian. But he sometimes had trouble. Reading to him often meant re-reading. "How profane I am," he said to Sabaneeff. "It is ridiculous that I had only four years of education at the Corps. What a *scandal* that was! I had to learn so much on my own about philosophy, ideas . . . There was no one in the home or in the Corps who could discuss such matters . . ." In the last years of his life, he complained to Schloezer, "I simply haven't enough knowledge. For my work, learning is indispensable. I don't want to be an authority, but I don't want to be a stranger in these fields. How awful it would be to do all this thinking on my own, only to find at the end that I have re-discovered America!"

In the middle of a conversation if someone expressed a certain thought, or if he read a passage in a book, he would cry out, "That's mine!" or

"I said that," even if the idea had been expressed in ancient Greece and printed before Scriabin was born. Scriabin could argue either way though, and he justified himself agilely. Other times he was pleased with his lack of education and consoled himself with it: "I don't have to break down in order to build up. That burden in others hinders them from action. I start straight from the beginning—to be logical and to be true at the same time is an impossibility. Here you must think illogically to arrive at the truth. In the life of the soul there will always be contradictions. In the end I can only rely on direct perception . . . ."

Often Scriabin used his sharp mind to prove perverse points. He well knew the difference between emotional and factual truth. Sabaneeff recalls a time when Scriabin asserted that pain can become pleasure.

"What about a toothache?" I asked.

Scriabin thought a while. "This is a question of distributing matter. All dissonances in music can be distributed in an artistic rhythm so that they turn into a vehicle of pleasure. I can caress a woman and make her discordant. I can hurt her and she will experience pleasure. Now the question is how to make external pain seem like internal pleasure . . . Now, what kind of a counterpoint can I write to a toothache?" And he laughed.

On another occasion Scriabin developed the thesis that "There are times in the life of mankind when murder is a virtue and to be murdered the greatest pleasure." Sabaneeff says here that "he said this with the conviction of one who had personally essayed such rarified satisfactions."

59

At the head of the list of Scriabin's friends now stood Prince Sergei Trubetskoi. Aside from his chair as reader in philosophy at Moscow University, Trubetskoi was also president of the Moscow Philosophical Society, an organization which sponsored lectures, readings, social gatherings, and even table-tipping séances by intellectuals, mystics, and mediums. Scriabin joined the society at Trubetskoi's behest, and he attended a number of their sessions. His signature on the membership roster and guest books attests to this.

Trubetskoi's influence on Scriabin was strong. His wife, Prakovya (1860–1914) (née Princess Obolenskaya), also loved Scriabin. She got along well with Vera, too. "The finest family on earth," Scriabin once exclaimed about them.

Trubetskoi regarded himself as a "concrete idealist," and a "mystical Christian." He hated, insofar as his elevated soul admitted to that emotion, what he called "abstract rationality," that is, reason and positivism. The fountainhead of his belief was that God is Love. He accepted this in the most profound sense, and the first step of his faith was his conviction of the divinity of Christ.

However, Trubetskoi was only a shadow, through whom shone a truer light, the figure of Vladimir Solovyov, who had exhorted Russia to be a nation of god-seeking, god-building, god-bearing and god-haunted "all-humans" belonging in an "all-unity."

Solovyov's and Trubetskoi's translations from the Greek made ancient myths and legends familiar. Part of Scriabin's everyday conversation too, was Greece. Amphion and Orpheus were alive in Scriabin's imagination.

Magical abilities were considered by Scriabin and his friends to be man's birthright. Once possessed by the ancients, he said, they had been allowed by moderns to fall into desuetude. Schloezer justified his attitude when he wrote, "If the assertion that the artist has power over matter sounds strange to contemporary ears, even absurd, the fact that the artist has power over our souls—no one will deny."

Scriabin's philosophy above all else wanted transubstantiation in music, to turn sound into ecstasy. He searched for musical ritual which would recapture ancient history's magical powers. To him the present was a "degeneration of what was *before*, the cult of real magic." "That's the magic I want to reestablish," he said. "In those mysteries of antiquity there was real transfiguration, real secrets, and sanctities." And, not even making an exception of Trubetskoi or Solovyov, he added that, "All our little saints of today have forgotten their powers of old . . ."

Scriabin went so far in this direction as to respect artifice, that extreme of fabrication, the "manipulation of reality into art," as he termed it. He idealized and idolized art for "how" it was made as well as for "what" was in its contents. His lips made a complimentary word "*beziskus-stvennosts*" (without artifice) pejorative. He said of Mussorgsky, in one generous moment, "the greatest talent Russia has produced," but that he was "too raw in *Boris*. . . . It is without artifice or art . . ."

There was some agitation against all this welter of mystical philosophy in Russia, and Scriabin's immoderateness of philosophy, in contrast to the respectability of his friends, alienated numbers of his adherents. Sabaneeff describes this in painful detail.

> I had heard various rumors . . . They said he was half-mad and wanted to unite music with philosophy.
>
> How so? I would think and then before me flashed the image of a tiny little man, elegantly dressed to the point of dandyism, pretentious, with passionate self-opinions and little education.
>
> Scriabin was beginning to be considered a degenerate, a decadent, a *réclamist* who used such methods as these only to draw attention to himself. Such was the opinion of many.

The public would change its opinion drastically—and Sabaneeff most of all.

60

IN THE summer of 1903 at Obolenskoe, Scriabin's neighbors were again the Pasternaks. Their houses perched on the same little wooded hill, separated only by a thicket of trees. The music from Scriabin's *dacha* "resounded and reverberated." Leonid Pasternak (1826–1945) was an Odessan Jew, the most sought-after and fashionable painter in all Russia, and an elected member of the Academy of Art. His friends and subjects were the great of the day—painters Serov, Vrubel, and Levitan; writers such as Tolstoi, Rilke, and Verhaeren; and musicians from Anton Rubinstein to Scriabin—nearly all of whom he sketched or drew (including Lenin, at a later date).

The mother, Rosa née Kaufman (1867–1949), a graduate of the Odessa Conservatory, had been a concert pianist until her marriage. Their son, Boris, poet and novelist, was then twelve and he fell in love with Scriabin.

Of the reams of documentation adoring Scriabin, none surpasses Boris Pasternak (1890–1960). In his three autobiographies, *I Remember*,

Safe Conduct, and *Childhood: 1905*, he wrote with precision and expressiveness. George Reavey lucidly speaks of "the whole elemental, paradoxical and almost superhuman personality of Scriabin" weaving its enchantment over Boris. "I loved music more than anything else, and I loved Scriabin more than anyone else in the world of music . . .

> Scriabin was my god and idol . . . Lord what music it was! . . . crumbling and tumbling like a city under artillery fire . . . brimful of ideas minutely worked out to a point that was indistinguishable from frenzy, and at the same time as new as the forest, breathing life and freshness . . . (The translation is David Magarshack's)

Leonid and Scriabin often went for long walks, and Boris followed like a puppy yapping at their heels. He was profoundly impressed by Scriabin's "charming elegance . . . fine breeding with which he avoided appearing serious-minded." He also noticed Scriabin's paradoxes as he argued with his father. The two artists agreed on "craftsmanship . . . about everything else they were poles apart." However, to Boris, Scriabin was always right. "I loved him to distraction . . . I was always on his side."

I Remember continues the eulogy (again the translation is David Magarshack's):

> Scriabin's argument about the Superman was a characteristically Russian craving for the extraordinary. Actually, not only must music be supermusic to mean anything, but everything in the world must excel itself to be itself . . .
>
> Scriabin with the means that were at the disposal of his predecessors renewed our sensation of music from its very foundation at the very beginning of his career. In the Studies of Opus 8 and in his Preludes of Opus 11, everything is already contemporary, everything is full of those inner correspondences, accessible to music, with the surrounding external world, with the way in which people of those days lived, thought, felt, traveled, and dressed.
>
> No sooner do the melodies of those works begin than tears start to your eyes . . . The melodies, mingling with the tears, run straight along your nerves to your heart, and you weep not because you feel sad, but because the way to your heart has been found so unerringly and so shrewdly . . .
>
> A generally acknowledged truth must wait for a rare piece of luck . . . Such a piece of luck was Scriabin. Just as Dostoyevsky is not only a novelist and just as Blok is not only a poet, so Scriabin is not only a composer, but an occasion for perpetual congratulations, a personified festival and triumph of Russian culture.

Boris decided to become a composer, and Yuri Engel was his teacher. This passion for Scriabin never left him. He never even minded when his idol played a passage of his (Boris') music in the wrong key, took his arm and put his hand on his shoulder and told him paradoxically that improvising was harmful, that one should aspire for simplicity like his sonatas ("notorious for their complexity"), that formlessness was more complex than form, and as for absolute pitch? Boris had been so happy that Scriabin did not have it, for it made the idol like the boy. When Boris mentioned their common weakness, Scriabin lost patience and said any piano tuner has it.

When Scriabin came late in the dark of Moscow, one evening to pose for a Pasternak drawing, Boris never forgot the moment, and it appeared as poetry in *Childhood: 1905* (translation by George Reavey):

> The doorbell rang
> And the sound of voices drew near:
> Scriabin—it was he.
> Oh where could I run
> From the footsteps of my divinity!

Safe Conduct (translated by Beatrice Scott) tells us more of the same year:

> On the way from school the name Scriabin, all in snow, tumbled from the concert bill on to my back. I brought it home with me on the lid of my school-satchel, water trickled from it on to the window sill. This adoration struck me more cruelly and no less fantastically than a fever. On seeing him, I would turn pale, only to flush deeply immediately afterwards for this very pallor. If he spoke to me my wits deserted me and amid the general laughter I would hear myself answering something that was not to the point, but what exactly—I could never hear. I knew that he guessed everything but had not once come to my aid. This meant that he did not pity me, and this was just that unanswerable indivisible feeling for which I thirsted. This feeling alone, the more fiery it was, the more it protected me from the desolation which his incommunicable music inspired.

And when Boris Pasternak died, Sviatoslav Richter played Scriabin music on the little upright piano next to the corpse all day and into the night.

In Obolenskoe Scriabin's friendship with Boris Schloezer deepened, and with it love for his sister, Tatyana. All was not philosophy between them, though it seemed so. In July, 1903 Scriabin wrote Boris: "I give philosophy little attention, having read only Uberweg." (This in itself was formidable. Friedrich Uberweg (1826–1871) was the author of the monumental, historiographical *Outline of Philosophy*).

Later in the month, when Boris (with Tatyana) visits the Scriabins in the country, he brings a present—*History of Philosophy* by Kuno Fischer. End of the month Scriabin writes, "I have nothing interesting to say about myself. I read, write, read, write, and that's how the time passes since your departure. It is with the greatest ease I devour the Kuno Fischer book. I want to read it all . . . If you could only know how I sometimes *need* to talk music and philosophy with you . . ."

Again Scriabin explained to Boris his neglect of philosophy: "I am literally sunk in work. I am orchestrating the symphony and composing piano pieces . . . I must finish 30 compositions in August, otherwise I cannot go to Switzerland. That is all I think of!"

On 6 September, 1903, he wrote: "I have not written you recently, because I have been wanting to fix the date more or less for my departure. Nothing must stand in the way of *that*! But *when*?! I am very busy, but only with music, that is, I am gradually getting my many pieces into some kind of order. Maybe I'll finish in a month! I am in desperation such as I have never known before! I convert myself into the cheapest of coins. I violate my inspiration."

By the end of August he had written Belaieff, "I wanted to send you some of the piano pieces, but it won't hurt to let them lie around for another 2 or 3 weeks. I have decided to give them to you all at once, personally, when I see you end of September . . . all 40 of them," he says, adding an extra ten to the figure.

25 September, 1903, Scriabin was still worried about his indebtedness to Belaieff: "I am so ashamed to abuse your kindness to me. You are on sound ground thinking ill of me, but I hope in a few days—perhaps 2 weeks at the most—to dispel your gloomy thoughts. Here's why I am late: Among the masses of music (40 pieces, as I told you), there are some very *big* things, such as a 4th sonata, a concert waltz fantasia, and so forth. They are complicated and need to be gone over especially carefully. I have had much trouble with them . . ."

He invited himself to SPb. "I'll stay in a hotel if you refuse me asylum."

And he ended the letter affectionately. "I kiss you warmly and remain your sincerely loving . . ." The next word comes from Belaieff: "Incorrigible Muscovite! 25 days have gone by without one word from you! What did you mean by 'very big?' And why don't you come to SPb *now*? Yes, because of our friendship I will keep your work a secret until you have finished. But wouldn't you like Liadov at least to rejoice with me?"

Scriabin's life had grown more complex. Now it was clear he had seduced Tatyana. His love became a source of inspiration for the thirty or forty piano pieces, it may be, and the Third Symphony, too, but most of all, Tatyana seemed an urgent cause for going abroad. He wished to relegate Vera and the children to Dresden, and asked Tatyana to identify her fortune with him in that land of freedom, Switzerland, in that city of Rousseau, Geneva. (He had forgotten Calvin also came from there.) Tatyana accedes, and the decision makes her ill.

To curry favor, Scriabin writes the Schloezer father (whom he has never met):

> I want to tell you of my joy in knowing your children. I find them good friends, interesting conversationalists, and fine connoisseurs. They afford an artist with many a delightful moment. I hope that their short sojourn in Moscow was only the beginning of our friendship. I sincerely hope to see them again as soon as possible. I remember our talks with such pleasure. Only your presence was missing from these occasions. I regret the great distance which separates us and prevents me from one of my greatest desires—calling on you in person. But happily, against space there is time. This fact gives me the hope that in the future I will overcome that obstacle. I live in this hope.

Scriabin's first note to Tatyana is undated, unaddressed, unsigned and secret. The only clue it contains is one sentence at the end, "Borya will tell you everything," placing the brother as conspirator. "Your frame of mind must be calm, CALM. The only thing you have to think about —and it *must* occupy all your time and attention—is your health. *All* the rest will come. With all my being I want what has been and what will be . . . How divine autumn is going to be!"

His second note to her, transmitted by conspirator Boris, is forceful. She was still ill from her decision to enter upon a disgraceful liaison with a married man: "How awful of you! Why do you doubt and upset yourself! You must be a good little girl and follow the doctor's orders to the letter. I live in one thought only—our trip to Switzerland. I am doing everything *possible* to realize this dream. And so, until our early and joyous meeting!"

Tatyana was susceptible. The philosophizing between him and her brother must have dazzled her. As a pianist with aspirations to become a composer, Tatyana's attraction to Scriabin finally overwhelmed her reason. After Scriabin's death, she submitted some fragmentary memoirs to Engel. They begin with her eighteenth year.

Dark, beautiful, shoulders held back, and a slight expression of pain or some indefinable inner distress almost permanently etched on her face, she told how she was taking the health cure and vacationing with her mother and brother in the Caucasus at the resort town of Pyatigorsk, famous for its thermal, restorative waters. Buyukli arrived to give a concert on 10 November, 1901. He played the Third Sonata.

> I dreamed of seeing the composer. In a year, my dream became reality. In November 1902, my brother and I went to Moscow and took furnished rooms.
>
> I was terribly nervous about meeting Alexander Nikolaevich. He came to us that first time late, around 9:30 in the evening. Instantly we were involved in a lively, warm conversation. He went to the piano at our request and my brother and I listened entranced. Everyone asked him to keep on playing and he did. Suddenly there was a knock on the door. The rule of the establishment was no music after 11 p.m. We were horrified. It was sacrilegious to stop Scriabin from playing! However, he just laughed and said if we wanted to hear him some more to come to his place. We did, and he played until two in the morning . . .
>
> I had come to Moscow primarily to find someone competent to help me with my composing. I was hardly bold enough to think of Scriabin in this connection. Imagine my joy when he proposed working with me. He liked my improvisations and my compositions.
>
> He did not teach often. His system was the same as he had been taught: "Write two measures," "Write four measures and a coda," "No parallel fifths," etc. When I did poorly, he was dissatisfied and I cried. I soon gave up my composing, for I was under his spell.

In personal conversations with Sabaneeff, Tatyana enlarged her account and described the courtship somewhat differently:

> "He was very nervous. There was no psychological connection between himself and Vera Ivanovna. They were strangers . . . The atmosphere in the

house was stiff as starch. Alexander Nikolaevich seemed to be visiting instead of being at home ... Then he said to me that it would be better were we to meet in my furnished rooms at the 'Prince' in Gazetny ... He followed this by saying that he was not suggesting this as a gentleman, and said that our acquaintance would appear to the world as dalliance."

61

HE LEFT for his near-annual trek to Petersburg for Belaieff's nameday celebrations of 1903. Belaieff was suffering again from recurrent stomach ulcers. Scriabin carried with him a portfolio of completed compositions for piano—thirty-six in number—covering a hundred sheets of music paper. He also brought with him the vast score of the Third Symphony almost finished. The group of piano pieces Op. 30 through Op. 42 contained the finest music Scriabin had so far written. They are, as Engel says, "diamonds of a very clear water," or according to Kashperov, "pearls for the piano ..." Nothing—both in quantity and quality— could have cheered Belaieff more.

His letters are unusually informative. He wrote Vera on 3 November, 1903: "It has not been appropriate for me to bring up such ticklish questions as business, but the beginning has been made. The bulk of the portfolio had the desired effect." He played the symphony for Liadov "who said he liked it very much, but I could see he did not understand all of it."

Belaieff devotes a formal Friday to a hearing of the symphony before the Board and other invited guests. "Last night," Scriabin wrote on 15 November, 1903, "I finally played my symphony for a group of Petersburgian composers and oh! what a surprise! Glazunov was in raptures. Korsakoff was most favorably disposed. And over dinner, *even* the subject of how well Nikisch would play it came up." (Taneieff recorded in his diary he thought it "a composition of talent.") "Thanks be to God all went well. It was like having a mountain lifted from my shoulders! Now Belaieff will publish the symphony with pleasure, and I am happy for this."

Best of all, Belaieff took to the Satanic Poem. "Imagine! Belyasha liked Satan!! I had to repeat the last part three times for him. "Afterwards, he impetuously handed him a wad of ruble notes without bothering to measure the new compositions against the debt. Scriabin sent the money instantly to Vera. "*Without fail* you must pay the rent." Vera told him a thief has robbed the attic and taken the children's clothes stored there. "Whoever stole them, may he catch cold and die!!!" Scriabin is too shy to pursue his need of money to Belaieff. If Vera needs more, he suggests she borrow from Aunt Lyubov.

Scriabin can scarcely relax in SPb. There is still finishing-up work before Belaieff can send the pieces to the printer. As usual, Scriabin has brought them exquisitely written, but without proper markings, He works, but Belaieff's home was conducive more to pleasure than concentration. "Yyadoff" (Liadov) drops over everyday at three and sits until late suppertime. By then other guests begin to arrive. Belaieff sent Scriabin to hear Nikisch conduct. The program is usual fare—Wagner, Tchaikovsky, Rimsky.

Belaieff is in considerable agony this November of 1903. He plans to return in May to the Lamana Sanitarium in Dresden, where his ulcers had been "cured" once before. Belaieff telegraphed Franz Scheffer, head of the Leipzig office, to find out all details of living costs and to start looking for a six-room apartment for the Scriabins. "He knows, and I have told him," Scriabin explains to Vera, "that aside from him I have no other source of income. He evidently wishes to undertake my financial support. He is altogether an angel." However, Scriabin has not been entirely frank. He has not spoken of Tatyana to Belaieff.

Vera wrote Scriabin on 8 November that he will receive "an excellent letter." One week later, Scriabin calls Vera a "horrid little black dog" for not writing often. It is all right for *him* not to write, he says, because he is working so hard "my head swims . . ." Then he replies to the promised "excellent letter." It is from Margarita Morozova, his erstwhile student. She was now widowed from the wealthy landowner Morozov, and was plunging into good works—promoting concerts, financing a publishing house called *Path*, and the like. He had instructed Vera to cultivate her; soon according to Scriabin the two women had "drunk their brotherhood (*Brüderschaft*) together."

Morozova's letter informed Scriabin that, knowing of his genius, his need to go abroad, and his financial hardship, she would give him a "pension" of 200 rubles a month. She enclosed the first installment of this open-end promise, "Here is my token of friendship." "She really is sweet!" Scriabin wrote Vera, "God grant her health. Even if she re-marries to an idiot, I will be pleased to forgive her." Then he adds more soberly, thinking of his future away from Vera, "I am so happy FOR YOU. That money is *for you and the children*. The news from Dresden is good. An apartment costs 1,200 to 1,500 marks a month. Servants are the only luxury there. They are all spoiled . . ." Yes, he would like to return home to Moscow and Vera sooner, but "Belaieff holds me here by my teeth . . ."

Scriabin informed Belaieff of the Morozova stipend, after he returns to Moscow. Belaieff asked if the good news cannot be shared with Liadov: "He will rejoice with me . . ." Scriabin answered, "Tell Anatol Konstantinovich, but IN SECRET." Belaieff also asked for more details. Scriabin hedged saying he had received 200 rubles, "And that's all . . . but probably it will come every month . . ." Belaieff continued his stipend, and asked if Scriabin would like him to put in writing a guarantee of 200 rubles a month.

That long November visit with Belaieff was the last. Belaieff's condition worsened. Neither May in the sanitarium nor a meeting with the Scriabin family in Dresden ever came. On 15 December—Scriabin wrote the year as "903"—he posted his last letter to Belyasha.

> I was very grieved by news of your illness. Why didn't you tell me specifically what is the matter? Surely not your stomach again? Even though it will make you angry I am going to tell you that a few days ago I talked with one of the very best doctors here about how to *cure* your ailment, and also about your weakness for pie pastry. He was horrified, and said that diet means not only *refraining* from certain foods but strictest *moderation* at all times. And as for those meat pies . . . well, I don't need to go into that any further. You'll come to grief. I told him, too, that it wasn't the stomach but the intestines and he answered *no matter what* it is, you must eat less. Now, I won't interfere anymore.

Nor would the chance arise.

He carried this letter around in his pocket for four days. He added a postscript apologizing for his "absent-mindedness . . ." I can't understand how this happened." Belaieff was dying when he read this final expression of Scriabin's devotion to him, and how many times, one wonders, had

Scriabin written identical words excusing his thoughtlessness? The ulcers had abscessed, and the doctors operated. The operation was a success, then suddenly Belaieff's heart gave way on 28 December, 1903. At the age of sixty-seven Belaieff died. His illness seemed a psychosomatic indictment of his gruff, enthusiastic, affectionate exterior. His death was followed in six days by that of Peter Jurgenson, the publisher whom Belaieff had first rivaled, then surpassed.

Scriabin was sunk with grief. He did not write a letter of condolence. He was unable to attend the funeral. When the month's stipend of two hundred rubles arrived—sent by Belaieff's businessman brother, Sergei, and executor of Belaieff's will—Scriabin answered formally and ignored the bereavement.

In the Findeizen letter, 1907, he could utter only this: "I met Mitrofan Petrovich Belaieff in 1892. [The date is wrong.] He instantly exhibited a most forthright and fatherly solicitude towards me. He accompanied me on my first concert tour to introduce my compositions abroad. This drew us even closer together. I have, I must confess, most affectionate memories of Belaieff. His loss was a very great blow to me, in all truth."

✐ XVII ✐
MIDDLE MASTERWORKS

62

THE THIRD Symphony was the first masterwork belonging to 1903, and sparked though it was by the opera's philosophy, still it was the last to reach final form. The first was the Fourth Sonata, Op. 30, and it marks Scriabin's transition from early works to his "Middle Period." Never had Scriabin worked faster. This sonata was jotted in its entirety in two days. The dreamlike, Prelude, Op. 37 No. 1 (*mesto*, "thoughtful and melancholic") took half an hour to write. The momentary yet massive Prelude, Op. 37 No. 2 (*maestoso fiero*, "majestic and proudly"), more of an étude than a prelude except in brevity, was composed in an hour. Even the two large Tragic and Satanic Poems, Opp. 34 and 36, were each drafted in three days' time.

All these middle masterworks were brand new in form, content, pianism, and free of Chopin's hegemony. Here began those patulous Scriabinic harmonies that astound with their subtlety. He bolstered the very timbre of the piano with repeated chords, rippled basses, octave leaps or what Samuel Randlett in his doctoral thesis on Scriabin's pianistic development calls "snaps," thick trebles of triads as melodies, double-noted arpeggios, chromatic inner textures of tenor melodies (played by the left-hand thumb), chords and melodies patterned in fourths, fluttery pedaling to keep the polyrhythms and tonal combinations translucent, slow releases of the pedal to catch after-resonances and keep their reverberance. He was already writing notes which did not exist as keys on the piano—a low G# (Prelude, Op. 39 No. 4) and soon, a high D (Sixth Sonata).

There were specific moods demanding these novelties, and here too, the content expanded. Opalesque satanism, for example, was one. It flickered like an underblaze. And misspelled as Scriabin's Italian occasionally was, he still used it meaningfully—*con fiducia* (trustingly), *elevato* (elevated), *esaltato* (exalted), *agevole* (actively), *ardito* (ardently), *con voglia* (with will). This music created a unique vocabularly of astonishment. Its evolution had been almost imperceptible. Such a gradual break with the conventions of preceding music was rare among early twentieth-century composers. Neither Debussy nor Schönberg moved from the known to the unknown, the familiar to the unfamiliar, the consonant to the dissonant, with equal inevitability or naturalness. The seams between Scriabin's classicism and modernism are tightly sewn.

The Fourth Sonata is a short, focused, quasi-sonata, consisting of two movements—*andante* and *prestissimo volando*. Thematically, it is twofold. The rising intervalic opening melody, which Scriabin once called "the striving upward toward ideal creative power," has a tail to its comet— a brief motif of "languor or exhaustion after effort." The finale (marked *focosamente* or "vehemently") is this beginning apotheosized *fortississimo*.

A quintessential step beyond its predecessors, the sonata's chordal structure is hollow spaced, light and airy. The form relentlessly progresses in a single direction. "My goal is maximum musical thought placed within a minimal form," Scriabin once said, and he used the Fourth Sonata to exemplify his conciseness. Both structure and sonority are crystalline. The shape of the whole piece is that of "A" growing, increasing, waxing into a final and ultimate "A⁺," spaced with subsidiary rises and falls. The pressure grows from quiet to grandiose, sustaining one single line of tension.

Scriabin will follow this structure of gradually evolving moods in all future sonatas, from languor, thirst, or longing (invariably slow, soft, vague, mysterious perhaps, and certainly indistinct, as if to induce the auditor's attention), through struggle, depths and heights, or battle (usually a skittering *allegro* with speed to disrupt tranquility and excitement), through flight, dance, luminosity, or ecstasy (each marked as such, in French). The chain is a series of lifts, ascents and upsurges, finally bursting into fragmentation, dematerialization, dissolution—a last and final strengthening of freedom. This is the original meaning of *nirvana*, a "blowing out" or "dispersal." Such "dematerialization" is a very great state of activity and the antithesis of inertia. It thereby abandons the force of gravity and breaks down even the restraint motion imposes. Marshall McLuhan described life in "three stages—alarm, resistance, and exhaustion," but Scriabin begins his music at the end and carries it through these "stages" arriving at a vertical rather than horizontal conclusion. Scriabin henceforth substituted his own forms and obeyed these in strictest symmetries—two measures by two, four bars by four. He began preferring the octave divided evenly and equally into half, that is, C-F#-C (two augmented fourths), rather than the imperfect and arbitrary imbalance of a fifth and a fourth.

Occasionally he deviated from the four square into hexagonals of musical phrases. ("Towards the Flame," Op. 72 is one example.) The pejorative designation for this practice was "paper music."

However, to dismiss it lightly is like looking at a chemical formula of an explosive without understanding its consequences. Scriabin counted his number of measures exactly. "I need to be exact so as to make the form crystal clear," he said. The small rigid units anchored the listener's mind and ear and somehow freed the understanding for the flowing textures and their musico-ideological conceptions. Yet for all this, Scriabin's music from the Fourth Sonata on *sounded* even more improvised than before. It seemed like an outburst of inspiration (which it was) and so loose in form as to be disorganized (which it was not).

The Fourth Sonata is accompanied by a poem in free verse. The impetus of Scriabin's inspiration overflowed into literature, and as two trees may have a single root, similarly the words express the music. He wrote the poem in French, poor French at that, almost as if his heart was already living in Switzerland. "In general," he once said to Schloezer, "I live only in and for the future . . ."

The poem follows the sidereal music exactly. It leads us from the faint shine of a far-distant star into a flashing sun. Scriabin's search for the sensation of light, the driving energy of this our universe, continues. Here, like a nova increasing its brilliance millionfold, the star theme magnifies itself into a sunburst of sound.

> In a light mist, transparent vapor
> Lost afar and yet distinct
> A star gleams softly.

How beautiful! The bluish mystery

Of her glow
Beckons me, cradles me.

O bring me to thee, far distant star!
Bathe me in trembling rays
Sweet light!

Sharp desire, voluptuous and crazed yet sweet
Endlessly with no other goal than longing
I would desire.

But no! I vault in joyous leap
Freely I take wing

Mad dance, godlike play!
Intoxicating, shining one!

It is toward thee, adored star
My flight guides me

Toward thee, created freely for me
To serve the end
My flight of liberation!

In this play
Sheer caprice
In moments I forget thee
In the maelstrom that carries me
I veer from thy glimmering rays

In the insanity of desire
Thou fadest
O distant goal

But ever thou shinest
As I forever desire thee!

Thou expandest, Star!
Now thou art a Sun
Flamboyant Sun! Sun of Triumph!

Approaching thee by my desire for thee
I lave myself in thy changing waves
O joyous god

I swallow thee
Sea of light

My self-of-light

I engulf Thee!

In 1904 when the middle masterworks were finally published, the *RMG* reviewed them. The critic was his good friend from Zverev days, Chernaev, but now he no longer understood:

> Mr. Scriabin has now given us four sonatas. His is, indeed, "Music of the Future!" This composer loves to abuse with his complicated rhythms and harmonies. He is so artful with his contrapuntal devices that they are sometimes nearly formless and incomprehensible. . . .

Continuing, he comments on each: The Funeral March in the First is a bit of Mussorgsky's *Khovanshchina*; the Second, "very beautiful"; the Third, "interesting and musical in the highest degree, but embroiled and occasionally without poetry." The Fourth lost him completely—"tangled, extraordinarily difficult, pompous, formless, melodically unclear."

63

THIS FOURTH Sonata poem was coeval with Scriabin's first "piano poem." Liszt originally introduced the word "poem" into music, but he applied it to those orchestral pieces which were neither symphonies nor even "preludes," another of his words. "Poem" to Liszt described a program of events or adventures of fact or soul. Scriabin, however, used the designation in his piano music to mean something more fleeting—a spell of enchantment, a passing and inexplicable mood, even a tender fragrance rendered in sound. Very rarely do his piano poems (unlike his huge symphonic poems to come) tell a psychical or philosophic story. Usually, they merely weave a texture of languor, sweetness, aimless wandering, a floating in air or on flames. Most always they are ethereal and elusive (*inafferando*).

Scriabin defined his vocabulary of titles in the middle works. "Prelude" means fragment, a sketch of an idea which could be and sometimes ought to have been developed into something more extended. Like a splinter, sharp and pointed, complete within itself, these preludes are parts of a larger, but rarely expressed whole. "Etude" now suggests a difficulty, but never a virtuosic one. Here the germ idea expands into a brief, more musical than technical complication.

Scriabin's first Poem, Op. 32 No. 1, in F♯ major, remains his most widely known composition. In it he flung magical distributions of tones into that unknown nowhere he so loved, and whence he evoked such startlingly felicitous sonorities. Pleasing quietude caresses the ear here. The beginning is marked *con affetto*, or with affection. Sabaneeff calls the Poem "an erotic kiss . . . a kind of sexual dissolving in waves of sensation." Magic and affection are present, certainly, but where? Is it in the symmetry?

The limpid, placid second measure, for example, is the heart of the Poem. The chord is, conventionally, a dominant ninth with a less conventional lowered fifth. Analyzed for its symmetrical proportions and schematic dynamics, the measure opposes two equal intervals of minor sevenths (c♯-b; e♯-d♯). Within each frame lie two converse unequal pulls, one of a half and the other a whole tone.

Viewed another way this chord composes a cluster of hidden enharmonic major thirds (c♯-e♯; g-b; b-d♯). Or again, it may be forced more artificially into the famous "mystic" or "Promethean" chord, an accretion of various augmented, diminished and perfect fourths—c-f♯-b flat e-a-d (c♯-f♯-b e♯-a♯-d♯)—for which Scriabin was noted in his day. Scriabin wrecked the usual terminology, and Dr. A. Eaglefield Hull described Scriabin's "favourite chord, as a dominant thirteenth with a flattened fifth and a major ninth, eleventh omitted!"

The second section of the Poem fragments this chordal structure into rhythmic sequences of three against five. The chordal symmetry of the dominant ninth opens into minor sevenths again, but with the converse pulls being equal minor thirds.

Theorists over Scriabin asserted that all his later music was built on the basic "mystic" chord. Perhaps the Poem and the root chord of the Fourth Sonata (b-e♯-a; d♯-g♯-c♯) started this, but actually very little of his music was so conceived. The first hints of fourth chords rather than triads appear in Liszt's third "Mephisto Waltz" and his *"Valse Oubliée,"* both pieces Scriabin knew and loved. Scriabin, however, thought primarily in terms of modes or scales. He arranged his vertical structures of harmonies, according to his final sketchbooks, from linear arrangements. His symmetry was of course, it must be said, unconscious or intuitive in large part. His erratically enharmonic spelling shows this. He was guided more by the grip of the keys under his fingers than any intellectualization after the fact. This feeling of the inherent symmetry of Scriabin's harmony is essential to pianists. It balances the weak and strong vibrations and decrees how they should sound under one's fingers.

Advanced harmony of this sort even flavors the Waltz, Op. 38, the last "valse" Scriabin ever wrote. He intended it originally as a splashy, "Grand Concert Valse Fantasia." However, he wrote or released for printing only one section—a theme exquisitely feathered. Its resonances evaporate almost as soon as sounded. They echo like a memory of how a waltz once sounded. "Play it as if you were dreaming it," the composer once told a student. He called it a "dream vision" (*snovidenie*), a mood wrapped in a wreath of unreality.

Some poems of this period warranted specific titles, the Tragic (*Tragique*) and Satanic (*Satanique*), for examples. Both are near-sonatas or first movements of something larger. Twice again in later life Scriabin would write major works which were complete in themselves but truncated studies and should have continued into larger creations ("Poème-Nocturne" and "Towards the Flame"). The Tragic Poem in temperament reverts to the Byronic outburst of *pafos* in the Third Sonata. Man against the gods, nature, himself. "Why is it tragic?" dense Chernaev asked himself and answered, "Hard to say. But the music is original, especially the middle part. A whole tempest in itself! Maybe we can look for the tragic element somewhere here?"

"Tragedy" to Scriabin meant the buffetings of life, their grand thunder and storm, the whirlwind around the counterpoise of man's defiance. Tragic really means "epic," full of "rough masculine colors," as Danilevich phrases it. The Tragic Poem's beginning onrush of fluttering, repeated, descending chords marked *festivamente* (joyously) and *fastoso* (pompous) is surely the court scene from the opera. The middle section, a trumpet melody, marked *irato fiero* (angry and proud), seems likely to be the poet-musician-philosopher's rebuke to the courtiers. The whole of the Tragic Poem is perplexingly written in the bright key of B flat major.

64

THE SATANIC Poem with its odor of brimstone and sulphur is one of Scriabin's strongest compositions. The composer himself enjoyed it, and performed it as often as any piece in his repertoire. One reason was its quick appeal. It is accessible to a general public.

The story is simple. The devil mocks a pair of lovers. His laughter, indulgent at first, gradually becomes exultant as he destroys love. (*Faust* in miniature.) Scriabin perversely contrasts love and the devil's mockery. The passion here is sickly sweet, insincere, and false. Satan is ironic, sarcastic and sardonic. His laughter is poisonous and bitter.

Theoretically, the Satanic Poem was written in the key of C major. The broad, clanging opening establishes the dominant ninth with raised fifth as homebase, and it endures until the piece actually ends—at last— on a C major chord. This central harmony is melodically derived from symmetrically converse pulls or steps downwards in the bass—d, c$\sharp$, c; and upwards in the treble—g flat, g, and g$\sharp$.

No other composer, including Liszt, ever flavored so much of his music with evil. The theory of demonism had been well established before Scriabin, but he more often surrendered his angel within to the demon possessing him without. There was the "Satanic-Abbé," as the Russians called Liszt of the "Mephisto Waltzes," "Malediction," and "Dance of Death." A thousand words were in use—Lucifer, Mephistopheles, Prince of Evil, The God Infernal, Beelzebub, Asmodeus, Anti-Christ, Chernobog (Black God). Mussorgsky called "Night on Bald Mountain", "Satan's cortège", and Balakirev rebuked him for writing music that "glorified Satan"; Pshibyshevsky had written *Satan's Synagogue*, Lermontov *The Demon*, Liadov *Kikimora*, Sologub *The Little Demon*, and dozens of other studies of evil and spirits of darkness came from the minds of writers and artists.

From the time of the Satanic Poem, Schloezer admits that Scriabin was spoken of as "a sickly talent," a producer of "immoral art," and an artist brimming with "sinful colors." Schloezer converts these accusations into "demonstrations of the power of art to cleanse the soul." "Art beautifies and transfigures all," he wrote. He called Scriabin's satanism "a yea-saying" to disperse doubt. Goethe's *Faust* said "Yes" to Mephistopheles. "He had laid the curse of anathema on Satan."

Sabaneeff took grave exception to Schloezer. "I could hardly be mistaken ... Scriabin was peculiarly attracted to moods of sin, corruption, and perversity ... Any artist is both sorcerer and saint. Scriabin himself mixed the satanic and the saintly, black and white magic. He was a holy man and a wicked wizard. He justified himself on the grounds of artistic contrast ..."

Scriabin spoke of this: "My *Poème Satanique* isn't true evil. It is an *apotheosis of insincerity.* Everything in it is hypocritical and false ... Satan is not really himself there. He's just a little devil. Not in earnest. In fact, there's a lot of the parlor about him. He's genteel, and rather sweet ... say, a guest in the home ..."

The Etudes, Op. 42 are dazzlingly pure pieces of sheer musicianship. Despite their immense pianistic problems, they are devoid of obscurity. Only lyricism and clearest emotion rise from them.

No. 1, *presto*, is a circular study of rippled chords metered in nines against fives. It ends in D flat major, but begins on one of Scriabin's symmetrical chord constructions of equidistant, alternating perfect fifths and minor sevenths.

No. 2, discussed earlier, has a series of three successive études all in F# minor. No. 3, "the mosquito" is a bagatelle, a study in measured, limited trills. No. 4, a singing *andante*, is a masterpiece of the slow étude form. Imbued with sweetness, its never naif sentiment flows translucently. No. 5, marked *affanato* (breathlessly), is the largest and most gloomcast étude Scriabin ever wrote. He himself played it in performance more than any other. Its theme (a contraction of major thirds (a-c#; e-g#) into minor thirds (a#-c#; e-g) appears three times in the same key in succession. A songlike interlude twice separates this spiral from the main body which changes its pattern into more intricacy, elaboration and higher tension.

No. 6 in D flat major is an exalted melodic study subtended with again, a restless meter of three against five. The melody, over a texture of thickening harmonies, grows, flowers, fades and crumbles, evolving according to a pattern of increase and diminution. No. 7 in F minor is a short, two-page agitated flutter of somber colors, metered in threes against fours.

No. 8 in E flat major is a pianistic display of complex rhythms, complicated harmonies, and Scriabin's characteristic descending melodic line. The interlude of song is deep, profound, one of Scriabin's most intense inspirations. Again the flutter of wings as in the beginning, and Op. 42 and this first period of Scriabin's now masterful writing finishes. Only the gargantuan symphony remained to be tidied for publication.

65

THE THIRD Symphony in C major, Op. 43 is titled "The Divine Poem" (*Le Poème Divin* or *Bozhestvenaya Poema*). The longest work Scriabin ever wrote, it is also gigantic in its scoring: four flutes, three oboes and English horn, three clarinets and one bass clarinet, three bassoons and one contrabassoon, eight horns, five trumpets, three trombones and one tuba, tympani, tam-tam, and glockenspiel, two harps and the usual string section. Its 207 pages of printed score require forty minutes of non-stop playing. By November, 1904, Vera had laboriously copied the manuscript and Lev Konyus was making the piano transcription for four hands, but even after two years' work invested in the music, Scriabin continued making changes. He completely rewrote the harp part, for instance, after hearing Glazunov's newest symphony in 1904.

The grandeur of "The Divine Poem" resides in the breadth of its musical conception and scope of the emotional philosophy without chorus or excessive number of movements. Sabaneeff saw this symphony as a "colossal biography of Scriabin's creative soul. . . . a picture of his cosmic plan."

"The Divine Poem," the first of his symphonies to be designated by the word "poem" and the first to dispense with Italian and turn to French for markings, divides into three movements: "Struggles" (*Luttes* or *Borba*) opens with a "divine and grandiose" theme. The "I" states itself in the opening measure. The "being" dares to assert itself and differentiates itself from a state of "non-being."

Schloezer said, "It almost says 'I am' (*Ya yesm*)." This "I am" theme, as it came to be known, is like a smile on the face. Musically it bears a strong affinity with the phallic "Sword" theme of Wagner's Niebelungen Ring.

Scriabin, while not admitting this, still always called that Wagner theme, "Will," and would invariably and denigratingly observe, "It is in the classical harmonic plan, though."

The nervously syncopated main theme of the *allegro* is marked "mysterious and tragic." Schloezer once pressed Scriabin to define this as "Mysticism." Scriabin acceded. "I am" represents the Man-God, while "Mysticism" stands for the Slave-Man. Their interplay titles the first movement as "Struggles." The "I am" becomes "affrighted by its own audacity. The spirit or soul sinks into an abyss." Now confident, now obsessed by fear and doubt, this force runs the gamut of its emotions—an intoxication with life, joy of man's liberation, the human spirit within the Universe in all its contrasts. A promise of freedom, a distant, faraway happiness flickers intermittently through the passages of despair. The first movement then concludes "proudly and triumphantly." (It is so marked.) The yearning towards the heroic becomes decisive. The several themes have all been woven in sonata form within a sonata form.

The second movement, "Sensual Pleasures" (*Voluptés* or *Naslazhdenia*) is the first overtly sexual page of Scriabin's music. For the New York performance in 1907, he authorized a translation of that title as "Ecstasies." This slow movement consists of shifting, changing enticements—trilling birds, tremulous steps in sylvan dells—nature, so to speak, as in the Third Sonata; but here the Spirit revels in physical sensation as well. "These comfort and console man . . . Yet, out of the depths of his being rises the sublime. The flutes affirm the soul's belief in the sublime." He uses Glazunov's system of doubling instruments and opens the movement with the winds. "I wanted the effect of an organ, a far-off organ," he once said, admitting that he had not yet caught the pure timbres of each orchestral instrument. However, the solo violin is passionately used to convey the human "I" and its longing for union with nature and its self-annihilation in orgasm.

As the second movement evolves, the singing initial theme is voluptuously transformed "with evergrowing drunkenness" (*avec une ivresse toujours croissante*). The theme of "voluptuous sensuality" is subsequently designated "with overflowing drunkenness" (*avec une ivresse débordante*).

Here, Scriabin was stopped for a long time in the score for lack of four measures. Schloezer tells the story, and it describes clearly how the creation of music came first, and only later followed by a program. Scriabin at this point wanted to link the section showing an increase in sensuous excitement with the return or recapitulation of the smoothly caressing flow and quiet of the beginning. He needed four transition measures. At long last he conceived a trombone fanfare which he then marked "with sublime upsurge" (*élan sublime*). This satisfied his esthetic sense and afterwards he began to speak of the passage in psychological terms. He called it, "the Soul's protest against those sensuous images ruling him."

The last movement titled "Divine Play" (*Jeu Divin* or *Bozhestvenaya Igra*) is the Soul released, the "I am" in untrammeled action throughout the Universe, the sublime joy of free activity. "The Spirit is now released from its former ties of submission to higher force," Scriabin wrote, "it creates its own world by its own creative Will." In this ecstatic *allegro* Scriabin's Soul creates aimlessly. It soars in flight and light. The ancient Stoics called the activity of creating the world, "divine senseless play," and Scriabin clung to the phrase which he had first discovered in the opera. Here too in the "Divine Poem" joy is disembodied. Meaning and purpose are dissolved in floods of sensation.

Long after its composition Scriabin had occasion to say to Sabaneeff, "I truly love that finale even now. Although, of course, it is along classical lines . . . This was the first time I found light in music, the first time I knew intoxication, flight, the *breathlessness* of happiness." Like Van Gogh of the same period, he was able now to say that he had found in art "not its rays, but the sun itself."

These specific passages of light in the Divine Symphony are marked "luminously" (*lumineux*). They are musical sparks, beacons of light which literally flash from the score. As the final movement draws to a close, they become even more emphatic. "Luminously and more and more flashing" (*lumineux de plus en plus éclatant*), he marked them.

Scriabin's language, that vocabulary he used so repetitiously in conversation and music was now manifest: "Flight or uplift" (*vzlyot*), "fluttering" or "hovering" (*porkhayushchii*), "light" (*svet*). Sabaneeff called his speech "a strange language that mixed science and terms used by the intelligentsia with the most poetical and impressionistic expressions."

Scriabin also loved this composition because of its contrapuntal complexity. The "fusing of my themes was now conscious and deliberate," he said, whereas in the First and Second symphonies the success had been more purely intuitive and less successful.

342 SCRIABIN

Sometimes he reminisced bitterly over that period of life in which he composed "The Divine Poem," in Obolenskoe 1903. Vera's father was staying with them. "Do you know what the atmosphere was like then? I was working one day, and the second theme of the finale had just come to me. Ivan Christoforovich shuffled into the room wearing house slippers and his dressing gown. 'Who knows? Who knows?' he muttered, 'Something may come of all this after all . . .'" Scriabin burst out to Sabaneeff. "Wasn't that nice of him! By then I had already had two symphonies *performed.*"

No wonder that for much of the time, Scriabin kept a brandy bottle on the little upright, ready to "release his musical inspiration," or, more truthfully, to deaden both internal and outside torment.

VOLUME TWO

Sketch of Scriabin in 1909, drawn by the celebrated portraitist
Leonid Pasternak, father of the writer, Boris.

Scriabin's manuscript for "Desire," Op. 57 (1908).

First page of manuscript of the Poem, Op. 63 No. 1 (1912).
Written on sketch paper with a draft of another composition.

First page of the manuscript for the Seventh Sonata, Op. 64
(1911), with the marking "Prophetically" as an instruction for
performance.

The first page of the Tenth Sonata, showing Scriabin's musical calligraphy at its most exquisite. 1913.

BOOK III

Only those who have felt the happiness of being in the presence of genius can know the ineffable impressions I retain from my closeness to Scriabin.

We loved that winged soul, loved even his errors and limitations. They were either touching or charming. He infected all of us around him with an enthusiasm for his beliefs and the beauty of his dreams. Even if you did not believe him, you at least wanted to.

Only when the sun went out so suddenly, were we able to face full force what we owed to him. None has inspired since, as he then inspired.

LEONID SABANEEFF in *Reminiscences of Scriabin*

✒ I ✒

INTRIGUE

I

BEING PUBLISHED was a composer's livelihood in the nineteenth and early twentieth centuries. Publishing and patronage were indispensable to any musician's tradecraft—what fellowships, commissions, and artists-in-residence appointments are to careers now. The present-day composer may be printed in immense quantities; however, if others do not perform his material, he cannot earn his living, let alone support a family.

Scriabin could not have played enough concerts, nor appeared in a sufficient number of salons, to maintain his household in Russia or abroad. He was also suffering at this period in his life—the years 1903–1904—from an aversion to public appearances. Fertile creativity was responsible for this strong feeling. But it was also profoundly, and inexplicably, emotional as well. "Why don't you interpret your compositions for the public?" his friends would ask, hoping this would alleviate his financial difficulties and hasten the actualization of his plans for living abroad. He answered invariably with annoyance, "I cannot!" He had to be published.

After Belaieff's death in December, 1903, the firm's Advisory Board turned into the "Board of Trustees for the Encouragement of Russian Composers and Musicians." The presences of Fyodor Groes, head of the Petersburg office and Belaieff's chief financial adviser, and Nikolai Artsybushev, who soon would take over the chairmanship of the Board, enlarged the triumvirate of Rimsky-Korsakov, Liadov and Glazunov. This intriguing faction unsympathetic to Scriabin, or possibly jealous of Belaieff's excessive affection for him, was now quite complete. The first week of February, 1904, Groes sent Scriabin an official letter signed

9

"The Executors of the Belaieff Estate," terminating the system of monthly advances. Payment would only be made after the composer approved first proofs. Meanwhile Scriabin had given up his apartment and auctioned his furniture. He had entrusted his precious piano given him by Belaieff to Morozova.

Dumbfounded, he instantly wrote two letters on 15 February. To the "Executors," he groveled, "The Belaieff firm has published my compositions for 10 years . . ." (He began incorrectly, as usual. The period was eight years.) "Taking all this into consideration cannot the Committee find a way to continue the terms, if not forever at least for a few years?"

To Liadov he wrote more intensely. Crushed by receiving only a curt, official announcement, without private, informal word or warning from his "dear Anatol Konstantinovich," he explained how it was with Belaieff's consent that he relinquished his professorship at the Conservatory, how Belaieff had guaranteed him full support while abroad and had offered to draw up a contract to that effect and that Scriabin had demurred at the formality, and he tells a lie (forgetting that Belaieff had spoken to Liadov about the very matter)—"This is between us, please, but the Morozova stipend was unknown both to him and me at the time." He points out how this two hundred rubles a month, "the one source of revenue I have outside composition," could never sustain his family of four children and nursemaid *even in Switzerland.*"

"I realize that according to the rules you are right," he pleaded. "But you would be executing Mitrofan Petrovich's wishes were you to continue arrangements as they are. You would not be making an exception for me personally, but for him. . . . Forgive me my agitation, but you understand how vitally important it is for me to resolve this matter. The symphony is undergoing drastic revision, and therefore cannot be sent for two months . . . The situation is very, very painful. It might even interfere with our friendship!!! And once again you will scold me for coldness and egotism! Well, forgive me. I won't ever again be so . . ."

Four days later, on 19 February, 1904, Scriabin left for Switzerland without waiting for Liadov's answer, and without Vera. His letter pricked the Trustees' conscience though, and until September he continued to receive the Belaieff 200 rubles monthly. He thanked the Board faithfully each month.

Scriabin received the Glinka Prize for his Third (300 rubles) and

Fourth (200 rubles) Sonatas. The presentation—the first since the "well-wisher's" death—was made openly in Belaieff's name. The other recipients, making the balance of the 3,000 rubles total award, were Arensky (D minor Trio), 500 rubles; Liapunov (E flat major Concerto), 500 rubles; Rachmaninoff (C minor Concerto), 500 rubles; and Taneieff (C minor Symphony), 1,000 rubles.

Scriabin was grateful. He wrote Vera in Moscow that "A wart may not be much of a thing in itself, but it's a big addition to the end of one's nose. What thanks I give for the 500! I had not expected that much." Scriabin telegraphed Groes that he would accept the money. Then he annoyingly wrote Glazunov urgently asking him what procedure to follow or whom to address himself to now that Stassov was no longer intermediary.

Glazunov replied only that "I have played your 4th Sonata very often and am enchanted with it. . . . It is original, full of ravishing colors, and its thoughts are expressed with such clarity and compactness . . ." Then he goes on to chat about his twelve years of insomnia which he has just conquered. He wishes Scriabin the "best of fame and health."

2

AGAINST THE Belaieff publishing house intrigue, Scriabin wove a counterpoint of love fantastical in its duplicity. Even if both funds had been canceled, he would still have had to leave Russia. He saw to this by a scandalous indiscretion. In January, 1904, he seduced one of the prettiest dark young girls at the St. Catherine's Institute, a former student of his named Maria Bogoslovskaya, whom he called affectionately "Marusya." As always acting with ostensible honor, he proposed that they elope. Marusya, in all the believing virtue of her teens, agreed, but the news leaked out. Her family promptly sent her away in hiding. Other parents of young ladies at the Institute protested. Scriabin had already resigned, but their gossip was piercing.

There seemed small humiliation for Scriabin in the ire of the philistines. On the contrary, he was pleased. He revealed the affair to all his friends, including Vera, who promptly told all his enemies. His disingenuous haste recalled his pristine attempt to force Natalya into marriage. But this behavior was now truly foolish for a thirty-three-year-old man, and immensely complex in motive and meaning. When Morozova wrote him she was worried Marusya would force him in some way to redress the wrong, he answered off the point: "It may be that your fear has some basis but it seems to me that you exaggerate the danger of M. It really is not necessary to fear friends and enemies. I know a greater danger which, although it cannot stop my creative activity, can obstruct the practical realization of my ideas. I mean Safonoff..."

Before leaving for Switzerland, Scriabin disburdened himself to Safonoff. He told him he wanted to leave Vera, and planned to do so once he settled her in Germany, sparing her the disgrace of abandonment in Moscow. He confessed his love for Tatyana and informed Safonoff that he had arranged for her abroad as his mistress. Safonoff was shocked. The absurdity also struck Safonoff.

There were questions of the children. Divorce was impossible. If Scriabin loved Tatyana so much, then how was it possible for him to have considered Marusya? Even Scriabin called that event "a filthy scandal to be avoided . . . for Tatyana's sake." Safonoff cautioned Scriabin against "excessive openness" with people, particularly gossips such as Morozova.

Her stipend to Scriabin had purchased his intimacy. She was now a confidante, and more. He asked her to act as a go-between with Safonoff. "Find out if he really disapproves of me. I cannot accept the idea that he opposes the facts of my life as they are . . . Don't let him SUSPECT what you are up to."

Just as he once made Vera and Morozova good friends, now he tried the same with Tatyana. Morozova was studying piano with Medtner (after Scriabin's departure), but he arranged for Tatyana to play his latest compositions for her. "You can work out the Third Sonata on your own . . . but it would be good if Tanya deciphered the harmony of the other pieces for you."

He extracted a promise from her to come to Switzerland and act as duenna. In other words, Tatyana will remain hidden from Vera until Morozova arrived. Then the two ladies could pretend to have come together. He wrote them both: "Write me General Delivery in Geneva, using only the initials A.N.S." Scriabin was unwise to involve Morozova in so much of his life. She was clearly idle-minded, rather stupid, and loose-tongued as Safonoff knew, despite her generosity. Certainly she was unreliable . . . slow in her payments to him, capricious in her plans, and at the last minute that spring postponed her coming to Switzerland.

Vera and the children reached Geneva ten days after Scriabin himself, on 13 March, 1904. After three days in a hotel together, Vera found them a little chalet in the village of Vézenaz on the southwest shore of Lake Geneva. The house was poetically named "Villa Les Lilas," after the lilac bush blooming each spring in the house's tiny garden. Les Lilas was owned by a genial couple named Calendret, and to reach it one could either take a boat from Geneva across the tip of the lake or, less scenically, a drab, twenty-minute tram ride.

Vera wrote Zinaida Monighetti on 24 March: "Our *domik* is charming enough, adequately furnished and with sufficient dishes. We have a small but lovely garden, and our view of the lake and the mountains is superb . . . Sasha has a room in the attic. An upright is there (we could not find a grand in all Geneva) and he can be alone there . . ." Scriabin spent his time searching for an apartment suitable for Tatyana.

Scriabin spoke well of Switzerland. "Here is true freedom . . . land of freedom . . . New ideas can flourish here . . ." And later writing in the Findeizen letter of autobiography (26 December, 1907) he said tortuously, still justifying his continuing absence: "I have preferred to live abroad because our Russian life, and particularly Moscow where we do not know how to adjust ourselves to the present, is little suited to my practicing those disciplines so needed for my tasks . . ." Switzerland at this time was crowded with Russians—political refugees seeking haven, the sick needing European medical skills, and maecenas-tourists. A man could live à la russe there without missing the homeland's language, food, culture, or feeling. Eventually Scriabin would concur with Dostoevsky, who found thirty years before that the Swiss were "dishonest, vile, incredibly stupid and intellectually backward."

Scriabin's chief concern was getting Tatyana to Switzerland. He had left part of the Morozova money with her. Now began a series of careful instructions. Wool-gathering Sasha was surprisingly authoritative as travel guide and keeper of the purse. His first letter was posted 14 March, 1904, from Geneva so that the Vézenaz postmaster would not see its addressee.

Tanya, I get quite frightened when I think of how you are going to bear up under this journey to Switzerland. You cannot imagine how tiring it is! First go to Berlin, and if you feel all right, that is, if you slept the first two nights, then you can chance going straight on through to Geneva (via Frankfurt and Basel). If you are very tired by the time you get to Berlin, then you *must* stop over, even if only for 1 day. The best train leaves Berlin at 8 in the morning from the Anhalter Bahnhof. The trip is fairly expensive: 37 rubles 60 kopecks from Moscow to Berlin, and from Berlin to Geneva, 84 marks, that is, around 40 rubles, which means in all 77 rubles. So with food and stopovers it comes to about 100 rubles.

See how well versed I am in business matters? Yes, and there are living expenses to be reckoned with. It is hard to find any tolerable place for less than 5 francs a day, or 150 francs a month. The best thing is for you to leave as soon as possible without waiting for spring in Moscow. It is already warm here and the trees are turning green.

I look for an apartment all day long, but have seen nothing suitable yet. Tanya, write me please *immediately*. I am very worried about your health. I want terribly to see you as soon as possible.

I kiss my good and wise and kind Bobika, Bobochka, Bobusha, Bobinka [Boris Schloezer, her brother]. You cannot conceive how much I long for you . . .

On 28 March, he wrote of the same concerns, this time from Vézenaz. Tatyana, flustered by her momentous and dangerous decision, still does not comprehend:

Tanya, I thought I had sent you the most detailed possible instructions for the trip to Switzerland, and suddenly I see that I hadn't. How useless I am! I will try once more and if this time I fail, I will give up all hope—to my great sorrow —of being a decent guide! Here goes: In Moscow buy a 2nd class ticket for *BERLIN* and a reserved seat for the first night (to Warsaw). The train reaches Warsaw at 10 in the night, I believe. You must go from the Moscow station to the Berlin station (that is what they call the one for Vienna). Now there are two ways of doing this: 1) the connecting train, but it is dreadful in every respect, on top of which it is sometimes *LATE*!! (incredibly) and 2) by horse carriage. I advise you to take this second choice. It is pleasanter and what's more important, reliable. At the Vienna station you absolutely *MUST* buy a sleeper ticket *international class*. Now this is expensive, but you will be able to sleep even better than you would at home. If when you arrive in Berlin (early morning) you feel able to continue the journey, then wait a few hours and come on the train which goes directly to Geneva. It leaves Berlin during the day but I don't know at what time (they will tell you at the station). It arrives in Geneva next day at 7 in the evening. If you are very tired on your second day, then stay in Berlin at the Central Hotel opposite the station. It has an elevator and the rooms are very cheap but nice.

Tanya, dear, obey me. Spend these few days before your departure *prudently.* Do *NOTHING.* Take walks, if it isn't damp. Go to bed early and *sleep!!!* Remember that you have an exhausting journey ahead of you. I will be fretting constantly, until I see you in Geneva. Write me several times en route, even if only from Warsaw and Berlin. In Germany don't step out of the train. It stops for only a minute and you could be left behind!

Please don't come if your health doesn't permit. It would be better to wait a few days. Inform me *IN TIME* of your arrival at Geneva. I will try to meet you, but it won't be easy . . .

He was careful not to sign these letters to Tatyana. Later that year in December, after Scriabin has gone to Paris leaving Vera in Switzerland and Tatyana has gone to her relatives in Brussels briefly to reconsider the embarrassment of life as a mistress, for a while he addressed letters to a Mme. Gallieaux at Avenue Louise for transmittal to Mlle. T. de Schloezer. Then afterward, he considerately disguised his handwriting to keep her family from knowing of their continuing relationship: "Dear, I am deliberately writing this way. I am fearfully worried about your health. Write me *INSTANTLY* to the *hotel.* It is faster, or if you can, send me a telegram. *WHEN* are you *coming?* You hear me? *INSTANTLY . . .*" He signs this "Your S." However, he forgets to put a stamp on the letter and the consternation over a postage-due letter alerted Tatyana's entire household of aunts and uncles. In reply, Tatyana asked him "not to subtilize . . . better write normally and stick a stamp on."

_II_ _

BREAK WITH VERA

3

DIVORCE IS a prolonged business of the heart. Its decisions are almost never reached clearly, particularly when one of the parties is undesirous as Vera was, and when the other tries to preserve as much as possible. Scriabin wanted everything as it had been before, except the marriage. He found Tatyana a room in the nearby village of Belle-Rive, twenty minutes away from Vézenaz. He could not, and really did not want to conceal her presence. With Vera, he had unfortunately and mistakenly decided on a course of honesty.

Tatyana was a frequent visitor to Les Lilas. Engel reported this at firsthand. He too was living in Switzerland, in Montreux that summer of 1904, as part of the Russian contingent. One day he went to Geneva to change some money. "Someone addressed me in Russian. I looked. It was Scriabin. He was charming and entreated me so insistently to come back with him to Vézenaz. I chucked my proper business and went with him. It was such a happy, amiable holiday time and all this affected Scriabin. Or was he simply latching on to a new face? Someone outside his home?"

Engel met Tatyana, whose presence Scriabin explained, was "due to ill health . . . she has to come to Switzerland." "Tatyana Fyodorovna Schloezer was present throughout," Engel observed, "even when he played me his compositions . . . She knew and loved Scriabin's music. She anticipated every note of it. It was she, not he, who paid attention to this or that detail in a piece. It was she who answered first when I made some comment or other. She, who resourcefully parried an oblique attack of mine, or who, when I was in ecstasy, joined in even more enraptured.

16

It appeared to me then that she had taken Alexander Nikolaevich well into the folds of her heart. His work and music had become hers." Vera was pliant, weak, and yielding. She asked only time to think. But instead of thinking, she turned tail and ran to her father, who had arrived in Europe on some legal business. Like many parents who have spent a lifetime ignoring their children, suddenly when the offspring is prostrate in defeat, Ivan Issakovich extended his helping hand. He turned his business trip into a holiday visit and lifted Vera directly out of the Vézenaz atmosphere into a tour of Nice, Naples, Rome and Milan. From the end of October to mid-November, 1904, father and heart-broken daughter journeyed together. Tatyana, over the tacit objection of Matilda, the newly hired governess for the children (recruited from among the local, indigent Russians), moved into Les Lilas.

Scriabin played dutiful husband by mail. "Dear Vushenka! I would not let Matilda Karlovna write to you today, because I want the first greeting you receive to be from me . . ." He was, however, off to a bad start due to his "eternal absent-mindedness." He wrote enviously of Vera "reveling in the luxuriant beauty of southern nature" while he and the children are "huddling around the dining room stove freezing." He sent this letter to Genoa, knowing full well she was in cold Nice. Then on 4 November he wondered, "Is it possible that my first letter did not reach you in Nice?" To make matters worse, he again wrote her, "Of course it is a pity about the oppressive fog which keeps you from enjoying yourself more fully. But I imagine it will not last long. . ." He posted this letter to Naples where she indeed was at the time . . . and quite warm.

Inattention was not his only unkindness. The letters bristle with gratuitous jibes. He said that Lev, now two years old, was surprised "not to find his grandfather downstairs, and he mentioned him several times . . .", but adds nothing about Vera being missed. He commented that Maria, the three-year-old daughter, did not cry over Vera's absence, but, strangely, hinting his early affair, he calls her "Marusya," instead of his usual diminutives. Then he referred to Vera's traveling habits: "Of course you did not sleep a single minute," and added, "Think as little as possible about us . . . The children are well. They are behaving themselves, at least that is what Matilda says," implying that he has little to do with them. Rimma, now aged six, has not been to school for two days:

"Tatyana Fyodorovna took her into town today."

In other letters he was informative without ulterior points to make: "The children are frisky ... Lev is being punished ... Rimma wants to write you herself. Tomorrow I'll make her do it ..." He faithfully sent kisses himself, transmitted those of the children, and forwarded bows, salutations and greetings from the governess.

He was working feverishly to finish last details of the "Divine Poem." He told Vera he had sent one rewritten part to "a harpist." Actually he only asked his former classmate, Nikita Morozov, for advice. He assured Vera that by her return the symphony would be finished and all she would have to do is "wrap it up for mailing." He worked, because he had decided to go to Paris and negotiate a first performance personally. The sooner it is in proofs, the sooner it can be played, he reasoned. On 6 November, he wrote, "Today at last I have finished the symphony, ENTIRELY I believe, but am afraid to say so. I worked on it all day long." Vera posted it to Leipzig on 22 November, one week after she returned to Vézenaz. He left for Paris the day after, with Tatyana. First though, he had what he hoped was a final discussion. It was not.

Within three weeks of separation, Vera communicated with Zinaida Monighetti:

He writes often, but does not say much. Only postcards. Still nothing is clarified definitely. He is renewing his old friendships. Musicians there are all greatly interested in him. He is constantly trying to arrange his symphony concert, but I don't know whether he will succeed or not. Nor do I know how long he will be in Paris. He wanted to return to us for Christmas, but I think he will remain there longer than that ... I am devoting my heart's all to music ...

Scriabin did return for the two weeks of Russian Christmas and New Years beginning 7 January, 1905, and stayed an extra week until 22 January. He wrote Tatyana on 9 January: "The mood of the house is precisely *as it should be*. If only you were over your cold, then I would be perfectly satisfied ..." Next day he said, "I can now make you *very* happy. Everything is arranging itself magnificently. MUCH BETTER than anyone could have expected."

On 4 July, Vera to Zinaida: "Sasha is here. He has come for all of 'one week.' ... If only I could believe, as you do, that Sasha will come back to me someday. This could be only if there were no rival. She grips him firmly and never lets go of him. He treats me with great love and tenderness. He worries over the children and me very much. And perhaps this is all to the good. Perhaps it will give me the shove to shake myself loose and make a person of myself. I have practiced all year and have made great strides, so much so in fact that Sasha advises me to appear in public this autumn. Of course, I will play only his music, as my goal is to glorify him."

4

It was essential for Vera to make a livelihood as a musician. Scriabin's fluctuating means could never sustain two households. Persuasively, he likens her to Teresa Carreño (1853–1917), Venezuelan pianist supreme among lady virtuosos. Occasionally an undercurrent of regret or fright at having been ruthless rippled through Scriabin's letters of advice and encouragement. Throughout he seemed to love her more than ever when living with her, as sometimes happens with estranged couples.

He wrote hastily on 23 November, 1904, en route to Paris for the first step of abandonment. A farewell, but not quite:

> I make my journey, and think of you all the time, my dear and good Zhuchenka! I could not sleep tonight, because of you! I will not rest until I hear good news from you that you are being SENSIBLE and conducting yourself wisely. Be a person. Hold yourself in check. Look at all the misery around you, all the unhappiness and you will not only find strength to bear up, but even to rejoice!

> Be nice now, my dear, my good one! I advise you to begin the reconstruction of your life INSTANTLY. First, work SERIOUSLY. I am not there, so no one can prevent you. Plot a schedule for every hour of the day. Practice 3½ hours or better still, 4. Also read constantly. You can get whatever you want from the library. This does not cost much, no matter how much it is. WALK 2 hours a day. Go to theater and concerts. Time will pass unnoticed, and then I will surprise you and give you a stiff examination, a very severe one! I will get you ready for a concert tour, if you wish! The pencil is finished, so I have to end whether I want to or not. Goodbye my dear, my beauty. Write me.

He forgot to sign the letter—or the pencil no longer wrote—but next day's letter again has no signature.

> I am in no state to do anything until I hear that you are feeling well and *are getting on with your affairs.* Remember, dear, work will give you all you want, *all*, I say—and happiness and fame too. How many times has someone worse than you, Carreño for instance, gathered laurels! You have now begun to play quite differently. Much more deeply, more maturely, incomparably more musically. I will do everything to help you along your way. I will even write Safonoff a special letter telling him about your abilities. Oh what hard days I have had, wanting my mind set at rest.

> Goodbye, my dear, dear, my darling friend. Just wait, I will cure your infection, and you will fly from me. You cannot conceive what happiness is in store for you. Life is a wheel. It turns and turns . . .

> 26 November, 1904

> Are you not ashamed of torturing me, dear Vushenka? You have not written one single word! I know nothing of what is happening with you! Have you received my letters? Are you well? I wanted to telegraph you, but remembered how you dread telegrams. I implore you to write me *IMMEDIATELY* and write as fully as possible. I kiss you, my soul.

Finally, Vera mustered strength and "her Sasha" answered with relief immediately: "I thank you for the letter, dear and good Vushenka. Now I can breathe easily—Vusha is well and the symphony arrived at the printers safely." He went on to say he cannot find a suitable place to live. The only place where it is "quiet and which has decent air" is the Champs Elysées, but he cannot afford that. The suburbs have no *pensions*; the hotels are "expensive and incommodious." So he will move in temporarily with his old friend and "protector of decadents," Gustave Doret. His place is in the country: "Doret is never here, and for *this* he rents an entire apartment."

At last Vera began forwarding Scriabin's mail. Safonoff, Igumnov, and Keneman had sent a round-robin postcard: "We love you Sasha. We cherish you and wish you all the very best." Igumnov played the Concerto in Moscow on 30 October (Russian time) at a big RMO concert. The reviews were less than comforting. Lipaev in the *RMG* found both music and performance "boring and monotonous." Kruglikov in *News of the Day* thought the concerto "pretentious, saying little as music . . .

without merit either in the solo part or in the orchestral accompaniment."

Learning of the separation, Scriabin's father had sent him a searing letter. Scriabin wanted to justify himself and "keep him from getting angry with me all over again," but he has misplaced the address. He wrote to find out where Papa is. Wifely, Vera answered, and reminded him to reply to Igumnov. "Tomorrow," he begged, "I simply cannot write more than one letter a day." Fearing that Vera would neglect her firstborn and his favorite, he asked her to take special care of Rimma.

Scriabin kept Vera informed of his life at a pace. But he spared her mention of Tatyana (who registered everywhere as "Mlle. de Schloezer"), even the relief of knowing that in a few days she would be leaving Paris. The time had not come for her to be seen in public with Scriabin. Vera was still remembered. Besides, Tatyana wanted to rethink her life and ensconce herself within her family in Brussels.

He saved one last hurt for Vera, like a rap in the teeth. After wandering around Paris tracking *pensions* as far in the environs as Belle-Vue, he settled for 5, rue de la Neva. Seven years before, Vera and he had honeymooned there. Yes, Scriabin made life a wheel . . . it turned and turned.

5

SCRIABIN was acutely lonely without Tatyana and needed the coddling comfort of luxury. He wrote Vera that he had to "scamper away from 5, rue de la Neva," because the *pension* was under new management and "You cannot imagine what tricks they were up to! Or how they fed me!" A few days later, he was so "exhausted from going hungry and freezing . . . searching for lodgings that I decided to comport myself in Papa's manner." Kindled by alcohol, he went to a good hotel, significantly perhaps, the Hotel de Lord Byron at 16, rue de Lord Byron. There, he said he would spend two weeks of "rest and luxury." He paid 11 francs a day for full *pension*, electric light, and heating. "This is unbelievably costly . . . Wine is included and I will not spend a penny more." (He returned to 5, rue de la Neva when Tatyana returned.)

Tatyana in the reality of her respectable family was constantly ill with a cold thinking about her anomalous position. Scriabin worried frantically. Now began a dual correspondence. He addressed his former wife one way, and in another wrote his wavering mistress. Only once had he strength sufficient to write them both the same day. Usually, he wrote Vera first; then the following day, repeated much of the same news more accurately to Tatyana. In general, to one he described the prosaic details of his life; to the other he would speak of love and dreams. "Today I dissipate," he wrote Vera on 5 December, and although his pleasures were paced by the hotel expenses, he spent nine francs for his seat to hear *Walküre* at the Opéra. He is jealous of her "in lovely Geneva weather . . . Paris is miserable, the air vile, not cold but damp . . . full of yellow mist and the stench of smoke . . ." To Tatyana: "Yesterday I heard *Walküre*. I had exactly the same impression as with *Siegfried*. The intention is always more than the achievement. As in *Siegfried* there are 2 or 3 moments of enchantment and all the rest is frightfully boring."

Morozova, characteristically late, arrived in Switzerland after Scriabin's departure, and took a lavish chalet in the village of Nyon near Vézenaz. She was consolation to Vera, and Scriabin used their friendship sometimes as a financial bridge between himself and his patron. In December, 1904, Vera's father returned to Vézenaz to stay again with his daughter.

5 December to Vera

I have received letters from Glazunov and Morozova, but nothing from you! What's wrong with you, Zhuchyokha! You want me to write often, but into a vacuum!

6 December to Tatyana

Tanishche, my good and dear one! Why so fainthearted! Tears! How shameful! I cry only tears of sorrow. We must *combat* conventionality. We must act. Never yield to being downhearted. We will always be together. Do not *forget THAT*! . . . I am not wasting time and am doing everything possible to realize my intention. Until then!! Don't *you* want to hear my 3rd Symphony? How I would like to talk forever with you, but I cannot. What grief!

Tatyana engaged herself with writing an article about Scriabin's music and program notes for the "Divine Poem." He encouraged her by saying that "it would be good to have the article in print before the New Year."

On 8 December he scribbles an open, indiscreet postcard to Tatyana (care of Mme. Gallieaux): "I am very worried about your health. *Somehow or other* you must get yourself fit for the journey here. Come quickly, but, dear, *BE CAREFUL. Do everything in your power* to keep from catching cold. Now, poisonous people have insulted my sweet baby. I can't fly there myself to rescue you. When you get ready to leave, write me *just a word or two* to forewarn me—either telegram or letter."

Her family evidently has heard gossip. Tatyana stood up to her family and decided forever to unite with Scriabin, regardless. She wrote now that she could "take the criticism of her uncle—that work-hardened bourgeois of independent means who sniggers at art and beauty . . ." Scriabin rejoiced over her letter. "I am in love with you, my beauty!"

12 December

Taninka, Tanyuka, what is happening? No news from you today! Can it be that you are ill! You DARE NOT, you hear, dare not fall ill. This depends ONLY ON YOU. You must know how needed you are, my delight, now so dear, so dear to me!

Now I am going to complain about the French. Fancy how they talk! Even Schmitt [Florent, (1870-1958)] and his ilk. Oh yes, they say, Russia is the country for music and has many great composers at the moment (that's right, not bad for a beginning, but listen further), and first place, of course, belongs to . . . Glazunov!!

Scriabin was so annoyed by this that he splattered dots over three lines of the letterpaper before writing Glazunov's distasteful name. "And such is the company in which I spend my time," he continued. "I don't want to contradict them. It is not worth the bother. Still, this is better than being with *your* relations! At least these are *ARTISTS* talking . . ."

Write me, Tanyuka, every day if possible . . . You do NOT KNOW how I look forward to your letters and HOW MUCH I WANT to see you as quickly as possible. However, I do not want you to come if you are ILL. I also worry about how I will set you up here! Everything is so expensive and squalid . . .

To Tatyana on 13 December, written in the buffet of the Gare St. Lazare, with his gloves on to keep warm:

. . . I am writing you for the last time. Day after tomorrow I see Tanyuka. Oh what joy! How much there is to say! I *need* you to make so many important decisions.

And on the day Tatyana joins Scriabin in Paris, he wrote to Vera:

> It is understandable for me not to have written in 2 days, but for you to count on my letters, that is not good. I am running about all the time as if possessed . . . I want a photograph of you very much. Send me the one of you with Rimochka. Kiss all the children. I am so happy Rimma is studying well. Don't worry about her learning at home, instead of at school. Think nothing of it . . .

✐ III ✐
ARRANGEMENTS

6

THE "TRIP" or "intention," as he called this Paris venture, and his running around "in a daze" or "as if possessed," meant elaborate, complicated, and debilitating arrangements for Scriabin to present himself and his music, namely the huge "Divine Poem," in a series of concerts. He went about this lengthy chore in extreme earnestness and with system. Such subsidiary duties beset any creator of sound: business negotiations and the drumming up of a public.

Scriabin called first on Belon, owner of a large music store in Paris. Then he went to concert manager Blondelle. "I cannot begin to say how delighted I am with their kindness and readiness to help me in every way." Blondelle, he said to Vera, "is *terrifically* interested." The Salle Erard was booked through the entire winter, but he promised to arrange something. One consideration was the size of the stage, which could not hold more than sixty musicians. Negotiations began as to whether they should enlarge the Salle Erard by building a platform over the front row of seats, or whether Scriabin should reduce the number of string instruments for the "Divine Poem." "Wouldn't it be better to rent a theater?" he wrote Tatyana in the end. "The orchestra would sound not too poorly in one."

Scriabin visited his friend Chevillard, who agreed to conduct, estimating the total cost at around 3,000 rubles. "No more, no less!" Scriabin moaned to Tatyana. Chevillard said that it would require five rehearsals at 400 rubles each "to be technically satisfactory. For an impeccable performance, eight to ten rehearsals. Nevertheless I have not lost heart and have already begun arrangements. *MY CONCERTS WILL TAKE PLACE!*"

He halved the estimate into "4,000 francs" for Vera, fearing her reproach at the exorbitance of his desire and ... vanity. Nor did he want her spoiling his financial arrangements with Morozova: "She wrote me a most lovely letter. She offers me money for concerts, but do not tell her that I received the letter—yet." He needed time to think over the undertaking. He also deplored the fact that an agent costs 500 francs, but "without him it would all be impossible ... However, I am *DETERMINED TO HAVE* one concert ..."

Perhaps with something less than forthrightness, Scriabin finally wrote on 13 December, 1904, a cozening letter to Morozova. She has not definitely agreed to subsidizing a concert, and the amount is far from clear, but he regards the prospect as a contract.

> I received your letter at a most unhappy time. It comforted me in two ways: First and most important, you generously showed me once again the extent of your friendship. Second, you restored the hope of my arranging a Paris concert. I will tell you the how and why. Please do not think I was counting on your support when I came to Paris. Here is the story. Every November ...

He now explained how for the past two years he had received 1,500 rubles (an exaggeration) from the Glinka Prize. To his surprise this year he had been awarded 500 rubles, no more. Claiming that the cost of the "Divine Poem" would only be 1,700 rubles, he reckoned, he said that that would have left only an additional 200 rubles to be borrowed from her. "See how I give you all these details? I could not be more direct or open. If you wish to help me, then I accept your assistance, but only on certain conditions. First, if this is the slightest inconvenience to you, then please do not bother. However, if it is all right, then please give me 1,000 rubles AS A LOAN. Next year, when I hope again to receive the prize, or better, at the first *opportunity*, I will return this thousand to you. Forgive me, dear Margarita Kirillovna, and do understand that it is only a feeling of delicacy which makes me raise these conditions. I am reluctant to inconvenience you."

In a later letter, he raises the thousand figure by "two or three hundred," adding, "See, how brazen I am! But *OF COURSE* I will *OWE* you this sum ..." Once again, when one thinks Scriabin most insincere, he proves to be honest. He wrote Tatyana at this time that he regarded the Morozova money "as a loan."

Once the concert became possible, Scriabin enlisted the aid of all his Paris friends. He played the "Divine Poem" at Belon's music store before a group of Doret's invitees, and made "masses of friends . . . Doret latched on to me and dragged me to dinner with some friends and then to a concert. I was bored stiff." For three days running Doret and Scriabin left the Hotel Lord Byron together at 11 in the morning and returned at 1 at night. "See what a hurly-burly life I lead!" he boasted self-pityingly to Morozova.

His most recent young friend was Viscount de Gissac, also staying at the Lord Byron. He was enamored of Scriabin, arranged for him to give a public lecture, and proposed that he write a column "when and what I feel like" in a philosophical weekly. Scriabin declined, however, because he felt he does not know French well enough.

On 28 December, 1904, Scriabin gladdened Vera and her father with a long letter:

> How is your little health? You have not written me in so long . . . All my business here goes well . . . Only one unpleasant matter. The hotel costs masses of money, but I am not in despair. I will extricate myself somehow or other . . . I have made several important friendships. I wrote you, I think, that I dined the other night with a French playwright who is very rich and a great admirer of Wagner. He is so taken with my compositions he is going to help me with the concerts. Yesterday I paid him a *visite de digestion* [a courtesy call paid the day after dining with a person of society]—I do not know how to spell that word, and now I am waiting for him here. Oh, I forgot to tell you his name—Amic. Have you heard of him?

He concluded the letter with a reproach and "warm greetings to the grandfather. Kiss, kiss the children for me. You are cruel not to want to send me a photograph of them!"

By "Amic" Scriabin meant Gabriel Astruc (1864–1938), an artist's representative, neither a playwright nor wealthy. As impresario he cornered the Russian artistic market—first Scriabin, then Diaghilev's ballet, followed by Chaliapin and his trainload of opera singers. Astruc, for a fee, managed those of Scriabin's Paris concerts that materialized. He proposed two possibilities to Scriabin. One, that Nikisch, not Chevillard, conduct the "Divine Poem." Second, that Scriabin tour Europe conducting his own symphonies. And from these ideas, Scriabin devised yet a third—based neither on fact nor feasibility—that he would tour as soloist in all-Scriabin programs conducted by Nikisch.

7

WHEN TATYANA joins Scriabin, their *pension* neighbor is an immensely sympathetic American singer, Florence Scarborough. As Russian Christmas approached Scriabin felt safe in leaving Tatyana in her care. Florence (not Tatyana) was to write to him constantly, as he wished to avoid Vera's hurt and watchful eye. Moreover, Tatyana is again ill in bed.

His Vézenaz letters began even before he left the station on his birthday (Paris time):

7 January, 1905

I cannot leave Paris without writing you a few words, dear Tanyuronka! I think about you all the time and about your health. Be good, my joy, and take care of yourself! Tell Florence to write me as soon as possible, today in fact. Goodbye, my sweet, forgive me for leaving you all alone and for not having a moment's peace until I hear you are well. Am in a frightful hurry.

10 January

Thank you for the letters, sweet, good, dear girl! I got them right away. I am as insanely happy now as I was worried then. You have recovered! You have moved into another room too! But the door of that room leads off into the hall and there is always a draft there. More, everyone who will come to see you will still be cold from the outdoors. This can give you a cold all over again. Please do not let Florence near you while she has her fur coat on. TAKE CARE OF YOURSELF. I am going to talk to Morozova now about the concerts. I will write you the result. I will write Florence myself. Tomorrow, however, I may not have a chance to write, but DO NOT WORRY!

10 January, again

Tanyurochka, what does this mean? Florence says: The little one does not feel so badly as *yesterday*. But yesterday she wrote me you were *better*. This means you are concealing something from me. That is AWFUL. Please always tell me the truth. Only then can I be calm. And do be careful as you PROMISED me. Think of your health and don't PINE. These two weeks will pass as a single instant, if you give yourself to dreams instead of fretting . . . I implore you to write me the truth and to be prudent!! I thank Florence from the bottom of my heart for her goodness . . .

11 January

I walked to Geneva [to post a card] as there was no carriage, and now I have to go back and I have 3 minutes. Do not worry ABOUT ANYTHING. All is well. Nikisch has AGREED.

12 January

Yesterday we talked until 2 in the morning. Vera is a miracle of stability and reasonableness. She will do anything I like.

I have not yet seen Morozova. Tomorrow I go and talk with her about the tour with Nikisch. I am almost certain it will come off, because Astruc is working very hard and has already got Nikisch to agree. You see how well everything is working out? Only one thing is lacking! Tanyuka's little health! How happy I would be to have a letter from you! Eat chocolate in all forms. And don't FRET. We will soon see each other! One week has already gone. The next is going faster still. Goodbye, my happiness, my dream.

On this same date, Vera dragoons Scriabin into sending season's greetings to friends. For one of the rare times in life, he observed this formality, and his postcards in 1905 must have surprised the Monighettis, Nikita Morozov, his aunt and *babushki*, and Keneman—the only ones who saved theirs.

17 January to Tatyana

Morozova, as usual, failed to show up yesterday. She sent a letter and will come tomorrow. Therefore, I do not know if I will be able to send you any money right away.

I will do so at the first opportunity. Meanwhile, borrow from Scarborough. She won't mind. I kiss you, my dear, and think of you all the time. Be at peace and happy.

18 January

Morozova was most sympathetic, but she did not offer any money. On Friday Vera and I go to see her again. She has invited us to dinner. There was no word from you today. I know it is difficult for you to mail letters and bothersome. I also know I will be with you on Sunday and it is already Wednesday! Goodbye, my dearest joy. Be quiet and WISE! I go to bed EARLY and I feel FINE . . .

On 20 January, 1905, Scriabin wrote an electric letter to Tatyana. In it much that had been formulating in his mind, both as music and thought, surfaced in terrifying expression. He has begun composing a Fourth Symphony, and the poem to this "Poem" as well. His philosophy is now concrete. The process of creation which this letter, again pencil written, reveals is arresting in its integrity and heart-whole sincerity. His psychic dependence on Tatyana is for the first time unveiled as out-soaring earth's statutes. She is his wings. The potency of his thought depends on her strength and their passion. The sexual connection is explicit in the letter's last lines.

> Tanyuko, it will soon be midnight. Everyone is asleep. I sit here alone in the dining room composing. I am going over the plan of my new composition for the thousandth time. Each time it has seemed to me that the canvas is painted, that I have explained the universe in terms of free creativity and I can at last become the playful, freely creating god! But then tomorrow comes and there are still doubts, still questions! Up to now everything has been schemes, plans, and patterns! A colossal structure such as the one I now erect needs total harmony within all its parts on a solid foundation. So, until everything comes clear in my mind, I cannot explain appearance totally from my point of vision. I am unable to fly. But I feel the time for all this is coming.
>
> Oh my darling little wings, set yourself aright! Sustain me in my unimaginable speed! Slake my scorching thirst for life!
>
> Oh how I long for the festive day! I am infinite desiring! There will come that day of rejoicing! We will suffocate. We will be consumed in flames. The world will burn with us in our bliss. My little wings, be strong. I need you! Oh how I need you!
>
> Soon I will be taking care of you in person! You will receive this note on Friday, my dearest, and Sunday night we will be together! Goodbye until then. May our mad rapture come soon.
>
> Until I arrive, do not do anything foolish. Do not go near an open window or any such thing. How happy I would be to find you well. Sleep deep. Learn how to fall asleep by the process of *calming* yourself.
>
> Tanya, do you understand what I want?
>
> Is the big room taken?

He repeats in another note that he arrives on Sunday night and wants the "big room." In eagerness to get away from Vera (or to be nearer Tatyana) he spends Saturday night, 21 January, at the Hotel de Genève.

His excuse was that the tram from Vézenaz does not leave early enough to catch the 6 A.M. train on the 22nd. Alone in the hotel, he dashed off two letters. A tragic sense of responsibility for Vera comes over him:

> Zhuchenka, my dear and good one. I write only these words to beg you once again to be sensible! I can only feel really all right with myself, if I know that my Zhuka is healthy and happy! Work, keep busy, dream of success, make plans and inform me of what you intend to do. When I come next time, you must show more progress . . .

He reverted to their early days of near-happiness by signing this letter "Your Tuka." Then he tore the sheet of hotel stationery in half and wrote to "Margrosha," as he now called Morozova intimately. He still hints for money, garlanding his prospects—the concerts in Paris—with success. Her money will be returned within a week from the "Divine Poem" performance alone, he says. He thanks her for her "unfailing faith, sincerity, deep friendship," and above all, for her understanding of his "situation," which she, conventionally and as Vera's friend, found distasteful. After his departure this time, Vera was so lonely she moved with the children to Morozova's villa in Nyon. He ended his letter to Morozova, "I am tortured thinking of the frightful thing I have done! Please, my dear, sweet and good person whatever you do, do not think ill of me because of this!"

Back in Paris he was needlessly cruel to Vera. He told her how badly he slept in Geneva, how shattered he was during the train trip, and for the first time, let her know that he has been staying all this time at 5, rue de la Neva—with Tatyana. He mentioned that he received a "most rapturous letter from F.I." (Tatyana's father) whom Vera had met in the Professor Schloezer days, and lamely adds, "about my compositions, of course." Scriabin stirred more ashes of love's fire when he asked her to ask Morozova about his letter. "Speak as if it comes from *yourself*. Please do this for me as I do not want to appear as if I am *pushing* her. You understand?" Morozova is keeping her own counsel.

Next day, 24 January, 1905, he leaves a note on his calling card for Tatyana. She is still asleep in the "big room," but he has concert errands:

> Tanyuka, my dear, I think of you and am with you every minute. I cannot compose. I cannot think of anything but my beloved girl. I will not be able to

be with you today. Forgive me, my divine one. I kiss you and madly love you, love you.

8

ASTRUC WAS enterprising, as only a man of forty who has not yet made his fortune can be. By the end of January, 1905, he negotiated with Nikisch yet a fourth idea—that he tour Europe playing all three Scriabin symphonies. Nikisch had already performed the First Symphony in Berlin, and had asked on his own initiative to have the Second sent to him. This cordiality between Nikisch and Scriabin's music did not, however, prevent Scriabin from sending the first galleys of the "Divine Poem" to the German conductor, Felix Weingartner (1863-1942). (He returned it with thanks, saying that he had had time to look through it "no more than cursorily.") Nor did this interfere with Nikisch's acquiescence to Astruc's proposal . . . for 10,000 rubles.

Scriabin wrote Morozova the "good news" on 28 January, 1905, and broached the subject of money: "I walked again in vain to the post office. You obviously have quite forgotten my existence (oh friendship!). I would not remind you of it but . . ." Astruc has asked for "money for disbursements." The music season was drawing to a close, and it was time to make all arrangements. "I fear he will begin to doubt the seriousness of my intentions . . . Nikisch has expressed his great readiness and even 'joy,' according to Astruc, to propagandize my compositions. Astruc assures me that I risk nothing, not even financially, in entrusting their introductory performance to this conductor so beloved of the European public. Therefore, sweet Margarita Kirillovna, I hope you will answer me immediately, if you can lend me the sum of 10,000 rubles you earlier earmarked for me for a year or two . . ."

Three days later he laments to Vera, "What kind of a friend is Morozova! . . . I cannot budge nor sign a thing, until I have some money. If only I could extricate myself from this existence of not knowing. I can go nowhere, nor see anyone, until my position is clear." On 5 February he wrote Vera: "Morozova sent me a letter full of friendly effusion and—excuses. She cannot give me the sum I asked for, because her finances are in a tangle and she is in *debt*!!!! She offered me 3,000 rubles with which to arrange one concert in Paris under Nikisch . . ."

He answered Morozova with a preamble: "Now, having spent so much time in Paris and disbursed so much money already, I would be foolish to leave without carrying through, without doing something toward publicizing my compositions and stabilizing my material situation. Therefore, I must avail myself of your kind offer and ask you to send the 3,000 rubles whenever you can, part of which to be sent on receipt of this letter, since it will be needed for initial expenses."

Morozova replied by sending 1,500 rubles on 7 February. Scriabin (without her asking) sent a promissory note for the total 3,000 rubles to be repaid within two years. On the 8th, he made a down payment to Astruc of 3,000 francs against the total 7,000 francs. (Astruc's commission was to be, safely, 25% of the gross receipts.) On receipt of this part payment, Nikisch formally contracted to conduct the "Divine Poem." On 9 February, Scriabin asked Vera not to tell anyone, not even Morozova, about Nikisch's fee. The money was to appear as being for other expenses.

The Théâtre Nouveau at the Châtelet in Paris was hired for 29 May, 1905, the soonest Nikisch was free. The program was set with the "novelty" to be sandwiched between Weber and Wagner. "It is his concert," Scriabin informed Vera, "and he will play several small things from his repertoire. I hope Nikisch playing music the public already knows will draw a bigger attendance than otherwise, and I can thus recuperate some of the colossal outlay of money. I also give a piano recital at the Salle Erard . . . I am doing everything in my power to get back a little of the money . . ."

Two letters placed in mid-February picture Scriabin's social activity. To Vera: "I have nothing to tell you, so this will not be a long letter [but it was]. Never in my life have I passed the time so monotonously and inanely. I do the symphony proofs 4 or 5 hours a day. Evening creeps up before I know it . . . composing is easier than correcting mistakes, that is, *finding* them. At dusk, I practice the piano a little. After supper around 9, I set out for the same old Solennikovs or Shaikeviches and I walk. The Viscount returns to Paris in a few days. On Monday, when I hope to finish the proofs, I will resume my rounds of social 'visits.' I have been invited a lot . . . Astruc is nice. He got me engagements to play in several well-known houses."

The glory of this period, aside from de Gissac, remained Doret. "He is an angel. I have never seen such a noble man. He is a true artist. He is really doing everything possible for my success. He has recommended me to all his acquaintances . . ." Camille Bellaigue (1858–1930), the most important critic in Paris, comes to hear Scriabin play through the "Divine Poem." "He was in raptures, and Doret says it is the first time in many years that he has seen him interested and what's more, moved!"

He litters his letters with names for Vera. He has met Ossip Gabrilovich (1878–1936), the pianist; Maria Muromtseva-Klimentova (1858–1946), the Bolshoi soprano; the Princess Marina Gagarina (1877–1924), Trubetskoi's sister; Vera Sorokhtin, who wrote under the name "Vera Vend"; Princess Braniovan; Maria Platonova, née Urusova (1846–1915); Countess Apraksina; the Polish historian Kazimir Valishevsky (1849–1935); Vasily Nemirovich-Danchenko (1844–1936) brother of the co-founder of the Moscow Art Theater (he talked about the Russo-Japanese War and "as always lies and sounds his own trumpet. I dislike him intensely"); Mme. Rostopchina, descendant of the famous Count who instigated the burning of Moscow to defeat Napoleon's troops; a Georgian princess named Eristova; and again their old mutual friend and playboy from Petersburg, Baron Alexander Fredericks.

This last rated six exclamation points both before and after his name. "As might be expected, Sashenka married a rich American and is now visiting Paris. What a woman she is!" Piqued, Vera wrote inviting him to a further description. Scriabin obliged in his next letter: "Fredericks' wife is old, ugly, extremely unpleasing, and must be evil. Poor Fredericks. He has sold himself. They live in most luxurious lodgings . . ."

Continuing, "I cannot begin to enumerate for you all the places I have been this week or where I plan to go. I'll mention only the more interesting . . ." He names the russophile society hostesses of Paris— Mme. Vullemain, Comtesse de Greffuhle, whose husband has an avenue named for him and "who sets the tone for all of Paris," and he meets Louis Diemer (1843–1919), French composer and founder of the Society for Ancient Musical Instruments, Louis Bourgault Ducoudray, composer and professor at the Conservatoire, Eduard Colonne (1838–1910), conductor, and finally, "Gissac is taking me to a ball at some duke's, called de Pomard, I think. I forget. Oh, how all this bores me!"

"In a word," Scriabin sums up his life in Paris, "I am surrounded at white heat by the most disagreeable salon sort of idle chitchat. If I waste masses of time this way, it is only to grab up a little money here and there. I cannot hope for pupils from Parisian salons, so playing is my only compensation." He closed cautioning Vera for the second time: "Do not write anyone that I am underwriting the Nikisch concert." Apparently Morozova now has been apprised of the situation: "Ask Morozova to keep her silence." He added a postscript that he "will send the Belaieff firm some ten pieces in ten days and you will be able to live three months off them." He asked in another postscript to see the prelude which Vera has composed. And again another caution: "How is your work? Remember that by October you must be on your feet fully armed!"

To Morozova he also expressed his feelings over his social life: "I am doing everything in my power to gain recognition. Each day I expand my circle with new acquaintances, much as it disgusts me, I still play in salons from time to time. It is unbearable. Among all those ignorant people I always find two or three who understand a little something of music, though. This mitigates the misery of the situation . . ." Still later, on 20 March, 1905, his nerves aggravated by the approaching concert, he exploded to her: "This stupid, empty life going to salons and performing before 'imbeciles' has plunged me into the last extremity of irritability. I want to compose my big piece! No matter how many acquaintances I make, they will not fill the hall—not even by half. Maybe a miracle can change things. The big concert is 29 May . . ."

As soon as Vera is back in Les Lilas her dear friend Vera Mirotvorseva, sister of Nadezhda Konyusa, joins her. He sent a hundred francs for both of them and the children to take a little Easter holiday in Montreux. He reproached Vera: "You are *obstinately silent.* Are you or are you not giving a concert in Geneva? Find out the costs so I can send you money . . ." Aunt Lyubov has written Vera a stern letter about Shurinka's behavior. Scriabin tells Vera to silence her on the subject of the separation by saying he will be in Vézenaz on 7 June.

As the concert drew near, his pace hastened. He made a salon appearance at the mansion of Mme. Robert Dumache on the morning of 30 March. "All of Saint-Germain was there, the highest French society . . ." *Figaro* reviewed it: "The great talent of the composer is accompanied by an artistic temperament of the first order. Both emerged in all their fullness . . . tender, full of melancholy and exuding Slavic passion. The composer's enormous success was only a prelude to his triumph. We are anticipating his next concert under Nikisch."

True to his word, Blondelle managed to get the Salle Erard for Scriabin and Scarborough (accompanied by Mme. de Fay-Jozin) for a joint introductory recital on 9 April, 1905. The financial obligations were undertaken by the Russian Art Circle of Paris, headed by the important lady-journalist, Ivan Strannik (1868–1935), née Anna Anichkova. Scriabin played the Second Sonata, four preludes, the left-hand Nocturne, three mazurkas, and his Concert Allegro. The American soprano sang a song by the accompanist, *Oh, quand je dors* by Liszt, "None but the Lonely Heart" of Tchaikovsky, and Scriabin's unique "Romance" for voice. The concert was reported in the American *Musical Courier* but nowhere reviewed. Scriabin quickly followed with a solo program at the same hall on 15 April, and this *was* reviewed briefly:

> The hall was filled with few enough people, however, we listened without any fatigue at all for two hours to many compositions by the talented musician Scriabin. Despite his youth he has already written much and over each piece hovers the impression of individuality and originality . . . The brilliant pianist was loudly applauded. . .

Soon after, he wrote Morozova: "I gave a concert the other day at the Salle Erard. It brought me only a most insignificant amount of money (a clear 180 francs), but it was enormously significant as an artistic success. The best yet for me with the Parisian public." To Vera he called it merely a "great success . . . the public was most select."

April 25 found him still railing against society: "I lead such a trying life preparing the way for this Nikisch concert. I add more and more acquaintances to my social list, but none of them is interesting. They have titles and big names, and nothing beyond . . ." To add to Scriabin's tension, the score of the "Divine Poem" still had not reached Nikisch. This was no cause for alarm to that merchant-conductor. He had been known to perform without having glanced at the score before a concert.

✍ IV ✍
REVOLUTION

9

In January, the Revolution of 1905 began in Petersburg with the infamous "Bloody Sunday" massacre by the Tsar's troops. A large group of workers headed by a priest marched on the palace to present a petition of grievances. Trigger-happy guards panicked, opened fire against defenseless, singing laborers, many of whom were carrying ikons. Hundreds were killed, and the world was outraged. This event—the beginning of the end—aggravated by the disastrous failure of the Russian Army and Navy against the Japanese, had enormous significance for Russians at home and abroad. Morozova, for instance, returned instantly to oversee her properties. On 28 January, Scriabin wrote her, "How are you and what effect has the revolution in Russia had on you? Aren't you happy? At last we are coming to life!" On 7 February, he wrote Glazunov more circumspectly, "Petersburg has experienced some turbulent times! You must have been quite worried."

All year long the turmoil continued. In February, Grand Duke Sergei, Governor-General of Moscow, was assassinated. In June, the crew of the battleship *Potyomkin* mutinied. By October, isolated strikes turned into a general strike.

By the end of 1905, nearly three million workers all over Russia had struck. Ninety percent of the country's industry had been crippled. There was no mail, no light or water, stores were not open, and food was rotting on docks and in stations. The Tsar renounced absolute autocracy, but too late. All "subjects" were advanced to the status of "citizens," but scarcely soon enough.

Scriabin wrote Vera on 12 April that Morozova "behaved very, very badly. She scampered back to Russia, skipping her promise about money. Surely she knows how I count on her help! I must write her and clear up this matter ..." So that month, Scriabin sent Vera 200 rubles from his own pocket, instead of the "friendship token" being given directly to her by Morozova. Much later, Tatyana wrote Morozova, "I beg you to tell us all you can. We take all news from Russia to heart. It is very near to us. As we read of what is happening, we suffer ..."

The musical as well as the financial and economic worlds were equally involved in the Revolution of 1905. One student at the SPb Conservatory, a spare time member of the Tsar's military music brigade, announced shortly after "Bloody Sunday" that he had participated in the shooting of the workers. The other students forced his expulsion. Rimsky-Korsakoff, liberal-minded director of the Conservatory, championed this side of the controversy. The Administrative Board, however, reinstated the student and fired Rimsky instead. Glazunov, Liadov, Blumenfeld immediately resigned in sympathy. All students went on strike and refused to attend classes. The Conservatory shut down.

The music revolt spread to Moscow like plague. Threats to bomb the Bolshoi Theater closed it for three weeks. The gallery booed Glinka's *A Life for the Tsar*. *Boris Godunov* was performed with the Insurrection scene entirely deleted. Rachmaninoff (then conductor) requested that all revolutionaries be expelled from the orchestra and he paid for this reactionary arrogance. His resignation was accepted, and he departed for abroad. He chose, so he is reputed to have said, "not to discuss political matters with a houseboy."

The military governor of Moscow, an admiral, bitterly moaned that he had only 20,000 troops with which "to suppress the Muscovites." Conservatory students vociferously attended the funeral of one of their student revolutionaries killed by government troops. Safonoff condemned their participation. Taneieff resigned in protest against him. Safonoff resorted to repressive measures. He expelled students, refused to listen to anti-Tsar talk, and threatened his professors. Such steps so entirely against the grain of all but the most hidebound opinions of the time resulted in his resignation being asked for, effective at semester's end. Ippolitov-Ivanov (1859–1935) succeeded him.

Safonoff left for a holiday in Europe to contemplate his future and look for new employment. He informed Scriabin that he would be spending a week in Paris and hoped to see him. This forced Scriabin into action. He exiled Tatyana from him. As it happened, it was time for her to spend Easter in Brussels. There was to be a grand reunion of the Schloezer family, including various maiden and married aunts scattered over Belgium and Holland. She was almost four months pregnant but had not yet begun to show. The Scriabin liaison was still secret.

Scriabin's letters to her in May 1905 exhibit a deepened love. His diminutives and name permutations were as countless as stars. He is clearly a man captured both in love and need. His life fragments without her. He wants her to regulate his existence. Yet, for all this, he still let her go away . . . without sufficient money for return fare. When he has to send her 20 francs, he calls her "odious." Often he was and will continue to be harsh with her. But "odious" for having asked for money? Or for not having asked him sooner? There is a clear hint of their having discussed the degrees of his cruelty. Most of all, his observations on Safonoff are knife-sharp.

1 May

My little flower! Dear, I came home half an hour ago and I sit here thinking of you. How are you faring on this trip? I fear you are train sick.

2 May

Tanyusha, dear, I am beside myself. There is no word from you. What does this mean? Please send a telegram. NOW. You hear? *Immediately* . . . Safonoff is in Paris and perhaps I see him tomorrow. I will report to you . . .

4 May

My angel, what joy you gave me with your sweet, sweet letter. How I love your aunts for tending to you like nurses. Today I breakfast with Gissac, dine with the Gagarins. Goodbye. Don't you think I disguise my writing well?

5 May

My little soul, my dear, please keep on writing every day. If you only knew what joy it is for me to wake up and see an envelope on the floor under my door with Tunina's handwriting! If you are this good throughout your stay in Brussels, then I will delight you when you come back! But if you are not, then I will not only be "kind of cruel" but "very cruel"! So be warned! . . .

8 May

My dear child, why didn't you write me sooner about money? I got your letter at half past twelve when I woke up. I dressed quickly and rushed out to change 20 francs into Belgian notes, but I could not. Today is Sunday and all banks and money exchanges are closed. I will send you 20 francs tomorrow by registered letter in my own handwriting. One day, somehow or other, man will devise a way of doing without money altogether . . . I am in a dreadful hurry. I have to wear a frock coat to Weingartner's concert.

I dined with Safonoff yesterday evening and I had a very long and truly interesting conversation with him. I'll tell you all about it when I see you.

Tunya, my joy, my dear, my little star, I am lonely without you, and am dying to see you. Six more days and then . . . TOGETHER! What bliss! Goodbye! Don't I alter my writing well?

8 May

Nyurochka, I am sending you this letter from the Gare du Nord where I saw Safonoff off. This is so you will get this letter tonight. I cannot tell you all right now how Safonoff and I are not only *reconciled* but are friendly once again. As far as I am concerned, I do not entirely trust his effusiveness, but it is not in my power to reject his affection. I must say he is either an infamous scoundrel or—a very queer fellow! I have much to tell you when we meet. I am sending you 20 francs, my odious one. If I ought to send you your fare, write me IMMEDIATELY, so there can be no delay about it. Cannot chat with you any longer. I am always hurrying, always late. I do everything on the run. When you come back, please organize me a little. I cannot continue living this way! Goodbye my Tanika, Tanila, be good, happy, and don't forget me. No letter from you today.

I composed all night long.

As token of Safonoff's sincerity, Scriabin would not long after receive word from him posted in Minsk: "Have just finished reading the first movement of your symphony and want from the bottom of my heart to congratulate you, dear one . . . I will be in Moscow tomorrow. I stand like Hercules at the crossroads. I am invited to SPb, but I want your free godlike world. I fear it is too late."

This rarely intimate note expressed his distress at leaving the Moscow Conservatory and perhaps comments on his entire life in Russia. As the future revealed, he did not take over Rimsky's post at the Petersburg Conservatory. He went into long and lonely exile in New York as director of the National School of Music in America on West 25th Street. For three years, from 1906 to 1909, Safonoff conducted the New York Philharmonic Orchestra. So prodigious was his reputation in this latter post he earned $1,000 a concert, as much as an opera singer. The afternoon ladies of New York were impressed by his massive hands and batonless conducting. (He introduced America to Mozart's "A Little Night Music.")

His tact with the sensitive American press was graceful. For instance, he rejected the American custom of wearing frock coats at matinée concerts. He appeared in full evening dress because of honor due music even in daytime. "It is neater, most comfortable," he explained and added to the reporters, "Now understand me, I am merely expressing my own views. I do not wish to cavil at any of the charming habits you have here in New York."

10

IT WAS a gullible world in 1905. Word had spread about Scriabin's "doctrine" or "teaching." He himself called it by such a religiously instructive term as *uchenie*. He fully expected something to "happen" when the "Divine Poem" was played. At last Scriabin's philosophy was to be blooded in actual symphonic test.

The first announcement of Nikisch's debut-reading appeared in French papers: "One composition of highest artistic interest will be the work of a composer who has roused the curiosity of the entire musical world, the Russian Scriabin, and his third symphony titled 'The Divine Poem.' This is a grandiose creation which transports you fantastically into another world and bases itself on a philosophical content."

Scriabin wrote to Morozova, 20 March, 1905, that the performance of the "Divine Poem" "will be the first public proclamation of my new doctrine, and it would be very bitter for me were you not to participate in such an important event in my life . . . You will hardly be able to hear the third symphony anywhere besides Paris! Certainly censorship will ban it in Russia for its title and text."

Nikisch rehearsed the Lamoureux orchestra of one hundred and two musicians at 9 in the morning on three successive days, 24, 25 and 26 May. Scriabin wrote Vera: "Yesterday I went to the general rehearsal of the symphony, and it went satisfactorily. Musicians and critics react to the symphony with great interest, although several of them say they are oppressed by its complexity. Now, the most important matter is to have a large audience for it. It appears that Nikisch is not as popular in Paris as he is in Russia or Germany. It would be good if I recuperate at least part of the expenses. After the concert I will write you about its success or failure."

The Paris première on 29 May was not without personal drama. Tatyana described the champagne supper party afterwards. Scriabin, beside himself with joy, could not keep from exclaiming to the waiter, "I've written a symphony!" The waiter replied, "*Bon bourgeois!*" (Good fellow). He continued, "I dream of an even greater symphony . . . all the peoples of the world will unite in the celebration of a great festival . . ."

Next morning after the concert Scriabin received a hand-delivered card from Vera. She had arrived uninvited and in secret to hear the "manifestation" herself. Scriabin answered on his own calling card by the same messenger: "Dear Vusha, Coming instantly. Getting dressed." She had found an inexpensive *pension* at 2, rue Soutenay far from 5, rue de la Neva, and would have returned the next day to Switzerland and the children, had it not been for another surprise.

Astruc informed Scriabin that all the money for the concert was spent. There would be no returns from the expenditures at all. Scriabin, blindly infuriated, challenged him publicly to a duel. On 3 June, 1905, Astruc sent a note to Scriabin frantically. He wanted to "*explain the misunderstanding between us in person*" and, better, he had 3,529 francs and 50 centimes "*in hand*" for him. In other words, half of the Morozova money for the concert had been regained.

Scriabin sent a note to Vera informing her that the duel would *not* take place. Simultaneously, he sent another note to Tatyana informing her of the same. Scriabin had been greatly embarrassed by the appearance on the Paris scene of the first Mme. Scriabina. As a matter of social propriety he spent nights away from both their *pensions*. Oddly enough, he was with Nikolai Sekerin, Natalya's youngest brother, who happened to be in Paris escaping the revolutionary risks in Russia. Scriabin informed the sensitive and jealous Tatyana of his companion, inexplicably. Now, Vera was free to return to the children in Switzerland.

The performance of the "Divine Poem" elicited wildly varied responses.

Gustave Doret dashed off a letter of testimony congratulating Scriabin
and saying the symphony "reinforced my rapture with your work . . ."
Engel, along with the large Russian population living in or visiting Paris
and still smarting from the ignominy of the Russo-Japanese War, attended the concert as a matter of nationalistic pride. They were "thrilled"
by it. Everywhere they loudly reiterated an adage to comfort themselves:
"In war we lose; in art, triumph." Riding this wave, Scriabin scheduled
another solo concert at the Salle Erard for 13 May (it failed to take place).
The Musical Courier of New York reviewed the "Divine Poem":

> . . . The composer was loudly called for from all sides at the conclusion of the
> symphony. When he appeared on the platform, part of the audience began
> whistling to indicate their higher praise . . .

The French interpreted the evening otherwise. Le Guide Musical, for
example:

> . . . The politely cold applause for the orchestra and conductor set the correct
> tone. But it went on a little too long and some hisses began. These latter were
> persistent. They had the last word.

Or Le Ménestrel (Minstrel):

> . . . Part of the audience demonstrated rather noisily against the composer,
> and the others applauded the directorial talent of Nikisch. Under these cir-
> cumstances, it was rather bizarre to bring M. Scriabin before the public in
> person.

Scriabin's own report a week later to Morozova seems to stand reliably
between the extremes of the critics and certain gushiness of the public:

> The concert as you have heard was a great success. Nikisch was on high and
> conducted beautifully. It is difficult to rouse the French to such a pitch of re-
> sponse. They are usually so chary of showing appreciation, particularly toward
> a long and complicated work. I assume there were some protests, judging from
> the few whistles, but they only incited the rest of the audience to greater
> declarations of enthusiasm. As for local musicians, they indicated their enor-
> mous interest, and I still receive letters of approbation from them. No doubt
> this concert will disseminate my musical and philosophical ideas, although
> materially the results were lamentable (half the public came free). Yes, that
> evening can be regarded as important.

It appears, incidentally, that the Nikisch name alone does not fill a theater here. Part of the reason too, was the heat. Another was the dreadful number of trivial concerts recently (such as the one given by Kubelik [Jan, violinist (1880–1940)]). These draw off most of the average public. Nikisch liked the symphony very much, and he is going to perform it in Berlin next season. He invited me to come then. That is all I have to say about my artistic adventures.

As it happened, another conductor presented the Berlin première of the "Divine Poem" at year's end, Oskar Fried (1871–1941) the German conductor and composer (in 1930 he emigrated to the USSR). That concert was given in aid of victims of a Sicilian earthquake and Fried played, according to Mark Meichik, "with an aureole of sympathy." Tatyana wrote Morozova on 4 December, 1905, "Do you know anything about the Third Symphony? We have only heard that some days ago it was played in Berlin. That's all we know. Was it played or not? And how did the Germans take to the 'Divine Poem?'"

Signale für die Musicalische Welt (Music World Guide) was cordial:

> ... After this symphony he can no longer be counted as just another "Russian with talent."

> Even after this first acquaintance one can certainly say that the composer is not afraid to leave the nest. Already he is fully capable of flying on his own. His physiognomy is wholly individual and has few features in common with other Russian composers—either in ideas, or in musical technique and orchestration.

> The music is red-blooded and can be appreciated without any programmatic explanation. A good sign, no doubt.

Musik simply stated that "... like all innovators, Scriabin is bound to gather adherents round him ..."

At the first Russian performance in SPb, 23 February, 1906, under Felix Blumenfeld, many had mixed reactions to the "Divine Poem." Sabaneeff's brother felt that speaking of "world souls" and "divine play" was absurd. "Some world it is," he said, "if the soul has to affirm itself like this!" Taneieff expressed "disbelief at the naturalness of the counterpoint," but confessed that "in one place, I almost wept ..." Later, he commented sarcastically regarding the "cock-a-hoop self-praise, *sublime, divin,* etc." "What," he said to Sabaneeff, "six notes to tell us that the essence of the Creative Spirit opens out before us? Six notes to express Divine Will? Surely it takes more than that!"

Many others, however, were profoundly affected and uncritical. Yuri Pomerantsev exclaimed to a friend, "You should hear Scriabin play the Divine Poem on the piano! Even *there* it sounds like the *perfect poem.*" He also attacked Blumenfeld's performance in a letter to Taneieff 24 February, 1906: "I heard that notably mediocre performance of Scriabin's *Poème Divin* . . . This 'remarkable' composition! Such wealth of musical truth—passion, *élan*, the richest melodies and contrapuntal intricacies. Even I who consider Scriabin a great master was simply astonished. He has taken steps which are past all belief. What luxuriant growth his music now shows. This was present when Nikisch gave it in Paris, I imagine . . ."

Earlier, on 26 August, 1905, Glazunov no less had sent an advance letter of praise to Scriabin:

> I have been studying your Third Symphony. I like it extraordinarily well. Several episodes are enormously attractive. I want terribly to hear it, but only if well played. Nikisch plays symphonies from memory; so in the future, I think, will he better attain a degree of perfection and better understand how to generate its numerous effects.
>
> I found several misprints while looking over the score, but only a few. Why did you change to German in the markings of the last part?

One of the last letters eighty-year-old Stassov would ever write was to Scriabin regarding the "Divine Poem":

> I was present at the triumph of your Third Symphony, *Le Poème Divin*, and was in rapture. At the rehearsal in the Noblemen's Hall on Wednesday the 22nd of February, it exerted its delight over the few who were present and who understand something of new music. The following day, Thursday the 23rd, it generated both surprise and deep feelings on the part of the large audience. The hall was filled to overflowing. And I think that you have added many admirers to your following! It could not and should not be otherwise.
>
> You have *grown* so much! You have already become a great musician. *No one has sent us* yet such a symphony of effects, scale, aspect, form and content.
>
> Naturally, there is not a little of *Richard Wagner*, but there is also much—an enormous amount—of *Alexander Scriabin*. What problems you set! What a plan! What power and what scale! So much passion and poetry in the second section! And the orchestra—so wonderful, mighty, powerful, sometimes tender and despairing, sometimes glittering! Yes, you have already many adherents and admirers among Russians.

Immediately after this Belaieff concert of the 23rd February, a lot of articles appeared in the papers. I will send you three of these . . .

The enclosures sent by Stassov were:

Our Life (by Mikhail Nesterov):

> . . . It is considerably better than his Second. There is more life and lift to it, more artistic finish. But is there not also a little of the superfluous, the stiff? Listening to the finale, one can say with certainty that Scriabin will soon again find new and powerful words with which he will sear humanity's heart.

Theatre and Art (by Alexander Schmuller [1880–1933], violinist, critic, professor at the conservatories in Berlin and Amsterdam):

> The C major Symphony, the most remarkable which Scriabin has yet written . . . complicated structure, searching harmonies, remarkable wealth of thematic material and artistic sequences in the development . . .

Russia (by Victor Kolomeitsev):

> The new work of Scriabin attests not only the development of his uncommon talent, but also his great erudition . . .

Scriabin answered promptly: "I offer you, respected Vladimir Vassilievich, my gratitude . . . You were the news-bearer of my first real success in Petersburg . . ." And to conductor Blumenfeld he wrote:

> Accept my sincere and deep thanks for the beautiful performance of my symphony. I learned of it from many newspapers and letters from friends. You accomplished a miracle performing it after only two rehearsals. This is incredible. What a pity I did not know sooner that you were conducting the symphony. I would have sent you its explanatory text. No doubt you did not know it was written on a philosophical basis . . .

Nikisch himself much later in a letter dated 6 February, 1908, to Baron Konstantin Stakelberg (1858–1925), conductor of the Court orchestra in Petersburg, who was contemplating playing the "Divine Poem" for the Tsar, described it as "very good . . . a most interesting composition, but there is nothing Russian in it."

V

DOCTRINE

II

In the Findeizen letter Scriabin wrote, "I left the Conservatory in order to devote myself exclusively to my ideas." A perusal of the Morozova correspondence of 1904–7 shows Scriabin's *uchenie* or doctrine to be deeply serious between them. Gone for the most part is his own personal suffering. No longer is composing a torture, but a radiant bliss. The magic of his mind has again transformed him and his social relations . . . for both good and for ill, as we will see later. He has begun calling his new music "my big work," "my important composition."

Scriabin was more *guru* to a pupil than *protégé* to patron. As early as March, 1904, writing from Vézenaz, he had said to Morozova: "How I want to share my musical and philosophical thoughts with you and I deplore being unable to do so as yet. That is why I rush you with your studies." In April, 1904, during a bereavement, he comforts her as a master would an adept: "What a pity we are not together so that I might try to console you. All of life is a series of such experiences. We must be ready for them. You will find beatitude and release only in constant victory over yourself and in uninterrupted activity there at the summit of the ascent. Don't look at everything with human, too human eyes. Face life in other ways, and it will disclose eternal happiness."

He continued with specific instructions: "It would please me much to learn that you are occupying yourself with philosophy. You need to absorb Kant as quickly as possible and then acquaint yourself a little with Fichte, Schelling and Hegel, even if only as part of the history of philosophy. The Überweg-Heinze History of New Philosophy is stolid, but very complete, important and *schematic*. Kuno-Fischer can tell you all

47

you need know about Kant. When you have assimilated all this, then it will be easier for me to work with you. You will then quickly grasp my own doctrine . . ."

He attended the second session of the International Congress of Philosophy, held in Geneva from 4 to 8 September, 1904, registered himself as a member, and attended lectures on these subjects: "What is Philosophy?" by Professor Stein of the University of Bern; "Fichte versus Schelling," by Xavier Leon; an explanation by the Geneva professor, Flouroy, of "panpsychism" which links the soul and body. Another lecture also on "panpsychism" was given by a Professor Strong of Columbia University. He, most agreeably to Scriabin, stated that the physical body was a "manifestation" of the soul hidden within it, and that the "evolutionary drama" of the material world was no more than "psychic evolution" of objects themselves. One musician, who ran into Scriabin by accident on the streets of Berlin that year, recounts that his first words were "not a greeting, but about Kant."

The stern teacher was capable of reproach. On 13 December, 1904, he wrote Morozova from Paris:

> I am angry with you for your mood! Once again you seem to have forgotten all our conversations! You talk of 'awareness' and 'knowledge' and say nothing of 'creativity.' One would think you satisfied locked in a closet all your life studying nothing but dry matter. WHAT doubts have you? Live with faith in yourself and your powers. Come quickly, and I will cure all your illnesses . . .

When Morozova missed the SPb performance of the "Divine Poem," Scriabin was shocked.

> But you did not speak of the other thing, the really important matter concerning my future—the performance and its great success. I will send you the reviews. Their likes have never been seen before in Russia. To tell the truth (oh how naive and presumptuous of me!) I had thought you would avail yourself of that second chance to hear le Divin Poème. I was certain that you would! When it turned out that you were not the messenger of its joy, I was rather offended, and accused you in my mind of indifference to my work. There will be a time, dear Margarita Kirillovna, when every person (not just friends) will skip from one pole of the earth to the other just to hear a pause in a composition of mine! And you, a friend close as you, could not even spend one night in a first-class comfortable compartment to go hear the entirety of my best composition.

His sensitivity continues and when she misunderstands his doctrine in connection with the Revolution, he delivered on 1 May, 1906, another intellectual chastisement:

> I am endlessly happy my suppositions that you were indifferent to my creative work are in error. You will understand and excuse my jealous nature.
>
> As for coming to Russia. How is it possible for you to fail to see that I must not, especially now? The POLITICAL revolution in Russia in its present phase and the *change* which I want are different. Of course, this revolution like every other political agitation brings the beginning of *my* desired moment closer. I make a mistake in using the word *change*. I do not want the ACTUALIZA-TION or ESTABLISHING of ANYTHING. I want only the endless lift of creative activity brought about by my art. This means that before all else I must complete my important composition. Generally, dear Margarita Kirillovna, I have figured the practical side of my work thus: *MY* moment has not yet begun. But it approaches. There will be a celebration! Soon!

The word *pod'yom*, meaning *élan*, lift, ascent, and even exaltation, enters Scriabin's common vocabulary as bedrock to the word "doctrine" itself. While he is composing, it means "inspiration" of profoundly spiritual import. In his philosophy it is the surge of creativity within him. He was invariably pleased when Morozova benefits by his doctrine. This proves the efficacy of his method. She often found herself in a state of *pod'yom*, sensing an ascent in feeling, a kind of elation which is as symptomatic and alarming to psychiatrists as it may be enjoyable to its subjects. "I am happy to learn of your bright mood and the surge of spirit you are experiencing," he wrote on 20 March, 1905, and adds impiously for a cicerone, "It is the reverse from what I am undergoing at the moment, I am ashamed to say." On 6 June, 1905: "I am happy with all my heart that you are experiencing a lift and telling many others about it." Scriabin liked, indeed, pupils who passed to a wider public word of ecstasy his doctrine engendered. All was propaganda for his cause.

Engel describes Scriabin's messianic mania sympathetically. He first observed it in Switzerland that lovely spring of 1904 as they rode by boat home to Vézenaz. Not even his proselytizing and gross magnification could destroy his greatness in the eyes of those close to him.

> He suddenly began talking intimately with me. He spoke of his most heartfelt dreams and hopes. Afterwards it struck me how unusual it was for him to be

so open. But at this time he was, and willingly so. As an outsider I found it curious.

"Never before has there been such music," he said of the Third Symphony. He spoke of its "divine play" as the fundamental of creation, both for creating the world itself and in producing art. He spoke of the essence of art, of religion, of socialism—in a word, of everything.

He said that a fusion of all the arts was essential, but not in the theatrical, Wagnerian, sense. Art must combine with philosophy and religion to produce something indivisible. This was the new Evangel to replace the old outworn Gospels.

"I have an idea to create some kind of a Mysterium. I need to construct a special temple for it, perhaps here (he made a gesture towards the panorama of mountains) or perhaps far from here, in India ... But people aren't ready for it. I must sermonize. I must show them a new path. I have even preached from a boat, like Christ ... I have a little group of people here who understand me. They will come with me. There's one in particular, a fisherman. He's simple, but a wonderful fellow. I'll introduce you ..."

When Alexander Nikolaevich talked this way, it was truly awe-inspiring. How appealing and beautiful! But when you thought of such things coming from a man on a boat ride, who had bought a ticket and held it in his hand, then you began to wonder if he were out of his mind! But I had no reason to fear. Here was "a poet of God's mercy" in front of me. No actual fact of existence could touch his dream—thanks to the power of his concentration. To him the dream was real. This infected everyone else too.

Scriabin did not keep his word about the fisherman-disciple. Engel enquired about him though from Vera and others. Otto Hauenstein lived in La Bellotte, a few minutes closer to Geneva from Vézenaz. Again it was one of those odd relationships where a rough and burly man, twice Scriabin's size, was enamored of him. They were truly friends. "Voilà Alexandre," Otto would cry when he espied him on the street, and they would sit down to drink beer and talk affectionately until late at night.

When Scriabin was with Vera in Switzerland, he wrote Tatyana that Otto sent her his "warmest greetings." When he was with Tatyana in Paris and Vera was about to quit Switzerland, he cautioned her to be sure to say goodbye to Otto. In September, 1907, Tatyana and Scriabin spent two weeks in Otto's cottage as guests. In 1908, Otto signs a round-robin greeting from the Scriabins to still another adherent of the doctrine —Nemenova-Lunz. As for music, Otto's only recorded comment, when he heard Scriabin play the Third Sonata, was, "My, what a lot of noise Alexandre makes all by himself."

Engel interprets Otto and his entourage of fisherfolk as being "rather socialistic and therefore they willingly listened when Scriabin thundered against the existing order. 'There should be no money!' 'There must be no beggars!' 'Each must work at what he loves!' 'Only those must bring up children who want to!' etc. But," he sighs, "it is hard to say how they responded to Scriabin on the subject of the new art, his new Bible, and the like..."

Vera in a brief recollection spoke of Otto:

> He was really a good man. Older than Alexander Nikolaevich, but still he called him "mon vieux." They were on close terms, used tu with each other, and first names.
>
> Once when he was away from home all day, I waited and waited. At nightfall, I went to the tram which runs to Geneva. Perhaps he will return here, I thought. Suddenly, passing by a café I heard his voice. There were many people, simple folk, and there was Otto. They were all listening to Alexander Nikolaevich. He was excited and preaching with passion. That's where he was to be found!

Other converts of different social levels came to Scriabin's ideas. Some were his equals and some his superiors, even if by now he admitted no superior. In a letter from Paris, 15 December, 1904, he described for Vera an encounter during an evening party at the Solennikovs.

> I met a Russian priest there, and we immediately began a conversation about basics. I straightaway explained the purpose of my presence in Paris and he became so interested in my ideas that he is coming to the concert and nothing can stop him!! The evening ended with my having persuaded him to my way of thinking! 'Father! What are you doing being so friendly with a heretic?' I said. He replied, 'Never mind, it may be that I will begin to bruit you about even in books, for all you say interests me deeply and appeals to me!—the final goal of a general flowering and general beatitude.' Well, in short, we chatted on for half the night. Annushka [Solennikova] was our Mary Magdalene and prepared more tea and strawberries for us and, of course, kept modestly quiet. Truly, isn't that amazing! For the time being you are not to say a word about a priest joining my ranks. Tell no one. He ASKED me to keep this quiet...

The Solennikov family was eager to learn more of his doctrine, too. In fact so many persons had gathered around Scriabin by 4 March, 1907, that he wrote Tatyana, "I have a great plan for the summer! We will live as a whole colony and if everybody helps me, my work can quickly be accomplished."

Meantime, Gissac gave Scriabin a copy of *La Clef de la Théosophie* (Key to Theosophy). This mystical bible was written by Helena Blavatsky (1831-1891), née Hahn, who also wrote under the Indian pseudonym of Radha Roy. She founded the famous religious cult with innumerable branches still today—the Theosophical Society. On 5 May, 1905, in Paris, Scriabin wrote Tatyana his first reference to Theosophy: "I am reading an interesting book ..." Three days later he wrote again, "*La Clef de la Théosophie* is a remarkable book. You will be astonished at how close it is to my thinking ..." These are Scriabin's only specific references to Theosophy as such, although from now on more and more of his friends and adherents were drawn from the Society.

12

NOTEBOOKS

IN THE ferocity of his doctrine's growth Scriabin kept extensive notebooks. He incessantly worked out plans, schemes, world-enveloping mental processes. How does my mind work? he asked himself over and over. How and why do I create the whole world and all in it?

His notebooks record rambling, untried, untested, evanid thoughts. In passages he firmly expresses most final and resolute convictions. Many times the jottings are fantasies, free verse poems, and sound as if intended for librettos. The pendulum swings often between avowed goals and admission of shortcomings. Occasionally, he blurs into fanaticism, into biblical preachments like a copycat Christ. At times he writes as a mystagogue officiating at the mysteries of Eleusis.

For a tiny man, the lust for power pulsating through each word astonishes, as does his perpetual nagging at himself about "creativity." This was irrevocably a part of Scriabin genius. He could never stop inventing his brightly painted chords and honeyed harmonies.

The Scriabin vocabulary now became more idiosyncratic. "Creation," for example, combined the sense of procreation, artistic achievement, and the material fact of producing physical phenomena. Creating the world, as he says, is like a man taking a woman. "Consciousness," "cognition," "awareness," "knowledge," all the same word in Russian (*soznanie*) after his special and repeated use, almost turned synonymous with its homonym *sozdanie* or "creation."

Scriabin's megalomania—"I am god"—was and is offensive. Nor is it forgivable by its iterated counterbalance—"I am nothing." But his madness shows an earthbound man soaring and daring to aspire to suns, stars, universes and galaxies. Psychopathological as it was—this embracing of the whole world as a personal plaything—it also expands our consciousness. How extraordinary to read his cosmogony where life is a divine game and he the total player, and we watch as he annihilates time and space. How godlike he felt when he burned in flames of sexual, ideational, or musical "creativity".

Ecstasy begins to be a paltry word, incapable of explicating his ultimate emotion. How often he writes in these notebooks of joy, happiness, bliss, beatitude, and beyond into hyperbole. Scriabin expressed these waves of feeling hesitantly and irrationally in his journals, but managed to convert them into fact in art. Art, not science nor endless ratiocinations, was, after all, the alchemy of his salvation. And along the way of harnessing his thoughts, he annihilated death as well as he could. He grudgingly said, "I will die as a human being," but by this he meant only his corporeal self. The very thought of resurrection of the *flesh* was revolting to him.

Solovyov had preached self-assertion of the Will as the source of evil, as Buddha proclaimed desire the root of suffering. Scriabin deified both Will and Desire. It is through pain that man comes to know his limitations, he intoned as if having surmounted them. All must resolve into the one, he cried. Unity in multiplicity, he, like many other Russians, over and over again proclaimed. *Sobornost'* is the climactic union, the apocalyptic togetherness. Simultaneously, there is always the split and the splinter . . . the "you" for every "I," the "other" for every "one."

Here is the text of the first Switzerland notebook (1904). Its considerably beautiful language begins with the beginning of the world, not ours but his—strange and inverted, but desirable.

I begin my story. It is the story of the world—of the universe. I am, and there is nothing outside of me. I am nothing. I am all. I am one, and within me is multiplicity. I wish to live. I am life's palpitation. I am desire. I am a dream. Oh radiant world of mine, my awakening, my play, my blossoming (my disappearance) of unknown feelings is a playing stream. Ever, eternally, ever new, different, more powerful, more tender, new delight, new torture, new play. Not until I disappear, not until I am consumed. I am fire. I am chaos.

I am come to tell you the secret of life, the secret of death, the secret of heaven and earth.

Desires in me are vague, and dreams dim. I do not yet know how to create you. I only know that I wish to create. I create already. The desire to create is creation.

My soul thirsts to conquer you,

Oh frightening phantoms of stony truth. All that hinders life is suffering. Everything which facilitates life is pleasure.

Life is activity, striving, struggle.

Whatever may be my activity in a given moment (whether I am composing, or whether I am making love, etc.), I feel pleasure if there is an obstacle placed in my path but one not greater than my ability to overcome. If circumstances paralyze my energy, I suffer. From this point of view, pleasure and pain accompany every moment of our life, even if we try to disregard them.

You are the gamut of my rage. You are the tender lines of my caresses. You are the soft half-light of my dreams. You are the stars, the lightning flashes of my glance. You are the sun of my bliss. You are the expression in space of my sensation in time. Thus I speak—drowned in time, wrenched from space.

Oh life. Oh creative surge. Oh all-creating desire. You are all. You are bliss of grief (of pain), and the bliss of joy, and I adore you both. You are the ocean of passion, now stormy and tranquil. I love your lamentation, and I love your joy (only I do not love despair). I am free. I am *nothing*. I want to live! I want the new, the unknown. I want to create, to create freely, to create consciously, to be at the peak. I want to conquer with my creation of divine beauty.

I want to be the brightest light, the greatest (and only) sun. I want to illuminate the universe with my light. I want to swallow all and include (all) in my individuality. I want to give (to the world) pleasure. I want to seize the world as a woman.

I create the world by the play of my mood, my smile, my sigh, my caress, anger, hope, doubt. That which I wish, I wish *here* and *now*. For that moment the history of the universe and humanity are needed. And with this caprice, this passing wish, I create all history as I create all future. All is my wish, my dream, and I am aware of all this.

13

THE SECOND or "Blue Notebook" dated "Summer-1904" was written in pencil at the open-air café in La Bellotte, his rendezvous spot with Otto. Here we see deeper reflection, more insistent philosophical, architectonic dialectics. Something within him forces self-wonderment. Sores of sorrow have opened again, and this notebook is less fantastic, more reasoning if not exactly reasonable. It is false. In it he summons points to prove the impossible. He argues for and against himself with tempered equanimity, but for all this he only moves from pseudo-hypothesis to spurious conclusion.

Scriabin now encountered the writings of Wilhelm Wundt (1832–1920), father of experimental psychology, the first psychologist to write of those distant, instant psychic influences which fascinated Sigmund Freud.

Wundt, primitive as he now sounds, was concerned with recording that which can be observed. He wanted to observe the contents of consciousness, and defined psychology as the "science of immediate experience and all its subjective feelings and perceptions." Introspection was its method. The chief struggle of late nineteenth-century thought was for a marriage, or at least happy equation between faith and science and those different universes . . . the mind and body. The mental sciences bent to reconcile the new nature of physical knowledge. From Kant's *Conceptus Cosmica* to the safer road of science decamped a mass of minor and major minds. How, in short, could man turn beliefs and feelings into observable and demonstrable science?

The "Blue Notebook" quotes then disputes Wundt, but only after extracting all that is useful to his self-justification. In these pages Scriabin's stepwise logic is startling. Of particular interest is his converse with himself, as if he were talking to another person who also thought *he* was God and therefore has created the world, Scriabin's world . . . the "not-I." Towards the end, we find indication that Scriabin's mind has begun to play him tricks, that he can induce a "loss of consciousness," and fatigue and pain are close, too close, undifferentiable "states of consciousness."

(Psychology, Wundt) (page 21)

1) The inner or psychological experience is not in the same realm of experience as others. It is an instant experience.

2) Direct experience does not present a dead content, but a *conjunction or series of processes*. It is not composed of objects but of processes.

3) Each process has, from one viewpoint, an *objective content*. From the other, it is a subjective happening.

This is modern psychology's departure point. These three theses are accepted as axiomatic and on them rests the whole structure of psychology.

In themselves they are *not obvious* to us. Each experience supposes a *content*, which is *given* us, and a *perception* of this content. In the psychological experience we are given PROCESSES, given *objects* which we PERCEIVE as subjective occurrences. But in what way are these processes given us? In what way, basing our experience on these *subjective* occurrences, which are all we can affirm, can we arrive at these processes outside us? Where is the basis for such a conclusion? Where is the bridge?

The identity of object and subject in a psychological *experience* appears obvious to me. Seeing it thus, the experience ceases to be an *experience* (but becomes creativity). If we can affirm everything as nothing more than subjective occurrence, then it can be *only* as a result of our activity, of our one and therefore free and absolute activity.

Therefore the world is the result of my activity, my creation, my wish (freely imposed).

Why, then, is this world which has been created by me not such as I would like to have it? Why do I as an individual find myself in unpleasant situations? And why do I at the same time so love the world and am so attached to it that one thought of death can throw me into terror?

In order to explain that there is no contradiction here, I will turn to certain methods of procedure. First, I will posit that all that causes me to suffer is now set aside. In such a world as I have wished it I, as an individual, am in a most advantageous situation. *Nothing remains for me to desire.* And in this position I find myself *eternally* at peace. Is it possible to imagine anything more frightful than numbness of satisfaction? Are not the most terrible sufferings and all the tortures of the Inquisition better, that is less horrible, than this feeling of infinite satisfaction? Of course they are. I doubt if anyone ever thought of making such a choice, except those who are weary and weak and for whom life holds no value.

Thus, the seeming disadvantage of my position in the world in no wise contradicts the fact that I am author of it. Even if I consider it bad, *I have chosen the better of two evils.*

Further, if the world is my one and absolutely free activity, then what about this Truth which I do not feel within myself but which I have suffered for, sought and desired? All history of mankind is the same search for Truth. If I do not feel it within myself, and if elsewhere I can only affirm that which I create, then *there is no Truth.* There is no Truth! That for which so many geniuses have lived, for which so much blood has flowed, for which so many lives have been lost?

What then is all our life? It is only that which I experience, only that which I wish for, and strive after. It is play, my free play. This is the absolute value for me. However, why do I not feel free?

If the world is my creation, then the question of *knowing* the world resolves itself into the question of knowing the nature of free creativity. How do I create? Or first, what does it mean *that* I create? What constitutes the processes of my creativity?

In this given moment I sit at a table and write. I ponder the nature of free creativity. From time to time I stop this work, look at the lake, admire the color of the water, the shimmering play of its tones. I look at people passing by, at some more closely than at others. Then again I return to writing my thoughts on untrammeled creativity. I want to drink and ask for a lemonade. I look at the clock, and note that lunch time is drawing near. This reminds me of the sensation of hunger. I quickly leave Bellotte and hurry home.

All this I know. I *differentiate* it. In every moment I know some one thing. Sometimes it seems to me that I know several things at one time. Thus at the present time I often raise my eyes to the lake, and although I look at it inattentively, I am still looking at it and writing and thinking. But work suffers from divided attention. So I completely submerge myself in thoughts of creativity and nothing distracts me. Passing some time thus, I tire and begin to feel sick.

Something is thinking in me apart from my will. I attempt to control myself and stop work. I leave. I am so tired my thoughts are confused. Letters dance before my eyes. I *differentiate* objects but *not clearly.* When I rest, I again return to work and will profit from these observations of myself.

First of all, in the whole mass of experiences of sensation and thought, I notice something that links them together in general. That it is *I* who experiences all this. It is *I* who knows all this.

Secondly, in order to be aware of this, I *act.* I strain myself and make an effort. I expend a greater or lesser amount of *attention.*

Thirdly, if I were to stop *knowing* all this, that is, if my activity were to cease, then *all* would disappear for me.

Thus, it is that I am the *author* of all experiences. I am the creator of the world...

14

As the last Swiss notebook of 1905 deepened, this labyrinthine intellection moves again closer to other thinkers. Fichte had long ago placed man as a knowing and willing subject at the center of the universe. From there, he separated the I and the not-I, the Ego and the non-Ego, and differentiated objects from subjects, one state of consciousness from another, and the inner from the outer world. But Fichte held tight to the philosopher's reins. He pulled himself up abruptly, before exchanging cogitation for conviction.

Novalis too had written that "The seat of the soul is where the inner world and outer world touch. For nobody knows himself, if he is only himself and not also another. To take possession of one's transcendental I is to be the not-I of one's I at the same time . . ." And he believed profoundly in Ecstasy. In a book called *Novalis: Romantic Idealism in Germany*, by E. Spenlé, which Scriabin borrowed from a friend during his Swiss period, he underscored one passage and made a marginal notation: "Novalis reproaches Fichte for not making Ecstasy the basis of his philosophical system."

Eduard von Hartmann (1842–1906), another important German romantic known to Scriabin, thought that reason and will had once been contained within the unconscious and at the time of the fall of man, they separated. Thus, reason and will struggle against each other in man, and cause him to suffer. When they are silenced, the world can become quiet and reach the state of the original unconscious. To Scriabin, reason and will become the centripetal and centrifugal forces, and the longing for the quiescent unconscious is for Ecstasy, a final, post-coital dissolution of the world, an irreversible "stepping out" from the prostrate body.

Scriabin's dance "from center to center" leads his thoughts into "insane passion." He cultivates that special languor he first mentioned in La Bellotte. He discovers the rhythm of the universe, the swirling forces that push out and the suction that draws in, the Brahmanical breathing in and breathing out. He creates the world like Brahma and destroys like Siva. He creates us (humanity), destroys us, and becomes us. He is resurrected. He talks, too, at length about being a genius. Mankind is an extension of genius, but "There is only one consciousness. That is mine,"

He employs here his first theosophical word—manvantara, meaning in Sanskrit a period of evolution lasting many thousands of years or one complete cycle of humanity. There are, according to Hinduism, fourteen small manvantaras within this one great one of ours which extends broadly from Chaos to the end of the Solar system. Scriabin had been searching for a word of such breadth to incorporate his own concept of history. Scriabin's fantasy was now unmoored. After all, what was Theosophy but the search for the "God of Wisdom" himself.

The following notebook began with narcissism and patterns. He treats ideas as tones or rhythms to create joint musical and literary effects. The shapes of the stanzas imply the structure of future compositions. But more important are the forecasts within this document. He discovers happiness, that *pod'yom* in excess, through megalomania. "I will be your God. You will be mine, because I created you ..." The cleavage within his personality is as sharp as the manic-depressive swing, the schizophrenic split. And he talks of sexuality. In one place he uses "self-aggrandizement" as equal to "self-preservation" and the propagation of the race. "I gave birth to you ..." "Life is the act of love ..." "Consciousness without sensation is empty ..." But when he says sexuality the word "death" succeeds immediately. Sin is sweet, but he couples it with torment. A kiss is synonymous with laceration, orgasm with hell-fire. Sometimes his thought seems no more than a butterfly struggle against fear of death.

On one page two separate, disjointed paragraphs, clearly written at different times foretell the Fifth and Sixth Sonatas to come. The first passage (in a reworked version) was extrapolated from the final "Poem of Ecstasy" and printed as a heading for the exuberant, beckoning Fifth Sonata:

You have heard my secret call, hidden powers of life, and you begin to stir. The billow of my being, light as a vision of dreams, embraces the world. To life! Burgeon!

I awaken you to life with kisses and the secret pleasures of my promises.

I summon you to life, hidden longings, lost in the chaos of sensations. Rise up from the secret depths of the creative soul.

The other passage, one of blackest dread, explains the ambiguities of the strange Sixth Sonata, where its first unexorcized climax is marked *l'épouvante surgit*, "the frightening rises up." It also provides the future key to the triumphant, white Seventh Sonata:

> Peoples! Blossom forth, create, negate me and rise up against me. I resurrect all you terrors of the past, all monsters and all frightful, horrible visions. I give you full flower. Try swallowing me up! Lay open the dragons' pasture. Serpents! Twine round me, strangle me, and bite. Everyone and everything seeks my destruction and when all fall upon me, that is when I begin my play. I will conquer you by loving you. I will surrender and seduce you. But I will never be conquered, since I will never conquer myself.

One more paragraph verbalizes what one later day could be an epigraph for the beginning of the mighty Fifth Symphony, *Prometheus*, "The Poem of Fire":

> Something began to glimmer and pulsate and this *something was one*. It trembled and glimmered, but it was one. I do not differentiate multiplicity. This *one* was all with nothing in opposition to it. It was everything. I am everything. It had the possibility of anything, and it was not yet Chaos (the threshold of consciousness). All history and all future are eternally in it. All elements are mixed, but all that can be is there. It exudes colors, feelings, and dreams. I wish. I create. I differentiate. I distinguish unclearly. Nothing is delineated. I know nothing, but all seems foreboding and I remember. Instants of the past and future come together. Confused presentiments and recollections, frights and joys.

Scriabin's "doctrine" was extraordinarily depersonalized, remote and withdrawn from the realities of the world. But his feelings about it were severe and secretive. Once in January, 1906, when he parted briefly from Tatyana for the first time since they had set up housekeeping, he wrote this vicious, fearful note, and from it we learn again these notebooks were for no one's eyes but his, and also that he kept a little collection of erotic photographs:

> Tanyuka, I have found a scrap of paper and use it to repeat the instructions I have already left with you. Children must always be told the same thing

several times. So listen! lst. Be good and *watch out for yourself.* 2nd. Don't you *DARE!!!*—you pig of an animal—read my writings. If you do, you'll regret you were ever born!!! 3rd. If you find some photographs among my papers, don't destroy them in a fit of jealousy. The one exception is the postcard of Cavaleri [Lina (1874–1944), the opera star]. You can throw that away. I have already told you how I got it, and may have already performed that disposal operation myself.

Again I kiss you, my little crumb.

NOTEBOOK–1905

I am a moment in shimmering eternity. I am freedom's play, I am life's play, I am the playing streams of unknown feelings.

I am freedom, I am life, I am a dream, I am weariness, I am unceasing burning desire, I am bliss, I am insane passion, I am nothing, I am atremble.
I am play, I am freedom, I am life, I am a dream, I am weariness, I am feeling, I am the world. I am insane passion, I am wild flight. I am desire, I am light, I am creative ascent that tenderly caresses, that captivates, that sears, Destroying, Revivifying. I am raging torrents of unknown feelings. I am the boundary, I am the summit. I am nothing.

I am God!
I am nothing, I am play, I am freedom, I am life.
I am the boundary, I am the peak.

I am God!
I am the blossoming, I the bliss,
I am all-consuming passion,
    all engulfing,
I am fire enveloping the universe,
Reducing it to chaos.
I am the blind play of powers released.
I am creation dormant, Intellect quenched.

    All is outside me,
    I am multiplicity made one,
    I have spent freedom
    and only its gleam
    lives in me,

        blindly yearning
        from the center,
        from the Sun,
        from the spark.

SCRIABIN
62 SCRIABIN
62 SCRIABIN

My former divinity
   drives me now
   to freedom,
   to unity,
   to knowledge,
   to truth,
   to God,
   to myself,
   to life,
   Oh life, Oh creative surge (wish)!
      All-creating urge,
         from the center eternally from the center
   to freedom
   to knowledge!

An impulse disturbs celestial harmony. This creates the substance on which divine idea is then printed. For an instant the balance with lower degrees is restored. Then by a new impulse again, it is disturbed, etc., until the whole reservoir of powers finds its outlet in the activity of *all manvantaras*.

How beautiful is the vitality of your aspirations and how wrong you are, if you wish to destroy the opposition which gave them birth.
Love your enemies—they give you feeling. Rise against them and struggle. Love one another for their opposition. Fly freely on the mighty wings of your search. There on the summit of your feelings' flight, you will know oneness, you will know bliss and dissolution in me.
Your best friends are your enemies. They awaken in you yearnings of love.

Why do the flowers fade when hardly blossomed? Why are there limits everywhere? Why is there an end to everything, always?
And why are the cups of love and sexuality so quickly drained?
But death.

In the past all was search for me and *I myself* in youth was the seeking of that which I later became, that which *I created myself*.
My youth was the highest point of tension and of boredom with the world of grief.
My present is the highest point of bliss and freedom, victory over sorrow.
The future will be rest within activity. The past was a presentiment of me.

A God requiring worship is no God.

Note well!
My joy is so great that myriads of worlds could plunge into it without so much as ruffling its surface. World of mine, sing my freedom and bliss.
Accept me. Do not struggle, I am not a fearsome Divinity, but a loving one. Do not worship me, but only accept. I will release you from the fears which

bind your suffering hearts eternally. I will relieve you of doubt and obligation's oppression. I will bring you full blossoming. You are free and if you can, be as free as I. If you dare, then you will be equal to me. You can do all that you wish. Your activity is realization itself. No more will evil or envy dwell in your hearts. I will give you the everlasting sweetness of activity, the inexhaustible source of joy, of life, all in exchange for the momentary sweetness of sin and its fear of eternal torment.

Suffering or dissatisfaction with desire is an obstacle to the *development* of individuality.

The life of the individual is for the most part suffering. The strong man frees himself from it by activity, by struggle against an obstacle. The weak man perishes.

Life, in general, is freeing oneself through struggle in activity. We desire suffering. We desire power. The greatest power is the power of fascination, power without violence.

I suffer, I am blissful, I run, I wish that something was not—all this is individual and predicated on the condition of an *I* and *not-I*. This is because experiencing means to divide: to know the *not-I* and the *I* and the relation of the *I* to the *not-I*.

I am come to save the world from the tyranny of rulers and from the tyranny of the populace. I bring unlimited freedom and justice. I bring fullest development and the divine joy of creativity. The world longs for freedom and fears it, because at the same time it longs for the mainstay, Truth. Naive! All truth includes freedom, and freedom is truth. Fear not this bottomless emptiness! You say: If there is no truth, then why live? Whither are we going? How can we live? Are affliction and joy or greatness and ascent mere phantoms of fantasy? Fear not. I comfort you. All exists. All is. All that you wish. You create all that you wish. Can all this disappear, if you knew your power and your freedom? You wish to fly, then fly. Fly as you will, whither you like, and all round you is empty space!

I will die as a human being. But all in me that does not come under the jurisdiction of death is what creates time and space and all within them.

The growth of human consciousness is the growth of the consciousnesses of geniuses. The consciousnesses of the remaining people are splashes and sparks of the same consciousness. There is only one consciousness. That is mine.

The genius contains all the play of colors and feelings of other people. He embraces the consciousness of all those people contemporary to him.

You were not surprised when I told you You do not yet exist, but it was so. You have embraced unto yourself Understanding, Space and Time.

Here is a complex: Feeling, sensation, will.

You see before you a man and you can not believe what I say, but you can experience in your consciousness what I say. You experience it as a readymade formula. But that function which makes what I say—that is what you cannot experience.

You say to me: I am God because I experience it. No. That is because it is your awareness speaking which *I* have created with the power of my free creativity. That is what is in your mind, and you draw from that, not from it itself. When you say you are God, you ARE CONFESSING THAT TO ME. But you will not be God. You will only be like God insofar as you are My reflection. *I gave birth to you.*

I can affirm the following:
1. The world. It is my creation, my creative act.
2. My wish to live.
3. My desire for fullest individual development.

I can pose the following questions:
1. What is the nature (my) of creativity (free)?
2. How is life possible?
3. How can full individual development take place and is it possible for all?

Within me all human nature is conquered. Godlike Freedom! You have only to guard it.

The world is narrow for me—dim colors—like aromas.

Conditions for the possibility of experience. Without this there is nothing:
1. Freedom from all other things
2. Connection with all other things
This means
1. Individuality (multiplicity)
2. Divinity (unity)

If I could know everything, I would violate my individuality which exists only in isolation and as a relationship to all else.

15

AT TIMES, Scriabin's secret colloquies with himself failed. He turned to drawings and sketches. An outline, jotted as an *aide mémoire*, represented an entire complex of thought. Sometimes he drew on a tablecloth at dinner or over drinks, only to have the waiter take it away and wash it.

For his friends to whom he expounded ideas, if they could not hear his meaning, he drew so that they could see it. Schloezer wrote that "Each schema, each formula was for him like a little peg to hang his contemplations on, down here on earth. In an argument, he made drawings. 'There! Look at my scheme! All is clear, new, logical, and graphic. Now you *can't* find any fault.'" Today, without their accompanying verbal explanation some of the drawings are mystifying. Others, however, such as these which follow, illustrate the texts of the notebooks.

Drawing I shows the centripetal-centrifugal forces whose swirling vibrations and rhythm absorb time and space. The powerful flow forms a figure 8 and this, for Scriabin, locates God in the center. He himself is here, with the past and future placed (in space) above and below him (in time). His disembodied spirit freely rests at the still center on which the world turns.

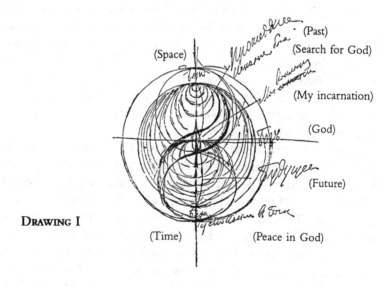

(Space)

(Past)

(Search for God)

(My incarnation)

(God)

(Future)

DRAWING I

(Time)

(Peace in God)

Drawing II reveals how the world appeared to Scriabin, the crucial points of the Swiss notebooks. This paper was a separate sheet sketched while talking with friends, perhaps at Otto's cafe.

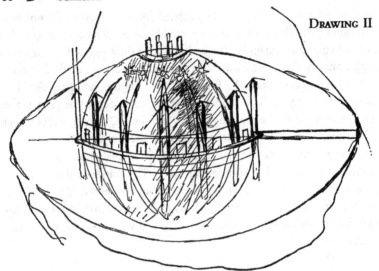

Drawing III is a "Scheme of Evolution" describing the progression from analysis to synthesis and how the breakdown and assembly are accomplished. Drawing from left to right, Scriabin traced the passive, inward turning, disparate and disorganized elements of life, the world and mind, and shifts them, of course through the power of his thought, into the desired goals of activity, organization, unity, and the step beyond—implied here as capital letters—Ecstasy, the ultimate answer to all questions and all activity of mind or body.

Drawing IV describes the refraction of unity into diversity and its ladder of contrasts. Fichte, Hegel and Schelling all might have diagrammed their thesis-antithesis-synthesis search for thought integration similarly.

We do not scoff at Haydn for saying that he felt God inside him when he composed *The Creation*. Nor are we averse to the philosophical mannerism Windelband calls "the naive ruggedness of following out single motives of reflection to their most one-sided logical conclusion"—the intellectual price of self-delusion. However, we cannot but regard Scriabin's notebooks as the weathervane of a man who wrote a paradox as glibly as a syllogism.

Still, we must not ignore a Russian penchant for claiming the deity for oneself: "I am God." Pushkin's teacher, Gavrila Derzhavin (1743–1816), wrote a poem on the theme, and a hundred years later so did symbolist

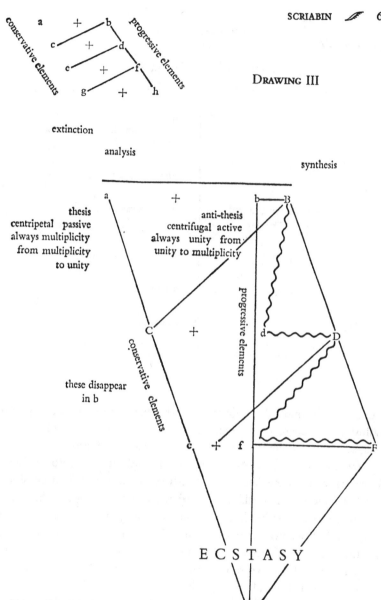

DRAWING III

Konstantin Balmont (1857–1918). Fyodor Sologub (1863–1927), another major symbolist, began one of his poems (around the same time as Scriabin's Swiss notebooks): "I am god of a secret world/All the world is/Only

DRAWING IV

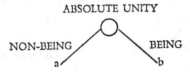

	ABSOLUTE UNITY	
NON-BEING		BEING
a		b

inertia	will to live desire to live, desire for the other, the new, *ENERGY*
center	from the center
striving toward the center	striving away from the center
peace	movement *ACTIVITY*
sleep	vigilance
	differentiation
non-distinguishing gravity constancy	distinguishing

one of my dreams." Even abroad, Charles Baudelaire (1821–1867) used hashish to be able to write "I am become God," and not a few latter-day drug saints have followed his lead in arriving at a godhead.

How easy to translate Scriabin's "wish" and "desire" into "drives." Scriabin's world-view falls easily into the linguistics of "compulsion" and "obsession." After all, he effaced reality and subrogated his false, sublime irreality. Scriabin half-stood in philosophy and science and asked What? and How? Psychiatry essays the Why? In those days this question was the concern of theologians. Had Scriabin delved more concretely into questions of his own motivation, he would have destroyed the very fantasies on which he ultimately subsisted.

Any discussion regarding the notebooks ends with a disputation regarding philosophy and music. Can the musician be a philosopher? Can the philosopher be a musician? Professor Ivan Lapshin is an authority here once again. In his book *The Legacy of Scriabin's Thought*, he begins by setting up the antinomy of "world-feeling of the artist" against the "world-understanding of the philosopher." He points out how philosophers Plato, Descartes and Rousseau were also musical theorists and dabblers in composition. He mentions Nietzsche's "tolerable piano playing," and his less tolerable *Hymn to Art* composed for chorus and orchestra. Pejoratively, he discusses Wagner's "foggy chatter about true essence." He cites further instances of the interplay between the two "arts," such as, Johann Herbart (1776–1841) played the piano; Schopenhauer performed admirably on the flute; Tchaikovsky relished Schopenhauer and, of course, Solovyov; Rimsky-Korsakoff liked Spinoza's pantheism.

Opponents to the interchange, however, ranged from Kant, who found music "tiresome and insistent" and for whom the singing of street musicians was a torment, to Beethoven, who diminished philosophy in a letter, "When I open my eyes and breathe, I know that music is far higher revelation than any wisdom or philosophy." Many others too disavowed any connection. Sculptor Antokolsky dismissed "the yardstick of rational and scientific study in measuring artistic intuition" as "putting the shoe on the wrong foot."

Even Rimsky-Korsakoff wrote in 1896 a letter to Findeizen sideswiping the trend Scriabin fostered: "Yes, I am a real Glinka-ist. Just listen with purely musical ears to contemporary cacophony with its formless, mindless, endless melody all justified by Kant, Schopenhauer, Nietzsche, or any redeemer other than a musical one. One must turn one's back on such frightful tendencies..." Another time he wrote, "the love of words in connection with music is a bottomless pit. Love of music all by itself suffices."

Part of this is a natural revulsion against the hugger-mugger of mysticism. Here too Lapshin summarizes the prime fallacies in Scriabin's thinking and classifies them as common to all mystics. He cynically heads his chapter with: "Mystics are good people, only they are apt to drool."

1. There is no difference between me and God, ergo, I am God.
2. There is no difference between the world and me, therefore, subject fuses with object.
3. There is no difference between space and time theoretically, therefore space and time are subjective forms of my acceptance of them. They will vanish in ecstasy and dissolve into one timeless, spaceless point of my making.

4. There is no difference between science and art, therefore highest art flows into and stems from highest knowledge.

5. There is no difference between the origin of sensation and the origins of art.

If you drain the hyperbole and the metaphor from Scriabin's mystical theories the music, rather than logic, remains.

Danilevich, springing into this breach, poses a shrewd question on the side of Lapshin. "How would it be possible for all that is potent and heartfelt in Scriabin's music to depend on irrational, idealistic deliria of Theosophical mysticism?" He answers himself. "I must disassociate myself from such an unbelievable conclusion. This would exclude all those profoundly progressive elements of his creative activity. No doubt much in his music was linked to philosophical idealism, but much of him opposed it too. He had to draw from more genuine sources."

Lapshin opposed this sentiment:

> Scriabin's philosophical ideas connect with his music. As his music expresses his emotional essence, so his philosophical notes translate his system of poetic images into a language of scientific-philosophical concepts.
>
> The philosopher tries to solve the world's riddle in words and ideas which are, after all, unfeeling concepts. Science builds on these concepts and evolves a system. The artist too presents us with his world. But he does it emotionally, not intellectually or consciously. The artist works from the center, but he has a *coefficient of refraction* and this can be found. It is demonstrable. Scriabin's notebooks are not accidental, haphazard excursions of a musician into a strange realm. They are organically linked to his artistic individuality.

During Scriabin's lifetime the most often asked question was what was the connection between his philosophy and music. In the Findeizen letter he answered precisely: "Most of my [musical] poems have a specific psychological content, but not all of them need program notes." He expressed himself on the subject clearly to Sabaneeff: "I can't understand how to write only 'music' now. How uninteresting it would be. Music, surely, takes on idea and significance when it is linked to one, single plan within the whole of a world-viewpoint. People just 'writing music' are like performers 'just *playing* music.' They are only to be valued when they are a link in a general plan. Music is the path of revelation. You can't imagine how potent a method of knowledge it is! If only you knew how much I have learned through music! All I now think and say, I know from my composing."

Schloezer, the artist's philosophical daemon, deserves a last word on the subject:

> His thought neither followed in the shadow of his art, nor did it precede it like a guidebook. Both activities were equal, direct, original, and single conditions of two purposes. They hinged on a personal and intuitive center.

✒ VI ✒
END OF VERA

16

ALONG THE doctrine way, Scriabin entirely lost the body nearest to him, Vera. She had written the Monighettis on 29 June, 1904: "Sasha reads a lot of philosophy and psychology and thinks all the while of his future compositions . . ." Soon after, she expressed herself bluntly to Morozova, "I cannot understand the world of philosophical omniscience where Alexander Nikolaevich now resides . . ." By November, he himself was forced to declare that he wanted someone who could "breathe the same philosophical air as I."

Vera continued to find his ideas increasingly "unbelievable and frightening," as she said everywhere. He announced his disaffection, saying "For the sake of art I must sacrifice a victim." 14 July, 1908, Vera struck at his inner circle by begging Morozova to persuade Scriabin to "discuss his doctrine with qualified persons . . . This is essential for Sasha himself, for if experts testify that he is saying something new and important, then his cause will be strengthened. If the opposite, then his eyes will open . . ."

The distance from Vera widened, but communication continued. On 12 June, 1905, he sent a most feeling letter before he leaves for Italy:

> My poor granny. The news that she is ill grieved me much. Auntie Lyuba writes that her trip to Switzerland must be postponed until autumn, because she simply cannot bring herself to leave that poor old woman. Vushenka, dear, pay attention to Lyalya's cough. Don't neglect her. She is weak. She can only get well summertimes. Rimma is a darling. Kiss her a lot for me and tell her that because she did so well in her examinations, I will send her a little book as a present. Tease Marusya for me, and spank Levka's behind.

"Aunt" Ida Schloezer, relishing the domestic trouble between the Scriabins that 1905 summer, arrived in Switzerland to visit Vera. Scriabin is naively "happy that you are no longer alone," but at the same time asked,

> Is it possible you two have not yet quarreled at least once? Kiss Ida Yulevna for me and beg her to stay longer . . . Soon I will do a little traveling, and by the end of the month or early July at the latest I will see you . . . I'm busy every day with farewell visits. Urusova is giving a lunch party in the Bois de Boulogne and I am invited. Tonight I play at the Apraksins. Now I go to Pierné to give him my song for *L'Illustration*. I long for a letter from you.

Gabriel Pierné (1863–1937), eminent composer, asked Scriabin for a little "melody" to be published in autograph form in the magazine of which he was music editor. Scriabin obliged with the old Natalya "Romance," which Florence Scarborough had recently sung. Pierné rejected this on the grounds that his readership was not used to "songs expressing complicated emotion." So next he sent a page-length piano piece, "Poem of Languor" (Op. 52). It is shaped like a bud opening out into a flower. Its erotic, even erectile meaning would have startled Pierné, had he understood. He published it and said, "Written expressly for *L'Illustration*."

Scriabin went to Italy to install pregnant, ailing Tatyana in a warm and gossip-free climate. They settled themselves in the tiny village of Bogliasco just outside Nervi, famous, unfortunately, as a health resort for sufferers with lung ailments. Russians thronged this area of the Italian Riviera. It was convenient, not far from San Remo, and only an hour from Genoa. Here too, Vera was unknown and for once not likely to turn up unexpectedly. Friendly Maria Nemenova-Lunz was present with her doctor husband, and it was she who found the Scriabins a place where they would live "for two months during the confinement." The house belonged to Signora Maria Canessa. The address: Via Avanazini 38, *presso la stazione* (near the station). It is now a tourist attraction with festivals of Scriabin's music.

Paris had upset Scriabin. He now called it "that frightful mess . . . how glad I am to be out of it . . ." In the same letter he promised Vera he would return to see her after two weeks, again in the hope of securing a divorce.

Tatyana, rosy with memory, recalled Bogliasco for Engel as "a veritable paradise on earth." The pocket-handkerchief garden had trees of cypress, olive, lemon and orange, she emphasized. The view was magnificent with the sea stretching right up to the garden gate. Cacti fenced their *domik*.

The Scriabins lived in a squalid, three-room apartment on the top floor of what was really a hot, miserable little house. One enormous, ungainly bed completely filled one of the rooms. "A disgusting little piano, the best the local café could produce, out of tune, and pitched a half-tone too low," was jammed in the bedroom to be near Scriabin at night, so feverish was his composing at this time, Engel says. A vulgar and brightly colored picture of a Roman Catholic saint hung on the wall of another room whose few pieces of furniture were covered monotonously in flowered cretonne. The village church next door tolled every time anyone died, and the bells rang often, too often, day and night in that town of ill health. It made Scriabin wince. Immediately behind were railroad tracks for the beach trains. As loads of swimmers arrived in Bogliasco hourly, the house shivered and shook, the rooms clouded up with dense, black smoke and gritty cinders.

Early in June, 1905, Scriabin had arranged for Belaieff monies to be sent to Vera. She was to take nearly all of the 700 rubles due him for Opp. 45–7 (and the advance), and only send him a hundred: "If Bogliasco has a post office where I can receive it . . . HIDE THE REST AWAY FOR ME for later use . . ." At last he went to Vézenaz on 2 July, again with full intention of saying real farewells and forcing final issues. He quarreled with Vera constantly. He saw Otto. He hated "Aunt" Ida all over again. Miraculously, he composed. He sneaked love letters to Tatyana, always full of solicitude for her health and extravagantly insistent with advice.

3 July

. . . My dear and good little one, I am in such despair at having led you into such heat. How will you endure these two months? Can't you put ice on plates in the room? Always keep the shutters on the sunny side of the house shut. My Tanyuka, sweet joy, my star, don't worry about a thing, because I love you, love you! You must BE HAPPY, because ahead of us lies only good. My journey here will be invaluable for us. The situation grows clearer and clearer and is settling. Vera is much calmer, talks readily, and often mentions you. I spoke with Ida Yulevna yesterday about Boris and you (both of you together, as I had to) with such language and in such raptures that she seemed thunderstruck. She said she saw me *for the first time* in ecstasy *OVER SOMEONE OTHER THAN MYSELF.*

Goodbye, my baby. Be sensible. TAKE CARE OF YOURSELF!! Eat well. THIS IS OBLIGATORY. *For the sake of our love* I implore you *DO NOT ECONOMIZE* on food. Dear, obey me! I am so happy that Vera has a lot of company. Nadya [Konyusa] and the children are also living at Calendret's [Les Lilas]. I am hurrying so I don't know whether you'll be able to decipher this.

5 July

I told Vera you were pregnant and she took it very sweetly. Sincerely so . . .

Yesterday and this morning I composed *MARVELOUSLY*. My only thought is how thrilled you will be. We will go straight into Genoa so I can play it for you on a good piano. Ida Yulevna is muttering again. It is abject misery going anywhere with her.

7 July

How happy I will be to see you. I'll be back Tuesday evening or Wednesday morning definitely. I cannot come any earlier and I'll tell you *why* when I see you . . . Don't get excited over every little thing. There is no cause for drama if people ask you how long you have been married. We decided on that little lie long ago to have peace. In truth we have appeared in society together with no serious consequences up to now. I kiss you.

10 July

I write only these two words to inform you, dear Tanyuka, that I leave tomorrow evening, and on Wednesday afternoon we see each other. What joy! Why have you suddenly begun feeling unwell? I am fearfully upset! Please be careful and don't get a cold. Sudden changes in temperature are very dangerous! Either do not go out at all or dress very warmly. At all costs I beg you not to excite yourself or worry if by any chance I am late by one day getting back. Do not come to any stupid conclusions. I simply have not been able to get the train.

On the 12th Scriabin left Vera, well behind schedule for Tatyana. Rimma had not been feeling well. The tension in the house must have been debilitating for the child. Her father's departure had been explained in as clear terms as possible to a seven-year-old. On the 14th, back in Bogliasco, Scriabin sent a shaming letter to Vera: "I wrote you a postcard while I was *en route* asking you to inform me of Rimmochka's health. Did you receive it? If so, aren't you disgraceful not to write me even a line?!"

Rimma began suffering severe pains in her stomach. The other children —Elena, Maria, and Lev—were dispatched across the lake to Anere, where Mme. Calendret, the landlady, had her own house and could care for them along with her children, out of the way and safe from possible infection. The very day Scriabin's letter arrived Vera had taken Rimma to the cantonment hospital in Geneva. The doctor diagnosed volvulus or "twisted intestines." Rimma died on 15 July, 1905. Vera telegraphed Scriabin. On the 16th he was again in Switzerland. Rimma, his favorite, the first born, was the first to die.

Scriabin was filled with mortification. His treatment of Vera may have led to this tragedy, but he dispelled the thought, using his doctrine and retreating deeper into his brain's bright world. A letter from Safonoff hardly helped Scriabin's hour of self-recrimination. He called Rimma's death "an act of Providence," a sign from on high that he "must not leave his first family."

Before going to the funeral, Scriabin dropped Tatyana a line: "Be sensible. I don't know when I can write, but will at the first opportunity . . . I am yours, I am yours." At the funeral Vera noted how "terribly shaken" Scriabin was. He in turn wrote Tatyana, "Vera showed more stability than I ever expected . . . I am not taking it badly, so don't worry about me." But here several words have been scratched out and the last line reads as if to himself, "Better not start any more. There is no time." His next letter: "You grieve me much. Don't worry on Vera's account. She is already somewhat calmer."

Scriabin had also to stay for the requiem mass held in Geneva's Russian Cathedral on the ninth day after death.

> Vera implored me to be there. She said it would be too heartbreaking for her to spend so sad a day alone, particularly after the separation from me which perhaps will be forever. But this is not the principal reason, of course. My presence is required here to help move the children. They have all come down with whooping cough and the doctor says they will get worse a little when we bring them back. Do not worry about poor Vera or the children. I am with Vera probably for the last time as she has DECIDED to go to Moscow in August. She has already written Safonoff asking him for work at the Conservatory. I am certain this will come about.

In a postcard to Tatyana, Scriabin said that he was still waiting for

Vera's ultimate answer for a divorce: "Until *that*, I don't know what I will do or how I will bear up." She never gave it.

17

NO SOONER is Scriabin back with Tatyana than a series of letters to Vera began, stranger for their continuity than finality.

26 July, 1905

I arrived safely, only I feel very tired and weak. Probably because of the heat. How are you, my little friend? Keep busy! Keep busy! Do not waste a moment. Not even you can imagine the results, if only you do this! Don't forget what I asked. Send me some music paper. In all it cannot come to more than 3 francs. I want to get down to writing some piano pieces . . . I want to write Auntie Lyuba today, but I don't know if I can overcome my usual aversion to letter writing. You write her for me, please, and set her mind at rest regarding me. Cross yourself for me at Rushenkina's grave. Write me Papa's address in full.

His next letter, 3 August, 1905, again rejoices that Vera's friends distract her.

Walk as much as possible. Take in new impressions, but don't forget work. Practice the piano more. You must not be lazy! I advise you to play. Do not laze about early in the morning, and by breakfast time you will have already worked for 2 or 3 hours. I am working very hard . . . I cannot tear myself away from composing . . .

He then relapses into absent-mindedness. He suggests that she leave the children for as long as possible in Konse (a nearby village); however, it now appears they have not yet left Anere. He had deceived Tatyana about staying on to move the children. He was, of course, sensitive to Vera's position, sending her back to Moscow with no guarantee of livelihood, and moreover did not dare offend either Vera or the nervous, frightened Tatyana.

6 August

Dear Vyusha, I just received your letter which I must admit vexed me a little.

Once more you are weakening. Again you begin to whine, instead of going on with the plan we arranged and heading straight toward it without being diverted by this obstacle or that. And why speak of trifles, as if the opinion of someone like Safonoff mattered? He in any case has never written anything bad about you. I am certain that when you get back to Moscow he will really do everything possible to find work for you. You ask how you can possibly move to Moscow with nothing "settled." But what have you that is "settled" in Geneva? Other than a cold winter and the necessity of leaving the children alone if you concertize, not to mention your loneliness! It is better for you to start your concerts in Russia where they already know and love me and are naturally curious. The risk is far greater abroad. In Moscow you will see so many friends and relatives who wish you well. Those surroundings are conducive to activity, and only in activity can anyone find full satisfaction.

You have masses of resources. I would suggest that you look deeper into life. Compare what you have by way of ability and training with what the majority of other people have—that will comfort and hearten you considerably. Once again as I have repeated so often to you: For life to be full and beautiful do not fear it, neither joys *nor sorrows*. One thing leads to another and all exists in relation to something else.

Be reasonable, my good little dear, and make the decision which I think is the only right one. Avail yourself of everything you can to hoe this row not alone but in the company of kind and concerned friends. Accomplish this with dignity (*NOT WITH SULKS*) and accept your responsibility.

Don't, please, make a drama out of your trip and claim you won't be seeing me. I have no intention of breaking with Russia; and I will be there much sooner than you could possibly imagine. I will never stop feeling for you, worrying about you, and advising you. You can count on that as experience has already proven. If you want to be even the least bit friendly, then give me some moral support by looking upon yourself as a person in your own right.

You ask if my mind is at ease. When I receive a letter full of moaning uncertainty, then of course I have no peace of mind. Peace, I say to you frankly, is absolutely essential to me at present for the success of the composition I have undertaken. I do not mean by this that you should hide your feelings from me. On the contrary, I want to be in a relationship with you of utmost sincerity. But to help me you must take yourself in hand. *ACTIVELY* work on yourself. Encourage yourself and show yourself that you are a serious person and not a piece of dirt! You understand me! If only you would fill yourself with good thoughts! I can't do this for you, but I kiss you warmly. Send me Morozova's address. I have a letter all written but cannot send it. I am grateful to you for the music paper.

The letter to Morozova, as Vera suspected, announced his removal from Vera's life:

What should have happened long ago has now actually come about. I am no longer living with Vera. I visit her and the children occasionally. I hope that at long last our lives can move on an even keel. Each of us is building life more harmoniously in accordance with our inclinations. We parted friends and are in correspondence with each other.

Vera has already informed you of the death of Rimma. It is terrible to lose a child, particularly for Vera. But this one tragedy took her mind off the other.

For some time I have been so exhausted and my nerves so unstrung that I am forced to be most quiet. I have worked all my life, but now in all this calm, my imagination blooms like a flower.

I am with my friend Tatyana Fyodorovna. She understands exactly what it is I need in order to compose. She tends to me with complete self-sacrifice and tenderness. She exudes the air I need to breathe. I am infinitely sad that you two have not become closer friends. When you come to know each other better, you will no doubt have the greatest respect and affection for one another.

I dare not invite you to Genoa, although it is only a little further from Moscow than Paris. How I would love to visit with you and share some of my new ideas with you.

Confronted with the realities of his impecunious position in Bogliasco, Scriabin discusses the practical side of life with Vera. The letter is postmarked 15 August:

As you have not written me recently, I am quite at a loss as to know what is happening with you. You will need a tidy sum of money for your trip to Moscow, but at the present time, despite all my wishes to the contrary, I simply cannot give it to you . . . If Ivan Christoforovich refuses to help you tangibly, I beg you to borrow temporarily.

Please not for one minute think that I am unmindful of your financial situation. I will do everything required of me. If Morozova sends money in time, then everything will be alright. I hope so. But with her unfortunately, I can never be sure. Therefore, do not be remiss. Take steps to be on the safe side, in case she dilly-dallies.

I hope to receive a long letter from you telling me exactly what the state of affairs is. I have been here 3 weeks and you have written precisely once. Not good, young person!

29 August, 1905, Morozova telegraphs Scriabin from her estate in Tver that sufficient calm has returned to Russia—and her affairs—and she will come to visit him in Italy via Switzerland. There is no mention of money so Scriabin jogs her memory.

She had sent the money to him already, and the thousand rubles arrived safely. Now he responds to her impending visit:

> I think rapturously of our joyous meeting soon to come. Of course, the quicker you come, the happier I will be; but in order to avoid any unpleasantness, I must tell you (confidential for the moment) that the end of September will see a small perturbation in our house which might dampen the delight of our visit with you. But all this will be over by the first week of October. Then Tatyana Fyodorovna and I will be overjoyed to receive you and spend all possible time with you. Be assured though, that I tell you all this only for *your* convenience. For us you are not a guest, so come when you like without thought of any other consideration. You cannot imagine how happy it will be for me to have you and Tatyana Fyodorovna together. She sends you warmest greetings and says that she felt a deep feeling of sympathy for you first time she met you.
>
> I was vexed by a letter from Vera the other day. She is wavering about going back to Russia. She must do this regardless. I am not thinking of a change of scene for someone who has suffered a loss. That always does good. But I mean her friends, of whom there are many. In Moscow she could also give lessons and lead a secure life. I trust that her indecision is momentary and that in the end she will come to her senses.
>
> Of myself I can say nothing new. I am working very much and very well.

Vera finally received formal word from the artistic committee of the Moscow Conservatory offering her a post as "Ordinary Professor in Piano," to begin 1 September (14 September, European time), 1905. Her decision having been made for her, she telegraphed Scriabin for her fare and money to cover the Vézenaz bills which must be closed out now. He answered quickly. The money he sends does not cover her last month's rent:

> At last you have your wishes: You have work and a position. Never doubt that you will quickly make a reputation for yourself as a fine professor. Don't take on too many pupils all at once. First, you are not used to it and will tire yourself terribly. Second, it would interrupt your own piano playing which under no circumstances must you do. Of course you will be invited to play with symphony orchestras and in chamber recitals.

Tatyana Fyodorovna Schloezer, sister of
Boris de Schloezer the musicologist-author,
became Scriabin's common-law wife. Their
affair began in 1903.

A postcard to Tatyana, dated 8
December, 1904. (See text.)

Scriabin at the time of the "Divine
Poem" and his friendship with the
Pasternaks.

Margarita Morozova, Scriabin's life-saving patron after the
break with the Belaieff firm
in 1906.

Left to right: Liadov, Glazunov and Rimsky-
Korsakoff in Petersburg, 1904.

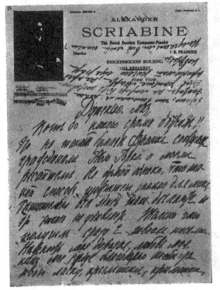

The first page of the 15 December, 1907 letter
to Tatyana from New York in which he apologizes for the flamboyant letter paper printed by
his manager, J. E. Francke.

His 30 May, 1907 letter to Altschuler signed "Pussycat" with an exclamation point.

Scriabin in Brussels, taken in 1909 in the drawing room of his garden house where he and Tatyana lived after a series of successful concert appearances. The photographer was Alexander Mozer, Scriabin's "electrical engineering" fan and professor, and inventor of the tastiera per luce for "Prometheus".

Scriabin snapped by Mozer one night during his composing "Prometheus" in 1910, in Moscow.

Scriabin in 1909. He autographed this Brussels photograph to a group of Moscow admirers of "contemporary music."

Robert Sterl, a German artist who accompanied Scriabin and Koussevitzky on their musical tour down the Volga in 1910, drew these portraits of Scriabin, who once said he would "awfully like to be like" the picture on the left.

Scriabin and Tatyana on the banks of the Oka River in 1912.

*Scriabin and Tatyana with their ill-fated son at Petrovskoe,
their summer home in 1913. Julian drowned six years later
at the age of 11.*

*Scriabin in Vilnius, near the
Polish border, in 1913 where he
performed with orchestra and in
recital.*

Now listen to me: Do not refuse to play other composers' compositions. If you feel they are beyond your powers, then ask Safonoff's help. But play, *WITHOUT FAIL*, this and that, here and there. You remember how well you played those little pieces of Scarlatti and Bach? For chamber music you should choose something from the classics (Schubert too). But not Beethoven. Once you played a Schubert trio, didn't you? Well, my little friend, I wish you brilliant success in all you undertake!

I am grieved at being unable to accompany you and the children. But never mind! I have no intention of cutting myself off from Russia, and so we will see each other. Until then you must write me in great detail and tell me all you are doing and all about the children. Incidentally, I am extremely worried about them. Please, dear Vushenka, look after them, attend to them more carefully, even though they are a strain on you! During the journey, do not let them sit in drafts, dress them warmly, and remember the difference in climate is tremendous. Rent an apartment in a good part of town.

I know you will want to be installed comfortably with electricity and a bath. You'll find such a place only in one of the new houses in Ostozhenka or Prechistenka. However, do not take any place which looks out over the Cathedral of Our Savior square. That may be a fine view, but it is damp and cold. Write me every last detail of your trip. I am not opposed to you moving in with Aunt Lyuba and the *babushki*. After all you will be at the Conservatory all day and the children will be alone. This, naturally, does not please me in the slightest. Oh there are so many little things I would like to say, but this letter cannot contain that much, and I am even afraid you won't get this as it is. I kiss you warmly, warmly, my little soul.

Bless you and the children. Be happy and brave for the journey!

Forever your Sasha

. . . Please don't stint either yourself or the children in anything, particularly *food*. Do everything necessary to make the trip *as much of a pleasure as possible*.

Around 12 September (25 September in Bogliasco), Scriabin received word, not from Vera first, but Aunt Lyubov. When Vera does write, he replies blisteringly. She had already reached Moscow on the 5th:

I heard from someone *else* that you and the children had arrived. Frankly, I am very worried about them. Please write *regularly*, even if you do not wish to write me often. Choose one day a week and set aside ten minutes just for writing me. This cannot be a burden. You write very little about yourself. Have you taken an apartment? If so *WHERE?* Is it nice? Expensive? Be very *careful* in looking for one . . . I forgot to tell you to get my piano back from

Morozova. This will give you two instruments. But do not let pupils play on it much. I say this only out of respect for Belaieff's memory. I would like to keep it in good condition for as long as possible. I can tell you nothing new about me. I am working a great deal . . . Are you playing? Much? Answer all my questions please, and add something about yourself too! Don't tell me any one thing in full detail, but tell me a little about everything . . . Tell Aunt Lyuba I will reply to her soon. Kiss the *babushki* and everybody for me. Write me about the weather and whether you and the children are going out for walks.

Send me pictures of the children RIGHT AWAY. I want them badly, particularly that one of Rimma and Lyalya *together.*

Vera did not write, nor send the children's pictures, nor even inform Scriabin of Prince Trubetskoi's unexpected death at this time. He wrote Morozova, "I am so very, very grateful to you, dear Margarita Kirillovna, for your help to Vera. I have not had a single letter from her from Moscow . . . We await the 'perturbation' from day to day, and I am sure that it will all be over by the time you arrive . . ."

Morozova came at the end of September. The "perturbation" politely waited. Gravid Tatyana and giddy Morozova hit it off together splendidly. In October new revolutionary strife precipitated her return again to Russia. (The turbulence delayed the 1,000 rubles Scriabin won for the 1905 Glinka Prize belatedly awarded his Second Symphony.) Scriabin announced the birth of the baby to Morozova on 26 October, 1905:

I am writing you just these few words to let you know of the happy event. At last the strain is over. The world is now richer by one beautiful creation with dark eyes. The little girl is adorable and healthy. Tanya is not doing too badly, although she is weak and worn from the suffering. By great good luck we found a marvelous midwife who took most excellent care of her.

Ariadna seemed almost as a replacement for the vanished Rimma. Her name, chosen from Greek mythology, perhaps unconsciously likening their escape from Vera to the theme of being led from the labyrinth. Scriabin nicknamed her *strekoza* or "dragonfly."

(Seeing far into the future, how sad it is to know that this bringer of joy would grow up in sorrow. She renounced her name, became a passionate Zionist, perhaps to vindicate her Jewish blood, married Dovid

Knut, the Israeli poet, and took the name of Sarah. She was also given another nickname late in life, this time by her own daughter when they were both living in exile in France—*trouble-fête* or "killjoy." In 1941 she was executed by the Nazis.)

Scriabin found the Morozova letter still in his pocket on 5 November, and adds a postscript of an excuse:

> ... the newspaper said that communication with Moscow was broken off and I decided not to send it out into the void. You cannot imagine how disturbed and upset I am by these events in Moscow. How I wish they would end, and quickly! ... Goodbye, my dear friend, I beg you once again not to leave me without news. You cannot think of the pleasure your letters give me! From 3 o'clock on I start listening for the hobble of our little old postlady. But so far, to my grief, in vain. Poor us! We are hermits ...

Tatyana, establishing herself in her new position as mistress-mother, addressed a formal letter to Aunt Lyubov informing her of her grandniece's arrival. She also wrote a chatty letter on 4 December to her now "intimate" Morozova.

> Unfortunately our circle is very narrow, restricted, and we feel quite cut off from the rest of the world. We console ourselves with plans for the future. Sasha is sunk in work. He is very tired, but he won't hear of taking a rest ... He sleeps badly. Everything gets on his nerves. Everything is such a trial for him.

The next two letters belonging to early 1906, are Scriabin's last words ever sent to Vera:

> 5 January
>
> At last communication has been resumed with Moscow, and I can expect news from you. Are all of you well? Have you survived those difficult days? Please write at the very soonest about yourself and the children.
>
> You will receive this letter during the holidays. Accept my good wishes and felicitations for the New Year. Kiss the children warmly for me. I would so much like to hear something about them. Is Lyalya going to school yet? She should be beginning to read and write. Have you begun teaching at the Conservatory? If not, when?
>
> I can tell you nothing new about myself, except that I am in difficulties over money because of the strikes ... I had to telegraph Papa to be kind and lend

me a little money for a short while. As soon as this comes, I will send it to you, of course.

10 January

I sent Mme. Calendret 150 francs. I would gladly send her all three hundred francs, but at present I cannot. I received the prize money, but most of it went on debts which had really piled up here—store bills, the midwife, doctor, and 500 francs to Papa. Moreover, I have to keep aside a large enough amount for us to move to Switzerland. We are finally thinking of living there permanently, after eight months of sitting here in Bogliasco because we had no money to do anything else. In view of this I would like to ask you to send Mme. Calendret the remaining 150 francs during the course of these winter months. I have already written her about this.

Before we can leave Bogliasco I have to pay the room up through the end of last year, at the very least 200 francs.

I just now received your letter where you mention your permanent passport. I will go to Genoa tomorrow for the notarized document of petition and send it to you straightaway. Goodbye. I kiss you and the children.

Sasha

The last service Scriabin performed for Vera was "husband's consent," as required by Russian law, for her to have a separate passport in her own name. In sympathy with Safonoff's earlier anti-revolutionary gesture, she now amid new strife had foolishly resigned from the Conservatory. Safonoff was suggesting the possibility of her coming to America, where together they might launch the young composer they both continued to believe in and love.

Scriabin wrote Vera once again, years later, sometime after his return to Moscow in 1910. This sharp, scrawling note of rebuke to her is full of underlinings, erasures, and changes, and he never sent it. He did not even finish its draft:

Dear Vera Ivanovna
Every time I ask you to send the children to my *babushki* so that I may see them, you reply with an invitation to come to you and see them there. I decline this with as much force as you propose it. I hold you responsible to the children for the consequences of my seeing them without your permission. I have this right, not counting the convenience of the children, to use my right to see the children without your concurrence.

18

EVEN AFTER Scriabin no longer wrote Vera, he continued to complain
and negotiate. 5 February, 1906, as he and Tatyana arrived in Geneva
from Bogliasco, he discussed Vera's last letter to him with Morozova:

We arrived safely, although Tanya has a mild cold. I just received a letter from
Vera in which she declines a divorce. Be so kind, Margarita Kirillovna, influence her. Your advice is enormously important to her. Explain to her that it
is better for her and the children to have a divorce. This way she would have
self-respect. And for us, a divorce is vital. If you could but know how weary
I am of all these worldly cares, and this goes for poor Tanya too. Be my friend,
and talk to Vera, my dear . . .

Further, on 18 March:

. . . I am no longer concerned with Vera, because her last letters and her actions
of the past few months have convinced me that she is incapable of deep feeling
for anything at all. And here you speak of her selfless friendship for me. I cannot
see how a refusal to give a divorce can be construed as unselfishness or self-
denial. Truly, Vera is not thinking of me when she puts me in an awkward
situation among those very people on whom I must count for helping me in
my work and amid whom I must, as you wish too, live in an acceptable atmosphere. Of course, in the last analysis I will do exactly as I plan. No scandal and
no pettiness can prevent me from the realization of my idea. It is a pity, though,
to waste my strength and time in battle over the trivial . . .

Neither does Vera's attitude towards Tatyana Fyodorovna show any friendship
for me. She knows perfectly well, and has said so more than once, that a better
matched pair of people could not be found anywhere. And you yourself
after closer acquaintance with Tanya in Bogliasco confirmed this, surely. In
the middle of all this however, she, Vera, acts most heartlessly towards Tanya.
She did not even ask if Tanya were alive after the birth of our daughter. Tanya,
on the other hand, when Rimmochka died wrote me a letter full of the deepest
and most heartfelt words for Vera. I passed this on to Vera, as instructed by
Tanya. So you see, in a word, you cannot speak of selflessness under the present
circumstances. She wants to have friendly relations with me and correspond
with me, while she completely ignores the very person who gives me happiness.
Where is the friendship, I would like to know? Therefore I am shedding no

tears over Vera. She has, as you write, many friends who sympathize with her and console her. I am, naturally, very happy about this and from the bottom of my heart I wish her well. I am worried about Tanya. She has suffered too much. It is time for her to rest and for me to care for her. Vera may not give me a divorce, and we will get along without it. But I cannot call such behavior anything but selfish.

There is only one way for Vera to show her friendship for me and that is to give me a divorce. She will lose nothing by this. On the contrary. And why take such revenge on Tatyana Fyodorovna? Tanya's only fault is that she loves me in a way Vera could not even imagine. You understand of course, that the divorce and the officialization of my relationship with Tatyana has not the slightest connection with my ideas. They are mere tickets of entry into that society on which I must depend until I become famous. Again I repeat that, regardless, I will actualize my dream. There is no question of the whole of my life being disrupted by this. The desired moment, however, will come more quickly, if those who consider themselves my friends would assist in removing these unnecessary obstacles in my path.

15 March:

Tanya is finishing a letter to you. By the way, you *must* write her as Mme. Scriabine. It would be unthinkable to address her in any other way here in Switzerland.

On 2 March, 1906 (Russian time), Vera gave her first all-Scriabin concert in the Little Hall of the Conservatory. No "Tatyana" music was included in her program of early works up through 1903, ending with the "Satanic Poem."

Morozova, more stupidly than innocently, expected Scriabin to rejoice at this "sign of friendship." But he answered her letter on 4 April (Swiss calendar):

You inform me of Vera Ivanovna's recital. Notwithstanding a certain propaganda significance, it is, under the circumstances (that is, without a divorce), no more than a public scandal for Tanya and me and the entire Schloezer family. The *LEAST* Vera could do would be *not to advertise* herself as my *WIFE*. If I were not so sure of your affection, I might think you would laugh at me for speaking so strongly on this matter. But poor Fyodor Yulevich [Tatyana's father, now in Moscow], already ill, was dealt a death blow by this concert. Now he is dangerously sick. Only Vera's egoism and heartlessness fails to perceive this.

Lipaev in *RMG*, 19 March, 1906, reviewed Vera's performance:

For some reason I always feel the same thing whenever I hear anything by Mr. Scriabin . . . The sweetness of his polyphony overwhelms me . . . his wailing and mournful song exudes the weakness of all our present-day dissatisfaction. Artist Scriabin is original in the highest degree. To understand him means to leave the hurly-burly of the masses and to renounce all that is banal and bourgeois . . . Thus it was with Mme. Scriabina's program of rarely played works by her husband. The concert was one of the most notable in recent times and very well attended.

Vera, like Morozova, thought her concert was a step towards reconciliation. And she took more steps in this mistaken direction through intermediaries. She saw the Monighettis often. The year before, Zinaida had written a letter asking Scriabin to remember his marriage vows. (Vera wrote her from Vézenaz, saying, "He received your letter forwarded to him from Paris. I have not read it. He hasn't showed it to me, but I am terribly grateful to you for writing it. I know the spirit in which it was composed . . .")

Zinaida interfered again and he answered on 10 April, 1906:

. . . Vera Ivanovna's concert under the circumstances, that is, without a divorce between us, and she refuses to give me one, is not only *not* a bright festival, but a ghastly unpleasantness. I find it strange that my friends do not wish to see the fact in this light.

I will tell you frankly now that I did not answer your last letter because it was too insulting to Tatyana Fyodorovna, and therefore to me too. I can understand it only by thinking that you simply have not realized, or possibly are unable to imagine, how much she means to me and how much she is in herself. I am not talking about her noble character which charms everyone of cultivation. No, that is not what I am saying. No matter what she may be in herself, she is my beloved wife. If my friends do not feel kindly disposed toward her—although it would be most unnatural of them not to feel so, since they know what great happiness she provides me—then, if they do not wish to insult me, they must show her due respect. You cannot write me a friendly letter ignoring the very person fate links me with closely and permanently. You must agree that such would indeed be strange.

It was good to know that a concert of my symphonies is being planned in Petersburg. But why doesn't the entrepreneur hire Nikisch for this? This would not only guarantee a good performance and the success of the symphonies, but it would cover the costs abundantly . . .

You cannot conceive how well Nikisch played the Divine Poem in Paris! Why don't you tell me, dear Zinaida Ivanovna, who is arranging these concerts? If you have found such a benefactor then it will be nice for me to inscribe his name in my heart and show him my gratitude. Who will conduct? Too bad the concerts won't be given abroad, say, in Paris or Berlin. In that case I could participate in them.

For many complicated reasons I cannot come back to Russia this year. First in view of the above circumstances, I do not wish to appear there without Tatyana Fyodorovna.

19

SCRIABIN'S MARRIAGE to Vera ended as it had begun with "Aunt" Ida. Instead of being loyal to her niece, Tatyana, Ida continued her mischief into the late years. She would invite Scriabin over to the Schloezers "to see the children." Vera would be there, and Scriabin would leave. Scriabin would later speak Ida's name only in a whisper, as if it were something indecent.

Aunt Lyubov and Belaieff originally had been correct in advising against marriage. Sabaneeff, who asked questions normally left in silence, put the matter this way in 1912: "What happened?" he said to Scriabin, "How could you have made the error of your first marriage?"

> Scriabin smiled and answered, "You know, I had very queer convictions in those days. I was young, a puppy in fact, and it seemed to me that at a certain age a young man *had* to get married without any question and that was that. I didn't love Vera in the slightest, and then there were all those other Schloezers including 'Aunt' Ida. They decided to marry me to Vera Ivanovna. They plotted it so cunningly . . . there was a whole scheme to it."

Scriabin volunteered the same story to Modest Altschuler. He was in the train facing Vera in the honeymoon compartment heading for the Crimea. Suddenly he looked at her. "She was a stranger. I had never seen her before. 'Is this my wife?' I asked myself. 'Is this my life to be?' In that instant I knew I could not love her and, worse, never would."

Sabaneeff also lards Scriabin's afterthoughts about Vera with further insights. One evening when Scriabin recalled the girl from St. Catherine's

Institute, he said, "In all truth, I have only really loved once, Marusya, but Tatyana knew better how to keep me in check . . ." Sabaneeff continues:

> Oh yes, she knew how to hold him, I remember that. No woman ever appeared on the Scriabin horizon. If one did, she was destroyed by all admissible and inadmissible means. Tatyana Fyodorovna liked to keep women away, and they surely liked to stay away from Tatyana Fyodorovna.
>
> Scriabin, that very feeling and passionate man, that Scriabin who had once led so wild a life, now was so domesticated. His "expeditions" were quite rare.
>
> Scriabin himself spoke simply and directly of his unfortunate domestic life with Vera, of its misunderstandings and lack of common interests. Like all people who have basically weak characters, he forgot all the good in his life with Vera and remembered only that which was dark and sad.
>
> "With her," Scriabin said, "everything there was *terre à terre*. There weren't even any material comforts. Mind you, I wasn't even able to work. I had not even a room to myself."
>
> I simply couldn't understand how he could color and distort this period of his life. I had the impression that Scriabin was unable to love devotedly or with any sort of necessary self-denial. In fact everything was construed so that he could "accept" love. He was submerged in himself, his work, and psychically there just was no room for love. Love to him was only a refinement of the erotic act, "a symphony of sensations" he called it, to awaken his own creativity. This symphony of sensations was essential for him, and without it there was no creative work.

Certainly, as the letters show, Tatyana was a tool of his creative labor, an instrument of his composition. "I need you . . . you *UNDERSTAND*! You are necessary to me."

✒ VII ✒
PLEKHANOV

20

HERMETIC AS Tatyana's picture of Bogliasco was, and Scriabin described their life as *"dolce far niente"* (the sweetness of doing nothing), still the pair was far from alone and not at all idle. Nemenova-Lunz, a pupil here, resumes her memories:

> I had not really known Scriabin at the Conservatory . . . On graduation day I had stood at the door of our classroom and wept tears of sincerity . . . The three months I spent visiting the Scriabin family everyday in Bogliasco will never, can never be erased from my memory . . . It was there that I saw for the first time the true Scriabin in all aspects of his genius.

Alexander Nikolaevich's mood during all this time in Bogliasco was extremely good and full of joy of living. He worshiped the sun. He never wore a hat. He thought the sun was good for keeping "the head fresh." His hat dangled from a button on his jacket. Little Italian boys encountering him along the beach would laugh and point their finger at *"signor senza cappello."*

Alexander Nikolaevich loved Italy and the hospitable Italians. In later life he often reminisced over Bogliasco. He described with great good nature the people downstairs [Mme. Canessa], and how they—accustomed to other kinds of music—must have suffered from his sounds. He worked all day long, and rested in the evenings in the tiny "salon" over glasses of chianti and lively conversation.

Occasionally we walked to those marvelous environs of Nervi—abandoned villas and ancient cemeteries. I remember a trip to Rapallo. We wandered around for a long time and finally chanced upon an old church. Scriabin in high humor characterized the group of fat monks there as "showing every feeling on their face save that of sanctitude." When we were thoroughly hungry, we went to a restaurant with a glassed-in veranda and a marvelous view of the sea in the distance. There in front of all the well-dressed customers, midst the elaborate furnishings, Scriabin lapsed into a childish and happy mood. He was lightheaded from wine and sun, and recalled his escapades with M.P. Belaieff in Paris. He sang humorous songs he remembered from Montmartre cabarets.

The embarrassment I felt when I was a student in front of a professor stuck with me for the first few days, but Scriabin was so fascinating and so direct, I forgot all about myself. I particularly wanted him to coach me in his compositions, but I did not tell him so or of my passion for his music. In those days, he was not yet so widely performed. In our evening conversations we often spoke of the fate of unrecognized geniuses. Other of our usual themes were art, religion, and especially philosophy.

My dream came true. We went through a number of his early and middle opuses together. I might describe his playing as "a blessing to the ear." Each time he played, he composed the piece anew. He could never repeat himself. This is why the lessons were not entirely successful. He never followed the printed page or his instructions of nuances. When I would point this out, he looked surprised. "Why? This way is so much better."

At the touch of his fingers, the ugly walls, the poor furnishings, the discordant piano, all disappeared and a mighty orchestra resounded. His inspired, extraordinary performance of such divine music was in truth a perpetual "divine poem." It is difficult to say what I felt in those days of Italy . . . He was so open, so childlike. His soul was as clear as the rays of the sun. All round him was light.

The most important personage in the Russian community of the Bogliasco area, and one with whom Scriabin formed a strange alliance, was the masterful genius of revolution, Georgy Plekhanov. Once again in a Scriabin relationship we find a profound intimacy, an incongruous elective affinity, physical contrast, and, in this instance particularly, intellectual antipathy. Professor Samuel Baron, author of the first English biography of this renowned man, Plekhanov, The Father of Russian Marxism, states no-nonsense facts that, "Almost singlehandedly Plekhanov launched the movement that was to culminate in the Bolshevik Revolution. He was one of the most cultured men of his time, the last of that line of gifted individuals in the history of the Russian intelligentsia."

Next to his disciple, Lenin, Plekhanov was not only the brainy architect of the Russian Revolution but its most powerful force. He had been that wild, terrifying, shouting voice of 1876 in the first popular demonstration in Russia held in front of the Kazan Cathedral. He was the first to translate Marx into Russian, first to mint the phrase "dialectical materialism" where historical rather than metaphysical interpretation of the past is fused with modern science. Plekhanov opposed terrorism and insisted that Revolution must come about through industrial workers and city dwellers. He thought the peasant too stupid. In this he differed from Lenin.

According to Yury Kamenev (*Leninsky Zbornik*, Vol. I, Moscow), Lenin was always accused (jokingly, of course) of being in love with Plekhanov. He called him his "beloved," spoke of his "infatuation," his "being enamored" even at the height of political differences with Plekhanov. After release from prison in 1898, Lenin went straight to Plekhanov hiding in Switzerland. They parted on the issue of timing. Scholar-philosopher Plekhanov wanted the Revolution to come "after the people are educated." Organizer and agitator Lenin wanted it instigated now. The press, when the two men took leave of each other years later, used the word "divorce." Lenin and his Bolsheviks won the Revolution of 1917, not Plekhanov and his Mensheviks. History delivered Russia to a firebrand, not to the intellectual.

This was the man who became close to Scriabin. Plekhanov had the same high pedigree as Scriabin, and the Tatar connection shows in his boyar name—ple-KHAN-ov. In one popular phrase of the day, he was a "repentant nobleman," or a Nietzschean "aristocratic radical." Engel interprets the Plekhanov-Scriabin relationship on the basis of a mutual "aristocracy of spirit." Both also had mistresses (and Jewesses) with whom they were defiantly living. (Plekhanov legally married only in 1908, after four children.)

In 1905 Plekhanov was nearing fifty and had passed his twenty-fifth year in exile as a "criminal of the state." His presence abroad dramatized the 1905 Revolution, and because of him Scriabin read Karl Marx's *Das Kapital*. Socialism, the muscles of social change, began to form part of his flaccid dreams, although he saw it as a spiritual move towards some further, higher, mystical plane. The central core of Marxist materialism was that "being determines consciousness," that is, thinking does not make a thing so. The development of social institutions is the result not of opinion but of already present facts. Scriabin phlegmatically insisted that "consciousness determines being."

Mark Meichik in his memoirs of Scriabin recalled how "a lot of mystic-romantics participated in the early Revolution of 1905. Some were real revolutionaries who went abroad to prepare for another revolution; but many of the intelligentsia, fearing a collapse of their routine life, ran away—either to 'abroad' or 'inside themselves.' These latter developed mystical theories, often with highly sexual overtones . . ." He was describing Scriabin at his most counterpoised to Plekhanov.

Drozdov reported a conversation where Scriabin said to him that his musical evolution "chimed in" with Revolution . . . "my art presupposes the coming revolution," he stated. And Drozdov has Mikhail Fabianovich Gnessin (1883–1957), the musician, corroborate this remark, adding, "I mention this without exaggerating it out of proportion. I, least of all, align Scriabin with politics and the Revolution's struggles. Let Scriabin's socio-political position remain obscure. However, my point is that it was unusual in those days for any musician to link creativity with revolution and Scriabin did." The pertinency of Scriabin to contemporary Russia persisted. In 1921, for example, Isadora Duncan, then living in Moscow, choreographed some Scriabin études to depict the famine then gripping the USSR.

Nemenova-Lunz recalled "how sincerely Scriabin felt for the democratic elements in Russian society." She wrote:

Alexander Nikolaevich's charm reached out as far as persons who even opposed his view of the world. G.V. Plekhanov first talked to Scriabin in Bogliasco with an air of condescension. His arsenal of erudition exploded Scriabin's intuitive propositions. Scriabin was not accustomed to quarrels which led so easily to offense. They grieved him, in fact. Next day, he would say that he would acquaint himself with all the authors quoted by Plekhanov, but added that he doubted they could change his thinking. Everyone who knew what active interest Scriabin took in all the latest tendencies in philosophy and other realms of knowledge, also knows how astonishingly fast he could fly to the heart of a complicated idea. His speed often surprised Plekhanov, who mentioned this to me on more than one occasion.

Quarrels were frequent enough in Bogliasco, not only with Plekhanov, but with two journalists who were also living there at the time. Often while walking along the Marina, we would stop at a tiny, open-air restaurant where a street orchestra supplied music. Alexander Nikolaevich would first look around suspiciously, because he was terrified of sick people and fearful for his own health. We would sit at a little table some distance from others and talk until late at night. We talked of the news from Russia . . .

The Italian papers, as is their wont, exaggerated everything by saying that tens of thousands of Muscovites were living in cellars. The change in Russia's political structure seemed to be a matter of days. All this made us very nervous, and I decided to return to Moscow, sad as it was to part from the Scriabins.

21

OF ALL Scriabin reminiscences, few are as penetrating as those written by Rosalia Bograd-Plekhanova. She brought a professionally sharp camera to photograph both men. Rosalia had been trained in medicine, but because of her liaison with Plekhanov, the régime withheld her diploma and her "certificate of excellence." In exile she began all over again and obtained her doctor's degree in Switzerland. She was then able to support Plekhanov and their family by practicing medicine. Plekhanov contributed to the household by tutoring children of the Genevan rich, and by writing (in his five fluent languages) for Socialist journals.

Plekhanov was an ill man suffering from chronic inflammation of the pharynx. Rosalia, with the apology of "permitting myself some digression to explain my thought," dramatically portrays the events which led the Plekhanovs not to Russia in 1905, but to Italy and Scriabin.

For Georgy Valentinovich 1905–1906 was a period of striving high hopes and at the same time, sad experiences. He worked and wrote and appeared before Russian groups in various Swiss towns. He yearned for direct action in the struggle itself.

Immediately after the Tsar's Manifesto of 17 October promising civil liberties (and a representative legislative body), we decided to return to the homeland. I relinquished my medical practice and prepared for the journey.

In November, all was ready but he fell very ill—the throat ailment again—and he lost his voice.

The specialists pronounced it grave, in view of his lung trouble, chronic since 1886. He said it might irreversibly turn into tuberculosis if Georgy Valentinovich did not immediately proceed to a warm climate.

Our passports were ready. However, we received a telegram that Plekhanov's brother was "ill" (i.e. arrested). Plekhanov, without a word, plunged into work. The situation in the homeland worsened and Plekhanov's temperature rose. It was imperative for him to escape the cold Geneva winter. I persuaded him with great difficulty to go to Italy.

The blessed sun of the Riviera, the glassy smooth sea, and the cloudless blue sky of Italy had magical effect on him. Nevertheless, I ascribed then and still continue to believe that Georgy Valentinovich's recuperation was due to Scriabin. He was attracted to this new friend's soft, harmonious, rather feminine nature, as well as to that twice-tender Scriabinic music. His great talent showed not only in music, but in the art of ideas and depth of philosophical interest. All this was restorative to Plekhanov and counteracted his soul-suffering.

They met one late November night, 1905, in the house of Vladimir Kobylyansky (b. 1874), one of the oldest Russian residents of Bogliasco, a revolutionary (real name, Vladislav Goldberg) and leading member of the Socialist Democrat Party. Because of a lung condition, he had come there and now acted as hospitable host to his compatriots. He was kind, sensitive, and informed. His wife was a musician, Olga Lunz (Nemenova-Lunz's sister-in-law), and Rosalia called her "clever, cultured, a delightful woman."

Rosalia records her first impressions of the Scriabins: "We were enchanted with both of them. Alexander Nikolaevich was refined to the point of femininity. His spiritual face with his naive and dreamy eyes reflected a universe of soul and melody. Tatyana was enormous beside him, but actually she was short in stature, with a sympathetic, but rasping voice. Her face was beautiful and animated, and her manners, gentle. In a word, both of them charmed us."

After first shaking hands and exchanging greetings, the conversation shifted to Government repressions which had crushed the actual revolution.

Alexander Nikolaevich was deeply interested in hearing of the heroic revolutionary struggle which had gripped the country. He at once expressed his feelings on the side of the revolutionaries. He seemed to want to put his strong sympathies in music. He went to the piano and played—études, valses, passages from his "Divine Poem," and went on to play bits of the "Poem of Ecstasy" on which he was working at the time. It was marvelous music which lifted us up into the realm of the ideal. His unique performance made a deep impression on all of us, especially Plekhanov.

We expressed ourselves in words of ravishment. Alexander Nikolaevich was obviously very pleased. Like a shy young girl in love, he told us that this music was of the Revolution too, that its ideals were what the Russian people were struggling for, and therefore he would give the Poem an epigraph. He decided then and there on "Arise, ye toiling people! Stand up!"

In Bogliasco we heard Alexander Nikolaevich play several times and noticed that he was always especially willing when asked by Plekhanov. Georgy Valentinovich played no instrument, but he loved music very much, listened well, and possessed a true musical intuition. He was acquainting himself with Scriabin's music for the first time. It calmed him and matched his mood. Up to then in general he had preferred the warlike, mighty creations of Beethoven, Berlioz, and Wagner.

Their walks together distracted Georgy Valentinovich from his gloomy thoughts. He and Alexander Nikolaevich had philosophical arguments in which two world-views were opposed—the idealistic versus the materialistic. The enthusiastic Alexander Nikolaevich was led by his mind into curious paradoxes, and Plekhanov would unravel him *per* Socrates. Once when we were walking we crossed a bridge. Below were huge boulders, and a stream of running water. We stopped and Alexander Nikolaevich propounded his credo: "We create the world with our creative soul, our will. There are no obstacles to manifesting our wills. The law of gravity does not exist. I can throw myself from this bridge and I will not crack my head on the stones. I will float in the air. Thanks to will power."

Plekhanov listened quietly, then he said, "Go ahead. Try it!" But the composer chose not to demonstrate.

Walking and philosophizing, Georgy Valentinovich sometimes teased. Scriabin would answer him in the same jocular manner. One glorious spring morning on the Marina of San Remo, we encountered Alexander Nikolaevich. Georgy Valentinovich grasped his hand.

"Good morning, Alexander Nikolaevich. What a marvelous morning! We are indebted to you for this incomparably beautiful sky, this vast expanse of sea. Thank you, thank you." Scriabin was embarrassed at first. It was unexpected, and though sensing the joke, he accepted the thanks quite as if he deserved them.

Alexander Nikolaevich was decidedly against any materialistic interpretation of nature or history. All the same he listened with great attention to Plekhanov and tossed questions at him. He was obviously trying to probe more deeply into what was for him a new view of the world. He even evinced a desire to study materialistic philosophy and asked for sources to read.

Scriabin, of course, never became a Marxist. But as Plekhanov himself later said, "Our daily arguments at every meeting not only did *not* alienate us from each other, but even contributed a good deal to our mutual closeness." Their friendship continued beyond Bogliasco into 1906 and Geneva.

✐ VIII ✐
1905-6 NOTEBOOKS

22

UNDER THE barrage of Plekhanov affection it is surprising that the Notebook of 1905 reflected virtually nothing of Marxist thought.

Scriabin read, underscored, and absorbed many of Plekhanov's writings, books and articles, and especially the notable *On the Question of the Development of the Monistic View of History.* This magnum opus (autographed to Scriabin "with sincere respect") traces the history of thought from French materialists of the eighteenth century through the German idealists on down to Marx. Plekhanov showed how each scheme of thought progressed only after social and economic conditions had first advanced and permitted it the luxury of intellectualization. Originally in 1895 the book had been called *In Defense of Materialism*, but to pass the Russian censors the title was changed.

In the main, Scriabin's Notebook sermonized as its author wrestles with himself. Sabaneeff recalled the same Scriabin but in 1911:

> How far he was from the austere ascetic who stands on a pillar like a statue. He was suspicious of asceticism. He loved life. He loved the feel of color, of sensations. He loved to immerse himself in a sea of sensations, in abundance, flowering, and growth.

> "You must experience everything," he often said. "Every sensation is a source of knowledge and therefore valuable. It is a great mistake to shrink from sensation. You must experience all sensations to the fullest. Then you can stop being interested. You remove yourself from them then."

> He illustrated this with an example from music. "Take a musician. If he is developed sufficiently, then a Strauss waltz can neither interest nor satisfy him. Take me, for instance, no classic music holds my interest. But this does not

mean that I deny myself it. No, simply that I do not *need* it. So it is with a man. In moments of development, he ceases to need much that formerly was indispensable."

And this explains why Schloezer could say Scriabin went "years on end without visiting an exhibition . . . was suspicious of contemporary art because it had lost its connection with religion and leaned to the abstract . . . and was only interested in literature and architecture and painting if they served his ends. If they were not useful to him, they did not exist."

The Notebook of 1905 is emotional. The title "Love! And Do Battle!" reflects more of Tatyana than the polemics of Plekhanov. He has, however, intensified the seesaw of his I and Not-I. In one brief fragment, he yields a point that the creation of the world is the work of the unconscious. In another section he suddenly finds himself as God alone and lonely. Toward the end, he almost surrenders for the first time to the possibility that another Man-God might be creating this world of his own and he, an illusionary Scriabin, is contained in it. The elaborate, restless ratiocination may have been a compromise induced by Plekhanov, or it may be a rationalist chink in his metaphysical armor. He wonders how an Ivan here and a Peter there came about.

However, the beginning is unvarnished messianism. God becomes only a word for "all being and beings." Of particular interest is the transition from fewer and fewer "death" references into greater clarification of "bliss" and "ecstasy." How characteristic of Scriabin, living in the shadow of sanatoria in Bogliasco to abolish death in his mind. In essence, Scriabin saw life, not death as the releaser, and its name is still Ecstasy.

> Love life with all your being, and you will be happy forever. Never fear to be what you wish to be. Never fear your desires. Never fear life, nor suffering, for there can be no greater victory over despondency than these. You must always be resplendent.
>
> If you are ugly and this weighs on you, then do battle, and you will conquer this *sickness*.
>
> If you are old and age *oppresses* you, it is the same, a sickness which you can conquer in battle by the strength of your wishing. Age is in time and is only a pleasant rest.
>
> Grow sumptuous. Develop all your talents. Study my laws of time and space and follow them exactly.

Look upon each unpleasantness only as an obstacle, as a *sign* that you have the *powers to defeat it.* Love people, *like life, like your own life,* as if they were your creation, and love them freely. *They are through me your creation.* Be divinely proud, and therefore never envy. Envy is a confession that you have been conquered.

If you fret and regret that you have no *talent,* then this is the sign that the seed of *talent* is in you. Let it grow and never doubt it.

Envy and despair equal *death.* Try to be like me and look at all life in general (in all its appearances) as if it were your own personal life. Rejoice in the creativity of other people since it is (through me) your own. *To receive is to create.* Try always to be simple and sincere, that is, never fear to want and *always* to do *what you wish.* In other words, do not fear *freedom. Abide by the laws* of time and space because they are *your laws,* provided that you experience me.

Oh, you my blind impulses, so searching, powerful, and tender, with your fearsome battle.
Tender, full of dread and temerity, full of implacable wickedness and harshness, tender forefathers of future strengths—cleverness and cunning. All of you are filled with thirst for growth and self-preservation. But you were blind and did not know that battle, not annihilation, was your growth.

And those who were strong and conquered easily grew weak; but the weak, accustomed to perpetual battle, grew strong. Their strength was that of cunning. You do not understand that each of you creates the other and you exist only together.

Theory of Knowledge:
1) Knowing means to identify with the known, means to experience.
2) Knowing can only be experience (one's own).
3) Knowing is to experience identical understandings.

Analysis of Reality:
1) Reality is a sphere of our sensations, a sphere of our experiences, our consciousness. Our immediate life, our activity and creativity is in it. It is the one proposition which we may assert as infallible.

In other words:
Reality to us is immediate only in the sphere of our sensations, psychic states, and we affirm no other reality. The expression "we know all *through the prism* of our mind" is incorrect. There is nothing, and can be nothing besides our mind.
2) Never propound or propose anything outside the sphere of consciousness. The objection that there are other people who also have consciousnesses which are closed to us in impenetrable spheres is incorrect. For me the

other person is a complex of *my* sensations. He exists only for me in my experiences as sensations. They say to me that I cannot negate, for instance, the experiences of other people who are other appearances.

Oh, what is coming! What is coming! I am on the road to Ecstasy! Finally I have found myself. What flights! What power of expressions! What a structure of sturdy logic and refined feeling. If my inspiration does not flag, then I will soon finish the text. It seems to me sometimes that I could with one leap . . .

The whole world is inundated by the waves of my being.

I wish to awaken in your consciousness a desire for insane, unlimited bliss. You are intoxicated by my fragrance, awakened by my kiss licking you and fluttering over you. You are made languid and feminine by the sweet tenderness of my proximity, are quickened by the lightning flashes of my passion. You will feel the glorious birthing of your dreams.

The moment of ecstasy stops being a moment (of time). It engulfs all time. This moment is absolute being.

Absolute being is the realization of the idea of God. Absolute being is the split second of eternity.

The concept of "two" is tightly joined with the concepts of "resemblance" and "repetition." The concept "other" is joined with the concepts of "different" and "novel."

In this actual moment in a given place in space, I am individual consciousness. I am my activity defining my relations with the outside so as to make my world. Generally speaking, I am God. I am awareness. Alone yet experiencing every other individuality. I am You; I am all. I will try to explain this better.

The material from which the world is made is creative thought, creative imagination. This brings us to an analogy with nature. The ocean is composed of many drops, each of which is a perfect creative expression as is the very ocean itself. The ocean creates fantasy—this means the ocean displays its drops in different colors. Further, only one drop is necessary for any one color, while the rest are needed only for the complementary colors. No color is anything except as a carrier for related colors.

This analogy gives us some understanding of individual creativity and its effect on the universe. What I am saying could only be said by a person living under certain conditions—in the 20th century, on the earth, etc. In order for my idea to be possible, I need the whole history of the universe which appears as a growth of consciousness from then down to my consciousness now. I construct the past which leads logically to this very moment, and I speak of the future. Predicting the future is only the structuring of logic. They say to me: Still, why are you *obliged* to be encased in your individuality? Why can't you change the surroundings you are in at will? Why can't you become me, for instance? Where does this "compulsory" proposition come from?

I answer: I cannot change my circumstances in a given moment in a given place, because I have *created* them. You do not need to be changed into me, because I am experiencing you in your individuality. If I wished to become you, and I was successful in so doing, then I would immediately forget my transformation and your past . . . All your relation with the outside world, which is all that makes your individuality, would become mine. Personal individuality is its own containment. It is the compulsory part of your proposition which you yourself have established, and it does not give you the right to include me. I know freedom, full individual freedom, and the position I find myself in is pleasant, indispensable and unique to me. Thus the world is given me as a real, in the ideal sense of the word, unity (*being as a whole*) and as real multiplicity (*individual being*). Unity is given to the consciousness instantly. We include in multiplicity learning about the nature of our individuality. This only appears to be connected with the outside world. The universe is an inner creative process (related to the creative beginning). Being as a whole wishes to be, because there is not and can never be any other principle for it but *being*. Being loves to be. Being is the will to live. The creative beginning is the will to live.

Let us analyze this will in itself. It is the one will. What does it mean to want to live? How is life possible? I can honestly affirm that I always want something. That means, of course, what I do not have. This is the most important and inflexible sign of life. Then man who wants nothing, definitely nothing, must die at once. He is like an atrophied organism, predestined for action but turned into a mechanism. The most important sign of life is the wish for new experiences. This is the single sign common to all living things. Biology tells us: an organism strives to preserve its life, to enlarge itself and to multiply. I add: An organism which does not evolve, that is which does not search either consciously or unconsciously for new experiences, atrophies and then dies out, degenerates and becomes unable to fight for its existence. Thus life is eternally different, eternally new. This means that the process of life (creative) has three phases:

1) Experiencing something, as a point of departure.
2) Dissatisfaction with the experience, thirst for the new experience and longing to attain the goal. This is the essence of creativity.
3) Attaining the ideal. New experience.

Do not forget that man *wears* his individuality like clothes on his body. Several philosophers confuse individuality with the soul. They think they are studying the soul when they are studying *individuality*, that is, how it acts in this or that given circumstance. *In essence* individuality differs from the soul. Philosophers forget that individuality is relationship between individualities.

I have already created you many times, world (how many living essences) *unconsciously*. Now I raise myself to conscious creativity. I created you, knowingly, so that I am now studying you.

23

SCRIABIN'S PRIVATE thoughts during early 1906 in Bogliasco and later in Geneva continue on the same plane as before. The Marxist explanation of history obviously ruffled Scriabin, so he repeatedly submits his own interpretation of the past. Again and again, he argues and weighs his solipsism.

The last pages of the 1906 Genevan Notebook are logical. They contain rational admissions and bend to the fact that he cannot at will change the circumstances of his life. He concedes that other consciousnesses may exist, but it is with half a heart and not quite real that he says this. His rationality dissolves in a schizophrenic question of "Who am I?" I am that which I want, but that is not the true "I." The suffering he feels when he loses an argument is well described here, "I want to win." Plekhanov had in the end reduced Scriabin to some intellectual misery, but not for long. As Man-God he ruled again.

I want to know the truth. And even before this, *I want to live.* I also have the *fact of my consciousness* wherein dwells the world in all its multiplicity of states and in which everything is unified. Knowing means identifying with the known. *I know the world as a set of states of my consciousness and outside this sphere I cannot exist.* I want to know the truth. This is the central figuration within my consciousness. Of this I am convinced. I identify with this conviction. Among the numerous states of consciousness some are close to the central state while others are scattered further apart. The central experience, so to speak, illuminates the universe in time and space and puts itself at the *center* as the *actual moment.* I affirm my *ACTIVITY.* In order to think and feel, in order to *create* the world, I exert certain powers, I act. If my activity stopped, I would sleep or die.

We must understand that the matter from which the universe is made is (our) imagination, (our) creative idea, (our) wish, and therefore, there is not the slightest difference in the concept of matter between the state of consciousness we call *"stone"* and the state of consciousness we call *"fancy."* Both stone and one's fancy are made of the same stuff. Both are uniquely real. They merely have different locations in consciousness. My contemplation of a stone is a psychological process achieved at the *present moment* and has a central location in the sphere of my consciousness. Our fancy is a process achieved in time's future; it is the contemplation of substance (process) separated from us by a larger or smaller interval of time, and therefore, it appears in vague outlines to us, like an object in the far distance from us. Intangible fancy is made from an unknown substance. In consciousness, *all is alive*. Everything, each idea has a *real* existence. The present moment is the central experience (the central figure). Around it the universe is distributed (like a logical sequence).

Every state of consciousness is a relationship to another state of consciousness. This means that its appearance is the negation of all else. In this negation I *relate* to the other, that is, *unconsciously* I struggle with the unconscious form of this other abiding in me . . .

Each state of consciousness is a determined point in vibrating motion. Vibration is the linkage of a state of consciousness to its single substance. By appearing to tremble and shake, they give us a scheme of opposites which resolves into vibration.

I recognize the world as a series of *my* states of consciousness. I can not leave this globe. I assert the fact of my consciousness, as well as that of my activity. Without this activity, everything would vanish for me. I classify my states of consciousness. I separate the world into nature, vegetable, animal, human, and man (one of people). *I understand from other people* that they feel and think what I do not feel and think. I also learn that they have many *states of consciousness* in their consciousnesses, just as I have *in mine*. They *contemplate the same world*, and they too are unable to leave the sphere of their consciousness. On the one hand, therefore, I ascertain the locked and *sealed spheres* of individual consciousness, and on the other, I ascertain the connection between them, as a carrier of *general states* which we call the universe. *All we people contemplate the same world*.

The following act of synthesis takes place in my consciousness: I connect one group of states to establish *my personality;* I connect the other to establish my *individuality;* and with a third, I establish the *not-I;* and with the fourth, I unify the I and the not-I; that is, I join together all my states of consciousness in one world and one *Universe*. The universe is an idea for me; a part of it is found in my consciousness and is an object of experience. The universe is an unconscious process. Part of it is accepted by me as an illumination of my consciousness.

God *as a state of consciousness* is *personality* appearing as the bearer of higher principle which is nothing and the possibility of all. It is creative power. The history of the universe is the evolution of God, the yearning for Ecstasy.

The universal consciousness in a state of activity appears as *personality, one enormous organism* which at any moment experiences a new stage of process called evolution. (At this basis lies the desire for absolute bliss. Life is an urge.) *Personality* is not constantly sentient in itself. For example, man does not feel all points of his body every moment, and still less does he experience earlier relationships of the past or yet those he will reach in the future. On the contrary, *precise accepting* or correct awareness is only of *ONE certain experience.* And so it is with the *God-personality* in the process of evolution. It accepts precisely the stage of evolution it experiences in a certain moment and does not feel all the points of its organism, that is, the universe. When it reaches the limits of its heights, the time draws near when it will communicate its bliss to all its organism. Like a man during the sexual act—at the moment of ecstasy he loses *consciousness* and his *whole organism* experiences bliss at each of its points. Similarly, God-Man, when he experiences ecstasy, fills the universe with bliss and ignites a fire.

Man-God appears as the bearer of universal consciousness.

If the personality acquires the ability to affect the outside world and can at will change the system of relationships between states at any given moment, then such a personality has seized godlike might. Such a personality returns the universe to its divine organism. This is the attainment of full harmony, the limit of creative urge, ecstasy. Such a personality will be in public demand, the demand to contemplate divine beauty.

The world will give herself to him, as a woman gives herself to a lover.

IX

BREAK WITH BELAIEFF

24

THE SCRIABINS were desperately poor in Bogliasco. Like the Plekhanovs, they wrote postcards instead of letters. They did not always eat three times a day. Scriabin had two women, two maidservants, four children, and himself to support. By the end of 1906 he would write, "I have been in great need. There were moments of despair . . ."

One pathetic slip of paper in Tatyana's handwriting shows how together they estimated 9,000 rubles would be coming in from the Belaieff firm "for present and future compositions . . . at official prices" and including Glinka Prizes. In piano composition, his output was slender. On 1 December, 1904, he had written Vera, "I am working on 5 pieces and that's all!" On 7 December he wrote Tatyana, "Tomorrow or the day after they are sending me a very good Erard piano and I will immediately begin composing piano pieces." Again on 12 December he told her "I am composing, I mean sketching 3 little piano pieces. They're not bad." And to Vera on 15 December, "Did I tell you I wrote four piano pieces? Very good. I work though, only in leisure moments." On 5 February, 1905, he promised Vera he will "send Petersburg 10 pieces within 20 days. You will be able to live for 3 months off them."

What actually happened was that, as a trial balloon, Scriabin sent Glazunov two page-long poems (Op. 44) demanding 150 rubles each. On 5 February, the advisory committee with Groes in formal charge and bumptious Artsybushev in secretarial power answered that "keeping in mind the highest amounts which the late Mitrofan Petrovich Belaieff paid you, 100 rubles per piece is correct." Scriabin accepted this with a brief note of protest to Glazunov to the effect that "In the future I ask the

Committee to set the honorarium for my works according to size, so as to avoid unpleasant discussion on the subject of recompense." At the same time he told Vera that, "Since I was afraid the Committee would not pay me as liberally as Belaieff had, I tested them by sending the smallest and weakest of my new pieces. As you see, I received the usual amount for them. I told you I had asked for 300 rubles. I did so on purpose..."

By August, 1905, Scriabin had sent eleven pieces, each shorter than the last. Among the first five (Opp. 44 and 45), there were three poems, all in C major, rich in sound, warm in melody, but only cautiously exploratory of newfound musical paths. One poem is called "Fantastic," and Scriabin used the word in the sense of "grotesque" or "outlandish." One prelude and the sweet "Albumleaf"—both in E flat major—revert to the conventions of the salon.

Opp. 46, 47 and 48 also consist of bits and pieces: "Scherzo" in C major that rises presto, like a sputtering firecracker; "Quasi-Valse" which sounds like a sigh; and four preludes, all in major keys, two in bland C major (the last of these like a festive sunburst of joy). These pieces are work-sheets—diatonic, triadic, held-over sounds which always resolve into the familiar. Their meters are for Scriabin shockingly simple—mostly 3/4 and never more compound than two against three.

He was, however, on his way. Later he said to Sabaneeff: "How can you express mysticism with major and minor? How can you convey the dissolution of matter, or luminosity? Above all, minor keys must disappear from music, because art must be a festival. Minor is a whine. I can't stand whining," and he would play some bars from Tchaikovsky. "Tragedy is not in the minor key... Minor is abnormal... Minor is *under*tone. I deal in *over*tones. Oh, how I want to break down the walls of these tempered tones." Soon he would.

(In compromise sometimes he hovered between major and minor keys, related or not. His tonalities often fluttered like millers batting their wings against light, until all concept of tonic-dominant harmony and conventional keys disappeared. The little prelude, Op. 74 No. 4, for one instance out of many, written in late 1914 not long before his death, is in dual tonality. It welds A major and A minor simultaneously together.)

In November, 1905, Scriabin sent off three more pieces, Op. 49. Again the inspiration was a single breath. The étude is like a harp in the wind, diaphanous and evanescent. The prelude is an angry, brusque bark at the world. The *Rêverie*, characteristic of that Russian dreaminess which Tolstoi described and perhaps glamorized as "a reflection on higher spiritual life," is the first time Scriabin titles a piano piece with an imaginative, interpretive, nonmusical designation. In Russian he called it *grozy*, suggesting idle, meandering thought. These dream-struck, contemplative notes are frequent in Scriabin's music.

On receipt of this manuscript, the committee sent a coldly official letter (composed by Artsybushev) saying they would only pay 150 rubles for all three pieces because of their brevity. Scriabin answered this letter of 12 December, on his birthday: "Sirs, I am insulted by your proposed payment for my last compositions, and seeing in this attitude on the part of the Belaieff firm a desire to break relations with me, I rise to the occasion by asking that my manuscripts be returned to me instantly." Three days later he wrote Groes again, having in his rage forgotten to enclose the necessary acknowledgment of the 1905 Glinka Prize.

On 2 January, 1906, the advisory committee wrote apologetically, and this letter was signed by friends Rimsky, Glazunov, and Liadov:

Rather than answer formally to your letter we are permitting ourselves to address you as a comrade whose compositions we value and hold dear. You took our proposal regarding the honorarium as an insult. Mitrofan Petrovich was the founder of the firm and as such had the power to pay fees as he willed. We, as directors of this firm, are responsible to the executors for the business we transact. While we feel fully justified in paying you 2,000 rubles for so complicated a work as your [third] symphony, we still do not feel we have the right to augment the honoraria for pieces as short as those you have sent us. You can see how highly we regard your compositions by looking at the Glinka Prize for last year. Therefore we beg you to retract your decision, the suggestion that we intended to offend you, and the breaking off of relations with this publisher. In the expectation of hearing from you, we are taking the liberty of holding your manuscripts here.

Indiscreetly, the committee sent the fatal Op. 49 off to be printed, and Scriabin found himself insulted again. On 5 February, 1906, he wrote his three friends:

I was astonished after your letter to receive *proofs* of my latest compositions. You obviously were certain that I would accept your conditions. I do not wish to make trouble with the printer, so I must leave these pieces with him, despite the inadequate remuneration and the inappropriateness of the action between publisher and composer. I do not understand what you mean by "augmenting the honoraria." The fact is you have reduced it by half. In the course of 12 [sic] years during the life of Mitrofan Petrovich and for two years after his death, never have I received less than a hundred rubles a piece, no matter how small. If you consider yourselves responsible to the executors for setting the fees paid composers, then such responsibility does not allow you to pass judgment on my compositions. I am happy that I was wrong about your intention to insult me. However, in view of the above-mentioned circumstances, I must begin negotiations with another publisher who will provide me with more normal arrangements. I trust that these business differences regarding the value of my compositions will not affect our fine personal relations.

The embarrassed committee immediately offered to destroy the plates or pay double for the three pieces. Scriabin accepted the 300 rubles on 14 February "with the understanding that this presents no obstacle to my entering into business arrangements with another publisher." Soon after, the committee sent Scriabin a reminder that he still owed Lev Konyus 200 rubles for the piano version of the "Divine Poem."

On 27 February, 1906, Scriabin wrote Boris Jurgenson:

I understand from my acquaintance, Maria Solomonovna Lunz, that you are interested in publishing my compositions.

I would like very much to be published in Russia and to return to your company which 14 years ago published my first music. I am sending you a list of pieces which are ready, or nearly so, for publication and for which I would like the following honoraria.

1. A large poem for orchestra with a philosophical program—4,000 rubles.
2. Two small pieces for orchestra at 300 rubles each—600.
3. Several little piano pieces at 200–300 each, according to length . . .

On the same day he sent a letter to Nemenova-Lunz, thanking her first of all for interceding with Jurgenson, and including a copy of this letter. As a customer of long standing she had spoken to the manager of the Peter Jurgenson music shop in Moscow, Fyodor Grishin. He in turn passed the message to Boris Jurgenson who expressed his agreement in principle, but had said he would like to hear from the composer directly. On 3 March he wrote that he would like to publish Scriabin again, but "your demands exceed my means."

Morozova sent her stipend and Scriabin answered on 15 March, 1906:

"You rescue me from very great unpleasantness and terrible depression. I have spent all my energy for months finding a publisher. I hope to arrange something and I am in touch with several, but have received no answer as yet."

In April, 1906, Scriabin approached Ernst Eberg, music shopkeeper and publisher in Moscow, but he did not reply. Another music printer, Yuly Zimmerman (1851-1922), did. He rejoiced at the opportunity of publishing Scriabin. But he would like to hear the music. Could the composer come to Russia?

In answer Scriabin sent him four pieces (later to be Op. 51—Op. 50 does not exist, because Scriabin forgot to count). These remarkably ingenious works are called "Fragility," "Prelude" (Lugubriously), "Winged Poem" and "Dance of Languor." This last and the "Danced Caress" (Op. 57, No. 2) were originally conceived as orchestral pieces, as indicated by the letter to Jurgenson. "I have worked hard and written three not so small piano pieces," he wrote Vera on 15 August, 1905, meaning Op. 49, "and two very small pieces for orchestra. Besides all this, I am making notable progress with my 4th Symphony." Who would consider publishing orchestral numbers that lasted only a minute each?

The big Fourth Symphony or "Poem of Ecstasy" was absorbing most of his creative effort anyway. Little piano pieces were an overflow. Neither of the venturesome flavors of "languor" or "wings" were matched with musical advance. Scriabin dipped back into the past—rejected pieces, even—for the sake of money. The lugubrious Prelude, Op. 51 in A minor is a case in point. It is soft, slow, triadic. Still, for all its conservatism, it has some psychical magic. Scriabin called it "the string breaker," claiming it could if played correctly, break the strings of the piano. It jangles with dissonance and overtones (when half-pedaled and the pedal slowly released to catch the harmonics). Scriabin never played it in public.

Zimmerman sent the pieces to a professor in Leipzig for an opinion. He advised against publishing them, and Zimmerman wonders if it would be better for all concerned, "including Mr. Scriabin's admirers," were he to write more "understandably and accessibly." He offered 25 rubles per "melodic waltz," if Mr. Scriabin will oblige.

Scriabin wrote frantically to all his friends about publishers. Meanwhile in search of emolument, he changed quarters. In February, 1906, the Scriabins left before the second summer of Italian heat could begin and moved to Switzerland. Geneva and Lausanne and Lucerne all had Conservatories where music at least—if not Scriabin's—flourished.

On 4 April, 1906, Scriabin in Geneva answered a Morozova letter more in pathos than anger:

> You wrote me that you wanted me in circumstances conducive to my ideas. The only thing is for me to be in a tolerable atmosphere for working. This means having a good publisher. Without one, I cannot even give concerts, and they require huge expenses at the outset anyway. Probably none of this has crossed your mind. Today I am going to be open and severe with you, as you are with me.
>
> Already now for several months I have not found a permanent residence and have been unable to work on my main composition, and I have not even been able to work at all really. In the mornings I sit down to compose little pieces, but the work bogs down, my thought falters, and I return again and again to one thing—the very sad specter of approaching want.
>
> Now, after having handed you this unpleasant pill to swallow and having turned you against me, I propose a request:
>
> Please advance me what is left of my stipend, that is to say, what you would send me on 1 July. Send all that to me now at the soonest. The rent date draws nigh, and that puts me in all sorts of difficulties. You surely know what a Swiss *propriétaire* can be like! You can send me the stipend for 1 December at the usual time.
>
> I am boundlessly mortified and even sick at heart to ask you this. But being without a publisher at this time leaves me helpless.

Morozova insensitively did not reply. In a letter to Nemenova-Lunz, Scriabin wrote, "Poor Tanya is unnerved and on top of all the sorrow so far, her father has taken a turn for the worse. I am not in a particularly happy mood myself. Work comes only with great difficulty. Write us, for we need moral support."

As a last resort in early June, Scriabin wrote one of his rare letters to Aunt Lyubov. He knows how skimpily that houseful of ladies lived, yet he must borrow money: "I will do everything possible to repay my debt to you as quickly as possible. Don't worry about me, dearest Auntie, and pay no attention to those disturbing things which are being said about me now. They upset me, of course. However, my mood is better, and I hope the concert I have planned will put me in a position to straighten out my material difficulties."

Sabaneeff reported that Moscow was rife with rumors. Scriabin had become paralyzed some said; others, that he was crazy. When the news of Ariadna's birth reached Moscow, one musician seriously assured Sabaneeff that "she had produced a monster, an animal so strange that it was preserved and placed in a museum. This proved Scriabin was a 'degenerate'." So much for his grandiose philosophy.

25

THE PLEKHANOVS had not yet reached Geneva, but Tatyana on her own found a tiny little house, "clean and commodious," as Rosalia would later describe it, at 2, Chemin de la Fontaine in the suburb of Servette. Scriabin immediately went about establishing himself musically and socially. In a letter to Nemenova-Lunz 27 February, 1906, he wrote: "I have paid several calls on professors at the Geneva Conservatory and was very warmly received by them. They are mostly Germans. Everyone expresses much interest in my projects. I must continue these rounds of social visit, this time with Tanya, because all the professors' wives want to meet her so much." (In March he will write Morozova, in a tirade against Vera: "Here's an example. Not a single musician in Geneva has returned my visit, although they received me most pleasantly. They have doubtless heard something scandalous. Cooperation with them is most important for me. But I am shunned.")

"We made one terrible blunder. We went to the local opera and saw *Louise*. I will leave the description of that amazing performance to Tanya." Tatyana in her letter omitted any reference to Charpentier, but she did describe how "well-settled" they were: "We are in a nice villa with a garden, and even have electricity. The city is quite near—12 minutes by foot, and the tram trip is nothing. After our palazzo in Bogliasco, we seem to be in paradise . . . Sasha has already composed two piano pieces which are so enchanting I am copying them out to send you immediately. You will see their marvel . . . Sasha is reading Plekhanov with passion . . ."

These pieces are the magnificent Poem and "Enigma," Op. 52 Nos. 1 and 2. Scriabin of the final period now emerges from the chrysalis in precise and expressive indications in French—"*avec langueur*," "*volup-*

tueux, charmé." In the veiled Poem (*voilé*), the root chord is transparently symmetrical. Scriabin's predilection for major thirds manifests itself. In the Poem he lines his melody with them. Even the modulations descend as if floating in air, at intervals of major thirds. He has only one timorous moment at the end—C major. Only two more compositions remained for Scriabin to write with a tonic ending—Prelude and "Ironies," Op. 56 Nos. 1 and 2. All the rest would soar or evaporate away, as does "Enigma," in abstractly evolved, demi-consonances of future sounds.

Why is "Enigma" called that? Scriabin had just composed it on the little piano in Servette. Tatyana came in.

"What's that?"

"What do you think it should be called?"

"I don't know. It's a puzzle." So it was titled *zagadka*, "puzzle" or as translated in French by the author himself, "*Enigme.*"

Its light, capricious charm, spaced with measures of sensual yearning, became a Sasha-Tanya theme song, iridescent with rays of desire transformed. Its strange and erratic sense of direction and faintly acid tonal arrangements appear in Scriabin's idiom for the first time.

Scriabin entered the publishing business himself in a shortlived venture of 1907. He privately printed 700 copies of these highly personal pieces (including a third, the 1905 "Poem of Languor," not to be confused with "Dance of Languor," Op. 51, he had written for *L'Illustration*). No wonder Tatyana wanted Nemenova-Lunz to have them instantly. They are early light after brief darkness.

When the Scriabins entertained in Servette, they served tea and little pastries. Guests walked in the tiny garden as they talked. Having heard of their financial state, Rosalia Plekhanova as soon as she arrived sent a note saying she very much wished to see them "*chez nous.*"

Alexander Nikolaevich came over straightway. He had a cold. He was worried and depressed. I asked, "What's the matter with you, dear Alexander Nikolaevich? Are you well?"

Our great composer became embarrassed and upset. He was in dire need after the death of Belaieff his publisher . . .

Much of this I now see was produced by Alexander Nikolaevich's sick sensitivity. It was painful to see him. He was so self-convinced, so proud, and so full of joy of living. Now, he was reduced to this sad mental state.

One small thing happened which characterizes Alexander Nikolaevich's attitude at that time. As he got ready to say goodbye, Alexander Paikes-Sokolov came in the hotel. He had energetically helped me plan benefits for refugees. I introduced them, "May I present Comrade Sokolov, Alexander Nikolaevich Scriabin." Scriabin corrected me, "Rosalia Markovna, I *too* am 'Comrade.'"

Rosalia asked him if he would agree to a concert in aid of the political refugees streaming into Switzerland as an aftermath of the 1905 Revolution. Persuasively she explained, "It would familiarize Genevan society with his music, as well as being invaluably helpful in filling the empty coffers of these poor emigrants. He readily agreed."

Saturday, 30 June, 1906, Scriabin made his Swiss debut as a pianist and composer. He was in fine fettle, but played a cautious program, short and full of established favorites.

Rosalia tells the story:

Student youths as well as comrades from among the rank and file of Russians living in Geneva helped me in the concert. We were convinced that it would be a great success and we decided to give 50% of the proceeds to Scriabin. I rejoiced in my heart that for once he could exist perhaps for two or three weeks without worry. This thought was hasty. Alas! Despite all efforts, tickets moved slowly. We reduced the price, so that students could afford them.

Our genial compatriot, Scriabin, however, was little known, even to the Russians themselves who were living in Geneva. We were a failure. Two days before the concert four tickets had been sold.

One thing alone remained to do. Discard all thoughts of making money and work only so that Alexander Nikolaevich would not appear before an empty house. I summoned the committee, explained the catastrophe, and suggested that all tickets be given away. We invited well-known names in the musical and art world, our Swiss friends, my patients even. We mobilized students to fill the seats. Some people accepted the free tickets merely as a favor to us. Scriabin was known in the musical heights, of course, but the general public neither knew nor would they understand him then.

The evening of June 30th, 1906 came. The Grand Hall of the Conservatory began to fill—but slowly. I was very upset. Henri Marteau [1874–1940], the famous French violinist, now teaching at the Geneva Conservatory, knew and highly prized Scriabin. He was sitting not far from me and was upset. I heard him whisper, '*Il retarde, Scriabine, il hésite d'apparaître devant un publique si niaise*' [sic] [He's late. Scriabin's afraid to appear before so negligible an audience.]

The concert started half an hour late, but the hall had gradually filled. The parterre was practically full. I breathed a little easily.

Alexander Nikolaevich came out alert and cordial. He won the public's sympathy instantly by his unaffected manner. He played waltzes and études, gentle as murmuring brooks. The Nocturne was masterful and the applause thunderous. Marteau was enchanted with the music and the playing. So were the students at the Conservatory who had helped fill the hall. Those who were cold to the music were our own Russian youth. They found it like Chopin but below the level of the great Polish maestro. They thought the left-hand Nocturne a charlatan's trick.

However, the concert did introduce Scriabin to Geneva audiences and as a great musical power. Unfortunately, it was a financial loss. We were only able to pay him 25 francs—exactly half the box office intake. The other 25 francs went to one needy family. Even now I blush with shame when I recall this. But, I will never forget the gratitude and moral beauty with which Scriabin accepted it.

Rosalia expatiated on life in Geneva:

During July and August, 1906, Alexander Nikolaevich waited impatiently for Georgy Valentinovich to return. He continued to work on Marxism and assembled a list of questions and doubts which he hoped to settle. He felt a deep and sincere attachment to Plekhanov, just stopping short of becoming a follower. He said to me, "I find Georgy Valentinovich too argumentative, too much the polemicist. If he didn't write his works so disputatiously, he would have more of a public. The didactic hazards switch a superficial reader away from the essence."

After this visit, I wrote Georgy Valentinovich, "He is looking forward to seeing you and is convinced it will have a deciding influence on his life." This shows that there was some contradiction in his *profession de foi*—philosophical idealism. Scriabin was at war with his own nature. As a thinking man he was drawn to Marxism because of its new viewpoint. He wanted to follow it through to the end and understand it. Thus armed, he would then propound that he was nearer the truth than Plekhanov. His quarrels with Plekhanov sharpened his wits and gave him intellectual pleasure, just as healthy sport gives joy to man's being and body.

I visited Alexander Nikolaevich and Tatyana Fyodorovna several times at their invitation, and usually with Madeleine Got, an acquaintance of my daughter's. Madeleine Got, a good musician, adored both the Scriabins and helped them arrange their little house. She became a great devotee of Scriabin and brought a talented sculptor of Geneva, Rodo, to them. However, this sculptor combined his great gifts with insufferable habits. He drank a great deal, and I feared such influence on the susceptible composer. Alas, my fears were well founded.

The strain of being without a publisher, poverty, perhaps even Ple-khanov's assaults of rationality on his mind, taxed Scriabin's psychic organism again. He was also homesick for Russia, according to Neme-nova-Lunz, who arrived that summer and took a lovely chalet at St. Beatenberg, a village high in the Alps near Bern and the Lake of Thun. He had asked her to bring him a samovar and he was "deeply happy with it. He joked to cover up his emotion and made a comically sad face. 'Now I can open up a shop,' he said, referring to his difficult financial position."

Perhaps he could have withstood his concatenation of emotions at this time by converting them into music, but he turned to drink because Rodo was there. Rodo (1863–1913), whose real name was August Niederchäusern, was a bachelor, a member of the "Salon" jury selecting art works and a gifted French sculptor. His bust of Verlaine is probably his finest work, but other representative examples can still be seen at the Rath or State Museum in Geneva.

Engel described Rodo: "Not of this world, this man, an occultist, full of mystic tendencies and extraordinary flights of fancy. Scriabin was attracted to him and loved to dine with him . . ." Dinner for Rodo, however, meant his ordering a 35 centimes plate, the cheapest item on the menu, and letting it sit while drinking the wine that came with it free. "The wine Rodo consumed," Engel prissily elaborates, "took more cognizance of quantity than quality." Scriabin avidly joined these non-eating, drinking evenings with Rodo.

In the middle of June, 1906, Plekhanov returned "thin and tired" from the Stockholm Congress and his political, underground travels, Rosalia wrote:

> I did not conceal his whereabouts from Alexander Nikolaevich, but told him frankly that Plekhanov was tired from the long journey . . . "When he comes," I said, "I will let you know immediately." The tactful Alexander Nikolaevich did not press, although he was most eager.

Plekhanov enquired about the "health and life of the Scriabins." Scriabin played him more and newer extracts of the "Poem of Ecstasy," announcing that "This music reeks of Revolution and the ideals for which the Russian people are struggling."

One anecdote recounted by Engel shows proud Scriabin throwing himself at Plekhanov's mercy. The pair had argued as to whether the artist should be aloof or engaged. Plekhanov rattled a newspaper in Scriabin's face. "Alexander Nikolaevich! Read this. Then tell me if I am not right. Haven't I proved that the artist can *not* just float in skyblue ether?!" The paper contained a number of front page articles about punitive raids against tribesmen, animal hunts, and the continuing Tsarist backlash of the 1905 Revolution. "Yes, you are right," Scriabin said, apologetic for his *hors de combat* mysticism.

Plekhanov and Scriabin often strolled together while Scriabin unfolded his philosophy, borrowing heavily, Rosalia said, from the Theosophists. Nemenova-Lunz also recalled how Scriabin's conversations were full of Theosophy and the personality of Blavatsky. He wanted to return to Russia where Theosophy had even more of a vogue than abroad. Even with the exposure of Blavatsky's occultism, which appeared headlined in every newspaper of the world, Scriabin was "unshaken . . . He attributed the exposés to personal grievances on the part of one member or other in the Theosophical movement."

In September, 1906, Rosalia witnessed a reverse side to the Plekhanov-Scriabin relationship: "I saw the soft and feminine Alexander Nikolaevich as unyielding and impassioned as Georgy Valentinovich himself, each in their separate realms."

She invited the Scriabins to a soirée. Madeleine Got, who had become Tatyana's inseparable companion, was also there. So was "a fanatic devotee of Scriabin," an émigré called Dmitri Petrov from Lausanne. Petrov had found a music publisher there who would print Scriabin for a small cost. (Nemenova-Lunz spoke warily of this: "Scriabin got the poor idea of publishing his own music. He was ignorant of all things practical, was gullible, and had to get out of this undertaking by the skin of his teeth.") Petrov told Scriabin how the musical world of Lausanne "greatly esteemed" him, that the director of the opera orchestra there referred to him as "*C'est un Beethoven contemporain*" (He's a living Beethoven), which probably did not please Scriabin.

However, Rosalia reported that "Alexander Nikolaevich was delighted with Petrov's gaiety and warm affection toward him and his family."

She continued her recollections of that party:

Madeleine Got sang an aria from Saint-Saëns *Samson et Delilah*. The center of interest, however, was Alexander Nikolaevich. He was especially entertaining that evening. He was outspoken and interesting. He played his best compositions, extracts of his new "Poem of Ecstasy," and delivered a whole lecture on counterpoint with demonstrations on the piano. We were all enraptured. We made a tight ring around him and showered him with questions concerning his new creative plans, philosophical ideas about music, and asked his opinions of his great predecessors Beethoven, Chopin, Wagner.

These opinions, I hasten to say, were all unfavorable. "That is in the past. There is nothing to be learned from them," he said.

I looked at Plekhanov. I saw that he was annoyed. Alexander Nikolaevich was discrediting his gods, Beethoven, Wagner. The pointed criticism of Chopin, whom Plekhanov found too personal, did not bother him. But Beethoven and Wagner! How can one speak of titans in that way!

For the first time we noticed something maniacal in Scriabin. He glowed with *folie de grandeur* [delusions of grandeur], a conviction in the "I." This cast a little cloud over our enchantment with him, the star-personality of the evening. But the cloud was dispelled as soon as the winged fantasy of the composer turned to the philosophical content of his compositions. We all listened to him with absorption.

Plekhanov never once took his eyes off Scriabin. He listened carefully to the development of that genius-composer's ideas. When Alexander Nikolaevich finished his explanations, Georgy Valentinovich thanked him and said, affectionately, "Alexander Nikolaevich, what you have just developed for us is pure mysticism. You have read, and even studied, as you yourself have said more than once, Marx and Marxism. Pity is that reading has no effect on you. You remain an incorrigible idealist-mystic, just as you were in Bogliasco."

The argument continued through supper. It was a tourney between Georgy Valentinovich and Alexander Nikolaevich, and it ended dramatically. Each participant passionately defended his point of view. Each stood fast. Idealism with its strange Theosophical face, and pure dialectical materialism.

Plekhanov was, in my opinion, merciless, and I was most upset. The presence of friends who loudly agreed with him only added fuel to the fire. One whispered to me, "What your husband is saying is good for Alexander Nikolaevich." No one took offense, but I nonetheless stopped the dispute first chance I could.

I proposed a toast to the success of Alexander Nikolaevich in America. Tatyana Fyodorovna, who also had been frightened by the turn of the conversation, answered with a toast to Georgy Valentinovich and to the triumph of Marxism in Russia. Passion subsided and the evening ended in a friendly way. Plekhanov and some friends escorted the Scriabins home. Scriabin was feeling tired. Returning, Georgy Valentinovich said to me, "What a talented and sympathetic man, and what an incorrigible mystic! His music is grandiose and stirring. It distills our Revolutionary epoch, but through the retort of an idealist-mystic mind or through his special temperament and view of the world."

We never saw the Scriabins again. We corresponded for a while. I remember receiving letters from Tatyana Fyodorovna from Brussels and Beatenberg.

26

SCRIABIN HAD not heard from Morozova in months. Now in penniless despair for lack of a publisher, he addressed himself to venerable Stassov. He would put matters aright in his favor. On 24 July, 1906, he wrote as his last recourse, subtly almost to the point of subterfuge:

Forgive me for turning to you for once for advice and help. I come to this decision only because you regard my music so kindly. It cannot be unknown to you that I have broken connection with the Belaieff firm, but what you probably do not know, or know only from the executors of the Belaieff estate, is why.

For two years after Belaieff's death no alteration or change was made in the honoraria I received for my compositions. Actually, it would have been natural to increase my fee, because my compositions are now very popular both in Russia and abroad. What happened was exactly the reverse! The last time I sent three piano pieces to Petersburg, the Committee informed me that they could not send me more than 50 rubles apiece. This was half the usual amount. The only reason they gave for this was the insignificant shortness of the music. However, I have not been criticized for this before, and never received less than a hundred rubles and sometimes 150 for pieces only 16 measures in length. All this can be verified in Mitrofan Belaieff's ledgers.

Furthermore, without waiting for my concurrence the members of the Committee sent those pieces off to the printers. I am quite willing to believe this, as they wrote, was a mistake and they offered me 100 rubles each piece because they felt they had to as there was no other way out of their predicament. But how can I send them my manuscripts after they have heaped such insults on me? And have I any guarantee that they won't propose 10 rubles for my next composition?! If I also tell you that I probably have been shorn of the support

I had been receiving from one person in Moscow, or surely will be since I have nothing from her in four months, then you will understand the horrifying position I am in.

I am thinking of giving a series of concerts this autumn, but until then I am at my wits' end as to what I should do. Maybe you will be so good as to advise me and recommend me to some publishing house. I have completed quite a large orchestral composition which is of greater importance in every respect than the Divine Poem. I do not know where to send it. I never thought that such a disaster would befall me. Even less did I ever dream that because of these difficulties I would be obligated to my comrades for my *art!* A.K. Glazunov surprises me! In the past he showed such sympathy for my music. As for A.K. Liadov, I simply cannot understand how he could have reached the point of impoliteness. He has not answered my last 3 letters.

In August, however, Morozova writes but sends no money. Scriabin answers on 9 September, 1906:

Finally, after four months of silence, you remembered my existence. I had begun to think you wanted to sever all connection. Now, all is clear: the events in Russia obscured my modest little self. So, Sashenka had to sit by the fire and spin! I don't want to be spiteful, although all my questions and requests cry like a voice in the wilderness. My big composition moves as well as it can under existing circumstances, and the existing circumstances are terrible. It's the same old story! I am still without a publisher! Again I am without livelihood. It hurts me to speak of this to you who give me my daily sustenance, but you understand that it is not enough for me to live on unless I have a publisher. And besides I am so humiliated to have to take from you all the time.

My fame has now reached a point where I can do a great deal. If it weren't for the false status of my married life, I would have long been on my way toward preaching my ideas. I have Vera Ivanovna to thank! Now I waste my strength for nothing. Be an angel, talk to someone about my business affairs. If only I could give a concert *series* (not just one solo recital as I did in Paris), then I would be all right. My technique is in fine shape, because I practiced every day all summer. In July I gave a concert in Geneva with enormous success and a profit of, just guess! 70 francs!! All the musicians here advise me to give another concert in the big hall, and I want to, provided I have the means to do so.

15 September he writes Morozova again, and for several reasons. One he entirely omits from the letter—Tatyana's father is dying and they must proceed to Amsterdam. Another is that he has decided to perform in America, definitely.

It depresses me to have to trouble you once more about sending me money in advance of the specified date. We must set out on a journey. 1st, Tanya must take Ariasha to her aunt in Amsterdam. She is good enough to want to take the little girl for the whole winter and thus free us from the expense and worry of her. Secondly, we have to leave right away for Paris where I will be able to find something to do, if no more than give piano lessons. Further, we must be ready to move from place to place concertizing. I am in correspondence with some impresarios regarding this, and one of them is as far away as America. What will come of all this I do not know, but I struggle on to the last extremity. We must leave Geneva. We are in a most awkward situation. It has reached the ears of certain musicians here that we are not married. And surely you know Swiss morals! Fortunately, several of the most intelligent people here are our friends, but they have no power.

I had to pay a number of debts with the money you sent on April 1, and we existed somehow or other on the rest for 4 months. Now we are living on promises to pay. If you could send me the 1 December money now, I would be infinitely grateful!

On 12 October, 1906, Scriabin wrote Morozova a last letter from Servette:

I am infinitely grateful to you for your speed in helping me. You are very, very sweet, and I cannot express all my gratitude to you.

R. Strakosch, a concert manager in Paris, secured two halls for Scriabin to play in that winter and joined him in Holland to discuss further details of the projected concert tour and Brussels' recitals. Scriabin wanted to use his "sparkling technique" in public again after Geneva. "I love the festival atmosphere after a concert," he often said. Before long he will have much of it.

The Scriabins reached 145 van Bree Straat, Amsterdam, where the favorite aunt, Aline Boty, lived. Another aunt, Henriette or "Tante Jette," also lived there. It suited Scriabin by its nearness to Brussels, and Tatyana, because she will not be lonely.

The fruit of the Stassov letter ripened within two months. Liadov wrote personally, beginning, "Ever dear and sweet Alexander Niko-laevich, as always!" Stassov had handed Scriabin's letter to the Committee asking from his authority that goodwill be restored. He counted on Liadov's well-known "tender love," and he was correct.

Liadov's letter of 18 September, 1906, continues after the greeting:

And why did you quarrel with us? We have always looked upon you as the *closest person* in this beloved enterprise of our late friend (especially yours and mine), M. P. Belaieff.

It had not occurred to us that the proposed honorarium of 50 rubles for the *very least* of your pieces could grieve you. If *you* could look upon the Belaieff business as something *apart* from yourself, you would see what others are paid. I think it is no secret from you that we are *not very rich*. We often have to turn various composers down simply for lack of money. We have cut our fees as low as possible.

Knowing you as well as I do, I could not comprehend how you could break with us *because of money*.

I, as the person in the wrong in this stupid affair, understand how hard it must have been for you to take the first step towards reconciliation. But we are glad. And you will receive one of these days, an invitation from the Board of Trustees to send us more compositions if you have some ready for printing.

I kiss you warmly.

Oh how I would like to sit and recall the past with you. Aren't you ever coming back?

Scriabin received this letter 1 October, together with the official invitation. No mention still has been made of money. Nonetheless, after waiting a little more than a week, Scriabin answered both letters. The first was a formal acceptance to the advisory committee, informing them that he was sending them "four compositions for piano" (Op. 51) and that "in a few weeks my big poem for orchestra will be ready." As usual, he grossly misgauged time.

"It is my best composition," he says to Liadov, and the letter glows heartily:

You cannot imagine how happy I am that everything was only a misunderstanding. Difficulty between us seemed monstrous. Of course, all will be forgotten, but I must tell you how hurt I was at your unjust judgment of me. Although it was a matter of payment, it is evident that it was not money which played the large part—it was *insult* . . .

How could I explain this change in evaluation of my work, when, at all costs, it is not worse? And too, *not a word was said* to me about the finances of the firm not flourishing. I was under the impression that Belaieff was one of the most successful firms in the world.

Never again will we speak of this sad episode. Indeed! Are you again my dear Anatol Konstantinovich?! Again?!! Yes, yes, of course, it could not be otherwise between us.

I want so much to see you and to ask you and tell you about everything that has happened these last three or four years. You know, don't you, that two years ago I separated from my wife so as to unite myself with Tatyana Fyodorovna, about whom you have heard me often speak. We have come to Amsterdam to settle our daughter, Ariadna, with her *babushka*. Then we set out for a concert tour.

The one thing I want is to arrange for some kind of financial security and live as a composer. Counting on the support of one's friends is trying . . . I dream of meeting you to speak of all I have been through but I won't bore you with this and for the present it is impossible.

Goodbye. I sincerely love you.

Scriabin gives two concerts in Brussels in November. Belgium was a country of mystical poetry to him—the symbolists Maeterlinck (1862–1949) and Verhaeren (1855–1916)—and it took to him well. The second concert at the big Salle Ravenstein on 21 November extended his conventional program as far as Op. 48, the octave prelude and its breathless fluttering mate in D flat major.

Le Guide Musical expressed this overall view:

M. Scriabine has a very original and distinguished talent, particularly alluring in restrained compositions. These are delicate sketches, full of Slavic soul with sentiments of unrest and melancholy. Scriabine is an accomplished master, a virtuoso. His performance is powerful, nervous, and sometimes vehement, but never does it lose charm. In sweet passages, he recalls Mark Hambourg.

Scriabin was playing marvelously well. Everyone now spoke of his "power," and although he was displeased to be compared to Mark Hambourg (1879–1960), a younger Russian pianist, he was glad to be "a virtuoso."

He wanted to send the score and Konyus's four-hand reduction of the "Divine Poem" to Pierné and two new conductors who had expressed interest—Bernhard Stavenhagen (1862–1914), a German pianist conducting the Hague orchestra, and Eugene Ysaÿe (1858–1931), Belgian violinist then conducting in Brussels.

He wrote Liadov while on tour, from Brussels.

> I am most upset and worried. I have just come from the Breitkopf store to see if they had the score of the Third Symphony from Leipzig. I ordered it a week ago. They want to play it in Amsterdam and Brussels. To my amazement, they told me that Leipzig said it was not yet for sale. What can this mean? Surely you can understand how important this is to me.
>
> Why haven't I been sent five copies of the transcription made by Konyus. It has been already a year since I answered that I would definitely undertake the expense myself. Konyus also wrote you to that effect. How is it possible that it is not yet published? Write me soon about all this. Please excuse my upset . . . Everything is turning my way, but I cannot afford to send scores to conductors.

Before he can receive an answer, he wrote again:

> I am in despair that I must trouble you again with a request. Of course, you already suspect that it concerns that metal which at the present moment I in no wise consider contemptible. I am greatly in need of it.
>
> This year my affairs have gone completely astray. I am seizing upon one desperate remedy—I am going to America where I have engagements. This is only to ask for something so that I can arrange things somewhat before this ocean voyage, and to have something during my first days there.
>
> I am thinking that perhaps you will agree to help me, first, send me the fee for the things I sent without waiting for first proofs, and second, give me a small advance of about 500 rubles. Soon I shall finish two small things for orchestra which I hope will cover this loan or at least the greater part of it. Also, my big poem will soon be completed.

The Belaieff Board paid him 100 rubles for each of the four little pieces (Op. 51) and gave them to him before receipt of corrected first proofs. (Liadov, however, could not resist making a notation on the invoice to Groes that "since Scriabin won't accept five kopecks per prelude which is all such short pieces are worth, we might as well pay him 400 rubles.") Further, they told Scriabin that he will receive 1,000 rubles, the Glinka Prize of 1906 for his "Divine Poem," but, please, will he neither divulge receiving the money or the honor in advance. They declined giving him a 500 ruble advance.

As to his earlier questions, the Breitkopf clerk was mistaken about the score. However, Konyus's transcription had been, it is revealed, lost in the mail en route to the printer in Leipzig. Scriabin answered Groes directly on 12 November, 1906: "I am surprised and grieved. I don't know what to do. You know how serious this is. It not only means time wasted for the committee and me, but what a disturbing shock for Lev Eduardovich . . . he spent five months on it and poured his soul into it. How could it have happened that you only learned of the loss a month ago? Surely you don't send valuable packages without being instantly informed of their safe arrival! I understand Konyus's agitation . . . What action is the committee going to take, and is Lev Eduardovich agreeable to doing it all over again?"

He writes in such excitement to Liadov's good news that he puts the month as December instead of November: "A word before leaving Europe to thank you again for your dear and cordial attitude. You cannot imagine the joy I felt telling me of the prize and the committee sending the money so quickly, particularly after the earlier letter which was so sad. I know full well how this was your doing, or rather the result of all your trouble on my behalf. I give you my profound gratitude . . . I kiss you."

But for all the exchange of affectionate words and "tender love," when a relationship has been so strained, it cannot bear another stress. Scriabin's return to Belaieff would prove to be temporary.

✐ X ✐
"THE POEM OF ECSTASY"

27

WAY BACK in July of 1904 Scriabin mentioned to Morozova that "a short exposition of my doctrine is to be published as a booklet, and so will the commentary on the Third Symphony." The "exposition" turned out to be a doctrinal poem. Its words and ideas were first formulated in the Swiss Notebook of 1904. Within a year the "text or program" of the Fourth Symphony, "The Poem of Ecstasy," Op. 54, had evolved.

The inception was dogma, but by December, 1904, the project had become more literary. A letter to Tatyana at this time reads with a poet's enthusiastic ecstasy:

> I have just written a monologue with the most divine colors. Again I am swept up by an enormous wave of creativity. I choke for breath, but oh, what bliss! I am creating divinely. I am working out a new style, and what joy it is to see it take shape so well! The very meter kindles the meaning. Sometimes the poem's effect is so potent that no content is needed. I am expressing what will be one and the same as music. I am writing it for you, my dearest joy!

If the Third Symphony was to have been a "manifestation," the Fourth was a "manifesto." However, behind this distillation of Scriabin's world-view there was something blunt—sex. The first draft in the Italian Note-book of 1905 labels the composition "Orgiastic Poem" (*Poème Orgiaque*). "Orgiastic" meant to Scriabin "orgasmic." Some of the actual passages of the poem are explicit, and so are the central pages of the music score (measures 507–530), marked "with a voluptuousness becoming more and more ecstatic" (*avec une volupté de plus en plus extatique*), although the line between physical and religious ecstasy has been blurred.

126

The word-outline of the "Orgiastic Poem" supposes a symphony of four movements, each with three to eight themes of specific designation and meaning:

I

1) Theme—sweetness of dreaming, the winged Spirit or Soul, desire to create, fatigue, thirst for the unknown
2) Flight to the heights of active negation or denial, Creativity
3) Elements of dejection caused by doubt
4) Endeavor of the conquering will
5) Man-God
6) Tranquility in motion

II

1) Spirit gives itself to love-dreams
2)
3) Doubt suddenly bursts in and the spirit is downcast
4) Protest is born
5) Struggle
6) Freedom in love and knowledge of oneness
7) Liberating yearnings burgeon
8) Man-God

III

1)
2)
3)
4)
5) Unification of the emotion of protest with the sweetness of dreaming
6) Last phase of the struggle, freedom coming with love

IV

1) Man-God. Knowledge of aimlessness, purposelessness. Free play. Intoxication with freedom. Knowledge of unity or oneness.
2) Consciousness of the world as appearances.
3) That which depressed spirit now rouses it into activity.

Such was the conception of the "Poem of Ecstasy," perhaps Scriabin's most famous symphony, which in final form consists of one movement lasting less than half-an-hour. It, together with its accompanying poem of three hundred brief lines, took nearly three years to perfect. Never had he worked so carefully, and many of his letters of 1905 refer to it. On arriving in Bogliasco he wrote Vera on 19 June, "I have begun composing. The heat doesn't bother me a bit. By the way, it is a fourth symphony . . ." Sometimes he worked on the stone table in the garden under the blazing Italian sun.

Nemenova-Lunz described the intensity of the "Orgiastic Poem" as she first knew it: "He worked with unusual ferocity and surprised me by his perseverance. Such hard qualities little matched his delicate appearance. In speaking of the non-musical elements at the root of this composition, Alexander Nikolaevich would get excited, his face changed, and he would repeat, 'This will be unlike anything I have ever done so far. It will be as I feel and see now—a great joy, an enormous festival . . .' "

Even when he broke the Bogliasco summer with a visit to Vera, he still could not stem the flow. He wrote Tatyana on 3 July, "I am changing the second theme of the poem for another more passionate one. It is exceptionally beautiful and broad . . ." Here he referred to the slow, third theme "*soavamente*" for clarinet (measures 19–22) (he still mixes Italian and French terminology).

On 6 August in writing to Morozova he made passing mention of his "ultimate work" (meaning the Mysterium), but said "I am working out a poem for orchestra. It is even bigger than the 3rd Symphony and prepares the soul to receive my next composition." On the 19th: "By the time of your arrival I will perhaps have finished my Poème Orgiaque and will play it for you." But he reaches a block. On 5 November he tells her, "Still I have not finished the Poème Orgiaque. Sometimes I think I will never get to the end. Fortunately, rain keeps me indoors . . ." Next day he wrote Vera, "I work a lot, but not well. I feel so tired. I just can't finish the Poème Orgiaque . . ." Tatyana herself expressed it mildly in a letter to Morozova of 4 December, 1905, "His Poème Orgiaque doesn't satisfy him yet."

The removal to Switzerland broke the hampering spell. 16 January, 1906, he wrote Tatyana, "I have composed some good little things for piano and also some verses." 19 February he told Nemenova-Lunz that "I have an Erard piano and am composing divinely," and a month later to Morozova, "I'll soon have the text of the Poème Orgiaque finished."

From Servette, an important letter dated 15 February is addressed to the music critic Emil Medtner (1872–1936). Medtner has started a new magazine *The Golden Fleece* in collaboration with some of the most exalted names in the history of Russian arts—painters Benoit, Bakst, Bilibin, Vrubel, Ivanov, Roerich, Serov, Sudbinin; writers, Andreev, Balmont, Blok, Bunin, Voloshin, Kuprin; and musician Rebikov. Medtner (not his brother Nikolai) invited Scriabin to write a regular music column.

Scriabin's answer is particularly graceful. He is flattered by the honor and the confidence expressed in him. He would like "to set out in search of the golden fleece in the company of such distinguished men," and will certainly write some articles about music, provided no date is fixed and the writing can be "casual." He can undertake nothing regular or fixed, because it would take too much time and distract him from his "main work." And he adds another more rejective reason, "The realms where I now study have no direct connection with music."

He wrote to Morozova again in March, 1906, "That text of the Poème Orgiaque will soon be ready," but added, "I will print it here as a separate pamphlet. This will cost only a trifle. I will send you a copy right away." In May he wrote her: "I already wrote you, haven't I, that I have finished the text to the Poème Orgiaque, and I want to have it printed here, as I am afraid to send the manuscript to Russia. Letters and packages get lost all the time. In any case it is very short, 10 pages, and it only costs a few francs to print . . ."

Between this letter and 30 May, 1906, the designation "Orgiastic Poem" had been dropped in favor of the "Poem of Ecstasy" (*Le Poème de l'Extase*). It was printed in Russian in an edition of five hundred copies by the Imprimerie Centrale on the Boulevard James-Fazy in Geneva. "Orgy," he felt, conjured up Venusberg or Walpurgisnacht music, and by altering the title ambiguously, Scriabin actually professed his philosophical and physical goal more wisely. Scriabin instantly sent copies (costing one franc each) to all his friends, including his aging Aunt Lyubov, who understood not a word of it.

Scriabin wrote Morozova on 9 September, "Yes, yes, I am delighted that my little pamphlet pleased you. All the more in that it outlines the main points of my view of the world. Pity is, I published it without commentary. It needs one for full comprehension."

In the Findeizen letter of 26 December, 1907, in speaking of his Mysterium he cites the "Poem of Ecstasy." "All I can say is that an idea of the content I want to give my main composition can be gleaned from the 'Poem of Ecstasy.' (Its text needs in turn a commentary, and I may publish such a thing separately.)" He never did, however. Later when arrangements for the first performance are being made in Petersburg between the Belaieff firm and conductor Blumenfeld, Scriabin is emphatic to Artsybushev: "I want the brochure of the Poem of Ecstasy sold in the lobby. If need be, I will send you several hundred copies." But regarding the actual printing, he changes his mind about this magisterium of the symphony: "No, I do not think the text should be printed with the score. Conductors who want to perform the Poem of Ecstasy can always be apprised that it has such a thing, but in general I would prefer for them to approach it first as pure music."

From the Swiss Notebook of 1905 the "I am God" declarations are truncated into a single "I am." Between the draft of the "Orgiastic Poem" and the finished text of the "Poem of Ecstasy," the Man-God disappears, only Spirit or Soul remains as a single thread throughout. The quotation marks around the hortatory middle section is still the voice of the impalpable prophet (Scriabin the Man-God as Ecstasy) guiding the disembodied Spirit naked in its unsheathed power. He has created Spirit, and by his strength gives all little spirits strength that they may become like His Spirit. All concludes in ravishment, sensation, irresponsible play, Ecstasy.

Spirit runs a strange gamut of feelings before reaching the assertion of freedom in the great "I am." The sting of serpents and the bite of hyenas (lines which caused Scriabin some ridicule: "How does he know what *that* feels like?" Muscovites chided) are part of the painful passage to Scriabin's orgasm and spirituality and . . . unconsciousness. The seizure of the world is in pain and pleasure, enveloped in aromas and touches, light and delight.

Schloezer answered one curious question which concerned the parallel yet mutually exclusive construction of the two Poems of Ecstasy. He wrote that from 1904 when "working as a poet again"—and at a time when certainly his musical yield was minimal—"he did not dare work on a musico-poetic unit. He feared losing the independence of his poetry. When he began working on the music, he was not concerned with matching the text precisely or strictly. The words did not comment on the music, and likewise, the music was not an illustration of the words."

Schloezer expanded this point for the *RMG*, 17 February, 1908:

> Scriabin and I worked together comparing text and music. I remember the
> pleasure and surprise he felt when the music was fully free yet followed the
> development of the text...

Scriabin loved his Poem. He would read passages of it to friends even
many years after his interest had changed from this aspect of his philosophy. He would say, "I would not write it this way now, however,
it was an experiment... but listen to its new rhythms."

28

THE POEM OF ECSTASY

Spirit,
Winged with thirst for life,
Is drawn into flight
On the summits of negation.
There, under the rays of its dream,
Emerges a magical world
Of heavenly forms and feelings
  Spirit playing,
  Spirit desiring.
Spirit creating all with a dream.
Surrenders to the bliss of love.
Mid the risen creations
It dwells in languor,
  From the height of inspiration
Calls them to flower.
And drunken with soaring
It is ready to sink into oblivion.

  But suddenly . . .
Trembling presentiments
Of dark rhythm
Break rudely into
This enchanted world,
  But only for an instant.
With light increase
Of divine will
It dispels

Frightening phantoms.
And it attained
Only desired victory
Over itself.
  Spirit playing,
  Spirit caressing,
Spirit calling hope of joy
Surrenders to the bliss of love.
Mid the flowers of its creation,
It lingers with a kiss
Over a whole world of titillation
Summons it to ecstasy.
Intoxicating it with breaths
Dazzling it with beauty
It is transported, it tittups,
Dances and whirls;
With a whole range of sensations
It is tormented, wearied.
Ready to sink into oblivion
  But again . . .

From mysterious wombs
The spirit confused
A formless host
Of savage terrors
Rises stormily
In menacing waves;

It threatens
All to submerge.

  Spirit,
Winged with thirst for life,
Is drawn into flight
On the summits of negation.
There, under the rays of its dream,
Emerges a magical world
Of heavenly forms and feelings.
  Spirit playing,
  Spirit suffering,
Spirit creating grief by doubt
Succumbs to love's torment
Mid the flowers of its creations
It lingers in torment,
  With whole earth shakings.
Calls them to death.
Seized with fear,
It is ready to sink into oblivion
  But then . . .

Bright presentiments
Of shining rhythms
Awake within it.
Sweet moment!
With rays of hope
Radiant again
It burns for life.
And marvelously attained
Is the power
  Of divine will.
It pierces
The dark abysses
With glowing glances,
It shouts with rage
And fury . . .
The battle blazes.
Yawning caverns
Of monster mouths
Flash menacingly
Passionate lightning streaks
Of divine will,
  All-conquering;
Radiant reflections

Of magical light
Illumine the world.

  Spirit,
Forgetting the beloved goal,
Drunkenly yields the struggle.
All enraptured,
Fully delighted
With free
Godlike play
The struggle of love.
In the divine loftiness
Of pure aimlessness,
In combining
Opposing desires
In single awareness,
One love.
Spirit learns
Its divine essence.
It knows that
Which desired struggle;
It desired only,
  And events
  Assembled round
  This wish
In harmonious order
Capricious emotion.
  Spirit,
Playing, changing
Vibrates the universe
Explaining
Affirming.
Desirous of victories,
It was victorious,
It is triumphant!
And to its beloved realm,
Joyous, it can return now.
But what darkens
The glorious moment?

ALAS!
IT HAS ATTAINED ITS
  PURPOSE.
It longs for past struggle.
Instantly it feels

Boredom, melancholy and emptiness.

But with thirst of life,
Again it is winged
Is drawn into flight
On the summits of negation.
There, under the rays of its dream
Emerges a magical world
Of heavenly forms and feelings.
And tormented by nothing
It can eternally
Surrender to
Favored dreaming

But why, O rebellious Spirit,
Again is Thy rest perturbed?
No disturbing rhythm
Overshadows Thee,
No dreadful phantoms
Haunt.
Only monotony's
Infecting poison,
The maggot of satiety
Devours feeling
With sickly cry
The universe resounds:
  Something else!
  The new!
Wearied of pleasure
Worn with pleasure
But not with life,
Spirit lifts into flight
To the kingdoms of grief and suffering.
And in its free return
To the world of dream and of excite-
ment
It comprehended miraculously
The idea of evil's
Mysterious abysses.
Again the dark caverns
Gape open
Again the mouths threaten to swallow
Again battle,
The girding of will
The wish to conquer all.

Again victory, again intoxication,
  And rapture
  And satiety.
With this increasing rhythm
Beats the pulse of stronger life!

O my world, my life,
My blossoming, my ecstasy!
Your moments each by each
I create by negation
Of earlier experience.
  I am forever
  Negation
  Again and
  Ever anew!
  More powerful
  Tenderer
  New torture,
  Fresh beatitude.

Delighting in this dance,
Choking in its vortex.
Unmindful of goals
Beloved aspirations
Spirit surrenders to playful
  drunkenness.
On powerful wings
  It speeds
Into realms of new discovery
Of Ecstasy.

In this endless change,
In this purposeless, godlike flight
  Spirit comprehends itself
  By its might of will,
  Alone, free
  Ever-creating.
  All-illumining
  All-lifegiving
  Divine play
  In multiplicity of forms:
  It knows itself
  As the palpitation of life,
  The wish to burgeon
  In the struggle of love.

Spirit playing
Spirit fluttering
By its enduring longing
Creating Ecstasy
Gives itself up to Love's thrill
Mid the flowers of its creations
It lives in freedom.

"I summon you to life,
Hidden longings!
  You, sunken
  In the somber depths
  Of creative spirit,
  You timid embryos
  Of life,
  To you I bring
  Daring!

Now, you are free!
Fragment and flower
Separately
Rise up one against another
Flee to the summits
That in sweetest bliss
You may know all your oneness
Annihilated within me!
Rise up one against another,
Strike against me,
Negate your love!
Turn against me, all people and
  elements,
All horrors lift up your heads
Try to destroy me,
Caverns of dragons' mouths
Serpents twist round me
Constrict me and bite me!

When all rises
  Against me,
  Then I begin
  My
  Play.

O waiting world,
Weary world!
You are thirsting to be created

You seek the creator.
Your tender sweet sigh,
  Calling
Has been wafted to me.
  I will come.
Already I dwell in you
O world of mine!

With mysterious delights
Of unknown feelings,
With myriads of dream and vision,
With inspiration's flame
With Truth seeking
With the forbidden wish
Of divine freedom.
O my beloved world,
  I shall come.
Your dream of me
Is being born
It is I.
Already I am manifest
In mysterious presence
  A barely perceptible
  Breath of freedom.
  Lightly,
  A wisp of dream
  The wave
Of my being
Has already seized you.
You are quivering already
I am your beloved freedom,
You my beloved world!

  I am come
  To dazzle you
  With the marvel
  Of enchantment repeated;
  I bring you
  The magical shiver
  Of scorching love
And unimaginable caresses.
Surrender to me in all faith!
I will drown you in oceans of bliss
And beloved kisses
And great heaving waves

But in our remoteness playing
Only the spray
Envelops you
And you insanely desire
    Something else!
    The new!

And then in torrents of flowers
I will lie upon you
With aromas and scents
I will bask languidly
In this play of fragrance
Now tender, now sharp
In the play of touches,
Now soft, now harsh
    And sinking into passion
You will
    Whisper:
    Again and
    Ever again!

Then I will plunge
With a horde of fearsome monsters
With savage torment and terror
I will crawl upon you with verminous
    nests of snakes
And will bite and choke you!
And you will want me
More madly, more passionately.
Then I will lie upon you
Under rays of celestial suns
And you will burn with the fires
    Of my emotion
    The holy
    Flames of desire
For the sweetest,
The most forbidden,
Most mysterious.

And all of you become a single wave
Of liberty and joy.
Multiplicity has created you.
Legions of feelings
Have elevated you
O pure desires,
I create you,
This complex unity
    This feeling of bliss
Seizes you completely.

I am the instant illumining eternity
    I am the affirmation.
    I am Ecstasy."

    The universe
    Is embraced in flames
Spirit at the summit of its being
Feels
Endless tides
Of divine power
Of free will.
Emboldened,
That which menaced
    Is now seduction
That which frightened
    Is now pleasure.
And the bites of panther and hyena
Are new caresses
    And the serpent's sting
Is but a burning kiss.

And thus the universe resounds
    With joyful cry
    I AM!

The "Poem of Ecstasy" as music sings one theme. Scriabin once said to Ivan Lipaev, "When you listen to 'Ecstasy' look straight into the eye of the Sun!" The brass—and the score requires eight horns in F, five trumpets in B flat, three trombones and tuba—timidly announces this theme of self-affirmation, a short ascending melody in fourths (T. 103) "*avec une noble et douce majesté*" (with noble and sweet majesty). It continues through all the vicissitudes of doubt and terror described in the poem's text, until it triumphs over the giantesque total orchestra climax of all instruments full blast. Its musical tension produces the resounding "I am," the orgiastic climax.

Its free sonata form consists of an exposition and development, with reprise and development almost identically paralleling each other. Harmonically, the entire composition sounds like a continuous suspension of dominant ninths, elevenths, twelfths. Passively languorous and emaciated at times, twisting and turning, dramatically fearful at others (the hyena bites and the serpent stings), strongly and unrelentingly building and increasing, slowing down only to speed, softening so as to harden, and passing through shudders of fleeting ravishment to the ear, *moderato avec délice* (with delight), *presque en délire* (almost deliriously)), moments marked *charmé* (as if enchanted), the "Poem of Ecstasy" continues unabated towards the beginning (T. 507) of the orgasm with the clarinet sweetly singing, and finishes in spirit and in flesh. All color disappears here. Only volume remains (the score calls for a pipe organ). Then a brief coda of weariness, and the end sees the composition's final resolution into C major.

XI

AMERICA

29

MODEST ALTSCHULER, Scriabin's cellist classmate at the Conservatory, and his businessman brother Jacob, suffering under the discriminatory atmosphere of Tsarist Russia, left their country in 1903. For the very reasons that would have kept the talented Altschulers home, Safonoff also exited to America.

Altschuler in America according to Engel:

> —put himself in a conspicuous and worthwhile position. He organized his own orchestra composed primarily of Jewish musicians who had like himself, emigrated. It was later to flourish, but in 1906 and 7 it barely existed. The pay for the musicians was scraped up any old how, even during intermissions. With it, however, Altschuler founded the Russian Symphony Society of New York whose concerts propagandized Russian music successfully.

Altschuler's orchestra, managed by the brother, aimed at "transplanting to the United States the musical culture thriving in Russia." By 1906 Altschuler was able to advertise in Moscow papers for orchestral scores. Morozova sent Scriabin the clipping, but his pride and modesty prevented him from answering. Someone else, probably Morozova again, suggested to Altschuler a formal invitation. He wrote, and Scriabin accepted.

Altschuler and Safonoff worked in close conjunction. The conductor of the Philharmonic could not invite Russians without fear of being accused of "favoritism," but he helped see that through Altschuler pianists Lhevinne, Rachmaninoff and Scriabin of Moscow came, as well as those Petersburg pianists, Hofmann and Gabrilovich, tenor Ivan Alchevsky, and violinist Alexander Petchnikoff.

Altschuler hired Carnegie Hall for his concerts, and Safonoff lent his prestige to fellow-Russians on every possible occasion. He conducted for Lhevinne's American debut on 17 January, 1906, in Rubinstein's Fifth Concerto. Although the Philharmonic forbade encores, the Russian orchestra allowed them. On this occasion Lhevinne played Scriabin's Nocturne, and Scriabin in America became known as "the composer for left hands." Safonoff told the press, "Of all contemporary composers, I recommend to you Alexander Scriabin. He is the most noteworthy."

In October, 1906, Scriabin cabled Jacob Altschuler authorizing him as his concert representative. At the same time he sent a letter answering various of Modest Altschuler's questions:

> I have just received your good letter, dear friend, and was very touched by all your concern for my success in America. Do not accept any engagements which pay so little that I would be embarrassed. You understand this, of course... I would like for my concerts to be as close to each other as possible, so that I will not have to be in America too long. I have ordered some photographs. I am very sorry, but I have sent all my reviews to other impresarios... Perhaps I can get a copy of L'Illustration which has my biography in it. Once again I send you my gratitude and sincere devotion.

What kind of an America would meet Scriabin? There was an undercurrent of anti-Russian sentiment that extended even into music. The powerful critic, Henry E. Krehbiel (1854–1923) of the *New York Daily Tribune*, an anti-Revolution conservative, had raised the question of where the money for Altschuler's Russian Symphony Society came from. He taunted this innocuous organization for its small attendance, lavish performances, and extravagantly imported performers. "It may very well be," he wrote ominously, "that there are higher influences than is generally suspected back of the movement to acquaint the Occidental world with the artists and art of the great empire of the Czar." When Altschuler and Rachmaninoff announced a joint tour of the larger cities of America (the plan fell through for lack of funds), Krehbiel renewed his question: "How could so expensive a venture even be contemplated?"

New York City was pretty much of an opera town. One night in December, 1906, someone counted that at that moment 6,702 people were listening to opera. Doings of stars made front pages; Nordica, Eames,

Gadski, Sembrich, Schumann-Heink were golden names. One night Melba earned $14,000; Farrar sang her first Marguerite and 2,000 people were turned away.

Religion, too, was a national preoccupation in America of those years. Mark Twain's book on Christian Science was a best seller. Mrs. Eddy, founder of the Christian Science movement, was being brought to court by her children for mental incompetence. Fakirs and fakers from India attracted throngs who listened to the message that money is pursued at the price of the true Self.

Now, the American public was to have a mystic-musician. Scriabin would bring philosophy from Russia. The time was right in one sense, but in another, the hard-boiled critics, Richard Aldrich (1863-1937) of the *Times*, Henry Theophilus Finck (1854-1926) of the *Post*, James Gibbons Huneker (1860-1921) and William James Henderson (1855-1937) of the *Sun*, and Leonard Liebling (1874-1945) of the *Musical Courier*, and, of course, Krehbiel, who was suspicious of everything foreign, regarded new musical messages with cautious reserve.

30

ON SATURDAY afternoon, 1 December, 1906, Scriabin sailed second-class from Rotterdam on the Holland-American steamship, the "Ryndam." The parting from Tatyana was particularly painful. She had fallen ill again. Scriabin was leaving her and the child in Amsterdam in the company of aunts and a cousin, Francine, who was married to a pleasant man called Morello.

The music of the "Poem of Ecstasy" was still crucial. It figured prominently in his letters, and there can be little question but that he was distressed at embarking while not having entirely finished the manuscript. But he was off to America to come back rich. He made it clear that Tatyana was indispensable to his music and psychic strength. However, the composing he began in America disputed this. He himself excused or explained it by the mental connection between them, telepathy, and her astral presence. He now believed they functioned together on a "higher plane" (a word he borrowed from Theosophy) and she in turn thought "as one with him."

Tatyana was unable even to come as far as the Amsterdam railway station to see him off for Rotterdam. His letters began instantly they are apart. After Bogliasco he addressed his letters to "Mme. Scriabine."

My dearest star. 3 minutes before the train leaves. Don't be sad, my little soul. Time will pass quickly, quickly. Kiss your aunts warmly and thank them once more for me. Take care of the money. Give it to your aunt for safekeeping. Farewell, my angel.

I write, as you see, from the steamer.

The steamer is excellent, huge, and very comfortable.
My soul. I think of you all the time. Be sensible and take care of yourself. You are your beloved's only treasure. In case of fire, don't even think of RISKING YOURSELF for the Poème de l'Extase. Better 10 poems of ecstasy be destroyed, than have your dear little face singed!

Be happy and live in the thought of our reunion. Time will pass fast, and this old billy-goat will return with his pouch stuffed with money. Then we will never again be separated.

His next two letters written on the "Ryndam" were not posted until the boat docked at Hoboken, New Jersey, on Tuesday, 11 December, 1906.

...I am with you all the time, my angel. I lie alone in my cabin and think of you my treasure. I lie down, because the boat pitches and tosses. Winter is always like this, they say.

How are you? My marvelous miracle, how I want to see you at the very soonest! I am constantly living in this hope. I feel so uneasy about you! Take care of yourself, my star, take care of your tired little heart.

UNDERSTAND THIS: I NEED YOU, if only you knew, stupid girl, how necessary you are to me!

Do not be too economical. If you or your mother want something, buy it.

The boat rocks. The slow motion is the worst of all. If it tires you to write to me, don't write MUCH but OFTEN. I cannot read what I have written. Forgive me, but the boat is rocking. I am sick.

Tasinka, my dear infant! In less than 24 hours I'll be in the New World! How time drags! Each hour is an eternity. The people on board are choice—both in kindness and stupidity. I have never experienced anything like it.

It is good that the boat is rocking and rolling. Much pleasanter than the company of these degenerates. It gives me a pretext to go to my cabin and exchange one great evil for a lesser one.

However, I am very wicked. These people have shown me nothing but the greatest kindness and affection. One evening I played in the saloon on a magnificent Steinway upright, and then became a "victim" of an unending ovation of rapturous applause. Each person felt it his duty to express personally his surprise and to pose me a series of questions about my "creativity." From this experience I have learned that success does not always bring with it delight. But none of this matters. May it be thus throughout my whole stay in the New World. Later we can make up for it one hundredfold.

I leave you now, Tasinka. I will pack my trunk. Tomorrow at 9 in the morning we face the American customs, and all has to be ready.

We have just arrived. Altschuler and an American met me and both were infinitely kind and sweet. I hasten to post this letter.

He gives Steinway Hall as his address. From the boat Scriabin sent two telegrams to Tatyana: one to say that he had arrived safely, and the other to ask her to cable him as to her health.

Altschuler and J. E. Francke, a free-lance concert manager from Steinway Hall and the man appointed to assist Scriabin during his time in America, met him at the pier. It was snowing, but Scriabin carried his hat in his hand.

Francke had done his work well. There were also reporters there. One from *Musical America* wrote that "his appearance has every indication of the scholar. He was reticent about expressing his impressions of American music. Wagner and Chopin, he said, were his favorite composers." Others asked him his opinions of Tolstoi, the Russo-Japanese War, and Gorky. The photographers photographed his left hand, "the nocturne's hand," as Scriabin said in English, and next day the papers announced the arrival of the "Cossack Chopin."

Altschuler and Francke installed Scriabin in the comfortable Lafayette-Brevoort Hotel on Fifth Avenue at Eighth Street. En route, Scriabin fell in love with New York and was impressed with the skyscrapers, but plunged into an account of his marital difficulties. "Modest," he began, "I must tell you everything, everything, in order to feel better . . ."

Altschuler arranged a reception at the Waldorf-Astoria in Scriabin's honor for 13 December, to be attended by "officers and members of the Drawing Room Club." A week later on Thursday, 20 December, he was to make his American debut with orchestra, and a solo recital possibly later. Those were the plans so far. Scriabin had come three thousand miles with nothing more than a guarantee of living expenses and one confirmed, non-paying engagement.

12 December, he wrote Tatyana:

> Again today no letter from you! How boring of you!
>
> Look here! Write oftener! If by this evening there still isn't a word from you, I will be furious!
>
> I am in frightful commotion here. I wrote you that Altschuler met me with an American. He is to be, it seems, my adjutant! He comes with me everywhere and yesterday evening he even took me to Safonoff and stayed there until it was time to fetch me home.
>
> About Safonoff. He is dearer than ever. He suggests that he will accompany me in the Concerto and replace Altschuler at the Russian Symphony (he conducts the Philharmonic). If the Concerto is a success then I will repeat it with the Philharmonic Society orchestra. As you see, things aren't going too badly so far.
>
> I am besieged by newspapermen. There were 2 of them this morning. They ask idiotic questions such as "What do you think of opera?" or "Has the Revolution had an effect on Russian composers?" The worst part is they fling all these ideas at you so suddenly and skip all logical sequence. One of the better ones is a lady of some years, a local poetess. She is more intelligent than the others. She asked about my philosophy and was deeply interested in it. She is writing a long article about the main points of the 3rd Symphony and the Poem of Ecstasy.
>
> Safonoff said there was nothing to be afraid of with the Americans. You can say what you like so long as what you say is not a direct or obvious infringement on their bourgeois well-being.
>
> Incidentally, Tasinka, imagine what lengths they go to to preserve their peace of mind. They EVICTED Gorky from this very hotel when they learned from the newspapers that the individual he had come with was not his wife!! Other hotels would not take him in! Think of that. We might have had the same thing happen to us. But what morals here! It's ghastly.
>
> Altschuler says that if Gorky had had a different whore in his room every day, and they had known ALL about that, they wouldn't have thought a thing of it or persecuted him to such an extent. That would have been natural. However, it is considered a crime now to live faithfully with a beloved woman out of wedlock.

I'll tell you more tomorrow. I kiss you, my precious and love you to the point of madness.

I am now taking the score [Concerto] to Safonoff. Tasyuka, when will I finally see your dear handwriting?

14 December

My little soul, my angel, thank you! What a joy your tender letter was for me! Small matter that you only cried once. It consoles my little heart to know that you miss me. Now I need no more of it, you hear? Do not *dare* to be sad any longer!

You know I am now terribly busy. I have to play and I have to talk to the reporters, go to concerts, make visits, but I don't forget you, not for a minute. I am doing all this for my Tusika. The more money I earn the more we can rest after all these perturbations. Now I want to take a trip with you after America. I dream of this all the time. Tuska, I am sending you the most stupid article by one reporter. He grasped nothing of what I said, twisted everything and wrote dreadful nonsense. Next time I'll send you other papers. There are articles about me every day.

A publisher here printed a thousand copies of my nocturne for left hand and it is already sold out. They play it on the player piano and my popularity is great but "on what a plane"!!!

Today they are photographing me in 1,000 poses.

17 December

Tasyuka, I am out of my mind with worry. 4 days and nothing from you. If I don't get any word today then I will telegraph you tomorrow. I have just come from rehearsing. The accompaniment was not very good because they were reading from handwritten notes.

My recital is on the 3rd of January. At the Symphony, besides the Concerto I will play a few short things. The left hand of course.

19 December

Tasichek. The concert is tomorrow. I smother my emotions, my dear, and try to think that all will go well. If it does not, will you stop loving me?

He sent her a near-hysterical telegram, though he can ill afford it:

AVOID CHILLS ABSTAIN FROM UNBOILED WATER.

31

On the night of 20 December, 1906, after the concert (which included Glazunov's Third Symphony and Rachmaninoff's "Gypsy Caprice"), William R. Steinway (1881–1960) gave a stag supper party in honor of Scriabin at the Café Lafayette in the Brevoort Hotel. Altschuler treasured the menu—handwritten in French and itemizing snails, sweetbreads and "bourgeois" onions—autographed by all the guests: W. Safonoff, Altschuler's brother, Lhevinne, and Ernest Urchs (1864–1928) in charge of Steinway's concert and artist department. Scriabin's signature cut across the *hors d'oeuvres*.

Next day Scriabin cabled Tatyana "Great Success." The day following he reported more fully:

... after the concert I was with Safonoff and the Altschuler brothers in a restaurant almost until morning. We drank a lot and I got up at noon dead. They are now dragging me by brute force somewhere. I spend all my time in somebody's house or at some club or other, and I do not know whose or where. I do not even know my hosts' names half the time. It is always the director of the Philharmonic or the Russian Symphony or musicians or just plain people all of whom, according to Altschuler, are useful for future concerts. Yesterday, between two engagements I managed to send you a telegram. I had hoped to write you before dinner, but what happened was that I did not dine at all and half-dead from hunger I was taken to Carnegie Hall for a Philharmonic concert where one of the directors had invited me into his box. I simply cannot orient myself and no matter how I arrange it I am always late wherever I go. What misery it all is!

Now, Tasyushenka, my daffodil, my dear, things seem to have sorted themselves out, more or less. I still don't know what the future holds. However, besides the recital in New York there is nothing definitely settled, but my success (BIG) according to Safonoff and Altschuler is a guarantee that engagements in the future will come.

I was more nervous than ever before, but played well despite. The piano, they say, sounded magical. After the Concerto, for the second part, I played the Nocturne for left hand, a mazurka and the D♯ minor étude. My soul, they are bothering me again. The phone is ringing.

The reviews were contradictory. Many were favorable; none was prophetic of future Scriabin:

The New York Daily Tribune. H. E. Krehbiel. 21 December, 1906

A kind sympathy for the work is invited by its directness and the absence from it of the unmeaning and pompous padding which fills so many pages in latter-day concertos. It has a spirited and rhythmically energetic finale, too, in which the solo instrument struggles valiantly against the orchestra, but is overwhelmed by the brazen cohorts at the end.

The Sun. W. J. Henderson.

The first movement of the concerto has one great merit. It is short . . . a very pretty and fragile piece of salon music.

. . . The last movement is not either polite or pretty and it compels the pianist to smite the keyboard very rudely indeed. The sentimental slow movement seemed to delight the audience . . .

Musical Courier. Leonard Liebling.

Mr. Scriabine's concerto is an eloquent, musicianly work, written with serious purpose, and not given to the slightest degree to meretricious display or catchpenny jingle of melody. The piano is given rather a subordinate role in the opening movement, which is treated in the symphonic style Brahms first made the fashion for modern concertos. Scriabine, however, is gifted with more direct expression than Brahms possessed.

The whole work is undeniably interesting, and has about it a flavor of freshness which speaks well for the originality of its composer. Mr. Scriabine played his concerto with an infectious enthusiasm which caught the fancy of the audience and won him a resoundingly cordial reception.

The New York Evening Sun.

Scriabine seemed to be built of wires and nerves, and the genuine excitement with which he played his magnum opus, a piano concerto, was infectious.

He danced and bounced up and down before the keyboard, but his skill in finding little windows in his orchestration for the piano's soul to shine through was fairly the work of a master.

The New York American.

Those who welcomed Alexander Scriabine—and there were many—had some knowledge of the romantic or sentimental facts attending Scriabine's appearance at the piano with Safonoff at the conductor's desk, and there was quite a little tumult of applause when the two came on together. And indeed it was a strik-ing picture when the grim and chunky Cossack and the long-haired, scholarly Muscovite stood bowing to the enthusiastic welcome!

Mr. Scriabine's playing last night showed an elegance of style, a buoyancy and an ingeniousness that were altogether charming ... Where Scriabine is exquisite, Rosenthal is majestic; he is brilliant where Rosenthal is bewitching. As a technician, Scriabine is all but faultless.

The New York Herald.

Mr. Scriabine displayed in his own concerto a crisp, sparkling touch, a bright but small tone and taste in the use of the pedals. His style, however, had elegance rather than authority.

The New York Evening Post. Henry Theophilus Finck.

His concerto for piano is a fluently written work, lucid, concise, not remarkable for melodic invention, but brilliant and effective in parts ...

The New York Times. Richard Aldrich.

Mr. Scriabine cannot read his title clear through this concerto to enter the field of more serious composition. He is evidently ill at ease in the large form and strives with little success to fill it with an appropriate or dignified content ... his style is brilliant, crisp, and clear; but he has not, so far as he showed last evening any considerable command of richness in depth of tone.

32

THE CORRESPONDENCE with Tatyana continued and the precious score of the "Poem of Ecstasy" became a source of antagonism, even fear, between them:

28 December, 1906

Write me about Bora. Why exactly has he gone to Petersburg? What is he doing there? Why has he ventured so near the Revolution? Has he moved there permanently or only for the nonce? Are your mother and her sisters getting along?

Tasik, I can tell you some very happy news. The Poem of Ecstasy pleased Altschuler beyond all expectations and he wants to perform it as soon as possible, that is, right now. He begs me to have the score copied and have it sent to him. Now do not get carried away!

It is *IMPOSSIBLE* to do this at present, and here are the reasons: First, I will not give it, that is you will not give it UNDER ANY CIRCUMSTANCES to anyone except to be copied *AT HOME.* That means you must find someone who is willing to come to your aunt's house. This would be either difficult to arrange or insanely expensive. Second, in its present condition the score is virtually undecipherable. I have not marked the instrumentation, the keys, the signs, etc. Even the devil himself would split his skull working over it. But no matter. He can perform it in the SPRING. As soon as I get back I will finish it and copy it out. *DON'T TAKE IT INTO YOUR HEAD TO DO IT!!!* I will copy it myself. You would see after 10 minutes on it that you would not get anywhere with it. We will be able to talk about this in a few weeks. How I regret I cannot say for you to go ahead with it. How foolish I was . . .

So many acquaintances that I have absolutely no time at all. A few days ago there was an opening of an exhibition and I left with more than 30 visiting cards in my pocket! . . .

I am in despair!! Why did I write you about the Poem. I am *out of my mind* with fear that you will think about transcribing it. Remember, it would be *MURDER* for you to sit in a bent-over position for so long!!!! Besides you cannot! I cannot write another letter to you. There isn't time, and I do not want to leave you without news. Be a good girl! Surely you will do that much for me!

Tatyana's mother had encouraged her son Boris to go to Petersburg where he could find employment more easily than in Belgium. He was not married, but he had to become self-supporting since his father's death. What Scriabin did not know was that already in May, 1901, Boris had pledged his loyalty to the Tsar. He would thus be quite safe during this period of reaction to the Revolution, nor would he run afoul of the revolutionaries who had been swallowed in the underearth of secrecy.

Soon Scriabin would help Borya. He wrote the editor of the powerful *Russian Musical Gazette,* Findeizen: "My *beau-frère,* Boris Fyodorovich Schloezer is a very talented journalist and a beautiful musician, but not a specialist . . . He could do an especially good article on musical philosophy (he's a doctor of Philosophy). I recommend him to you in fullest confidence . . ." Schloezer was hired and his first assignment was a survey of the musical and philosophical implications of Scriabin.

Francke in New York proved himself an able, if gaudy, entrepreneur. He had fancy stationery printed with Scriabin's personal letterhead ("The Noted Russian Composer-Pianist"), a dignified photograph, and a facsimile in Scriabin's marvelous calligraphy of the first two measures of a theme song—the left-hand Nocturne. His solo debut after the Concerto was scheduled for Thursday afternoon, 3 January, 1907, at the small but elegant and acoustically perfect Mendelssohn Hall, 119 West 40th Street. Tickets were being sold at the usual prices: one dollar, and a dollar and a half.

The next letters to Tatyana disclose her growing anxiety at being separated from him. Scriabin is morbidly rigid on two issues: one, that Tatyana remain in Amsterdam, leaving him alone in New York; and two, that she not meddle with his "Poem of Ecstasy." She is not even permitted to translate the text into French. (That chore will be awarded young Joseph Belleau, a Belgian adherent of Scriabin's doctrine. He put it into prose and Scriabin privately printed this French version in Lausanne.) Philosophically, a strange new covering of modesty now shrouds Scriabin's god within. He calls it "H E" in grandiose letters. No longer is *he* (the little Scriabin), god, or spirit, but H E is. Another self has taken over the inner Scriabin, but the egomania is merely recumbent.

28 December, 1906

Look at this disgrace!! The letter paper is how Francke informs New York's citizens of my recital. Please do not think this sort of thing has been done just for me. It is usual here and no one thinks a thing of it.

Do not unnerve yourself, my dear, my only treasure, my enchantment. I prostrate myself before the enormity of feeling you render him who *dwells within me*. You believe in him! H E is great, although I myself am sometimes poor, small, weak, and weary. But you truly forgive me that, for H E lives within me. I am not yet become H E but soon I shall! Have patience a little longer, and believe, believe. H E identifies himself with me. I work, and I have grown stronger. But you help me. Be strong!!!

Kiss my daughter tenderly. Now do remember that the Poem of Ecstasy cannot be performed here before March. So do not do *anything* with it. I repeat this again.

A letter describes his nervousness before a concert and how remarkably and artistically dependent he is on Tatyana's faith in him. Still he has his wits about him and does not wish Tatyana's presence. Kashperov explains Scriabin's reluctance toward Tatyana joining him as "poverty." They had not even enough money for a wet nurse. Tatyana's coming to America would abandon their child to starvation.

2 January, 1907

My recital is tomorrow. I am quite unsettled in mood, worried in fact. I am readier for concerts than I was even in Brussels; but still the demand here is for technique and technique to be better than Rosenthal, Lhevinne and all that ilk of tightrope walkers.

My soul, it is already 10 and I haven't eaten yet. I practiced for $3\frac{1}{2}$ hours nonstop . . .

3 January

My wings! Today you SERVED ME. I PLAYED VERY, VERY WELL. My little sun shed her light over me! My soul, surely you were with me today? Were you thinking about me? My success was very great, but the audience was not very great. The weather was revolting. Rain came down in buckets!

Oh Lord, what joy that you are not loving me any the less! Tasinaya, believe in my love and love me, love me. Today either new harmonies whispered new caresses to me or new caresses provided me with new harmonies. I have NOT YET FLOWERED to the full! Tusiki. Still there is more to come. Always there is more! You will hear. You will see.

Love to Ariasheckha. Never think that I don't *love* her! I WORSHIP *OUR CHILD*.

The concert went brilliantly. The critics were excellent and praised me to the skies. Now I must reap the fruits and accept engagements and give more concerts. But here's the catch. In order to go to other places, or even play in New York itself again, the next concerts have to be successful in a material sense (the first just covered expenses; I broke even). To do this I need publicity. And for that I need time. Francke tells me that if I stay here for another month, I'll make a good deal of money. And at the same time I WILL GO CRAZY FROM WORRY, if you want to come here *ON YOUR OWN*. How can my little child spend 8 or 9 days on a boat in the company of vulgar and brash people who might insult my Taska. And yet at the same time I am going out of my mind with desire to see you. Tasinka! Tasinka! What shall I do? Tell me, sunny girl! Be wise.

I will tell you one good thing. You cannot imagine how unbelievable this is! Imagine, Safonoff is on our side and he is going to write Vera about a divorce!!!

Isn't that a miracle? Ever since I've been here he has treated me like a lover. When I played him the 4th Sonata he wept tears of emotion and kept saying "it is genius . . . genius." All this is pleasant, but it COMPLICATES matters for *us*. It is unthinkable for you to come here using MY NAME. Here are people who know Vera and who wish to do me evil. On the other hand there are people here who know you as my wife.

Only one way is left. That would be to shunt you off to a side street and for you not to appear except in those places where you can appear as my wife. To do this, it seems to me, would be easy, once Vera agrees to a divorce. Tasichek, Tasyuk. What shall I do? They will ask you, why have you come to America? Have you acquaintances here? etc. What if they arrest you! Lord, what shall we do! Taseshesek, can you not be more patient? You know, everything here is 5 *times* more expensive than in Europe. I do not buy myself a *SINGLE THING. ONE DAY* costs 50 francs. I pay 4 dollars that is, 20 francs a day for a single room! Now, figure it out. You and your mother can settle for a little less, but all the same expenses are colossal! And if I go on tour, you will be sitting all alone in New York. How much will we see of each other?

If you come with your mother the tickets would be 1,000 francs! And in my opinion it would be unthinkable for you to come alone! And where will I put you! You will weep with loneliness, and I shall be quite undone! Won't it be better to wait one little week or two quietly with your aunts, instead of this TERRIBLE trip (you'll be seasick the whole time), and then you can come meet your little billy-goat and never be parted again from him!

If you are going to fall ill if you don't come then it would be better for you to come, but the trip will kill you. What will you do when the ocean rocks, my little one?

Maybe I should cancel my engagements and leave. But everyone would say what waste not to make use of the big success. Do not grieve, and wait for my next letter, no matter what.

You could say that you were coming here to take music lessons with Altschuler, or with me, or Safonoff, and that you have many acquaintances. But do not think of leaving until you get my next letter, and when you leave telegraph me the name of the ship. No matter how you try you will still be 11 days on the sea, even by fast boat!!! If you haven't enough money, borrow from your aunts, and I will send it to them. I say all this in the event you are stupid and crazy. If you are wise, you will wait just 3 weeks.

It takes *MUCH* STRENGTH for me to dissuade you from coming. You cannot begin to DREAM of how much I want to see you.

There is a hypnotist here called Feldman. I have very interesting conversations with him.

Here are excerpts from the American reviews of Scriabin's 3 January matinée recital. The program was:

Concert Allegro
Prelude and Nocturne for the Left Hand Alone
Six Preludes (Op. 11)
Three Mazurkas (Op. 3)
Sonata No. 3
Two Poems (Op. 32)
Three Etudes (Op. 8)
Waltz (Op. 38).

Musical Courier.

... Because of the dearth of good piano music since Liszt was gathered to his fathers, Scriabine's devotion to the instrument of the ivory keys should be thrice welcome, and it is so regarded by all those who know his compositions and have been following his gradual evolution from a mere imitator of Chopin to a creator of things original even if they are not great ...

The melodic sense is not too all prominent in Scriabine's compositions, but he holds the interest with his ingenious and highly cultivated manner.

The New York Evening Post.

... He played the opening number, an allegro de concert, with more body of tone than he used in his concerto. His famous prelude and nocturne for the left hand alone, he reproduced really beautifully with rich coloring ...

The general impression was that if Mr. Scriabine can curb his propensity of writing too much, he is one of the men to be reckoned with in the future.

The New York Times.

... The welcome was not by any means a demonstrative one, for he was heard by a very small audience indeed. While Mr. Scriabine is not one of the greater men of the musical movement in Russia, he is a man of gracious gifts who has done something as a composer very well worth doing.

As a pianist Mr. Scriabine has less charm than as a composer. He cannot bring out of the piano all it can offer in the way of richness, beauty, or variety of tone, nor does he always make it sing. His style is toward crispness, a little overdone, and a brilliancy that is a little hard. A more convincing interpreter than he himself is of his own music could make it sound even more ingratiating than he did.

But Safonoff was in the front row and he shouted "Bravo" all on his own several times.

33

THE AMIABLE first conductor of the recently formed Cincinnati Symphony in Ohio, Valentin Van der Stucken (1858–1929) (né Frank, born in Gillespie County, Texas, and a former pupil of Grieg), engaged Scriabin to play the Concerto twice, sandwiched between Beethoven's Fifth Symphony and Lalo's *Namouna* ballet, on 10 and 12 January, 1907. Scriabin's vacillation over Tatyana's insistence on coming to America now turned into strongest dissuasion.

In the meanwhile an ever-watchful Altschuler arranged for Scriabin to take to a cheaper hotel, the Wellington on 55th Street and Seventh Avenue, next to Altschuler's own modest apartment.

9 January, 1907, Cincinnati

Tanyuka. Here is where I now bend my efforts, my little droplet. Last year they played my *Rêverie* with great success and so my name is known. The conductor is Van der Stucken, a very sweet person and a talented musician. I hope he accompanies well. I am only afraid that one rehearsal, all they allow, is not enough.

I am afraid to tell you how much, how madly I want to see you because you might jump on a boat and turn up in New York. And I am now convinced more than ever that the climate here is not for you and that it is killing even for people stronger than you. If engagements pile up and I have to remain on for long, then I will risk sending for you, but under no circumstance come *alone*. Come with your MOTHER. Don't you dare come here alone! I won't meet you!!! I will send you back!!! As things stand I myself won't be staying here beyond the 15th of February. No, you just think about what we will do when we have some money! We can go to Italy! To Paris! We can have Ecstasy performed! Only now have I begun to see what you mean to me! Just think if it were not for you, do you think I could endure even one day of this idiotic life! There is only one side, apart from money, which comforts me a little in all this: I am becoming very well known and so it will be easier for me to propagandize my *real* compositions.

Soul, I haven't slept for two nights and tomorrow I have the rehearsal!! The concert is at 3 in the afternoon and again day after tomorrow . . . my eyes cannot see from fatigue.

I get 300 dollars for this concert, that is, 1500 francs. This is the third time here I have earned money. Yesterday I played at a salon for money (not much).

11 January

Only two words to kiss you my one and only joy and to say that yesterday and today I had a colossal success. Van der Stucken says that no one has ever been so well-received before. How good this is! Tomorrow I will send the reviews to New York, so Francke can use them to get more engagements. Maybe we will have some money! Do you understand now how happy we will be, you stupid girl? Little soul, I cannot talk much with you today. I have to pack, and tomorrow I play my two symphonies (first and third) for local musicians. Maybe they will be performed.

(On 7 February, Van der Stucken wrote Scriabin disappointingly, informing him that he could not perform the Third Symphony this season because his musicians were not yet experienced enough.)

To Tatyana:
16 January

HAVE FIRM OFFER OF ENGAGEMENTS THROUGH APRIL CONSULT DOCTOR FOR PERMISSION TO TRAVEL IN THIS CLIMATE IF AUTHORIZED COME WITH MOTHER TELEGRAPH DECISION WELLINGTON HOTEL BRING POEM OF ECSTASY CABLING 500 FRANCS TOMORROW

19 January

CONTRACT NOT SIGNED POSTPONE DEPARTURE LETTER FOLLOWS

On this day Scriabin too wrote a letter which, uniquely, has an exclamation point after almost every sentence:

Tasinka, I have some news for you which is not good! Imagine how well everything was going! Concerts in New York went brilliantly and even better in Cincinnati! Reviews were superb! I needed only to put all this to work for me and—become rich! Opportunity knocked! One management offered me a tour of 15 concerts at $150 per, that means, 750 francs each!

What could have been better! And because of Francke's stupidity the whole thing fell through! Now I am waiting for another proposal to turn up, but alas, it may not come! If within the next few days nothing is suggested, you will get a telegram announcing my return!

None of this really matters, my little bird! Do not despair! It only means we will see each other the sooner, the sooner! Once again we will be living side by side! My poor little one, somehow or other, I never seem to succeed in bringing you even a brief respite. I have only one thought and that is how hurt my little girl is—she who has already suffered because of and for me. Tasya, is it possible that I do not give you even a little happiness? Surely it cannot matter that we are poor little people now? Wait! Our fame will grow not by the day but within hours, and there will be money! Do not be sad if you have to cancel your boat ticket. I actually would be happier if you do not cross that frightful Atlantic Ocean and endanger your health in this New York climate. You cannot imagine what it's like.

28 January

You are really silly to fret when you haven't a letter from me. There is no news. However, I have some engagements, in Chicago, but not until March. I cannot afford to live here for two months although the honorarium is 150 dollars for the two concerts, but life here, you know, is dear. If nothing more comes my way, then I give up and fly back to you. If something comes, then you can come, although I AM OUT OF MY MIND WITH FEARS for you. Alone, on the boat! You will catch cold. FEBRUARY! THE ROCKING AND ROLLING! The PITCHING AND TOSSING! There will be frost in the cabin!! A DUTCH BOAT!! Not even the Express! If you are coming, however, then summon up all your prudence. I kiss you my precious!

Buy warm clothes.

As Scriabin was writing this "Don't come; Do" letter, undauntable Tatyana simply cabled him she was arriving on 7 February—alone.

She would pay for this disobedience. Altschuler described how at dinner Scriabin for no apparent reason would kick her under the table, hard and hurtfully.

Scriabin gave his repeat recital at Mendelssohn Hall on 30 January, 1907. He was still under contract to Francke, but because of his success the auspices of this recital were more distinguished—Theodore Steinway himself with, naturally, Urchs doing the management. Scriabin played:

Etudes (Op. 8, B♭ minor, A♭ major)
Preludes (Op. 15)

Impromptu (Op. 10, A major)
Prelude (Op. 11)
Mazurka (Op. 25, F major)
Prelude (Op. 17, No. 1)
Etude (Op. 8, D# minor)
Second Sonata
Album Leaf (Op. 45)
Waltz (Op. 38)
Prelude (Op. 39, No. 3)
Satanic Poem (Op. 36)
Four Preludes (Op. 33)
Waltz for the Left Hand Alone.

The demand for the waltz was so great Altschuler asked Scriabin later to send him a copy for printing in America, but Scriabin, after long thought, refused. It was the waltz Rozenov recalled and referred to earlier, and once it came up in discussion with Sabaneeff in 1911. Scriabin said in recollection:

"There was quite a to-do over me in America . . . The left-hand Nocturne always enjoyed a special success. Then and there I somehow remembered that I had composed a wickedly clever waltz for the left hand, after the manner of Strauss, full of virtuoso passages, octaves, and it was *ghastly!* I composed it so as to exercise my left hand when I was ill, and it was at a time when I was a worldly person. And so I decided to play this waltz for the Americans to see what would happen. I played it, and it brought the house down, could not have been better. Suddenly in the middle of this noise and applause, I heard one single, piercing hiss. It seems it was an acquaintance of mine, a Russian, who happened to be in town and came to hear the concert. He was expressing his disapproval for what he thought was disgraceful for me. And I too felt ashamed, and I never played the waltz again."

Here are the mixed reviews of the second New York concert, even less well-received than his first:

Musical Courier.

Alexander Scriabine's second New York recital lasted just one hour, and yet there were twenty numbers on the program.

The compositions are so short, so fragmentary, that they might aptly be termed musical epigrams. And yet, each holds a musical thought of more or less value and originality.

He is endowed with the artistic temperament, is poetic, intellectual, refined, yet is deficient in that *sine qua non* of piano playing, at which critics these days are wont to sneer—technic. It cannot be denied, however, that his playing is dainty and full of sentiment.

The audience gave the pianist a friendly greeting, and testified its pleasure. The concluding piece, a waltz for left hand, was played more effectively than any of the other numbers and was heartily encored.

Musical America.

. . . proved his masterly touch in the interpretation of a mood and his almost inexhaustible command of vivid and unhackneyed melody.

One wonders how it is that so mild-eyed an individual should be father to a Poème Satanique, but so it is, and to quite a diabolic furor did the climax ascend. . . . On each of his programs has appeared a work for "left hand only." This time it was a Valse, tremendously difficult and interesting as well.

New York Times.

. . . There are not many composers whose works can furnish forth an evening's program without danger of monotony. Mr. Scriabine is not one of these. His pieces were slight both in length and in musical intent. Many of them are lacking in originality or in striking musical thought.

New York Evening Sun.

. . . charming and there are felicitous phrases and turns of expression, as well as striking harmonic contrivances. There is often the definite expression of a mood. But they are all frankly salon music and they pall after a certain length of time.

The New York Daily Tribune.

. . . his list was made up chiefly of short pieces better fitten for enjoyment in the salon than a public concert room, but he gave central position to a piece, by courtesy called a sonata in G♯ minor . . . it made short-breathed phrases take the place of melodies, and aided by its composer's playing sounded jerky and spasmodic. But more successfully than before, Mr. Scriabine disclosed command of beautiful tonal effects.

The New York Evening Post.

. . . he appears as a competitor with modern French and German masters, in unexplored fields of harmony. As a pianist he has a fine sense of color, perspective and effective accentuation.

The Sun.

A small and thoughtful audience listened earnestly and applauded with much resolution. The music performed was of a gentle and sensitive kind which should not be subjected to the rigors of criticism. Most of it will be put away in cotton padding for safe return to Russia.

For America in 1907 a career could still be built on such poor notices. But now the scene had to shift to meeting Tatyana. Sabaneeff, by quoting an evening's idle chitchat dating to 1911, indirectly affirms Scriabin's conflictual feelings over her arrival. It would end his relationship with Safonoff. Tatyana could no more be concealed than Gorky's mistress had been. But there are, as always in the complexity of Scriabin's mind, reasons within reasons for the débacle at the end of the American tour.

Tatyana one night reprovingly spoke of "Your America" to Scriabin:

> He turned to me, "Tatyana Fyodorovna is anti-American because I wasn't there at the beginning, from the first second, so to speak . . . May I tell the story, please, Tasya?"

> He had telegraphed her that he would meet her at the dock. The steamer was late, time passed, but when it docked he was not there. Alexander Nikolaevich got tired of waiting and went to a café and because he had nothing else to do started eating and drinking. This eating and drinking went on just too long.

> "And when the steamer arrived," Alexander Nikolaevich recounted, "and Tatyana Fyodorovna should have been wrapped in felicity at our meeting, there I was, my hat at half-cock, looking completely independent and rampageous."

> He laughed from the bottom of his heart, remembering how furious and unsatisfactory their "reunion" had been.

34

ON 28 February, 1907 Altschuler at the fifth Russian Symphony Society concert played Scriabin's First Symphony (without the chorus). Tatyana and Scriabin were seated in one box at Carnegie Hall, Safonoff at another across the hall. Louis Stanley and Modest Altschuler described the background of the performance:

... The conductor was amazed that the score did not show the tempos and dynamics in which Scriabin played the composition ...

During the rehearsals Altschuler suggested a few modifications in the orchestration and the addition of ringing bells at the end of the scherzo. Scriabin agreed to the changes. The First Symphony won loud applause. The Scherzo with the effective bells had to be repeated. Altschuler pointed to the box where the composer was sitting and motioned to Scriabin to rise. "Even now," reminisces Altschuler, "I can see clearly Scriabin smile and his shining eyes look at me over the dark expanse of the hall."

Scriabin was already being remarked for enjoying his own music and his indifference as to how it was played, only so long as it was played. Altschuler too was notorious for changes in scores.

The reviewers criticized the First Symphony caustically:

The Sun.

... The audience fell upon the Scherzo with feet and hands and Mr. Scriabine was compelled to rise and bow many times, after which Conductor Modest Altschuler repeated the movement.

There is a factitious atmosphere of grief and woe in this composition. We cannot avoid the conclusion that the musician seeks to embody serious sorrows. It is as if he strove decorously to paint in tones some tumultuous tragedy in the life of a butterfly or to narrate the history of a cold, old crime misbegotten under the harvest moon by an erring katydid.

The New York Times.

... a tuneful work that shows the same short flights of inspiration evident in the piano pieces and the same felicitous turn of phrase. He has not the power of symphonic development, and is soon ended with the treatment of his themes, nor has he a wide command of the resources of the orchestra, but he writes agreeably without a slavish adherence to Russian formulas.

The New York Evening Post.

... The general tone of the work is cheerful in melody and coloring. The harmonies occasionally become turbulent; one is even reminded here and there of Strauss.

Musical America.

... He is an inexhaustible melodist, but when it comes to sustained development of themes he is at a loss.

Scriabin was engaged to play in Chicago at the Amateur Musical Club on 4 March, and the woman who met him at the train station was mortified by his beard. During the carriage ride to the hotel she averted her eyes. Chicago, however, afforded one letter to Tatyana, in which he speaks of a psychic upsurge. He has begun his next sonata.

35

FROM CHICAGO, Scriabin went to Detroit to play his concerto on 6 March. He substituted for Gabrilovich, who is ill. He returned to New York well in time for Altschuler's performance of the "Divine Poem." Louis Stanley recounts an incident at the start of the venture:

> When Safonoff learned of Altschuler's intentions, he expressed a desire to hear the Divine Poem. He arranged that Scriabin play it for him and the Altschuler brothers at his hotel, the Netherland, on Fifth Avenue. In the hotel lounge was a concert grand, and there, in the semidarkness Scriabin sat down and began to play the Divine Poem. He was excited, for he was not sure whether either of the conductors for whom he was playing would like his Third Symphony.
>
> He played on and on for three quarters of an hour and Altschuler recalls how the composer's slight figure seemed to grow to colossal proportions before his eyes. Scriabin finished. The three listeners were quiet for a while. Finally, Modest rose and announced, "I shall play your Third Symphony!" Safonoff, head lowered, murmured, "No, no. I prefer your First Symphony."
>
> As if to relieve the tension, Safonoff found the words to invite the three guests to his room for supper. There was little more said about the Divine Poem. The host seemed to be keeping back something from the others. Modest believes that Safonoff must have been brooding over the connection of the Divine Poem with Tatyana. Apparently prompted by his dark thoughts and darker emotions he began to tell a story of philandering by Richard Wagner.
>
> The German composer was supposed to have just finished conducting one of his operas. A beautiful, wealthy lady, impressed with Wagner's music, invited him to her house in the country for dinner and a weekend holiday. Wagner, intrigued, took along his favorite red silk pajamas. At the demitasses, Wagner whispered loudly, so that the husband overheard what he was saying, that he would come to the lady's room that night. The husband ordered the houseboy

to polish the floors of the corridor all night long. Every time Wagner opened the door to go down the hall to his hostess' room in his favorite red silk pajamas, he found the houseboy still polishing the floors of the corridor. Finally, Wagner gave up and turned in for the night. Early in the morning, the husband knocked at Wagner's door and asked his distinguished guest to leave forthwith.

When Safonoff finished he began to laugh. Scriabin's pale face grew paler. He leaped up from his seat and exclaimed, "What are you hinting at? Your lady is a fool. She should have considered it an honor that Wagner paid any attention to her at all." A quarrel ensued between Safonoff and Scriabin. They both shouted incoherently. Finally, Scriabin, incensed, swept to the floor the tablecloth with the drinks, the silver, and the remains of food, and without saying goodbye to anyone left the party.

The date for the Altschuler performance of the "Divine Poem" was 14 March, 1907, the sixth and last concert of the season for the Russian Symphony Society.

Tatyana sat with Scriabin at all rehearsals. Quietly the two listened somewhere in the darkness of the large auditorium. To Altschuler they seemed like little birds. Occasionally, he shouted into the darkness of the hall, "Scriabin, come here, tell me, how you like this tempo." Scriabin would approach the stage and looking at Altschuler with blissful eyes, he would say, "Marvelous, marvelous, Modest."

The orchestral changes suggested by Altschuler entailed much work for several nights. In the living room of Altschuler's home tables were put together and six copyists, working steadily, put the required changes into the orchestral parts. Altschuler rushed to one table, Scriabin to another, instructing the copyists. The odor of spaghetti, Tatyana's specialty, came in from the kitchen, whetting the appetites. Tatyana, red-faced from working over the stove, would frequently run out of the kitchen to join her Sasha. In spite of the night work, rehearsals began each morning at nine o'clock sharp.

At the end of the première of the Divine Poem, the audience responded with much applause.

The concert was followed by an intimate celebration. The Modest and Jacob Altschuler families, Scriabin and Tatyana, and Alfred LaLiberté, a French-Canadian admirer of Scriabin, went off to a second-floor restaurant on West 57th Street near Eighth Avenue. Safonoff was not there. He had not shown up backstage. The party was gay. Everybody made speeches. Scriabin was so overcome by the toasts that he called the waiter and ordered five bottles of champagne.

The performance of the "Divine Poem" created something of a sensation by its hundred players performing full tilt for an hour. It gained many admirers for Scriabin, and lost him many as well. The great Huneker, dean of American critics and only rarely reviewing at this time, commented to the *Evening Sun* critic in the intermission, "Sighing Alexander of the sad salon pieces has taken off his kid gloves at last." Safonoff had sat quietly in a box. The reports once again compounded confusion and inaccuracy:

New York Daily Tribune.

... a symphony, so called, of the extremely modern and most aggressive kind—a program symphony, obviously designed to out-Liszt Liszt (the father of the Russian symphonies) and out-Strauss Strauss, the Richard. Neither task is easy, but, as things are going in music nowadays, Mr. Scriabine went about it in the approved way. When you have nothing in particular to say, say it as bombastically as possible, and call in the aid of a voluminous program. Roll the waters with much blathering of brass and much literary ink; then, at any rate, if your message fails of understanding, you may claim relationship with the progressists in art and rail at the conservatives who are blind to the beckoning light ... It has indubitable strength ... it indicates a capacity to handle masses for which we had not given him credit. But, like the music which it imitates, it betrays that it was inspired from without rather than from within, and like much of that music it pursues the ugly and the painful, as if they were things to be wooed instead of to be shunned in art. It is simply the product of a fine talent lost in vagaries, like much of the music written by the cleverest composers today.

Musical Courier.

... It is not likely that there will be any insistent clamor for a repetition of the Divine Poem.

Musical America.

The main theme is good, the rest is "sound and fury signifying nothing." It is the work of a neurotic, a Fourth of July celebration in which every member of the orchestra has signed a Declaration of Independence and makes just as much noise as he possibly can.

The New York Times.

The magnificent undertaking has resulted in a pretentious and amazing phantasmagoria of tone in which an irreducible minimum of idea is spread out to intolerable lengths, tortured with all sorts of strained harmony, and presented in all the combinations and permutations of orchestral tone that time and space allowed. Mr. Scriabine has tugged long and hard at his bootstraps but his flight is imperceptible.

The Sun.

Let me confess that this first part of the symphony is its most successful passage.

... In vain does the program note tell us that the flute theme affirms the Soul's belief in the sublime. Mr. Scriabine knows as well as any other musician that a flute is never sublime.

No, that flute theme paints the thrills of the composer's spirit in the sheer joy of scattering little black dots with long tails on wide sheets of ruled paper. One could fill pages of newspapers with rhapsodizing about that extraordinary publication of inner life, but let it suffice to say that it has more convolutions than the "Symphonia Domestica" and that it is charged with more shrieking discords than anything that Vincent d'Indy ever conceived in his most abandoned moments. It was performed with deadly effect. When it was past, the audience called out Mr. Scriabine and took a good look at him.

Lawrence Gilman (1878–1939), reviewer for *Harper's Weekly* magazine devoted his column of 30 March, 1907, to Scriabin, although he deemed the "Divine Poem" a failure. Some years later he would find the "Poem of Ecstasy," however, an unequivocal, first-rate masterpiece.

... He has essayed a theme which would have taxed the genius of Wagner and of Richard Strauss, and he has, quite naturally, met defeat. His symphony afflicts by its monotony of mood, its lack of variety and contrast, its amorphous structure, and, above all, by the weakness of its fundamental ideas. It has some moments of splendor; passages that are impressive through their harmonic richness and poignancy and their orchestral plangency. But they are too infrequent to produce much effect upon the texture of the music as a whole; and, most lamentable of all, they are interspersed with passages that afflict by the emptiness of their unashamed sentimentality.

Altschuler considered the evening successful, and newspaper reporters began to call at Scriabin's hotel for interviews. Louis Stanley continues the story:

There they found a pretty woman with him, who was supposed to be his wife. They became suspicious. Only a year before, in April, 1906, Maxim Gorky had come to this country to raise funds for the Russian Revolution. He was greeted most warmly by Mark Twain, William Dean Howells, and many respectable American intellectuals and socialites. At the height of the enthusiasm over Gorky the New York *World* flashed front-page photographs revealing that Maxim Gorky had left a wife and family in Russia. The Gorky cause collapsed immediately, and Gorky and Mme. Andreyeva, ejected from three hotels in succession found themselves one night on the sidewalks of New York. The newspaper circulation and the Czarist régime gained the benefit from the exposure. Was another Gorky scandal in the making?

When Safonoff was asked who was the wife of Scriabin, he replied in strict honesty, "Vera." A reporter telephoned to Jacob Altschuler inquiring about the woman with Scriabin. Jacob denied there was anything amiss, but hurried straight over to Scriabin's hotel to warn him. If the story reached the newspapers, Scriabin, and perhaps with him the Russian Symphony, would be ruined. Scriabin and Tatyana had to confront the facts, and much as they would have liked to stay, they could convince themselves of no other decision than to escape without delay. While Sasha and Tanya began to pack, Jacob phoned the Cunard Line and reserved a good cabin for them on a boat leaving the next day to Liverpool via Queenstown. They departed from the United States forever.

But not before Scriabin telegraphed Glazunov frantically on 21 March:

MUST IMMEDIATELY LEAVE AMERICA PLEASE CABLE ME 600 RUBLES NEW YORK SENDING SIX COMPOSITIONS.

Tatyana's arrival had used up all the money he had earned. The six pieces turned out to be Opp. 56 and 57, "Prelude," "Ironies," "Nuances," "Etude," "Desire," and "Danced Caress". Some had been written earlier. Some were yet to come next month.

(The presto Etude was American-written in a new and magical style, but he had not dared try out an audience there. It takes 20 seconds, with its sharp symmetrical basis established in its last two chords. "Desire," however, one of these "new ways of making love," was assymetrical: two minor sevenths G—F; B—A, one increased by adding a bottom C to make an envelope of a perfect fifth, and its treble adds a D# an augmented fourth to encapsulate this final chord.)

Glazunov complied, but Scriabin did not send the manuscripts. When he did, excitement and confusion from the American emergency still clung in the air. He altogether forgot Op. 55.

The question will never be answered whether the immigration authorities or public pressure would have actually expelled the Scriabins. Was the precipitate flight Scriabin's own imagined fright? Scriabin carried with him a deep affection for America. Gorky, of course, was bitter and wrote anti-American stories such as the "Yellow Devil." Scriabin, in the Findeizen letter said: "I gleaned a very fine impression of America. In my opinion, the judgments Europeans usually make about America are often immature and one-sided."

Sabaneeff recorded more of another evening's conversation in 1911:

"America has a great future . . ." Scriabin said, "There is a very strong mystic movement there."

"It's a revolting, prosaic country, and has no future at all," Tatyana interrupted. "No, Tasya," Alexander Nikolaevich corrected, caressingly, "You don't understand. Not now, but soon it will have. That has to be so.

"There is so much that is interesting in America, in the sense of its frame of mind . . . They are producing a literature, and they will certainly have a contemporary music. After all, one writer like Edgar Poe counts for very much."

It is hard to say on what he based his "mystic" expectations about America. It seems to me that alongside the real America there was in Scriabin's mind an "ideal America" (just as there was an "ideal India" as opposed to the "real"). However, the way he always defended America must be acknowledged.

The Scriabins reached Paris, with 30 francs between them, and they would remain there, too poor to move until June, 1907. On 18 April, Safonoff sailed for Europe to spend the summer in the Caucasus. He passed through Paris without notifying Scriabin. Scriabin was glad. He felt that Safonoff after Tatyana's arrival had deliberately withdrawn support from him. Who, after all, told reporters who the "true Scriabina" was? He had even tried to alienate him from his other friend, Modest Altschuler. As for him, Scriabin now carried his photograph in his pocket.

✒ XII ✒

EUROPE AGAIN

38

IN APRIL, 1907, Scriabin dispatched this exuberant missive from Paris to Altschuler:

> Sweet one! I am writing half-dead from fatigue. Spent the day looking for a place to live. To my woe, we found nothing that was right. We await you with great pleasure. We hope you will not be coming alone. Only your forthcoming presence makes time bearable since we last saw your dear little "mug." Kisses. Pussycat

The Scriabins luckily located a small house at 24, rue de la Tour, in the Passy district near the Trocadéro, and rented the ground floor. On a street lined with sweet-smelling flower trees, the house itself too was surrounded by a garden.

Morozova has been silent again. He wrote her about "my great artistic success in the U.S.A." He also scathes Safonoff for not asking him to appear with the Philharmonic. "For the most part I was quite satisfied by the journey, although I was surprised that I was not properly presented before the public, not even by those who call themselves my friends. Some went so far even as to undermine my artistic reputation. It disgusts me to speak of this. I thank the Altschuler brothers. They comported themselves like angels. Modest Altschuler conducted the symphonies surprisingly well."

The greatest excitement in musical Paris of 1907 was the "Russian Season" of five concerts at the Grand Opéra—from the 16th to the 30th of May. Advertised as "Russian Music Through the Ages" and "Great Historical Concerts from Glinka to Scriabin" (the billing was alphabetical) with Chevillard, Lamoureux and Nikisch as conductors, these programs were organized by two Sergeis—Diaghilev and Taneieff. Taneieff, as artistic controller, had veto power over music and performers. Diaghilev, the impresario, supplied financing both from his own fortune and a now magnanimous Tsar's privy purse.

Diaghilev, editor-publisher of the "decadent" journal, *World of Art*, was indeed a high-minded maecenas. Massively fleshy, always carefully groomed, perfumed even, and with his hair touched up with black dye except for a distinguished sidestreak of white, he incarnated elegance both personally and for the Russian arts he promoted. His idea for the "*Saison Russe*" drew every Russian of means or musical importance. They swarmed to Paris to hear or be heard. Some, merely to be seen. Conspicuously present were Rimsky, Glazunov, Chaliapin, Blumenfeld, Rachmaninoff (he appeared in three capacities—composer, conductor, pianist), Felia Litvina (1861–1936), leading soprano at the Bolshoi. Unnoticed were two other Sergeis—Koussevitzky (with a new, millionairess bride) and Prokofiev. Little-known Stravinsky tagged along with his teacher, Rimsky.

Leading French musicians were hosts and they arranged elaborate hospitality. Yet the Russians spent whole nights talking with each other at the Café de la Paix, exactly as if they were back in Petersburg or Moscow. Scriabin, for instance, never met Debussy or Ravel. The French considered the Russians secretive and rude. High society entertained some musicians in salon fashion. The Russians attended one official dinner. There Diaghilev first coined a cliché: "If this hall burnt down, Russian music would come to an end . . ."

Morozova could not miss these Paris concerts. They afforded her an opportunity to travel, meet old friends, and be patriotic and stylish at the same time. Not least of these inducements was the chance to hear her protégé-master's music on grand scale. "How we will gossip," Scriabin wrote her in mid-April. "We have room to put you up, if you come alone. We know what an easy and accommodating guest you are, good and undemanding. Remember Bogliasco? Do not fear. It's not the same here. We are *much* more comfortable! Yesterday I telegraphed you for money. Forgive me for troubling you, but I am in dire need. My finances have for a long time been quite at an end. I have one piece of good news for me and for you (see what a modest little boy I am), the Poem of

Ecstasy will be played instead of my 2nd Symphony, and I am rushing to get it finished. I work day and night . . ."

At this grandest event in the history of Russian music abroad Hofmann played Scriabin's Third Sonata and Concerto on the program of 23 May. To end the historical panorama at its apogee of modernity, Nikisch scheduled the "Poem of Ecstasy" for 30 May. He conducted the Second Symphony instead, "more for the audience than for the music," as Stravinsky said about Nikisch in another connection. Twice Scriabin had written Altschuler the "Poem of Ecstasy" was ready. However much was in his head, it was not yet wholly on paper.

(The *Guide Musical* called the second movement of the Concerto "very sweet, refined, distinguished. The piano embroiders on the melody like the warbling of birds"; the Third Sonata, "imposing"; and the Second Symphony, "very rich, with tremendous surge of power."

Scriabin wrote Altschuler, who had bypassed Paris in May, hastening to enlist funds from Russia for his concerts in New York:

Dear little Friendlet! You just don't make sense. All the music world is here, and all wealthy music lovers too! You have gone to Moscow and Petersburg to spend your money fruitlessly. You're no better than I am, after all! Ha, ha! I received your letter just as I was seeing Taneieff off at the station for Petersburg. I could not talk to him about anything. M.K. Morozova diabolically *asked*(!) if she could help you. You will see her when you go to Moscow. The hope is very slight that she will give anything, and she said hardly anyone will respond to your request, because these are difficult times for everyone, My poor sweeeeeeet one! My fears about her attitude toward me turned out to be completely groundless. She was just as sweet as ever toward us. Her silence had been unintentional.

How suspicious I have become! All my musical comrades and their wives have been enchanting to Tatyana Fyodorovna—not like *some* of our mutual acquaintances! Nadezhda Nikolaevna Korsakova is a jewel! What a delightful family the Korsakoffs are! I am so happy we have all met again finally. Now I can believe in their goodwill and wishes.

And now you, all lewd, are coming here! How I want to pinch you and squeeze you. Ah, you, you, you! And I have finished the Poem of Ecstasy! Oh what labor this piece has cost me! How many sleepless nights! Come! We will go over it together. Here's to our early re-meeting! You hear? *SOON!* Until then I kiss you and Tanya asks me to send you warmest greetings.

Your pussycat

P.S. In a day or two I meet Oranovsky whom I hope will aid your concerts.
I will talk to him first opportunity, and tell him about you and your
concerts. Rest easy. I am doing all I can.

Mme. Rimsky-Korsakova ratified Scriabin's glowing impression with
her reminiscence (published in *Soviet Music*, No. 5, 1950): "Nikolai
Andrevich knew Scriabin's music as far as the Poem of Ecstasy, although
he never heard that piece performed by an orchestra. We spent a very
pleasant and interesting evening with the Scriabins. Alexander Nikolaevich
was feverishly working on 'Ecstasy.' First he read us the poem and then
presented the composition. He explained its orchestration, the meaning
of the different themes, and played various parts of it. Nikolai Andreevich
liked individual themes and passages of the music, but he thought the
entire composition would be somewhat monotonous, because of the
emphasis on one theme, the continuous spices of the harmony, and the
unrelieved tension in the mood . . ."

Tatyana wrote Nemenova-Lunz on 23 May, 1907, also of friendly
though not uncritical encounters: "Every musician is here and they are
all very sweet to us. We see them often. Rachmaninoff has become quite
famous and we are on good terms with him. Even when we disagree,
it is still pleasant. He believes that Sasha has chosen a wrong path!"
Rimsky, too, whenever Scriabin broached the subject of mysticism would
draw a zero on the tablecloth. During one quarrel Rimsky and Scriabin
sided against Rachmaninoff. The argument concerned the connection
between colors and sounds. Both Scriabin and Rimsky heard synesthet-
ically, that is, saw colors while they heard music. Scriabin felt his colors
like a blind man feeling his way on the piano keys. Rimsky responded
visually by keys. He saw E♭ major as blue; Scriabin saw the note E♭
alone as the steely glint of metal, the key as reddish-purple.

Rachmaninoff resisted the whole concept. His opponents tried to
prove that this quality, photism, was inherent in everyone, and that even
he used it unconsciously.

"Why then, in the cellar scene of your *Miserly Knight*," Rimsky said
in reference to the moment when the old baron opens his caskets of
gold and jewels, "do you make the key of D major predominate? It's
the color of golden brown."

"You see," Scriabin interrupted, "your intuition follows laws whose very existence you try to deny."

Von Riesemann reported this conversation at the Café de la Paix and has Rachmaninoff say somewhat sadly in self-justification: "I had to admit that the passage *was* written in D major, but I had a much simpler explanation. While composing it I must have borne in mind the scene in Rimsky-Korsakoff's opera *Sadko* where the people, at Sadko's command, draw the great catch of goldfish and break into the jubilant shout, 'Gold! Gold!' This shout is written in D major . . . But I could not prevent my two colleagues from leaving with the air of conquerors."

According to von Riesemann, Scriabin generated a number of arguments among Russian artists at the "Season." He was eagerly debated. "His behavior was free from all pose, but very original . . . He was the first who 'for hygienic reasons' gave up wearing a hat." And he talked of the "microphytes" crawling on restaurant tableware. His larger influence in Paris would be felt in the years to come. A decade later for instance, after Scriabin's quasar had entered the universe of European music, Erik Satie (1866–1925) began his multi-media fusions of music, poetry, colors, handwriting and painting.

The "Five Evenings" produced one serious altercation, this time between Scriabin and Diaghilev. It was Diaghilev's practice to send complimentary tickets to musicians. For one concert, Scriabin's tickets arrived late. During the intermission in the foyer he "delicately and diffidently" mentioned this inconvenience, "How late you sent the tickets . . . I almost missed them."

"Say 'thank you' that I sent them at all," retorted Diaghilev. "I could have just as easily *not* have." Engel, who was present, recounts the scene that ensued:

> It is hard to describe what happened to Scriabin. What had become of our gentle Alexander Nikolaevich! He threw himself at Diaghilev, screamed almost hysterically somehow without losing all dignity, "You allow yourself to talk to me this way! You forget art. *We* are artists! We create it, and you merely flutter and strut about its edges selling it. Without *us*, who would want to know *you*? You would be less than . . . than *nothing* on this earth!"
>
> Diaghilev was disconcerted but apologetic. He said, "Yes, Alexander Nikolaevich, yes. I meant no harm . . ."

His capitulation was as astounding to his friends as polite Scriabin's outburst was to his.

Diaghilev took his revenge, though. He later dissuaded Balanchine the choreographer from his Scriabiniana ballets. "It's not really very good music . . ." he said.

In Paris, Scriabin moved in his wonted high society. So busy were he and Tatyana they did not see daughter Ariadna until June, when Tatyana's mother joined them to keep house and help with the ménage. Tatyana was pregnant a second time. On 30 May, Scriabin pictured his gilded life for Altschuler and showed how obliging he is:

> Dear friend, you surely have forgooooooootten your arithmetic! You know now of course that I cannot help you, because Taneieff left Paris for Petersburg or somewhere else, maybe London. I don't know. We saw him 2 or 3 times, and the last time was the day of the fifth concert when my symphony was played, and he explained to me then that he was leaving Paris the next day.

> I have spoken to Morozova constantly about you and showed her your photograph, and described your talent.

> However, I am frightfully angry with you. I simply *cannot understand your actions.* If you were here we would not be separated for a minute. I would introduce you to *everybody!* Stop this sour note! I am now waiting in Paris for a millionaire, a certain Oranovsky, in whom I place some hopes, if not more, for you. If you come here I will introduce you to Shaikevich, to whom I have already spoken. He himself is not a millionaire, but he knows masses of rich people in Paris. If you stay more than a month in Russia you won't find me here, because on the first we go to Switzerland . . .

> P.S. Seriously, you have grieved me most terribly. I had so wanted to be of service to you. I waited for you up to the last minute. Even during my symphony I looked for you in the audience, thinking you were keeping your arrival a surprise. *NO!!* not a sign of you! You didn't appear. Deeeeevil take you!!! I kiss you.

In a Morozova letter he writes on 13 June, 1907, after receiving money ("You are sweet, sweet!"), that he would have written sooner but for spending the day with Sergei Shchukin who introduced him to Dmitri Merezhkovsky (1865–1914) the writer, and Minsky (1855–1937) (pseudonym for Nikolai Vilenkin), a poet.

He raises here again the idea of publishing his own music at his own expense. Doret has put him in touch with E. Fromont of Enoch Editions in Paris. They print ten pages of music for 100 rubles. "The printing is cheap, but the distribution of the music for sale is very difficult." Although stacks of uncirculated music are valueless, he says, "Let's try it and see."

39

MID-JUNE, Scriabin wrote Jacob Altschuler:

> ...I am very sad Modest failed in Russia. But OF COURSE he should have been in Paris.
>
> On the 1st or 2nd I received 2 letters from him in Petersburg saying that he was waiting for Safonoff! Why Safonoff?! Better not speak of that! The thought infuriates me!

(Altschuler had not been unwise. Through Safonoff he raised 15,000 rubles.) Scriabin continued his letter with gossip, hopes and aspirations. Diaghilev says he will present Scriabin and Atlschuler in joint concerts, despite the fight. He lost 100,000 francs on the Russian Series. The opera house had been filled to overflowing, but "artists like Nikisch and Chaliapin cost a lot...I read a great deal, and prepare myself for work. I finished the Poem of Ecstasy, and it is to be played here next year. I want to play it for Modest."

Mid-July, the Scriabins leave for St. Beatenberg, Nemenova-Lunz's favorite Swiss resort, and they rent there the rather lovely Schmoker chalet. His first letter goes to Modest Altschuler:

> I simply cannot understand what you mean! I wrote you 2 letters, one to Petersburg, the other to Moscow (to be forwarded to Taneieff). I also telegraphed you my address! I have been here more than a week! Come immediately, fast as you can! Life here is divine and quite cheap! There is a spare room in our châlet. Telegraph me quickly that you are coming.

To Morozova, in early August he wrote:

> Here we are, three weeks in this divine spot. Unfortunately, neither Tanya or I can fully take pleasure in it. The days pass like minutes and I realize with horror that soon it will be time to return to Paris. You know what comforts

us and really profits from the village life? Arochka. She is growing up and getting stronger each day. What a pity the poor thing hasn't longer to play on grass.

And how are your children? I think that only the Russian countryside is ideal. Children after they have been ill always get well there. You no doubt know that Maria Solomonova Lunz is here with her husband and this brightens our lives. She is going over all my latest compositions with me during her stay, prior to introducing them to high society in Moscow. My latest pieces are so complex in mood that I am happy to have the chance of communicating some of their finer points to someone as talented and dedicated to my art as she. Are you playing? By the way where is Medtner summering? And will you be studying with him? If Russian country life has not completely taken your mind off us, write just a few words.

On 16 August, Nemenova-Lunz herself described this period in a letter to her friend Leonid Nikolaev (1878–1942), pianist and composer: "If only you could hear the Fifth Sonata he is writing, the preludes he has already written, and oh how he plays, and how he teaches me! Scriabin's last pieces embark on a brand new period of unexpected harmonies and original forms. He's copying out the Poem of Ecstasy for the printers and it will be performed in Petersburg this winter...I practice a lot, take regular lessons from Scriabin, have learned 12 of his pieces, of which 2 are not published. And I have also learned from him a Tausig Waltz, Schumann's Humoresque and Waldstimmer [Forest Murmurs], and a Chopin étude and waltz. I am in ecstasies over his interpretations, especially in the waltz."

She enlarged these impressions in her memoirs:

Scriabin loved the "working-out" of the Strauss-Tausig Waltz and felt that it was airy, rapturously alive, and elegant. He played it incomparably coquettishly and capriciously. All the difficult passages sounded like lace. Never once did he break or interrupt the Straussian *luftpausen* [pauses for breath].

That summer of 1907 in Switzerland, we were all light-hearted and gay. Alexander Nikolaevich enjoyed himself like a child. He skillfully pirouetted around chairs, recalled scenes from his Cadet days, and laughed at each joke told by the well-known cellist and orchestra conductor, Modest Altschuler, who was staying with Scriabin. In free times, he wandered off into the mountain forests. Alexander Nikolaevich would comment on how sad it was that even the oldest trees in Switzerland advertised pensions. On the whole Scriabin did not like the Swiss, cheerful as they are. Nor did he like their hotel-type or châlet style of life.

In June, 1907, the Belaieff firm agreed sight unseen but on Rimsky's recommendation, to pay Scriabin 1,500 rubles for the score of the "Poem of Ecstasy" and his reduction of it to two pianos four hands. (Lev Konyus ended up by doing it.) Scriabin asked for an advance in July. The Board had to decline, but compromised by saying they would pay the amount in full immediately upon the first performance scheduled by Blumenfeld at the Belaieff Russian Symphony concert in February, 1908. To hurry matters, Scriabin wrote on 9 August he was sending the "Poem of Ecstasy" direct to the printers within twenty days.

In Beatenberg both Altschuler and Scriabin labored hard over the final instrumentation of "Ecstasy." "He wants to perform it for the first time with all accouterments of luxury," he wrote Morozova, "with light effects . . ." He also tells her that without waiting for approval, he had 500 exemplars printed of his Op. 52—Poem and "Enigma." Nemenova-Lunz, he assures her, "knows all the music stores in Moscow and has promised to help get them on the market . . ."

Siloti, who is organizing a concert series in Petersburg (with his wife's money), has meanwhile written Scriabin to ask for proofs of "Ecstasy." He wants to begin his series with its première. He would pay more than Blumenfeld for first Russian rights.

Artsybushev on behalf of the Belaieff series accepts Siloti's proposal and asks Rimsky in "Ecstasy's" stead and as a novelty for excerpts from his new opera *Golden Cockerel*. He concurred, but said: "My consent is not an obligation for you to perform my music. I have doubts as to the wisdom of eliminating the Poem of Ecstasy. It is an obscene piece and a very long one. It is not even easy to perform. However, do bear this in mind: Scriabin, wearing as he may be, is interesting." In other words, think again. Artsybushev did, and "Ecstasy" remained—for a time—Blumenfeld's property.

Scriabin telegraphed on 4 October: SENDING SCORE IN FIVE DAYS INFORM BOARD. He reassured the firm again on 15 October that only eight more days are needed. He is making a few changes. But on 2 December, he had found an entire section displeasing to him. He wrote an apologetic letter to Artsybushev: ". . . Now I have learned by experience that I can never set a deadline. In creative work it is unthinkable . . . If you want to be kind, please drop me two lines saying that you, Glazunov, and Liadov are not furious with me." They were.

The bulky package whose postage to Leipzig Scriabin had to borrow was finally mailed on 3 December, 1907. Both Tatyana and Scriabin depict the final travail. Scriabin to Artsybushev: "I am frightfully unstrung. Everything comes out of me with great difficulty. I literally stayed at my desk for 16 hours nonstop (no exaggeration). I was so tired after going over the final version of the score, I slept 12 hours without once waking up."

Tatyana to Nemenova-Lunz, 5 December:

> Sasha received a telegram from Petersburg asking for the score as soon as possible. We immediately began a scurrying I can only describe as *tremendous!* I say 'we,' because as it turned out, I am happy to say, I had much of the work to do on it. We stayed up until 5 each morning and then rose again at 7! You can imagine what that was like! Day before yesterday at long last the score was posted. We were so exhausted we could think only of one thing—sleep, sleep, sleep.

Never again would Scriabin send music to the Belaieff firm, although he contemplated briefly sending them the already printed Op. 52, Poem and "Enigma."

Blumenfeld began rehearsals, but could not cope with such music by himself. (Nor could Siloti.) He telegraphed for help in the emergency. Scriabin replied tersely: CANNOT COME REGRETS GREETINGS. The performance was canceled. (The first world performance of the "Poem of Ecstasy" was Altschuler's in New York City on Thursday, 10 December, 1908. In Russia it took place 19 January, 1909, with Hugo Warlich conducting the Court Orchestra of St. Petersburg. Sergei Prokofiev, who attended "Ecstasy's" debut sitting next to composer Nikolai Myaskovsky (1887-1950), mentions how embarrassed both of them were at not understanding either the music or the meaning.)

At summer's end in Beatenberg, the specter of where to live rose again. He began rationalizing against Paris in early September to Morozova: "Life in Paris is fearfully expensive; the climate rotten. The air in the areas where we could find an apartment big enough for us at a reasonable price is frightful. Mostly, I find it impossible to work in Paris, because you cannot make any noise. You have to wear house slippers after 10 at night." He chooses Lausanne partly because he is now printing his music there and, as he continues his letter: "Everything in Lausanne is healthier, cheaper, and quieter. It is very convenient, being only 7 hours from Paris, so I can arrange a concert tour from there ... If you would care to underwrite publishing music on my own and therefore enlarge its scope, I would be very, very grateful for the help. Please talk to Maria Solomonova Nemenova ... Write me meantimes, care of Otto Hauenstein."

Altschuler does not receive the money he expects before leaving for America. He cables, but to get to the steamer in time he borrows from Scriabin, who dips into the last remains of the Morozova stipend. On 17 September, still in Beatenberg, Scriabin sends out a cry of distress to her: "I telegraphed Altschuler at the steamer and again to New York, but no reply. Now the season is over here. It is cold and damp, and my credit is exhausted. I don't even know how we are going to eat. I am infinitely ashamed to ask you for money. Wouldn't this have to happen just when I took every precaution so as to have enough money for every step of the way? I could not possibly have foreseen *this*!"

After Morozova obliged by telegram, Scriabin wrote, "I cannot express my joy. During those last days we felt we were going to be buried there forever. Almost everyone had already left . . ."

Once the Scriabins reached Lausanne, they took an apartment for 75 francs a month in a complex of dwellings around the tiny Square de la Harpe in "C" building, where Edward Gibbon (1737–1794) once lived. Scriabin described it as "pretty good, charming, adequate space, and for the same amount of money as we paid in Paris we have two extra rooms larger than any there. We even have conveniences—a bath and electric light. Life here simply cannot be compared with Paris as far as economy goes. Most important, nothing interferes with my work. I can pound on the piano all night long."

For the first time in their married life, Scriabin and Tatyana were established as a real household and in good readiness for the child expected in February. Scriabin continued his letter to Morozova: "Mama is with us, and she adorns our life endlessly and lightens our burdens. She takes over all household chores, which means that now Tatyana has leisure to help me with my musical and literary preoccupations." Boris finally married and comes with his wife, Polina, to visit them.

Scriabin gave his first Lausanne concert on 1 November, 1907: "A great artistic success. I was never better received anywhere." Scriabin played twice again in Lausanne, on 11 April and 12 July, 1908. Neither program included works of the superlative direction in which he was now moving. His music was growing fecund and *in flagrante delirio*, as it were. Not only "Ecstasy" but the Fifth Sonata were perfect cases in point.

40

MOROZOVA DAWDLED a month and a half before writing Scriabin in early December, 1907. He responded instantly with his first announcement of the Fifth Sonata: "The Poem of Ecstasy took much of my strength and taxed my patience. So now are you imagining me giving myself over to rest, something I have wanted for so long? No, not at all! Today I have almost finished my 5th Sonata. It is a big poem for piano and I deem it the best piano composition I have ever written. I do not know by what miracle I accomplished it . . ."

On 8 December, Tatyana informed Nemenova-Lunz, "We go out a little, having caught up on our sleep. We begin to look normal again. Sasha even has begun to compose—5th Sonata!!! I cannot believe my ears. It is incredible! That Sonata pours from him like a fountain. Everything you have heard up to now is as nothing. You cannot even tell it is a sonata. Nothing compares to it. He has played it through several times, and all he has to do is to write it down—a matter of three days work, then I copy it, and we send it off to be printed . . ." in Lausanne.

Its ecstatic genesis, the triadic, chordal section *presto con allegrezza* swirling around the key of F♯ major (page 4) came to Scriabin in Chicago. (In one sense these passages are transformations of "Fragility" and make of it a preparatory étude.) Nevertheless, the actual writing took only six days, from 8 to 14 December, 1907. Five months later all magnificent eighteen pages were back from the printers in a beautiful edition of 300 copies, costing Scriabin 300 francs.

Another December letter went to Altschuler, who has in time repaid his debt:

> You ought to be executed. I spend all my time these days thinking of ways to kill you in the most horrible possible fashion! Tanya says the best thing would

be for us to come TOGETHER all over again to New York and cause you trouble a second time! That would kill you all right. Well, blessings on you, for if you write to me all will be forgiven!

I congratulate you and all yours this New Year's, and wish you *parantèle-fond* [much money] and all accompanying good! I will say nothing about me, because I do not know what might interest you after this long time. However, I will inform you of the main news. I may be going to Russia. They are organizing big concerts for me in Moscow and Petersburg to play the 3rd Symphony and Poem of Ecstasy. If you arrange our trip to America for February, this probably will take place in March. We'll make a convenient date, so as not to miss the season over there!

You will not recognize the Poem of Ecstasy! There is so much that is new in it! Both in the details of the music and the orchestration! I think it is pretty good! Those past days I was not at all able to stop myself. I have opened newer and newer horizons in the orchestration. You will be amazed at what you see in my next composition! I do wish I had some connection with an orchestra and orchestral musicians. My imagination is enormous, but imagination is not always enough. At times I need to play on the instrument I am writing for! Well look at me. I meant to scribble 2 words and here I have prattled. Sleep well! I kiss you and once again *SHOUT!!!!* and beg!!!!! for a letter! Oh, you, you, you . . . Write!!

Some societies of some sort asked for my autographed photograph to publish in magazines—in Chicago and in Canada.

The correspondence over the "Poem of Ecstasy" continues in all directions. To the printer in Leipzig he writes, "Yes, on page 93 I want the 8 horns with their bells held high in the air." And again to Altschuler, "In 2 or 3 days I will send you a short résumé of the poem which I ask you to put into English. I would like it in the program notes to help auditors understand the content of the Poem. You're going to have many troubles, my poor dear one, during rehearsals! The score is 10 times more complicated now than the 3rd Symphony . . ."

Through unfortunate timing the American introduction of "Ecstasy" sank as heavily as if it had been weighted with lead. That same night Toscanini at the Metropolitan conducted Wagner for the first time, and even more disastrously, on the same Russian Symphony program nineteen-year-old violinist, Mischa Elman, made his debut. After the Tchaikovsky concerto Elman was recalled to the stage a dozen times, and Altschuler twice began the final number on the program (the *1812 Over-*

ture) but still the audience did not stop cheering. There was little critical time left for Scriabin.

The *New York Times* ignored him, and the *Herald* merely noted that "all the music was warmly applauded." The *Tribune* said: "Scriabine's composition . . . had its rapturous moments but it left the hearers unconvinced." The *New York Evening Sun*, 11 December, 1908, waxed specific:

> The nerves of the audience last night, as it happened, had been worn and racked as nerves are seldom assailed even in these days. Scriabine's "Poème de l'Extase" was the cause.
>
> Certainly it conveyed a sense of eeriness, and uncanny connotation. Most of the time the violins were whimpering and wailing like lost souls, while strange undulating and formless melodies roved about in the wood-wind. A solo violin spoke occasionally, growing more and more plaintive and finally being swallowed up in a chaos of acid harmonies with violins screaming in agony overhead.
>
> It all seemed far more like several other things than ecstasy.

Altschuler afterwards lied to Scriabin. He wrote that there had been no reviews at all. Scriabin crackled: "What swine not to write about 'Ecstasy.' ")

The desperation of his poverty in Lausanne contrasted senselessly with the "Poem of Ecstasy" being out in the world and the Fifth Sonata already born. Finally, in December, 1907, Scriabin begs from Glazunov once more:

> I turn to you with a big request. I am conscience-stricken at troubling you, but there is no other avenue open. I have spent all my money. Perhaps I have 2 francs. I have nowhere to go for more. In a few days I must pay the rent for 3 months, and it will be catastrophic if I do not. The prize this year was not awarded me, and I am not to receive any money for the Poem of Ecstasy until January, and N.V. Artsybushev says perhaps not until the beginning of February. So please lend or advance me 300 or 400 rubles until March. I would be infinitely grateful. If you yourself cannot, then speak, please with Nikolai Andreevich or Anatol Konstantinovich. Please manage somehow, and if it is possible, telegraph the money to me.
>
> You cannot conceive how nervous and overwrought I am. We expect an addition to the family in the very near future, which will complicate matters. I am dreadfully tired, as I have recently been working like a Negro, sometimes for more than 15 hours a day. I am now finishing a big poem for piano. I can

compose nothing more, because I am crushed by my moods and dreadfully anxious.

To Morozova he writes in equal panic. His dismay at not winning the Glinka Prize of 1907 and some of it going to lesser composers so revolts him that he puts quotation marks around their names, as if he were handling insects with a pair of tweezers.

Yesterday to my enormous grief I found out that I will not win the prize this year. It is divided this time between Korsakoff, "Witohl," "Cherepnin" and Taneieff. The Poem of Ecstasy unfortunately did not meet the deadline, but there were piano pieces I had counted on which went unrewarded. Can you advance me just 300 rubles so I can live until February? We unfortunately have a mass of extra expenses. You know, I am sure, that we expect a little one for whom we must provide. Tanya must be especially looked after as she is fearfully weak, anemic, and I do not know how she is going to live through this "perturbation." Let's work it out this way: If Petersburg does not send me anything, then I will send you a one-word telegram saying "envoyez" [send]. I hope that this brevity will not offend you. It is for economy's sake. Thus, send me BY TELEGRAM 300 rubles, and deduct it from the March stipend.

The Belaieff firm advances Scriabin 300 rubles, chargeable against the "Poem of Ecstasy" and with the request that he dispatch the proofs quickly. Scriabin thanks the committee by saying he will send four pieces in February, but he does not and fortunately will not need to. He could not have, even had he wanted. They did not exist.

Fortunes presently bettered themselves. At the end of January, 1908, Welte-Mignon and its rival player-piano company, Phonola, invited Scriabin to Leipzig. Their roster eventually numbered 5,000 rolls made by masters such as d'Albert, Leschetizky, Sauer, Paderewski, Strauss, Leoncavallo, Fauré, etc. The paper spools, with the notes, speed, and pedal punched on them, crude as they were, immortalized many titanic performances in those early days when the phonograph was too primitive to catch the piano sound. For one week's sessions, Scriabin received 1,500 francs. He recorded the Second and Third Sonatas; Preludes, Op. 11 (G flat major, E flat minor, C# minor, G# minor), Op. 17 (D flat major, B minor), Op. 22 (G# minor); Etudes, Op. 8 (D# minor, A flat major); Mazurkas, Op. 25 (F major, E minor, C# minor); Op. 40 (F# major); Poems, Op. 32; Albumleaf (Op. 45); and "Desire," Op. 57. His erratic uptempos are astounding, today. He frequently disregards the musical sense the page gives. As lessons to the inside of Scriabin's mind, these records are invaluable, though not for the concertgoer. His mood reflects in the playing.

He writes Tatyana twice:

> Tatuk, just returned from a quartet evening where I hoped to meet some Leipzig musicians and get acquainted. In vain. There was not one famous soul among them. My soul, how are you?
>
> I am thinking of you every second all the time and I am reproaching myself! It is too much that while I fondle my little flower, I torture her with my capricious behavior and my stupid character. I have grown unbearable!
>
> Oh how bored I was at the concert listening to Beethoven, Brahms, and Mendelssohn! I have become a stranger to everything, and to everyone— except you! It's frightening! Tasuk, if only you were happy! Enough of this! Sleep well.

A January concert of Scriabin music—with the "Poem of Ecstasy" as centerpiece—which Morozova and the directors of the Moscow RMO hoped to arrange, was definitely off. Morozova could not raise sufficient funds. She was desolate, but Scriabin sighed with relief. It was not the time to return to Russia, as he wrote his suddenly diligent patroness.

February brought happiness: the "Poem of Ecstasy" was at last in print (he received 3,152 francs); and the baby arrived. He wrote Morozova: "Only a few words to inform you of the happy event. In the middle of the night a son, Julian, was born to us. You can imagine how happy I am that everything ended well. I admit I was quite worried for Tanya . . ." Later: "He was born skinny, but has now put on a little weight . . ." Scriabin nicknamed him "Mouton" (sheep). Only one grey cloud darkened. One of his pair of *babushki* died: Maria, sister of Scriabin's grandmother. For the new life, one hostage in death.

Again the question of coming to Russia is raised, this time by Artsybushev planning for next year. Scriabin answers: "It would be very agreeable, but there is one matter I did not want to mention but which unfortunately, I must. The answer determines my answer. Remuneration. Since the Belaieff concerts are very dear to me because of Mitrofan Petrovich, I have not spoken of material matters. But surely you know the expense that a trip to Russia entails. I ask you to write me the maximum you propose; then I can give a precise answer." Artsybushev offered a fee of 300 to 500 rubles (aside from a similar amount of royalty), and Scriabin's answer was "Yes."

They set 31 January, 1909, as the date for his return to Petersburg. ("I hope no misunderstanding with Moscow arises out of this . . .") The program was scheduled with "Ecstasy," of course, and Artsybushev promises it will be the only piece rehearsed. Scriabin writes:

> The conductor has a terrible time sorting out all the details of this complicated composition. Altschuler told me that he would not have been able to decipher the score had he not heard me play it several times. The use of the instruments is new, there is much polyphony, and sometimes it is difficult to know the intention of the composer and to decide which voice should lead. To indicate all this in a score is impossible. Therefore I can say that half the success of 'Ecstasy' depends on the performance. It is essential for me to be present at rehearsals of 'Ecstasy,' and Blumenfeld insists on it too.

> I will play the 5th Sonata uninterrupted in one movement although it has masses of tempo changes. These cannot be listed on a billboard advertisement as movements. Why not just put 'solo' and then the details can be given on the program? If I write something new over the summer then I would like to play that too, but I don't want to commit myself to a more definite program at the moment.

The Fifth Sonata, Op. 53, whose completion burst so unexpectedly out of tiredness, shines with the high intensity of a vapor lamp, like a glorious afterthought to "Ecstasy." That stanza describing the creative spirit which exhorts hidden strivings of timid creatures into the boldness of life gives the fission coherence and direction. An imperious, imposing three-note summons (leaps of minor sixths) (page 6) commands these mysterious forces encased within man. The *allegrezzo* sections are the divine play—the exquisite revel—which comes with liberation. Some of Scriabin's most ardent music sings in the slow passages of the beginning *languido* (languid) and later the *meno vivo* (less fast) themes.

The last two pages, among the most expansive in piano literature (no piece before covered so many keys or spanned the keyboard as widely), are marked *con luminosità* (luminously) and *estatico* (ecstatically). For the first time Scriabin is unquestionably successful in light and ecstasy. Radiance bursts from the piano. An unusual cluster composed of perfect fourths—G♯-C♯-F♯ and A♯-D♯-G♯—emerges softly on page 9, measure

15, and the sonata is spangled with scintillas of symmetries and asymmetries forming unusual vibrations, but the climactic chord—symmetrically formed from two minor sevenths enveloped by perfect fifths—appears like flames seen on wings the instant an airplane crashes the sound barrier.

The Fifth Sonata with its continual harmonic exfoliation moved Scriabin profoundly and spiritually. He said that for the first time he found a composition outside himself. He saw it as "an image," a "sound-body" of three dimensions with colors from another plane. "I am a translator," he cried to Schloezer. His problem was how to render it from concealment into palpable life, to transfer it into corporeal music without losing its original sensation. He did not want his own shadow to dim its quartz-clear image. Schloezer says that while he unraveled his vision, he constantly felt he was impoverishing and simplifying it. This dismayed him.

"In those moments when the power weakened," Schloezer wrote later, "he would again summon the original conception, the idea-picture. This he called 'contemplating things in their oneness,' or in Theosophical terminology, '*se placer sur le plan de l'unité*' (placing oneself on the plane of unity)." Scriabin's creative process worked now: "First moment—intuition of the whole, the act of synthesis, harmonious unity. Second moment—act of analysis, the breaking down of the vision seen by the intuition. Third moment—reconstruction, creation of a new whole, harmonization on another plane."

In composing the Fifth Sonata Scriabin was again akin to Haydn, who said through tears of ecstasy over *The Creation*, "I could not have made it myself. It was not I who produced it . . ." Or Mozart who sometimes heard a composition as a single sound ("*wie ein einziger Laut*"). "H E" within Scriabin was creating on its own. This composition had to be privately printed. How could he trust such inspiration to a coarse Artsybushev or a Belaieff firm sans Belaieff? Self-publication was, of course, not unusual for Russians. Both the wives of Tolstoi and Chekhov had pleaded with their husbands to publish their own works on their own terms (and profits).

41

THE LUCK of February, 1908, lasted all year. Inspiration renewed itself with April sunshine and he began "the text of my next work—for the stage." He is drawing closer to the Mysterium, his ultimate composition to which he has obliquely referred as "my main work." Now he named it for the first time openly.

"Ecstasy" received second place (700 rubles) for the 1908 Glinka Prize (Rachmaninoff's Second Symphony beat it), and not to be outdone by Petersburg, Moscow RMO invited Scriabin for three appearances. He refused to play his Concerto, however: "It's a childhood composition . . . unsuitable for me now . . . I don't like it any more." He preferred to expound his doctrine and its doctrinal music. Emil Cooper (1879–1961), Russian-born, English conductor (then engaged by the Zimin Opera and later the Bolshoi), arrived in Lausanne for briefing on "Ecstasy." He is to guest-conduct its Moscow première 21 February, 1909, and initiate a "Scriabin Week."

Scriabin in Lausanne also attracts pupils. "We music-make much and often . . ." When the "Ecstasy" manuscript comes back from the printers with proofs, he gives it to the Canadian LaLiberté. Meichik is coached before playing the debut of the Fifth Sonata, and his own first public appearance, 18 November. One day Meichik began playing Beethoven's "Moonlight Sonata." Scriabin hurtled in from another room: "For the love of God, stop! I can't abide such music . . ."

Into Scriabin's Switzerland life strode also another person of momentous import, Serge Koussevitzky. Olga Monighetti had spoken to him about Scriabin's anguish over a publisher. She had met Koussevitzky's new Gentile wife socially, but more important, the Monighetti household had always received Jews.

Olga made a special note of this in her Recollections:

> I was most disturbed when I read in Sabaneeff's book that there was anti-Semitism in Scriabin's later home. He was never so. All his friends at the Conservatory were Jewish, except Kolya Averino, and he regarded them with love.

Olga was the driving catalyst both men needed before they could meet and be mutually useful. Koussevitzky telegraphed Scriabin at Ouchy, June, 1908. Could he come and see him? Yes. And Koussevitzky, driven in a shiny, chauffered limousine—the first automobile Scriabin ever rode in and the first Moscow, later, would see—came riding through the narrow village streets like a mustachioed savior in armor.

Koussevitzky in contrast to Scriabin was musically and socially at the perigee and a much disliked man. He had twice married, this second time to, and possibly, it was said, for money. Natalya Ushkova, his bride, was heiress to a fairytale fortune in tea, chemicals, factories and ordnance plants in the Urals. One account asserts that her tea interests alone accounted for a gross income of 38 million rubles a year. Koussevitzky, who (after being baptized) played doublebass at the Imperial Bolshoi Theater, had a salary of 100 rubles a month. According to orthodox civil and religious law, half the fortune was the groom's; he used it widely to establish his position.

Sabaneeff describes Koussevitzky cruelly:

> . . . He looked like a barber with his little mustache. He was hated because he was a *parvenu*, a *parvenu* into the Moscow *bourgeoisie*. Yet he was spurned by musical circles because he was representative of the *bourgeoisie*. They hated him for marrying a millionairess. They said it was only so he could pay Artur Nikisch to teach him conducting.

If money incited resentment, Koussevitzky's every action aggravated his enviers. Sabaneeff elaborates, "He leased a palace . . . lavish and tasteless . . . guarded by a parade of liveried lackeys and French bulldogs . . . thirteen servants." Even Ferruccio Busoni spoke ungratefully of his stay with the Koussevitzkys, "I was looked after like a tame monkey." Tactlessly and in utmost ostentation Koussevitzky displayed his wealth by planning a Moscow "Palace of Art" with the symphony hall building to bear his name. He rented one of Moscow's large, three-acre amusement parks with three auditoriums for a series of music, opera and ballet programs. However he was of great service to art. He organized "Koussevitzky Concerts" and hired as soloists Leopold Godowsky, Fritz Kreisler, and Scriabin. He imported Richard Strauss and Claude Debussy to conduct festivals of their own music. And most pertinent to Scriabin, he founded in Berlin a new music publishing house on 30 April, 1908, with a capital of half a million rubles. He incorporated this as the "Russian Music Edition" (*Rossiiskoe Muzykalnoe Izdatel'stvo*), which Russians quickly punned into "Russian Music Mockery" (*R. M. Izdevatel'stvo*). Each piece of music was stamped with "*fondée par* (founded by) *S. et N. Koussewitzky.*"

Koussevitzky invited Scriabin to be on the advisory board. Rachmaninoff had already accepted, and soon he would ask Medtner. The discussions in Ouchy touched upon this first, and on solo appearances second. Koussevitzky offered Scriabin 1,000 rubles a concert to appear with his orchestra. Scriabin accepted with alacrity.

Scriabin overflowed with plans. He spoke of tactile symphonies. He called incense an art which joins earth and heaven. He described the Mysterium. He explained this great final, cataclysmic opus as synthesizing all the arts, loading all senses in a hypnoidal, many-media extravaganza of sound, sight, smell, feel, dance, décor, orchestra, piano, singers, light, sculptures, colors, visions. Koussevitzky bought rights to it then and there. He tendered an offer of 5,000 rubles a year for five years, the time Scriabin estimated it would take to complete the Mysterium. In return he would publish all his compositions during the next five years at excellent royalty terms.

Sabaneeff explains:

> Scriabin was an acknowledged genius, regarded as the leader of the left-wing modernist school of Russian composition. Koussevitzky had an extraordinary instinct for doing the right thing artistically and this guided him through all his subsequent career. He had merely raised the stakes.

And he praises him. "Others were afraid to play so much Scriabin then— the piano music was too difficult, the orchestral pieces too complicated, but Koussevitzky took the risk and he hit the jackpot!" Engel sums the successful meeting between the two men simply: "Scriabin no longer had to tremble at the thought of tomorrow morning, and Koussevitzky had snared for his Edition and concert series a star of first magnitude."

Scriabin did not even mind how quickly Koussevitzky foisted intimacy by using *ty*. The wives were harmonious and when the Koussevitzkys invited them to spend two months in Biarritz, the last resistance capitulated into affection. It was the first time any Russian residing in the homeland had extended hospitality to Tatyana as "Mme. Scriabina."

Koussevitzky confirmed the agreement in writing, adding: "If you see Rachmaninoff by any chance, do not mention the terms. This conversation is outside the realm of the composer. I think it best if we keep our arrangements for your honoraria over the first five years strictly between ourselves."

Scriabin never got the name of Koussevitzky's publishing firm right. He innocently called it the "Self-publishing Firm of Russian Composers." "I am participating in it. How pleasant for me! Rejoice with me!" he wrote Morozova telling her that he no longer needed her stipend and that he was at last financially independent. "My fortunes have taken a turn for the better, and beginning 1 January, I need not trouble you further about sending me money ... I want to express to you my sincerest and deepest gratitude for providing me over these past years such kindly help. You know how vital it has been for me. I shall never forget your kindness toward me. I hope, dear Margarita Kirillovna, that the cessation of our 'business' dealings will not give you a reason for writing us less often, even if you haven't answered my last two letters! Oh dear, I simply cannot keep from being reproachful! What an insupportable person I am!"

Nor would he fulfill his obligation and pore over the music submitted to Koussevitzky's house for publication. Ossovsky, who later joined the advisory board, found Scriabin "indifferent to all alien music and very weak at reading from the written page ... He accepted or rejected at sight, without analysis." Scriabin's approach was "to open the doors of the firm to innovation ... the most important thing was to ascertain if the composer had a creative principle, if so, find it, and evaluate the work according to adherence to his principle which, in turn, gives birth to his style." However the first music published by the Russian Music Edition was conservative, a symphony by Goedicke, a quintet by Catoire, piano music by Medtner, aside from Scriabin (Fifth Sonata and three pieces, Op. 52).

The Scriabins dismantled their Lausanne apartment. Tatyana took the children and her mother to Belgium. After Biarritz they will take up residence in Brussels, a more expensive city than provincial Lausanne. Now Scriabin can be seen—with honor—there in Tatyana's home town. He explained their decision in part to Morozova: "Brussels unites one's preference for being in a capital, yet it is quiet and cheap, almost like living in a village. Besides it is near Paris and London where I will often be traveling. We think we will settle down in Brussels for a long time to come, and we hope that at last our long life of suffering is ended. Mama feels at home in Brussels and it is particularly convenient for leaving the children with relatives when we are absent. In this way we can travel with some peace of mind ..."

The Scriabins enjoy themselves in Biarritz and remained through August. "We feel somewhat better and ascribe this not purely to the climate," Scriabin wrote Morozova appreciatively of the Koussevitzkys, "but also to the fact that we have been so enchantingly and cordially entertained by our friends. They surround us most touchingly with every solicitude."

In Brussels Tatyana's family finds them a little private apartment at 45, rue de la Réforme. "Work is marvelous here—no bothersome neighbors and no outside noise ... I work from morning until 7 in the evening, and then after dinner we go out somewhere or friends or relations come to us." They begin their social life. It is noteworthy this time not for its caliber of snobbism (Paris), nor for music (Geneva and Lausanne), but for its sincerity and intimacy. Scriabin's circle widens, largely due to Theosophy. He forms here attachments of thought, mysticism, and sympathy which will endure until his death.

Emile Sigogne, professor of elocution and a student of languages, was a friend. He was an outright Theosophist and enrolled the Scriabins in the Brussels branch of the society. Characteristically, Scriabin misnamed it as a "psychological society ... we intend to go to its meetings eagerly." Engel described Sigogne—"They loved each other"—as having the soul of a Hellenist while Scriabin was Hinduist. In their conversations they agreed constantly on socialism, art's potency, and linguistic problems. Together they worked on an absolutely new language for the Mysterium. It had Sanskritic roots, but included cries, interjections, exclamations, and the sounds of breath exhaled and inhaled. Much of this was plotted on Sundays, when they sat at a favorite café drinking wine.

F. A. Gevaert, a pioneer in color film and author of *The Musical Problems of Aristotle*, was also a friend. So was Jean Delville, painter and Theosophist. He had recently written a book called *The Mission of Art* which expressed exactly what Scriabin had felt earlier. "Art and literature have lost their sense of the divine ... The Line [meaning outline or scheme] in all Nature's objects is the signature of God . . ." The sculptor Serafim Sudbinin (1867–1944) made a bust of Scriabin. Djane LaVoie, a young Canadian girl, later married to impresario Siegfried Herz, came to study with the "*maître*," as Scriabin was now called.

There was also a young man, Alexei Podgaetsky, a Russian who studied piano at the Brussels Conservatory. Already he was bald, his mouth a little curved, and he splattered his conversation with French, halted every four words with "*n'est-ce pas?*" and spoke of "astral planes," "auras," and Blavatsky as casually as one asks for a glass of water. Later he was briefly an actor at the Kamerny (Chamber) Theater in Moscow under Alexander Tairov (1885–1950) where Scriabin saw the Indian classic *Sakuntala*. Podgaetsky became a true friend, although he had been horrified at first when his teacher at the Conservatory told him that Beethoven meant nothing to Scriabin. However, on hearing for himself the first Scriabin concert in 1906 he was captured. Podgaetsky took on Scriabin's prejudices—he began hating Schubert, and mocked the horrible whistling figure in the scherzo of Tchaikovsky's Fourth Symphony. In exchange for such loyalty, Scriabin was always "simple and warm." Their friendship never flagged.

Even surrounded by his loving phalange, Scriabin was not an easy person, Engel testifies. "He had only to read a page of Blavatsky and under her flag claim the cargo as his own. The cargo, often as not, was of a disputatious and aggressive nature. Scriabin simply asked for trouble in those days, screeching a battle cry against all whose thoughts were different from his. He sometimes shocked. Later, in Moscow, he became more reserved . . ."

The Scriabins went out fairly often, now. Sigogne took the Scriabins to *Siegfried* performed by the local opera. Tatyana, who naturally reflected Scriabin's views, found the performance "acceptable and we left satisfied . . ." A chamber music evening by her cousin fared less well. "Lord, forgive us our sins. We went to a Beethoven quartet, so endlessly long and heavy we nearly died . . ." Another time, "*Salomé* impressed us better than we expected. It is charlatan's music, of course, but not without beauty and temperament, albeit somewhat coarse. Its impact depends on Wild's [sic] superlative drama. The opera was put on very well and the performances were excellent . . ."

By the end of 1908 the commotion over returning to Russia started.

Scriabin needed a thousand rubles. "Passports alone take 400 rubles," and he wrote Altschuler: "Alas, sweet friend, my trip to America cannot take place for several reasons. I grieve deeply!! Who knows, perhaps next year our desires will come true under better circumstances." He tells Altschuler how much he would like to hear his "Ecstasy" performed by him ("If only I could fly there for one night!"). "I kiss you tenderly and wait for a letter from you, you hear, and write me even though you no longer need me now. O businessman! [in English]" The major reason he had to stay in Europe was to sort out his "family situation," which meant to get a divorce before going back to the homeland. But in this he was quite mistaken.

Vera reads about Scriabin's impending return and immediately gives two "Scriabin Abends," one in SPb, the other in Moscow. The critics were not unanimously kind. *RMG* said of the October recital:

> Scriabin demands a colossal technique and particular concentration and memory. He is difficult to get into one's fingers, because there are never any automatic passages to assist the pianist. He also requires an enormous reservoir of energy. All this Mme. Scriabina manifested in much abundance, and she played several encores. Her performing individuality is, in fact, surprisingly attractive. She is a very musical and intelligent pianist.

> This is not enough, however. He must be played with a tissue woven of nerves and impulse. Mme. Scriabina is deficient here ... The packed house indicates the interest in Scriabin's music.

> However, in the second section, the pianist got control of herself and in the third positively attracted with her art; so the evening may be judged a serious success ... The sounds spoke all the time of a great talent, capricious, nervous, daring and fantastic, ranging easily from fieriness, pathos, and cold irony ... but to end the program with Op. 51 ["Fragility"] was really a little enigmatic.

The Moscow concert of 30 November included some "later" music learned from Nemenova-Lunz's manuscripts. The *RMG* now criticized her piano (a poor Bechstein from the Grossman store), found "Enigma" Debussy-like, the twelve études, Op. 8 "uneven ..."

Vera's concerts almost spoiled 1908 and all its good fortune for Scriabin.

XIII
HOME

42

THE TRAIN with the Scriabins in a modest second-class compartment arrived in Moscow at 9: 50 in the morning of 14 January, 1909. They were met by Koussevitzky's butler, Fyodor, who whisked them away to the mansion in Little Glazovsky Lane. Once settled, Scriabin said to his friends, "Come visit us"; but Sabaneeff points up once more Moscow's antagonism to the Koussevitzkys. "It was not so easy. Not everyone dared venture into that house. Scriabin must have felt locked away in a fortress, cut off from all . . ." As for the Monighettis, they could not go to the Koussevitzkys as long as Tatyana was there. Vera was their constant visitor.

Scriabin was now thirty-eight, tiny as ever (among musicians only Wagner was smaller), frail and pale. His eyes were hazel (to Sabaneeff), grey (to Drozdov), blue (to Eaglefield Hull), but they had a special look these mature years. "Something animal," Sabaneeff said, "but soft, not wild or savage." "Drunken-looking," Schloezer remarked, "but not the drunkenness which is a coarse parody of that true drunkenness—Dionysian ecstasy." Often Scriabin stared absent-mindedly upward. Almost always in company there was a half-smile on his face. Schloezer found it sometimes "mocking and childlike."

His skin was "a little greenish," through his lanuginous face. His beard was not flowing or extreme. His mustaches were still "officer-like," and on concert days he stroked them wickedly upwards. Scriabin was extremely conscious of his hair. "Hair washing was a crisis in the home . . . always," Vera had said. By now his hairline had begun to recede slightly. "What's this? I'm beginning to go bald! What a scandal!" he

190

would exclaim at the sight of a fallen hair. He brushed his hair to hide his imagined premature baldness. He always carried a little comb in his pocket. "His morning toilet," Sabaneeff reports, "took him as much time as it takes a girl in love." Before entering a salon he peered in the hallway mirror for a maddeningly long time. Scriabin was not remarkable in his appearance. Eyes did not follow him when he walked in public, unless you knew who he was.

The contrast between Scriabin's nature and his bold mustaches and beard puzzled everyone. Drozdov commented that "his grooming lacked the 'bridegroom' look," so painfully characteristic of officers, but Sabaneeff's brother, professor of organ at the Moscow Conservatory, called Scriabin a "cockroach," because of the reddish-grey color of his beard coupled with his restless, nervous movements and antennae-like mustaches.

As he had been from the beginning, he was a voguishly dressed dandy. "*Epatant*" was a word most consistently used then about him, and it meant not so much a "stunning" man as it did a man who was stunningly outfitted. Drozdov called him always "indescribably elegant in dress coat and suit . . . *épatant.*" He rarely dressed casually. Even at home he lounged in high-fashion clothes.

Scriabin's good manners and mannered tenderness, his modest and apologetic air struck anyone within their range. "He was warm, open-hearted, sincere. Soft voiced, his tone in conversation was intimate, almost confidential," according to Drozdov.

Of the several sketches recalling Scriabin's return to Russia, none is more charming than Sabaneeff's:

> How elegantly polite and delicate he was! And by those very qualities people surrounding him with friendship were placed at a distance. It always struck me how through politeness he could put a million kilometers between himself and his conversational partner of the moment. Politeness and gentlemanly manners seemed to protect him from psychic disruption . . . Everyone was sweet to Scriabin's face when they were with him—even those who minutes earlier had made the most appalling allegations.

Although Scriabin's face had begun to crease a little—"the imprint of creative experience etched on his countenance," Drozdov said—he still looked like a boy. Nemenova-Lunz called him her "40-year-old child." Like a growing boy, he lacked too, all placidity. He could not sit still in a chair for half an hour. He constantly jumped up. Sometimes at this period he talked too loudly. Or he ran about the room "so full of life," his friends said, but it was also a little too close to being like a jack-in-the-box with springs loose.

Yes, Scriabin was a nest of nervous gestures and compulsive habits all his life. He washed his hands constantly, often after merely shaking hands. He wore gloves inside the house. He feared bacteria, contagious germs, everything. "Money fell on this letter. Hold the paper by the edge. The 4th page is most infected," he wrote Tatyana from London on 21 March, 1914. Rozenov remembered how at Zenino when Sasha was served a soft-boiled egg, he said, "But it's uncooked! What if the hen were tubercular?" He fidgetted, fretted, fussed, fumed and drummed his fingers. He jiggled his knees, pinched the bridge of his nose as if sinus pained him, shuddered if any food fell from the plate to the tablecloth and refused to eat it even if it was bread. If a doctor prescribed medicine, he invariably took beyond the dose. In winter he put on an overcoat to open a window, slipped into gloves to receive or give money to a tradesman. He was particularly restless sitting beside women. He was terrified of their gossip. In summer he was afraid to sit on grass, and he shared with Rachmaninoff a horror and hysteria at cockchafers. He bolted at claps of thunder.

For someone who was so rarely ill, thanks to his mental discipline and psychosomatic control, people found it strange to see how quickly his spirits sank at the slightest suggestion of ill health. If he coughed, he would ask, "I have something serious . . . Could it be consumption?" And this was the person Sabaneeff caustically notes who dreamed in terms of being "a man of great soul drawing millions to him for the final Festival . . ." And all this existed under a covering of total charm and utter sweetness, and shining through beamed a formidable intellect.

On 26 January, the Scriabins proceeded to Petersburg. On 31 January, 1909, Scriabin would play "Desire," "Danced Caress," and two preludes, followed by the weightier second half of the program—the Fifth Sonata and Blumenfeld conducting the orchestra in the "Poem of Ecstasy." Scriabin's curious friends and enemies crowded the rehearsals at the Maryinsky Theater.

During one evening party afterward there was an incident with Liadov.

Scriabin with (left) his friend and biographer Leonid Sabaneeff, and the photographer Mozer, in the summer of 1913 at Petrovskoe, Alexander Siloti's country place rented by Scriabin.

Sabaneeff, Scriabin and Tatyana during the same summer.

Scriabin with his friend the Lithuanian poet Yurgis Baltrushaitis, at Scriabin's summer place, Grivo, near Podolosk. Summer, 1914.

Scriabin in 1914.

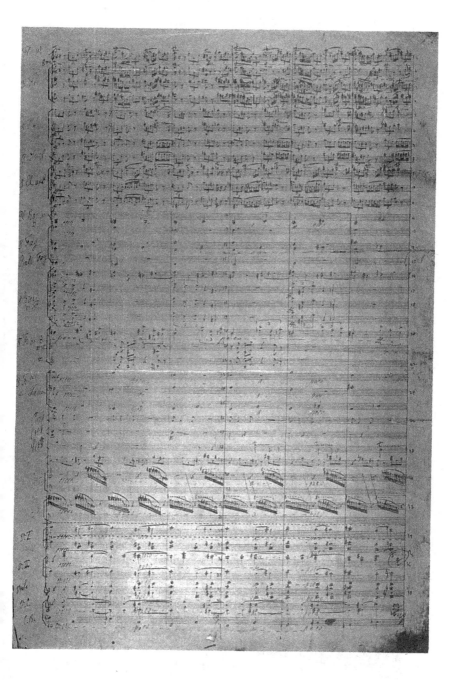

A page from the score of the "Poem of Ecstasy"; another instance of Scriabin's fine calligraphy. (Courtesy of Mme. Alfred LaLiberté.)

A trick silhouette-photograph by Mozer of Scriabin at the piano in his Moscow apartment in the last years of his life.

Scriabin's last apartment, now the Scriabin State Museum. The lease expired on the same date as Scriabin's own death, April 14, 1915, in Moscow: Eastertime.

The bedroom (before the Correggio nudes were restored).

The kabinet or study-work-room where Scriabin did much of his final composing on the "Prefatory Action" and the Mysterium, his cataclysmic opuses to end the world and its present race of men. The oval portrait is Scriabin's mother painted by her brother. The saint over the composition table is by Sperling.

The dining room where Tatyana served modest suppers of meat pastries, cakes and dry Georgian wines.

Scriabin's funeral procession. Taneieff and Rachmaninoff were in the cortège, and the crowds were so large that tickets had to be issued for the church service.

Scriabin's grave high in the Sparrow (now Lenin) Hills where Russia's celebrities are buried. In the background is the Novodevichi Monastery, built in the sixteenth century to commemorate the fall of Smolensk to Grand Duke Vasily III.

The high-flown discussion had been about "the ultimate meaning of art and new aesthetic directions." Scriabin, carried away with his self-appointed mission of bending the world to his artistic arc and flushed with what he called his forthcoming "Russian triumph," cried out "pathetically," as reported by Ossovsky: "I am the creator of a new world. I am God!" At this point, the gentle and loving, handsome and balding Liadov tapped Scriabin's shoulder, "And just what sort of god are you? A cock-of-the-walk, that's what!" Scriabin was struck dumb. He lost his half-smile for the moment, and the other guests laughed nervously.

For the actual performance Scriabin inadvertently forgot to leave complimentary tickets at the box office for Liadov, and the performance was sold out. Scriabin apologized later (28 April, 1909): "Forgive me, a thousand times I ask forgiveness. I was so grieved not to see you at the performance. I was, I must admit, offended. Now, it is all in the past . . ."

Scriabin played two encores that night (one, the Waltz, Op. 38). *RMG* wrote that the audience "listened without understanding much, but not being bored either . . . Some people demonstrated by leaving the hall before 'Ecstasy' began. It is clear that the name of Scriabin awakens curiosity, and it is also clear that his music very much disenchanted some while it made others take him more seriously. Scriabin builds a structure in the 'Poem of Ecstasy' which is original, complicated, and with places of surprising beauty and brilliancy. It is more difficult to speak of the piano music. As music it is very intimate, not for a large hall, particularly when the composer himself is performing. It is mostly note-sketches for moods. Scriabin's musical characteristics are *spasmodic*, original and nervous and strange to unaccustomed ears. His success was imposing, although whether this is superficial or sincere is as yet hard to tell." The tight-minded *Russian Word* (SPb) surprisingly praised Scriabin. Speaking of the music's "enormous impact . . ." the critic concluded: "In thought and in orchestral complexity, the 'Poem of Ecstasy' is the most daring composition in contemporary music, and this includes Richard Strauss. It is a brilliant score."

Before leaving SPb the Court proposed Scriabin as superintendent of the Imperial Chapel. Such a sinecure carrying with it government quarters and emoluments for life, required the composer to write periodically a short choral composition honoring an official occasion. The post had been held in turn by Rimsky-Korsakoff, Balakirev, and the recently deceased Arensky. Scriabin declined and never met the Tsar.

Scriabin was invited to return to Petersburg for a solo recital to be given on 16 March, 1909, *en route* back to Brussels. Meanwhile, on 4 February he returned by the Sevastopol train to Moscow and the Koussevitzky mansion. Tatyana fell ill and was confined to her bed. The preparations for "Scriabin Week" in Moscow began.

43

THE MOSCOW practice sessions were thronged, and the dress rehearsal of "Ecstasy" looked more like a public performance. Scriabin sat in a box. Sabaneeff recorded how "his face seemed tragic and doomed, a look which was emphasized by the strong unblinking hall lights. During the rehearsal he was nervous, would suddenly stand up, prompt, and then sit down again.

"Listening to his music, his face froze strangely. He closed his eyes, and displayed an almost physiological voluptuousness. He opened his eyes, looked as if he wanted to take flight, and in moments of tension in the music, he breathed heavily gripping his chair with both hands. I never saw a composer react so intensely."

Saturday afternoon, 21 February, 1909, in the Great Hall of the Moscow Conservatory, Emil Cooper began the "Divine Poem," followed by Scriabin playing the Fifth Sonata, two preludes and a mazurka. The program ended on the "Poem of Ecstasy." Tuesday, 24 February, at 9 in the evening, the RMO presented a chamber concert beginning with Zolotaryoff's new Sextet and followed by Scriabin performing Fifth Sonata, two poems, Op. 32, "Desire," "Danced Caress," "Enigma" and "Satanic Poem." On 8 March, Cooper conducted the RMO orchestra (this time to benefit the widows and orphans of musicians) repeating "Divine Poem" and "Ecstasy," while Scriabin played a series of preludes. In reply to public demand, he gave an extra, solo recital at the Synodal School Hall on 12 March of conventional music, almost as if to remind Moscow of who he used to be:

Two Etudes, Op. 8
Three Preludes, Op. 11

Prelude, Op. 15
Two Preludes, Op. 17
Two Mazurkas, Op. 25
Third Sonata
Four Preludes, Op. 37
Albumleaf, Op. 45
Quasi-Valse, Op. 47
Waltz, Op. 38

The liberal *Russian Gazette,* the "intellectual's passport," reviewed the first concert: "Yesterday a large public assembled . . . Audience reaction to Scriabin's music is far from unanimous. A minority applauded ecstatically and called for the composer again and again, presenting him with wreaths and flowers. The majority, however, were stumped. Yet even this is a step forward toward Scriabin's recognition by a 'large public.' In its day his Second Symphony elicited catcalls. Now, after the 3rd symphony and the Poem of Ecstasy, and even after the 5th Sonata, there was nary a whistle, although we did hear some expression of dissatisfaction around us. In any event, Scriabin has upset the musical audience of Moscow as no one else has in a long, long time."

The ovation of that evening had been genuine. The orchestra tapped on its music stands. Backstage in the artists' room, Wilhelm Gericke, conductor of the Vienna opera visiting Russia, fell on his knees crying, "It's genius, it's genius . . ." Taneieff was there too.

"How did you like 'Ecstasy'?" Scriabin asked him.

"My impression?" Taneieff turned red in the face, then forced a smile. "I felt as if I had been beaten with sticks." Scriabin was silent. As for the Fifth Sonata, "It doesn't have an ending. It just stops. That's all . . ." Next day, Taneieff sent a copy of his counterpoint to him affectionately inscribed not only to Scriabin but to Tatyana as well. Old Nikolai Kashkin reviewing for the *Russian Word* (Moscow) took Scriabin's philosophy to task: "This music speaks for itself. It is a lively artistic organism despite its long and deadly program notes. There can be no doubt in my mind that this music was *not* written to a scheme . . . Scriabin's music is a thousand times richer than its supposed content, thought, or poetry and all program notes containing such. It would be best in the future for him to devote himself solely to his powerful talent, and not to cast side glances at lifeless philosophical plots . . ." He added, "As for the 5th Sonata, I did not understand it at all . . . The 3rd Symphony was brilliantly performed and the audience gave the composer a rapturous ovation . . ."; and he raved over the piano recital, regarding Scriabin both as composer and pianist as "elegant . . . a true artistic nature . . . real feeling."

To Grigory Prokofiev in the *RMG* fell the lot of summarizing the "Scriabin Week" thoughtfully and, according to his lights then, percipiently:

> This week revolved around our little brown musical bear, and he stirred up discussion and posed once more the question: Where is Scriabin leading us? Even in his most off moments we still know that we are in the presence of a great talent and an artist . . . Try correcting his musical grammar or logic, and you will find the mistakes in *you*, not him . . .
>
> Is not his music the music of the future (in the best sense of these abused words)?
>
> I think Scriabin cannot be understood in our time, but he will be in the future when people's hearing, their ears, will be able to take in the sounds. At present this cannot be done. "All is possible. No limits to the Creative Spirit." No! No! No!! There *are* limits, and they are by determined our physiological reception and acceptance. Our ears cannot absorb a long chain of uninterrupted dissonances. We simply cannot *hear* the excellence of Scriabin's music even in the ending of the 4th Sonata or the finale of the Fantasy Sonata. In all the 5th Sonata there is not one single consonance . . . Thus it receives no approbation, because it surprises yet fails to delight . . . The Cooper and Scriabin recital however was very successful. It elevated the level of the audience and widened the musical horizon.

A second critic reported in the *RMG*:

> In my view, after Op. 47 he is off the track . . . The center of the concert was the remarkable Third Sonata . . . It is sincere, full of drama and poetry of purest water . . . His playing is tied to his musical countenance. It may not have those bright rays of light such as tonal beauty, strength, and variety, but regardless of all this, I have never heard such growth and development, such lift as Scriabin gave the D♯ minor étude. The emotional side of his playing is always shining and attractive, and although you know you are not exactly listening to a pianist, you obediently follow him into all the flights of his soul. As I have said, is there any pianist who can perform with such energy and *élan* in dramatic pieces and with such poetry in the slow sections! I shall never forget the andante of the Third Sonata and the Poem, Op. 32 No. 1!

Because of notices such as these, talk now devolved on returning to Russia permanently. Scriabin was making a host of friends and adherents. Let us, one fan said, give lie to the saying that a prophet is without honor save in his own country. Alexander Koptaev (1868–1914), music critic and biographer, became a satellite and received this word from Scriabin: "Your sweet letter touched me very, very much, and I thank you for its feeling of closeness to me. My greatest satisfaction is to render happiness. I hope that your expectations at my concerts were in part met . . ." In another letter to him, "I am terribly happy you are composing new pieces and ascribe your inspiration to my music . . ."

He wrote (after receiving a fan letter) the brilliant composer Fyodor Akimenko (1876–1945), former pupil of Balakirev, to send his compositions to Koussevitzky's publishing house—"they give the best terms possible." Vladimir Derzhanovsky (1881–1942), editor of *Music* and on the editorial staff of *Contemporary Music*, asked Scriabin to recommend pianists who play his music best. He names only Meichik, who "possesses a very big artistic temperament," and Nemenova-Lunz, who "is more modest than she should be. She beautifully plays those compositions of mine which do not require large hands . . ."

Medtner proposed making a collection of articles on Scriabin for his new magazine. It took Scriabin six months to get around to having a photograph taken, and only then by a disciple, Alexander Mozer, Professor of Electrical Engineering at one of Moscow's *technikums*. Scriabin suggests "Klaus Wolfram," the correspondent in Germany who has already written about him for the *Peterburgischer Zeitung* (Petersburg Times), and he errs on the name. He calls him "Claude Wolfram," but it is, anyway, a pen name for Ernst Pingoud (1888–1942).

Goldenweizer asks permission to organize a Scriabin Society in Moscow, and Scriabin replies conditionally, "provided Vera Ivanovna does not participate . . . To invite her will encourage her and impede my divorce . . ." To Nemenova-Lunz on the same subject he wrote: "Even to raise the question is incredible, and still more unbelievable is to ponder the question seriously in your presence! I am amazed that my opinion on the matter was even asked, and I admit I was grieved and angered greatly. Such unpleasantness can ruin my peace of mind (and I need this very much). A circle of a few friends, perceptive souls, who understand my creative activity can assist the realization of my ideas, far more than a whole crowd. But now again about Vera Ivanovna, I repeat..." And here Scriabin's followers asked themselves a spiritual question: In the final celebration of Scriabin's ecstasy, in that unification of all people in the "all-humanity of the universal" Mysterium, would Vera be present?

Scriabin was elected to an honorary membership in the Petersburg RMO on the occasion of its fiftieth anniversary in January, 1910, along with Godowsky, Hofmann, Ysaÿe, Hans Richter, Elgar, Saint-Saëns, Sgambatti, Humperdinck, etc. To cap his honors, Groes and Artsybushev are no longer his disbursers. Now they rent and hire his scores, agent for him and book his concerts in the Belaieff Series. They will have galling moments when they pay 700 rubles for the right to perform his Fifth Symphony which Koussevitzky published. They also invited Scriabin for another return concert in SPb on 20 February, 1910.

As for other old friends, one night the Koussevitzkys, somewhat possessively, prevent Scriabin from dining with Morozova. They take him to the theater and have arranged supper afterwards. Zinaida Monighetti asks Scriabin for complimentary tickets to his solo recital—a note on his calling card will do, she says—but Scriabin answers that he has no Russian calling cards. He extends half a hand of friendship by saying, "If you do come here to collect the card [in French], you will see NO ONE but me." And they met uneasily. He played for her. He returned her call alone.

At last, on 19 March (1 April), 1909, the Scriabins arrived back "home" in Brussels. As Scriabin wrote Liadov, "We returned to our quiet life and I am working very hard, disregarding how poorly I feel and weary... Soon I will finish the text of Mysterium and, if you like, I will send you a copy when I write it out..." Tatyana described the Russian trip for Nemenova-Lunz: "We have been through so much these last three months! We have oh so many remembrances of Moscow and Russia, and nearly all of them are pleasant. The concert in Petersburg was one continuous ovation. The audience shouted at the end 'Give us another concert, Scriabin,' 'Thanks,' 'Bravo!' A delegation came to the house to ask for another repeat concert, and when they didn't find Alexander Nikolaevich, they left a most touching note..." Scriabin himself wrote her saying, "I feel badly and am greatly fatigued..."

Koussevitzky was emotionally reassured by the Russian successes, and he stokes the furnace of Scriabin's ambition. He proposes taking him to London and, *mirabile dictu*, persuades him to play the Concerto. (The trip did not eventuate.) Later that summer, Scriabin, Tatyana, and students LaLiberté and Rita Loctot all send Meichik a picture postcard. Scriabin writes on it in the afterglow of victory: "You are sitting there in Weimar with Liszt, Wagner and Goethe. But I assure you, dear Mark Naumovich, we are much better than they!"

There were, inescapably, repercussions from the Russian visit. One letter to Olga Monighetti (12 July, 1909) regards Tatyana and another, even more stern, on that and similar subjects went to his father (2 December, 1909).

> Respected Olga Ivanovna ... I value friendship very highly and have not forgotten the sweetness of your family. If our relations were broken for a spell, then that to my deep sorrow was due to you. Tatyana Fyodorovna shares all my sympathy and attachments, and I am convinced that on closer acquaintance with her you would understand how offended I have been by your attitude towards her. Oh well, let's not recall the past. Better to think of the renewal of our friendship.

He tells her that they are staying in the city of Brussels for the summer, because after having rented a *dacha* he learned that three children in the area had whooping cough. Naturally, they could not go there. "But fortunately, or unfortunately, summer in the city is cold and rainy, and perhaps pleasanter than the country ..."

> Dear Papa, I received your letter after such a long interval and was very happy, but as usual, happiness does not last long. How stiff and cold your attitude toward me. I imagined that when you wrote me to come to Russia alone that you knew I would not take your advice. I must say, to Russia's credit, that my country acted towards me as was fitting, and I say this even with all my touchiness. Never once had I occasion to be displeased by the treatment accorded Tatyana Fyodorovna. As for the worthless opinion of strangers, your reproaches are completely unjust. I cannot be rebuked. I should be very sorry if our presence in Moscow humiliated anyone. I can do nothing about that, since I cannot exile those many persons whose presence in Russia humiliates *me*.

> We are not only going to go to Moscow again, but next year we are going to move there and remain perhaps for a long time. Artistic work summons me thither.

> Everything you write, dear Papa, leads me to believe that you want to extricate yourself and your family from seeing us because of our illegal situation— *which is not of my making*. Instead, you should be helping us out of this position

and respect your own true feelings, which you believe in but which are so rarely shown in our century. Not only do you not respect the lofty personality of Tatyana Fyodorovna, but you insult her doubly by hinting that she is my enemy and advises me falsely, and by refusing to extend greetings from Mamochka and my half-sister to her.

You are turning your family against me when you should be teaching them to read Russian art in my countenance. You talk all the time to me about family, but all your actions force me to think I have no family. To withhold your embrace—like so many others—from Tatyana Fyodorovna and your grandchildren until we get married is something I might expect from strangers, but *not* from my own father, my own family. Oh yes, I expected (naively) something *more* for her. She has shared my life without thought of herself and has accepted my misfortunes which, as you know, have been numerous.

If I am not mistaken the point of your letter is to get me to understand all this, and I hasten to set your mind at rest saying that up till now I had thought it my duty to call on you with my wife. Now I would consider it indelicate. Farewell, dear Papa.

44

THE LETTERS of spring, summer and winter of 1909 and extending as far as the beginning of summer 1910 convey all the intensity of his hard labor. Tatyana tells Nemenova-Lunz on 17 April of the afflatus: "Alexander Nikolaevich is composing a lot. Once again it is new; again infinitely beautiful! He feels himself overflowing with creative energy and in a state of uplift. I am supremely happy just watching him at work!" In August she wrote Meichik: "Alexander Nikolaevich is working like the very devil!"

He, himself, thinking he was writing the Mysterium at first, now speaks to Monighetti as: "I hope soon to finish one major composition;" to Koptaev: "All summer I never left my *kabinet,* neither hunted nor fished [not that he ever had] and only very rarely took my customary walks." However, to Alexander Khessin (1869–1955), a Nikisch pupil who was conducting "Ecstasy" in Berlin on 2 December, 1909 (*RMG* reported merely that "the symphony was beyond his powers"), the "composition" is reduced in size: "I would come there for a few days with the greatest of pleasure, provided my most urgent work (a poem for orchestra and piano) does not keep me chained to my worktable for the next three weeks."

The first time Scriabin titled this new work was to Artsybushev on 20 November, 1909—*Prometheus*, "The Poem of Fire" for orchestra and piano. He again utters its name on 5 December, 1909, to Koptaev: "I am working like a madman on Prometheus—successfully these past days, although I am right tired . . . have not left the house in more than two weeks . . ."

The music of Prometheus was begun in Russia, before he left for Brussels, according to Olga Monighetti's memoirs:

> One afternoon he played his early compositions. He stopped suddenly and asked, "Are you telling me the truth when you say this is good? Does not beauty really reside only in complexity? No! Here, listen to this, I'll play a little fragment from my latest composition—it isn't written down yet, still in my head! It will be a Poem."
>
> He began to play, not taking his eyes from my face, looking for the answer.
>
> "I don't like it," I said frankly when he had finished.
>
> "That was because you didn't understand at all."
>
> "That's very possible," I honestly agreed, "but I feel that music must first of all be sincere, direct, born of inspiration—then it is irresistible, but such far-fetched complexity leaves me cold."
>
> "Do you really think this is farfetched? Listen. Here are 5 themes: the first . . ." He began to sing in a bass voice the themes one after the other. "Here the second meets the first, here the third comes in . . . the fourth opposes it. The first comes again, already changed, it dominates all of them and engulfs them. Listen, aren't they beautiful? Don't they move you?"
>
> "Yes, the themes by themselves are lovely, but to weave them all together thus is cacaphonous and tires the ear." Scriabin repeated the fragment several times obviously trying to implant it in my ear and in my stupid head. But it was useless.
>
> "Well, do you still not like it?"
>
> "No, I don't, Skryabochka, it isn't suitable for the piano! It would be a different matter for orchestra. There all the themes could be differently colored and interwoven to make a wonderful pattern, but on the piano my ear cannot follow. It gives the impression of a contrapuntal mess, and says nothing to the soul. It's algebra!"

"You're an impertinent girl and nothing more! How dare you say that to me!?" The words were strong, but the tone was gentle, so that I was not frightened. Scriabin began absent-mindedly to let his fingers move over the keys, fixing his eyes somewhere inside himself.

"Yes," he said suddenly, "you are right. It isn't for piano. It must be for orchestra. What marvelous colors! What a combination of colors in these zigzags, like tongues of flame! It will be stunning!!" He jumped up from the piano and said: "I must run now!"

He came back from the hallway, his eyes burning, as they did when he was seized by some wonderful, powerful idea or dream: "I am getting it. These color sounds, I can see them!"

Later on hearing *Prometheus* I recognized this passage which had produced our argument, although it was changed.

She continues the story with another aspect of Scriabin's theoretical discussions, one which concerned the purity of *Prometheus'* sounds:

He wanted to construct a new instrument. The piano could not make the sounds he wanted. He was extraordinarily depressed by the skeptical attitude toward his idea of creating a new instrument which he met on all sides, both from representatives of the musical world and even from his closest friends. One time I was playing when he came in.

"What a beautiful piece!! And what a lovely tone!" he said standing at the door.

"Yes, a wonderful étude and I adore the key of D♭," I answered as I stepped forward to greet him.

"No, what I meant was that you had a lovely touch. Why do you like D♭, is it different from other major keys?" He seemed amused, and I smiled. "But isn't it all the same to call it C♯?"

"Oh no, no. Quite different!" I even frowned.

"But my dear, it is enharmonic." He quickly took my hand and led me to the piano. "Different?" he asked me. "Now you will understand why I must have another instrument. You still won't admit enharmonics?"

"No, Sasha, I can't admit it ... but there is a difference between C♯ and D♭!"

"There," cried Scriabin with joy, "I said so! And they laughed at me, what kind of new music can it be if it demands a new and special instrument! Come. Listen. Enharmony is only for the tempered instrument, the piano. Yes? But it is arbitrary. It is incorrect. There is another tuning, and I hear it. I am not alone. The orchestra could do it, but it is tied to too many tempered instruments, and all musical literature is based on the tempered scale. But I must have another. Here, this chord . . ." He sat at the piano. "This chord sounds cacophonous, and why? Because the piano is tempered and the augmented second sounds the same as the minor third. Can that be correct? The *seventh:* a dissonant interval? But enlarged and it becomes an octave—a purely consonant interval. Diminished and it becomes a sixth again, a consonant interval! And the inverse is true! You want a consonance, let us say for example, a minor third, but it sounds dissonant, because it is an augmented second. Why don't they understand? What Utopia is there? What newness in that? What is original about it? It is frightful that no one supports me!" His face was tortured. "I simply do not know what to do about the practical side of it all. I need someone who knows the mechanical aspect and who would understand me."

We stood a long time debating. Scriabin took the pencil and made some figures and sketches. I made a scheme for the keyboard: as far as I remember, there were two variants: the first octave a row of white keys making up pure, major and minor intervals, numbering 11 keys. All augmented and diminished intervals belonged to a row of black keys, numbering 14. But the octaves were too big for the hand, and playing the chromatic scale difficult.

Prometheus, "The Poem of Fire," Op. 60, his fifth and last symphony, "my beloved composition," he called it, is scored massively, embracing every sonority. Although the piece is in no sense a concerto, the piano is a solo instrument flamboyantly integrated within the orchestration. The chorus is supposed to be robed in solid white, and originally, when *Prometheus* was a section of the Mysterium, the audience was to be similarly dressed. It sings vowel sounds. Each vowel had a connoting color for Scriabin, though less fixed and different from Arthur Rimbaud (1854–1891) and his famous poem ("Black A, white E, etc."). To Scriabin the choral hum (with which it plunges into the music's ending) is a pearly blue, the color of moonshine; E is violet; A, steel with violet in it; and O, pearly white or sometimes red.

At the top of the *Prometheus* score is a two-note part written for the *tastiera per luce,* Mozer's keyboard of lights or color organ, which projected appropriate colors on a screen and in the audience atmosphere synchronized with the music. The upper line of notes denotes the root of the harmony (*Prometheus* begins on A—green and F♯—blue). The lower color-melody inches by whole tones to symbolize involution and evolution, the sustaining breathing in and out of the cosmos. The polarity throughout shifts between F♯ as a dominant or central key with A as the tonic or resting point. The entire work lasts a half an hour and is a giant suspension of a thousand discords and distorted harmonies. It resolves at the last moment on F# major, unexpectedly.

"It's the tonality of A," Scriabin once said to Sabaneeff, and he reduced all of *Prometheus* to six tones (A, B, C#, D#, F#, G). He played various chords and themes out of this, adding, "There is no difference between melody and harmony. They are one and the same. I have followed this 'prynciple' strictly in Prometheus. There is not a wasted note, not a wedge where a mosquito could get in and bite!" The arrangement A, D#, G, C#, F#, B, the so-called mystic chord of fourths augmented, diminished and perfect, opens the piece. It is the Ur-chord of many chords in *Prometheus*. Its distribution is so wide, releasing such unusual resonances (G lies at the bottom, which throws the ensuant overtones out of line), that Scriabin used to defy anyone to repeat it after him by ear.

At last, Scriabin had written color-music actually adding visual effects. Koussevitzky at his first performance of "Ecstasy" strung garlands of little electric light bulbs over the proscenium arch. ("Frightfully vulgar," Scriabin mumbled to his friends, "but never mind.") But *Prometheus* was a coordination of color and light, a pioneering triumph of specifics. Coincidentally in the same year, A. Wallace Rimmington (1854–1915), Professor of Fine Arts at London University, published his book, *Colour Music*: "The Art of Mobile Colour." He had also constructed his own color organ. Dividing the spectrum-band like a musical octave, Rimmington used a piano-like keyboard to play these colors, but unfortunately like subsequent other instruments, such as those of Thomas Wilfred and I. J. Belmont, it was of no use in the concert hall or as an adjunct to the controlled performance of formal music. (These early uses were, as at present, more concerned with color painting as an independent art.) But long before all these experiments, there had been in the eighteenth century a Jesuit priest who invented a color harpsichord. Rousseau believed in it. Composer Ernest Grétry (1740–1813) even wrote a supportive essay on "The Analogy Between Color and Music," and espoused the "inseparability of these two senses and arts, since both belong to the natural order of things."

Scriabin's scale of colors was arbitrary and personal, and although man, any man, can see in the neighborhood of 8,000 colors, his choice was restrictive. He worked on a scheme of fifths in cycles, and since red and orange are closest colors, they had to be his C and G, etc.

Red	Orange	Yellow	Green	Blue	Violet	
C	G	D	A	E	B	F#

He tried to match the physical logic of the spectrum. But no infallible correlation is possible, since the level of vibration between sound and sight is too distantly at variance. Apples cannot be counted as pears, neither logically nor scientifically, except in an extra-sensorial realm of intuition. It is impossible to process music through some chamber box of mathematics and have it come out lighted color. Under drugs, photism is a frequent manifestation, but the connection remains in the province of imagination and as material for the artist. No two people see the same colors every time for the identical tone.

Here is Scriabin's color scale for *Prometheus'* lights:

C	256 vibrations per second	Red
C#	277	Violet
D	298	Yellow
D#	319	Steel
E	341	Pearly white: (alternately described as moon-
F	362	Dark red shine, frost color, bluish pearl)
F#	383	Blue
G	405	Rosy orange
G#	426	Violet purple
A	447	Green
A#	469	Steel (the glint of metal)
B	490	Pearly blue or white

No sooner was this set than Scriabin was dissatisfied. He explained to Sabaneeff that he had indeed wanted "to augment sounds with the parallelism of light. But *now*, I want counterpoint. The lights pursue their melody, and the music goes on with its. Now I want a contrapuntalism of all the different lines of art . . ." He cited Wagner as an example of someone who did not understand color at all: "Take the 'Magic Fire Music.' He could not possibly have seen colors, because he uses the wrong tonality to begin with, and he repeats the same music each time in a *different* key. He felt no specific color, so the tonality is never right. The color of fire would have to be orange, that is to say, G. So his *Feuerzauber* goes to E and F and simply *never* to G. And take the sunrise in 'Twilight of the Gods.' He paints the *white* light of day once in C major (red) and next time in B major (blue)!"

Prometheus has almost never been done well with colors. The first performance was by Altschuler in New York, where the colors flashed feebly on a white movie screen hanging over the orchestra at Carnegie Hall. Two colors invariably blurred into a murky neutral grey. And Scriabin himself never saw a performance with color, except in his inner eye and Mozer's little hand machine—a circle of light bulbs. Once after Scriabin's death *Prometheus* was given at the Bolshoi. The colors were projected on a screen again, but his intention was to bathe the hall in light and pervade the very air and atmosphere.

The Rochester Philharmonic in New York with pianist György Sándor performed *Prometheus* with full colors in 1967. Alex Ushakoff, a film producer and designer of space simulations systems for astronauts, developed a light modulation device which scattered the correct colors throughout the entire auditorium.

Prometheus as a plot reeks of Theosophical symbolism and is Scriabin's only composition so heavily inflated with such paraphernalia. It exhales Brussels and the dense, mystical air of that city. Delville's cover design for the score shows a lyre ("the World," symbolized by music) rising from a lotus bloom ("the Womb," mind or Asia). In the center over the Star of David ("really the ancient symbol of Lucifer," Scriabin said, encompassing all religions) is Prometheus' face. Delville, and perhaps Scriabin, had joined a secret cult within Theosophy called "Sons of the Flames of Wisdom." They worshiped Prometheus, because those fires, colors, lights were metasymbols of man's highest thoughts. Fire was Prometheus' stolen gift to man, and it lay deep within hearts. A riddle as archaic as Rurik lives today: "What sleeps in stone, is awakened by iron, goes by wood, and flies faster than a falcon?"

To Scriabin, Prometheus had further symbolism beyond Theosophy's haziness. Lucifer was the "Light Bringer" or "Ferryman of Light," according to the Bible, and Satan was the "Disobedient Rebel." Sabaneeff's program notes, which Scriabin authorized for the first performances of 2 March, 1911, (Moscow) and 9 March (SPb), with Koussevitzky and Scriabin appearing on the platform together, state that "Prometheus, Satanas, and Lucifer all meet in ancient myth. They represent the active energy of the universe, its creative principle. The fire is light, life, struggle, increase, abundance, and thought. At first, this powerful force manifests itself wearily, as languid thirsting for life. Within this lassitude then appears the primordial polarity between soul and matter. The creative upsurge or gust of feeling registers a protest against this torpor. Later it does battle and conquers matter—of which it itself is a mere atom—and returns to the original quiet and tranquility, thus completing the cycle."

Prometheus to Scriabin was humanity's arch-rebel and arch-martyr. He suited mankind and the Revolution, and was, in fact, Marx's favorite myth. (He made an annual pleasure of re-reading Aeschylus's *Prometheus Bound*.) Prometheus was a Titan; Satan an angel. Both fell from heaven. Both left a false paradise of gods or God to help the earth. Both made man wiser than the gods themselves, for they described man's freedom from and superiority over the gods. They ripped the veil from the selfishness and jealousy that gods bore towards men.

Scriabin also commented on the similarity of Prometheus and Christ. (He copied Turgenev in this, rejecting one for the other: "For my part, I prefer Prometheus or Satan, the prototype of revolt and individuality. Here I am my own master. I want truth, not salvation.") Were the historical Christ ever to be disproved, Scriabin said, his provenance in Greek legend would still stand eternal. Prometheus gave enLIGHTenment to man, was silent under suffering, was nailed to Mt. Caucasus, and forsaken by a woman; only women witnessed his dying agonies. Five hundred years before Christ, Aeschylus' words had deified Prometheus for uniting the divine with human nature.

Prometheus is the greatest symphony Scriabin ever wrote. It dazzles with its sparkling genius, its glimmering tongues of flame. Every phrase is as remarkable as summer's first light on a spring day. Some passages emit sparks and flames, many of which are of dark, opalescent hue and others wound the eye with their sharp colors. Nothing in orchestral literature approaches its shimmering brilliancy and scintillant novelty. Its sheen is brittle as icicles, its heat blistering, and mixed in are soaring, surging themes—some seven different ones—of almost naked exaltation.

The symphony begins with Chaos, the inchoate ooze of the formlessness of the world—blue and green inertia of matter. The opening chord sounds the "active beginning," that mythical Prometheus which serves to open the symbol on this first state of consciousness. Here the orchestra represents the Cosmos as it was before Karma, before lives have been lived and deeds accumulated predestination. Out of this long sustained chord dimly rises the melody of the Creative Principle. Then, a muted trumpet sends up the Will theme (blue vanishes). Languor ensues, and the "contemplative" harmonies of the theme of Reason appear. Over this sweetly sings a solo flute—"the dawn of human consciousness" (green flashes back over the blue, and shortly vanishes). The piano (Man) enters imperiously, almost marchlike, and expresses its firm existence (the color of steel). At the second repetition of the end of the piano's initial figure, the color of glowing red envelops both piano and orchestra.

Almost immediately the piano changes into the "Joy of Life" section (the blue of chaos is obscured by the sun-color, yellow). Here (T2 in the score) Sabaneeff speaks: "Delight in the procreative act, magical action, enchantment, hypnotic and at the same time, vehement with mystical passion." (Critic Grigory Prokofiev asked regarding this juncture, "What musical theme can express *such* gradations of feeling?") Sex too emerges (T4) and it is immediately associated with sorrow—the first sad note of the music—but gradually it turns into passion, ravishment, ecstatic delight (as marked in the score). After the appearance of "intense desire," the solo violin sings of human love (pearl blue and blood red). Man now asserts himself, singing the beautiful cry of self-realization, "I am!" (T9). Scriabin described this passage as the "Ego," and it is a majestic glorification of the Creative Principle heard at the very beginning.

The center climax is reached (T15) with an ecstatic orgy of harmonies —scattering, falling and sinking. Soul descends into matter. The reprise begins at midway point with red waves enveloping the music's "tones of blood." As the mystery of this struggle and mystical complexity clarifies itself, the yellow of the sun begins to glow "joyously" (T30). The yellow persists until the sun becomes the moon again, and moonshine's pearly blue dominates. The Chorus, representing myriad forms of life in multiplicity, now emerges. The world's beginning and the original blue mix into moon color. The final cosmic dance of atoms begins (T54). The piano issues lashings of (violet and blue) fire which sputter and sear the mind's ear. The music becomes delirious. The coda is lost in vertigo. Although the world is now formed, life's symbols expressed, and man has been fired with wisdom, the color of *Prometheus* ends as it began— veiled in blue mystery.

Prometheus lost Scriabin some friends. Safonoff said, "It makes the air heavy and irritates the nose." One woman in the audience at the first performance had a heart attack. Sokolov called it "sick." Solovyoff found himself "undoubtedly negative." Dinoël wrote that he relaxed only when the orchestra tuned up for the rest of the program—"At last a perfect fifth." Nikolai Bernstein reviewed it as "hopeless, chaotic noise . . . This poem of fire is a burning example of anti-art innovation . . ." And young Stravinsky wrote Derzhanovsky that the Prometheus period of Scriabin's music displeased him in general. Even worshipful Koptaev had been shaken by it—"chaotic . . . a doctoral dissertation on musical bravado . . ."

As for exigent Liadov, Ossovsky speaks for him:

> He loved that which was high and fine in Scriabin, like so much that was in his own music. He loved much in Scriabin and found it close to his own personality and necessary to himself. Grace and clarity were decisive factors in his fascination for Scriabin's music. But after the Fifth Sonata, a shroud fell over Liadov's eyes and it grew stronger, the nearer Scriabin came to his ultimate attainments.

> I remember at the rehearsal of Prometheus, Liadov was sitting next to me nervously shaking his head and saying: "Frightful, how frightful this is!" And in the artist's room afterward Scriabin asked, "Well, how was it?" Liadov answered, "You know, I could never get accustomed to those fourths in the horns in the beginning." And only that. Sensitive Scriabin smiled embarrassedly and asked no more. Liadov simply could not find aesthetic scales to weigh such music. He was lost.

> Is he not going in the wrong direction, is he not lost? This doubt tortured Liadov. In November, 1911, the Board of Trustees after long debating and wavering, decided to award *Prometheus* the annual Glinka Prize of 1,500 rubles. The protocol was signed and the committee went home as it was already very late at night. The following morning at an unusually early hour for Liadov, he phoned me (I was a substitute member of the Board and had strongly ratified *Prometheus*). He said, "Can you know how badly I slept last night? The thought won't leave my mind of how fine it will be when in two weeks we hear Scriabin has been taken to Udelnyi [an insane asylum along the railroad to Finland].

However, many saw *Prometheus* as a masterpiece. Koussevitzky called it a "fact of history" and gave it nine rehearsals at unprecedented expense. He constructed a new instrument for the finale's bells—of low diapason but lighter and more portable, and remarkably loud, sharp, clear-pealing. To ease the audience into understanding, he printed program notes—a first time in Russia. Koussevitzky, however, was so unskilled as a conductor that the general services of Eduard Napravnik (1839–1916), conductor of the Imperial Opera in SPb, were prevailed upon. Scriabin wrote him a formal letter of appreciation.

B. Tyuneev of SPb in *RMG* called *Prometheus* "a bridge between what *is* and what *will* be . . . this bright start, grandiose in its measure, shows that his meridian has not yet been reached . . ."

Grigory Prokofiev of Moscow also wrote in the *RMG*:

> If a sensation was wanted, *Prometheus* got it. But aside from this, it is a major event in the history of art . . . magnificent moments . . . Scriabin's gifts and daring have already taught us much, and often the pure Scriabin sounds caress our ears. So this leads me to believe that the Poem of Fire harmonically speaking is a "burst of eternity," a new conquest by man's genius. It is a step forward in the direction of his Mysterium which will bring all influences to bear on man's psyche in order to attain ecstasy. *Prometheus* is a first experiment towards this abnormal excitement of the organs . . .

> And how was *Prometheus* received? On the cold side. There was no ovation from the packed house, but no noisy protests either. The majority were silent. The minority was not especially active. The concert began with a performance of Scriabin's 2nd Symphony, and it was entirely successful in Mr. Koussevitzky's hands and excellently played.

The *Prometheus* gust of inspiration also brought with it the great and final piano music. In the midst of his orchestral creating, he laid aside his thoughts to autograph a music book. The result was the "Feuillet d'Album" (Albumleaf) Op. 58, a signature for all the magical, new, undreamed of, previously unheard sounds of Scriabin at his most advanced and unusual. This little fragment is a study in piano pedal blurs (the unbelievably long pedaling is marked by Scriabin), and against them fall droplets of pearly, translucent, musical water. Scriabin himself felt that his extraordinary piano effects were the result of his astral or nonphysical being. Actually it was his superb technique exploring ultimate sonorities and balancing tones within harmonies. As companion piece came the wondrous Poem, Op. 59 No. 1. Its harmonies are rigidly symmetrical in minor sevenths and perfect fourths, yet softened by sweet grace and melodic atmosphere.

From now on, not a slip of Scriabin's pen will mar a page of his music. An artist-sorcerer has reached his pinnacle.

45

SCRIABIN WITH all his family, including Tatyana's mother, returned in January, 1910, to live permanently in Russia. After a two-week stay with the Koussevitzkys they found an apartment in a house owned by Oltarzhevsky in the Arbat on Little Tolstoi Lane. They had brought with them all their European furniture, but the larger quarters left the place looking unfurnished. The glassed-in bookcase now contained Barth's *Religion in India* and Arnold's *Light of Asia* in French, and Balmont's Russian translation of Asvogoshi's *Life of Buddha*. The carrot-colored rug, the rocking-chair near the piano, a corner cabinet, long-stemmed vases with purple-stained lips, were *art moderne*. The Russians expressed their disapproval of this "decadent" Brusselian West. Formerly their furniture had been a satisfactory "neutral bourgeois."

Vera welcomed the couple back with an all-Scriabin program on 14 January. On 7 February, she and Safonoff played the Concerto. Then possibly out of shame, she left for Berlin. "Claude Wolfram" kindly praised her "sensitive playing" in the First Sonata, but was baffled at not finding "the composer of 'Ecstasy'" throughout the whole evening. *Signale* saw Beethoven and Chopin in the "Funeral March," questioned the "striving for heroics . . . However, we must be grateful to Mme. Scriabina for acquainting us with the fine and lovely things her husband has given the world." She and Safonoff also performed two other concertos, by Scharwenka and Liapunov. After her return, the eight-year-old son, Lev, died. Vera and Sasha meet in the church without speaking. Scriabin, long alienated from his children, does not go to the interment.

1910 was Scriabin Year. January and February inaugurated six fabulous Moscow "Koussevitzky Concerts." On 31 January, Koussevitzky directed the "Divine Poem." He conducted the First Symphony with full chorus on 21 February, and while he did not at first "achieve the nervous inspiration of an ecstatic orgy," as Grigory Prokofiev stated, he nevertheless succeeded wherever and whenever the music itself succeeded.

Oskar Fried conducted the "Divine Poem" on 12 January in SPb and repeated it in Moscow, 31 January. 10 February Cooper conducted "Ecstasy" and the First Symphony in Moscow. 21 February, Leonid Kreutzer (1884–1953) conducted the Second Symphony. (Tyuneev spoke at this late date of "its protesting Slavic soul . . . the new shores whither Russian music must hie itself . . .")

On 20 February, Glazunov conducted the First Symphony with full chorus (*Prometheus* was not ready) in Petersburg, and Scriabin played Preludes, Op. 11 Nos. 1, 2 and 24, Etude, Op. 42 in D flat major, and his brand new Albumleaf, Op. 58. (Glazunov ended the program with his own "Prologue in Memory of Gogol.") Scriabin encountered bad reviews: "The First Symphony smells of youth . . . the new Russian school tries to wipe its nose with the handkerchief of Western authority . . . the piano pieces were insignificant. This is not music but mannerism. God save Scriabin from it! His gift deserves a better direction . . ." 13 March, Nikisch conducted "Ecstasy" in Moscow, and the reviews blasted him for not knowing the score. He flew "off in all directions—in one, looking at the clouds; the other going backwards; and yet a third going down, drowning in the water."

However, after an initial flutter of discontent it was soon evident that Koussevitzky was the master of them all. He began to electrify Moscow's musical world with his magical renditions of Scriabin. He found a haven for his own arhythmical talents and expressiveness, and few ever matched him. Only perhaps the Russified Englishman Cooper and later, Albert Coates (1882–1953) (conductor at the Maryinsky Theater in SPb), approached the shimmering Scriabinic mystery as well.

On 28 March (13 March, Russian time), Scriabin and Koussevitzky traveled to Berlin. Koussevitzky conducted "Ecstasy" this time with full "ecstatic orgy." The small impression of Vera's recital was "revoked," the critics gleefully announced. Scriabin was called to the stage and the whole evening wildly applauded. When Koussevitzky went on to play "Ecstasy" with the London Symphony, he warned the orchestra, "You may not like this music now, but in a few years you will remember with pride that you were the first to play it here." After a successful performance, Koussevitzky proclaimed, "Those few years passed in a day." Criticism now became like gnat bites, and no more irritating.

The *RMG's* "What's Written about Music in the Papers" reprinted an interview of 28 March, 1910, on the occasion of the one hundredth anniversary of Chopin's birth. Scriabin and Hofmann, now on fame's par, were asked their opinions:

> A writer on "*Le Matin Russe*" (Russian Morning) visited Mr. Scriabin in Moscow, who formerly bowed down to Chopin, and the composer of "Ecstasy" offered the following:

> "Chopin is colossally musical. In this he is without a peer amongst all his contemporaries. With his gifts he could have become the greatest composer in the world; but unfortunately the musical quality was not matched by equal intellect.

> "The history of music knows many such cases, where these two sides are not in accordance. That man of genius, Berlioz, was a bad musician. He foresaw much but he did not know how to clothe it in worthy musical form. Yes, and Beethoven—even he shows himself less mighty as a musician in the Ninth Symphony in which the realization is far inferior to the idea of genius which it embodies. Chopin, furthermore, was restricted by nationalism. He didn't know how to write anything universal, anything beyond the national.

> "It is astonishing in Chopin that there was practically no evolution in him as a composer. Almost from the first opus here was a finished composer with a clearly defined individuality. His was a haughty high-strung nature, which was revealed in its entirety in his creative work."

In April, 1910, Koussevitzky effected one of the gaudiest ideas ever conceived in the maecenas-studded history of Russian music—a complete tour of all the major towns along the Volga from Tver to Astrakhan. He hired some sixty members of the Imperial Bolshoi Orchestra, rented a Volga steamboat called, almost significantly, "The First," and engaged four distinguished soloists—Scriabin, Violinist Mogilevsky (b. 1885), Tenor Damaev (1878–1932) of the Zimin Opera, and Cellist Erlich (1866–1924). With an eye on the international press, he invited the fine German journalist, Ellen von Tideböhl, to cover the enterprise for Germany and America, and another German as well, artist Robert Sterl (1867–1932), to sketch the boat trip and concerts for publicity and posterity. Sterl was also hired to do portraits of the soloists. The Russian press was not given cabins on the steamer, but it was arranged for reports from the local newspapers to be reprinted in Moscow and SPb. Scriabin asked for his friend Mozer to photograph the tour, but Koussevitzky declined for lack of space. Tatyana, however, accompanied the group.

Koussevitzky prepared two programs—the first exclusively of foreign music; the second, more popularly, of Russian music. The group played nineteen concerts in eleven cities, and for many provincials it was their first music. Certainly it was the first time that they had heard a great orchestra.

At noon on 26 April, the party took the Nikolaevsky train as far as Tver. They boarded ship, and early next morning departed. That evening they reached Uglich monastery (where Boris Godunov murdered Dmitri the Pretender). Von Tideböhl watching Scriabin recorded his every action —how he listened to birds, admired the shoreline and the glittering silver of the Volga, the green branches and blossoms. Uglich's Byzantine cupolas of gold with crosses turned rose-colored by the setting sun thrilled Scriabin. "He was walking beside me and at once a great emotion reflected in his face: 'O religion! O holy faith!' he exclaimed. 'What worlds of beauty and delight lie in such confidence and trust in God!'"

There was a bell which accrued benefit to the body and soul of anyone who struck it. (It rang of its own accord when Dmitri was killed.) Now Scriabin whispered: "O how wonderful, a divine voice of the past speaks to us of mankind's eternal union. There is no space, no time in the universe. Everything surges into the infinite." Tideböhl describes how from the vibration of the bell, everyone fell even more silent listening to Scriabin. He found in bells a symbol of the eternal and enduring elements of the universe, although the ringing itself does not last long. "There is concord and unity in their bright and harmonious sound," he said. "I can always work more intensely after hearing them . . ."

Scriabin played his Concerto eleven times, invariably with success. He added streams of encores after each performance. Tideböhl remarked how strange it was, hearing the same piece of music night after night, to find he played it differently according to his mood. She also mentioned his extreme nervousness before the concert.

On the 30th, they reached Kostroma, visited Ipatievsky monastery where Mikhail Romanov had lived and the plot of *A Life for the Tsar* is set, and heard another peal of bells. This time Scriabin made an elaborate harmonic analysis of the reverberating sound. Scriabin and Tideböhl often discussed Nietzsche. She was reading *Birth of Tragedy*. Scriabin told her of his indebtedness to the book for its elaboration of the Dionysian concept of abandon, pleasure, and rapture. "It strengthened my own doctrine." He also gave her his own autographed copy of poet Vyacheslav Ivanov's *Among the Stars*, a book of abysmal obscurity, but Scriabin admired it as an exercise in philosophy, aesthetics and criticism and for its flavor of Nietzsche and Dionysian mythology.

One night at dinner in the boat's saloon a member of the company praised a politician because he had risen to so high a post. This incensed Scriabin who rose from his seat "extraordinarily angry." "Politicians and bureaucrats are *not* to be praised. Writers, composers, authors, and sculptors are the first-ranking men in the universe, first to expound principles and doctrines, and solve world problems. Real progress rests on artists alone. They must not give place to others of lower aims . . ." On safer days, they discussed the Mysterium "synthesizing odors . . . touching . . . textures of scents . . ."

In Astrakhan, at the mouth of the Caspian Sea, on 16 May, Scriabin toasted Koussevitzky in champagne for the epoch-making journey. "It has been magnificent, but I am tired of doing nothing! I long for my home in Moscow where I can give myself over entirely to work." On the 19th, on the return trip at Saratov (where he must have pondered his mother's early life there thirty-nine years ago), he and Tatyana took the train back to Moscow. She was pregnant again. "The company felt his absence very much," von Tideböhl concluded.

The Scriabins spent the summer at an estate called simply "Mark," a few miles along the Savelov railway line east of the city. Scriabin worked quietly. 27 June, the newspapers carried an announcement that the Mysterium will soon be finished and as *Prometheus* was built from six tones like the Pleiades, the Mysterium will be hitched to a constellation of nine. With the winter season Scriabin was invited to the Fiftieth Anniversary of the founding of the Moscow RMO, where Cooper conducted his "Divine Poem." Scriabin was sent only one ticket, which he furiously construed as an insult to Tatyana. Publisher Boris Jurgenson now re-entered Scriabin's life as peacemaker. He personally sends an extra ticket.

Diedrichs, concert manager and dealer in Bechstein pianos, also entered Scriabin's orbit. He will manage all his engagements on condition he give up the Steinway. On 22 November, Scriabin played an important concert of astoundingly short pieces in Petersburg:

Preludes, Op. 13 (C major)
Op. 11 (G# minor)

Op. 37 (F# major)
Op. 39 (G major, A♭ major)
Op. 16 (B major)
Op. 31 (E♭ minor)
Op. 48 (C major)
Etudes, Op. 8 (B minor, D♯ minor)
"Fragility," Op. 51
Mazurkas, Op. 3 (E♭ minor)
Op. 40 (D♭ major)
Fourth Sonata
Poem
"Enigma," Op. 52
"Poem of Languor"
Fantastic Poem, Op. 45
"Desire," Op. 57
Polonaise, Op. 21.

He, Koussevitzky, and Diedrichs telegraphed Tatyana: CONCERT BRILLIANT HUGE CROWD ENORMOUS SUCCESS FEELING MARVELOUS MISSING YOU DRINKING YOUR HEALTH HURRAH.

Scriabin returned to Moscow the following day. Diedrichs sent a telegram to Tatyana telling when Scriabin will arrive and added reassuringly: I CAN INFORM YOU THAT WE WERE BOTH VERY GOOD LITTLE BOYS AND DIDNT EVEN DRINK PEPPER WINE FOR OUR HEALTH.

The day after Scriabin's triumphant concert, the Belaieff firm gave an enormous banquet celebrating the 25th anniversary of its founding. Scriabin pretended he had to return to Moscow, and all the guests regretting his absence sent him a cordial telegram: THE FRIENDS AND ADMIRERS OF THE GREAT ARTISTIC GIFTS OF ALEXANDER NIKOLAEVICH SCRIABIN WHOSE NAME HAS ADORNED AND ENHANCES THE BELAIEFF MUSIC PUBLISHING HOUSE SEND HIM THIS HEARTFELT GREETING AND EXPRESS THEIR REGRET THAT HE IS NOT PRESENT AT THIS AMICABLE GATHERING IN MEMORY OF MITROFAN BELAIEFF ON THIS JUBILEE . . . The message is signed illustriously—Glazunov, Liadov,

Cui, Siloti, Sigismund, Blumenfeld, Cherepnin, Scheffer, Jurgenson, Witohl, Artsybushev, Lavrov, Groes, Ossovsky, Kalafati, Nikolaev, etc.

Diedrichs worked out with Scriabin's old Zverevian friend, Matthew Pressman, a brief tour of Russia for 1911: Three recitals (of early works only) for 1,200 rubles in Novocherkassk on 6 January, 1911; Rostov on the Don, where Pressman was Director of the Rostov Music School, on 8 January; and in Ekaterinodar on 10 January. Podgaetsky accompanies Scriabin on this tour, while Tatyana awaits the new baby. Scriabin sent Tatyana one worried letter:

Have just finished a divine breakfast and am drinking your health. I think of you all the time and talk about you with Podgaetsky. He is infinitely dear and is a calming influence on me. I am nevertheless agitated, fearfully agitated about your health. You are so nervous, so thin, and your dear little face looked so tortured this morning.

Please tell the porter to mark me in Rostov on the Don. This is very important because otherwise I would have to pay a 500 ruble fine [for leaving the city without notification, a restriction placed on all Russians].

The concert in Novocherkassk went brilliantly and the audience was amazing. On stage I thought of you many times as my guardian angel and this gave me much strength. Before the concert I was out of my mind with fright, and I tortured poor Podgaetsky as usual. Today I am calmer, and am now afraid that I may get to like appearing on the platform!

Pressman recalled some episodes with Scriabin on tour:

In Rostov on the Don we arranged that after my work which finished at 8:00, we would go to the movies. Promptly at 8:00 Scriabin arrived. In those days, motion pictures were shown in twos: first a long picture, and then a short comedy. I suggested that we go to the best picture house in town, but Scriabin said that the title of the long picture at the other theater sounded more interesting. Having no other reason than to show Scriabin the best picture house, I did not argue. We saw the first picture; the comedy began. From the very beginning Scriabin began explaining to me: "And in a moment this will take place, and in a moment he will jump over the fence, etc." This astonished me, and I naturally asked "How do you know?" At first he said nothing, then laughed and confessed: "To wait until 8:00 without doing anything would have been boring, and since I like the cinema very much I went to the very movie house that you wanted me to see, and the comedy there was the same one as here. That's how . . ."

Pressman continued:

He was always frightfully nervous before a concert and this in turn prevented him from playing his music in all its beauty. He would get lost and forget. I remember when he was playing the Poème Satanique in Rostov he forgot and hesitated a little, and even improvised. Coming off the stage into the artist's room he rushed toward me in agitation asking if the mistake had been very apparent to the audience. My assurances had no effect on him.

"But you noticed it?" he asked in despair.

"I noticed it because I know the piece well and play it," I said trying to console him.

"There, you see. You noticed it."

The whole evening after the concert, he kept returning to that incident and could not be pacified. Scriabin himself attached no great significance to his concerts. He rather looked upon them as a means to reinforcing his pocket-book which all his life was a source of worry and never full.

Marina, their third and last child, was born on 17 January, 1911. He called her "Doll" or "Marochka." Scriabin left again. In February, he toured abroad in Berlin, Dresden and Leipzig, and wrote Tatyana:

Please be careful . . . most important of all is to observe every rule of cleanliness. I beg you keep watch over the wet nurse and make her scrub herself with a brush . . . There was no place in 2nd class so we are in first in a coupé. Good luck!

I did not write you yesterday [from Dresden] because Sterl met me at the station and wouldn't leave me for a second. We dined together, then drank tea at some café, and I played for him in my room until I was exhausted. He was no sooner gone than I was in bed, dead from fatigue, thinking of my dear child and went sound asleep. I spend today again with that dear man. We are going to his studio now, then he comes with me to choose a piano for the concert, and then we go dine I don't know where. We talk all the time (in German!!!) about art and Theosophy (rather, the Mysterium). He is terribly interested in my Mysterium. He is quite a sensitive and quick person. How is Marochka? I remember her dear little face so well and when I get back I probably won't recognize her, she will have grown so fast. Tell Ariasha I beg her not to cause her mama any trouble and to behave. Kiss her hard for me and also Mouton. Kiss your mama for me, although she doesn't need it . . . I carelessly brought the keys to the cupboard and writing table with me.

Tatyana at first had answered in "a very inspired and lyrical mood," but she feared that were he not in an identical and receptive mood, he would not understand her mystical transport. He reproved her:

> Tatyusinka, naturally, I am very angry with you for tearing up your letter. Please NEVER DO THAT AGAIN! Anyway, I thank you for the sweet letter you *did* write me. What a portrait Sterl did of me! He drew an ideal being with soft oval face and a very complicated expression in the eyes. I would like awfully much to be like it in person!

From the Park Hotel, Scharlottenburg, Berlin, Scriabin informed Tatyana that "I am composing well! How is that possible?!"

> What joy! Five letters from you all at once! How I will thank you and answer all your kisses when I finally see you! It pains me to want to get home fast and be unable to. I have just come from Leipzig where I had a big success, although I played worse than in Dresden. My right hand has begun to hurt a little. The public did not notice though.

He telegraphed her his arrival time on 16 February (Russian time): IF IT IS COLD DO NOT MEET ME.

The German trip was a triumph. The important Leipzig newspaper, *Neueste Nachrichten* on 25 February, 1911, called him "a most elegant pianist with the lightest technique, a master of the pedal and a virtuoso of the left hand..." The *Hamburger Fremdenblatt* (3 March) said: "He displayed really marvelous art, both in controlling the instrument and in his profound interpretations...Healthy music of discerning, robust, and inspiring strength." And the *Allgemeine Musik Zeitung* (3 March) perversely noted: "His *first* significance is as a splendid pianist."

On his return a gargantuan rupture burst wide the friendship of Koussevitzky and Scriabin. There was a check for a thousand rubles to cover the entire Volga tour in the quarterly payment of Koussevitzky's Mysterium money. The *Prometheus* performances in which the two men had appeared in public so happily were paid on the same niggardly basis— one hundred rubles a concert.

"A scandal," screamed Scriabin over the telephone passing the flash-point of anger. "I received more when I was a student in Conservatory." Koussevitzky lost his temper.

"You are worth no more!"

Scriabin considered Koussevitzky an employer, leader of the orchestra, but servant of the soloist and a slave of the composer's music.

"I would not perish without *you*," Scriabin cried, "but certainly you would perish without *me* to build your reputation on!" Since this confirmed what he knew was true, Koussevitzky raged all the louder. Scriabin's conceited tone of voice was the breaking straw. Koussevitzky hung up the receiver, sat down, and sent Scriabin a bill for all monies advanced him.

Friends on both sides fanned the flames of enmity by their opinions, intrusions, and mere listening presence. The consensus wanted Koussevitzky to have his come-uppance. Joseph Koussevitzky (b. 1896), doctor and pathologist, wrote in an unpublished memoir that Scriabin offended his brother all along by refusing to treat him like an artist. He consistently relegated him to the background, and Koussevitzky, after all, was a virtuoso, a conductor, and a man who "owned an orchestra all his own and a music publishing firm." He felt that he was well in position to talk "eye to eye... he was boss of the outfit... he invited performers to participate in his concerts on his terms and he paid them on his terms..."

Arthur Lourié simplified Koussevitzky's side of the story on the basis that the conductor had been unable to go all the way toward becoming "a Scriabin fanatic—and this was indispensable to the maintenance of a close contact with the composer." But Scriabin's version as quoted by Sabaneeff differs, and rings true to on-the-spot fact:

> I said to him when he asked for so much money back, "Who are you? and now compare it with who *I* am."... And do you know what he said? He said, "I've done a lot for you." *He*... done a lot?! I said that he and all his ilk ought to rejoice at the chance to work with creative artists like me and not carry on so disgracefully. Ludwig of Bavaria would have endured anything from Wagner. That rankled him. He answered, "Ludwig was only a king, and I am an *artist*." Those were *my* words he spoke... my very words that I had said to him long ago when I told him that the calling of an artist was higher than a king's. And he threw my own words back at *me!* All to serve his own purpose...

Of course, Scriabin considered money from Koussevitzky as a creative subsidy, a gift against labor, no more to be repaid (were it ever possible for an artist to repay) than the Morozova fund or Belaieff's stipend. He wrote Koussevitzky that he now released him from any obligation he might feel toward him and in view of the hard personal relationship now arisen, Koussevitzky was free of any commitment to him. One hotheaded draft of a letter never sent has been found. It chokes with fury. He has scratched out, erased, crossed with lines and x's, abbreviated, but the gist reads: "...no answer to letters...writing clarification...as of 1 April consider myself free...if not agreeable to you my address..." Scriabin assumed that Koussevitzky's silence erased the matter.

Scriabin, still whimpering from the impecunious, Belaieff-less years would not have been so courageous, had there not been the possibility of rapprochement with wealthy Siloti. The Scriabin-Koussevitzky scandal traveled as fast as telegraph wires could carry it, and the news fed Russia's musical trenchermen for a year and more. Matthew Pressman even forgot his own personal troubles with the Rostov on the Don RMO (he wanted local autonomy in the school and concert series control) to act as intermediary between Scriabin and Siloti. When Scriabin finally telegraphed his release—the wish was greater than the fact—on 11 May, 1911: FREE ACT QUICKLY GREETINGS, Siloti quick as an arrow to its target proposed a "Scriabin Cycle in SPb": 1,000 rubles to play *Prometheus* on 5 November; 1,200 rubles for a pair of solo recitals, 31 October and 7 November. With still more enthusiasm at the prospect of capturing a prize, and with uncanny subtlety, he transmitted a message from his cousin Rachmaninoff, who had just been appointed permanent conductor of the Moscow Philharmonic (a post he held until 1913). Rachmaninoff would pay 700 rubles for a Moscow concert slated for 10 December, where Scriabin would play the Concerto under his direction and he would conduct the First Symphony (the "swine" one) without chorus.

Scriabin accepted everything. To Rachmaninoff he wrote: "My only regret is that it is the Concerto and not *Prometheus* which reunites us." When Siloti invited the Scriabins to stay with them in SPb during the tourney, Scriabin took a snide swipe at Koussevitzky and his hospitality. "How pleasant for an artist to be the guest of an artist. I hope closer acquaintance with me will not disillusion you too much...I will also gladly give you the manuscript of any orchestral pieces I might write this summer, before sending them to be published, but naturally I cannot vouchsafe the sort of composition they will be..." To Pressman he writes that Siloti "has the soul of an artist!... In advance I can even taste the sweet repose of being in the company of dear and cultured people..."

Another bee flies to the open honey pot. Liadov writes Scriabin on Thursday, 13 May:

> To us all has come word that you have definitely broken with Koussevitzky. The Board of Trustees has instructed me to write you that they always treasured and still treasure your music. They therefore invite you to publish again with us. Please answer.
>
> I rejoice that you are negotiating with Siloti. He is an excellent person with a deep artistic soul. The better you know him, the more you will love him. I can imagine how revolting and ruffling this whole affair with Koussevitzky has been for you and Tatyana Fyodorovna. Money is the lowest thing in the world. And yet, how can we do without it?

Scriabin guardedly answered on the 15th, the day before leaving Moscow for the summer:

> The call from my dear old friends touched me deeply. Tell the Board that I am moved by their kindness and say that in principle I would be very glad to return to the firm, but can only do so when my position with the firm of K is definitely clarified. This will be very soon, I hope, because I await the reply to a letter of inquiry . . .

Fortunately, for the interests of accuracy, one short exchange of letters speaks precisely of the Scriabin-Koussevitzky altercation. Siloti wrote on 1 July, 1911:

> A rumor reached me today, spread by Koussevitzky, who is angry that we have joined together, that I will never get a single piece of new music from you because you belong to him under eternal contract. Did you give him such a promise verbally or in writing? And unconditionally? Is your obligation only to give him first rights on purchasing new and future compositions, or does it include *first performance* rights as well? If no official mention has been made of *performances*, then K rejoices before his time. You then have the rights of FIRST *performance*, and afterward you can sell the pieces to him. Sale and performing are two different things! The only inconvenience is for the orchestra playing from manuscript instead of printed pages. Incidentally, the parts for Prometheus have not yet appeared in print. I have studied the score closely. God bless it! What an amazing piece it is!

Siloti wrote again: "Now that our 'concert' arrangements are settled, now only can I say to you that your Prometheus pleases me *TERRI-*

FICALLY! It is a *colossal* composition, just what I expected from you. Prometheus is so full of colors that one's head spins. My dream now is that you will be pleased with my performance! I approach it like all big works. It is clear and simple, but requires a very good and careful performance. Perhaps I will be able to communicate my enthusiasm to the musicians in the orchestra."

One reply from Koussevitzky to Scriabin—the only Koussevitzky letter on the subject in existence—is dated 10 August, and presents a written, calmer version of the disputation:

> The direct answer to your questions Alexander Nikolaevich, [the *ty* is gone], is the same as in former letters which you could not have received, because you seem to have forgotten our verbal agreement where for a five-year period you are to be published solely by the Russian Music Edition. This clause could not be omitted from our agreement, because during this five-year period you received a guarantee of 5,000 rubles per year to enable you to work on compositions to be completed in due course and obviously to be published by the Russian Music Edition.
>
> At the time these general terms were being laid down, they seemed perfectly in order, because we could not set dates as this could only depend on you. The relations now existing between us demand more specific terms. Those conditions are no longer satisfactory. For instance, over the past three years you have written Prometheus and two piano pieces [Op. 59], and the honorarium for these, including the 5th Sonata and two other pieces [Op. 52—three pieces] you gave to the Edition, does not exceed 3,000 rubles. This means you have in excess of 13,500 rubles, and must by some means or other begin repaying this balance of payments. The best thing for us would be to work out with N. Struve as intermediary some solution acceptable by both sides when I return to Moscow. I have selected Struve because he was the only person present at our verbal agreement.

Choking through his rage at one of the frustrating letters preceding this cordially couched ultimatum, Scriabin had written Sabaneeff on 1 July, "I received a letter from K so upsetting in its oddness, its baseless claims, that I still have not come back to my senses. I am in a fury!" And now, rich Koussevitzky is adamant toward the poor composer. On 10 September, Scriabin actually sent a packet of cash to Koussevitzky who, refusing to accept the insult and certainly not desirous of letting his golden composer slip through his fingers, sent Struve to return it. At year's end and New Year's beginning, when Scriabin gave Koussevitzky a series of unflawed masterpieces—Sixth and Seventh Sonatas, Poem-Nocturne, and two venturous little pieces, "Mask" and "Strangeness"—all rinsed in the very dye of genius and innovation, Koussevitzky respectfully honored them with a payment of 10,500 rubles. He tendered an account showing that Scriabin now owed him 3,000 rubles worth of music. Scriabin, however, placing still higher value on the music, considered the account closed and never sent the Russian Music Edition another piece of music.

Scriabin could no longer bring himself even to utter Koussevitzky's name or patronymic. He called him "he" or "that man" for the rest of his life, if the painful subject arose. In letters to Siloti he secretively used the code letter "N." Koussevitzky in a fit of disgust destroyed all correspondence from Scriabin, a remarkable gesture for that self-conscious era when everyone thought everyone else a genius and that the future held high stakes of fame and value for all of them. The Soviet Government enquired in vain of Mme. Koussevitzky for Scriabin memorabilia among her late husband's papers and effects. There was nothing, not a single souvenir even, of happy, early times.

Koussevitzky still continued to perform Scriabin. He announced in May, 1911, two conjunctive cycles: One, all nine Beethoven symphonies; and two, all five of the Scriabin symphonies (with another soloist at the piano for *Prometheus*). (He also conducted his first Stravinsky at this time.) The reputations of both Scriabin and Koussevitzky grew apace. In 1912 Koussevitzky made another grand Volga tour—with Meichik at the piano. Continuing into the future, it can be said that Koussevitzky after the Revolution worked for the Bolsheviks until 1920, when he resigned his post as head of the State Orchestra and left the USSR. In 1923 he came to America. On his first appearance with the Boston Symphony Orchestra in October, 1924, he climaxed a dazzling program with the "Poem of Ecstasy." No one listening to that night's incandescent rendition of a favored masterpiece would have thought anything had ever gone wrong.

Still pursuing the future, in 1941, when Koussevitzky hailed Shostakovich as "the second Beethoven," Rachmaninoff who, according to biographer Moses Smith, never stopped treating Koussevitzky with the disdain usually meted him in Moscow, drily cracked in a reference to Scriabin, "Not the first time he's found a second Beethoven . . ." Koussevitzky, still an apostle of Scriabinesque ideas, received the press at

Lenox, Massachusetts, on his seventieth birthday, 26 July, 1944, at the height
of World War II. His prepared speech announced "Music can save the
world!" Scriabin had said this of his Mysterium. And Safonoff too, another
broken relationship, also made pronunciamentos à la Scriabine. When
he first lectured in England (in English) in 1915, his subject had been
"Music's Power Over Life."

46

SUMMER OF 1911 the Scriabins went a hundred miles away from Moscow,
to Ryazan Province. There was an estate named Obratsovo-Karpovo,
on the railway line to the Urals, a short walk from the placidly wind-
ing Oka River. Their train stop was Stupino, scarcely the size of a
village. "We are in a veritable paradise—and for Russia, an unusually
beautiful spot," he wrote Pressman. To Sabaneeff, "There are two trains
a day, you have to signal before they stop, and we will send horses to
meet you. Write us if you are coming, but allow four days for the
letter..."

First, before the Scriabins leave, Pressman passes through Moscow
on his way to thresh out his conflict with the Petersburg RMO. The
Scriabins meet him at the station during the train wait. Publisher Boris
Jurgenson was also there, so they cannot speak of his difficulties with
Koussevitzky beyond a certain point. Anyway, it is Pressman's hour.
Scriabin sides with him and calls his opponents "unrestrained and stub-
born people ... it is necessary for *you* 'the third bell' to ring!" (Pressman
won.)

Von Riesemann was also in the party at the station supporting Pressman and in an aside, Pressman asks him to speak appropriately to Jurgenson about publishing Scriabin again. He does, and immediately after the
first Siloti concert of the cycle that autumn of 1911, Jurgenson initiates
business discussions. By March, 1912, the contract is signed giving Scriabin
enormously favorable terms—6,000 rubles a year, payable in lots of
1,500 rubles each in March, June, September, and December. This increase
in money matches the rise in Scriabin's standard of living. He had become,

as Sabaneeff states it *"pervosortny"* (first class) and had added to their style of life a French governess and a maid.

The Petersburg cycle went sensationally well. Usual comments were made regarding Scriabin's "living-room music," how the hall was too large for his performances, and how extraordinary it all was. The *RMG* wrote of *Prometheus*: "The composer had tremendous personal success . . . the public is unquestionably intrigued by his music. He knows how to rouse curiosity and feed our hopes . . . Where is this artist leading us? What are these strange and (apparently) daring-demoniac songs really singing? Is it a rapture or a nerve massage?" Not a word was said about Siloti's conducting, which was never more than barely adequate.

For his piano concerts, Scriabin turned to an unadventurous, but not quite provincial program first, and in the second program added the already familiar Fifth Sonata, introduced the four American pieces (Op. 56), and the stunning Albumleaf. The shorter the composition the better the audience responded. Invariably he had to encore the little pieces.

When the Scriabin-Rachmaninoff concert in Moscow at the Great Noblemen's Hall was announced, press and public scoured for trouble. Their friendship always crackled with rivalry because of their close similarities. Both were Muscovites, pianists, composers, and they were almost the same age. They had grown up together, studied with the same teachers, and both were celebrated, having received national and international accolades. Only their inspirations and aspirations were different, and this fomented all the more competitiveness among their separate factions.

On 10 December, 1911, the hall was overflowing with excitement. Scriabin played many encores. The second half of the program was Rachmaninoff conducting Rachmaninoff. The audience was wildly demonstrative. The critics were fiercely partisan, both as to opinion and in their loyalty to one favorite or the other. Grigory Prokofiev found Scriabin's tone weak. The nationalists and Slavophiles behind Rachmaninoff on one side jeered the cosmopolitan internationalists who had nominated Scriabin their leader. Rachmaninoff riffled through books on ethnography and songs. He incorporated folk rhythms and vocal intonations in his music. Scriabin looked away from anything so *terre à terre.*

All his life Scriabin resented charges of being un-Russian. For one thing it was not true. For another, he himself felt Russian. In one early letter to Belaieff, he had snapped about Rachmaninoff, "Is it possible that I am not a *Russian* composer merely because I don't write overtures and capriccios on Russian themes!?" On another occasion he stated his platform more formally to Asafiev: "Russian music is not confined to the narrow ranks of 'nationalism' in the sense that Western Europe means the word. It is of course nationalistic, but all the same it has to breathe the atmosphere of *inter*nationalism."

After the Moscow concert he spoke again to Asafiev in a glow of warmth towards Rachmaninoff: "You want Russian music? Then don't look for Russian peculiarity and exoticism. Take the notes of something by Rachmaninoff. Listen to it with your eyes and then hear Rachmaninoff play it on the piano. The same notes, yes, but the quality is entirely different. Unquestionably beautiful, no argument, convincing, everything sings. This proves that reading with your eyes you already hear the instruments, the music hidden in the human voice and even the rhythms are human breathing. Isn't *this* then the secret of Russian orchestration? And I am not the only one who has it . . ." Scriabin emphasized. Quarrels, like psychology, are double-edged. If Scriabin had once been chided and continued to be chided, so was Rachmaninoff. He played Chopin "as if the *rue de la Paix* were overrun with troikas . . ." Heinrich Neuhaus said.

Through October and November, 1911, Scriabin played twelve concerts. Even with Jurgenson's terms in the offing, he was compelled to concertize. He received 300 rubles a concert. Pressman, of course, helped him. "Oh exploiter," he wrote him regarding a tour of the south, "but I must accept." He appeared as far away as Vilnius, Minsk, Tambov, and in Odessa at the Union Hall, and Taganrog at the Commercial School there. Pressman invited him to make his headquarters for the tour in Rostov with him, but Scriabin is discreet: "It is quite probable that I will come with Tatyana Fyodorovna, and you will understand that we will stay in the hotel so as not to embarrass you . . ." However, at the last minute, his companion once again was Podgaetsky.

Between January and April, 1912, Scriabin gave seven concerts. For the Rostov program, Pressman begged him to repeat the SPb program, but Scriabin refused. "It is impossible to play the 5th Sonata for them . . . It is complicated and hard for even the public in Petersburg to understand." Then he moaned, "I not only must play early pieces, but play them as if I like them!"

Scriabin had difficulties on tour. Sometimes people called out for *Prometheus*. They wearyingly demanded the left-hand nocturne and the D# minor étude. Once he started playing before the provincial governor arrived, and dismayed petty officials stopped him in consternation. When friends took him to a house of prostitution in Rostov, he waited outside, much to everyone's surprise. Sabaneeff acknowledged that giving concerts was "curiously unpleasant" for Scriabin, but "they widened his scope of experience and enhanced his reputation as more than a composer or pianist and musical leader even . . . He became an individual of far-flung note."

Scriabin had played badly at the Rachmaninoff concert, and not entirely because of nerves. He hints this in a letter to Zinaida Monighetti, 17 December, 1911—the last he would write any member of that dear, once-treasured family:

> You advise me not to kill myself traveling, not to burn the candle at both ends, etc. You talk about all this and say that there will be nothing left of me if I go on dissipating my nervous and physical strengths in this way, and that this makes everyone who *loves me* truly sick at heart. Do you not see that in such a surmise you are really saying that I am not surrounded by my true friends and that the people around me completely ignore my peace of mind and body, do not see, do not want to see my slow death and that they exploit me for their own egotistical ends. (Indeed, only such a supposition could permit you to interfere in my private life.)

> Your letter is directed against the person nearest me and accuses her of crimes against my work. You show a desire to destroy my belief in her devotion to me. I would like to remind you that such an attempt on your part before while we were abroad led to a break between us. Tatyana Fyodorovna shows her devotion to me and to my art every minute of her life, and not in words but in deeds. My *true* friends are the first to understand this. Do not suffer in your heart for me. Rejoice! That is what I *should* have!

> I regret that I was incautious enough to tell you I was tired, if that gave you the right to come to such a pitying conclusion. You ask me what my recent cooling off toward you means. Surely you have guessed that the attack you launched against Tatyana Fyodorovna when her mother and her aunt called on you could hardly bring us together! Do you not understand how your letter today spoils those good relations which *could* exist between us? But you destroy them.

> If I had to play a concert today, I would probably play incomparably worse than I did on 10 December—all because you have agitated me to such an

extent. Incidentally, your evaluation of my last appearance surprised me very much. I could prove to you that I played very well, had you not come with your mind already made up that I was a damned soul. Enough! I am very upset, and this is injurious to my health . . .

The saddest part is that the Monighettis were correct in their assessment of Scriabin's career. Concerts—and he gives more and more of them as he grows more and more renowned—conflict with his compositions. While the latter wax greater, they become fewer. The end of Scriabin's life is all concerts—a sin against the "HE," his mystical muse, to whom he had for so long sedulously given himself.

47

WHILE SCRIABIN thought over his Mysterium—in conversation, schemes, plans and poems—and sketched its themes, motifs and moments, fragments of the music kept shaping into sudden and individual entities. His work over the 1911 summer produced two sonatas, and he presided over their construction like a book of discipline. Scriabin glibly postscripted a letter on 16 November to Siloti, "Am finishing 6th sonata." A month later he says, "And here's some news which may be pleasant for you! The Sixth Sonata is finished except for some unimportant details, and I burn with eagerness to play it all the way through for you."

The Sixth Sonata, Op. 62 is a netherstar. Its dark and evil aspect embrace horror, terror, and the omnipresent Unknown. "Only my music expresses the inexpressible," Scriabin boasted, and called the Sixth's sweet and harsh harmonies, "nightmarish . . . fuliginous . . . murky . . . dark and hidden . . . unclean . . . mischievous." When he played excerpts for friends, he would stare off in the distance away from the piano, as if watching effluvium rise from the floor and walls around him. He seemed frightened and sometimes shuddered. Its mood directly inherits the inchoate, incomprehensible, unformed chaos of the dark beginning—the Void.

Regarding the Seventh Sonata, Op. 64, Scriabin addressed a letter to Pressman on 19 January, 1912, saying, "I hasten to copy the sonata and will send it to the printers in a day or so." In February, Tatyana wrote

Vera Siloti, "You doubtless know that Alexander Nikolaevich has finished his 7th Sonata and will play it on the 21st at his *clavierabend*. He will repeat it for Petersburg in April . . ."

Musically the Seventh Sonata, with triadic jumps blasting into luminosity, succeeds the Fifth. Here for the first time Scriabin defines his "set" or "series"—a central chord or cluster of two minor thirds separated by a perfect fourth. For density, he subdivides the inner interval into halves or, because of the artificiality of the piano scale, near-halves. His first program bills the key as "F#," but the chromaticism is so intense there can be no signature at the beginning. His chords are so full of unconventional sounds that tonic and dominant disappear.

One of several "bell themes" of the Mysterium, a pealing burst of quivering and fulgurous resonances (requiring four staves), serves double duty for the parallel climaxes in the Seventh Sonata. A so-called "glimmering theme," intended to suggest a shimmer of unfocused light, appears near the end of the sonata (p. 20, marked pianissimo and "flashing with light"). This first appears on another pitch (p. 6) where Scriabin calls it "sparks from the fountain of fire . . ."

This period in Scriabin's life was unique in reconciling simultaneously two such pieces of music. One descends from the heavens; the other rises like subterranean mephitis. The total traffic of the Sixth is satanic. Its harmonies scratch with perfect fourths and fifths, but even in the loudest sections, there is no burst or breakthrough. The chords sound like undusted surfaces, powdered and soft as flesh. His "set" here is a condensed chord of concentrated minor thirds. Hidden little sub-themes of two tones only— "*charmes*" (spells) or "*appel mystérieux*" (mysterious call)—darken and defile, scarify the music.

Scriabin himself feared this Sixth Sonata, and never played it publicly. (Bekman-Shcherbina gave its première in Moscow, 6 March, 1912.) Writing in October, 1912, he asks Siloti to choose any sonata he should play "except the 6th." He also shows his bias: "No matter what, I must repeat the 7th and," as an afterthought, "play the 3rd since I didn't give it last year. Or did I?" (In this same letter he approves the performance of *Prometheus* omitting the chorus: "It is tolerable, provided there is STILL THE ORGAN PART . . .")

None of Scriabin's music ever pleased him so much as his Seventh Sonata. As his favorite piece he played it repeatedly in concert and in private. He considered it "holy," marked some passages "*très pur*" (very pure), and thought its sonorities "beatitudinous" or "saintly." He himself subtitled the sonata "The White Mass," to dramatize its sacerdotal character, and to him its performance was ritual. Sounding the tocsin of Theosophy, he spoke of its ". . . purest mysticism . . . total absence of human feeling . . . complete lack of emotional lyricism." At last Scriabin felt he had reached his sainthood and manifest dematerialization. Schloezer said he had now "stripped all fleshly garment and returned to pure spirituality in his music."

The opening theme is heaven's autocratic "call." The second, but primary theme (p. 4) is man's sensual reaction, and is to be played "with celestial voluptuousness" (*céleste volupté*). Changing and evolving, it is repeated continuously, and ultimately returns (p. 18) "with radiant and ecstatic voluptuousness" (*volupté radieuse, extatique*). The theme is the same; only the elaboration differs.

Scriabin liked to talk as he played for intimates, almost as if dictating to a stenographer. He began the Seventh Sonata once for Sabaneeff saying, "Perfumes, like clouds, are here . . . already this music approximates the Mysterium . . . listen to this quiet joy . . . it's so much better than Prometheus . . ." When he reached the second theme he said: "All is born here . . . the waves lift . . . the face of the sun dispels the clouds . . . Listen to how it burns, how it grows and grows, more and more . . ." (Pianist Richter feels the first pages are "hot and stifling . . . suffocating in their heat . . .") Then explaining that the "clouds" were "mystic clouds," not tangible ones, he unexpectedly skipped ahead to point out passages of "flight." "Here melody flutters overhead . . . wings . . . here is maximum flight in music . . . How it lifts and soars in heaven itself . . ." In the summer of 1912 Scriabin informed the musical journals that he was writing a symphonic picture to be called *Icarus*. "It will depict the flight and fall of the mythological hero. To give the illusion of fluttering wings, Mr. Scriabin is incorporating into his orchestra a new instrument— a propeller," reported *RMG*.

The "glimmering theme" or "fountain of fire" leads into the "last dance and dissolution." "Trumpets of archangels herald it . . ." The vortical dance spins giddily in disequilibrium. Scriabin adored the chaotic fortississimo of the crashing final pages: "Everything here is mixed, blended," he said here, playing as if a thousand bells had gone wild. "This is real *vertigo!*" Scriabin was transported. He whispered his emphasis as he played, "This is truly holy. Here is the *last* dance before the *act* itself, before the instant of dematerialization. *BY MEANS OF THIS DANCE* all is accomplished . . ."

The Sixth Sonata neither ended Scriabin's satanism, nor did the blessedness of the Seventh Sonata purge. Immediately after, he wrote two Poems (Op. 63) subtitled "Mask" and "Strangeness" invoking evil's deceptive, illusory world. He marked "Mask" as *"douceur cachée"* (hidden sweetness), and a subsidiary passage—a miniature peak—*"bizarre."* He wanted "Strangeness" played with *"fausse douceur"* (false sweetness), so its corruption pullulates. Masked, he now advanced toward heaven and hell, into good and evil.

Sabaneeff enquired about this juxtaposing of God and Satan in music. He theorized that, "The 'spirit of evil' plays a sad role in Christian theodicy, but for Scriabin it was not something wicked or bad at all. He was sympathetic to it and called it the 'creative spirit.' It was that which created everything from the world itself to the Poem of Ecstasy.

" 'Satan', he said, 'is the shivering of the universe which cannot gather all together in one place or unify. It is the principle of movement.' And never once," Sabaneeff consternates, "did he mention God in connection with the creation of the world. To Scriabin it had been the work of Satan or Lucifer. God dwelled only in the nothingness . . .'"

As *Prometheus* and the Albumleaf had been the divide in the stairs which laddered his music from the middle period into its final ultimate, so too did the first public performance of the Seventh Sonata crack public opinion wide open. Two unequal but equally vociferous factions stand pat now for the rest of Scriabin's lifetime. On 21 February, 1912, at the Great Noblemen's Hall in Moscow under the auspices of the Philharmonic Society, Scriabin played the first of his supreme, latter-day programs of music:

Preludes, Op. 11 (C major, E minor, C# minor, G# major, Eb minor, D major, D minor)
Etudes, Op. 42 (C# minor), Op. 8 (Ab major, D# minor)
Third Sonata
Poems, Op. 32
Prelude, Op. 48 (C major)
"Dance of Languor," Op. 51

"Desire", Op. 57
"Enigma", Op. 52
Albumleaf, Op. 58
Seventh Sonata, Op. 64

Scriabin perplexed critics in both capitals. Some were angered, even his old friends. Engel writing for *Russian Gazette* commented, as usual, on the "rubato, free, tense, nervous playing, hesitating in places, capricious, full of new harmonies and melodies . . ." And calling the music "great suns of small universes," he reiterated the old charge:

> Chopin knew better and played only in salons. Perhaps Scriabin does not understand himself, or perhaps his management is capitalistic and makes more money from producing *en gros* rather than from a *lieder* or *clavier abend*. What a pity and waste.
>
> Scriabin's tender and finely soft piano gifts were barely audible. You never felt there was any gunpowder, only smoke from a powder flash. One sees the smoke from the muzzle of the gun, but was there ever really a shot? If there was, we did not hear it. But the powder charge *is* in Scriabin's music, such as Op. 8, the dramatic Third Sonata, but only when we hear it played by other hands. Listening to Rachmaninoff or Medtner, you think that no one could play their music better, but this is not so with Scriabin. Others play his compositions more *powerfully*, and not just in the sense of force.
>
> He played the 7th Sonata for the first time. It is not yet printed so one cannot study it, but it was the "nail of the evening." I can say nothing about it from my first impression. After all the beautiful music Scriabin has composed up to now, one wants to believe everything will be lovely. But belief without fact is death. The 7th Sonata gives me no immediate idea of living beauty, only one of originality and complexity. At least, so it seemed from first hearing.

Grigory Prokofiev reviewed the Moscow performance in *RMG*:

> Without looking at the sonata more closely, it is difficult to say anything definite. Its form is so condensed, its writing so ethereal, and its harmonies so far from the ordinary that we could not grasp it during its rendition. It has something endearing about its soaring flight, but for our planet, it is too flighty, too ephemeral. The volatility of the sonata is unpleasant. Even the very beginning in the first theme where the rhythm struggles toward something more concrete or corporeal, is shot through with flight. It is strange how the more flying the music of Scriabin is, the more monotonous his playing. If he continues on this path, he will not be able to play his earlier compositions with enough poetry and power. He played "Desire" and "Enigma" astonishingly and incomparably.

RMG in SPb said the Seventh Sonata's first effect was one of something "obscure, indistinct, foolish even" and recalled *Prometheus*.

Yuri Sakhnovsky, former friend at Zverev's, used his column in *Russian Word* to launch a major destruction of Scriabin. He had sided with Rachmaninoff at the 10 December, 1911, concert, but now he used his artillery of words—"decadent and degenerate"—to denigrate Scriabin and his music. All the more extraordinary was this attitude coming from the *bon vivant* (he weighed 260 lbs.), handsome, brilliant and wealthy Sakhnovsky. He lived, as von Riesemann said, "in an uninterrupted stream of orgies . . . lewd in the absolute sense of the word." But Scriabin's musical "obscenities" as they became more and more incorporeal incited him to damnation.

Ossovsky recalls how the viciousness of this article "released a terrible stream of emotions" and sent Sakhnovsky to the musical gutter-fringe. It was by Russian standards libelous and particularly hurtful for a musician, since he was important and on the RMO's board of directors. "Even Liadov could not rest after reading the article. He telephoned friends and acquaintances, started arguments at gatherings, and asked people to protest against so unworthy a reception of Scriabin."

Sakhnovsky was never stilled. As late as 25 January, 1914, he continued in the same vein. Here is his last vitriol:

> Standing as a decadent, Mr. Scriabin all the same tries to stand on his own feet. He writes endlessly long orchestral compositions and, in reverse, exceptionally short piano pieces. Formerly we laughed at composers when they could not devise a melodic phrase longer than a sparrow's beak. Now, Mr. Scriabin flaunts them before us. He does not even write phrases, but compositions which are shorter than a bear's tail. His short musical fictions have sounds not at all appropriate to their titles as "Poem," "Sonata." But these poems, preludes, or sonatas are as alike as two drops of water—they have one mood, as if the author has fallen into a quagmire and cannot extricate himself. This music obviously makes a strange impression even on Mr. Scriabin's few admirers who gathered together last Sunday at the Great Noblemen's Hall. They looked at each other in confusion not knowing whether to applaud or even whether Mr. Scriabin was playing his own compositions. Even if some found themselves in harmony with the music, others did not and did not even know if the "pieces" were finished. To the great joy of all, each of the 3 parts of the program lasted no longer than 15–20 minutes and there were entr'actes. In the end all's well that ends well and thus the concert of Mr. S. kept its public for less than 2 hours. For this delicacy, we thank the composer.

The last composition sent Koussevitzky was the superlative Poem-Nocturne, Op. 61. Its breathless themes and passages tumble one after the other with gentle grace. Like constant changes in a dimly lit mirror-room, they flash and vanish, disappear and reappear. The range is prodigal.

Scriabin played another magnificent program on 10 December, 1912, in SPb. For the first time he performed all twenty-four preludes of Op. 11 exactly in their printed order. He devoted the second section to the Seventh Sonata, pausing for better aural contemplation before and after it. The third section presented "Fragility," "Mask," Poem (Op. 59) and Prelude (Op. 59 "savage and bellicose," for the first time), Poem-Nocturne (for the first time), and ended with the popular "Satanic Poem."

On 9 February, 1913 Scriabin and Siloti appeared together: First Symphony, *Prometheus* with the composer at the piano, and an interlude of Scriabin playing solo, Poem, Op. 32 No. 1, the sixteen-measure Prelude, Op. 39 in A♭, Poem-Nocturne, and "Strangeness."

The Dutch conductor Willem Mengelberg, after touring Russia, brought Scriabin home with him in 1912. He engaged him for three concerts in Holland and one in Germany (26, 27, 28 October and 1 November) playing *Prometheus* and the Concerto with the Concertgebouw Orchestra of Amsterdam. Scriabin telephoned Rachmaninoff to see if 600 marks a concert was sufficient. Rachmaninoff urged him to accept. At first the plan was to omit the chorus, but Scriabin so enchanted the lady-chairman of the Dutch Choral Society she volunteered her chorus of 500 voices!, and during the curtain calls loaded him down with flowers.

Scriabin and Tatyana, pouches stuffed with Jurgenson and concert money, holidayed in Beatenberg the summer of 1912. Their intention was to rest three long months, then spend three weeks in Brussels with Tatyana's relatives and his friends. He would leave her there in a villa outside town, "Les Charmettes" in Genval, while Bryanchaninov, living in England—his new home—accompanied him on the Holland tour.

On 12 June (Swiss time) Scriabin greeted Sabaneeff, who had recently married and produced a son. "I salute you from the clouds of space. It is marvelous here, clean air, quiet. No music; only the cows produce art here—with their tinkling bells! ... " Within two weeks he wrote in different vein: "I now inform you of something pleasant for me, perhaps of indifference to you, and quite painful for all defenders of the classical faith: A composer whom you know has written three études! In fifths (Horrors!), in ninths (How depraved!) and . . . in major sevenths (the *last* fall from Grace!?). What will the world say? . . ."

These Beatenberg compositions turned out to be the astonishing Etudes, Op. 65—the last of Scriabin's total of twenty-six études and the first new compositions for Jurgenson. They blossom with romanticism. The first, in major ninths, requires massive hand-spread, and few pianists can negotiate its chromatic, glissando-like, ascending sweeps. In between these displays of technique and velocity come slow, soft-sweet sections tugging at the tightness of structure. If the pianist macerates these, the music becomes soggy and senseless. The second, in major sevenths, is a poetic study of lingering sonorities, and the swift, clanging étude in fifths is remarkably easy. Scriabin never played these études. Was he afraid of the ninths' difficulty?

Of the successful Holland concerts, Bryanchaninov contributes one amusing story. They left for the station. Scriabin was aghast that he had left his comb—a little cheap one—in the hotel. He started to go back for it, but suddenly found it in his pocket. The odd thing, Bryanchaninov recalled jovially, was that he hadn't wanted to use it, nor did he, when he finally found it.

✒ XIV ✒
FINALE

48

MOSCOW, EARLY November, Vera again started the season with a concert of Scriabin music. Tatyana found a wonderful seven-room apartment on the second floor of a fine house in the Arbat, No. 11 on Great Nikolo-Peskov Lane (now Vakhtangov Street and leading off Olga Knipper-Chekhova Lane). Scriabin signed a two-and-a-half-year lease, in Russian custom. It expired 14 April, 1915—the day of his own death.

The apartment was fit for a seigneur. It had an imposing entrance, a wide hallway with a wall telephone. Sabaneeff gives us the number: 3-36-30, and it still has not changed. The sitting room with three windows looked onto the quiet street. Tatyana hung curtains matching the carroty rug. Her mother brought an armoire for clothes, but it was so bulky it had to stay in a corner of the hallway. The first room, as you enter, was Scriabin's workroom, far from the children and servant quarters. Next came a large sitting room. But guests all preferred sitting around the table in the dining room. The parlor furniture was worn and its springs bulged up through the upholstery. "I've just ordered an antique sofa," Tatyana said one night to Princess Shakhovskaya, "it will soon be ready."

"How can you order an antique?" the princess asked.

Tatyana's mother was the apartment housekeeper and managed the children. Like Scriabin, she always spoke French with them. Only the nurse spoke Russian. He caressed his children, Sabaneeff noted, "in an abstract, theoretical way ..."

A change had come over Scriabin—the man, *père de famille*, celebrated musician. He was tender, and it came into the open particularly in the new apartment. Was it the congeniality of the apartment itself? Or was

237

it that commodious sense of enough money, abundant fame, and a reaction from shortage and contumely? Once a man becomes a master, life becomes simple. His work speaks, and his daily life becomes unimportant, dissolving into routine meetings, ordinary gatherings, day-to-day functions of no particular pain or value. Joy is in the products of art.

Engel explicitly describes this new, almost colorless aspect of Scriabin:

> The word "home" took on for Scriabin a much greater meaning than before. Now one could really call him a homebody. As before, he loved people, but now he preferred his friends to assemble around him and so it happened—virtually every day and often until the late hours of the night. He loved all the "trappings" of home life—a table covered with baize, glasses overflowing with wine, sitting beside the samovar, Tatyana serving tea, in a word, he loved all these celebratory reminders that life is a feast and festival.

> After dinner he loved distraction taking his thought from his work. He played Patience, mixed light conversation into it. He played chess. He loved ancient bric-à-brac. He liked his circle to dress well and look neat and handsome. He was sensitive to outward elegance, but the outer was mixed with the inner and by no means did he concern himself with physical appearance or looks alone. His exterior countenance merely divined an inner person.

Aside from family, Scriabin had many friends constituting a jealous inner and a less possessive outer circle. The inner circle called almost nightly for conversation and a light supper of pastry cakes and drink. Often he napped after dinner, until these guests arrived around 10. His pet intimates were Podgaetsky forever, Mozer of course, and coming from Petersburg, Alchevsky, who gave him some potted palms which lived as long as Scriabin himself. Physician Vladimir Bogorodsky, an eternal student, felt he had attained ultimate knowledge in payment for attending the Scriabins professionally. There was also Sperling, the vivid painter, gloomy and cold, self-encased, whom Scriabin called "black," because his eyes were so deep. He was allowed to sit next to him while he composed. Zhilaev, however, would later be evicted from the circle. He once said, "Better to write sonatas than trifling poetry." Alexander Krein, pianist and composer, Gnessin again, Bryanchaninov, when he was not in England, and of course, Sabaneeff. Goldenweizer was often invited, too. For one reason, Scriabin always checked him in chess—in two moves.

Scriabin's apartment became a mecca for an outer circle of foreign visitors—Gordon Craig, Coates, Cooper, Hanako, Isadora Duncan,

Pablo Casals, Ferruccio Busoni (who was specially partial to the Ninth Sonata). Scriabin's Russian callers were equally distinguished: Meyerhold, Tairov, Merezhkovsky, and the Lithuanian Chiurlionis, who painted sonatas and called his *vernissages* "concerts." Scriabin went to one, enjoyed it, but said astutely, "he doesn't want his dream to become *reality*. There's no *real* power there." Symbolist, imagist, futurist and acmeist poets, including the great Essenin, also paid visits, and so did the old aristocracy. There was an entire pitter-pat of princes and princesses at his feet—Gagarins, Volkonskys, Vorontsovs, Shakhovskois, the widow Trubetskaya, as well as Bryanchaninov's "Serene Highness" and Count Alexei Tolstoi (1882–1945), novelist and playwright, who trimmed his beard in the style of a coachman.

Of all these, Scriabin's heart was closest to the symbolist poets. He loved them, and they were useful. The whole literary temperament of Russia revolved around symbolists. They were also known as "Decadents" or, as Chekhov sourly said, "Knaves dealing in spoiled goods." Silence had followed Turgenev and Tolstoi and Dostoevsky after their massive output from 1860 to 1890. Now, most writing in Russia focused on poetry. These men gathered at the Journalists Café on Stoleshnikov Lane in Moscow, or at Scriabin's apartment, anywhere where they could talk and talk and talk.

There was Vyacheslav Ivanov, "lightly burned, neither young nor old, with bearlike eyes that looked out from the side of his head. From the fountain of his mouth, a high tenor voice poured out the most learned, delightful monologues and conversations," or so Alexander Blok, (1880–1921), an even greater poet, described him. Scriabin said of Ivanov, "He is magnificent . . . I am close to him . . . we are alike . . ." Like Scriabin, he turned his gaze toward Indian mysticism and East-drenched Theosophy.

Taciturn Jurgis Baltrushaitis (1873–1945), translator of D'Annunzio and Byron, was "a man of great kindness and great gloom," according to Ilya Ehrenburg. When he spoke it was as sparse as his pruned poetry. He became the first ambassador from Lithuania to the USSR after the Revolution, having risen from a peasant family, and Boris Pasternak was hired to tutor his son. Also in the group were Andrei Biely (1880–1934), author of *Saint Petersburg*, and Valery Bryussov (1873–1924), critic, and intellectual poet, disciple of anthroposophist Rudolph Steiner. He took cocaine, became a Communist, wrote a novel on witchcraft. Scriabin composed a sonnet celebrating Bryussov's safe return from the Front in January, 1915.

> Dear conqueror and lover of the world/So far from you and strange/I, attentive to my own enigmatic fate/Cannot, alas, attend your feast today.

This compliment would be repaid. One of the dozens of poems written about Scriabin's death was by Bryussov in the *Russian Gazette*. Above all other poets, however, loomed fabulous Konstantin Balmont, giant, red-headed, dominant leader of the whole symbolist movement. "I am the refinement of Russian speech. Who is equal to me in power of song? No one," he wrote in a poem, and no one disputed the fact.

The symbolists wrote often about Scriabin. Their words were a prolonged testament of faith in his genius. What Balmont, for instance, said was quoted everywhere in Moscow and Petersburg salons. His most famous phrase was, "In fact when Scriabin plays, there is no piano, only a beautiful woman. He is making love to her." After *Prometheus'* synthesis of arts," Balmont sang with poetic rapture in a pamphlet of enormous beauty and near-incomprehensibility, *Light and Sound in Nature and the Color Symphony of Scriabin* (Koussevitzky, having bought a book publishing house, printed it in 1917):

> Scriabin is the singing of a falling moon. Starlight in music. A flame's movement. A burst of sunlight. The cry of soul to soul . . . A singing illumination of the air itself, in which he himself is captive child of the gods. A strong tenderness; a mighty invincible sweetness . . . All his music is light itself.

Both Balmont and Scriabin shared love of the sun and light. In 1903 Balmont had written a masterful poem beginning, "Let us be like unto the sun," and Scriabin brought the sun itself into sound. And Bryanchaninov too was a sun cultist. He made his servants on his estate stand and pray facing the sunrise every morning.

Compositions by younger composers were brought to Scriabin's desk for approval or help. Prokofiev, who like Scriabin eventually wrote ten piano sonatas, overheard Liadov at the Belaieff office say one day, "What's happening? Everyone tries to write like Scriabin." And he quotes himself in his autobiography, writing to conductor Vasily Morolev, "I am overjoyed at your delight in the 'Divine Poem.' It is truly an astounding composition. I spent all winter arranging it for 2 hands and showed all of the first movement to the author himself."

However, behind Scriabin's façade of politeness, his judgments were contemptuous: Akimenko ("decorative"), Stanchinsky ("strips the nerves"), Prokofiev ("trash"), Medtner ("mixed-up styles"), Rachmaninoff ("boiled ham"). And Stravinsky? Of him, next year.

49

BRYANCHANINOV DREW closer to Scriabin as the years advanced. He was, in fact, his longest standing friend. As high a value as Scriabin placed on himself, and he continued to detest what he called *amikoshonstvo* (familiarity, from the French for "friend"), Bryanchaninov used *ty*, and was the only one in the intimate circle to do so. Tatyana said *Vy* to him, or formally, "Alexander Nikolaevich." Bryanchaninov's influence was unusual, and because of it Sabaneeff and Schloezer noticed Scriabin's nature entering a new phase. An almost reactionary encroachment of aristocratism and hierarchy and hieratical thinking colored him. Scriabin favored aristocratism in music too, according to Engel. "No need to transform every experience into music. That would be humdrum. Only the special, the exceptional, the ecstatic is necessary."

Where once Scriabin had been pro-American, now he was pro-English. His favorite hotel in Petersburg was "Hotel Angleterre." He was fascinated by the class system in England. He called it "order." How important it is, he felt, for the oldest son to be "lord," the second son to enter the Church, the third to become a lawyer. "This establishes organization. It makes the development of creative strength possible and intensifies it." He attributed England's economic, political and geographic "success" to this. When introducing Bryanchaninov, Scriabin would say, "You know, a friend of Parliamentarians." Indeed, in England Bryanchaninov was often feted in the House of Commons, though doubtless he would have preferred the House of Lords.

Two other factors also influenced Scriabin. Mme. Blavatsky had lived in England, and the present head of Theosophy, Mrs. Annie Besant, the

Indophile, was an Englishwoman. England, most of all, was becoming by 1913 fanatically fond of Scriabin's music. On 1 February, 1913, Sir Henry Wood performed *Prometheus* in London. Rosa Newmarch composed the program notes and took the occasion to write Scriabin:

Dear Master: We have heard your Prometheus! We heard it even twice! I personally heard it 4 times, counting the rehearsals at which I was present. It is impossible to speak of "success" in the usual sense of the word. But I can tell you that the impression was quite shaking, strange and the work aroused unusual interest. This was surprising for London, where we take slowly to new experiments. The hall was packed, but not with the usual audience of free tickets to musicians. THIS WAS THE UNDERSTANDING PUBLIC, composed of people who really love music and who buy the cheapest seats several weeks in advance.

I will tell you about everything. Perhaps it will amuse you. Studying your Prometheus I became more and more interested in its psychological plan. Having written a small article about this, I gave a lecture at my club and invited 50–60 people to study with me the contents of Prometheus. The result was very curious. In the discussions which followed with Wood, the Times critic and several others, the idea arose of repeating your work twice in one program. This idea was unheard of for England, but it quickly took root. It was announced in the papers within two days. Naturally it caused a lot of opposition. You will understand that, won't you? "Why such an honor to a Russian symphony, and not British? What a frightful precedent! Wood loves a sensation! This Mrs. Newmarch disturbs the good old order of London concerts. Mad, she is quite mad!!" etc., etc. But we were firm.

After the first performance there was fortunately no apathy. Several whistles (virtually unknown here) along with sincere and spontaneous applause. But I doubt that the work was to the audience's taste and I think that the applause was due to Wood and the orchestra rather than for your Prometheus. Finally, after the Beethoven concerto and before the repetition of your work, a good part of the audience left in great haste! I must tell you, that knowing the London musical public, I was more surprised at the great number who stayed for the second playing. (You see I am telling you only the real truth.) After the indifferent and/or antipathetic group left, Sir Henry began again. Second time, everything went *much better* than the first. One felt a sincerely charged atmosphere. The orchestra was in fine mettle. The impression was splendid and lovely. The applause was really warm and rapturous. Wood had to come out three times (after novelties, this is quite unusual).

It may interest you to know that among those I noticed who remained were Bernard Shaw who was one of the most enthusiastic and applauded with all his strength, and the artist John Sargent who cried out loudly: "We want to hear it a third time!!" As for the critics, we will send you several reviews which show little understanding. In the majority of cases our press is most unenlightened, so be prepared for stupidities.

Forgive me for this long letter, but perhaps it will interest you, and also forgive me for the mistakes since I am writing so quickly. You have expressed something new, ideal, deeply moving, especially arousing curiosity; although I am not yet convinced that it will become music of my soul and heart, I thank you very warmly for all that your work has awakened in me. I think also that you have made rapturous friends here . . .

Siloti asked to repeat *Prometheus* (with Scriabin at the piano) twice at his concert of 9 November, 1913. For the first time too there would be general admission. Heretofore, entrance to Belaieff concerts and the RMO had been by subscription, which meant an exclusively musical, select and limited public. Scriabin answered him on 7 June, 1913, saying he had overcome his objections to presenting *Prometheus* before the public at large. However, "I say to you frankly that double performances of *Prometheus* are not to my liking. One performance or the other will suffer, I am sure. It is impossible to give equal inspiration twice over."

The Scriabins spend the summer of 1913 on an estate called "Petrovskoe," owned by a German named Baer, in Kaluzhsky Province along the Syzrano-Vyazma railway line to the south. The rundown *dacha* was enormous, with a porch of gigantic columns the size of the Parthenon, nestling in the middle of an overgrown park. Baltrushaitis was their nearest neighbor.

Suddenly and incredibly Scriabin finished three sonatas all at once—the Eighth, Ninth, and Tenth. He spent the end of the summer laboriously correcting proofs, making last-minute changes of perfection on perfection. He returns them to Jurgenson with a note saying, "We have been very satisfied with our summer. It was excellent in every respect. The weather is still holding up beautifully." There can be no explanation for this amazing surge of music. He had often said in the course of the year, "I have much to do . . . I have no right to pause or rest," meaning that the Mysterium was growing urgent. It used to annoy him to be reminded that he was overdue according to his own estimates and promises.

The Eighth (Op. 66) resembles the Seventh in its sublimity and chockablock chords. The Ninth (Op. 68), satanic twin to the Sixth, ends with a nightmare march of Gothic visions, ghosts, and distorted horrors—the most raucous page in all Scriabin. The Tenth (Op. 70), the "Trill Sonata," is radiant music. Its harmonic symmetry based on major thirds shrinking swiftly into minor thirds sets up a vortex of interior diminution constantly raised by lifts and tremolos. Scriabin used to amuse his guests by playing the first three measures of the Tenth, following it with the scale of G major. "You hear," he would say, "my music lies between the tones." And certainly the scale sounds as wide and gaping as teeth in a pumpkin.

The Eighth Sonata is the longest of all Scriabin's one-movement piano sonatas. Again, he never played it in public, possibly because he could not commit it to memory. He proudly played its majestic, gorgeously blooming harmonies derived from five fragmentary melodies governing the entire composition and successively stated within the first five measures. These supposedly represent the elements of earth, air, fire, water and the mystic ether. Woven together they form a cobweb of gossamer filigree. "And you say I have no counterpoint after hearing this?" he would say defiantly to friends. "Note well how all the notes of the counterpoint are harmony. They are not at war with each other as in Bach. Here they are reconciled." Regarding the center of the melody in the third measure, he said, "See how I break mood within the one phrase." And playing the figure rising to a "B" and emphasizing the end of the rise and following it with "B♭" and the descending figure he would add, "Listen to the tragedy born out of such a dissolution . . . in two notes I alter hope into despair." And that same half-step descent appears in *Prometheus'* opening theme. There Scriabin called it, inflatedly, "the most tragic episode of my creative work." He also felt the behemoth harmonies in the Eighth were "drawn from Nature, as if they had existed before, like the bells in the Seventh Sonata . . . bridges between harmony and geometry, life visible and life unseen . . ."

Podgaetsky dubbed the Ninth Sonata the "Black Mass." Scriabin especially loved its second theme (p.4). In conversation he called it "dormant or dreaming saintliness," but in his usual confusion between passion sensual and passion supernal marked it in the score as "nascent languor." This theme develops evilly, as the notation reads, "a sweetness gradually becoming more and more caressing and poisonous." Its ritual is perverse. The rite is a spitting at all that is holy or sacred. If the Seventh exorcizes demons, the Ninth resummons them. Corruption, perversity, diabolism recurs. From the velvet of the Eighth, these harmonies of the Ninth clash in discordant minor ninths to replace dead and dulcet octaves.

All summer long, Scriabin remained indoors, unless Sabaneeff, Sperling, Schloezer, Podgaetsky or Bogarodsky came to visit him, and then he would take walks. He read a new mystic magazine *Testament* and Kappa's *Life of Wagner*. ("I had thought Wagner more aware of himself. It seemed to me that in his plans he ought to have had more conscious will.") Scriabin had noticed little of the countryside or nature and had ignored his green surroundings. Unprotesting, he walked, though he tired easily, and he talked constantly, as if desperately eager to communicate his least thought. Sabaneeff records one day at Petrovskoe. He picked a theme:

"All plants and little animals are expressions of our psyches. Their appearance corresponds to movements of our souls. They are symbols, and oh! what wonderful symbols. Surely you feel that an animal can correspond to a caress in sex. What kind of a caress is it that makes this caress? I'll tell you. For example, a bird is a wingéd caress. You know, I see these birds fluttering up above and I feel very clearly their *identity* with my own inner movement—a kiss with wings poised inside me ready to take flight.

"And there are kisses of torment. Animals symbolize also our inner bestiality. Their color is due to our animal motions which change into caresses. There are tiger kisses, or you can kiss like a hyena or a wolf. Note all this well. The symbol is very important. What a mistake to think animals are only animals . . . Why does a mouse have bad associations for us? If you see a mouse in a dream it means misfortune is coming. Why? Because it has had another existence and brings with it meanings from its other-life.

"My Tenth Sonata is a sonata of insects. Insects are born from the sun . . . they are the sun's kisses . . . How unified world-understanding is when you look at things this way. In science all is *dis*-unified, not made into one. It is analysis, not synthesis."

He now strained his eyes as if looking for something in the distance. His face was smiling, but he was very serious:

"Otherwise how could the whole world be invited to the Mysterium. Animals, insects, birds, all must be there. How could they be, if they were not part of *my* being? And if they exist, then I have the power to send them where I like. I distribute them today as I scatter my caresses, sow seeds with my kisses.

"What happiness to tear the world apart with millions of eagles, tigers, to peck at it with kisses, to give pain and again to caress . . .

"And on the last day, in that final dance I and everything else—by the end of the Mysterium—will be different. No longer people, but all will be animal caresses, bird, snake . . . kisses."

Now, his face looked dreaming, exactly as it did when he played those final prestississimos of vertiginous and delirious codas to his later sonatas, Sabaneeff continued:

"One thing in Nature always strikes me deeply. Plants, flowers, trees. They cannot move. They are a chorus singing the juices of the earth and the rays of the sun. But the animal world is all movement, from slow to fast—zigzag. This is a true dance of movement to honor the immobile world of plants. Does this contrast not strike you too? In nature, animals represent activity, the male. The growing world is the female, material, will-less and passive. Here again is polarity. Do you suppose there is some act between them possible—a polarity act? Sex. Yes, I must take walks more often. It is useful. Much opens up in me which I had not observed before."

50

NIKOLAI, IMITATING his father, ordered his son to a grand, summer's end reunion of all the Scriabins in Switzerland. Tatyana was not included. Nikolai merely stated that they would talk about her privately when they meet again in Lausanne (Ouchy) where he has now retired. Peace will be made and Scriabin's marital status finally accepted by his father. Uncle Mitya will be there. Uncle Alexander's sixteen-year-old son, Apollon, also arrives there, and Scriabin is attentive to him, as a late memoir will show. Aunt Lyubov and the mother are too old to travel, and Uncle Nil stays behind with them.

Certainly these were inducements beyond the peremptory invitation, and Scriabin accepts without a fight. He has grown domesticated, gentler. Even the tone of his letters softens. His handwriting has changed, still grandiose with large letters, but the pressure on the pen is light and the ink comes out pale. Scriabin is guilt-ridden still and aware of his sickly excesses. He could have overruled his father, brought Tatyana, but Nikolai as a matter of fact was reflecting Scriabin's own desires. As a man coming to terms with himself he wanted to discover his other family *en masse*, be in it without tension, and he needed respite from Tatyana herself.

Scriabin was abroad with the Scriabins for three weeks September and October, 1913. During his absence, plans for founding the Scriabin Society honoring him as a musician and somewhat as a prophet flourished among both inner and outer circles in a skein of intrigue, secrecy, and prejudice. He writes Tatyana:

> En route. After four hours I am in Warsaw, my thoughts still in Moscow! Dearest, I am so sad that you are not with me! Why didn't I insist and if I had been firmer—had you agreed—we would be together enjoying this journey! I will not forgive myself this weakness . . . The people in the train have not bothered me. I read and write, but most of all *think*. You see, you keep me from working! Go to the theater with your mother. See Mlada [Rimsky's new ballet-opera] . . . Kiss your mother, and assure her I am not the monster she thinks. Kiss the children, and ask Marinochka to forgive me.

> Tutochka, what horror! I just found this letter in my pocket. That means I sent you a blank piece of paper! Forgive me, child. How sharply and painfully I felt our parting!

And from Lausanne:

> Papa and mama met me at the station and exhibited great joy. Both of them kiss me and woo me. Papa and I talked until 1 in the morning, but don't be angry, child. I promise you there will be no more of it. We talked a lot about you and our affairs. He said much that was conciliatory. I am pretty well and tomorrow start work. They are bringing me an upright tomorrow, which I rented for 3 weeks, not bad.

> . . . I did not tell you I am sharing a room with Apollon. It is directly over papa's. The others are full. But I am very well off. The bed is marvelous and in absolute darkness, and that is all I need.

29 September.

> Dear, you are such an angel. You spoil me! Three letters from you today! Thank you. Yesterday (Sunday) I took advantage of the marvelous weather and went boating on the lake. Yesterday, I worked in the morning, but I cannot say I worked very well. I did add somehow to the second part of the text. From today on I am going to stick to my timetable and work mornings to 12:30 and again from 5 to 7.

> We go to Arco on Saturday, and pass a few hours under Italian skies, spending the night in Milan.

Tusinka, all that you write about the concert tour and the Society is very agreeable. Does Saradzhev [Konstantin (1877–1954) violinist and conductor] have to be in it? And aren't Baltrushaitis and Podgaetsky invited? Think all this out and consult with Vl. Vas. [Bogorodsky]. Take each step with great care, otherwise a mistake is hard to set right. One more thing: Is it convenient for you to have the meetings in our place? The Society should be set up without our exact knowledge. However, I say all this merely for you to take each detail into consideration. Decide everything for yourself. I am sure you will do the right thing. Now I must get to work. I kiss you hard, hard, hard. I think about you all the time. Take care of yourself! Strength is so necessary! So much still lies ahead of us! Kiss mama and the children. How are they? I am waiting for a letter from Ariana and Yulochka.

Do not misconstrue this trip of mine in any way! It was only because of my mother whose grave I have never visited, not even once! That is the only reason I have come here. And no matter what, I still cannot forgive myself for having come without you!

Papa and mama kiss you warmly. I haven't seen them this morning yet, but they gave me that message *yesterday*.

Have you received my first letter (the one with the blank paper)? I sent it from Bern.

Igor Stravinsky was living in Clarens, an hour's train ride from Lausanne. He has heard that Scriabin was in Ouchy, and on 30 September invites him to visit him: "Yesterday I played your 7th Sonata again and my opinion has not changed. I await you eagerly so I can show you and tell you what I like so especially in it . . ." Scriabin declined, so Stravinsky came to him instead, on 6 October. Stravinsky wrote a friend, "I am spending some time in Lausanne and saw Scriabin (he's with his father). I was so surprised to discover that he does not know my compositions. He spoke about them as if by hearsay, entirely in the words of others . . . He played me his last sonatas and they pleased me incomparably . . ." Scriabin wrote Tatyana: "Tusiki, I am so guilty before you. Forgive me! I haven't written you for three days! Yesterday Stravinsky (composer) prevented me from chatting with my little soul. He's here in Switzerland, came at 12 and stayed until 7."

Stravinsky later detested Scriabin, or so he said. "A man without a passport . . ." he cried, harping on nationalism. "Emphysema," implying a gas swelling or inflation of nothing into emptiness, he declared. In time though, after Stravinsky identified himself with serialism, he recognized

Scriabin as a harbinger of his future. In George Perle's words, "Scriabin ... may be considered the first to exploit serial procedures systematically as a means of compensating for the loss of the traditional tonal functions."

When Scriabin eventually looked at Stravinsky's music, he dismissed it. "*Minimum tvorchestvo*, a minimum of creativity . . ." his favorite phrase of condemnation, ". . . the sad part is that all such music actually expresses something frightfully successfully." He continued, "but the 'something' is just frightful." He called *Petrouchka*, "Very Rimsky-Korsakoff . . . only it's wiser, less naive. How *busy* it is," and using another favorite word, this time of praise, "How sweet (*milo*) . . . Except it's just a toy, a plaything, if you take it as a whole . . . The Coachman's Dance is charming, absolutely excellent . . . You see the coachman before your eyes, *Ach, ty, shto-ty, shto-ty*," and he imitated the rhythm energetically to the syllables of a popular song, "I'm a Soldier of the 9th Regiment." "But . . . all the same, what a mass of *insolence* resides in such music. *Minimum tvorchestvo* . . ."

To Tatyana, October, 1913, from Lausanne:

I am so sad! Is it possible that you are angry with me for that forgetfulness? . . . My soul, I took this piece of paper thinking to write you some of the new episodes in my text, but I read through them and saw that they must still be changed a lot, and therefore I defer . . . I have worked most productively these last three days. I dare not hope for more than that it continue. The poem blooms magnificently. But, please, for the time being, not a word to anyone about it!

You write me that Sabaneeff has gone to Jurgenson! He was invited in what capacity? Member of the firm? Company publicist? Is that suitable? In the meantime, if Sabaneeff looks there for his material means, then it is almost impossible not to ask him to be the founder of the Society. You must think this over very carefully. It seems to me that those behind this enterprise must be close to the spirit of my art. True there are some rich people among them, Polyakov for example. Why doesn't Nikolai Sergeevich [Zhilaev] address himself to my work with more finances? By the way, it is only TO YOU that I express this opinion, and I do not want to interfere in the least. If you are in the position to advise, do so, please, as from *you*. I must stand absolutely apart for the time being. I will begin to lead only when the Society is completely organized. I hold it in reserve as an instrument with which to realize my ideas.

Please not a word, not even to Zhilaev, about what I am writing to you. In principle, there is no me in this matter. I must leave you. Papa and I are going on a boat ride. Thank you for your kisses. They warm my heart. Kiss our dear children. How glorious our children are to us. Julian made every one laugh with his imitation of "strikers." Can't you take a picture of them? I hope you have already been photographed? I wait impatiently for the pictures. A big kiss to your mama. Kiss my grandmother and aunt and Uncle Nil.

7 October.

As you see, Papa and I did not go to Arco on Saturday, and here's why: Minister of Foreign Affairs Sazonov [Sergei (1861–1927)] is coming to Lausanne and Papa has to be here. We decided that I would stay here until tomorrow, and then go onto Germany and Russia from Arco! That means we will see each other several days earlier than we thought. What joy! Here is what I plan on doing. Three days, that is, until Saturday, say, I will stay at Lake Garda. Then I go to Munich for two days to see the opera. On the 1st I leave for Berlin and by the 3rd or 4th of the month I will be at the Russian border! Soul, my joy, we will be so happy!

I received a telegram from Keil [concert manager for Diedrichs] proposing a concert before some Society (I did not understand what one) for 1,000 rubles. You probably know which Society (I don't think Keil would telegraph me without your knowledge), but I agreed. If I am wrong, that is if Keil did not get in touch with you about this engagement, then telephone him and ascertain the details and what the aim of the concert is.

13 October, Riva on Lake Garda.

I have just returned from Mamina's grave, and before everything else, my dear, my little one, I want to share with you the complicated feelings I felt. They were complicated and *new* feelings for me. I regret you did not know the precise time I was going to be at the cemetery, because you would have then, I am sure, simply SEEN all that I experienced at that beloved grave. Dear little daughter, I have suffered much these days, and the visit to Arco disturbed me greatly. I will speak of this only when I see you!

It is divine here! A veritable paradise. The trees are in bloom, palms just as in Nervi but also there are the majestic mountains, and the lake makes even Lake Geneva pale by comparison! This is not an exaggeration! How shameful, how painful that you are not here! When we come abroad this spring, I'll show you it. I get dressed now. Byebye [in English].

30 September, 1913, from Munich.

Today I very much need your love! I am composing constantly, and am in such a state of nerves! The more I am blessed and the poem manifests itself to me perfectly, the more . . . no, better not say anything about the state I am in, you will despise me.

O, if only I could FINISH one part at least. But alas, that is still a long way away.

Tanyushka, in a few days we will see each other!! Do you realize what that means? I would fly to you right now, but it is better for us both that I work as much as possible and put my loneliness and quiet to good use.

His last message to Tatyana from abroad is a telegram from Warsaw announcing his arrival at 3:40 P.M. on Saturday 3 October (Russian calendar): WEAR YOUR FUR COAT.

51

SCRIABIN INTRODUCED the Ninth Sonata to Moscow on 30 October, 1913. In November and December he played six concerts in southwest Russia—the provincial program and a sprinkling of short novelties. On 12 December, in Moscow's Great Noblemen's Hall, he played a huge, magnificent program:

Etude, Op. 8 (B♭ minor)
Mazurka, Op. 3 (E♭ minor and C♯ minor)
Preludes, Op. 15 (E major)
            Op. 22 (C♯ minor and G♯ minor)
Impromptu, Op. 14 (B major)
Second Sonata
Ninth Sonata
Tenth Sonata (first time)
Preludes, Op. 37 (B♭ minor, F♯ major,
                B major, G minor)
"Fragility," "Winged Poem," "Dance of Languor," Op. 51
"Nuances," Op. 56
Prelude, Op. 67 No. 2 (first time)
Poem, Op. 69 No. 1 (first time)
Waltz, Op. 38
The critics found the new things "unfamiliar and dissonant."

G. Prokofiev in *RMG* mentioned how he always anticipated hearing Scriabin's new works, because until he hears the author's interpretation he himself dares not attempt "even an approximate diagnosis." Yet, he goes on to complain:

> Scriabin never does full justice when he performs any of his major pieces for the first time. He was not at all convincing in the 10th Sonata. Only in the future can he illuminate us and it in all its harmony and beauty . . . In essence, the harmonic structure of the 10th Sonata is closer to contemporary ears than the 6th, 7th, or 9th, but this simplicity does not gladden, because the harmonic whole is beyond the scope of our hearing and eludes our sensibilities. The 9th Sonata's monolithic mood and laconic form is immediately comprehensible. It wins out when placed next to the 10th. The author played the 9th this time with particular feeling. After the two sonatas, the composer was cordially and warmly applauded. Were these sonatas closer to the auditors' comprehension? Or was the audience encouraging a talent in which we are accustomed to believing and which of course needs response from the audience? I cannot judge or answer, but the question, I think, is worth asking.

After this concert Scriabin said, "Finally, I feel I am beginning to do remarkable things . . ." Others thought so too, and soon he accepts an invitation to play in London—one performance of *Prometheus* in Queen's Hall under Wood on 14 March, 1914, and two recitals in Bechstein Hall on 20 and 24 March. Otto Kling initiated the discussions, although the distinguished concert managers, Ibbs and Tillet, would make the arrangements.

In early correspondence, Scriabin answers Kling's requests: "I recently played my 9th and 10th sonatas, both very difficult, and so it is certainly agreeable to me and a great pleasure as well for me to play my very latest works this spring . . . I have only the one Concerto—I played it on the Volga trip, you remember—but it will be new to London. It will also give the public some relief from the complicated harmonies in Prometheus . . ." He has trouble with the Tenth Sonata, and only gives London the Second, Third, and Ninth Sonatas.

January and February, Scriabin tours the south of Russia playing provincial programs. He risks the Ninth Sonata once in Kharkov, a city of some musical sophistication. Now, once more Scriabin leaves Tatyana, this time for five weeks abroad in England, with interpreter-companion Bryanchaninov. Scriabin carries under his arm the text on which he has been laboring. The Mysterium has now become, by a process of self-limitation, the Prefatory Action, a preliminary to the vast and ultimate work. His enemies mockingly called it the "Safe Mysterium."

The Prefatory Action would still be a stage work of immense proportion and conception. Bells suspended from the clouds in the sky would summon the spectators from all over the world. The performance was to take place in a half-temple to be built in India. A reflecting pool of water would complete the divinity of the half-circle stage. Spectators would sit in tiers across the water. Those in the balconies would be the least spiritually advanced. The seating was strictly graded, ranking radially from the center of the stage, where Scriabin would sit at the piano, surrounded by hosts of instruments, singers, dancers. The entire group was to be permeated continually with movement, and costumed speakers reciting the text in processions and parades would form parts of the action. The choreography would include glances, looks, eye motions, touches of the hands, odors of both pleasant perfumes and acrid smokes, frankincense and myrrh. Pillars of incense would form part of the scenery. Lights, fires, and constantly changing lighting effects would pervade the cast and audience, each to number in the thousands. This prefaces the final Mysterium and prepares people for their ultimate dissolution in ecstasy. These ideas rushed through Scriabin's head, and somehow he felt that practical and mystical England would fructify these dreams. England was, after all, the steppingstone to India.

Due to Theosophy and his inherent Eurasianism, he was as caught by India as a fly in a web of imagining. He undertook yogic breathing exercises and bought himself a topi and a white cotton tropical suit. He thought that India would revive his soul, would awaken new feelings and ideas, and heighten his receptivities. It seemed to him that he would see the world from a new slant. He said that he did not conceal from himself the fact that contemporary India with its cities, railroads, Europeanized intelligentsia and industry was not in conformity—at odds, even—with his dreams. But despite this, he convinced himself that through it all he could find the old and authentic India. "I need only a hint, a push," he said, almost as if whistling to keep up his courage of conviction, "Geographical India does not interest me . . . only India herself . . . with those feelings, those experiences which the *real* India expresses and embodies in space."

To Scriabin, India was a land of sages, sadhus, magical and mystifying attainments, not the chicanery of its mango tricks and thieving beggars. There were the perfumed tropical flowers he needed, the succulent and savory tropical fruits he hungered for, having never had them. He wanted —and in England bought—a plot of Indian ground in Darjeeling at the foot of the Himalayas where snow moderated the heat and where the sunsets and dawns could be incorporated into his Prefatory Action. "I know that all depends on me and my finishing the text first, then the music. After *these* all else will come. The means and the people to be involved will come . . ."

The Mysterium still existed, for he would never abandon its exalted vision. It was to be the history of the universe . . . of the human race . . . of the individual soul. The Mysterium must transfigure and accomplish all the macrocosmic and microcosmic processes of our era. Like the Prefatory Action, it too was a work of art to be performed in a theatrical manner, but it was more mystic and liturgical. Not a musical drama, nor an oratorio, neither presentation nor re-presentation, but a "direct experience."

The universe would be completely destroyed by it, and mankind plunged into the holocaust of finality. But in this act of unity, the sons would become the father. Soul and matter would separate under the highest tension induced by the music's vibration, and man would be transfigured into an endlessness deeper than the deepest ocean. Male and female would vanish in a trice. All of us would be immersed as Scriabin said another time, "into an ecstatic abyss of sunshine . . . The one Father flashes into the consciousness of all. All would experience voluntary sonhood, divine essence, sacrificial or martyrical nature. But the father would not yet *be*, because there would still be man, free, conscious, and numerical." At the end of the seventh day, the Mysterium leads mankind to the threshold of death. The inexpressible, the unutterable begins. A loving return to God, the birth of God, the blessed immersion within Him, the joining with Him, the resurrection, the reception by His sons would be effected and this manvantara then concludes. The act is crowned. A brand-new race of purified, purged, clarified and spiritually advanced men is born—Scriabin among them—to repeat this monster act all over again, but on a higher plane. Strangely, the Prefatory Action speaks of death, premonitorily as it happened.

Letters to Tatyana begin on 18 February, 1914, from Klin *en route*

to Petersburg where Bryanchaninov has booked tickets to Europe for
7 P.M., 20 February. Scriabin's thoughts are various, not least of which
is concern for his latest achievement, "Toward the Flame" (*Vers la
Flamme*) Op. 72, a poem for piano (although at first he thought it for
orchestra, then as a sonata). It is composed essentially of two notes—that
familiar descending half-step—which crackle like lashing flames, sputtering and sparkling over an embroidery of nine against five compound
meter. The piece as a whole is like a Roman candle of increasing, mag-
nifying blazes, until it becomes consumed in its own flames. Trills no
longer suffice for Scriabin's frenetic pianism. He now writes spasms of
eight clustered, shaking and quivering notes.

> Am comfortable in a sleeper, alone in a big compartment, and feel not badly
> if I could get rid of my worry over your state of health. Set my mind at rest
> and ask Vl. Vas. [Bogorodsky] to look at you and send for another doctor,
> if he thinks it necessary. Most of all, do everything he says, and stay in bed for
> as long as possible.

> I am also fretted by the thought of poor granny. How happy I would be to
> know that she is better. I cannot remember did I give mama the *manuscript*
> (music). If not, ask her to put it in the *chest of drawers* (in the *bedroom*) and
> hide it, keep it [*Vers la Flamme*] under lock and key.

Hotel Angleterre, SPb, 20 February, 1914.

> I spent the night I arrived with Borya and next day got up very late, set
> out for Vera Pavlovna [Siloti]. I practiced and spent the rest of the day with
> the Bryanchaninovs. We sat around until three o'clock. God only knows when
> I got to bed, and again rose very late.

Continental Hotel, Berlin, 9 March (European time).

> First I am missing you very much and if it were not for Alexander Nikolaevich
> [Bryanchaninov] with all his care and concern and his touching understanding
> of me, I do not know how I would survive this journey. He is truly sweet, and
> I am glad that fate has drawn us even closer together. I am astonished how all
> my most daring projects find such spirited response in the souls of those people
> who look so cold and measured. He talks all the time about the Mysterium,
> about our trip to India, and how he is going to help me in every way!

> They have brought me a piano. I must practice for an hour, then Alexander
> Nikolaevich and I will dine and go to some light comedy. Struve has invited
> me for blinis tomorrow.

Hotel Astoria, Brussels, 11 March.

I am going further and further away from you all the time! We will finally be in London this evening! We loafed around Brussels for these past two days and managed to see everybody. . . . Talked a lot with Delvil [sic] about the journey to India.

At 10 in the morning on 12 March, Sir Henry Wood and Mrs. Newmarch call on Scriabin at the Welbeck Palace Hotel. They go together to the Bechstein studios to hear Scriabin's instructions and tempos regarding the Concerto and *Prometheus*. Next day Scriabin began a letter which continued over several days. It contains the first mention of what was to cause his death only a year later.

15 March

. . . God, what days! I cannot believe they are now in the past. First, until I got to London I had not known that the symphony concert was in the afternoon, so I had to buy a frock coat. Fortunately Alexander Nikolaevich knew a well-known tailor who made one for me in 24 hours. The rehearsals (two in one day) were just more of a tiring and nerve-wracking experience. On top of everything, a little sore appeared on my lip and gave me great pain. We went to the doctor who lanced it and drained the abcess of some sort of liquid hoping it would go away. He said that these sores come from colds or more often, nerves. Mine did not go away and I had to appear before the English public for the first time with a swollen lip! And although I have never given a concert under such disastrous circumstances, NEVER have I had such a gigantic success. I am so happy about this I am unable to write of it. Rejoice only, and do not upset yourself over my lip. I am staying in bed all day today trying to let this pimple come to a head. Now is when I long for our dear Vl. Vas. He could rid me of this unwanted intruder in a second. Greet him. I receive your letters all the time! They are on the night table beside me and I sneak glances at their dear words, wondering should I or should I not reread them again.

Tomorrow reams of stuff is going to appear about the concert. Alexander Nikolaevich has already written a detailed report of the concert and sent it to *Link*. You will be pleased! . . .

His next London letter was dated 18 March:

Child, I am so sorry not to have sent you a telegram saying I arrived in London! Forgive me the unhappy minutes, or worse, hours and days I unwittingly caused you! In fact, the evening we arrived in London I was especially thinking of you and missing you. Poor Tutik, how I torture her with my failings. I nearly died of shock and shame when I received your last letter. I am just now coming again to my senses. Only *I* could have done such a thing.

All the critics were on my side, and already I have several engagements for next year. But I cannot yet say "it's all over but the shouting." There are still two concerts more to go.

I am sitting in my little room alone before the fireplace waiting for Alexander Nikolaevich. We are going to spend this evening together playing chess. Never fear, we do not go out on the town. Alexander Nikolaevich is very circumspect here.

19 March

My child, forgive me, forgive me, dear, I am to blame and again I am not. I have not forgotten about you NOT FOR ONE SECOND. When I *see* you I will give you the details of the two days A. N. and I spent in Brussels and you will see that a long letter would have been impossible. What I do need to be abused for, however, is the fact that I did not send you an arrival telegram. I am still torturing myself because of that.

To my horror, I find I must have received at least three letters from you before you received my first one from London. It will tell you of the first days in London—they were almost like a nightmare, and they are painful to recall.

Since this is now in the past I can inform you that they found that my pimple was a large furuncle. The blaggard sat right under my right mustache. The most horrible thing was that the sore formed on the very day of the concert. Imagine what it was like for me on the stage. Imagine too how strange it was not to feel any pain while I played and then to be totally apathetic to everything afterward. I greeted people like a machine and could only think of getting back into bed as quickly as possible. As luck had it though, Alexander Nikolaevich talked me into going with him to the theater that evening. I was very ill in the theater. Next day I could not get out of bed. The doctor was called, and he decided it was a furuncle and suggested a treatment (not a cure). I could not have done without the Sisters of Mercy who came and changed my bandage every two hours for 3 days. What made matters worse was that I do not have a piano in my room. It seems that good hotels in London refuse "musical" guests, and quite disapprove of music. So here I am looking extremely silly with a bandage and having to walk to Bechstein's (fortunately, only across the street) to practice for 2 hours in one of the private rooms. This means that I have had only 8 hours to prepare for my concert tomorrow. I suffered frightfully while practicing and the pain stopped yesterday for the first time. Today I am in great shape and were it not for having lost part of my right mustache (the important part right near the nose), then I could say with some accuracy that I am back to normal looking. Altogether I was in bed for only one day, but I must admit I was quite frightened.

21 March

I am sending you a whole dossier on Prometheus. Take the trouble to read *all* the reviews and choose the best only to give them for reprinting. It would be best to do this through Boris Petrovich [Jurgenson] who gives the RMO all gleanings from the London press. So, I am reduced to this sort of indecorous business, but I have been awfully hurt by the RMO, what with Sakhnovsky at the head of the list! . . . I have a mountain of letters asking for my autograph . . . Tillet tells me I must comply with Londoners' requests for these, and it will take me all of 3 hours to be their victim. Where am I to find the time? I saw London in all its magnificence today for the first time. It was the first good day. A. N. and I went around in a taxi.

24 March

Tomorrow A. N. and I spend the whole day in Cambridge. Two professors who are interested in my light symphony and in my theories in general have invited us. We ought to have a very interesting discussion. Furthermore, we will see the sights of Cambridge and the university.

My second piano concert is day after tomorrow evening. If it goes as well as the first then I will be very happy, although that will mean I will have no time to practice. Today, for example, I devoted half the day to writing letters, and the rest I spent with A. N. at Parliament where, as you probably have heard, there is a stormy debate going on about the Irish question. Although I do not understand the language, it was very interesting to me to see the English in a crisis. On Friday I dine with some Theosophists. The dinner is arranged by Weed, a man who has been secretary of the Theosophical Society for 32 years (ever since it was founded). Last year he left the Society for reasons which cannot be written in a letter. At his house I will meet the woman in whose arms Blavatsky died. The dinner promises me much. Alexander Nikolaevich gathers more and more information about India every day, seeks out interesting and well-informed people concerning occult matters, introduces me to them, and keeps me roused to action.

Professor Charles Mayer of Cambridge reported Scriabin's visit in full in the *British Journal of Psychology* (Vol. VII, 1914)—an article on color-hearing—and Sir Henry Wood and Professor Wallace Rimmington together work out a plan for performing *Prometheus* with colors next season.

Ibbs and Tillet scheduled concerts for Liverpool, 9 February, 1915, and again London on the 13th, but the outbreak of World War I in September intervened.

The atmosphere generated by Scriabin in England was electric. An international press attended the concerts, and many acclaimed him. "The new direction in art," said the German *Allgemeine Musik Zeitung.* "Only Scriabin interprets his works so enchantingly," wrote America's *Musical Courier.* Bryanchaninov wrote in *Link*: "Scriabin conquered London. It is difficult to overcome the English, but once they yield, they do so entirely, unconditionally, and there are no more steadfast enthusiasms than those of the English."

The *London Times* observed:

> The first appearance of Mr. Scriabin brought a very large audience on the tiptoe of curiosity ... His playing with its velvet touch, its exquisite precision of phrasing, and its effortless energy of rhythm, made the whole Concerto full of charm and freshness ... Everyone must have felt that Prometheus was a different work from the one we heard twice a year ago, not only because the composer's commanding playing replaced the painstaking and painsmaking efforts of the courageous pianist who came to the rescue last year, but because the London Symphony orchestra and Sir Henry Wood had studied the music. Before it seemed a patchwork of incongruity, now it was wonderfully clarified.

> The audience recalled Mr. Scriabin and cheered him so loudly that some few of the dissenters were forced to assert their opinion a little rudely.

Again on 16 March, another critic of the *Times* wrote with more qualified praise:

> We feel certain Mr. Scriabin is working upon a perverted musical theory which he has succeeded in justifying to himself, but is not likely to justify to others. If this is so, though the performance of his work will be damaged by it, as Turner's has been damaged by the composition of his colors, that does not prevent us from realizing the extraordinary vividness of his imagination and fertility of his musical mind.

Musical Standard:

> The large audience with a noticeable proportion of the younger generation who flocked to Queen's Hall ... received Mr. Scriabin with an enthusiasm which must have gratified him exceedingly. As pianist and composer Scriabin creates an atmosphere of his own, and whether or not one is in sympathy with

his theosophical ideas, there can hardly be two opinions as to the exquisite delicacy and subtle phrasing of his pianoforte playing, nor as to his rare gifts as a composer.

Musical Times:

The flow from abroad! Schönberg, who had been imported to conduct his Five Pieces for Orchestra; and now Scriabin. It was the completest of triumphs . . . many recalls.

For his solo recitals, Scriabin fared less well. Ibbs promised a third recital if the second went as well as the first, but it did not, though in the hearts of a chain of Londoners Scriabin became an immortal—Eaglefield Hull, Montagu-Nathan, Alfred Swan, George Woodhouse, and Ernest Newman.

Scriabin played 20 March, 1914:

Preludes, Op. 13 (C major)

Op. 11 (G# minor, E minor, C major, C# minor, B♭ minor, E♭, B minor, D major, D minor)

Mazurkas, Op. 3 (B♭ minor, F# major)

Etudes, Op. 8 (F# minor, A♭ major (lento), D# minor)

Third Sonata

Poem, Op. 32 No. 1

"Winged Poem," Op. 51

"Desire," Op. 57

"Strangeness," Op. 63

Albumleaf, Op. 58

And on 26 March, 1914:

Preludes, Op. 35 (B♭ major, D♭ major)

Op. 17 (D minor, C minor)

Op. 11 (E♭ minor)

Op. 16 (B major, G# minor, G♭ Major, E ♭ minor, F# major)

Mazurkas, Op. 25 (F minor, E minor)

Fantasy Sonata

Two Poems, Op. 32

Poem, Op. 69 No. 1

"Mask," Op. 63

Prelude, Op. 67 No. 1
Poem, Op. 69 No. 2
Ninth Sonata

London Times, 21 March:

Mr. Scriabin charmed a large audience at Bechstein Hall by his exquisite music, playing one delicate trifle after another till the audience became a little apathetic. Not till he had reached *Etrangeté* did they feel they had got, as the Americans would say, "right there," and its piquant phraseology and brilliant playing roused them to demand an encore. It was curious to find the *Poème Ailé* modeled on Chopin's Etude in F, Op. 25. The Third Sonata, the largest work on the program, was the most interesting with its vigorous finale. The first movement is tedious by its insistence on one rhythm, but the finale (which follows two movements, both quite slight) is built on big lines, and the composer's masterly interpretation created a deep impression.

The subsidiary critic of the *Times* of 27 March was harsher.

Mr. Scriabin began his second recital last night with a number of those little pieces which it would only be possible to enjoy in comfort if one could kidnap the composer and insist upon a recital all to oneself by firelight. They are too slight for the concert hall, with its persistent punctuations of applause . . . He followed them by a Second Sonata with a vague andante and an exceedingly brilliant presto. The latter gave us full flavor of his technical command of the piano. The second of the Poèmes (Op. 69) with its wild arabesques persistently hitting on what used to be called "wrong notes," entertained the audience immensely, and they asked for and got its repetition. The 9th Sonata was disappointing. One would have expected at least that it would have given wider range of tone and color than it did, and the 4-note phrase which is its principal theme hardly seems worth the elaboration it gets. However, the audience wanted more, and Mr. Scriabin satisfied them by playing *Etrangeté* which was one of the events of last week's recital.

The *Musical Standard* regarded the first recital "dainty" (the preludes), "Satanic Poem" ("nothing distinctive about it"), Third Sonata ("slender material . . . very little of interest except for the last movement"), but found "consummate playing which alone would have aroused enthusiasm. *Etrangeté* attracted most attention. The compositions are charming and charmingly played, and as such they win our admiration if they do not astonish us." And the second recital:

What is color in music? Scriabin is telling us something about it in his showy compositions ... His effective display again arrested our interest. The group of dainty preludes showed how easy it is to be effective without being ponderous and his mazurkas were as vivid and energetic thrown at us without restraint. The Chopinesque poem and Sonata hardly prepared us for the final three items, fireworks undeniably, and labeled Op. 67, 68, and 69 with their squibs and Catherine wheels of most vivid color.

In order not to be alone, Scriabin's strongest childhood fear still remaining, he waited three days in London for Bryanchaninov to finish up his business details. In Paris, however, they parted anyway on 4 April at the Palace Hotel near the Gare de Lyon. "Alexander Nikolaevich said he would come back to Russia with me if I insisted, since he felt so guilty towards me, but he would feel uncomfortable knowing he still had material pertaining to the present political situation to collect for his journal. There was nothing I could do, so I freed him. Now I am flying all by myself to my precious Tusyavost."

He wants to see Tatyana alone to discuss India, the Prefatory Action, the English success, their life in general, and make love. He had suggested SPb. Moscow is overcrowded. Conversation there with Tatyana in a houseful of children and with friends and doting relatives would be impossible.

And how I wanted to spend at least one day alone with you, just us TWO. How can we do this? Think of something! In any event come meet me at the station *ALONE*, I implore you, my joy, we must be alone. This is very necessary for me! I have so many ideas, so many kisses ...

I will bring you some new verses! I think that I will finish the text this summer and will begin to finish part of the prefatory action synthesizing all arts together. God, how much I have to tell you that is interesting. Our trip to India is settled. I have even bought some of the necessary clothing.

Tusyavost, our material situation is somewhat better than I had thought, but only a *little*. You cannot conceive how much London the monster gobbled up. I cannot complain about this though, because next year my expenses in England are guaranteed. But until then I will be bringing home only around 500 rubles out of an earned 1,400. I am bringing with me all the bills, so that I can go over them and study them and next time won't make any mistakes. True, I am bringing back a lot of things, two new trunks, for example, which will last us a long time. But we will talk about all this when I see you. I mentioned this only because the conversation came around to India, and I want you to know what to count on. In any event, things are not hopeless. We must be economical only for this summer.

I want so terribly to go to India. I will never travel again without you!!

As soon as he is back in Moscow he writes Siloti to postpone his concert appearances for a year, because of India.

> To concertize immediately after India, that is, to go directly to Petersburg is very dangerous. The doctor says that two weeks in a moderate climate is absolutely essential to prevent a lung collapse. So by your freeing me from participation in your symphony concert in January (the only engagement I have in Russia for that month) and giving me the possibility of spending February (European calendar) in England, I can defer my return to Russia until a month later. I am so happy that you understand what it means to me to go to India. Your active interest deeply moves me. If I have the slightest chance, I will of course write some small things for your symphony concerts. I myself would like that very, very much.

52

SUMMER, 1914, WAS shrouded in cerements of approaching war ... for almost everyone, that is, except Scriabin. He was thoroughly happy and invulnerable in divinity's sheath. In May he took a *dacha*, "Morovich," four miles from Grivno along the Moscow-Kursk railway line and near Podolsk, where he had summered before near Moscow. The atmosphere was conducive to "concentrated work." The house was isolated. There were no neighbors known to or friendly with the Scriabins. There were no pretty walks to take. The roof leaked when it rained. In one room downstairs stood a little upright. Scriabin rarely touched it.

Scriabin worked on the Prefatory Action upstairs on a big open balcony flooded with morning sun. He sat there training himself for India. "It was astonishing how he could endure such great heat. Under the rays of the sun he seemed to blossom." wrote Schloezer, who spent that surprisingly hot June with them. Life was regular to a degree of regimen. Scriabin and his guests—the usual disciples, Sperling, Bogorodsky, Podgaetsky and now Grechaninov—rose early. After coffee, he paced in the garden, talking or rather thinking out loud to anyone beside him. Then he worked until lunch at 1 o'clock, after which he rested or walked again, and resumed work.

After supper he read. His library was in keeping with his text and almost exclusively poetical—Balmont's *Vertograd* or "Green City," which he loved especially, Ivanov's *Cor Ardens* and Zelinsky's translation of Sophocles' dramas, to help him with the theatrical aspect of the Prefatory Action. He asked Schloezer to bring him the complete *Theory and Practice of Poetic Art* by Fyodor Tyuchev (1803–1873), Russian lyric poet and contemporary of Pushkin. Tyuchev's famous line, "An uttered thought is a lie," was the diametric opposite of what Scriabin was determined to accomplish. He wanted to strike the truth.

His habit that summer was to read lines from his text slowly, almost didactically. "Doesn't this seem rational?" he would ask. "Is it not a versified proposition of a theoretical structure?" Or, when he would match vowels and consonants in particularly felicitous configurations, "How about this principle of orchestration?" Scriabin was acutely aware of his limitations in poetry. "Texts trouble me. I feel myself a master in music, and I am at ease. But I now must master the technique of verse. I cannot permit my text to be worse than its music!" Scriabin brought nothing of Theosophy with him, no books of Blavatsky or any other "mystic." He had moved on, in the way he had earlier left Nietzsche, Wagner, and other determining influences.

Before the summer he wrote his last music. "Two Dances," Op. 73, resemble each other like brother and sister. No. 1, titled "Garlands" (*Guirlandes*), is a passage from the Mysterium where he invokes flowers, dancers waving garlands in the air. In sound though, the music trembles like a chandelier of spiky, circular, tinted lights, crisp petals from some glass flower of translucent fragrances. "Dark Flames" (*Flammes Sombres*), its contrasting mate, is subdued, somber, and thoughtful. Its lambent colors are embers, even during the middle section where you can feel dancers' skirts swirling around a fire. The fire here is dark, dark as the music's mood. "You hear," he often said, "this is not music any longer . . . it's something else . . . It's the Mysterium."

The five preludes, Op. 74, his final opus, point a new direction in Scriabin's composition. Page-long as they may be, they still cast a very long shadow. They are composer's études, studies in secret complexity hidden behind transparency. There is counterpoint, layers of melodic lines coagulated into chords of blending tonalities. No. 2, his favorite, is quite simple on the surface, combining F♯ minor and C major in a long sustained cry of the heart over a droning bass of open fifths in pendulum repetition. "Sad . . . as if torn . . . vague . . . undecided . . ." are some of the other preludes' markings, and the last reintroduces in new form a new kind of *pafos* "proud and bellicose." Scriabin is the defiant conqueror of body and soul's mortality.

In June the proofs of Op. 74 reached Grivno, but Scriabin could not bother. They lay unopened in their package. Schloezer had to persuade him to play them. When he did, he talked. "Listen to their simplicity, and yet, how complicated they are psychologically . . ." He saw No. 2, marked only "slow and contemplative," as a desert: "An astral desert, mind you, and here is fatigue, exhaustion (the descending chromatic line). See how this short prelude sounds as if it lasts an entire century? Actually it is all eternity, millions of years . . ."

With Op. 74 Scriabin said he created music which could be played to mean different concepts. "It is like a crystal, the same crystal can reflect many different lights and colors." And he explains the contradiction between the titles and sounds of the "Two Dances." Once he played the Prelude, Op. 74 No. 2, twice, and asked the difference. Sabaneeff could not answer, but he knew that the piece the second time had lost "every trace of caressing eros which once shadowed it. The warmth was gone." "Yes," Scriabin whispered. "It is *death* now. It is death like the appearance of the Eternally Feminine which leads to the Final Unity. Death and love . . . I call death 'Sister' in my Prefatory Action, because there must be no trace of fear about it. It is the highest reconciliation, a white radiance . . ."

Scriabin rarely went into Grivno, but when he did, it was for the mail, not the newspapers. The war burst upon Scriabin and his house guests unexpectedly in 1914, despite all the clouds of preparation. Scriabin's concern with death had been musical. Now it was worldwide actuality. He would be more affected by death before the year is out. Liadov died, and so did his father. Nikolai was buried in Lausanne, but no members of the family could travel abroad. Uncle Vladimir also died early in 1915, perhaps from sorrow at being too old to serve in the Army.

The news of the war shocked Scriabin. He floundered momentarily, because he had not foreseen it and had no explanation for it in his Mysterium of the human cycle. Offhand he said that it was a sort of "spiritual renewal for people, even though it destroyed them materially." As the struggle intensified, he announced that war was "a spiritual upheaval enacted on another plane of being," a cosmic struggle reflected on earth.

Schloezer, however, read the papers avidly each day for facts. Scriabin had to make an effort to tear himself away from his work on the text and sketches of themes for the Prefatory Action and come downstairs and listen. After a gliding comment, he raced back upstairs.

Bryanchaninov commissioned Scriabin to interpret the educational significance of the War for his journal. Scriabin obliged after he had sorted out his thoughts, and in March, 1915, his comments were widely reproduced in England and Russia. He wrote:

> The masses need to be shaken. In this way they can be rendered more perceptive of finer vibrations than usual. How deeply mistaken it is to view War merely as discord between nations. What the meditating prophet and the creative artist standing at center feel in their moments of inspiration is expressed at the periphery. But the masses do not receive it. They make the idea subservient to the rhythm of their individuality and its development. However, periodically creative energy accumulates and erupts at the periphery. In this way the race evolves . . . Upheavals, cataclysms, catastrophes, Wars, Revolutions, all these shake the souls of peoples and force them to perceive the idea hidden behind the outer event . . . The time has now come for me to cry out to all those capable of new conceptions, to all artists and scientists who unconsciously create history. They have new problems to synthesize, newly differentiated arts to unify, new experiences to seek out . . . Thinking now of the War I am inclined to ascribe the enthusiasm for my *Prometheus* in England not so much to its music as to its mysticism.

In private Scriabin and his followers could not help feeling that the war was a prefatory action in itself to his Mysterium. At summer's end everyone returned to Moscow. He said to a Petersburg correspondent who visited him, "My one dream now is to see and hear the Prefatory Action on which I have worked ten years. The day of its performance will be the happiest day of my life."

Over the winter season, Scriabin's hands were "dreadfully out of shape." However, he practiced all day long for a week and gave a concert in Moscow, at the Great Noblemen's Hall on 22 November, 1914, organized by Moscow University in aid of "Families of Reserve Officers Killed in the War." The program introduced the Prelude, Op. 74 No. 2. Some critics complained that he played too little from his most recent music, but the *Russian Gazette* stated that "As usual for a Scriabin concert, the higher the opus number the colder the public. Still, it was a *succès d'estime*. The Seventh Sonata is a 'laboratory experiment'. Only the early works and the marvelous Poems, Op. 32, warmed the hearts of the large audience . . . The new prelude appears very interesting. It moves slowly, dimly, secretly beckons, but it is a quiet little orchid. It had to be repeated at the end of the program along with a whole row of early favorites which electrified the public more than all the other music. Mr. Scriabin played beautifully."

Jurgenson and Scriabin held long conferences as to how to print the Prefatory Action. Special marks would indicate the different arts and separate types of print would denote sounds, mime, lights, movements and processions. Rimsky-Korsakoff's son, organizer in Petersburg of a new concert series, "Contemporary Music," invited Scriabin soon after on very generous terms to appear, but Siloti refused to release him. He himself telephoned Korsakoff and said, "Rachmaninoff, Casals and Scriabin are mine, mine, mine!" On 27 January, 1915, Scriabin again played a fine recital in Moscow. The tickets cost from 8 rubles 10 kopecks down to 55 kopecks, the highest any pianist at the time drew. The concert was arranged by Princess Maria Trubetskaya, wife of the Russian representative in Serbia, and half the proceeds went to the Serbian Red Cross.

Preludes, Op. 13 (C and G major)
        Op. 31 (E♭ minor, D♭ major)
"Winged Poem," Op. 51 No. 3
Preludes, Op. 48 (C major)
        Op. 39 (A flat major)
Poem-Nocturne, Op. 61
Prelude, Op. 49 (F major)
Mazurkas, Op. 40 (D flat major, F# major)
Fourth Sonata
Poem, Op. 59 No. 1
"Mask," Op. 63
Albumleaf, Op. 58
"Dark Flames," Op. 73 (first time)
Prelude, Op. 74 No. 2
"Enigma," Op. 52

"Desire" and "Danced Caress," Op. 57

Satanic Poem, Op. 36

Grigory Prokofiev reviewed the occasion in *RMG*. Kashperov, editor of Scriabin's letters, astutely cites this review for diametrically contradicting every problem Belaieff outlined to Safonoff at the beginning of Scriabin's career. This was Scriabin's final public performance in Moscow.

> The second concert of A.N. Scriabin went with great success. The lingering impression is one of something ravishing. This "something ravishing" is composed of numerous elements, chief among which is Scriabin's own enchanting performance.
>
> To someone who lures a wealth of tonal possibilities from the piano, Scriabin's playing may seem a monotone with its continuous sharpness, even clanging mezzo-piano. Nor do Scriabin's fingers produce massive sounds, it is true; but the Scriabin tone itself its marvelous. Even more important is the fact that this sound is eminently suited to Scriabin music and Scriabin mood.
>
> Here we notice another surprising secret: His ethereal sounds cannot quite fill the hall. But don't forget that he is a wizard with the pedal. He achieves extraordinary effects.
>
> Another of his ways of captivating the audience is the very strong impression he gives of improvising. He breaks the chains of strict rhythm and makes the rhythm sound anew every time he plays, filling his performance with freshness. Never has he played his Fourth Sonata with such mastery and sincerity as he did yesterday. And with what power the theme of the second part resounded! And for all this, the actual sound was not great. The secret here is his energetic rhythm.

In February, 1915, on the 21th and 16th, he gives two successive concerts in Petersburg for Siloti.

> Waltz, Op.1
> Preludes, Op. 15 (C# minor, E major)
> Impromptu, Op. 10 (A major)
> Mazurkas, Op. 25 (E minor, F major)
> "Fragility," Op. 51
> Quasi-Valse, Op. 47
> Albumleaf, Op. 58
> Etude, Op. 42 (C# minor)
>
> Seventh Sonata

Two Poems, Op. 69
Prelude, Op. 74 No. 2
"Strangeness," Op. 63
Two Poems, Op. 32
Ninth Sonata, Op. 68

The second repeated the Moscow program with the Tenth Sonata replacing the Fourth.

The concerts were unusually successful and finely reviewed. Karatygin, critic for *Speech*, wrote of the 12 February recital, "The public was huge. The ecstatic ovation accorded the famous composer made him play many encores. There was no end. He played with passionate rapture, lift, fire and unusual enchantment . . . nervously and with exaltation." Of the 16 February recital, he said, ". . . an enormous success like the first. The audience would not leave. An entire fourth part of encores was added to the program. The 10th Sonata was capital. He played it absolutely wonderfully. There are a few pianists in the world who have better technique then Scriabin, but none can give the inspiration that he gives . . ."

In March, 1915, Scriabin toured the provinces playing an advanced program in Kharkov which included "Toward the Flame," and in Kiev his second recital featured "Dark Flames," Prelude, Op. 74 No. 2, and the Ninth Sonata. He wrote Tatyana on 3 March, 1915, a letter which took four days to reach Moscow because of the war ("How boring it all is!") "In Kharkov I had no strength or self-possession on the stage," and in Kiev when the second concert was requested and the agent guaranteed him 600 rubles if the take was over 1,200 rubles, "I was too weak even to resist 500 rubles . . ."

The box office for the first recital was 3,000 rubles, and Scriabin is horrified to realize that the manager made 2,000 rubles off him. "Just think, I *could* be bringing home 4,000 rubles altogether. But still we are not about to fall into rack and ruin. Do not regret. It's not worth it. I played well, as I rarely do, and the reception was like Petersburg itself. Fancy, the Kiev Conservatory brought me a wreath!! How times change!" He and Reinhold Glière (1875–1956), the composer-director of the Conservatory (later at Moscow Conservatory), became friendly.

Scriabin asks Tatyana about the children—"dragonfly," "mutton," and the "doll." He tells her that he does not dress until noon—"I have brought your habits with me."

Scriabin's last letter to Tatyana from the tour was dated 7 March, 1915:

> Why do you write me so little about yourself and the state of your health? I can only write you two words today. I have to go to the bank, get my ticket, buy a few things, and most of all run through the 3rd Sonata. I've put it on the program. All yesterday I only got to practice one hour. This evening I have to go to the Conservatory. I am tired of music.

But that night he sent a telegram accepting an engagement to play in Warsaw.

Popular demand again recalled him to Petersburg. He played there for the third time since February, on 2 April, 1915, the last concert of his lifetime:

Preludes, Op. 35 (D♭ major, B major)
        Op. 37 (B♭ minor, F# major, B major, G minor)
        Op. 39 (G major)
Mazurka, Op. 25 (E major)
Etude, Op. 8 (B♭ minor)
Waltz, Op. 38
Third Sonata
"Nuances," Op. 56
"Dance of Languor," Op. 51
Two Preludes, Op. 74 Nos. 4 and 1
"Garlands" (first time) and "Dark Flames," Op. 73
Prelude, Op. 74 No. 2
"Strangeness," Op. 63
Fourth Sonata

Never had he received higher accolades. Ossovsky found him playing at his "most inspiring and affecting." Ellen von Tiedeböhl wrote for *Etude* Magazine in America that "his eyes flashed fire and his face radiated happiness." Grigory Timofeev in *Speech*, 4 April, 1915, asked simply, "Is there any need really to speak of the pianist's success or of his great public?" After the concert, Schloezer said to him that he had noted a "possession of the soul," a state in which he seemed "illuminated and in the power of strange forces." Scriabin replied that during the Third Sonata, "I completely forgot I was playing in a hall with people around me. This happens very rarely to me on the platform." Usually, he elaborated, he had to watch himself very carefully, look at himself as if from afar, to keep himself in control.

53

The final, though incomplete text of the Prefatory Action (translated by George Reavey):

Once again in you the Pre-Eternal wills
Acceptance of love's paradise
Once again the Infinite wills
To know himself in the finite.

Choir
In the lightning soaring, in the dread explosion,
In love's creative surge,
In its godlike breathing
There's the innermost aspect of the universe.

The ardor of the instant gives birth to eternity,
Lights the depths of space;
Infinity breathes with worlds,
Ringing sounds envelop silence.

The great comes to pass
And sweet delightful love
Is born anew!

In burning hearts
Our Pre-Eternal Father
Weds with death!

Female Voice
To you many-lighted, U U, to you impulsive
My answering moan, U U, my cry of summons.

Male Voice
Who are you, arisen in holy silence,
In white beams calling to me?

Female Voice
I am the bright joy of the ultimate achievement
In the white flame I am the incandescent diamond

I am the ineffable bliss of dissolution
I am the joy of death, I am freedom, I am ecstasy!

Male Voice
Impart to me how I may soar to you desired one
That drives me mad with the shimmer of your beams
Where stands your palace, illuminated with magic light.
Hear my prayer and reveal to me the mystery of death.

Female Voice
Heed me variegated light, the abysses of life lie between us,
Life with its delusions, agonizing dreams;
Multicolored spaces have divided us
Amid the wondrous radiance of star-bloomed adornment.
To enthrall me, you must pass through them
Overcome them and break down at your journey's end.

Male Voice
But I do not see my way in the starry firmament,
I don't see, blessed one, those spaces, those abysses.

Female Voice
Like me, they're your dream, your willing.
You must see the light, hear your prophetic voice,
And you will know, you will behold in your languor
The flowering worlds dividing us.

You fill everything with yourself
I am not when you are there
When in the beams of your dreaming
As an image of new beauty
I, in shimmering play, appear
Thereby dooming to life
Swarms of reveries, choirs of dreams,
Assemblies of glittering worlds.
There is no I, no I, only you exist,
You fill everything with yourself.

(Solemnly)
Speaking within you, I call upon you
From radiant heights from divine exhal-
ations
And appealing to the creative will in you
I demand sacrifices and solemn vows,

So that in your infinite striving you may
Come to know the bliss of another
timelessness.
Three deeds you must perform, Pre-
Eternal,
Make three sacrifices in intoxicating
mutability.

The first sacrifice—is a dream of me;
You must forget caressing sleep
And rush into the abysses that have
separated us
And thus given us wings for the feat of
love.

Male and Female Voices
O divine deed, all-starry dance,
In you we shall prove victorious over the
abyss,
In you we, who have been torn apart,
shall discover ourselves,
In you we shall blissfully die in each other.

Female Voices
You have begun your dance. From the
peak of exhalations
I behold you in motion, O Lord;
I distinguish the colors of the surrounding
spheres—
Of the bridal garments adorning you.

You live already and, moving towards me
Lives bear you away from me
With intoxicating dreams around you
Shimmering and froth, illumining and
sound.

Male Voices
In my movements I am bound

By the crude texture of my apparel,
Yet I soar, obliged to you
For all the energy of my fiery hopes.

Female Voice
If the cry of my joyous call
Had not sounded in your soul,
You would not have created, O Sweet
Lord, the beginning of all beginnings.

You are all-yearning for me
And because of that the night
Of the abysses will assist you
To overcome all things in your creative
striving.
Behold: Seven angels in ethereal garb,
The purest harbingers of your deathless
glories,
Fiery soaring pillars, the beaming heads
Of your dazzling sparkling orbs
Shall come to serve you in divesting your
holy raiments!

They are the heaven-dwellers,
Fire-bearers,
Rulers of destiny,
Builders of the world,
Preservers of frontiers,
Warriors against God,
Destroyers of walls.
They are yours, these children tearing you
apart,
Fathered by you in an agitated breast.
Your path towards me lies in their
negating dawn.
Come in their aspect and perform your
deed!

They are the builders of a radiant cathedral,
In which the drama of the universe will
take place,
Where in a languorous dance, in being
wedded to me
You will attain to another desired world.

I am Your will, I am the dread instrument
Of Your great achievements.
Through my strength you pour down
dreamlike
Intoxications into crystals of creations.

And I am your dream about the future
universe,
One of the links of dual existence.
I enthralled you, but soon I shall be in
thrall

In your wreath I'll be a wondrous star.

Lightnings of the will, we thirst for
achievements.
We'll be incarnated in the blows of deci-
sion.
In the roar of explosions and in the
thunder of wrecks
We shall live boldly in dreams,
We shall serve both dark and light.

We are the bright fumes of divine thought,
Through contemplation we'll be incarnated in pure souls.
Through us you enthrall the spirits of
darkness and negation
And anew you'll bind together fractured
dreams.

We are the beaming assembly of flame-
thoughts
And of pure lights, of token-lights,
For you—of the world of yearning
dreams,
For the earth—of the feast of rejoicing
stars.

We are born through your desire to
distinguish,
We are awakened by the gleams of
heavenly fire,
We are the waves of feelings, the world
of aspects and delusions,
Sounding on sunbeam-strings, we enthrall
all things.

We Are The Waves of Life

Waves,
The first ones,
Waves,
The timid ones,
The first
Murmurs,
The timid
Whispers,
The first
Quivers,
The timid
Lispings.

Waves,
The gentle ones,
Waves,
The swelling ones,
The tender
Mutations,
Mounting

Foam-flurries,
The gentle
Soarings,
The impulses
Of rising spray.
We are—all of us—a single
Current, directed from out of
Eternity towards the instant
On the way to humanity,
Down from transparency
Towards a stony gloom
So that we may imprint upon stone
In fiery creativeness
The image of Your Divine Countenance.

Waves,
Waves,
First
Waves.
With waves,
Waves,
Stirring ones,
Waves,
With waves
Kissing
Waves.
What's this sweet bliss
That is roused in the waves
By the flaring snow
Of the foaming rollers?
What is the mystery
That lures us into the valleys
From the boundless heights
To the schism of life?

Awakening Feelings

The tender delight
Of touching for the first time
The mysterious sweetness
Of moist lips kissing,

The sweet moaning
Of first languorous moments,
The first ringing vibrations
The calls of our inclinations.

The tender caresses
Of the first glimmers—
The mysterious tales
Told by amorous lights.

The Waves

Having grown heavy—sodden
In a downpour of sensations,
We have become absorbed
In the current of life.

Into the valleys of languor
Waves come surging.
In clouds of desiring
We have been clothed

In cloud-bondage
Closer to the perishable,
Pour down you frothing waters
Lower and lower.
Sweet is the perishable world,
For only on what is perishable
Can your image be
Imprinted

Sweet is the perishable world,
For only in what is perishable
In the manifest world
Can you go on living.

All the more invested,
The waves U foaming,
All the more manifest,
The tender bondages,

All the more loving, all the more pleasur-
able,
All the more languorous, all the more
joyous,
All the more torturing, lovely,
Sensuous, corporeal;

O our captivity,
Sweet captivity,
Everywhere present, for us,
Most inevitable,
Enveloping us on all sides,
Become our bodily clothing.

The Wave
You gleamed, and swooning sweet-
ness
Poured through the moist body,
And I soared full of languor,
Towards you in dreams.

Born of the dark elements,
A wave merging with other waves,
As in a languorous dream,
I now take leave of my sisters.

And in your sweet turbulence
I am the most wingèd of the waves.
In my bold flight I am your joyous,
Your divine laughter.

I am the love that stirred within you,
You are the light that stirred within
me.

I am a wave, become self-aware,
As though in answer to your play.

Into the super-terrestrial spheres of
the spirit
Where the thread of life originated,
Where your ethereal palaces are
I soar to implore you:

Awaken like the consciousness within
me,
Awaken, o golden beam!
Heed my conjurations
And merge with me—in a wave!

Listen to the tender whispering of
foam
About our one and only mutual
destiny
And about our imitability
In our striving towards you.

A long time with your shimmerings
Have you gleamed before me, im-
mortal sunbeam,
And have lured and called me
With your lights.

I would have remained impersonal
And would not have become a wave
If the extraordinary gleams
Had not given me existence.

O, fall, spread in caresses,
Spill over your blessedness,
You gain knowledge of yourself
through the tales
Told by fractured sunbeams!

Sunbeam
Only in the garb of a threatening
cloud
Solemn and fatal could I
Meet you, abandoning
My godlike dream

The Wave
In our dreams, which rush to the
heights
Like illusions, clothe yourself
Wrapped in their mists,
Do not descend closer into the valley.

Choir
All covered in the breathing
Of the yearning dream about the
wave
And drunk with its sweet fragrance
In sweet sleep,

In transports of burning love,
In the power of a single thought,
The sunbeam drooped in a lightning
 cloud
Above the loving wave.

The Wave

I soar towards you, my courageous
 one,
An instant more—I've risen higher
And into the valley languorously
 moist
I plunged in tender foam.

O, sacred instant of creation
Blessed instant, fiery instant,
You've manifested to me the re-
 flection
Of death pale white and fatal.

You've roused in me the awareness
Of existence one and dual.
I am henceforth the combination
Of "I" and an alien "not-I."

Delicate textures come to life,
The textures of feelings—my ap-
 parel,
And rebellious they speed into the
 distance
Far away from the opening eyelids.

The smoky walls of dungeons
Melt and drown and break apart,
And crowds of lives—carriages
Rush into the depths.

In a world of sacrificial love
I became a royal union.
I overflow with settled strength,
I came to know the ardor of my
 blood.

O all-powerful desire,
You are living—and you are not I.
Our passionate caresses are still
 living
In multicolored existence.

You and I and our swoonings
Are a world of discovered wonders,
Of dreamlike intoxication,
Of the life of slumbering skies.

The miraculous combinations have
 come to pass.
The circle was completed, and there
 was born

The fruit of the marriage of wave and
 sunbeam,
The starlit countenance of the
 universe.

Kindled by the sacred instant's
 lightning,
The dreams of creation flame, and the
 wave,
With bewitching consciousness im-
 prisoning inspirations,
Is all given up to the contemplation
 of distinctions.

He shines in the sun, the God of the
 ruling light,
And gleams in stars in fathomless
 night.
In space the wave hovers like a royal
 planet
Enveloped in a shroud of cloudy
 pearl.
And the sunbeam caresses U of the
 first chosen union
Awakening in a mirage of dazzling
 wonders
Are identified with the multicolored,
 many-faceted
With the bridal adornments, the
 brocade of her veils.

The Mountains

We are the frozen impulses of
 amorous rages.
We are the petrified billows of
 stormy caresses,
The explosion caught arrested by the
 enchantment of cooling
Snowy peaks, valleys and rocks.

The Meadows

We're the warm breathing of lips
 that did not meet,
Secreting in ourselves all the delights
 of poisons.
By the fragrance of flowers we are
 awakened here
We have begun to stir with rustling
 grasses.

The Forest

We are the soaring pillars of twilight
 cathedrals.
We are richly garbed in green
 rustling sounds.
We hide crowds of enigmatic

creatures.
Into us pour mysterious languorous lights.

The Desert
Having identified myself as a desert in space,
The dry sultry kiss of a sunbeam and the earth,
Having driven out the forest life from my region

And hating the living songs of streams.

I am a winged caress, I flutter bird-like,
And I come to life as a savage lacerating beast.
As a writhing, crawling snake I have awakened,
I, voluptuous one, as the darling of the moist elements.

54

SCRIABIN'S FLAW for all his existence was a lack of a sense of ending. The finale of the First Symphony was poor beyond belief. *Prometheus*, alas, for all its supernal sound has no true ending either. It, rather than the Fifth Sonata, merely halts. The conductor must cover the deficiency by slowing down gradually in a quasi-conclusion, almost as soon as the exalted chorus begins with its massive, heaving sigh. So too with his concentrated preludes. Some are too short to have begun before they end. Scriabin did not believe in endings. As one dealing in eternal verities, he could not. Music in his aesthetics was a continuum. His time measurement had no yardstick. Philosophically, the past and the future were jumbled.

So too, Scriabin's death was an unfinished misadventure. Its timing and senselessness were all wrong. That spring of 1915 in which so many words had been planted, so many thoughts had been voiced, and so much fame and glory accorded, was brought meaninglessly to an end.

The concert in St. Petersburg had been reminiscent of London—all recognition, excitement, novelty. On Saturday, 4 April, he returned to Moscow, and noticed once again the little pimple on his upper right lip. He pointed it out to Dr. Bogorodsky. His temperature rose. On Tuesday the 7th, he took to his bed, and he canceled his Moscow concert for 11 April, although the posters were already pasted up throughout the city. The pimple became a pustule, then a carbuncle and again a furuncle. Bogorodsky was astonished at its color. "Like purple fire," he said. Scriabin's temperature soared to 106° and remained steadily there all day on 10 April. He called in Dr. Shchelkan, a specialist from the University.

The newspapers issued daily reports on Scriabin's condition. His friends gathered in the apartment. Podgaetsky donned a white nurse's jacket and dispensed the medicines Scriabin had been prescribed at set intervals. Poet Ivanov waited vigilantly, dropping by the apartment when he could. His wife sent a "brew of drinking yeast" to reduce the inflammation. Tatyana's lips were tight, but she held to her remarkable composure. She telegraphed for Boris to come, and she spoke with distress of his absence in the south. Princess Gagarina and her stately sister, Mme. Lermontova, stood helpfully to one side. Aunt Lyubov kept wringing her hands and saying, "But he was always so careful of infection!" The newspaper *Russian Morning* assigned Sabaneeff to write Scriabin's obituary.

Once Sabaneeff arrived at the apartment on 11 April he realized the gravity of the situation. Now crowds of acquaintances lined the stone stairway, standing, wondering, waiting for the latest bulletin. The piano was open and the white music notebook for the Prefatory Action stood in the rack. For the first time Sabaneeff was taken into the bedroom. It was half-dark with the shades drawn. Scriabin lay in one of twin beds, rare for those days of "matrimonials." Half of his face was covered with a sheet. His mustaches and beard were hidden. His eyes, shot through with suffering, stared out, but he was calm. Sabaneeff took his hand. It was like touching a burning stove.

"What a *scandal* I am making . . ." Scriabin muttered. His voice was strange. The swelling was so great he could not pronounce consonants.

"Of course, this will pass . . . I always said that suffering was necessary . . . I was right in what I said. I *have* overcome it. You know, I feel quite all right now, even through the pain . . ."

He asked about Sabaneeff's wife, and Sabaneeff thought to himself, "A gentleman even now. He does not forget manners even at a time like this."

Dr. Shchelkan decided that an incision must be made. The infection had spread through the blood stream.

"I cannot do it," Dr. Bogorodsky said, "I am too close a friend. I simply cannot."

Shchelkan in turn called a leading surgeon, Professor Doctor Spizharny. Bogorodsky refrains from telling Tatyana of the operation. Son Julian, the little "sheep," passes by. Tatyana pats him on the head absent-mindedly at first. She runs her finger along the birthmark on his forehead and says, "I'd always find you, if you got lost. I'd know you from this." Sabaneeff left before the incision is made.

The incision produced no pus, surprisingly. The doctor cut deeply a second time. A blood test revealed both strepto- and staphylococcus. On Sunday, 12 April, another surgeon, Professor Martynov was summoned. He pronounced Scriabin's condition "serious but not hopeless . . . yet." He slashed the lip again.

Sabaneeff arrived this time to find Scriabin in a state of mild delirium. Scriabin did not remember seeing him the day before. Now his single concern was that he would be "disfigured." Sabaneeff was slightly shocked to find him thinking of his external appearance. Tatyana cut their meeting short. "He is wandering. This means his temperature is rising." And to Scriabin she said as if talking to a baby, "Quiet now . . . Now sleep." On Monday, the thirteenth, the swelling reduced remarkably. Scriabin felt well. "I want to go compose something at the piano," he said.

Sabaneeff's editor telephoned the Scriabin apartment.

"Is he dead yet? How's the obituary coming? If you don't get it in on time, I'll have one written on the subject of *you*. This is the most important news item in Moscow. I'll give you 350 lines." Sabaneeff cried out in dismay, "But he's still alive!"

At noon Sabaneeff was again allowed in the bedroom. Scriabin and he held hands looking at each another. "You see, I am resurrected. Whatever suffering I endured for a few days, the worst of it was not the pain, but the hallucinations, the frightening thoughts, the visions. I could not understand them. What did they mean? The pain was not so hard to bear. I am convinced that suffering is necessary, because of its *contrast* . . ." He again asked Sabaneeff if he would be disfigured from the incisions.

"I hurt here," he said, pointing to his chest. "What does that mean?" Bogorodsky interpreted it was "pain from nerves . . . the nervous depression which follows a raging fever." Suddenly, Scriabin screamed, "This pain is unbearable . . . If this lasts I won't be able to *live* . . . I can't bear it . . ." Then after tossing and turning in agony, "This means the end! But this is a catastrophe . . ."

A lung specialist, Dr. Pletnev, was summoned. Pleurisy had set in. Blood poisoning was coursing throughout Scriabin's entire body. Intractably and inexplicably, a simple spot had grown into a terminal ailment. Scriabin's ordeal with death intensified. At midnight, he complained he could not breathe. He grew more and more delirious. Once he shouted out, "Who is there?" Those were his last words to Sister Death.

Mme. Lermontova, standing vigil at the head of his bed, handed him a piece of paper and a pencil. He seemed to realize that he was now expected to write his last words. He lost consciousness. Quickly, a priest was sent for. At 3:00 A.M. he received extreme unction and he died at 8:00 A.M. Tuesday, 14 April, 1915.

Merkulov, the sculptor, came to take a death mask, but Scriabin's face was too scarred. He made a cast of his right hand and ear instead. At noon, Mass was performed over Scriabin's body. Now it lay in an oak coffin strewn with strong scented flowers. Again that night at 8:00 another Mass was said. The sidewalk outside the Arbat house was thronged. Schloezer struggled through the crowd. He arrived too late. The funeral was held on Thursday, 16 April, at 10:00 in the morning. It was Easter week. The bells rang out all day long—three times a day for the three Masses, and each time anyone pulled a rope to release his sins. Sunshine glowed brilliantly. Only on the day of the funeral did the weather change—light rain with flakes of snow. The occasion was a social affair. Tickets had to be issued to The Church of the Miracle Worker in the Great Nikolo-Peskov Lane, near the apartment itself, in order to accommodate the public.

The obituaries began: "Yesterday Moscow buried the composer A. N. Scriabin. Almost all of Moscow's musical world, many artists, writers, painters, a mass of young students, and many devotees all gathered to pay last tribute to the composer. Already by 10:00 A.M. a great crowd of admirers had assembled in the Church. The crowd grew continuously and entrance became impossible. The Church was decorated with trees and tropical flowers. The coffin of the deceased was submerged in wreaths and flowers . . . At 10:30 A.M. the liturgy for the dead began . . ."

The music was specially chosen. Only the most beautiful voices of the Synodical Choir were selected, and they sang, as Rachmaninoff later commented, "with particular beauty, well aware of the distinguished public attending this funeral." Modern religious works by Kastalsky were sung, as well as one ancient Russian setting of the Lord's Prayer consisting only of the D minor chord and its dominant distributed in nine and ten part harmonies. Archbishop V. Nekrasov delivered a final oration. He praised the "divine will to freedom," concluding dramatically: "Say not that 'He is no more,' say rather, 'He was!'" As the coffin was carried through the streets, rows of people lined the sidewalks. Taneieff, one of the pallbearers along with the inner circle, caught a severe cold. It soon turned into pneumonia and within weeks he too was dead. Scriabin was buried in fashionable Novodevichy Cemetery, where the opening scene of *Boris Godunov* is laid, high in the Sparrow Hills. Over the cloister walls, nuns could be heard in their endless singing.

For Scriabin's intimate circle, the passing was tragic. Sabaneeff may have earlier complained:

> In the frightening, luxuriant, spiritual hothouse of Scriabin's private life, the heady atmosphere was poisonously sweet—like an opium den. The most infectious and dangerous flower was the idea of Scriabin's own self-deification. This thought was never expressed *en toutes lettres;* but it always hovered about us and we were always vaguely conscious of it.

But now he wrote, "Our sun had gone out. Without warning, we, the satellites, were left suddenly with no planet to orbit . . . What a wicked and unaccountable trick of fate. Scriabin is dead and with him all those grandiose schemes . . ."

The newspapers were filled for weeks with memorial testimonies, formal obituaries, spontaneous poems, sonnets, words of condolences to the writers themselves and to the public at large.

Nikolai Evreinov (1879–1953), friend, playwright, creator of "theater in life," composed his grief in this poem:

> The sooner the flesh of genius dies, the sooner the soul returns to freedom.
> Our bodies are a prison, a grave.
> In truth, death is our resurrection.
> The awesome day for Scriabin, imprisoned here on earth, was a celebration.
> With death ends the tragic controversy
> His soul of godlike colors, his majestic powers, heroic doubts . . .
>
> Scriabin is dead.
> It is well for him but awesome for us—who were lured by his genius.
> The prisoner grew weary.
> And still we are left with the riddle of life.

The great, hardheaded Plekhanov wrote Bogorodsky a long obituary letter:

Although it is my conviction that Scriabin posed art an insurmountable problem, it also seems to me that he put this very error to very great use. His spiritual interests enlarged the scope of his art...Without all their appanage, the weight of Scriabin's artistic gift might have been the less.

Everything relating to this remarkable man's development has significance. It is to be studied as a document of mankind . . .

And soon veneration set in. Critic Asafiev, in a spate of enthusiasm,

> The proud idea of Scriabin as man-god places the human soul in the center of the universe like the sun. He did not turn towards the sun like sun-worshiping Orientals. He wanted to be absorbed into it, to become it, to fuse with the Sun itself... He has yet to become a legend, for people finally will believe only in legends.

But Scriabin in his lifetime had become a legend. Asafiev himself began his monograph on him with a flattering, allusive line from Pushkin's *Mozart and Salieri*, "You are God."

Stories of enmity between Scriabin and Rachmaninoff now ended with Scriabin's death. Almost immediately, he and Siloti performed the Concerto as part of a memorial program. Rachmaninoff alone made a grand tour of Russia playing nothing but all-Scriabin programs. He gave the proceeds to Tatyana, who was now impoverished. These concerts were also significant because Rachmaninoff, like Scriabin, had never performed any piano music in public other than his own. Scriabin's death started this tremendous career. Provincial audiences of 1915, who were lost in "international" innovations and preferred more Russian-sounding music, would sometimes shout for the familiar. "Play something of *yours*!" Staunch Rachmaninoff would mumble, "Only Scriabin . . . tonight . . ."

Without Scriabin, life continued and so did death. Tatyana had a vision. She saw Scriabin's face in a medallion. A medium was called, and it was computed that in 33 years (1948) Scriabin would reappear in this world. Soon after in 1919, she went to the warmth of the South to stay with Kiev friends. Julian, the son who had already composed four little preludes—musical extensions of Scriabin's last Opus 74—drowned swimming in the Dnieper River. He had just turned eleven.

Tatyana returned to Moscow and became guardian-caretaker of the

Scriabin Museum, their old apartment. She had the "look of someone whose whole life is in the past with nothing ahead of her," Sabaneeff said. She became profoundly mystic, not radiant like Scriabin's Ecstasy and "I am," but dark and brooding. She draped herself in black veils, rarely spoke, table-tipped, used Ouija boards, all to search for Scriabin. She was, as usual, constantly ill. One day in 1922, sitting in his old rocking chair, she got up suddenly, fell, struck her head and never regained consciousness.

Vera, two years earlier, had died falling in the same way exactly. For a longer time she had been lonely, with no one either to hate or to love.

CATALOG OF SCRIABIN'S WORKS

Dates of composition appear in parentheses.

---

* There are no Opp. 50 and 55.

3. 10 Mazurkas (1888–1890)

1. B minor	6. C♯ minor
2. F♯ minor	7. E minor
3. G minor	8. B flat minor
4. E major	9. G♯ minor
5. D♯ minor	10. E flat minor

4. *Allegro appassionato*, E flat minor (1887–1893)
5. 2 Nocturnes (F♯ minor; A major) (1893)
6. First Sonata, F minor (1893)
7. 2 Impromptus à la Mazur (1891)
   (G♯ minor; F♯ minor)
8. 12 Etudes (1894–1895)

1. C♯ major	7. B flat minor
2. F♯ minor	8. A flat major
3. B minor	9. C♯ minor
4. B major	10. D flat major (Thirds)
5. E major	11. B flat minor
6. A major	12. D♯ minor (*Patético*)

9. 2 Pieces for the left hand alone (1894)
   1. Prelude, C♯ minor
   2. Nocturne, D flat major
10. 2 Impromptus (F♯ minor; A major) (1894)
11. 24 Preludes (1888–1896)

1. C major	13. G flat major
2. A minor	14. E flat minor
3. G major	15. D flat major
4. E minor	16. B flat minor
5. D major	17. A flat major
6. B minor	18. F minor
7. A major	19. E flat major
8. F♯ minor	20. C minor
9. E major	21. B flat major
10. C♯ minor	22. G minor
11. B major	23. F major
12. G♯ minor	24. D minor

12. 2 Impromptus (F♯ major; B flat minor) (1895)
13. 6 Preludes (1895)

1. C major	4. E minor
2. A minor	5. D major
3. G major	6. B minor

14. 2 Impromptus (B major; F♯ minor) (1895)
15. 5 Preludes (1895–1896)

1. A major	3. E major
2. F♯ minor	4. E major
5. C♯ minor	

16. 5 Preludes (1894–1895)

1. B major	3. G flat major
2. G♯ minor	4. E flat minor
5. F♯ major	

17. 7 Preludes (1895–1896)

1. D minor	4. B flat minor
2. E flat major	5. F minor
3. D flat major	6. B flat major
7. G minor	

18. *Allegro de concert*, B flat minor (1895?–1897)
19. Second Sonata (*Sonate-Fantaisie*), G♯ minor (1892–1897)
21. Polonaise, B flat minor (1897–1898)
22. 4 Preludes (1897–1898)

1. G♯ minor	3. B major
2. C♯ minor	4. B minor

23. Third Sonata, F♯ minor (1897–1898)
25. 9 Mazurkas (1899)

1. F minor	5. C♯ minor
2. C major	6. F♯ major
3. E minor	7. F♯ minor
4. E major	8. B major
9. E flat minor	

27. 2 Preludes (G minor; B major) (1900)
28. *Fantaisie*, B minor (1900–1901)
30. Fourth Sonata, F♯ major (1901–1903)
31. 4 Preludes (1903)

1. D flat major–C major
2. F minor
3. E flat major
4. C major

32. 2 Poems (F♯ major; D major) (1903)
33. 4 Preludes (1903)

1. E major	3. C major
2. F♯ major	4. A flat major

34. Tragic Poem (*Poème Tragique*), B flat major (1903)

35. 3 Preludes (D flat major; B flat major; C major) (1903)
36. Satanic Poem (*Poème Satanique*), C major (1903)
37. 4 Preludes (1903)

    1. B flat minor   3. B major
    2. F♯ major   4. G minor

38. Waltz, A flat major (1903)
39. 4 Preludes (1903)

    1. F♯ major   3. G major
    2. D major   4. A flat major

40. 2 Mazurkas (D flat major; F♯ major) (1903)
41. Poem, D flat major (1903)
42. 8 Etudes (1903)

    1. D flat major   5. C♯ minor
    2. F♯ minor   6. D flat major
    3. F♯ major   7. F minor
    4. F♯ major   8. E flat major

44. 2 Poems (C major; C major) (1905)
45. 3 Pieces (1905)

    1. Albumleaf, E flat major
    2. Fantastic Poem (*Poème Fantasque*), C major
    3. Prelude, E flat major

46. Scherzo, C major (1905)
47. *Quasi-Valse*, F major (1905)
48. 4 Preludes (1905)

    1. F♯ major   3. D flat major
    2. C major   4. C major

49. 3 Pieces (1905)

    1. Etude, E flat major
    2. Prelude, F major
    3. *Rêverie*, C major

51. 4 Pieces (1906)

    1. Fragility (*Fragilité*), E flat major
    2. Prelude, A minor
    3. Wingèd Poem (*Poème Ailé*), B major
    4. Dance of Languor (*Danse Languide*), G major

52. 3 Pieces (1905–1907)

    1. Poem, C major
    2. Enigma (*Enigme*)
    3. Poem of Languor (*Poème Languide*), B major

53. Fifth Sonata, F♯ major (1907)

56. 4 Pieces (1908)
    1. Prelude, E major
    2. Ironies, C major
    3. Nuances
    4. Etude
57. 2 Pieces (1908)
    1. Desire (*Désir*) (1908)
    2. Danced Caress (*Caresse Dansée*)
58. Albumleaf (*Feuillette d'Album*) (1911?)
59. 2 Pieces (*Poème*; Prelude) (1910–1911)
61. *Poème-Nocturne* (1911–1912)
62. Sixth Sonata, G major (1911–1912)
63. 2 Poems (1912)
    1. Mask (*Masque*)
    2. Strangeness (*Etrangeté*)
64. Seventh Sonata ("White Mass") (1911–1912)
65. 3 Etudes (1912)
    1. B flat major (Ninths)
    2. C♯ major (Sevenths)
    3. G major (Fifths)
66. Eighth Sonata (1913)
67. 2 Preludes (Andante; Presto) (1912–1913)
68. Ninth Sonata ("Black Mass") (1913)
69. 2 Poems (1913)
    1. Allegretto (3-4)
    2. Allegretto (6-8)
70. Tenth Sonata (1913)
71. 2 Poems (1913)
    1. Fantastic (*Fantastique*)
    2. Dreaming (*En Rêvant*)
72. Poem, Toward the Flame (*Vers la Flamme*) (1914)
73. 2 Dances (1914)
    1. Garlands (*Guirlandes*)
    2. Dark Flames (*Flammes Sombres*)
74. 5 Preludes (1914)
    1. Douloureux, déchirant
    2. Très lent, contemplatif
    3. Allegro drammatico
    4. Lent, vague, indécis
    5. Fier, belliqueux

Posthumous Works

PIANO

Canon, D minor (1883; published 1928)
Nocturne, A flat major (1884; published 1911)
Mazurka, B minor (1884; published 1893)
Mazurka, C major (1886; published 1893)
Valse, D flat major (1886; published 1929)
Sonata-Fantasy, G♯ minor (1886; published 1940)

TWO PIANOS

Fantasy, A minor (1889; published 1940)

VOCAL

Romance (1894; published 1924)

INDEX OF PRINCIPAL NAMES

I and *II* refer to the two volumes in this edition.
Vol. II begins after p. 342.

A CATALOG OF SELECTED
DOVER BOOKS
IN SCIENCE AND MATHEMATICS

Astronomy

BURNHAM'S CELESTIAL HANDBOOK, Robert Burnham, Jr. Thorough guide to the stars beyond our solar system. Exhaustive treatment. Alphabetical by constellation: Andromeda to Cetus in Vol. 1; Chamaeleon to Orion in Vol. 2; and Pavo to Vulpecula in Vol. 3. Hundreds of illustrations. Index in Vol. 3. 2,000pp. 6⅛ x 9¼.
Vol. I: 0-486-23567-X
Vol. II: 0-486-23568-8
Vol. III: 0-486-23673-0

EXPLORING THE MOON THROUGH BINOCULARS AND SMALL TELESCOPES, Ernest H. Cherrington, Jr. Informative, profusely illustrated guide to locating and identifying craters, rills, seas, mountains, other lunar features. Newly revised and updated with special section of new photos. Over 100 photos and diagrams. 240pp. 8¼ x 11. 0-486-24491-1

THE EXTRATERRESTRIAL LIFE DEBATE, 1750–1900, Michael J. Crowe. First detailed, scholarly study in English of the many ideas that developed from 1750 to 1900 regarding the existence of intelligent extraterrestrial life. Examines ideas of Kant, Herschel, Voltaire, Percival Lowell, many other scientists and thinkers. 16 illustrations. 704pp. 5⅜ x 8½. 0-486-40675-X

THEORIES OF THE WORLD FROM ANTIQUITY TO THE COPERNICAN REVOLUTION, Michael J. Crowe. Newly revised edition of an accessible, enlightening book re-creates the change from an earth-centered to a sun-centered conception of the solar system. 242pp. 5⅜ x 8½. 0-486-41444-2

ARISTARCHUS OF SAMOS: The Ancient Copernicus, Sir Thomas Heath. Heath's history of astronomy ranges from Homer and Hesiod to Aristarchus and includes quotes from numerous thinkers, compilers, and scholasticists from Thales and Anaximander through Pythagoras, Plato, Aristotle, and Heraclides. 34 figures. 448pp. 5⅜ x 8½.
0-486-43886-4

A COMPLETE MANUAL OF AMATEUR ASTRONOMY: TOOLS AND TECHNIQUES FOR ASTRONOMICAL OBSERVATIONS, P. Clay Sherrod with Thomas L. Koed. Concise, highly readable book discusses: selecting, setting up and maintaining a telescope; amateur studies of the sun; lunar topography and occultations; observations of Mars, Jupiter, Saturn, the minor planets and the stars; an introduction to photoelectric photometry; more. 1981 ed. 124 figures. 25 halftones. 37 tables. 335pp. 6½ x 9¼. 0-486-42820-8

AMATEUR ASTRONOMER'S HANDBOOK, J. B. Sidgwick. Timeless, comprehensive coverage of telescopes, mirrors, lenses, mountings, telescope drives, micrometers, spectroscopes, more. 189 illustrations. 576pp. 5⅝ x 8¼. (Available in U.S. only.)
0-486-24034-7

STAR LORE: Myths, Legends, and Facts, William Tyler Olcott. Captivating retellings of the origins and histories of ancient star groups include Pegasus, Ursa Major, Pleiades, signs of the zodiac, and other constellations. "Classic."—Sky & Telescope. 58 illustrations. 544pp. 5⅜ x 8½. 0-486-43581-4

Chemistry

THE SCEPTICAL CHYMIST: THE CLASSIC 1661 TEXT, Robert Boyle. Boyle defines the term "element," asserting that all natural phenomena can be explained by the motion and organization of primary particles. 1911 ed. viii+232pp. $5\frac{3}{8}$ x $8\frac{1}{2}$.
0-486-42825-7

RADIOACTIVE SUBSTANCES, Marie Curie. Here is the celebrated scientist's doctoral thesis, the prelude to her receipt of the 1903 Nobel Prize. Curie discusses establishing atomic character of radioactivity found in compounds of uranium and thorium; extraction from pitchblende of polonium and radium; isolation of pure radium chloride; determination of atomic weight of radium; plus electric, photographic, luminous, heat, color effects of radioactivity. ii+94pp. $5\frac{3}{8}$ x $8\frac{1}{2}$.
0-486-42550-9

CHEMICAL MAGIC, Leonard A. Ford. Second Edition, Revised by E. Winston Grundmeier. Over 100 unusual stunts demonstrating cold fire, dust explosions, much more. Text explains scientific principles and stresses safety precautions. 128pp. $5\frac{3}{8}$ x $8\frac{1}{2}$.
0-486-67628-5

MOLECULAR THEORY OF CAPILLARITY, J. S. Rowlinson and B. Widom. History of surface phenomena offers critical and detailed examination and assessment of modern theories, focusing on statistical mechanics and application of results in mean-field approximation to model systems. 1989 edition. 352pp. $5\frac{3}{8}$ x $8\frac{1}{2}$.
0-486-42544-4

CHEMICAL AND CATALYTIC REACTION ENGINEERING, James J. Carberry. Designed to offer background for managing chemical reactions, this text examines behavior of chemical reactions and reactors; fluid-fluid and fluid-solid reaction systems; heterogeneous catalysis and catalytic kinetics; more. 1976 edition. 672pp. $6\frac{1}{8}$ x $9\frac{1}{4}$.
0-486-41736-0 $31.95

ELEMENTS OF CHEMISTRY, Antoine Lavoisier. Monumental classic by founder of modern chemistry in remarkable reprint of rare 1790 Kerr translation. A must for every student of chemistry or the history of science. 539pp. $5\frac{3}{8}$ x $8\frac{1}{2}$.
0-486-64624-6

MOLECULES AND RADIATION: An Introduction to Modern Molecular Spectroscopy. Second Edition, Jeffrey I. Steinfeld. This unified treatment introduces upper-level undergraduates and graduate students to the concepts and the methods of molecular spectroscopy and applications to quantum electronics, lasers, and related optical phenomena. 1985 edition. 512pp. $5\frac{3}{8}$ x $8\frac{1}{2}$.
0-486-44152-0

A SHORT HISTORY OF CHEMISTRY, J. R. Partington. Classic exposition explores origins of chemistry, alchemy, early medical chemistry, nature of atmosphere, theory of valency, laws and structure of atomic theory, much more. 428pp. $5\frac{3}{8}$ x $8\frac{1}{2}$. (Available in U.S. only.)
0-486-65977-1

GENERAL CHEMISTRY, Linus Pauling. Revised 3rd edition of classic first-year text by Nobel laureate. Atomic and molecular structure, quantum mechanics, statistical mechanics, thermodynamics correlated with descriptive chemistry. Problems. 992pp. $5\frac{3}{8}$ x $8\frac{1}{2}$.
0-486-65622-5

ELECTRON CORRELATION IN MOLECULES, S. Wilson. This text addresses one of theoretical chemistry's central problems. Topics include molecular electronic structure, independent electron models, electron correlation, the linked diagram theorem, and related topics. 1984 edition. 304pp. $5\frac{3}{8}$ x $8\frac{1}{2}$.
0-486-45879-2

Engineering

DE RE METALLICA, Georgius Agricola. The famous Hoover translation of greatest treatise on technological chemistry, engineering, geology, mining of early modern times (1556). All 289 original woodcuts. 638pp. 6¾ x 11. 0-486-60006-8

FUNDAMENTALS OF ASTRODYNAMICS, Roger Bate et al. Modern approach developed by U.S. Air Force Academy. Designed as a first course. Problems, exercises. Numerous illustrations. 455pp. 5⅜ x 8½. 0-486-60061-0

DYNAMICS OF FLUIDS IN POROUS MEDIA, Jacob Bear. For advanced students of ground water hydrology, soil mechanics and physics, drainage and irrigation engineering and more. 335 illustrations. Exercises, with answers. 784pp. 6⅛ x 9¼. 0-486-65675-6

THEORY OF VISCOELASTICITY (SECOND EDITION), Richard M. Christensen. Complete consistent description of the linear theory of the viscoelastic behavior of materials. Problem-solving techniques discussed. 1982 edition. 29 figures. xiv+364pp. 6⅛ x 9¼. 0-486-42880-X

MECHANICS, J. P. Den Hartog. A classic introductory text or refresher. Hundreds of applications and design problems illuminate fundamentals of trusses, loaded beams and cables, etc. 334 answered problems. 462pp. 5⅜ x 8½. 0-486-60754-2

MECHANICAL VIBRATIONS, J. P. Den Hartog. Classic textbook offers lucid explanations and illustrative models, applying theories of vibrations to a variety of practical industrial engineering problems. Numerous figures. 233 problems, solutions. Appendix. Index. Preface. 436pp. 5⅜ x 8½. 0-486-64785-4

STRENGTH OF MATERIALS, J. P. Den Hartog. Full, clear treatment of basic material (tension, torsion, bending, etc.) plus advanced material on engineering methods, applications. 350 answered problems. 323pp. 5⅜ x 8½. 0-486-60755-0

A HISTORY OF MECHANICS, René Dugas. Monumental study of mechanical principles from antiquity to quantum mechanics. Contributions of ancient Greeks, Galileo, Leonardo, Kepler, Lagrange, many others. 671pp. 5⅜ x 8½. 0-486-65632-2

STABILITY THEORY AND ITS APPLICATIONS TO STRUCTURAL MECHANICS, Clive L. Dym. Self-contained text focuses on Koiter postbuckling analyses, with mathematical notions of stability of motion. Basing minimum energy principles for static stability upon dynamic concepts of stability of motion, it develops asymptotic buckling and postbuckling analyses from potential energy considerations, with applications to columns, plates, and arches. 1974 ed. 208pp. 5⅜ x 8½. 0-486-42541-X

BASIC ELECTRICITY, U.S. Bureau of Naval Personnel. Originally a training course; best nontechnical coverage. Topics include batteries, circuits, conductors, AC and DC, inductance and capacitance, generators, motors, transformers, amplifiers, etc. Many questions with answers. 349 illustrations. 1969 edition. 448pp. 6½ x 9¼. 0-486-20973-3

ROCKETS, Robert Goddard. Two of the most significant publications in the history of rocketry and jet propulsion: "A Method of Reaching Extreme Altitudes" (1919) and "Liquid Propellant Rocket Development" (1936). 128pp. 5⅜ x 8½. 0-486-42537-1

STATISTICAL MECHANICS: PRINCIPLES AND APPLICATIONS, Terrell L. Hill. Standard text covers fundamentals of statistical mechanics, applications to fluctuation theory, imperfect gases, distribution functions, more. 448pp. 5⅜ x 8½. 0-486-65390-0

ENGINEERING AND TECHNOLOGY 1650–1750: ILLUSTRATIONS AND TEXTS FROM ORIGINAL SOURCES, Martin Jensen. Highly readable text with more than 200 contemporary drawings and detailed engravings of engineering projects dealing with surveying, leveling, materials, hand tools, lifting equipment, transport and erection, piling, bailing, water supply, hydraulic engineering, and more. Among the specific projects outlined-transporting a 50-ton stone to the Louvre, erecting an obelisk, building timber locks, and dredging canals. 207pp. 8⅜ x 11¼. 0-486-42232-1

THE VARIATIONAL PRINCIPLES OF MECHANICS, Cornelius Lanczos. Graduate level coverage of calculus of variations, equations of motion, relativistic mechanics, more. First inexpensive paperbound edition of classic treatise. Index. Bibliography. 418pp. 5⅜ x 8½. 0-486-65067-7

PROTECTION OF ELECTRONIC CIRCUITS FROM OVERVOLTAGES, Ronald B. Standler. Five-part treatment presents practical rules and strategies for circuits designed to protect electronic systems from damage by transient overvoltages. 1989 ed. xxiv+434pp. 6⅛ x 9¼. 0-486-42552-5

ROTARY WING AERODYNAMICS, W. Z. Stepniewski. Clear, concise text covers aerodynamic phenomena of the rotor and offers guidelines for helicopter performance evaluation. Originally prepared for NASA. 537 figures. 640pp. 6⅛ x 9¼. 0-486-64647-5

INTRODUCTION TO SPACE DYNAMICS, William Tyrrell Thomson. Comprehensive, classic introduction to space-flight engineering for advanced undergraduate and graduate students. Includes vector algebra, kinematics, transformation of coordinates. Bibliography. Index. 352pp. 5⅜ x 8½. 0-486-65113-4

HISTORY OF STRENGTH OF MATERIALS, Stephen P. Timoshenko. Excellent historical survey of the strength of materials with many references to the theories of elasticity and structure. 245 figures. 452pp. 5⅜ x 8½. 0-486-61187-6

ANALYTICAL FRACTURE MECHANICS, David J. Unger. Self-contained text supplements standard fracture mechanics texts by focusing on analytical methods for determining crack-tip stress and strain fields. 336pp. 6⅛ x 9¼. 0-486-41737-9

STATISTICAL MECHANICS OF ELASTICITY, J. H. Weiner. Advanced, self-contained treatment illustrates general principles and elastic behavior of solids. Part 1, based on classical mechanics, studies thermoelastic behavior of crystalline and polymeric solids. Part 2, based on quantum mechanics, focuses on interatomic force laws, behavior of solids, and thermally activated processes. For students of physics and chemistry and for polymer physicists. 1983 ed. 96 figures. 496pp. 5⅜ x 8½. 0-486-42260-7

Mathematics

FUNCTIONAL ANALYSIS (Second Corrected Edition), George Bachman and Lawrence Narici. Excellent treatment of subject geared toward students with background in linear algebra, advanced calculus, physics and engineering. Text covers introduction to inner-product spaces, normed, metric spaces, and topological spaces; complete orthonormal sets, the Hahn-Banach Theorem and its consequences, and many other related subjects. 1966 ed. 544pp. 6⅛ x 9¼. 0-486-40251-7

DIFFERENTIAL MANIFOLDS, Antoni A. Kosinski. Introductory text for advanced undergraduates and graduate students presents systematic study of the topological structure of smooth manifolds, starting with elements of theory and concluding with method of surgery. 1993 edition. 288pp. 5⅜ x 8½. 0-486-46244-7

VECTOR AND TENSOR ANALYSIS WITH APPLICATIONS, A. I. Borisenko and I. E. Tarapov. Concise introduction. Worked-out problems, solutions, exercises. 257pp. 5⅜ x 8¼. 0-486-63833-2

AN INTRODUCTION TO ORDINARY DIFFERENTIAL EQUATIONS, Earl A. Coddington. A thorough and systematic first course in elementary differential equations for undergraduates in mathematics and science, with many exercises and problems (with answers). Index. 304pp. 5⅜ x 8½. 0-486-65942-9

FOURIER SERIES AND ORTHOGONAL FUNCTIONS, Harry F. Davis. An incisive text combining theory and practical example to introduce Fourier series, orthogonal functions and applications of the Fourier method to boundary-value problems. 570 exercises. Answers and notes. 416pp. 5⅜ x 8½. 0-486-65973-9

COMPUTABILITY AND UNSOLVABILITY, Martin Davis. Classic graduate-level introduction to theory of computability, usually referred to as theory of recurrent functions. New preface and appendix. 288pp. 5⅜ x 8½. 0-486-61471-9

AN INTRODUCTION TO MATHEMATICAL ANALYSIS, Robert A. Rankin. Dealing chiefly with functions of a single real variable, this text by a distinguished educator introduces limits, continuity, differentiability, integration, convergence of infinite series, double series, and infinite products. 1963 edition. 624pp. 5⅜ x 8½. 0-486-46251-X

METHODS OF NUMERICAL INTEGRATION (SECOND EDITION), Philip J. Davis and Philip Rabinowitz. Requiring only a background in calculus, this text covers approximate integration over finite and infinite intervals, error analysis, approximate integration in two or more dimensions, and automatic integration. 1984 edition. 624pp. 5⅜ x 8½. 0-486-45339-1

INTRODUCTION TO LINEAR ALGEBRA AND DIFFERENTIAL EQUATIONS, John W. Dettman. Excellent text covers complex numbers, determinants, orthonormal bases, Laplace transforms, much more. Exercises with solutions. Undergraduate level. 416pp. 5⅜ x 8½. 0-486-65191-6

RIEMANN'S ZETA FUNCTION, H. M. Edwards. Superb, high-level study of landmark 1859 publication entitled "On the Number of Primes Less Than a Given Magnitude" traces developments in mathematical theory that it inspired. xiv+315pp. 5⅜ x 8½. 0-486-41740-9

CALCULUS OF VARIATIONS WITH APPLICATIONS, George M. Ewing. Applications-oriented introduction to variational theory develops insight and promotes understanding of specialized books, research papers. Suitable for advanced undergraduate/graduate students as primary, supplementary text. 352pp. 5³/₈ x 8¹/₂.
0-486-64856-7

MATHEMATICIAN'S DELIGHT, W. W. Sawyer. "Recommended with confidence" by *The Times Literary Supplement,* this lively survey was written by a renowned teacher. It starts with arithmetic and algebra, gradually proceeding to trigonometry and calculus. 1943 edition. 240pp. 5³/₈ x 8¹/₂.
0-486-46240-4

ADVANCED EUCLIDEAN GEOMETRY, Roger A. Johnson. This classic text explores the geometry of the triangle and the circle, concentrating on extensions of Euclidean theory, and examining in detail many relatively recent theorems. 1929 edition. 336pp. 5³/₈ x 8¹/₂.
0-486-46237-4

COUNTEREXAMPLES IN ANALYSIS, Bernard R. Gelbaum and John M. H. Olmsted. These counterexamples deal mostly with the part of analysis known as "real variables." The first half covers the real number system, and the second half encompasses higher dimensions. 1962 edition. xxiv+198pp. 5³/₈ x 8¹/₂.
0-486-42875-3

CATASTROPHE THEORY FOR SCIENTISTS AND ENGINEERS, Robert Gilmore. Advanced-level treatment describes mathematics of theory grounded in the work of Poincaré, R. Thom, other mathematicians. Also important applications to problems in mathematics, physics, chemistry and engineering. 1981 edition. References. 28 tables. 397 black-and-white illustrations. xvii + 666pp. 6¹/₈ x 9¹/₄.
0-486-67539-4

COMPLEX VARIABLES: Second Edition, Robert B. Ash and W. P. Novinger. Suitable for advanced undergraduates and graduate students, this newly revised treatment covers Cauchy theorem and its applications, analytic functions, and the prime number theorem. Numerous problems and solutions. 2004 edition. 224pp. 6¹/₂ x 9¹/₄.
0-486-46250-1

NUMERICAL METHODS FOR SCIENTISTS AND ENGINEERS, Richard Hamming. Classic text stresses frequency approach in coverage of algorithms, polynomial approximation, Fourier approximation, exponential approximation, other topics. Revised and enlarged 2nd edition. 721pp. 5³/₈ x 8¹/₂.
0-486-65241-6

INTRODUCTION TO NUMERICAL ANALYSIS (2nd Edition), F. B. Hildebrand. Classic, fundamental treatment covers computation, approximation, interpolation, numerical differentiation and integration, other topics. 150 new problems. 669pp. 5³/₈ x 8¹/₂.
0-486-65363-3

MARKOV PROCESSES AND POTENTIAL THEORY, Robert M. Blumental and Ronald K. Getoor. This graduate-level text explores the relationship between Markov processes and potential theory in terms of excessive functions, multiplicative functionals and subprocesses, additive functionals and their potentials, and dual processes. 1968 edition. 320pp. 5³/₈ x 8¹/₂.
0-486-46263-3

ABSTRACT SETS AND FINITE ORDINALS: An Introduction to the Study of Set Theory, G. B. Keene. This text unites logical and philosophical aspects of set theory in a manner intelligible to mathematicians without training in formal logic and to logicians without a mathematical background. 1961 edition. 112pp. 5³/₈ x 8¹/₂.
0-486-46249-8

INTRODUCTORY REAL ANALYSIS, A.N. Kolmogorov, S. V. Fomin. Translated by Richard A. Silverman. Self-contained, evenly paced introduction to real and functional analysis. Some 350 problems. 403pp. 5³/₈ x 8¹/₂. 0-486-61226-0

APPLIED ANALYSIS, Cornelius Lanczos. Classic work on analysis and design of finite processes for approximating solution of analytical problems. Algebraic equations, matrices, harmonic analysis, quadrature methods, much more. 559pp. 5³/₈ x 8¹/₂. 0-486-65656-X

AN INTRODUCTION TO ALGEBRAIC STRUCTURES, Joseph Landin. Superb self-contained text covers "abstract algebra": sets and numbers, theory of groups, theory of rings, much more. Numerous well-chosen examples, exercises. 247pp. 5³/₈ x 8¹/₂. 0-486-65940-2

QUALITATIVE THEORY OF DIFFERENTIAL EQUATIONS, V. V. Nemytskii and V.V. Stepanov. Classic graduate-level text by two prominent Soviet mathematicians covers classical differential equations as well as topological dynamics and ergodic theory. Bibliographies. 523pp. 5³/₈ x 8¹/₂. 0-486-65954-2

THEORY OF MATRICES, Sam Perlis. Outstanding text covering rank, nonsingularity and inverses in connection with the development of canonical matrices under the relation of equivalence, and without the intervention of determinants. Includes exercises. 237pp. 5³/₈ x 8¹/₂. 0-486-66810-X

INTRODUCTION TO ANALYSIS, Maxwell Rosenlicht. Unusually clear, accessible coverage of set theory, real number system, metric spaces, continuous functions, Riemann integration, multiple integrals, more. Wide range of problems. Undergraduate level. Bibliography. 254pp. 5³/₈ x 8¹/₂. 0-486-65038-3

MODERN NONLINEAR EQUATIONS, Thomas L. Saaty. Emphasizes practical solution of problems; covers seven types of equations. ". . . a welcome contribution to the existing literature. . . ."—*Math Reviews*. 490pp. 5³/₈ x 8¹/₂. 0-486-64232-1

MATRICES AND LINEAR ALGEBRA, Hans Schneider and George Phillip Barker. Basic textbook covers theory of matrices and its applications to systems of linear equations and related topics such as determinants, eigenvalues and differential equations. Numerous exercises. 432pp. 5³/₈ x 8¹/₂. 0-486-66014-1

LINEAR ALGEBRA, Georgi E. Shilov. Determinants, linear spaces, matrix algebras, similar topics. For advanced undergraduates, graduates. Silverman translation. 387pp. 5³/₈ x 8¹/₂. 0-486-63518-X

MATHEMATICAL METHODS OF GAME AND ECONOMIC THEORY: Revised Edition, Jean-Pierre Aubin. This text begins with optimization theory and convex analysis, followed by topics in game theory and mathematical economics, and concluding with an introduction to nonlinear analysis and control theory. 1982 edition. 656pp. 6¹/₈ x 9¹/₄. 0-486-46265-X

SET THEORY AND LOGIC, Robert R. Stoll. Lucid introduction to unified theory of mathematical concepts. Set theory and logic seen as tools for conceptual understanding of real number system. 496pp. 5⁵/₈ x 8¹/₄. 0-486-63829-4

CATALOG OF DOVER BOOKS

TENSOR CALCULUS, J.L. Synge and A. Schild. Widely used introductory text covers spaces and tensors, basic operations in Riemannian space, non-Riemannian spaces, etc. 324pp. 5⅜ x 8¼. 0-486-63612-7

ORDINARY DIFFERENTIAL EQUATIONS, Morris Tenenbaum and Harry Pollard. Exhaustive survey of ordinary differential equations for undergraduates in mathematics, engineering, science. Thorough analysis of theorems. Diagrams. Bibliography. Index. 818pp. 5⅜ x 8½. 0-486-64940-7

INTEGRAL EQUATIONS, F. G. Tricomi. Authoritative, well-written treatment of extremely useful mathematical tool with wide applications. Volterra Equations, Fredholm Equations, much more. Advanced undergraduate to graduate level. Exercises. Bibliography. 238pp. 5⅜ x 8½. 0-486-64828-1

FOURIER SERIES, Georgi P. Tolstov. Translated by Richard A. Silverman. A valuable addition to the literature on the subject, moving clearly from subject to subject and theorem to theorem. 107 problems, answers. 336pp. 5⅜ x 8½. 0-486-63317-9

INTRODUCTION TO MATHEMATICAL THINKING, Friedrich Waismann. Examinations of arithmetic, geometry, and theory of integers; rational and natural numbers; complete induction; limit and point of accumulation; remarkable curves; complex and hypercomplex numbers, more. 1959 ed. 27 figures. xii+260pp. 5⅜ x 8½.
0-486-42804-8

THE RADON TRANSFORM AND SOME OF ITS APPLICATIONS, Stanley R. Deans. Of value to mathematicians, physicists, and engineers, this excellent introduction covers both theory and applications, including a rich array of examples and literature. Revised and updated by the author. 1993 edition. 304pp. 6⅛ x 9¼. 0-486-46241-2

CALCULUS OF VARIATIONS, Robert Weinstock. Basic introduction covering isoperimetric problems, theory of elasticity, quantum mechanics, electrostatics, etc. Exercises throughout. 326pp. 5⅜ x 8½. 0-486-63069-2

THE CONTINUUM: A CRITICAL EXAMINATION OF THE FOUNDATION OF ANALYSIS, Hermann Weyl. Classic of 20th-century foundational research deals with the conceptual problem posed by the continuum. 156pp. 5⅜ x 8½. 0-486-67982-9

CHALLENGING MATHEMATICAL PROBLEMS WITH ELEMENTARY SOLUTIONS, A. M. Yaglom and I. M. Yaglom. Over 170 challenging problems on probability theory, combinatorial analysis, points and lines, topology, convex polygons, many other topics. Solutions. Total of 445pp. 5⅜ x 8½. Two-vol. set.
Vol. I: 0-486-65536-9 Vol. II: 0-486-65537-7

INTRODUCTION TO PARTIAL DIFFERENTIAL EQUATIONS WITH APPLICATIONS, E. C. Zachmanoglou and Dale W. Thoe. Essentials of partial differential equations applied to common problems in engineering and the physical sciences. Problems and answers. 416pp. 5⅜ x 8½. 0-486-65251-3

STOCHASTIC PROCESSES AND FILTERING THEORY, Andrew H. Jazwinski. This unified treatment presents material previously available only in journals, and in terms accessible to engineering students. Although theory is emphasized, it discusses numerous practical applications as well. 1970 edition. 400pp. 5⅜ x 8½. 0-486-46274-9

Math—Decision Theory, Statistics, Probability

INTRODUCTION TO PROBABILITY, John E. Freund. Featured topics include permutations and factorials, probabilities and odds, frequency interpretation, mathematical expectation, decision-making, postulates of probability, rule of elimination, much more. Exercises with some solutions. Summary. 1973 edition. 247pp. 5³/₈ x 8¹/₂.
0-486-67549-1

STATISTICAL AND INDUCTIVE PROBABILITIES, Hugues Leblanc. This treatment addresses a decades-old dispute among probability theorists, asserting that both statistical and inductive probabilities may be treated as sentence-theoretic measurements, and that the latter qualify as estimates of the former. 1962 edition. 160pp. 5³/₈ x 8¹/₂.
0-486-44980-7

APPLIED MULTIVARIATE ANALYSIS: Using Bayesian and Frequentist Methods of Inference, Second Edition, S. James Press. This two-part treatment deals with foundations as well as models and applications. Topics include continuous multivariate distributions; regression and analysis of variance; factor analysis and latent structure analysis; and structuring multivariate populations. 1982 edition. 692pp. 5³/₈ x 8¹/₂.
0-486-44236-5

LINEAR PROGRAMMING AND ECONOMIC ANALYSIS, Robert Dorfman, Paul A. Samuelson and Robert M. Solow. First comprehensive treatment of linear programming in standard economic analysis. Game theory, modern welfare economics, Leontief input-output, more. 525pp. 5³/₈ x 8¹/₂.
0-486-65491-5

PROBABILITY: AN INTRODUCTION, Samuel Goldberg. Excellent basic text covers set theory, probability theory for finite sample spaces, binomial theorem, much more. 360 problems. Bibliographies. 322pp. 5³/₈ x 8¹/₂.
0-486-65252-1

GAMES AND DECISIONS: INTRODUCTION AND CRITICAL SURVEY, R. Duncan Luce and Howard Raiffa. Superb nontechnical introduction to game theory, primarily applied to social sciences. Utility theory, zero-sum games, n-person games, decision-making, much more. Bibliography. 509pp. 5³/₈ x 8¹/₂.
0-486-65943-7

INTRODUCTION TO THE THEORY OF GAMES, J. C. C. McKinsey. This comprehensive overview of the mathematical theory of games illustrates applications to situations involving conflicts of interest, including economic, social, political, and military contexts. Appropriate for advanced undergraduate and graduate courses; advanced calculus a prerequisite. 1952 ed. x+372pp. 5³/₈ x 8¹/₂.
0-486-42811-7

FIFTY CHALLENGING PROBLEMS IN PROBABILITY WITH SOLUTIONS, Frederick Mosteller. Remarkable puzzlers, graded in difficulty, illustrate elementary and advanced aspects of probability. Detailed solutions. 88pp. 5³/₈ x 8¹/₂. 0-486-65355-2

PROBABILITY THEORY: A CONCISE COURSE, Y. A. Rozanov. Highly readable, self-contained introduction covers combination of events, dependent events, Bernoulli trials, etc. 148pp. 5³/₈ x 8¹/₄.
0-486-63544-9

THE STATISTICAL ANALYSIS OF EXPERIMENTAL DATA, John Mandel. First half of book presents fundamental mathematical definitions, concepts and facts while remaining half deals with statistics primarily as an interpretive tool. Well-written text, numerous worked examples with step-by-step presentation. Includes 116 tables. 448pp. 5³/₈ x 8¹/₂.
0-486-64666-1

Math—Geometry and Topology

ELEMENTARY CONCEPTS OF TOPOLOGY, Paul Alexandroff. Elegant, intuitive approach to topology from set-theoretic topology to Betti groups; how concepts of topology are useful in math and physics. 25 figures. 57pp. 5³/₈ x 8¹/₂. 0-486-60747-X

A LONG WAY FROM EUCLID, Constance Reid. Lively guide by a prominent historian focuses on the role of Euclid's Elements in subsequent mathematical developments. Elementary algebra and plane geometry are sole prerequisites. 80 drawings. 1963 edition. 304pp. 5³/₈ x 8¹/₂. 0-486-43613-6

EXPERIMENTS IN TOPOLOGY, Stephen Barr. Classic, lively explanation of one of the byways of mathematics. Klein bottles, Moebius strips, projective planes, map coloring, problem of the Koenigsberg bridges, much more, described with clarity and wit. 43 figures. 210pp. 5³/₈ x 8¹/₂. 0-486-25933-1

THE GEOMETRY OF RENÉ DESCARTES, René Descartes. The great work founded analytical geometry. Original French text, Descartes's own diagrams, together with definitive Smith-Latham translation. 244pp. 5³/₈ x 8¹/₂. 0-486-60068-8

EUCLIDEAN GEOMETRY AND TRANSFORMATIONS, Clayton W. Dodge. This introduction to Euclidean geometry emphasizes transformations, particularly isometries and similarities. Suitable for undergraduate courses, it includes numerous examples, many with detailed answers. 1972 ed. viii+296pp. 6¹/₈ x 9¹/₄. 0-486-43476-1

EXCURSIONS IN GEOMETRY, C. Stanley Ogilvy. A straightedge, compass, and a little thought are all that's needed to discover the intellectual excitement of geometry. Harmonic division and Apollonian circles, inversive geometry, hexlet, Golden Section, more. 132 illustrations. 192pp. 5³/₈ x 8¹/₂. 0-486-26530-7

THE THIRTEEN BOOKS OF EUCLID'S ELEMENTS, translated with introduction and commentary by Sir Thomas L. Heath. Definitive edition. Textual and linguistic notes, mathematical analysis. 2,500 years of critical commentary. Unabridged. 1,414pp. 5³/₈ x 8¹/₂. Three-vol. set.
              Vol. I: 0-486-60088-2   Vol. II: 0-486-60089-0   Vol. III: 0-486-60090-4

SPACE AND GEOMETRY: IN THE LIGHT OF PHYSIOLOGICAL, PSYCHOLOGICAL AND PHYSICAL INQUIRY, Ernst Mach. Three essays by an eminent philosopher and scientist explore the nature, origin, and development of our concepts of space, with a distinctness and precision suitable for undergraduate students and other readers. 1906 ed. vi+148pp. 5³/₈ x 8¹/₂. 0-486-43909-7

GEOMETRY OF COMPLEX NUMBERS, Hans Schwerdtfeger. Illuminating, widely praised book on analytic geometry of circles, the Moebius transformation, and two-dimensional non-Euclidean geometries. 200pp. 5⁵/₈ x 8¹/₄. 0-486-63830-8

DIFFERENTIAL GEOMETRY, Heinrich W. Guggenheimer. Local differential geometry as an application of advanced calculus and linear algebra. Curvature, transformation groups, surfaces, more. Exercises. 62 figures. 378pp. 5³/₈ x 8¹/₂. 0-486-63433-7

History of Math

THE WORKS OF ARCHIMEDES, Archimedes (T. L. Heath, ed.). Topics include the famous problems of the ratio of the areas of a cylinder and an inscribed sphere; the measurement of a circle; the properties of conoids, spheroids, and spirals; and the quadrature of the parabola. Informative introduction. clxxxvi+326pp. 5³/₈ x 8¹/₂.   0-486-42084-1

A SHORT ACCOUNT OF THE HISTORY OF MATHEMATICS, W. W. Rouse Ball. One of clearest, most authoritative surveys from the Egyptians and Phoenicians through 19th-century figures such as Grassman, Galois, Riemann. Fourth edition. 522pp. 5³/₈ x 8¹/₂.   0-486-20630-0

THE HISTORY OF THE CALCULUS AND ITS CONCEPTUAL DEVELOP-MENT, Carl B. Boyer. Origins in antiquity, medieval contributions, work of Newton, Leibniz, rigorous formulation. Treatment is verbal. 346pp. 5³/₈ x 8¹/₂.   0-486-60509-4

THE HISTORICAL ROOTS OF ELEMENTARY MATHEMATICS, Lucas N. H. Bunt, Phillip S. Jones, and Jack D. Bedient. Fundamental underpinnings of modern arithmetic, algebra, geometry and number systems derived from ancient civilizations. 320pp. 5³/₈ x 8¹/₂.   0-486-25563-8

THE HISTORY OF THE CALCULUS AND ITS CONCEPTUAL DEVELOP-MENT, Carl B. Boyer. Fluent description of the development of both the integral and differential calculus—its early beginnings in antiquity, medieval contributions, and a consideration of Newton and Leibniz. 368pp. 5³/₈ x 8¹/₂.   0-486-60509-4

GAMES, GODS & GAMBLING: A HISTORY OF PROBABILITY AND STATISTICAL IDEAS, F. N. David. Episodes from the lives of Galileo, Fermat, Pascal, and others illustrate this fascinating account of the roots of mathematics. Features thought-provoking references to classics, archaeology, biography, poetry. 1962 edition. 304pp. 5³/₈ x 8¹/₂. (Available in U.S. only.)   0-486-40023-9

OF MEN AND NUMBERS: THE STORY OF THE GREAT MATHEMATICIANS, Jane Muir. Fascinating accounts of the lives and accomplishments of history's greatest mathematical minds—Pythagoras, Descartes, Euler, Pascal, Cantor, many more. Anecdotal, illuminating. 30 diagrams. Bibliography. 256pp. 5³/₈ x 8¹/₂.   0-486-28973-7

HISTORY OF MATHEMATICS, David E. Smith. Nontechnical survey from ancient Greece and Orient to late 19th century; evolution of arithmetic, geometry, trigonometry, calculating devices, algebra, the calculus. 362 illustrations. 1,355pp. 5³/₈ x 8¹/₂. Two-vol. set.   Vol. I: 0-486-20429-4   Vol. II: 0-486-20430-8

A CONCISE HISTORY OF MATHEMATICS, Dirk J. Struik. The best brief history of mathematics. Stresses origins and covers every major figure from ancient Near East to 19th century. 41 illustrations. 195pp. 5³/₈ x 8¹/₂.   0-486-60255-9

Physics

OPTICAL RESONANCE AND TWO-LEVEL ATOMS, L. Allen and J. H. Eberly. Clear, comprehensive introduction to basic principles behind all quantum optical resonance phenomena. 53 illustrations. Preface. Index. 256pp. $5^3/_8$ x $8^1/_2$.   0-486-65533-4

QUANTUM THEORY, David Bohm. This advanced undergraduate-level text presents the quantum theory in terms of qualitative and imaginative concepts, followed by specific applications worked out in mathematical detail. Preface. Index. 655pp. $5^3/_8$ x $8^1/_2$.
0-486-65969-0

ATOMIC PHYSICS (8th EDITION), Max Born. Nobel laureate's lucid treatment of kinetic theory of gases, elementary particles, nuclear atom, wave-corpuscles, atomic structure and spectral lines, much more. Over 40 appendices, bibliography. 495pp. $5^3/_8$ x $8^1/_2$.
0-486-65984-4

A SOPHISTICATE'S PRIMER OF RELATIVITY, P. W. Bridgman. Geared toward readers already acquainted with special relativity, this book transcends the view of theory as a working tool to answer natural questions: What is a frame of reference? What is a "law of nature"? What is the role of the "observer"? Extensive treatment, written in terms accessible to those without a scientific background. 1983 ed. xlviii+172pp. $5^3/_8$ x $8^1/_2$.
0-486-42549-5

AN INTRODUCTION TO HAMILTONIAN OPTICS, H. A. Buchdahl. Detailed account of the Hamiltonian treatment of aberration theory in geometrical optics. Many classes of optical systems defined in terms of the symmetries they possess. Problems with detailed solutions. 1970 edition. xv + 360pp. $5^3/_8$ x $8^1/_2$.   0-486-67597-1

PRIMER OF QUANTUM MECHANICS, Marvin Chester. Introductory text examines the classical quantum bead on a track: its state and representations; operator eigenvalues; harmonic oscillator and bound bead in a symmetric force field; and bead in a spherical shell. Other topics include spin, matrices, and the structure of quantum mechanics; the simplest atom; indistinguishable particles; and stationary-state perturbation theory. 1992 ed. xiv+314pp. $6^1/_8$ x $9^1/_4$.   0-486-42878-8

LECTURES ON QUANTUM MECHANICS, Paul A. M. Dirac. Four concise, brilliant lectures on mathematical methods in quantum mechanics from Nobel Prize-winning quantum pioneer build on idea of visualizing quantum theory through the use of classical mechanics. 96pp. $5^3/_8$ x $8^1/_2$.   0-486-41713-1

THIRTY YEARS THAT SHOOK PHYSICS: THE STORY OF QUANTUM THEORY, George Gamow. Lucid, accessible introduction to influential theory of energy and matter. Careful explanations of Dirac's anti-particles, Bohr's model of the atom, much more. 12 plates. Numerous drawings. 240pp. $5^3/_8$ x $8^1/_2$.   0-486-24895-X

ELECTRONIC STRUCTURE AND THE PROPERTIES OF SOLIDS: THE PHYSICS OF THE CHEMICAL BOND, Walter A. Harrison. Innovative text offers basic understanding of the electronic structure of covalent and ionic solids, simple metals, transition metals and their compounds. Problems. 1980 edition. 582pp. $6^1/_8$ x $9^1/_4$.
0-486-66021-4

HYDRODYNAMIC AND HYDROMAGNETIC STABILITY, S. Chandrasekhar. Lucid examination of the Rayleigh-Benard problem; clear coverage of the theory of instabilities causing convection. 704pp. 5⅜ x 8¼. 0-486-64071-X

INVESTIGATIONS ON THE THEORY OF THE BROWNIAN MOVEMENT, Albert Einstein. Five papers (1905–8) investigating dynamics of Brownian motion and evolving elementary theory. Notes by R. Fürth. 122pp. 5⅜ x 8½. 0-486-60304-0

THE PHYSICS OF WAVES, William C. Elmore and Mark A. Heald. Unique overview of classical wave theory. Acoustics, optics, electromagnetic radiation, more. Ideal as classroom text or for self-study. Problems. 477pp. 5⅜ x 8½. 0-486-64926-1

GRAVITY, George Gamow. Distinguished physicist and teacher takes reader-friendly look at three scientists whose work unlocked many of the mysteries behind the laws of physics: Galileo, Newton, and Einstein. Most of the book focuses on Newton's ideas, with a concluding chapter on post-Einsteinian speculations concerning the relationship between gravity and other physical phenomena. 160pp. 5⅜ x 8½. 0-486-42563-0

PHYSICAL PRINCIPLES OF THE QUANTUM THEORY, Werner Heisenberg. Nobel Laureate discusses quantum theory, uncertainty, wave mechanics, work of Dirac, Schroedinger, Compton, Wilson, Einstein, etc. 184pp. 5⅜ x 8½. 0-486-60113-7

ATOMIC SPECTRA AND ATOMIC STRUCTURE, Gerhard Herzberg. One of best introductions; especially for specialist in other fields. Treatment is physical rather than mathematical. 80 illustrations. 257pp. 5⅜ x 8½. 0-486-60115-3

AN INTRODUCTION TO STATISTICAL THERMODYNAMICS, Terrell L. Hill. Excellent basic text offers wide-ranging coverage of quantum statistical mechanics, systems of interacting molecules, quantum statistics, more. 523pp. 5⅜ x 8½. 0-486-65242-4

THEORETICAL PHYSICS, Georg Joos, with Ira M. Freeman. Classic overview covers essential math, mechanics, electromagnetic theory, thermodynamics, quantum mechanics, nuclear physics, other topics. First paperback edition. xxiii + 885pp. 5⅜ x 8½. 0-486-65227-0

PROBLEMS AND SOLUTIONS IN QUANTUM CHEMISTRY AND PHYSICS, Charles S. Johnson, Jr. and Lee G. Pedersen. Unusually varied problems, detailed solutions in coverage of quantum mechanics, wave mechanics, angular momentum, molecular spectroscopy, more. 280 problems plus 139 supplementary exercises. 430pp. 6½ x 9¼. 0-486-65236-X

THEORETICAL SOLID STATE PHYSICS, Vol. 1: Perfect Lattices in Equilibrium; Vol. II: Non-Equilibrium and Disorder, William Jones and Norman H. March. Monumental reference work covers fundamental theory of equilibrium properties of perfect crystalline solids, non-equilibrium properties, defects and disordered systems. Appendices. Problems. Preface. Diagrams. Index. Bibliography. Total of 1,301pp. 5⅜ x 8½. Two volumes. Vol. I: 0-486-65015-4 Vol. II: 0-486-65016-2

WHAT IS RELATIVITY? L. D. Landau and G. B. Rumer. Written by a Nobel Prize physicist and his distinguished colleague, this compelling book explains the special theory of relativity to readers with no scientific background, using such familiar objects as trains, rulers, and clocks. 1960 ed. vi+72pp. 5⅜ x 8½. 0-486-42806-0

CATALOG OF DOVER BOOKS

A TREATISE ON ELECTRICITY AND MAGNETISM, James Clerk Maxwell. Important foundation work of modern physics. Brings to final form Maxwell's theory of electromagnetism and rigorously derives his general equations of field theory. 1,084pp. 5³/₈ x 8¹/₂. Two-vol. set. Vol. I: 0-486-60636-8 Vol. II: 0-486-60637-6

MATHEMATICS FOR PHYSICISTS, Philippe Dennery and Andre Krzywicki. Superb text provides math needed to understand today's more advanced topics in physics and engineering. Theory of functions of a complex variable, linear vector spaces, much more. Problems. 1967 edition. 400pp. 6¹/₂ x 9¹/₄. 0-486-69193-4

INTRODUCTION TO QUANTUM MECHANICS WITH APPLICATIONS TO CHEMISTRY, Linus Pauling & E. Bright Wilson, Jr. Classic undergraduate text by Nobel Prize winner applies quantum mechanics to chemical and physical problems. Numerous tables and figures enhance the text. Chapter bibliographies. Appendices. Index. 468pp. 5³/₈ x 8¹/₂. 0-486-64871-0

METHODS OF THERMODYNAMICS, Howard Reiss. Outstanding text focuses on physical technique of thermodynamics, typical problem areas of understanding, and significance and use of thermodynamic potential. 1965 edition. 238pp. 5³/₈ x 8¹/₂. 0-486-69445-3

THE ELECTROMAGNETIC FIELD, Albert Shadowitz. Comprehensive under- graduate text covers basics of electric and magnetic fields, builds up to electromagnetic theory. Also related topics, including relativity. Over 900 problems. 768pp. 5³/₈ x 8¹/₄. 0-486-65660-8

GREAT EXPERIMENTS IN PHYSICS: FIRSTHAND ACCOUNTS FROM GALILEO TO EINSTEIN, Morris H. Shamos (ed.). 25 crucial discoveries: Newton's laws of motion, Chadwick's study of the neutron, Hertz on electromagnetic waves, more. Original accounts clearly annotated. 370pp. 5³/₈ x 8¹/₂. 0-486-25346-5

EINSTEIN'S LEGACY, Julian Schwinger. A Nobel Laureate relates fascinating story of Einstein and development of relativity theory in well-illustrated, nontechnical volume. Subjects include meaning of time, paradoxes of space travel, gravity and its effect on light, non-Euclidean geometry and curving of space-time, impact of radio astronomy and space-age discoveries, and more. 189 b/w illustrations. xiv+250pp. 8³/₈ x 9¹/₄. 0-486-41974-6

THE VARIATIONAL PRINCIPLES OF MECHANICS, Cornelius Lanczos. Philosophic, less formalistic approach to analytical mechanics offers model of clear, scholarly exposition at graduate level with coverage of basics, calculus of variations, principle of virtual work, equations of motion, more. 418pp. 5³/₈ x 8¹/₂. 0-486-65067-7

Paperbound unless otherwise indicated. Available at your book dealer, online at www.doverpublications.com, or by writing to Dept. GI, Dover Publications, Inc., 31 East 2nd Street, Mineola, NY 11501. For current price information or for free catalogues (please indicate field of interest), write to Dover Publications or log on to www.doverpublications.com and see every Dover book in print. Dover publishes more than 400 books each year on science, elementary and advanced mathematics, biology, music, art, literary history, social sciences, and other areas.